A HISTORY OF
THE METHODIST CHURCH
IN GREAT BRITAIN

VOLUME THREE

General Editors

RUPERT DAVIES

A. RAYMOND GEORGE

GORDON RUPP

A History of THE METHODIST CHURCH *in Great Britain*

VOLUME THREE

LONDON
EPWORTH PRESS

First published 1983
by Epworth Press

Enquiries should be addressed to
The Epworth Press
Room 195
1 Central Buildings
Westminster
London SW1H 9NR

7162 0387 1

Typeset by Gloucester Typesetting Services
and printed in Great Britain by
Richard Clay (The Chaucer Press) Plc
Bungay, Suffolk

CONTENTS

PREFACE

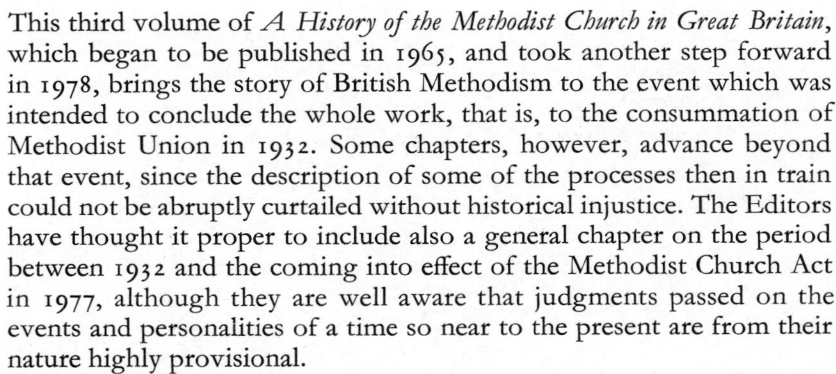

This third volume of *A History of the Methodist Church in Great Britain*, which began to be published in 1965, and took another step forward in 1978, brings the story of British Methodism to the event which was intended to conclude the whole work, that is, to the consummation of Methodist Union in 1932. Some chapters, however, advance beyond that event, since the description of some of the processes then in train could not be abruptly curtailed without historical injustice. The Editors have thought it proper to include also a general chapter on the period between 1932 and the coming into effect of the Methodist Church Act in 1977, although they are well aware that judgments passed on the events and personalities of a time so near to the present are from their nature highly provisional.

The fourth volume, now in preparation, will contain a full bibliography for the complete work, and a collection of documents necessary for the close study of Methodist history.

The absence of any treatment of the crucial theme of Methodist missions from the first two volumes accounts for the extended treatment which the Editors felt it right to give the subject in this volume. Dr Allen Birtwhistle's historical studies, and his own experience on the mission field, especially qualified him for the task of writing the required chapter, a task which he undertook with characteristic enthusiasm. Unfortunately failing health became a growing impediment to a labour of love in which he courageously persisted until his death. His son, Mr John Birtwhistle, gave generously of time and skill in editing the manuscript, and the Editors wish their gratitude to Allen's widow, Harriet, and to John Birtwhistle to be recorded, while the article itself is a testimony to the ministry of one who was himself within a great Methodist and missionary tradition.

The chapter on 'Methodism in Ireland' was originally written by the Rev. R. Lee Cole, who died without being able to revise his work. The passage of time has made a virtual re-writing necessary, and this has been carried out by Dr Eric Gallagher, who acknowledges his indebtedness to Mr Lee Cole.

The British Methodist Conference, the Overseas Division of the Methodist Church, the Irish Methodist Conference and the Joseph

Rank Benevolent Trust have helped to overcome the financial difficulties of publication by generous subventions.

The Editors wish to thank the Rev. Gordon Wakefield for his advice throughout their work; Mr Herbert Rees for preparing the volume for the press with meticulous attention to detail; and Miss Linda Graham, who has prepared the Index under great pressure.

March 1982

RUPERT E. DAVIES
A. RAYMOND GEORGE
E. GORDON RUPP

ABBREVIATIONS

H.M.G.B.	*A History of the Methodist Church in Great Britain* (London 1965–).
L.Q.H.R.	*The London Quarterly and Holborn Review* (London 1932–1968).
N.H.M.	*The New History of Methodism*, ed. W. J. Townsend, H. B. Workman, and G. Eayrs, 2 vols. (London 1909).
Wesley:	
Journal	*The Journal of John Wesley*, standard edn. in 8 vols., ed. N. Curnock (London 1909–16).
Letters	*The Letters of John Wesley*, standard edn. in 8 vols., ed. J. Telford (London 1931).
Works	14 vols., 3rd edn., ed. T. Jackson (London 1831ff.).
W.H.S. Proc.	*The Proceedings of the Wesley Historical Society*, 1899– .

PART ONE

I

Methodist Missions

N. ALLEN BIRTWHISTLE

1. The First Half-century: 1786–1838

THE very nature of the Methodist Revival made it impossible that its energies could be confined to one small country or even to its own Societies. It has been suggested that the great missionary outgoing of the following century, which was a common feature of all evangelical groups and denominations, owed much to the warmth, and perhaps more to the Arminianism, of the Wesleys and their followers. Perhaps no words of John Wesley are more frequently quoted than his famous claim: 'I look upon all the world as my parish.' Yet his own caution when it came to initiating missions to non-Christians overseas – springing, perhaps, from memories of his own experiences in Georgia and certainly strengthened by a shrewd estimate as to the prospects of immediate success for such ventures by comparison with the harvest waiting to be gathered at home – led him at times to be less than exuberant about some of the schemes proposed by his colleague Dr Thomas Coke.

The nineteenth century was, however, to see a conjunction of favourable influences that made an unprecedented missionary explosion almost inevitable, and produced that heroic and now often neglected figure, the 'missionary'. Livingstone's 'I beg you to direct your attention to Africa' speech in the Cambridge University Senate House in 1858, and the prolonged applause that greeted it, would have been as unthinkable a century earlier as it would be today. Factors which made some such event likely at the time were the colonial expansion which influenced the outlook and philosophy of the whole nation, and a widely accepted theology which took seriously not only the place of Christians in the world but also man's desperate state in the light of eternity.

Such were the forces that eventually produced the Methodist Missionary Society. This was to become the largest Protestant missionary society in Europe, as its sister in America is the largest there.

Where does a great river start? At that point in the hills where a tiny stream begins to flow from the wet springy soil, or in those clouds where moisture condenses and begins to fall as rain?

Various moments have been claimed as the beginning of the Methodist Missionary Society. Was it in 1758, when Nathaniel Gilbert, a distinguished lawyer and Speaker of the House of Assembly in Antigua, was visiting England and heard a sermon by John Wesley in a house on Wandsworth High Street? Two of Gilbert's Negro servants were with him then, and they were converted; Wesley baptized them. But why not go further back to the day in 1744 when John Wesley wrote his *Earnest Appeal to Men of Reason and Religion*? It was that document, falling into the hands of Nathaniel Gilbert when he was lying ill in Antigua, which convinced him by its logical approach, and made him decide to sail for England with the main purpose of hearing John Wesley preach.

A better case could be made out for another moment in Nathaniel Gilbert's life. He returned to Antigua, and there are few more dramatic events in Methodist history than that of a Sunday in 1760 when the bell was rung calling together the slaves from his estate. As they came in from the canefields he did not address them from the veranda, but invited them into his home, and when they were seated in the drawing room he told them what Christ had done for them and for every man.

But we can hardly claim this as the beginning of world missions consciously backed and supported by Methodism. (We cannot properly use the term 'the Methodist Church' for that period.) The Methodist Conference had not sent Nathaniel Gilbert as a missionary to the West Indies. Like many another pioneer of Methodism overseas, he was a layman acting on his own initiative. Soldiers, sailors, ship's carpenters, traders: these were the sort of men who established the first Methodist Societies in other countries, led Class Meetings, and preached the Word. The Conference did not usually seem to be aware of what such pioneers were doing; so, if we define our task as deciding when the Methodist Conference first established a foreign mission, we must look to other people and other times.

We are seeking two distinguishing marks. This beginning must not be an individual enterprise, however noble. It must be the first collective and officially recognized effort. And it must be a mission to what would then have been called 'the heathen overseas'. Quite early on, the Conference had designated as 'missionaries' those preachers who were sent to Ireland and Scotland and the Shetland Islands and what they called 'the Norman Islands' – Jersey and Guernsey. But these do not fall within our field. Nor do the acts of the Conference in sending men much further overseas to America. The *Minutes* for 1769 carry a fascinating record. Nestling among statements about the Connexional debt on new buildings, we find this gem, cut in the usual question-and-answer style of Wesley's minutes:

> *Q.*13. We have a pressing call from our brethren at New York (who have built a preaching-house) to come over and help them. Who is willing to go?
>
> *A.* Richard Boardman and Joseph Pilmoor.
>
> *Q.*14. What can we do further, in token of our brotherly love?
>
> *A.* Let us now make a collection among ourselves. This was immediately done, and out of it £50 were allotted towards the payment of their debt, and about £20 given to our brethren for their passage.

'Willing to go.' How often that emotive expression, and its companion, 'Let us go in the name of the Lord', were to be heard in the following century! They sum up precisely the response of that great company of those who published the word given to them by him whom they called the God of Missions. But these 'missionaries' to New York were sent to their own kith and kin who were fellow Methodists. So we cannot claim 1769 as the date for the founding of the Methodist Missionary Society.

Nor can we look for its beginning to the *Plan of the Society for the Establishment of Missions among the Heathens* put out by Dr Coke, probably in the latter part of 1783, though on paper it had the marks we are seeking. There was to be a mission to non-Christians, in the British Dominions in Asia. And as far as organization went, there was to be a membership consisting of those who contributed at least two guineas a year (at a time when many a labourer earned less than a shilling a day); and a general meeting of subscribers with power to set up a committee, appoint a secretary, and prepare and send out missionaries.

The first of these general meetings was to have been held at 11 West Street, London, on Tuesday, 27 January 1784; but there is no evidence that it ever took place. More than likely, Wesley vetoed it. He probably disapproved of it on two grounds. In the first place, by its proposed constitution the Society would have enjoyed a measure of autonomy which would have enabled it to act without the restraint of Mr Wesley and his Conference. Secondly, it is clear that Coke had in mind a mission to India, while subsequent events revealed that Wesley intended that he should found a Methodist Church in America.

With such a clash of inclinations it is not surprising that Coke went West, not East. Within three weeks of the date that had been proposed for the first general meeting at West Street, Wesley records in his *Journal*:

> I desired all our preachers to meet and consider thoroughly the proposal of sending missionaries to the East Indies. After the matter had been fully considered, we were unanimous in our judgement that we have no call thither yet, no invitation, no providential opening of any kind.[1]

But if the door to the East was firmly bolted by Wesley, it seems clear that this was the occasion when he opened up with his colleague the American proposals. Certainly, events now moved rapidly. By the middle of April, Coke was writing to Wesley accepting the idea. In July, the Conference appointed Coke, Whatcoat and Vasey to America. In Bristol at the beginning of September Wesley ordained Whatcoat and Vasey as deacons and then as elders, and set apart Coke 'as a Superintendent'.[2] On 18 September they sailed and on 3 November they arrived in New York. At Christmas 1784 the most important Conference of Methodist preachers ever held in America assembled in Baltimore and made Asbury a bishop.

In a later session the Conference acknowledged the success of John Baxter's work in Antigua. When Nathaniel Gilbert died and his brother left the island, two of the members, both women, kept the society together until Baxter came out from England. A handwritten list of *The Names of the Local Circuit* carries the entry:

Time of commencing preaching	*Name*	*Occupation*	*Residence*	*Departure*
1771				
Decr 23	*John Baxter*	*Shipwright*		*Went to Antigua*

He had been working with the Navy at Chatham, and in 1778 was posted to the Government dockyard at English Harbour, Antigua. By the time Coke arrived in America, six years later, Baxter's free time was completely absorbed in caring for a membership of more than 1500, all but three of them Negroes. The American Conference agreed that Baxter, who was not present, should be made an 'Elder', and they appointed another preacher, Jeremiah Lambert, as his colleague. Lambert was a sick man, and died before he could go to Antigua, but their two names appear under this station in the *Minutes* of the English Conference of the following year.

Still we cannot claim that this marks the beginning of the Methodist Missionary Society. The entry under *Antigua* in the Stations for 1785 was simply a record of the decision made by the American Conference.

[1] *Journal*, vi, 476.
[2] *H.M.G.B.*, ii, 145–6.

English Methodism had not appointed Baxter and Lambert, did not support them with financial grants, and accepted no responsibility for maintaining their work.

After all these plans and pilot schemes it was inevitable that sooner or later one of Coke's contrivances would get into orbit. His big day came in March 1786, when he received a letter from Wesley commending his project entitled: *An Address to the Pious and Benevolent, proposing an Annual Subscription for the support of Missionaries in the Highlands and adjacent Islands of Scotland, the Isles of Jersey, Guernsey, and Newfoundland, the West Indies, and the provinces of Nova Scotia and Quebec.* Though he had to postpone for thirty years his plan to evangelize India, keeping his hopes on ice throughout that period, the resilient doctor knew that here at last was the support he needed for beginning a mission to non-Christians. The significant thing was that now he could take men to work in the West Indies. The Methodist Missionary Society was launched.

Again events moved quickly. Wesley's letter of approval was dated *n*2 March 1786. The day after it came, Coke published it along with the *Address*. Once again it was at Bristol that decisive action was taken. Not surprisingly, the Conference, in view of Wesley's backing, approved the plan, agreed that part of the money raised by the appeal could be used for the work in Antigua, and concluded the list of stations with the entries:

> 86 *Antigua*, J. Baxter, William Warrener; 87 *Nova Scotia*, William Black, J. Mann, F. Garretson, J. Cromwell; 88, *Newfoundland*, John McGeary, John Clark, W. Hammet.

Warrener had told Wesley a year before that he was 'at his and the Lord's disposal, to go to America or wherever he might be wanted'. When Coke told him where he had been stationed, he went to see Wesley, and asked, 'Sir, is it your desire that I should go to Antigua?' Wesley replied, 'It is,' and to this Warrener said, 'I have nothing more to say. I go in the name of the Lord.'

Once again the Conference decision to send men overseas was followed by ordinations. On 28 July, Joshua Keighley (appointed to Inverness), William Warrener and William Hammet were ordained as deacons, and next day ordained as elders.[3]

Few missionary maiden voyages are more justly famous than the one that began at Gravesend on 24 September 1786. With Clark, Hammet, Warrener and Coke on board, the ship sailed into such violent storms that the Captain had to change course and instead of heading for Newfoundland turned south for Antigua. With torn sails, and seams wrenched open by the heavy seas, they limped into harbour at St John's

[3] Diary, in *Journal*, vii, 192–3.

on Christmas morning. Famous, too, is that moment when the little company walking from the quay met Baxter with his lantern on his way to take the early morning service.

How fluid the situation was in America and the West Indies at that time, and how ready Coke was to improvise and take the initiative to meet it, may be judged from the fact that in January 1787, a few days after landing in Antigua, he was sailing for other islands in the archipelago, taking the whole staff, Baxter, Clark and Hammet, with him. Clark he left to work at St Vincent, Hammet at St Kitts. Other islands were led to hope that they too would soon have their missionary.

Coke had no qualms about redirecting men who had been designated by the Conference for work in North America and switching them to serve Negro slaves in the Caribbean. 'It is impossible to have any doubt concerning the will of God,' he wrote. 'All is as clear as if it was written by a sunbeam.' It is the spirit that animates so many pioneers. But what seemed so clear in the West Indian sun did not shine so brilliantly in England; and Wesley was not a little disgruntled to discover that promises of help to Newfoundland and Nova Scotia had been broken.

One swift result of Coke's arbitrary activities was that later in the same year, 1787, the American Conference took the West Indies off their stations. The enterprise had grown too big for their resources, and the English Conference now assumed complete responsibility for Baxter. In 1788, they doubled the staff at Coke's disposal by appointing five recruits to the West Indies; and on his second visit, in 1788–9, Coke more than doubled the number of islands which they served. In the *Minutes* of the Conference of 1789, held at Leeds, these missionary appointments appeared in a separate list for the first time. After the Home Stations, which included those in Ireland, we read:

> *THE WEST INDIES*: 1 *Antigua*, Matthew Lumb, John Harper; 2 *St Christophers*, William Warrener; 3 *St Eustatius*, George Skirrit; 4 *Nevis*, Thomas Owens; 5 *St Vincents, in the Carribee* [*sic*] *Division*, John Baxter; *in the English Division*, Robert Gamble, John Clark; 6 *Dominica*, William McCornock; 7 *Barbadoes*, Benjamin Pearce; 8 *Saba*, William Brazier; 9 *Tortola*, [and] 10 *Santa Cruz*, William Hammet.

The total membership in these islands, as recorded in the *Minutes*, was 3,433, Antigua claiming 2,670.

Soon the present pattern began to emerge. In 1790 the Conference appointed a 'Committee for the management of our affairs in the West Indies'. There were to be nine members: Thomas Coke, stationed in London; Alexander Mather, supernumerary, in London; James Rogers, in London; Henry Moore, in Bristol; Adam Clarke, in Dublin, along with John Baxter, William Warrener and Matthew Lumb in the West

Indies. This was a talented and experienced body of men; but, with communications and travel as they were, it was not likely that they could work together effectively, still less exert any kind of control over a determined leader like Coke.

Yet it was a start in the right direction. The Conference in 1799 resolved, regarding the West Indian Missions: 'We, in the fullest manner, take these Missions under our care, and consider Dr Coke is our Agent.' The *Minutes* now, for the first time, record the membership in Africa: 223 in Sierra Leone. And the following year the Conference decided that accounts showing what money had been raised and spent at home, and all expenditure overseas, should be presented to itself or to a Committee which it had appointed.

Rudimentary as it was in some respects, the structure of the Missionary Society had been erected.

The first half-century of the Society's existence saw an amazing pace of growth. From 1786 – when, as we have seen, the Conference finally and formally shouldered its overseas missionary responsibility – to the centenary in 1838 of Wesley's Aldersgate experience, Methodism was transformed from what had been in the main a minority proletarian movement largely confined to England into a considerable and almost world-wide organization.

The theologian may be permitted to see here the activity of God in his world through the inspiration and guidance of his Holy Spirit. At the same time, the church historian will point to the vision and initiative of one man, Dr Thomas Coke, and the desire of many dedicated laymen abroad who wished to continue for themselves, and make available to others, the system that had completely changed their lives and sustained their spirits ever since. The secular historian will not fail to mention other factors, equally important in making possible such swift development. Just as the spread of Methodism was helped in the eighteenth century by the introduction of cheap printing and by the discovery of new ways of lighting city streets and public buildings after dark, making evening meetings which did not clash with parish church services a popular novelty, so now there were new forces at work which facilitated the movement of men and ideas at the very time when all this missionary activity was ready to burst out. Steam locomotion by rail and sea, more efficient rail services, and the development of the telegraph, were as helpful to the missionary as to the colonial administrator.

A generation that is growing up to regard even the struggle of colonial peoples for liberation and self-determination as past history may find it difficult to enter sympathetically into the exuberance that impelled our ancestors. But it is essential to appreciate their mood if we are to understand that of the missionaries, which was closely allied to it. No doubt the colonies provided some younger sons of aristocratic families, and ambitious men of ability from other strata of society, with a way of making a quick fortune and of living at a higher standard than they could expect at home. But few in fact became fabulously rich. Many lost their lives at a time when the nature and causes of tropical diseases were so little understood that few reliable cures were known. There are reminders of this in the couplet,

> Take heed and beware of the Bight of Benin,
> For few come out, though many go in,

and in the names 'the White Man's Grave', given to the West Coast of Africa, and 'Elder Dempster's Graveyard', for the part of the homeward journey from that coast where the ship came into the chilly north-east trade winds and men debilitated by malaria often swiftly succumbed. There was a famous reply from the Colonial Office to the Governor of Sierra Leone who wrote asking what were the pension arrangements he could expect on retirement: 'The question has never previously arisen.'

The fact is that the Colonial Service offered far more than a hope of speedy gain. There was immense curiosity about countries such as Africa, which, apart from some coastal regions, was almost totally unknown to Europeans until the journeys of Livingstone. There was the prospect of almost immediate promotion to a position of considerable responsibility. The dangers of the situation and its novelty presented an irresistible fascination to those who loved adventure. And there was a deep concern, amounting to compassion, for people regarded with good reason as less fortunate than ourselves. It is easy to make fun of all that lay behind such a phrase as 'the White Man's Burden', which epitomized this outlook. In our day, when the excitements of colonial service no longer provide the same outlet for the energies of aspiring and well-meaning young people, it is not difficult to jeer, from the comfortable vantage-point of an armchair, at those who were moved by idealism to work for the unprivileged and the oppressed. Of course there are many dark pages in the history of our colonial empire, many evidences of unworthy motives and wrong-headed acts, but for many who staffed the administration the concept of service was a warm reality. Long before self-government came to Nigeria, the dedication and loyalty of those key men in the administration, the District Officers, to the people of their own area, was summed up in the saying: 'If all the Africans were to leave the country today, war would break out between the D.O.s tomorrow.'

The day of Western political domination over what were once colonial territories is over, and perhaps no one regrets the fact. But we have not ceased to exert an irresistible influence there. The introduction of Western technology, apart from anything else, for better, for worse, ensured that the expansion of our ideas and ways should continue, so that in comparing the situation of the missionary now with what it was in the early nineteenth century, the significance of the end of colonialism can be over-estimated. What is important is the fact that the Church today, in the West as well as in the East, lives in a non-Christian world. This was not true a century and a half ago. Talk about older and younger churches now becomes less and less significant. All are as young as atomic power and as old as the first Whitsuntide. But early in the nineteenth century, when Western colonization and missionary expansion went hand in hand, both had much of value to offer from the base of a relatively stable society.

Even so, the accusation, often aimed at the early missionaries, that they were handmaids of white imperialism, is as irrelevant and distorted as the myth that all colonial authority was devoted to unrelieved exploitation. The difference between the pace of political advance and the relatively slow response to evangelism shows this, as does the record of missionary opposition on so many occasions both to colonial governments and colonial capitalism.

There certainly was no confusion about all this in the minds of missionary supporters in 1838. That year at the annual meeting of the Wesleyan Methodist Missionary Society, the chairman, John Hardy, said:

> We have heard, too, lately, of an intention, on the part of some persons, to colonize certain islands [New Zealand] in which your Missionaries have occupied a distinguished station. I hope that never will take place. The evils of such a step have been demonstrated by one of your Secretaries [Mr Beecham], by arguments which, I think, no reasonable man can resist. We all know, from experience, that colonization is too often followed by tyranny and oppression; and we, unlike the Jews with respect to the Canaanites, have no commission to extirpate any nation. To evangelize is one thing; to colonize another. The colonist goes 'with arms of mortal temper in his hands'; with the musket, the bayonet, and the gunpowder; but your Missionaries go with the 'sword of the Spirit, which is the word of God'. I trust they will be permitted to go unmolested. Nothing can be greater than their disinterestedness in that cause. They cannot be suspected of any objects of ambition: they go poor and defenceless, to make many rich; whereas colonists generally go to make many poor, in order to enrich a few. To Christianize countries like these is indeed a great object of ambition, and it deserves from Christians all the credit which I trust it receives.

'There have been three eras of missionaries', it has been said, no doubt with the modern outgoing from the West in mind; 'the first were pioneers and dictators, the second paternalists, and the third are here to serve.'[4] In fact, the divisions have never been as clear-cut as this comment would suggest, but there is an element of truth in it, and in the period 1786–1838 we are dealing in the main with the first of the three categories, the pioneers, whether or not they were dictators.

Between the 1786 of Mozart, Kant and Pitt the Younger and the 1813 of Napoleon, Beethoven, the English Romantic poets, and Robert Owen (with his theories of how to influence character), the story of missions sponsored by the British Methodist Missionary Society is dominated by a great burst of activity in their oldest field, the West Indies. As we have seen, the apostolic visits of Coke in the 1780s had left a curving chain of island stations, 500 miles in extent, on the eastern side of the Caribbean Sea. By 1789, this sunlit crescent in the Lesser Antilles could show a membership of nearly 3,500. At the turn of the century the numbers were more than three times greater. Work had begun, not only in the tiny island of St Bartholomews, but also 800 miles to the east in the much larger island of Jamaica. From Jamaica to Barbados, two outposts of the field, is a journey of almost 1,200 miles, and Bermuda, which had also been reached, is 1,500 miles north of Barbados.

An article in the *Methodist Magazine* for January 1800, apparently by Dr Coke himself and entitled 'A Short Account of the Success of the Methodist Missionaries in the West-Indies', describes the position in language which conveys the mood and outlook of the day:

> We have been engaged but thirteen years in this blessed work, and yet the Lord has graciously given us about eleven thousand souls, besides those who in that time have been safely lodged in Abraham's Bosom. All of these, as far as we, who are no discerners of the heart, can judge, are truly awakened to a knowledge of their fallen state: They have forsaken their outward sins, yea, even the most favourite of all – Polygamy; and are earnestly seeking salvation through the Blood of the Covenant: and a very considerable part of them are happy in the love of GOD. In the Love-feasts and Band-meetings in St John's in Antigua, Basse-Terre in St Christopher's, Charleston in Nevis, Kingston in St Vincent's, Kingston in Jamaica, etc., I have been charmed with the testimony which the believing Negroes bore for Jesus Christ. One after another, with the utmost order, they gave an account in their Negro-dialect, of the work of grace upon their souls in its different stages, with as much clearness and perspicuity as any Believer in Europe: and their own masters confess that they are the best and most faithful Servants which they possess.
>
> We have now 2,800 in Society in Antigua, above 1,800 in St

[4] Richard & Helen Exley, *The Missionary Myth* (London 1974).

Christopher's, 500 in Nevis, above 3,000 in Tortola and the other Virgin islands, 100 in Dominica, 2,000 in St Vincent's, 44 in Barbadoes, 130 in Grenada, near 600 in Jamaica, and 120 in St Bartholomew's. All these we are not ashamed to call Members of our Society.

Inclusive of the above, we have between fifty and sixty thousand under instruction, of all of whom we are in hopes that we shall be able in time, through the Grace of GOD, to give a good account. And the Lord has been pleased to raise up about fifty Preachers among the Negroes.

We have also opened a new Mission among the Negroes in Bermuda, of which Mr Stephenson, our Missionary in that Island, gives us a pleasing account. Mr Turton, who has introduced the Gospel into St Bartholomew's, has been appointed for Providence Island to which we have had strong and repeated invitations. We are also establishing a Mission among the French Negroes in the Island of Jersey having undertaken that arduous task. In short, the success which the Lord has been pleased to give us, exceeds our most sanguine expectations; and the prospects before us are of the most pleasing kind.

Indeed they were, and we may balance this survey of the Caribbean area in 1800 with one missionary's account of how he put in his time there. Charles Hodgson is writing from Tortola, on 8 February 1808, to Mr William Myles. Having described the grim state of the people before Coke and Hammet arrived – 'surely, if ever there was a place where souls were perishing for lack of divine knowledge, it was Tortola' – and told how, single-handed, he performs 'the office of judge, magistrate, and minister unto nearly two thousand people', he writes:

I shall now proceed to give you an account how I spend my time for one week, that you may judge whether I am idle or not. On Sunday morning, at six, we meet the classes; at ten read prayers, and preach, and conclude about twelve. From that time until four in the afternoon, I am employed in settling disputes and reconciling differences; besides marrying, baptizing, admitting new members into the society and excluding those that walk disorderly. In the evening, at six o'clock, I preach again. On Monday morning, at five, I preach, exhort, or read some portion of Scripture. In the afternoon, I set out into the circuit, at night preach on P.W.'s estate. On Tuesday morning I proceed for Frenchman's Key, dine there, then take a row-boat and set off for Joevandyke, an island to the north of Tortola. In this passage we experienced several disagreeable things. 1st. The sun beams hot upon us all the time, which always gives me a most violent *head-ache*. 2ndly, A strange current runs between the islands, which is ready to swamp the boat every *pull*. 3dly, when the wind blows, the water rises to such a degree, and breaks over the boat, that we get wet thro'. By the time we arrive there it is the hour for preaching, so that just as we land, sick with the motion, and often wet, we have to scramble up the mountains *one thousand* feet above the level of the sea, before we get to the chapel, and then there is no place where we can get the least refreshment, without clambering up another mountain; for this country is something like the Alps, mountains rising one above another. I have been ready to die for thirst before I could get a drink of water. When the negroes have done labouring in the plantations (which are here chiefly of cotton) they come from the different parts of the island to our little chapel, and bring us some refreshment with them, which is generally fish and yams; and, after preaching, we sleep upon benches in the chapel; yet, I bless the Lord, notwithstanding all this barrenness of outward things, we have some precious feasts of spiritual things. I have heard such sound Christian experience upon the top of this mountain as I little expected to hear. Wednesday, we recross to Frenchman's Key, experiencing the same disagreeable things in our return as I have before described; we preach there in the evening, and stay all night. On Thursday morning we return to the head place in the circuit, and preach in the evening. On Friday we visit another part of the circuit, called Fat-hog Bay, and preach and sleep there, and return to town on Saturday, to prepare for the duties of the Lord's-Day. But the places I have mentioned do not make half the circuit; we have to visit a whole group of islands all round Tortola; and sometimes when we are crossing from one to another huge sharks will play round the boat.

Hodgson ends his letter by mentioning one or two signs of progress and saying, 'I believe I am just where the Lord would have me to be, and I rejoice that my labour is not in vain in the Lord.' At least he could have claimed that he had gone some little way toward observing Wesley's advice to his helpers: Never be unemployed; never be triflingly employed.

In some parts of the West Indies there were greater hazards to be faced than the inconveniences which Hodgson described. That almost casual remark in the survey of 1800 about Stephenson's appointment to Bermuda is a reminder that the work did not always go forward smoothly. Stephenson went to Bermuda in 1799 because a British officer, appalled by the condition of the people there, had written to Coke begging him to send a missionary to help them to raise their living and moral standards. From the start it was clear that the officer's account had not been exaggerated: nor did it cover all that Stephenson had to contend with. He was immediately attacked by some of the white members of the community who resented his intrusion and hated the thought of anyone trying to educate and elevate the slaves. Within a short time of his arrival he was arrested, tried and condemned for a breach of the law in preaching without a licence. He was imprisoned for six months, fined £50 and required to pay the costs. When he came out of gaol he was expelled from the island and the mission came to a temporary halt.

It was eight years before Joshua Marsden came to pick up the threads and found that with other men in power the climate was a little more congenial. Even so, on 20 May 1809 he was writing to Joseph Benson, the Connexional Editor, about the 'hurtful weeds of prejudice, with which the place was completely overgrown', and which prevented black and coloured people from entering those private houses where he usually preached. He was building a chapel to overcome this difficulty. The Bishop of London had waded into the fight with a flurry of pamphlets, but no one in authority seemed to be taking much notice of them. Perhaps, says Marsden philosophically, it is better that the Methodists never had noble or influential patrons:

> it brings back the state of the Primitive Church, when religion stood upon its own bottom. It is not patronage, it is not money, nor titles, but genuine grace, holy zeal, and primitive simplicity, that must support and promote the cause of God.

There are two other points of interest in that letter from Marsden. The first is an appeal that Benson should do his best to send him a few Testaments: 'Many of the Blacks and Coloured people can read a little, and this Island abounds with extremely poor white people', so the want of them is 'inexpressibly great'. He had made the same plea at greater length a month earlier in a letter to the Book Steward, Thomas Blanshard, where he showed himself to be most forward-looking on the whole topic of Christian literature, a reminder that from the start it was the policy of missionaries to train their people to read and think. Hodgson wrote from Tortola: 'I can assure you that the people speak better English here than the majority of the people in London' – a view no doubt entirely congenial to a Yorkshireman – and they 'will reason and talk with the Preacher in a manner that would amaze you'.

The second issue Marsden raises is equally modern in tone. He has seen from the *Minutes* of the previous Conference that some of the stations in the West Indies are vacant.

> What, do the funds fail? or will none of our zealous young men come forward in so noble and blessed a cause? Can we sing, 'O! for a trumpet's voice, on all the world to call!' and yet not be willing to come and call the poor, forlorn Blacks from darkness to God's marvellous light? . . . Shall the sailor, the merchant, the adventurer,

> the traveller, the soldier, do more for a living for interest, speculation, knowledge, or honour, than we for the glory of God?

The *Methodist Magazine*, in the issue of which for January 1810 this letter appeared, was more or less compulsory reading for members of the Societies at home, and it is impossible to overestimate the effect of appeals like this on young people at the time. There was little else to read in many homes; certainly nothing else that opened a window on such an exciting scene as those lovely palm-beached islands that in our day have become one of the world's major tourist attractions. That the missionaries enjoyed an almost totally open-air life, not only in their boats and during their journeys on foot but in those airy buildings constructed to capture the breeze as well as to provide a welcome shade, is revealed by some who confessed that on their return to Britain they found their houses intolerably stuffy and the whole scene, one suspects, a little dull. Their letters to Coke reveal a constant puzzlement as to why they were not joined by many more recruits. Though they often begin with some such introduction as, 'Having heard of a vessel being about to sail for London, I take the opportunity of answering your very kind and welcome letter', they do not seem unduly aware of a sense of isolation. How could they, when those they went to serve greeted them with the enthusiasm that Hodgson describes in a letter written from Tortola on 15 December 1807:

> The people knew me to be their PARSON (for this is the title they give us) as soon as I landed and the news flew thro' the town like lightning. I soon heard from all quarters: 'The Parson is come! The Parson is come!' The news soon reached the Chapel, and out the people came. Three or four got hold of each arm, some behind and some before, and I was led in triumph thro' the streets that were on our way to the Preacher's house. And all the windows of the houses were filled with people to see the Parson pass by.

Hodgson goes on to say how grateful and humble such a carnival of a welcome from 'this affectionate people' made him. He was the only minister in all the Virgin Islands, but the load of caring for thousands of people was lifted a little by the gracious way in which he was received by the Governor.

Encouragement of this kind from men in authority was far from the normal experience of missionaries in many of the other islands. Stephenson's harsh reception in Bermuda was matched, for instance, in Nevis by that of John Brownell. Writing from that island on 12 May 1797, he told how 'several great men were ringleaders' of the severe persecution that had hit the young church there. During services they had burst in, waving weapons and creating a riot. It all came to a head when they had set fire to the chapel and struck Brownell with a club when he was on his way to make a report to the magistrate. He presented a written complaint to the President and Council, and later was heard with patience and courtesy. He says that they 'would have given me satisfaction; but I freely forgave the persecutors what was past, on condition that they pledged their honour to trouble us no more'. Apart from this magnanimity, the most remarkable aspect of the whole episode was that Brownell could add: 'During this time of persecution the Society flourished amazingly. Numbers flocked to the Chapel; and I trust to Christ; insomuch that we were obliged to enlarge our chapel.' Looking back on the failure of an earlier attempt to gain protection from the magistrate, and the way 'our friends hung down their heads, and did not wish to interfere, while our enemies triumphed greatly', as a result of this encouragement, his diagnosis was that it was 'generally believed that we were connected with Mr Wilberforce to destroy the slave-trade'.

The technique often used to hamper the missionary was to prosecute him for preaching without a licence, while the same people refused to allow a licence to be issued; but the persecutors did not always have the best of it. John Shipman, who was appointed to Jamaica in 1814, describes the strategy employed in Montego Bay, a port twenty miles west of Falmouth where he was stationed.[5] Once again laymen took the initiative. A Mr Jones, a gentleman from Chester who had been connected with Methodism, and a Sergeant Waugh of the Royal Artillery, then stationed there, wrote to Shipman asking for pastoral help at the Bay. A handful of members still met, though it was twenty-three years since a missionary named Daniel Campbell had been driven away by persecution. Shipman went to Montego Bay at the time when the court of quarter sessions was sitting, and applied for a licence to preach, but a majority of the magistrates were against him and the application was refused. Remembering how he had emerged successful from a similar struggle at Kingston, Shipman returned to Falmouth and waited for the next sessions. The night before the court was to sit again he slipped into Montego Bay unnoticed, having arranged with Jones that a few friendly magistrates would be on the bench. The court was formed with only one of his opponents present, despite whose angry protests the licence was granted.

There the matter might have ended, especially since within a week the sole objector died. But others who shared his views were undeterred and they attacked on a new line. Now that Shipman had his licence to preach, a house was bought and adapted for worship. But when it was to be opened, the magistrates discovered that they had legal powers to prevent its use because Shipman was not in possession of the property

[5] *The Missionary Child*, pp. 10ff. (see below, n. 34).

at the time when his licence was issued. Neither party was willing to give way and they were clearly on a collision course. The magistrates expected a riot and asked the commanding officer at the fort to provide a detachment of soldiers to support the civil arm. This put Sergeant Waugh in a dilemma. He asked Shipman what he should do and was told to do his duty as a soldier. With a fine gesture, which he afterwards thought to have been a trifle rash, he added, 'Blow my brains out, if your officer commands you to do so.'

When it came to the event, Shipman took the heat out of the situation and there was no violence at all. The people assembled for the opening ceremony, with the Chief Constable present holding a warrant to prevent the building from being used for worship. Shipman began the service, was interrupted by the Constable reading his warrant, and then read his licence to show that he was recognized by the authorities as a minister. He then told the congregation that the house was not yet licensed for public services, but that it soon would be, and he asked them to leave quietly. Within a short time he visited the magistrates in their homes, reasoned with them, and won their support, so that at the following sessions one of them indicated their approval, and the house was registered.

While, in spite of official opposition, Methodism was making rapid progress in the West Indies, there were the first signs of movement in the great Continent which had been the Negroes' original home. As in other parts of the world, no ordained minister or missionary of the Society was in at the beginning. We find George Middlemiss, a soldier stationed at Cape Town, writing to a Mr Story, a friend of his in England, on 16 September 1807, telling of 'the glorious work which God is carrying on in the hearts of some individuals of the several regiments in this Colony'. About a year previously, a few of the soldiers had begun finding out how many of them were Methodists, or at least willing to form a Society. In one regiment there were thirty-four, though many of these were Presbyterians. In Middlemiss's own regiment there were two, and in another one. It was enough to make a start. They met to get to know each other, and agreed to continue meeting 'at a distance from the town where we built, with stones, a small sanctuary'. They held prayer meetings there for a time and then on weekdays they were able to use a large Quaker meeting house in the town. Doctrinal difficulties, apparently with the Presbyterians, caused some to leave the group, but from then onwards all was harmony and their numbers began to increase. By the time Middlemiss was writing this letter, they had held two love-feasts, regular class and band meetings, and some watch-night services at the time proposed by the Society. 'But we are short of books. We would thank you to send us some Hymn-books, Bibles and Mr Wesley's Works for our Instruction. We have collected a small sum of money for that purpose. Please to write by the first packet.'

A similar appeal for Bibles by a newly formed society was later to lead to the arrival of the first Methodist missionary on Cape Coast, now part of Ghana, in West Africa. Before then there had been developments in Sierra Leone. Eight months after George Middlemiss had written from Cape Town, a letter was sent to Adam Clarke by one described in the *Methodist Magazine* for December 1808 as 'Mingo Jordan, a Preacher of Colour at Sierra Leone'. It, too, tells of growth, this time among the coloured population:

> I have the pleasure to inform you, that on the 11th of June 1805, I went into the Maroon's town to preach, and continued there until ninety-six days were expired, before I met with any success amongst them, having much difficulty with the settlers.[6] But the Lord enabled me to stand the heat and trial of that day.
>
> The first Maroon that was converted was John Harding. Since then the number amounts to 20, who have followed his glorious example. On the 19th February 1808, 20 persons came to be baptized, which was accomplished on the 22nd. On the 23rd instant they began to subscribe two cents each per week, for the further promoting of the gospel of Christ. The Maroons still continue to meet in Class and walk in the fear of God, and give evidence that they are on the way towards salvation. The converted Maroons give their love to their Rev Fathers and Brethren in Christ Jesus and hope that their souls are in health as ours are . . .
>
> Dear Fathers and Brethren in the Gospel of our Lord Jesus Christ, write to us the first opportunity, and, for a token of love, please to send us some Hymn-Books, and the Preachers will be thankful for any wearing apparel that will be suited to the work.
>
> From Christmas-Day to April the 12th, the number of settlers converted is about 28. And the whole number of members in society, as near as we can say, amounts to about 100. Mr Warren[7] is here, and very useful to us. My love to you, though unknown by face. I write to you in the love of Christ, hoping that you may answer my Letter.

Such reports remind us that the number of missionaries deployed at any time in the last two hundred years has appeared minute compared

[6] The first settlers were a few adventurers from England, and a number of coloured persons from Nova Scotia. Later, from time to time, Negroes freed by the British Navy were brought there, and land was allocated to them under the supervision of the colonial government.

[7] Henry Warren: not to be confused with George Warren, who was sent by the Society in 1811; see p. 18, below.

with the enormous task they have undertaken.[8] In 1808, when Marsden was in Bermuda, Middlemiss at the Cape, and Jordan in Sierra Leone, the total number of Methodist missionaries officially stationed overseas was eighteen. All of them were in the West Indies. By 1813, when Warren had been two years in Sierra Leone and six men had been appointed to open the work in Asia, that number had barely doubled. What sort of a force was this to undertake a world mission? But the project does not submit to arithmetical evaluation. Those early missionaries, and the great company that followed them, would have had no hesitation in ascribing it all to the activity of God in the hearts of men. But that does not prevent us from observing something of the method by which that activity was made effective. The little company of the Missionary Society's agents were more often than not sent to a situation where a beginning, however small, had already been made by a group of laymen who already knew something of Methodism. Also, the Wesleyan system, as they called it in the early nineteenth century, with its class meetings that resembled living cells in the realm of biology, was self-propagating and admirably adapted for rapid growth without the loss of intimacy and of distinctive characteristics that mere increase in numbers often brings about. The whole regime of piety, in the best sense of the word, based on a fellowship of Bible study, outgoing service, and a life of faith and prayer, together with the rules which made of the societies disciplined bodies of free men, ensured that growth, even in isolated and difficult situations, was usually healthy and in harmony with the rest of the Connexion.

When George Warren, the first Methodist to be sent to Africa by the Missionary Society in London, arrived in Sierra Leone, this foundation had already been laid by settlers who had been brought into membership in North America, so that he stepped into a familiar situation. His letter, dated 6 December 1811, to Mr Francis Collier tells how he had 'landed at Sierra Leone on the 12th of November, at 5 o'clock in the afternoon, having been out from Liverpool 52 days, without touching at any place in our way from that port to this settlement'.[9] At first, not surprisingly since they crossed the Bay of Biscay in winter, they had a rough time with severe storms, heavy seas, and a head wind that made progress extremely slow. They were a whole week beating about in what he calls the Irish Channel, and after a month they were still off the coast of Spain. A good following wind helped them on their way for ten days. Then they were delayed by the other extreme of weather, and

[8] In some degree this can also be said of the number of officials deployed to administer the British Empire even at its zenith. Only a highly disciplined corps of men could have undertaken, and to some extent have succeeded in, the care of such vast areas and large populations.

[9] The Superintendent on the Helston Circuit in Cornwall, where George Warren had been his junior colleague in 1810.

time after time lay motionless, waiting for a breeze. The cramped conditions, monotonous diet and lack of news, which were inevitable ingredients of travel at that time, were relieved for a few days when it looked as though they might be captured by a French privateer, but patience must have been needed. Still, this kind of journey gave time to adjust to the change of climate, and for those who could put up with their own company there was time to think, time to read and pray.

This journey that Warren was making marked the beginning of official Methodist missions in Africa: it also showed that the Society had the imagination to send with him three teachers to open the first of our many schools in that continent.

When the party finally arrived at Sierra Leone they had a gracious welcome from the Governor, the Chaplain of the settlement, and others; and while they were being entertained in the home of a merchant in the settlement, Gordon, one of the Local Preachers who had taken a lead in the local Society, came in, saying that this was what they had long been praying for. He could have added that they had repeatedly written to Dr Coke asking him to send a missionary. It was on a Tuesday evening that they had disembarked. On the Thursday Warren met the Society and read them a letter from Dr Coke. The membership was 110, out of an estimated population for 'Sierra Leone and its environs' of around 4,000. There were three Local Preachers, two of them acting as Class Leaders, and six other Class Leaders.

It was not persecution but fever that brought Warren's work to an abrupt close, eight months after his arrival. On 12 June 1812, malaria claimed the first of so many missionary victims on the West Coast. Two years passed before the right man was found to replace him, and then William Davies and his wife began their brief spell of service for a Church that still felt the loss of their first missionary. They too died of malaria.

One of the grimmest and most glorious chapters of missionary history had begun. When Richmond College was founded, thirty years later, there was to come a unique tradition for filling these gaps which so impressed Dietrich Bonhoeffer that he used it to rally the pastors in Germany who were struggling against the state. 'I am not asking you to do or suffer anything new,' he told them. 'This has always been the way of the witness. What, over there in Richmond College there are boards[10] with the names of the Methodist missionaries who died on the field, and when one fell there was another to take his place.'

The intricate process by which the protozoa causing malarial infection are transmitted by the anopheles mosquito had not entered anybody's wildest speculations. The work on this by the English physician in India, Sir Ronald Ross, came at the end of the century, and when it

[10] Now displayed in the main committee room of the Mission House in Marylebone.

had been confirmed the Colonial Office sent a letter to British residents in the tropics. Oliver Griffin, later to be Chairman of the Western Nigeria District, used to tell how he received that letter while ill with malaria at Oyo, and how he got up from bed to take a hammer and break all the water-pots, half sunk in the soil, which surrounded his house to collect rain from the roof and provided ideal conditions for breeding mosquitoes.

The very name 'malaria' indicates that in the time of Warren and Davies it was thought that the dank air near swamps was the culprit: there was much talk about the deadly climate of the West Coast. In the nineteenth century the disease was probably in a particularly malignant phase. Missionary after missionary died about three weeks after landing. If they survived their 'seasoning fever', they might live for a year. Towards the end of the century, this virulence seems to have been modified a little so that there were fewer early deaths, even before the mosquito had been blamed. The improvement may also have been due to a wider and more systematic use of quinine.

Between the arrival of Warren and that of the Davieses in Sierra Leone, much had been happening at home. It all came to an apex in 1813 with Coke's departure with a team of missionaries for Asia, and the resulting effect on the Church at home, now deprived of his tireless advocacy and money-raising tours. It was this introduction of local organization in support of the funds that led to the mistaken idea that 1813 marked the beginning of the Methodist Missionary Society.

Coke's *Plan of the Society for the Establishment of Missions among the Heathens*, which he launched abortively in 1783, had India in mind. It attracted twenty-five subscribers, who gave a total of £66 3*s*. 0*d*., and Coke wrote to one of them, Fletcher of Madeley, asking him 'to get a few subscribers more'. As we have seen, Wesley poured cold water on the scheme. His mind was on the thousands of Methodists in America who were without adequate pastoral care and were denied the sacraments. When Coke published his revised appeal three years later, he explained that,

> the providence of God has lately opened to us so many doors nearer home that Mr Wesley thinks it improvident to hazard at present the lives of any of our preachers by sending them to so great a distance and amidst so many uncertainties and difficulties, when so large a field of action is afforded us in countries to which we have so much easier admittance.

It was an expression of loyalty to his leader. We may suspect that in spite of all the uncertainties and difficulties Coke would have been willing to go. There never has been a moment when prudence could not say that it was inconvenient to begin a major venture of evangelism, but there was wisdom in Wesley's argument, and Coke bowed to the force of it.

Coke also referred, however, to 'a principal gentleman in the province of Bengal' who was ready to give him support. This was Charles Grant, by all accounts 'one of the noblest of the servants of the East India Company, a man of utter integrity and of superb courage and determination'. The year after Coke wrote his preamble, Grant was promoted from being Commercial Resident in Malda to membership of the Board of Trade in Calcutta with the supervision of all the East India Company's trade in Bengal. From this he retired in 1790, and served in the House of Commons as a member for sixteen years. In 1813, when the Company's Charter was revised, his good influence proved invaluable. He was strongly in favour of allowing Christian missionaries free entry into India, and this was of immense importance to the team who landed there soon afterwards.[11] Their immunity from arrest and deportation as 'interlopers' was in large measure due to his efforts in the House to gain more liberal terms in the Charter. Grant had no illusions about the difficulty of Coke's scheme on other grounds. He knew that there would be opposition from Hindu and Muslim alike, but he was convinced that the enterprise was right and that, under God, Christianity would go forward in India, just as it had against heavy odds in the Roman Empire. In a letter to Grant dated 25 January 1786, in which he acknowledges the letter mentioned in the preamble to his revised appeal, Coke writes: 'As soon as the present extraordinary calls from America are answered, I trust we shall be able to turn our thoughts to Bengal.'

In the thirty years that elapsed between the publishing of Coke's first *Plan* in 1783 and the moment when he sailed for Ceylon in 1813 he had not been entirely idle. Not only had he established those missions in the West Indies and Sierra Leone that we have mentioned; he had also been acting as the more or less perpetual President of the Irish Conference, and had begun to organize the home mission. In addition, he had dealt with letters both from places where missionaries had been appointed, including Nova Scotia, New Brunswick and Newfoundland, and from many others urging him to include them on the stations. And some energy had been expended on abortive attempts in places that had appeared to promise good prospects of success. So, when the Conference of 1808 re-opened work at Gibraltar by sending William Griffith, it was with memories of what had happened there four years earlier. The McMullens and their young daughter had arrived at the Rock in

[11] On their way to Ceylon they spent a month at Bombay, the Harvards remaining rather longer. During that period they were not idle, and as a result a request was made that a missionary be sent to Bombay.

September 1804, only to find the population in the grip of a disastrous epidemic of yellow fever. Like malaria, this disease is also transmitted by a mosquito *aëdes aegypti*, though at the time it too was thought to be caused by 'tainted air'. The child went down with it immediately. In October the parents died. Astonishingly their daughter recovered and returned to England to be cared for in the home of Adam Clarke. Later she was to marry the Rev. John Rigg and became the mother of Dr J. H. Rigg, a famous principal of the Westminster Teacher Training College.

The Conference of 1813, meeting in Liverpool, gave Coke the long-sought permission to begin work in Ceylon, and provided a young team of six men, two with their wives, to go with him. Characteristically, he lost no time in getting off the mark once the decision had been taken: he went straight back to London to find a ship. None was going to Ceylon. Then they must reach Bombay and re-embark to complete their journey in another vessel. Even so, there was no ship with enough berths available for all nine to travel together. So Coke, with Clough and the Harvards, sailed on 29 December in the *Cabalva*, while Lynch, Erskine, Squance and the Aults joined the *Lady Melville*. At sea there was some danger of attack from the French fleet, which had recovered from its defeat at Trafalgar, so the English ships sailed in convoy. 'The sight of such a floating city is very agreeable; and were it not that the lagging ships, which must be frequently waited for, lengthen out the voyage, would be peculiarly desirable.' When they were completely becalmed they were at least safe, and boats would pass from ship to ship.

In his study cabin, Coke single-mindedly employed himself 'in reading and writing Portuguese, excepting my hours of meditation, which, indeed, I can hardly except; for my chief study is my Portuguese Bible'. Ever since Ceylon had been visited in 1505 by the Portuguese, and even more when it had been assigned to them in the famous bull of Pope Alexander VI, their cultural influence there had been extensive. So Coke translated some fifty hymns into the language, wrote new ones, and prepared sermons and prayers in Portuguese for use when they arrived. All seemed to be going well.

Then, winter gales in the Bay of Biscay smashed some of the ships and some were 'more or less dismasted'. One after another they were lost in the storm. The crews of battered vessels fired distress guns but the tempest made it impossible to reach them. Even on ships that were still seaworthy, sailors were swept from their posts in the rigging and were killed by falling on deck or lost overboard. Through all this, Mrs Ault had become so weak from tuberculosis that her only hope was thought to be in reaching tropical sunshine – although she remained 'quite happy and resigned, always pleasant and cheerful'. On 10 February she died. Unable to join the *Lady Melville* for the awesome ceremony of burial at sea, Coke knew what was happening by watching the ship's flag. It was flown at half-mast when Mrs Ault died, and raised topmast high when they began to read the lesson: I Corinthians 15. Every other ship in the convoy repeated the signals.

The next time they were all becalmed, the younger men, Harvard and Clough, went over to visit Ault. Coke, who was now sixty-seven, felt that climbing rope ladders into little boats tossed by the Atlantic swell was more than he could face. 'I am so old, that I dare not venture up and down the sides of ships but as little as possible.'

Coke's *Journal* as printed in the January number of the *Methodist Magazine*, 1815, comes to an abrupt end, for a warship was able to take away correspondence for England and he sent what he had written. The story is taken up by letters that stunned the Church at home. Coke had been found dead in his cabin. Three weeks sailing from Bombay, just north-east of the Seychelles, the little band had lost their leader. Their bewilderment and shock still come through the account of how they shared the news and cared for one another in their desolation.

Among Coke's papers there was nothing authorizing them to become his successors or to draw money for their support, but Captain Birch introduced Harvard, who had been chosen by his colleagues to represent them, to Thomas Money and other merchants in Bombay. Coke had been bearing a letter of introduction to Money, and this, with the Captain's assurances, released the financial resources they needed. Birch, who also presented Harvard to the Governor, had formed a tremendous respect and affection for Coke, and this stood the young men in good stead during those first vital days in India. A new charter might have been granted by Parliament, in a more tolerant vein than its predecessor, but it takes time to alter the attitude of a community that is touchy about its privileges and its profits. The six wrote of Birch in their joint *Letter* to the Committee:

> He felt as a tender friend for us all . . . He ever partook of our feelings, and always assured us that we had not so much to fear as he thought we dreaded. His report of us to his Excellency the governor, to Mr Money, and many other gentlemen, before an unfair statement of our case could circulate, prevented troubles, expenses, and afflictions, which otherwise we must have fallen into.

All this goodwill reached further than Bombay. Money and some of his friends who shared his concern for the welfare of the missionaries wrote letters to Ceylon to prepare their way. When the party, who had left the Harvards behind in Bombay for a while, finally reached their destination on 29 June, to their surprise they were met by a formidable group of people, including the Governor and Lord and Lady

Molesworth, who were in a position to give them considerable help. Government House was their home until they were able to find accommodation. The main church at Galle was put at their disposal for services.

In the same spirit that would certainly have animated Coke, they began work immediately; and they were not content to confine themselves to their own kith and kin. The authorities suggested various places where their ministry was needed, and where schools, supported by government grants, could be founded. From these, after prayer and consultation, they selected six: three in the Sinhalese-speaking south and three in the north, where the language was Tamil. The appointments were made by ballot. Lynch, Squance (ill with consumption: 'there is now little hope of his recovery'), and Ault were to go north; to the south went Clough, Erskine and Harvard (who took up his work at Colombo in March 1815, and mastered Sinhalese and Portuguese so that before the end of the year he was fluent enough to preach in them). The Methodist Church in Ceylon had been planted.

By going to Asia, Coke at once increased the financial and staffing liability of the Society and removed its sole recruiting and fund-raising agent. Incredibly, for years he had done all that is now done by the Home Organization Department, in addition to being its sole collector in the circuits and being responsible for finding, selecting and sending out candidates. With his departure an entirely new era began. The Church was compelled to find completely different ways of attracting men and money.

Providentially the right man appeared. Jabez Bunting was then stationed in Leeds. On 6 October 1813, between the Conference which in July had agreed that Coke should be sent to Asia, and the day, just after Christmas, when he sailed, the first Methodist Missionary meeting was held in the Old Chapel at Leeds, known then as the Boggard House. The idea was first mooted by George Morley, superintendent of the Leeds Circuit, which already had a tradition of supporting mission work; but the design and subsequent development owed all to Bunting's organization and judgement.

Bunting was to transform the Missionary Society, drawing from Methodist thrift and sobriety the financial means of expansion. His 'first master-stroke of policy', as Thomas Jackson recalled it in the *Methodist Magazine* for October 1863, was to find the right chairman, so disarming 'censure in some high quarters where it was most likely to be severe'. 'Few men of leading influence in the Connexion would like to come into collision with a man whose reputation stood so high as that of "Banker Thompson", who so honourably represented Methodism in the House of Commons.' He also invited widely-known and well-loved senior ministers to move and second no fewer than eighteen resolutions (though not all were to be spoken to) so as to enlist the sympathies of a large body of men in behalf of the missionary cause, and publicly to pledge them as its supporters.

Not only was this the first Methodist Missionary meeting; it was the first public meeting of any kind, other than those for worship, prayer, Bible study or testimony, ever to be held by Methodists. Some of those who took part in that gathering were full of trepidation, their nervousness arising from their inexperience in speaking at such an assembly. When the example was followed by the Halifax, York, Sheffield, Cornwall and Newcastle Districts, there were those who were apprehensive on quite different grounds. In his biography of Robert Newton, written from Richmond College over forty years later, Thomas Jackson pointed out:

> . . . many were the searchings of heart which these proceedings excited. Some thought that public meetings might generate a spirit of unhallowed levity, which would be highly injurious to the cause of spiritual religion. Others thought that such publicity would be given to foreign missions, and such an interest in their favour created, that they would be supported at the expense of every other Christian object. In these circumstances timid men were afraid to speak, and afraid to act.

There were three outstanding men, at that time all stationed in Yorkshire, who certainly were not too scared to get into this fight. Foremost among them, of course, was Jabez Bunting himself, who not only organized that meeting in the Leeds Old Chapel but used it to launch the first District Missionary Society. By 1833, as leader of a team of 'Resident Secretaries for our Missions', he had been given overall responsibility for the work overseas.[12] In the following year, when the Wesleyan Theological Institution was founded, he was 'appointed to the office of President of the Institution, under such arrangements as may render his acceptance of that office convenient to himself, and compatible with the retention of his present situation as Senior Secretary of the Wesleyan Missionary Society'. Such a double appointment was unique, and the power that Bunting was able to wield, enhanced by his being from time to time elected either President or Secretary of the Conference, was undisputed. He brought to his advocacy of missions that same force and clarity which were characteristic of all his sermons and speeches. His powerful style rejected all embroidery, giving the impression of a balanced whole, broad in conception, relentless in

[12] His colleagues in this work were John Beecham and Robert Alder. Elijah Hoole, who soon was to become one of the secretaries, was 'Agent of our Missionary Committee for the Irish Schools'.

concentration on the truth as he knew it. 'He stood erect, and scarcely ever deviated from this attitude . . . No gesticulation was allowed of any description, and almost the only motion observable was that of the head, and the wonderful glance of his piercing eye.'

If Bunting could have pointed to no other outcome of the Leeds District meeting, he could at least have taken credit for bringing Richard Watson's outstanding talents into wider notice. For a while Watson had been out of the ministry, and he had only recently returned to it. He distinguished himself by a memorable sermon on Ezekiel's vision of the Valley of the Dry Bones which ensured his appointment three years later as what would now be called the Home Organization Secretary of the Missionary Society. Perhaps more than anyone else he was the man who took up the torch that fell from Coke's hand. That, at any rate, is how his contemporaries saw him. Soon after he had been moved from Hull to the Mission House, charges against Wesleyan activity in the Caribbean area drew from him *A Defence of the Wesleyan Methodist Missions in the West Indies: including a Refutation of the Charges in Mr. Marryat's "Thoughts on the Abolition of the Slave Trade &c." and in Other Publications*, which was published in 1817. The work there was being hindered by the bitter struggle over the emancipation of the slaves. For instance, when in 1816 the slaves in Barbados rebelled, the planters in their panic, and perhaps not surprisingly, blamed those who had spread Christian teaching among the Negroes. Excessive and unjustified restrictions were imposed. Chapels were closed and missionaries were prohibited from preaching. Slaves were not allowed to meet for prayer, and their marriages were not recognized as legal. It seems probable that this situation was largely responsible for the famous *Instructions* which were issued to Wesleyan missionaries. Of these, the fifth was of cardinal importance. It warned missionaries 'against meddling with political parties or secular disputes', a line that would not win the unanimous support of missionaries or their subscribers today. The interpretation of that rule was always difficult, especially in an explosive situation like that of South Africa.

Without doubt, Richard Watson was the most distinguished Methodist author of the first half of the nineteenth century. In his *Institutes* he was the first to bring the theology of the Connexion into a coherent system. He wrote a *Life of Wesley* and a *Theological Dictionary*. He became notorious for his attacks on the slave-trade, and was always a formidable opponent in debate. When George IV read his reply to Southey's *Life of Wesley* he exclaimed, 'O my poor Poet Laureate!' Watson served as General Secretary of the Missionary Society from 1821 to 1825; was elected President of the Conference in 1826, and returned to the Mission House as General Secretary from 1832 until his early death the following year. Bunting had been his colleague there from 1821 to 1823, and when Watson died he returned to serve there until 1851.

If Watson brought wide scholarship and aesthetic sensitivity to his powerful missionary advocacy, Robert Newton with his strong sense of humour and his superb speaking voice was unquestionably the man of the people. His fine masculine style drew large crowds and he came to be regarded as the most effective champion of our missions. Like Bunting, he too was to become four times President: in 1824, 1832, 1840 and 1848; and he too was often elected to be Secretary, so that these two friends virtually controlled the Conference over a considerable period, despite increasing resentment.

Ministers moved quickly from circuit to circuit at that time. Although in 1813 Newton was stationed in Wakefield and so was readily available for the meeting in Leeds, only a year earlier he had been transferred from the bracing heights and brusque company of Holmfirth in the West Riding to the cheerful elegance of Hinde Street, 'where gentlemen and ladies, with their glittering equipages, and attended by liveried servants, were seen moving in all directions'.

It was Coke who set Newton on fire as a missionary advocate. Coke used to call on anyone who was likely to help forward his plans for evangelism overseas. In the coach which he used to hire at his own expense to save time and energy when making these calls, he was usually accompanied by a colleague in the ministry. During a year in London, Newton was often the one who went with him. This experience – together with Coke's determination to start work in Asia, his pleadings with the Conference, and his departure in his late sixties to Ceylon with six young colleagues – had an enormous influence on Newton and made him, to his life's end, a devoted and successful advocate of the missionary cause. Along with Bunting, Watson and that great scholar Adam Clarke, he was to form part of what was arguably the ablest and most effective team of speakers and administrators that the Missionary Society has ever known.

Their work contributed to the change whereby Methodism, from being an eighteenth-century Connexion of Societies, became a nineteenth-century Church. The primary concern was still salvation and holiness attained by the grace of God and maintained in the fellowship of like-minded members, but that other consuming passion of the earlier period, loving care for the unprivileged and the poor in Christ's name, was now related to the new age of machines and travel, industry and commerce, not only in Britain but increasingly overseas. It was a liberal and liberating process that drew men's minds away from concentration on their own affairs to those of people far away whom most of them would never see. The question, Who is my neighbour? took on a wider scope. Adam Clarke and Richard Watson, with Robert Newton to provide the lighter touch, were attuning Methodist teaching and missionary advocacy to the mood of the new England, which was rapidly turning from farms to factories, offices and shops.

To read the letters and journals of the missionaries of the 1820s alongside articles about the home Church published in the *Methodist Magazine* of that period is to be impressed by the coherent pattern which they all present. Not only was there a joy and fellowship about their religion that in part explains why they were willing to go into frightening situations; there was also a relentless logic and an uncompromising, almost ruthless, attachment to the truth as they saw it, which would not let them escape from the practical implications of their beliefs: Christ died for all. Many millions still do not know what God has done for their salvation; they will never know unless someone goes and tells them. I have had the inestimable privilege of hearing this news; I am well and strong and able to go; here am I, send me!

Their religion and their lives were one. To watch them at their work is to find theology coming alive and philanthropy springing from faith. It is also to see in action, a century-and-a-half ago, what many are now saying Christians should be doing in the community where they live. From the beginning, a great part of a missionary's time in this period was taken up in raising the whole standard of life among his people. This involved caring for their health by teaching hygiene and using preventive medicine, feeding their minds as well as their bodies, and imparting skills.

For the converts, too, religion and life came to be seen as one. Nowhere was this more true than in South Africa. The letter written by George Middlemiss from Cape Town in September 1807[13] was not the only appeal that had come from those barracks. Time after time, the most pacific of creeds, with the possible exception of Buddhism, has been introduced into new countries by military and naval men. This has been particularly true of Methodism. Sergeant Kendrick, of the Twenty-first Light Dragoons, carried on the work which had been started by Middlemiss. Kendrick had reached the Cape in 1806 as a soldier in the British army of occupation. He had been converted in Leeds during the ministry of that same George Morley who later was to be one of the prime movers in starting the auxiliary missionary society in that District.[14] Before leaving England, Kendrick had become a Class Leader and a Local Preacher and he gave what pastoral help he could to his fellow-soldiers. On 22 April 1912 he wrote from Cape Town to William Rudd of Woolwich, telling him that a previous society had broken up for various reasons, so that 'about June 1809 . . . four of the regiment to which I belong, and about three of the 93rd met for

[13] See p. 16, above.
[14] See p. 24, above.

the purpose of forming the Society afresh'. Kendrick was appointed leader. He reckoned that there were more than 60 in the Dragoons, more than 80 in the 83rd Regiment, about 18 in the Artillery and 14 in the 93rd, 'all of whom experience the love of God shed abroad in their hearts'. Ten of them were exhorters.

Kendrick soon realized that with all his professional duties there was more to be done than he could manage, and a full-time chaplain was needed. So, on 30 December 1812, he wrote to a friend a letter which Findlay and Holdsworth[15] rightly regarded as one of the historic documents of the Methodist Missionary Society. 'In the name of the Methodist Society at the Cape of Good Hope' he pleads their weakness and asks that their request for a preacher be 'laid before Dr Coke'. Kendrick died before he received a reply, but his request received the response he hoped for in the words of a terse resolution passed by the Conference of 1813:

> The Conference authorizes and appoints Dr Coke to undertake a Mission to Ceylon and Java, and allows him to take six Missionaries for that purpose, exclusive of one for the Cape of Good Hope.

John McKenny was the man sent. He arrived in Cape Town in 1814, intending to serve not only the soldiers there but also the Negro slaves. This would have been no small assignment. When slavery was abolished in British colonies during 1834, the estimated number of slaves in the region of Cape Town was almost forty thousand. But McKenny was not allowed even to begin. The Governor, Lord Charles Somerset, blocked the way by invoking a regulation, taken over from the Dutch, which empowered him to refuse anyone the right to hold religious services. There was an Anglican chaplain for the soldiers. The Dutch did not like the idea of any ministry to the slaves. McKenny was not needed.

Faced with this vigorous opposition, McKenny folded up. Writing from Cape Town to Francis Collins on 28 March 1815, he says that he has little satisfaction in sending news because he has nothing pleasant to tell:

> Notwithstanding there has been, ever since my arrival, a most delightful opportunity of preaching the word of life to many who desire to hear it; yet I have been obliged to be silent to the present, and must remain so until I hear from home.

When he did hear, it was to receive permission to leave South Africa only a few months after arriving there, and to join the others in Ceylon where there was opportunity enough to keep him busy. In 1816,

[15] G. G. Findlay & W. W. Holdsworth, *The History of the Wesleyan Methodist Missionary Society*, 5 vols. (London 1921–24), iv, 240.

however, the Conference sent Barnabas Shaw, and the date of his landing, 14 April, may be regarded as the true beginning of the Methodist mission to South Africa, a land in which the London Missionary Society and the Moravians were then the only Protestant missionaries. In the same year, John Henry Schmelen, of the London Missionary Society, visited Cape Town and told Barnabas Shaw about opportunities north of the Orange River in Great Namaqualand where he was serving. When he found Shaw anxious to fulfil that part of his commission which related to Africans living inland, he proposed that they should join forces. Barnabas hesitated on one ground only: Would it be right to take his wife to such a lonely, difficult and dangerous place? Jane's reply was simple and final: 'We will go with you,' she said to Schmelen, 'the Lord is opening our way to the heathen.' So the first Methodist thrust into the interior began.

A month of rough trekking by ox-wagon, in a general direction over rough country rather than following a road, brought them to the Olifants River. On the other side, as they were passing through the Karroo Desert, they met a party of Africans travelling south. They had come from Little Namaqualand on their way to ask that a Christian teacher would come and live with them. There could not have been a clearer call. While Schmelen returned to his station alone, Barnabas and Jane Shaw went with the seekers. Their new house at Lily Fountain was a hut without door, chimney or window; with neither chair nor stool; and where they slept on the floor. From there Barnabas wrote, in a vivid and moving style, a stream of letters which from June 1817 onwards were published in the *Methodist Magazine*. In that same month, June 1817, Shaw baptized the first two converts. For ten years he and Jane gave heroic service in Little Namaqualand; then in 1826 they returned to the Cape, where he died in 1857.

Into the pioneering situation opened up by Barnabas Shaw came the dynamic William Shaw (no relation). He was twenty-two, and a glance at his portrait shows a man of high intelligence, vigorous and alert. It is no surprise to find that forty-five years later in 1865, having returned to the home work in 1856, he was elected President of the Conference. With his courageous and imaginative leadership he was just the kind of man the young church needed in fluid conditions which were so full of potential and where everything depended on wise decisions promptly taken and firmly carried out. Within a few months of his arrival he was telling the Missionary Committee in London that Salem, where he was stationed, was the key to development along the coastal plain. He had a vision of a chain of Wesleyan Mission Stations beginning near the border of the colony, and extending along the coast country of Kaffraria to Natal and Delagoa Bay. The map showing Circuits of the Methodist Church of South Africa which was published to mark the 150th anniversary of the beginning of the work is a complete vindication of his judgment. The main strength of South African Methodism today lies along that chain of stations from Port Elizabeth to Lourenço Marques, with considerable penetration inland, which William Shaw visualized soon after landing and subsequently helped to found. Later, at the time of the Kaffir War, he was to withstand the formidable Dr John Philip, who laid the blame on the Colonists; whereas Shaw was convinced that the fault lay with the Colonial Government and its unstable policy. While he was home on furlough in 1835 he appeared three times before the House of Commons Select Committee on Aborigines, to whom he was asked to give his views on this difficult situation. Sir George Cory, in *The Rise of South Africa* (London 1910–30), ii, 98, wrote:

> Of the honoured names among the 1820 settlers, it is doubtful whether there is one which is worthy of being held in greater veneration than that of the Rev. William Shaw.

Shaw had come to South Africa with those 1820 settlers at the expense of the Government. They would have provided him and his wife with special accommodation on the ship, but the couple insisted on sharing the same conditions as those to whom they ministered. The scheme made it possible for parties of not less than a hundred families who could agree to form a settlement to take with them a minister of whatever denomination they chose. Apparently the only group from any church to take advantage of this offer were the Methodists of the Queen Street Circuit in London, along with their friends from other circuits and some members of other denominations. William B. Boyce in his *Memoir of the Rev. William Shaw* (London 1874) tells how the manager[16] of the Queen Street party (later known as 'Sephton's Party') applied to the Missionary Committee for an ordained minister, but the request was refused. They then advertised on the cover of the *Methodist Magazine* 'and of course found that no respectable, accredited preacher would be willing to go out, unless duly sent and in connexion with the authorities of the Wesleyan body at home'. Several lay preachers answered the advertisement, among them William Shaw, who had been refused entry into the Methodist ministry in England because he was married.

Immediately there were difficulties. The first response of the Missionary Committee was distinctly cool, and the candidate himself sensed that some of the members thought 'that to send a young and inexperienced missionary with a Body of British settlers going to a new and untried country, would entail no small amount of trouble and

[16] A layman, Edward Wynne, who as it turned out was unable to sail with the party because of his wife's illness: the leadership passed to Hezekiah Sephton.

disappointment'. Shaw, who had preached his first sermon in the army, had become a schoolmaster and Local Preacher. He now felt called to offer for missionary service overseas and after being examined at what were then called the Quarterly and District Meetings, he was asked whether he had any 'encumbrance'. This was a delicate way of inquiring into his matrimonial prospects. William Shaw was encumbered. As Boyce puts it, 'having entered into a matrimonial engagement with Miss Ann Maw,' he 'stipulated that if sent abroad he should go as a married man, although willing to conform to the rule which very wisely enjoins a single life on all probationers labouring in England'.

Twenty-one years later, when Thomas Birch Freeman offered himself for a post in West Africa, he was told that he could not go unmarried and he had to look around somewhat urgently for a suitable mate. But the policy in 1817 was quite the reverse, and the President, John Gaulter, in the rather high-handed style that was perhaps not uncommon at that time, summarily decided against William Shaw's acceptance for work overseas on the terms that he had stated. There followed one of those chains of events which are individually fairly trivial, but which change the course of a man's life and so, in Shaw's case, that of many others too. He fully expected that although he had been rejected for missionary service he would be placed on the list of reserve for a home station, should a vacancy occur. No word came through, but he decided to wait until Christmas before taking action. No call to a circuit reached him. In reply to an inquiry the President declared that William Shaw's name was not on his list. 'Our fathers, with many excellences, were not all of them exact men of business,' is Boyce's comment. So arrangements went forward for the marriage. At the last moment a letter arrived from a minister asking him to fill a vacancy and saying that the appointment had the sanction of the President and the Secretary of the Missionary Committee. By a blunder on the part of a village postmaster it had been delayed ten days. If it had come even a little earlier, the marriage would have been deferred and William Shaw might have spent the whole of his ministry in home work; as it was, the marriage with Ann Maw took place on 30 December 1817.

William had just celebrated his nineteenth birthday. We may be willing to accept his biographer's *apologia* when he says that,

> the bridegroom, though young in years, was never, strictly speaking, *a young man*, and the bride was some years his senior. Both of them were prudent, steady Christians, constitutionally cheerful, yet with minds free from all the illusions of romance, looking forward complacently to a life of labour, supported by the sense of duty, and by the consciousness that whether that life was to be spent in the care

> of a school or in the more important labours of the Christian ministry, they would be working for Christ.

But the fact is that some of those who went to difficult and dangerous situations overseas seem to have been very young, and the hesitation of the Committee was more likely to have been on the ground that he had gone through with his marriage after receiving the call to a circuit, rather than of his immaturity.

The second impediment to his going to Africa two years later was in some ways even more formidable. It was raised by his mother-in-law. Before their marriage, Ann had enjoyed a full social life, often going to card parties and dances near her home in Lincolnshire. Life with William was quieter in that respect, but she had known all along about his desire to be a missionary if the way should open. Now she became the focus of an intense emotional conflict which only costly sacrifice could resolve. Her widowed mother put up a spirited opposition to their South African project and would not hear of her leaving the country. Torn between two loyalties, Ann was compelled to compromise. William wrote later:

> Our greatest trouble was that the only condition on which the aged Mrs Maw would consent to part with her daughter was that we should leave our first-born child, then an infant, with her and his aunt, so that if we 'perished in the sea, or in the deserts of Africa', they might at least have this relic of a lost family remaining, to whom they might show kindness and love for our sake.

Something of the cost is revealed by William's restrained comment: 'Whether it was right for them to ask, or for us to consent to such a sacrifice, will be differently viewed by different minds.' The book has yet to be written that will tell us what view was taken by such *children*.

Such was the situation confronting the Missionary Committee in 1819 when William Shaw, not yet twenty-one and already married, offered to be their missionary in South Africa. It seems to have been the advice and advocacy of George Morley,[17] who had become the superintendent of the Queen Street Circuit, that finally persuaded them to agree.

The appointment gave him a unique position. When Barnabas Shaw had arrived at the Cape in 1816, he had found an established community in which the Dutch were served by their *predikants* and the English soldiers by their chaplains. It did not seem to have occurred to anyone to provide ministers for the slaves. The missionaries of the Moravians, and later those of the London Missionary Society, had served the Bantu people well inland; later still, they were joined by workers of the

[17] For Morley, see pp. 24, 28, above.

Glasgow Missionary Society. The Dutch Reformed Church was not without a sense of missionary vocation, but it drew a clear distinction between a *predikant*, who is a pastor in the home church, and the *zendeling*, the missionary, who is given inferior status. William Threlfall, in a letter to his colleagues at Delagoa Bay, said that Barnabas Shaw was on a good footing with the Boers and that they respected him as a missionary, but did not think him a proper person to baptize their children. 'We met a Boer going to the Cape from the Camies Bergen with his children that they might be baptized by a *Predikant* (at least a distance of 400 miles).'

The status of William Shaw was quite different. He came in a dual capacity. Ordained[18] and Received into Full Connexion with the British Methodist Conference, and appointed as chaplain to Sephton's Party of Settlers, in the eyes of the Boers he was a *predikant*: at the same time he was also a *zendeling*, designated by the Missionary Committee as a missionary, acting under their authority and commissioned in their service. According to Methodist discipline, of course, this was the only way in which he could appear on the Stations if he were to accompany the settlers as their chaplain. It placed him in a very strong position. The enhanced prestige of being accorded by the Dutch the position of *predikant* was a minor advantage compared with the fact that since he united in his person the two functions of chaplain to Europeans and missionary to Africans, these two sides of the Church's work were seen to be one. We find him writing of a meeting in 1822:

> One thing that contributed to make it more than ordinarily interesting was the presence of several of our Hottentot Society, who spoke with considerable propriety and feeling of the work of God in their souls. Mr Barker, who favoured us with his presence on this occasion also, was requested to interpret, for the benefit of the English persons present, what was said by the Hottentots in Dutch. All of every class were much gratified and, I trust, edified on the occasion. For my own part, I cannot describe what I felt while sitting in the pulpit, and beholding before me Europeans and Africans in a mixed group, formerly too rare a sight in this colony – hearing them tell, each in his own tongue, the wonderful dealings of God towards them.

[18] At this period, men going abroad as missionaries were ordained by the laying-on of hands, so that they might celebrate the sacraments in the countries to which they were appointed. William Shaw was ordained, along with Titus Close, on 25 November 1819, in St George's Chapel in the East. Close was about to leave for Madras. Many of the Sephton's Party of settlers and their friends from the Greater London area were present (see *H.M.G.B.*, ii, 153–4, esp. 154, n. 31). 'It was a solemn service,' wrote William Shaw. 'I had never witnessed a Wesleyan Ordination, and scarcely knew what was expected from me on the occasion. When called upon, however, I spoke in the simplicity of my heart, reciting an outline of the circumstances connected with my early conversion to God, and the reasons which induced me to believe that I was moved by the Holy Ghost "to take upon me the office, duties, and responsibilities of a Christian Missionary".'

Apostolic words to describe a Pentecostal event these may be, but they also emphasize that the men sent to the Albany District were completely identified with both groups in the community – colonists and Africans – and that they were evangelists and pastors, missionaries and ministers, to both. In the District Meeting the work of the church in all its aspects was viewed as a whole. This had another, unforeseen advantage. What was ecclesiastically convenient was not only theologically sound but also politically effective. William Shaw and the colleagues who joined him later were deeply involved in the local affairs of the Colony and those parts of the interior which were their mission field. By their regular visits to that chain of stations which came into being as a product of William Shaw's vision and energy, they gained an unrivalled knowledge of African life and customs. As a result, the letters they and many other missionaries in other countries wrote home have proved to be mines of information for historians and anthropologists. But at the time their special knowledge, arising from their close contact with the people, was often of immense practical importance. So, in South Africa, when crises arose as in the clash between the colonists and the Xhosa between 1820 and 1840, Wesleyan missionaries held a uniquely impartial position. It was because William Shaw was the acknowledged leader of a team of such men that he was able to exert the moral authority which earned Sir George Cory's admiration.[19]

'That chain of stations' came into being because William Shaw always regarded Salem, the English settlement where he and the settlers with him began in 1820 at ground level, simply as a stage towards a Kaffir mission. Within a few months of arriving in the country he wrote in 1820 from Salem to the Missionary Committee:

> This station will be the key to Kaffirland, a country abounding with heathen inhabitants. Certainly the present is not the time for penetrating that country; but I hope the present turbulent spirit of that people will soon begin to subside, and then I should wish to see a Wesleyan Missionary ready to take advantage of the opportunity to enter and proclaim upon their mountains 'good tidings, and to publish peace and salvation'.

Towards the end of 1823 it looked as though they could begin to build the chain of stations that William Shaw had envisaged from the border of the Colony along the coast country of Kaffraria to Natal and Delagoa Bay. We have seen that Ann was a woman of courage and strong character; now she was to take part in an incident that has inspired the South African Church ever since. Barnabas Shaw wrote on 10 July 1823 saying that the moment had come for William to put his plan into action. There would still be a minister and a number of Local

[19] See p. 31, above.

Preachers to look after the settlers. The members at Graham's Town were feeling strong enough to build a chapel.

When they almost finished loading the wagons to set out, news came through that the Kaffirs had made frightful raids on the frontier farms. Their friends urged them to stay. Nothing could be done for such a warlike people. They would be robbed and murdered. The Missionary Committee might not be able to send a replacement for a long time. 'I cannot say that these suggestions and remonstrations produced no effect on me,' William wrote; 'I felt my mind burdened and oppressed with a load of care and anxiety.' William's wife matched his own devotion and would not let him turn back.

As we look back over the first half-century of Methodist world mission, we find rapid and confident growth, dominated at first by the vision and courageous initiative of one man, Dr Coke. Towards the close of the period, the great burst of activity in our oldest missionary area,[20] the West Indies, continued. Talboys opened a station in British Guiana in 1815; Brown and Catts began in Haiti in 1817, and Raynar in the same year in Tobago; Wilkinson entered British Honduras in 1825. Developments in West Africa saw Morgan opening up in the Gambia in 1821 and Dunwell on Cape Coast during 1835. In Asia, Hoole was appointed to Mysore in 1821. Further afield, Leigh went to New South Wales in 1815; and after a preliminary visit to New Zealand three years later, he was transferred to work there in 1822. Horton arrived in Tasmania in 1821, following upon a forced visit by Carvosso during his journey to New South Wales a year earlier. Western Australia had to wait until 1839 for its first missionary, Smithies; but Tonga had been reached in 1822 by the Lawrys, whose brief stay was followed by the establishment of Thomas and Hutchinson there in 1825. Fiji received Cross and Cargill from Tonga ten years later, in 1835.

As we have seen, it would be quite wrong to suppose that the whole of this swift outreach was initiated by missionaries sent officially from Britain. Time after time, it was laymen emigrating or serving abroad who began a movement which soon developed to the point where it needed the full-time care of a trained minister; though, almost to the end of the period, any preparation that was given was what we would now describe as in-service training. We have already seen how Sergeant Kendrick appealed to Coke from South Africa for a chaplain to serve the many soldiers who were already meeting in class, and how, even earlier, Nathaniel Gilbert and John Baxter began the work in Antigua. That process, with many variants, was reproduced in other countries. A few English Methodists resident in Madras round about 1816 began meeting for prayer and fellowship. Sometimes they read Wesley's

[20] See p. 10, above.

sermons. When they heard about the arrival of Coke's team of missionaries in Ceylon, they asked that one might be spared for the mainland. Lynch was sent to them, and so the great development in South India began. Some 20,000 free settlers and deported convicts in New South Wales were for many years served, as regards religion and pastoral care, by a few chaplains and teachers, sent in the main to look after the officers of the establishment and their families. Two of the teachers were Methodists who were so shocked at the degraded level of society around them that they wrote home urgently pleading for a Wesleyan missionary to be sent to Australia. The picture they painted was forceful, and the home Church responded with a splendid appointment: Samuel Leigh arrived at Sydney on 10 August 1815. Here he made his headquarters, and from that base he moved around a vast circuit, establishing outstations which later themselves became important circuit centres. So, in spite of initial difficulties with the Governor, he laid the foundations of what became the great Methodist Church in Australia. In 1818, Samuel Marsden, an Anglican clergyman in Sydney, and Samuel Leigh visited New Zealand. They saw enough of the need among the aboriginals for Leigh to launch a special appeal during his furlough in England; and when he embarked, with the wife who shared in his arduous work and journeys, on 18 April 1821, he returned to found a Wesleyan mission in New Zealand with the backing of the Conference.

Keeping pace with this rapid growth overseas was an equally significant development of the supporting organization at home. The *Methodist Magazine* for June 1825, in a synopsis of the Society's Anniversary report, proclaimed the spread of Missionary Associations:

> By this means information on the moral condition of the world, and the state of the work of God in foreign lands, has been very widely diffused; and from these minor streams a large confluence of contributions poured itself into the general fund . . . To accomplish fully the vast, and in many parts the yet unattempted work which lies before us, the whole church of CHRIST must be roused to take its equal share of labour and sacrifice; nor have any means more efficient as yet been pointed out to us, by the leadings of divine Providence, than those which, in every instance, have been so successful – the calling together of the friends of CHRIST in public Assemblies, to lay before them the condition of mankind, to point out the signs of the times, to exhibit actual success as incitements to exertions more commensurate with the case, and to engage their systematic co-operation, in counsel, in prayers, and in liberalities.

Clearly there is an element of propaganda here: the more lethargic places could 'emulate the ardour and liberality of those churches placed nearer to the sources of religious intelligence'. The report also demonstrates two important and persistent characteristics of the Society: the economy with which the Connexional system operates in raising large funds, and the value, as an instrument of adult education, of well-organized and well-informed committees and public meetings.

It took time to build what was later called the Home Organization Department – a system that was far more than a machine for collecting money, though that was done with astonishing efficiency. The Church had to be educated about its responsibilities towards 'the deplorable condition of many nations of the earth yet destitute of evangelical light and privileges'. The sheer geographical and anthropological facts were hardly known to anyone at the beginning of the nineteenth century. Expedition after expedition went out from Britain to look for the source of the great River Niger. At the General Meeting held in the Exeter Hall, London, on 30 April 1838, the Rev. John Hawtrey spoke of the ignorance of other countries which then prevailed:

> Though the combined forces of the great Captain of our salvation have been called into this field of labour and of contest against the powers of darkness, comparatively little ... has, up to the present time, been done. We have yet but approached the confines of the enemy's territory. It is but little we know of the interior of Africa; it is little we know of the empire of China; it is little we know of even our own immense colonial possessions in the eastern world.

In our own time, historians and anthropologists have discovered the rich mine of information buried in the archives of our missionary societies. At their best, the missionary pioneers, men and women, knew and understood the people, identifying themselves with them, in a way that few traders or government officials (in many places the only other categories of British residents) could ever do. Certainly they had their ear to the ground and were able to write home with fewer inhibitions than those who were making official reports.

Another gradual aspect of teaching the home Church about its overseas evangelical obligation was to provide the corpus of missionary hymns which became so prominent and effective a feature of public meetings arranged by the societies. Some had already been written by the beginning of the first half-century, in 1786. These included 'The Lord will come, and not be slow', by John Milton; 'The heavens declare Thy glory, Lord', and 'Jesus shall reign where'er the sun', by Isaac Watts; and Henry More's 'On all the earth Thy Spirit shower'. John Wesley himself had contributed 'Eternal Son, eternal Love', and Charles such well-known favourites as 'See how great a flame aspires', and 'Head of Thy Church, whose Spirit fills'. The hymn by Charles Wesley which has stood first in every major collection of hymns published for

Methodists, 'O for a thousand tongues to sing', is far more world-wide in outlook as it was first printed than it is in *The Methodist Hymn-Book* of 1933. Before verse six of the 1933 version, 'See all your sins on Jesus laid', was one which completely changes the merely personal application. It read:

> Look unto him, ye nations, own
> Your God, ye fallen race;
> Look, and be saved through faith alone,
> Be justified by grace.

By the end of our period, 1838, Benjamin Rhodes had written 'My heart and voice I raise'; Jonathan Friedrich Bahnmaier's 'Spread, O spread, thou mighty word' was waiting to be translated by Catherine Winkworth, and two of the most popular of all – 'Thou whose almighty word' by John Marriott and 'From Greenland's icy mountains' by Bishop Heber – were becoming known.

Still to come were rafter-splitters like Priscilla Jane Owens's 'We have heard a joyful sound', emotive favourites like 'O Church of God, arise', by Annie Matheson, 'Christ for the world, we sing', by Samuel Wolcott, and Charles Edward Oakley's 'Hills of the North, rejoice'. To this group belongs Bishop Coxe's 'Saviour, sprinkle many nations' – altered in the 1933 *Methodist Hymn-Book* to 'Saviour, quicken many nations': surely the original, with its reference to the sprinkling of *one* nation by Moses at Sinai, is better. Similarly, most missionary hymns for children were written after 1838. It would be hard to overestimate the effect on recruitment for work overseas and support from the home base of Basil Mathews's 'Far round the world Thy children sing their song', Percy Dearmer's 'Remember all the people who live in far-off lands', or those gusty rousers, 'I think, when I read that sweet story of old', and 'When mothers of Salem', not to mention 'Hear the pennies dropping'.

The annual missionary meeting, when these hymns were given a vigorous rendering and powerful speeches were made, in a period which lacked the impact of radio and television, provided an immense impetus for the cause and often aroused tremendous enthusiasm. Behind the public façade there grew up a matching pyramid of committees from Conference, through district and circuit, to local church level, which provided a superb instrument of adult education and – in the original and inoffensive sense of the word – propaganda. If the vast sums of money raised by the Methodist Missionary Societies in subsequent years were gathered at a financial cost in terms of administrative and advertising expenses so low as to be the envy of all other charities in the country, this was because the Connexional system of voluntary workers – connected by personal links through committees to headquarters – opened channels of communication at the minimum of expense.

And the sums gathered were vast, especially when we allow for the comparative values of our money then and now. By 1840, the income from Contributions and Legacies was £90,182, though the accumulated deficit for 1838, 1839 and 1840 had risen to £42,939. The following year saw the total rise above £100,000 for the first time.

The 1840 figures are of interest, since for the first time they include the Christmas offerings given and collected by children and young people, though Juvenile Missionary Societies are on record as far back as 1816, the year in which the Methodist church in Colombo, the oldest in Asia, was built. As far as records tell, the first of these Societies was begun at Wesley's Chapel, City Road, London, in May 1816. A manual of rules was published: the object of the Society was to raise subscriptions in aid of the missionary work first established by the late Rev. J. Wesley and the late Rev. Dr Coke and others. All collectors were to be under thirty years of age. A meeting was arranged for the third Tuesday in every month, when collectors were to hand in their money. Other churches in the London East Circuit were approached and invited to form branches of the J.M.S. On the third Friday of each month, the weekly Prayer Meeting was to be for missionary work, and extracts from the 'Missionary Notices' and letters from missionaries were read. The same year saw similar societies springing up in Leeds, Hull, Halifax and Kingswood School.

The Juvenile Christmas Offerings, begun in 1840 as part of the attack on the growing debt, and successful from the start with a total of £4,721 7*s.* 4*d.*, from then onwards have a special place in each year's report. In 1841, Joseph Blake, a Methodist shoemaker at Harrow-on-the-Hill, encouraged children to collect small sums weekly. Half the total raised was to be used overseas, and half at home. With the entry in the Report under Harrow for that year there is the modest item: Juvenile Books, £6 2*s.* 5*d.* Eastcote and Pinner in the same circuit made a similar contribution of £2 0*s.* 0*d.* So began the Blake System, which later was taken up with the Christmas Offerings into the Juvenile Missionary Association, which made a magnificent contribution to the Society's funds.

Even more important than the gifts they gathered, later to exceed £200,000 a year, was the educational value of the J.M.A. to the children. As early as 1844 the first magazine was published for them with the title *The Wesleyan Juvenile Offering*. In 1879 this was to be combined with *The Home Mission Record* in the more attractively named *At Home and Abroad*. By then, the Juvenile Collectors were raising more than £30,000, and many missionaries abroad and devoted workers at home had heard their call to service through the J.M.A. and those missionary sessions which became a memorable part of Sunday School life.

It was towards the end of April or the beginning of May each year, at the Annual General Meeting of the Wesleyan Methodist Missionary Society, that the Church was given an account of activities undertaken and accomplished abroad and financial affairs at home. These gatherings were the culmination of a series of meetings and services held during the preceding days and they were in themselves great fund-raisers. Those who packed the Exeter Hall for such gatherings looked forward to the moment when Dr Bunting announced: 'Dr Newton and the Collection'. In 1838, for example, there was a deficit, and the bogy of retrenchment, so often to raise its head in the future, menaced the work. By the end of Dr Newton's second sentence there was 'cheering from all parts of the Meeting', and money was being handed to him on the platform.

The same note had been struck at the very beginning of that meeting by the Chairman, a member of the Church of England and a Member of Parliament, John Hardy. He was standing in for another Anglican, J. P. Plumptre, 'the excellent and highly respected Member for East Kent', who was at the funeral of his eighteen-year-old daughter. Hardy began by recalling words often quoted at a time when the average expectation of life was far lower than it is now, and when many illnesses were nursed at home: 'in the midst of life we are in death'. He went on to ask 'this immense assemblage', 'Be ye also ready?' and explained that he meant, 'ready, not only in reference to the salvation of your own precious souls; be ready and alert to carry on your exertions for the salvation of the souls of those myriads who are daily, as unexpectedly as she whose loss we deplore, passing from this mortal world into a spiritual and eternal state of being'. He rejected all 'rumours of a "Stoppage of supplies" '.[21]

It has been mentioned in passing that the Chairman and the one who would have taken the chair had it not been for his family's bereavement were both Anglican laymen. The same was true of the deputy chairman, Henry Pownall, who took over when John Hardy had to leave; and the resolutions (on which the annual meetings of those days were based) were seconded by men like the Right Hon. Viscount Barnard and Viscount Sandon, who described himself as 'a devoted son, however unworthy, of the national Church of England'. The massive inter-denominational unity as regards evangelism abroad which characterized the period is seen also in the fact that the *Methodist Magazine* for 1838 carried not only a full account of the General Meeting of the Wesleyan Methodist Missionary Society, but lengthy reports on similar events organized by the Church Missionary Society, the British and Foreign Bible Society (the servant of the others and a notable meeting-ground for birds of the same Evangelical feather), the London Missionary

[21] He went on to make that distinction between evangelizing and colonizing which we have quoted earlier, p. 9, above.

Society and the Baptist Missionary Society, as well as the Religious Tract Society, the Sunday School Union and the Irish Evangelical Society.

Rapid missionary expansion was not a characteristic confined to Methodism, but was a common feature of all the main denominations of the Church in Britain during the period. It would appear that reaction to the militant atheism of the French Revolution not only gave an impetus to the spread of Methodism among the poorer classes, but by the new life it brought to the rapidly developing Wesleyan Societies it infused a fresh evangelical zeal into the Nonconformist bodies. An energetic though not very large evangelical group in the Church of England was in complete harmony with the movement. More concerned with the salvation of souls than with doctrines of church order, and numbering among their members some of the most influential laymen of the time, during the first four decades of the nineteenth century they exerted a powerful influence on the home government and the Colonial Office. It has been observed[22] that over many generations, large numbers of Britain's

> most vigorous children have been able to find an outlet for their energies in overseas trade, military adventure, colonial expansion and missionary service, yet all in such a way as to enrich rather than impoverish her domestic life since England remained large, metropolitan and attractive enough always to remain as 'home'.

How true that is in terms of the life of the Churches. It would be impossible to overvalue the feed-back into the home Churches of exciting news about Christian advance in ever new countries.

From 1818 onwards, the Secretaries of the various Societies met, at first quarterly and later monthly, for discussion on current problems and the exchange of news. This precursor of the Edinburgh House committees of the Conference of British Missionary Societies was first held regularly at Church Missionary Society House, and later in the different missionary headquarters in turn. Later in the nineteenth century this united wave of evangelical effort had in some measure receded, but it has never been completely damped down and, along with biblical scholarship, it has been an area of real church unity in spite of 'our unhappy divisions'.

Whatever may have accrued by way of organization and finance from all the eloquence and activity we have surveyed, no one lost sight of what it was all about. At the heart of this, the most effective era of Christian missions, was the firm conviction that the destiny of mankind is to live in the presence of God as his partner. There was an acute sense, not only of the dereliction, but also of the unnecessary

[22] By Daniel Jenkins, *The British: Their Identity and Their Religion* (London 1975), p. 60.

deprivation of their natural birthright, suffered by those who were regarded as living and dying in darkness.

The missionary impulse sprang from the belief that the conversion of the world was an important part of the purpose of God. As early as 1744, in his last sermon preached before the University of Oxford, on Scriptural Christianity, John Wesley had shown how this began in the individual soul, spread from one to another, and then became victorious, covering the earth. The belief of many was that the Son would glorify the Father when the lost sheep, his own for ages lost, should be brought home; and the lost sheep were the people of all nations – Red Indians, East Indians, Tartars, those who lived in 'the heathen parts of the Russias, and the inhabitants of Norway, Finland, and Lapland'. More distant nations, and inaccessible islands were to be reached, 'all Israel too shall be saved', and the victory of Christ would be complete.

This was an out-going, world-minded vision. As Charles Wesley expressed it:

> O for a trumpet voice,
> On all the world to call!
> To bid their hearts rejoice
> In Him who died for all;
> For all my Lord was crucified,
> For all, for all my Saviour died.

2. Years of Grace: 1838–1885

The year 1838, the centenary of the conversion of the Wesleys, was indeed a year of grace. Thomas Birch Freeman, perhaps the most famous Methodist West African missionary, arrived on 3 January, while on 28 April John and Hannah Hunt embarked at Gravesend for their eight-month journey to Fiji. The normal tour to those islands in their day was of twenty years' duration, and though John died when they were only half-way through their stint, in those ten years he had made a superb contribution to the tiny church there, so that even in recent years when a visitor to Suva mentioned his name the immediate reply was, 'The man who gave us our Bible'.

The Hunts left when Methodism was on the eve of celebrating the centenary of the founding of its first Societies and the nation was preparing for the coronation of the Queen. Membership of the Methodist Societies had increased steadily during the previous eight years; chapels and schools had sprung up all over the country, and the funds of the Connexion had never been in a more healthy state. A special Centenary Fund of at least eighty thousand pounds was to be raised, for two main purposes:

1. In the First Place, – To the erection and preparation of suitable premises for the accommodation of those Students who, after satisfactory evidence obtained by the Conference, as heretofore, of their sound conversion to God, their solid piety, and their divine call to the Christian ministry, shall be received into the *Wesleyan Theological Institution*, whether such students be designed for Home or for Missionary Service:

2. In the Second Place, – To the provision of commodious premises in London for the use of the Wesleyan Missionary Society, adequate to the greatly augmented and augmenting extent of its multifarious and important business.

Amongst further purposes for the fund, the Centenary Committee resolved to provide,

a WESLEYAN MISSIONARY SHIP, for the purpose of forwarding Missionaries and Missionary stores, as may from time to time be found necessary and expedient, from New South Wales and Van Diemen's Land to our Mission-Stations in New-Zealand, in the Friendly Islands, in the Feejee Islands, and in other Polynesian groups; – such a ship being exceedingly wanted, both for the comfort of the Missionaries labouring in those islands, and for the general advantage and security of the Missions themselves.

The scheme was first made public at the Conference of 1838, meeting in July at Bristol. By November of that year, £47,000 had already been received or promised. In the end, the total raised was £222,589 – 'beyond the most sanguine expectations that its friends had indulged'.[23] Few protests were heard against the raising of this fund, which had such obvious value for the growing Church, and which by its very success brought encouragement and new vigour to the Societies; but there was one critical voice. It was that of William Martin, the eccentric Newcastle inventor, brother of John who in his day was one of London's most popular painters, and of Jonathan, the lunatic Methodist who on 21 February 1829 had set fire to York Minster. 'They are turning very rich in worldly store,' wrote William of the Societies, 'they have now a great deal of pride among them, which they endeavour to hide by the cloak of religion.'

Although there were some who were uneasy about the first objective of the fund, the provision of suitable premises for training ministers did not arouse the definite and sometimes bitter opposition which had been faced by those who, a few years earlier, had proposed that such an institution should be established.

By 1838, the quality of the first students, and the advantages to the

[23] Cf. *H.M.G.B.*, ii, 22.

Church of their training, were beginning to be recognized, and it was possible to use more than £70,000 from the Centenary Fund for building a Theological Institution in two branches: one at Didsbury, Manchester, and one at Richmond, Surrey.

The second claim upon the Centenary Fund was 'the provision of commodious premises in London for the use of the Wesleyan Missionary Society'. The Society had first occupied an office at 4 City Road, not far from Wesley's Chapel. Then premises at 77 Hatton Garden were bought. By 1838, that house had become inadequate as the home base of the Society, and another set of premises was bought with the grant of £30,000 received from the Centenary Fund; £15,000 being the price of the premises, and the other £15,000 the cost of adapting them for their new purpose. Number 24 Bishopsgate had housed the City of London Tavern, 'a very beautiful mercantile residence, which was since the Fire of London, built for Sir Roger Hudson, by Sir Christopher Wren'. The Wesleyan Centenary Hall, as it came to be known, was not a bad bargain at £15,000, even at the currency values of those days. In addition to the building itself, which had cost more than that sum to erect, the purchase included 'splendid pier and chimney glasses, chandeliers, several thousand ounces of plate, about 2,000 dozen of the finest Port, sherry, Madeira and other wines'. It became an extremely valuable asset, but those who were responsible for buying it did not escape the lash of the fly-sheet authors, any more than did those – largely the same people and predominantly Jabez Bunting – who spent money on the two branches of the Theological Institution. They were accused of 'tricking out Methodism as a thing to be admired by the world'.

For forty years the City of London Tavern, having had a face-lift that provided it with a new Corinthian-pillared façade, but with the minimum of internal reconstruction, served well as missionary headquarters. During that period it was the scene of many meetings. An annual sermon was preached by the President of the Conference in the Assembly Hall. From time to time sales of work were held there. Perhaps the most memorable of these took place in June 1851, when the newly converted members of Tonga and Fiji sent as a thank-offering many articles they had made themselves. These included 'temple clothes and mats, spears and clubs, shells and bowls, costumes, idols and musical instruments'. An engraving made at the time shows our Methodist ancestors in top hats and swallow-tail coats for the men, and the women in coal-scuttle bonnets, lace shawls and crinolines, crowding round the stalls. That they bought generously is clear from the financial success of the event.

But by the end of that period it was clear that once again the work had outgrown the accommodation which the building provided, and in addition the building had become costly to maintain. The next twenty years were spent in considering various schemes; in 1897 it was finally decided to move the Home Organization Department to premises near by, in Carlisle Avenue, off Aldgate. Work was begun on this scheme in 1900 and completed, at a total cost of around £76,000, by 1903. The whole amount was paid off in twenty-one years from rent received from the National Bank of India, to which some of the earlier building had been leased. Nearly forty years later, when the time came to move into yet larger premises, the proceeds of the sale of 24 Bishopsgate more than covered the cost of building a new Mission House in Marylebone.

The third main objective for which the Centenary Fund was raised – the Wesleyan Missionary ship – was also of immense benefit to the Society. It is hard for us to realize how isolated at this period were the men and women who went to the Antipodes. Some living on small islands on their own resources were from time to time reduced to at best real hardship, and at worst near-starvation. It was reported that one family was down to a single cracked cup when a boat came in. For those in Tonga and Fiji the journey from home could take at least eight months. Visits from English vessels were so infrequent that it could take anything up to two years or more to receive an answer to a letter sent to the family. When a ship did get through, the anxiety was immense. Will there be letters for me? The value to the missionaries of a ship that could make regular voyages, taking essential stores and returning with goods that could replenish the stalls at the next Mission House sale of work, was obvious. The first ship bought for the purpose was the *Triton*. It was purchased early in 1839 with a grant from the Centenary Fund, and immediately steps were taken to fit it out for its first voyage to the South Seas. An appeal went out, through the 'Missionary Notices' in the *Methodist Magazine*, for help in this costly project. There was a request for

> A PINNACE, – ready to be built on arrival at the Friendly Islands, to act as companion to the Missionary ship, for the purpose of visiting such shores and islands as may be inaccessible to large vessels, in consequence of the reefs and shallows which frequently obstruct navigation among the islands of the South Pacific.

There were requests, too, for ship's tackling, sea-stores ('such as are required for the comfort and support of seamen and passengers during a long voyage; and would also prove an acceptable supply to Missionary families, who have seldom an opportunity of obtaining European articles of food, and other comforts'), a tent, furniture ('including *earthenware*, *tinware*, and *ironmongery*. Many of the houses of the Missionaries are almost destitute of these articles; and it is desirable that, to as great an extent as possible, the use of them should be introduced among the converted natives'), clothing ('for men and boys, women and girls; including *blankets*, *flannels*, *prints*, *calicos*, *remnants*, *tapes*, *threads*, *buttons*, *etc*. Articles of clothing are in great demand among the Christian natives of the South-Sea Islands. They are very acceptable as rewards to those natives who perform valuable service to the Missionaries; and are among the most attractive articles which can be offered in return for the supplies of food and labour, for which the Missionaries are dependent on the natives'), medicine and surgical instruments ('these also are in great demand; and many of the Missionaries possess a sufficient knowledge of medicine and surgery to use them to great advantage'), bells ('for the use of Mission chapels and schools'), and stationery, etc. ('writing and printing paper, school-books, slates, pencils, maps, scripture and other prints, charts, compasses, etc.').

The response to this appeal was swift and generous. Not only was the *Triton* 'entirely freighted with stores and presents for the various Missions which she will visit', but the gifts exceeded the vessel's capacity and the overflow had to be sent on to Sydney by another ship, to be taken on by the *Triton* when she had discharged a part of her cargo. She sailed in September 1839 from Bristol, and the *Methodist Magazine* did not fail to point out that Richard Boardman and Joseph Pilmoor, described as 'the first Methodist Missionaries', had embarked for America from that same port seventy years earlier. On the evening of 4 September, ten days before the vessel actually left the basin, which in those days was right in the centre of the city, a valedictory service was held in St Philip's Chapel,

> on which occasion the Missionaries who were preparing for embarkation, in the presence of a crowded and deeply-interested congregation, gave an account of the motives which induced them to leave their friends and native-land, and to engage in Missionary work, and were then solemnly commended to God in prayer.

The President of the Conference, Theophilus Lessey, conducted the service. He and Jabez Bunting delivered 'suitable addresses to the Missionaries, of considerable length'. Apparently the crew were in complete sympathy with the passengers and the work to which they were going. As the writer of the article said, they

> are chiefly pious men, who have engaged in the service especially from love to the cause of Missions. A pleasing instance of their zeal occurred shortly after the vessel left the river. Thomas Ingledew, the Steward, brought a Missionary-box upon deck, and placing it on the binnacle, respectfully solicited subscriptions from those present for the Wesleyan Missionary Society.

These consisted of 'a select number of friends' who 'accompanied the

Triton for a considerable distance down the Channel'. Bunting baptized the captain's child, who had been born on board the previous day.

The earnings of the *Triton* were set aside year by year. 'A moderate sum, less than was previously paid for the occasional hire of vessels, was charged to the several Districts which were benefitted [*sic*] its services.' This money, along with the proceeds of sale of the *Triton*, enabled the Society to build and equip a new, larger and swifter vessel, seven years later. This ship was named the *John Wesley* and it sailed from Southampton on 21 November 1846. Both vessels, on their maiden missionary voyages, ran straight into foul weather and had to turn back for shelter. One of the missionary secretaries, John Beecham, conducted the first religious service on the *John Wesley* in the afternoon of Sunday, 15 November. The appointments of the missionaries who sailed on that first voyage were:

> Mr. and Mrs. Harris and child, with a female attendant, are to remain at Sydney. Mr. Kirk is for New-Zealand. Mr. Adams, who has spent three years as a student at the Richmond Branch of the Theological Institution, goes with his wife to the Friendly Islands. In the same District will be placed Mr. and Mrs. Daniel, Mr. and Mrs. Davis, and Mr. and Mrs. Amos. To Messrs. Daniel and Davis, who are acquainted with the art of printing, is confided the management of the press,[24] the operations of which have been suspended since the removal of Mr. Kevern[25] in consequence of the failure of his health, while Mr. Amos, who has had a thorough training in the Glasgow Normal Institution, with his wife who has also been accustomed to tuition, is designed for the school department of the work. Mr. and Mrs. Ford, with their two children, and Mr. and Mrs. Malvern and

[24] On this voyage a large proportion of the cargo was 'paper, to be used in the printing of translations of the sacred Scriptures and elementary books, in the dialects of New-Zealand, and the Polynesian Islands, where the Society's Missions are established'. It is hard to escape the conclusion that in the early days of missionary pioneering, when the small number of converts may not always have made heavy demands on a missionary's time in the way of pastoral care, he was freer to get on with the work of providing that Christian literature in the language of the people which became so valuable to his successors. Later on, many missionaries, realizing the urgent need for such literature – either new, or revised in the light of a better knowledge of the vernacular – were so pressed by other duties that they were unable to devote much of their energy to this work.

[25] George Kevern had sailed in that first missionary voyage of the *Triton*. So vulnerable, in the early days, was the work in many areas that it was often largely dependent on the health of one or two key people. The *Triton*, in September 1839, flew a banner with the inscription: 'The Wesleyan Missionary Society's Centenary Ship A.D. 1839', and below that the dying words of John Wesley: 'The best of all is, God is with us.' These words were also in the minds of those present on deck when John Beecham, before the launching of the *John Wesley*, preached that short address, 'more especially applicable to the officers and crew of the vessel, and several engaged in fervent prayer and supplication. It was a season of gracious influence; and the language of the hearts of most present was that of him whose name the vessel bears: "The best of all is, God is with us!"'

child are to proceed to Feejee. The medical skill of Mr. Harris will be especially valuable during the voyage, should sickness be permitted to occur.

The benefits of the Centenary Fund had come just at the right time to strengthen the work overseas. One of the most dramatic periods of missionary expansion in the whole history of the Church was about to begin. Our world is much changed from that of the great missionary half-century. Then, colonization and missionary expansion went hand in hand. Today the Church is no longer supported by the power position of Western society. The paternalist attitude has been rejected. Missionaries in India had a feeling of intense relief in 1947 when at last the British raj was ended and the Gospel could be offered in its own right without the support or hindrance of sheltering beneath the flag. At times the current attitude of our people works more against missionary involvement than in its support. The spiritual state of the Church in those countries which a century ago could properly be described as 'receiving' seems more healthy than at home, so that some are left wondering whether we have anything to offer. No such qualms afflicted Coke or Bunting, Freeman or Hunt. A hymn by Charles Wesley which was not included even in the famous 1779 edition of the Methodist Hymnbook sums up the attitude of those young people, fearless and capable of thinking on a large scale, who were willing to go, in the name of the Lord, whatever might be the consequences:

My God and Lord, Thy counsel show,
What wouldst Thou have Thy servant do
Before I hence depart?
How shall I serve Thy Church, and where?
The thing, the time, the means declare
And teach my listening heart.

Master, be Thou my might, my mouth,
And send me forth to North or South,
To farthest East or West;
Be Thou my guide to worlds unknown:
Rest to my flesh I covet none,
But give my spirit rest.

My rest on earth to toil for Thee,
My whole delight and business be
To minister Thy word;
For Thee immortal souls to win,
And make the wretched slaves of sin
The freemen of my Lord.

Perhaps one of the most profound differences between a Christian today and his counterpart a century ago is that he no longer lives in a relatively stable world. It is true that a society where basic values were shared and accepted, often with less pressure than some of our contemporaries seem able to believe, had its weaknesses and hypocrisies. But it was a world of clear-cut distinctions: right was right and wrong was wrong. Fundamentalist the average Methodist of the period may have been, but he had all the strengths of that position: he believed in God; he read his Bible; he said his prayers; and he gave liberally to the Cause.

Christians then were not a peculiar sub-culture, with a language totally incomprehensible to their workmates. Even though their motives and experiences were not always understood, they had not been pushed to the margins of society as we often seem to be today. The fact is that, while it could be claimed that the Victorian missionary went from a Christian to a non-Christian culture, he now goes from a predominantly secular society.

In two other ways there has been a major change. The first is the increased number of young people in further and higher education. This has meant that there are more educated minds among missionary candidates, at any rate in the academic sense, and that the age at which they offer is, on the whole, higher. William Shaw was 'proposed as a candidate for the foreign work' to the Conference of 1817 when he was nineteen years of age. We have also seen with what maturity of judgment and strength of character he took over his work in South Africa. The older, more academic, candidate of today may often be less experienced in some important areas of life than those young people of the past. In the second place, England in the period we are considering was rapidly changing from rural to urban life. From less than ten million in 1801, the population rose to thirty million a century later and at the half-way mark, in 1851, when the population approached twenty million, for the first time in our history as many of our people lived in towns as in villages.[26] The great majority of the early missionaries went from country life in England to country life overseas, and that was a great advantage to all concerned. It may well be that nearer our own time the biggest change that a missionary has had to face on taking up an appointment abroad, has been the townsman's difficulty in adjusting to the pace, point of view and rhythms of the village.

[26] The world's population is said to have doubled between 1830 and 1930: another thousand million had been added by 1960, and yet another thousand million by the year 1974. It is estimated that by A.D. 2000 the total will be over six thousand million. It is in the light of these figures that the Roman Catholic missionary policy for the coming decades has been formulated. Since the increases have, on the whole, been greater in the non-Christian communities than among Christians, the *proportion* of the world's population that is Christian is probably less than it *was before the great period of missionary expansion in the nineteenth century*.

The period under review, 1838–1885, opens with the full emancipation of the slaves in British West Indian territories (August 1838); covers the opening of China to foreigners, and therefore to Christian influences, by those treaties (passed in 1845) with certain European and American countries which sowed the seeds of later trouble; saw the handing over of responsibility for Methodist missionary work in Polynesia to the newly constituted independent Australasian Wesleyan Methodist Connexion (August 1854),[27] witnessed the grim events of the Indian Mutiny (1857) and the jubilant proclamation of Queen Victoria as Empress of that sub-continent only nineteen years later (1 January 1877); and heard Livingstone's memorable speech at Cambridge in 1858, which gave enormous impetus to missionary recruitment.

On the more domestic Methodist level, the period begins with one of the missionary secretaries, John Beecham, joining Coates, of the Church Missionary Society, in a vain battle to prevent the colonization of New Zealand (1838), and ends with Freeman preaching the Jubilee sermon commemorating fifty years of Methodism in what is now called Ghana (February 1885).

Of great significance was the minute of the General Committee, 13 October 1858:

> Resolved that the subject of Female Education in India is regarded by this Committee with lively interest. They rejoice in the help which has been afforded by many Ladies' Societies in London and elsewhere, and look favourably on the project for organizing those Societies more extensively for the promotion of Female Education in India and in other parts of the Mission Field.

WW, as the Women's Work section of the Missionary Society came to be affectionately called, was officially launched, though we have to go back to the summer of 1834 for the laying of the keel. What has been claimed as one of the most important afternoon teas in history had come to an end. The Rev. David Abeel, an American missionary on his way home from China, had been speaking. He had broken his journey in London to deliver a message from some Chinese women: 'Are there no female men who can come to teach us?' In response, the interdenominational Society for Promoting Female Education in the

[27] The Australian Connexion was established at the Conference in Birmingham, England, on 9 August 1854, and Australia held its first Conference in January of the following year. From the start it accepted full responsibility for New Zealand, the Friendly Islands (Tonga), and Fiji, though the Church in Britain continued to recruit candidates for that area. In February 1863, the *Methodist Magazine* carried the following statement under a report from the Wesleyan Missionary Society:

> FIJI
>
> Four Missionaries are requested for this successful Mission, who will be sent as soon as practicable. It would be a wise economy to send a larger number, so as to occupy the whole of the islands now willing to receive the Gospel.

East came into being, and under its wing a Methodist daughter of the manse, Mary Twiddy, sailed for Ceylon in 1840. Eighteen years later, the Rev. Dr Elijah Hoole, the senior Secretary at the Mission House, and his wife spent the evening with the lay treasurer of the Society, Thomas Farmer, Mrs Farmer, and their five daughters. They had met to discuss a letter received by a Miss Farmer from Mary Twiddy, by then married to the Rev. Peter Batchelor in Negapatam, South India. Mary, too, had a question to ask: 'Can we Methodists not have a Society of our own to find and support women missionaries?' Hoole was convinced that it could be done, and the above quoted Resolution was the result.

No time was lost in putting the decision into effect. The first committee, officially opened by Dr Hoole, who made a general statement of the plan and then retired, met on 20 December 1858. Mrs Hoole was appointed Foreign Correspondent and Miss Farmer Home Correspondent. It was agreed that a periodical, known as the *Occasional Paper*' should be issued. A circular drawn up by the General Secretaries went to every Circuit in the Connexion. It began by acknowledging the previous services of Methodist women in the common cause and described them as 'able and zealous fellow workers in almost every town and city in the kingdom'. The circular then went on to say that, valuable as these isolated, desultory, and occasional operations had been, they 'might be combined in one system and fostered into vigorous and regular action'. By this means, assurance would be given 'to the female labourers in the foreign field that their circumstances, being understood and appreciated, would receive due consideration in the application of the means which may be placed at the disposal of the Ladies' Committee'. For the first time, the women of Methodism had the right to decide how money they had raised should be spent.

The first aim was to secure recruits and money in order to staff Girls' Schools, many of which had been started by missionaries' wives. The first year's income was £320. And the Roll of Honour began:

1859	Susannah Beal	Belize, British Honduras	died	1860
1860	Mary Scott	Negapatam, South India	married	1860
	Miss Tookey	Fiji	returned	1864
1861	Eleanor Lamb	Verulam, Natal	returned	1868
	Isabel Vera Eacott	Jaffna	returned	1864
1862	Mary Gunson	Canton	died	1864

In 1868 the first Indian Biblewoman, Sanjivi, was appointed.

Among the treasured portraits now hanging in the Mission House is a fine picture of Caroline Wiseman, wife of the Rev. Luke Wiseman. She attended her first meeting of what had come to be known as 'the

Ladies' Committee for the Amelioration of the Condition of Women in Heathen Countries, Female Education, etc.' She was a woman of some spirit, and on returning home after the meeting she announced with heat to her husband, one of the General Secretaries of the Society, that she would never go to another. 'Oh, yes, you will,' he said, 'and in a short time you will have made another thing of it and a much larger one.' That was in 1874. Within a year she had been widowed, and in 1876 she was appointed foreign secretary. Until her death in 1912, Mrs Wiseman fulfilled her husband's prophecy, ruling over the councils of the Ladies' Committee with a genius for organization and a gift for oratory that inspired the whole Church. Under her influence, over two hundred women sailed for work abroad, and the income of what came to be called the Ladies' Auxiliary increased from £2,500 to £23,000.

It was not only in the realm of Women's Work that the laity were taking a greater responsibility for the financial and administrative affairs of Methodism. For many years they had been admitted to the Conference when money matters were being discussed, but it was not until 1878 that, in addition to a Pastoral Session, a properly constituted Representative Session was held. It dealt with such important items as the Committee of Privileges, Foreign Missions, Chapel Affairs, Home-Mission and Contingent Fund, and Schools. While it may not be possible to substantiate J. R. Green's statement in his *A Short History of the English People* that Methodism 'gave the first impulse to popular education', it is certain that Methodists were in the forefront of the Sunday School Movement, and that the removal of religious tests from the universities enabled them to go ahead with secondary education. By 1875 the Leys School had been opened at Cambridge under the headship of Dr W. F. Moulton,[28] and five years later David Hill, home from his work in China, appealed to the boys to consider becoming medical missionaries. His visit had at least two memorable results. One of the scholars, S. R. Hodge,[29] had hoped from the age of six to become a minister, and had been equally certain that he did not want to be a doctor. David Hill's presentation of the need changed all that and Hodge went to China, so becoming the first of many old Leysians who were to serve as medical missionaries overseas. He had entered the school in its second term just before his seventeenth birthday, became senior prefect at the age of twenty, and left in July 1880, having stayed on at the Leys to be prepared as a candidate for the ministry, the first

[28] The Rev. William Fiddian Moulton, biblical scholar and older brother of the Rev. James Egan Moulton, who himself revised the New Testament in Tongan.

The records of the British and Foreign Bible Society demonstrate that Methodists have played an outstanding part in providing the people of many countries with the Bible in their own languages.

[29] See Derek Baker's centenary history: *Partnership in Excellence: A Late-Victorian Educational Venture: The Leys School, Cambridge 1875–1975* (Cambridge 1975), pp. 194, 198.

Leysian to enter those ranks. He died in China in 1907. The other notable result of David Hill's visit was the formation of a school missionary society in 1881 which opened staff and boys to the claims of the wider world.

For the rest of this section we shall look into the example of an outstanding individual, Thomas Birch Freeman, as a telling instance of the matrix, commitment and life-patterns which are disclosed in the missionary. Mindful of the great company of those whose names have little or no memorial, we may none the less learn from the more fully documented life-stories of the common faith which sustained them through exhaustion, hardship and danger.

It was largely due to Freeman that in the early decades of the twentieth century Methodism was virtually the official Church in what by then was called the Gold Coast. Aggrey, who once said, 'I am a humble product of the self-sacrifice of those who came out to the white man's grave', came from Anomabu, Ghana. Freeman and his son had ministered there and had seen what could almost be described as a mass movement. In making that statement, Aggrey was deeply conscious of the heroic self-giving of those who survived for such brief periods on the West Coast, but he must also have known how much he owed to the one man who was able to give more than half a century of service to his people.

When Freeman and his wife landed at Cape Coast Castle, Ghana, on Wednesday 3 January 1838, they found themselves without missionary colleagues in their new work. They received a great welcome from the Africans who had come down to the beach to meet them, and much friendly help from the few British residents – traders and the Acting President – who felt sympathy for them, as they came to a house of death. They had expected to find George Wrigley at work among the Methodist Societies on the Coast, but just before they landed they were told that he had died in the previous November. So all five of the first Methodist missionaries to Ghana had gone down before the rigours of the climate. Wrigley's term of thirteen months was, in fact, the longest period of service of the five.

The first to land had been Joseph Dunwell, on New Year's Day, 1835. He had come out in response to a dramatic appeal from a group of young African men. In 1830 they had started reading the Bible at a government school at Cape Coast, and had met for discussion and study. Governor McCarthy had founded this school to train African civil servants, and it was directed by Joseph Smith, an African who probably came from Freetown with McCarthy. He was a Christian, and began by reading the Bible to his students; but their questions soon carried him out of his depth, and with his simple and litetal methods of exposition he was unable to help them with their problems. One of the young men, William De Graft, was soon in revolt against his teacher. After studying the Bible and thinking about it for himself he arrived at views similar to those of Luther, and developed methods not unlike those of Wesley and the Holy Club. The group he founded was known as 'A meeting or society for Promoting Christian Knowledge'.

The whole approach of De Graft's group alarmed Joseph Smith. He denounced them to the Governor on the grounds that their teaching was seditious since it might foment further strife in a country which was already suffering from quarrels, not only among the Fanti chiefs but also between the Fantis of the Coast and the warlike inland kingdom of Ashanti. As a result, De Graft and two others were sent to prison. Though they were later released, their prospect of working for the government as civil servants had gone, and they found work in the trading stores. Unlike the others who stayed at Cape Coast, De Graft settled further west at the coastal town of Dixcove. He kept in touch with his group, now known as the Bible Band, and heard that because of their increasing numbers they were short of Bibles. So he asked an English captain called Potter to bring some out on his next voyage from home. Potter was different from the rough type of man who at that time usually took charge of ships bound for the West Coast of Africa. When he was at home in England he used to worship with the Methodists, and he gave some part of each day to his devotions when he was at sea. Not only did he bring the Bibles that De Graft asked for; he went from Bristol to London to meet the Missionary Committee and offered to take, at his own charges, the books and a missionary. The man they sent was Dunwell, and in six months he was dead.

In that short spell he accomplished astonishing results, perhaps the most valuable of these being the reconciliation which he was able to bring about between Joseph Smith and William De Graft. He drew up plans for the first church to be built in Cape Coast, visited the three coastal towns of Saltpond, Winneba, and Anomabu and started on plans for churches in these places as well. Dunwell was responsible for the conversion of two Ashanti princes who were presented by Jabez Bunting to the Methodist Conference of 1840. In fact it would appear that he exhausted himself by working early and late, visiting the people in their homes, and preaching in the open air. When Governor Maclean buried him on 24 June 1835, he did so in the presence of a silent crowd of Africans who had just begun to realize what it meant to have a missionary among them.

For the next fifteen months Smith and De Graft were the joint leaders of the young church, and it says much for the quality of their leadership that the Methodists not only held their own during that time but increased their numbers. Their impact on the life of the people was strengthened too, as was seen by the change from indifference to vigorous and hostile opposition on the part of the local priests. Then George Wrigley and his wife arrived. He began to build the church that Dunwell had planned, and she cared for the women and girls, notably by opening a Domestic Science school where many of the girls who later became the wives of teachers and evangelists were trained.

The Wrigleys had been at work four months when they were joined by the Harrops. They landed in January 1837 and immediately they were fully engaged in the work. Taking little notice of warnings about the climate, and often leaving themselves no time even to eat, they were ill within a few days of their arrival, no doubt with malaria; Mrs Harrop died exactly three weeks after landing. Mrs Wrigley collapsed through the shock caused by this sudden blow, and three days later she too was dead. Harrop died within the next hour. It was events like these that earned the West Coast of Africa the title of the White Man's Grave.

When the facts were made known at home, along with Wrigley's appeal for volunteers to fill the vacant places, Freeman knew immediately that he was called of God to serve in Africa. He was under no illusions as to what he faced:

> Woe is me if I preach not the Gospel, and woe unto me if I am not prepared to forsake home, and friends, and all I hold dear to me to preach that Gospel, to the heathen . . . If I hesitate to go to a sickly clime at the command of the Lord of Hosts, because in so doing I may risk the shortening of my days in this life, cannot He who bids me go strike me here while surrounded with all the advantages of this sea-girt isle?

Freeman was the son of an African father and an English mother. They were not well off, and the father, who was a gardener, died when the boy was only six years old, so the mother, with three other children, had a struggling time. After some training as a botanist, Freeman was appointed head gardener to Sir Robert Harland, at Orwell Park near Ipswich. Quite early he joined the Methodists and while working for Harland became a local preacher. It was common for local preachers, in the country at any rate, to exercise a pastoral as well as a prophetic ministry, and Freeman regularly visited the people in their homes. This brought him up against the vicar, and Sir Robert gave him the choice: his job as a gardener, or his work for Methodism. Without hesitation he held to his calling as a preacher, and left Orwell Park.

Within three months dramatic changes had taken place in his life. He offered his services to the Missionary Society with Wrigley's appeal in view, and was gladly accepted by the special committee called to meet him at the Mission House in Hatton Garden. There were two events that had to take place before he could sail: he had to be ordained, and he was asked to get married. This second requirement indicated a change of policy. At first it had been thought that the climate on the West Coast was too lethal for women to be sent there, so men like Dunwell went alone. It then became clear that men in such difficult conditions, with extremely heavy work-loads, needed someone to look after them, and that women had their own different and important contribution to make. Whether or not Freeman had up to then entertained any romantic ideas, he promptly married Elizabeth Boot, Sir Robert Harland's housekeeper. The ordination of missionaries was another matter. This had been the practice, from the very beginning, on the grounds that the men were going to parts of the world where the authority of bishops of the Church of England had no force, and where it was essential that the missionaries could administer the sacraments.[30] Freeman was ordained in Islington Chapel, Liverpool Road, London, on 10 October 1837, and married to Elizabeth on the following Tuesday.

They sailed from Gravesend soon afterwards. Freeman's journal declares him to be 'composed and prepared for leaving my Native Land': 'Send me forth, I beseech Thee, in Thine own strength and make me and my beloved partner a blessing to the poor benighted and opprest Africans . . . Help me, O Lord, to live in the enjoyment of vital Religion, that I may know how to feed Thy sheep in the wilderness, through Christ Jesus my Lord.'

They arrived at Cape Coast to the sympathy and welcome we have described. Freeman soon fell into the courteous ways of Africa. He showed infinite patience with the endless ceremonies, salutations and palavers, so that Africans often said with delight, 'He understands our customs.' In addition to deep personal piety, and a passion to preach the Gospel, he showed sound practical judgement. Not every newly appointed minister shifts the site of the manse immediately on arrival in his new circuit without asking the permission of the stewards, but that is what Freeman did. He moved the Mission House from a damp, swampy, mosquito-ridden area to a dry hill, with immense benefit for everyone who had to live in it. One other notable feature of his character was his courage. He soon had need of all the fortitude that he could muster, for less than six weeks after they landed, Elizabeth died.

For a while his chief enemy was loneliness and his main solace was his work. He believed in giving people something to do. The people had built the Cape Coast Chapel within six months of his arrival, and three months later it was packed for the first missionary meeting held in Ghana. At the Quarterly Meeting held on 11 June 1838, the day after the chapel was opened, he began to implement the policy he had advocated

[30] See p. 34 n. 18 above.

in the first letter he wrote to the Missionary Committee after his wife's death. He was impressed by the insecurity of life for Europeans on the Coast and urged the importance of training an African ministry. At that first Quarterly Meeting, William De Graft was accepted as a candidate.

In the meantime Freeman had been visiting other towns in the region and in the vicinity of Winneba; he had been impressed, as a gardener, by the many hundreds of acres of fine soil which could be brought under cultivation. But once the chapel at Cape Coast was opened, and the work there established, his mind turned to an exciting area inland to the north. He was fascinated by the Ashanti people and their capital city, Kumasi. Under the heading 'Intention of proceeding to Ashantee', he wrote to the committee at home saying that apart from their disposition he saw no obstacle to the introduction of Christianity to that nation. He explains that it would be costly to visit Kumasi, as much as £30 or £40 for a missionary, though it would cost a merchant, who would not live as simply, more than £200. There is no time to be lost. There is a friendly feeling between the Government of Cape Coast and the King of Ashanti, and the Governor has promised to put him under the protection of the Fort whenever he is ready to start. Mails between England and West Africa are, he points out, infrequent, so perhaps they will not mind if he takes the first chance that presents itself of going up country without waiting for their consent.

Five months after that first missionary meeting he makes one of the most memorable entries in any missionary's diary:

> 30th January 1839: Deeply sensible of the difficult and dangerous nature of my undertaking and not ignorant of that eternal Source from whence I must receive all my strength both of a Physical and Spiritual Nature, I left Cape Coast for Coomassie and reached Annamaboe at noon.

The sonority of this statement was matched by the dignity and determination with which the journey was begun. The President of the Council, G. W. Maclean, who had taken the chair at the September missionary meeting, provided an escort of an African sergeant and a private, and letters of introduction to the King of Ashanti. Eighteen carriers took Freeman's loads on their heads through two hundred miles of forest paths. He himself was carried on a travelling chair. But the party was held up by many frustrating delays and it was not until 1 April that they arrived at Kumasi, having been two months on the way.

They were given a royal welcome. One Ashanti messenger after another, each carrying gold-covered symbols of office, came to meet them as they approached the city:

> As soon as we arrived at the market-place, I got out of my little travelling chair, and walked through the midst of an immense concourse of persons, a narrow path being kept clear for me, paying my respects to the King and his numerous chiefs and captains, who were seated on wooden chairs, richly decorated with brass and gold, under the shade of their splendid umbrellas, some of them large enough to screen twelve or fourteen persons from the burning rays of the sun, and crowned with images of beasts covered with gold, surrounded by their troops and numerous attendants. I was occupied for half an hour in walking slowly through the midst of this immense assembly.

After Freeman had been taken to a seat, the vast concourse, including, finally, Kwaku Dua the King, filed past him with salutations. Many carried objects of great value made of silver and gold.

> In this ostentatious display, I also saw what was calculated to harrow up the strongest and most painful feelings – the royal executioners, bearing the bloodstained stools on which hundreds, and perhaps thousands of human victims have been sacrificed by decapitation and also the large *death-drum*,[31] which is beaten at the moment when the fatal knife severs the head from the body, the very sound of which carries with it a thrill of terror.

He was soon to hear its grim message:[32] 'King, I have killed him; King, I have killed him,' because a few days later the King's brother died and many victims were sent on into the next world to help him there: twenty-five one day; fifteen the next. It horrified Freeman until he realized that these practices sprang from an intense awareness of the reality of the spirit world. He could see the vision of a happier future: 'A brighter day is approaching when the death-drum shall give place to the Bible.'

The funeral rites caused considerable delay before Freeman was able to speak with Kwaku Dua, though the King had been sending him valuable gifts as a sign of his good will. When the two men did meet, nothing was said about the purpose of the visit, but Freeman left feeling that to establish friendly relationships had been well worth while. It was high time for him to be returning to the coast: the rainy season had begun, and he was anxious about the young churches he had left behind; so the journey to Cape Coast began as soon as he had left the King's house. A violent tornado did not halt the party. They knew that

[31] The death-drum was decorated with the skulls of human victims, including that of Governor McCarthy (of Sierra Leone and what is now called Ghana), who in 1824 had advanced into Ashanti with a small force, and had been defeated and killed.

[32] Since the languages of West Africa are tonal, depending on the rising and falling of the voice for the meaning of their words, it is possible, by tightening and slackening the skin of a drum, to convey messages and salutations.

the swollen rivers were rising fast and would soon become impassable: 'I again resumed my journey under rather trying circumstances, being almost without food.' Later: 'My sleeping place, it is true, was a very bad one (such as an Englishman would hardly put a pig in), but I laid me down in conscious security and slept in peace.' And, as so often at dramatic points in the journal, he concluded by quoting a hymn of Charles Wesley's, 'How do Thy mercies close me round!'

Back at the coast he had a busy year in front of him. The spectacular journeys he made must not blind us to his continuing ministry: baptizing, marrying, preaching, meeting classes, building churches, founding schools; by patience and friendship, with vision and faith, winning love and respect, he reaped an amazing harvest. Just when the burden seemed to be growing too great, new colleagues arrived. 'On Monday the 13th January, 1840, about four o'clock in the afternoon the Brig *Osborne* arrived from England having on board Bro^{r}. and Sister Mycock and Bro^{r}. Brooking. I went down and met them at the Castle, and how shall I express the joyous satisfaction with which I hailed them on their arrival.' The new men brought with them a letter from the Committee urging Freeman to return on furlough, but he saw that it was necessary for him to stay another two or three months. The Mission House was under repair, as also was the burnt-out chapel at Anomabu. New chapels were under construction at Komenda, Abasa, and Saltpond. He was extending the girls' school at Cape Coast. Most importantly, he wanted to watch over his colleagues during their first attacks of fever. When he sailed in the brig *Maclean*, on 27 March 1840, with William De Graft, whom he was taking to England for further training, the Governor came on board to see him off.

He was surprised, on arriving home eight weeks later, to find himself already famous. This furlough was going to be no rest. A week after landing, Freeman was speaking to the Committee at the Mission House on the state of the work in Ghana. They decided to send back with him six new missionaries, to take advantage of the opportunities in Ashanti, but made one condition: the men would go if £5,000 could be raised immediately to cover the cost of their passages and their keep for the first three years. So the appeal for the Ashanti Fund was launched throughout the Connexion. Already a few hundred pounds had come in as a result of the publication of Freeman's Ashanti journal. Now his journal began to consist largely of meetings he had addressed and the astonishing sums that were raised. There are familiar and famous names among the churches where he preached: almost the first was Wesley's Chapel in City Road, London; Brunswick at Leeds and Nicolson Square, Edinburgh, followed later. He went not only to large towns: Belfast, Bristol, Bradford – almost every main city was on the list – but to little villages too, and they also gave liberally. De Graft went with him. Freeman spoke of the need, and De Graft was a living proof of what the Gospel, in a brief time, could do for Africa. Before Freeman left at the end of the year, the required total had been reached.

Freeman attended the Conference of 1840 at Newcastle-upon-Tyne. The journey from London by rail took two whole days. After all, it was only fifteen years since the Stockton and Darlington line had been opened and passenger train services had been inaugurated. He was to make a journey from London to Leeds in September, and of this he says in his journal: 'At noon I left the Docks, and the following morning at half-past one I retired to rest in Leeds 195 miles distant from London, so much has the introduction of Steam and Railroads annihilated time and distance.'

Two events at the Conference moved Freeman deeply. The Ordination Service reminded him of his own vows, and the signing of the Journal in the presence of 'the President and the venerable Fathers' impressed him with a sense of the brevity of human life: 'I cannot expect under the most favourable circumstances which I can imagine ever to meet all these aged worthies again on this side of the grave.'[33]

Another of Freeman's train journeys took him from Bristol to London, this time on his honeymoon with his second wife, Lucinda Cowan. His diary mentions the wedding quite suddenly, though there is no previous mention of Lucinda, and indeed up to the day of the wedding he was still travelling around the country speaking on behalf of the Ashanti Fund. Less than a month later they left England for West Africa, taking with them as a gift for the King of Ashanti a phaeton which had been inspected by Queen Victoria and Prince Albert.

Dr Jabez Bunting conducted a memorable ordination and valedictory service for men and women who were returning with Freeman. It was held on 1 December 1840 at Great Queen Street Chapel, and the other Secretaries of the Society took part: Hannah, Alder, Beecham and

[33] That year, while Conference discussion was dominated by a dispute between the Canadian Conference and the Mission House in London, the *Methodist Magazine* carried two lists of APPLICATIONS FROM VARIOUS MISSIONARY STATIONS WHICH, IN WHOLE OR IN PART, HAVE BEEN REFUSED BY THE WESLEYAN MISSIONARY COMMITTEE, CHIEFLY IN CONSEQUENCE OF THE WANT OF FUNDS.

The Wesleyan Methodist Missionary Society has always been a 'faith mission' in the sense that it has been annually committed to its work, and has spent the greater part of its yearly income, long before the necessary money has been received. The list of needed recruits and grants was followed by an important article pointing out that almost sixty additional missionaries were required. If the letters appealing for the services of each man and the support of each grant could be presented in detail, 'all our friends would at once decide that the request should be complied with'. Then came five suggestions as to how income could be increased to meet the new opportunities: 'The augmentation of annual subscriptions', 'The increase of annual subscribers', 'An improved working of the "Collector" system', 'A more systematic and diligent attention to the management of Branch Societies', and 'Special Considerations for the liquidation of the debt of £20,000 to be solicited by persons having Cards for that purpose'. The income of the Society went up from £90,182 in 1840 to £101,688 in 1841.

Hoole. The newly-appointed missionaries were Mr and Mrs Thompson Hesk, John Watson, Mr and Mrs Samuel A. Shipman, William Thackwray, and Charles Walden. Bunting presented William De Graft with a Bible. The following day they took formal leave of the General Committee and 'the Wesleyan ministers of London and its vicinity'. There was no exaggeration in the *Methodist Magazine* account of their last few days in England:

> Never was a Missionary party dismissed from the shores of England with a more intense feeling of interest and sympathy. All acknowledge the very arduous and difficult character of the Mission, as well as its important bearings on the welfare of the human race, and one of the boldest efforts yet made by the church in modern times, to introduce Christianity and its attendant blessings to the independent Negro states of interior Africa. Thousands of prayers have been offered in behalf of these Missionaries and their undertaking; and we do not doubt that they will be constantly remembered at the throne of grace, by those who are concerned for the prosperity and extension of the kingdom of Christ.

This sense of being held in the prayers of the home Church was one of the distinguishing features of the Methodist missionaries of this period. How could they fail to be encouraged and supported, during times of danger, distress and difficulty, by the memory of such valedictory services as that at Great Queen Street of which the report says: 'At the close of the service the whole congregation appeared to unite most fervently in the prayer which was offered up in behalf of the Missionaries, and for the success of the Mission, by the Revd Dr Bunting.' Nor was it merely the evangelical enthusiasts of the home Church who saw the significance of this part of the Society's work. The Select Committee of the House of Commons, which sat, in 1842, to receive evidence relative to West Africa, recorded its sense of the importance of this mission:

> We would here acknowledge the great services rendered to religion and civilisation on this Coast by the Wesleyan body; they have even established a friendly communication with the barbarous court of the Ashantee; which promises results important in every way; and, indeed, little in the way of instruction would have been done without them.

When the party arrived at Cape Coast, on 1 February 1841, they found to their relief that there had been no deaths among their colleagues, though the Mycocks were in poor health and went home a month later. The Hesks went with the Freemans to Anomabu and were stationed there. The Shipmans[34] were sent to Accra, and Walden stayed at Cape Coast. A little later, Thackwray went up country to Dominasi to develop a model farm which Freeman had planned since that first interior journey when he had perceived the potentialities of the rich Fanti soil. Brooking was now free to go inland to Mansu, two days on the road to Kumasi, and an excellent outpost for keeping in touch with the Ashanti mission when it could be founded. A school had been established there. De Graft had been appointed an 'assistant missionary' and he returned to his work at Winneba. Watson went to Dixcove, where years before De Graft had begun to build up a church.

The plan was that after the rainy season Brooking and Walden should go with Freeman to Ashanti and that they should be stationed there, but soon tragedy overtook the new workers. Every one of them went down with 'seasoning fever', and Thackwray died on 4 May, three months after landing and having been ill only a week. Walden died on 29 July. Thackwray's death was followed by Lucinda's illness. From 1 February to 7 August, when he wrote, 'My life hath been in one incessant whirl', there is no entry in Freeman's journal. Now suffering from malaria himself, when he heard that a ship bound for Accra had come in, he took Lucinda away, hoping that the drier air there might do her good. On 25 August, less than seven months after entering the country, she died. Three days later, Mrs Hesk died, and on 17 September Hesk returned to England. From the start his health had caused anxiety. Faced with the fact that, of the twelve missionaries who had formed the staff of the Gold Coast and Ashanti District earlier in the year, seven were either dead or had returned home, Freeman could write in his journal: 'My soul is borne above the water-floods, and my strength is equal to my day. The Son of God is with me in the fire and he keeps my mind in perfect peace.'

Years later, Freeman married an educated African woman and they had four children. One of them was also called Thomas Birch Freeman. He entered the ministry and worked alongside his father, but before then there were to be spectacular journeys and bitter discouragements. Soon after Lucy died the two Ashanti princes returned from England, and since Freeman had been planning to revisit Kumasi he arranged that they should make the journey together. The King sent a hundred and sixty carriers to help the princes to bring their boxes. Freeman had nearly as many for his and those of Brooking. They had to hack a road

[34] Shipman survived for two years before he died on 2 February 1843 at the age of twenty-five. His father, who had been a missionary in Jamaica, where Samuel was born, and where three other children of the family died, wrote an account of his own service overseas and that of his son, in *The Missionary Child: a Memoir of Samuel Annesley Shipman, by his father* (London 1846). This slim volume, dedicated to the children of Wesleyan and other ministers, conveys something of the pride and joy as well as the anguish of the families of those pioneer missionaries who died on the field.

through the dense forest wide enough to take the phaeton, which, for part of the way, was dismantled and carried on the porters' heads. There was an even more enthusiastic welcome than on his first entry to Kumasi, with the exchanging of gifts: a gold tobacco pipe and wild beasts for Queen Victoria, and another pipe for the Missionary Committee. But the most satisfactory outcome was the permission granted to Brooking to stay on when Freeman returned to the coast.

Abeokuta, five hundred miles away in what is now called Nigeria, was the next great African town that Freeman visited. Some of the slaves who had been released by British warships while on the way to America in Portuguese vessels were returned to West Africa and landed at Freetown, Sierra Leone. Some of them bought a ship and began to trade along the coast. They did brisk business at Badagry, then pushed on to Lagos, and recognized it as the port where they had been shipped as slaves. Full of joy at hearing their own language, they went inland to Abeokuta and found their relatives. They themselves were now Christians, having been converted in Freetown, and they wrote to the missionary there, Thomas Dove, pleading that missionaries be sent to their people. He passed the request on to the Mission House in London, and the secretaries wrote to Freeman asking him to go and see what was happening. He landed at Badagry on 24 September 1842, the first Protestant missionary to enter Nigeria. By the end of November, Freeman and his helpers had put up the Mission House, the first European home in Badagry, and a small bamboo chapel. It had meant searching in the forest for timber and bringing it by canoe down the creeks. Some of the great trunks had to be driven into the ground to act as piles for the foundations of the buildings in the swampy soil.

While all this was going on – building, preaching, and preparing the way with the people for De Graft's work when he should leave – Freeman was in touch not only with Shodeke, King of Abeokuta, but also with Gezo, King of Dahomey. To Shodeke he sent a message by the hand of James Ferguson, the Sierra Leonean who had led the trading expedition which had started the return of so many of his people to Abeokuta. In reply, Shodeke sent a present of a pony and harness with a note of welcome which must have been written by one of those who had been educated in Sierra Leone:

TO THE ENGLISHMAN AT BADAGRY, –

I THANK YOU FOR YOUR KIND PROMISE THAT YOU WILL VISIT US IN THIS COUNTRY. I SHALL BE GLAD TO RECEIVE YOU, AND BY THE BLESSING OF GOD NOTHING SHALL HARM YOU. I REMAIN,

YOURS TRULY, SODAKA
KING OF UNDERSTONE

UNDERSTONE,[35] OCTOBER 1842.

[35] The English translation of Abeokuta.

As soon as the buildings were reasonably complete – he lived in a tent all the time he was at Badagry – and when Shodeke sent an escort of fourteen men to guide and help him, Freeman set out on yet another forest journey. When he arrived at Abeokuta to a tumultuous welcome, he held the first Christian service ever conducted in the town. Shodeke showed his desire to be helpful by having a small mud hut constructed, 'because he will need somewhere to put his god for the night!' The King joined Freeman at his travelling-table, and so they held a service. 'I gave a brief address, which was explained to the King in the vernacular tongue.'

As a result of this visit, Freeman pressed the Missionary Society to send eight men immediately to Abeokuta and Badagry. It was eighteen years before one man arrived, and it is hard to avoid the conclusion that the major reason for the delay was Methodism's preoccupation with its own domestic and divisive conflicts. Shodeke meant what he said in the room allotted to Freeman after the public reception:

> My people told me they were sure their friends in England would not neglect them; but I feared you would not venture to come so far. Now I see you and my heart rejoices; and as you have now come to visit us, I hope the English will never leave us.

Later, Shodeke was murdered by the Ifa priests for being so friendly to the Christians. It was not only the white missionaries who made sacrifices for the Gospel in West Africa.

Freeman turned next to Dahomey.[36] Gezo, her King, was the great slave-raiding despot who was the most powerful supporter of the Portuguese in that traffic. It meant another gruelling if uneventful journey through the forests and villages, and a similar pattern of royal reception and generous gifts. One new feature was the company of women soldiers, armed with guns and cutlasses, who surrounded Gezo. But in spite of their threatening appearance, the King proved more friendly than Freeman could have hoped, and he actually asked that a missionary should be stationed in his port of Wida.

This first visit of Freeman to Nigeria and Dahomey had profound historical effects. The account of the slave trade which he gave to Governor Maclean on his return to Cape Coast resulted in the sending of an African sergeant to Badagry to take its people under British

[36] He had first to return to Badagry. That journey began like a royal triumph and ended in delight. Shodeke went with him in a hammock to the outskirts of Abeokuta through crowded streets where people shouted, 'Goodbye! Come again soon!' He arrived at Badagry on Christmas Eve, to find that Townsend, of the Church Missionary Society, had recently arrived on his way to visit those Sierra Leoneans in Abeokuta who were members of the Anglican Church. There is something symbolical about the meeting of these representatives of the two Societies which have worked so well together since that time in Nigeria; and they began the long association with a combined service.

protection. To the Portuguese slavers this was a sure sign that Britain meant business as regards the slave trade, and the action provoked attacks on Badagry from Lagos which led to the events of 1851, when Britain bombarded Lagos and replaced its ruler by one who opposed the traffic. Just as significant was the consent which Freeman gained from Gezo for the re-establishment of a British fort at Wida. This was another key position used by the slavers, and in 1842 it had been the subject of questions in the Parliamentary Select Committee on the West Coast of Africa. But perhaps the most remarkable effect of Freeman's visit was unknown to him at the time, though it was mentioned with astonishment by travellers who went to Dahomey a little later. An explorer called Duncan, who was there three years after Freeman, discovered that as a direct outcome of the missionary's visit Gezo had deprived his provincial chiefs of the right to offer human sacrifices.

At home too, the publication of Freeman's Badagry – Abeokuta – Dahomey journal had a profound effect. The Missionary Committee described this as one of the most interesting and important documents they had ever had the privilege and honour of submitting to public attention. The occasion was made the opportunity of calling the Church to prayer. It was suggested that the monthly prayer meetings of November 1843 should be given throughout the country to the reading of brief extracts from the journal, thanksgiving for the success which had so far been seen, and intercession for Freeman and his colleagues. It was also used to remind the Church of the need for more generous giving to supplement the already depleted Five Thousand Pound Fund, and to answer those whom Freeman called 'cold-hearted sceptics' who complained at the sacrifice of life which was the real cost of the work at that time.

The fact is that Freeman, fighting as he was on a 500-mile front, was setting a pace that was too hot for the home Church. These pioneering travels were followed by years of arduous and successful service which everywhere opened ground that he could not resist the temptation to enter. On his second furlough in 1844 he was depressed by his reception: 'Met the Committee. They received me kindly, but grumbled very much about expenses. This is very trying, but I trust I have acted for the best in my transaction of business on the West Coast of Africa.' Once again he toured the country and £5,500 was quickly subscribed; but, back on the coast, trouble began to build up for him. As he went on with his work of visiting the societies, building up the membership and opening schools, the Church was spreading so quickly that he found he had gone too far for those at home to follow. The year 1855 saw him enlarging the Cape Coast Church because of the increased congregation, and in the following year six new churches were built and eight hundred new members baptized. But the stations at Wida and

Lagos involved him in financial difficulties. He had opened them on his own initiative, seeing a unique opportunity and accepting it as a call from God, in the hope that the very nature of the situation would arouse interest and support in England. It did not. He was left with the burden of the new expenditure, and the Committee firmly refused to let him go on without restraint. They had work to care for in other parts of the world, and claims from other countries they could not meet. In 1851 they had refused support for George Piercy, who felt so strongly the call to work for the Society in China that he went there at his own expense. Instead of increasing their grants to the work in West Africa, in 1856 they sent William West to be the financial secretary to the mission and Daniel West to examine the state of that Church and report back to London. Though it meant that financial responsibility had been taken away from him, he welcomed both men and co-operated fully in their investigations. Daniel West, at the end of his tour, informed the Committee:

> God has, by means of His servants, wrought a great work. We have good chapels and schools and houses, and large attentive congregations . . . The whole country is open to us. In many villages and towns through which I passed, one uniform state of feeling was evident – one desire earnestly expressed: 'Send us teachers and missionaries'. Oh, that we had the means.

The man who had been sent to enforce rigid economy, and even retrenchment, was so impressed by his visit to Lagos and Abeokuta that he advised the Committee to enlarge the staff by putting a missionary there. Freeman always felt that if Daniel West had reached home, subsequent events would have taken a very different course; but West died in the Gambia, and the Committee had only his letters to judge by.

Though the report on the spiritual state of the Church was excellent, it was a different picture when it came to finance. Freeman himself was astonished when William West had completed his analysis. There was never any suspicion that Freeman was anything but scrupulously honest, but there was abundant evidence that in handling money he lacked method, and the annual cost of his District was a revelation to him. Yet we cannot escape the conviction that when Freeman resigned in face of the facts, the failure of the home Church to afford him adequate financial support was at least as powerful a factor as his own inefficiency with accounts. His letter to the Committee, in which he asked to be relieved of his responsibilities as Chairman and General Superintendent of the mission, was entirely without rancour. With his accustomed courtesy, he accepted the judgment passed upon him, but he could not help making some defence of his policies over nearly three decades:

> I will not attempt to offer my weary toils for so many years as an apology for any part of these difficulties. I ought to have minded what the world calls *the main thing* in these matters, and been more quiet and calculating and less impassioned; but in one sense it has been unfortunate for me personally that one single passion has absorbed my life – namely, the extension of our work, and in the midst thereof I have overlooked and neglected matters of expenditure.

The paragraph in his letter where he refers to his future is typically unresentful:

> In standing aside I should not deprive the mission of any services I may be able to render, and I would most willingly act as a local preacher[37] under Mr William West or any brother who may fulfil the duties of General Superintendent. I would aid the work by every means in my power.

As a proof that this was no idle offer, only a month later he went with William West to help in the opening of a new village chapel.

A tough letter was sent from the Wesleyan Conference at Liverpool in 1857 and signed by the President, Francis A. West, after Freeman's case had been considered in the light of 'the Report of the Deputation appointed by the previous Conference to visit the Mission under your care, certain Minutes of the Missionary Committee relating to those Missions and the Report of the Missionary Committee of Discipline'. It begins with severe censure for having exceeded the expenditure authorized by the Committee. The Conference is prepared to

> believe that this most censurable conduct has originated partly in thoughtlessness and partly from a false and exaggerated confidence in the resources of the Missionary Committee; and also that you have expended the immense sums of money which have passed through your hands for purposes generally connected with the Missions under your care.

For these reasons and because he personally has not made his 'responsible office a source of individual emolument, nor acquired private property at Cape Coast or elsewhere', his case has been 'considered more favourably than it might have been' and his 'standing in the ministry continues unimpaired'. But he is relieved of administrative responsibility, and the letter concludes: 'The debt owing by you personally to the Society you will be required to repay.'

Freeman lived under the shadow of that rebuke for the next sixteen years. He preached regularly, and devoted himself to the welfare of the

[37] Not as a lay preacher, but as a preacher 'in local connexion', as opposed to a missionary who was regarded as being based on the Church in Britain.

Gold Coast people. He retained the warm friendship of the missionary staff, though he was compelled by the rules of Methodism to retire from the ministry when he accepted from Sir B. C. C. Price, the new Governor, the administrative post of civil commandant of the Accra district. It was an exacting assignment, though the salary would enable him to comply, at any rate in some measure, with the requirement that he should repay his debt to the Society. The area he had to control included Christiansborg, along with all the territory that had once been Danish. Christiansborg had been desolated by bombardment sanctioned by a previous governor because of rioting. Its buildings had been flattened and its streets were deserted, but when Freeman took charge the people returned and rebuilt their homes.

They were full years. With characteristic tact he composed tribal differences. He built a house near Accra and turned his hand to market gardening and the running of a model farm. He continued his botanical studies, corresponding regularly with Kew Gardens, and wrote a novel called *Missionary Enterprise No Fiction* based on his own experiences and totally without rancour against the committee at home or those who had taken over his work in Africa.

It was inevitable that sooner or later such a man should return to the life which he loved and to which he still felt irresistibly called. On 1 September 1873, when he was sixty-four, he started his second period as a minister in West Africa. At such an age, thirteen years of Circuit work still lay before him. Freed from the financial and administrative responsibilities of District office, he was able to devote himself to a new chapel going up, and to pastoral work among the increasing number of members. One day, while he was taking special services at Cape Coast, his wife had to send for him to take charge of a movement which had suddenly developed at Anomabu. The people had begun to crowd the church night after night, and the numbers increased until the building could not hold them. At two services held on one day in 1875 he baptized nearly three hundred members. One service was at Saltpond, the other at Anomabu, and both had to be held out of doors because of the crowds. In Asafa, a seaside village near Cape Coast where a quarter of a century earlier there had been bitter persecution of Christians by the priests of animism, he baptized in one day two hundred and fifty people. He introduced camp meetings. They were a new idea on the Gold Coast and they were immediately popular. Crowds of over a thousand came to hear the old man, whom they loved and called Father Freeman, as he offered the Word of Life. In 1877 more than three thousand people were baptized and Freeman was responsible for half of them. In December of that year he was writing to the Mission House to say that they had sent him only 1,710 class tickets and the Anomabu Circuit now had about 2,500 people meeting in class.

Three further events came to cheer and vindicate him. His son Tom, child of his third marriage, was ordained and worked with him, first in Accra and later in the Anomabu Circuit. Then came a request from the Missionary Committee in London to take part in a tricky inquiry in Lagos. It was reassuring to know that he had regained their confidence, and his knowledge and shrewdness helped bring about agreement.

The third event was the Jubilee of the Gold Coast Mission in 1885. Great gatherings were held in every circuit. As people looked back over the fifty years since the landing of Dunwell, they realized what a vast difference the Christian message had made to their country. From being public meetings addressed by speakers, the services passed into testimony. One after another rose to say what God had done in their lives, and what they would give in return so that even greater things might be seen in the future. More than £16,000 was promised. Chiefs who had not officially renounced the old religion but who respected the new faith and acknowledged how it had changed their people made generous gifts. From that group of young men who, half a century ago, had met to read their Bibles, the Church had grown to a District with seven strong circuits.

Freeman was asked to take full charge of the celebrations at Cape Coast, and on Sunday, 1 February 1885, came the supreme moment of his life when he preached the chief sermon of the anniversary at the morning service. As early as three o'clock in the morning the church had been crowded for a prayer meeting. It had been enlarged more than once since he first built it, and the pulpit from which he spoke was not far from the grave of his first wife. Beneath that pulpit and in the soil around it were buried men and women who had died while serving with him during the earliest days. Moved with emotion, the old man 'with great energy and eloquence, drew upon his rich experience, contrasting the past with the present'. The text was the missionary favourite: 'What hath God wrought!'

In old age, Father Freeman was a dignified figure. A very tall, straight, stately old man, with silvery hair, graceful manners, and a splendid presence, he was kind and courteous to all, and wherever he went he was loved. Children ran after him in the street and when he went out it was usual to see two or three of them holding his hands. Soon after the Jubilee he retired and his strength failed. He and his wife lived on a meagre pension in a small house near Accra until he was in his eighty-first year. Then Price, the Superintendent of the Accra Circuit, invited them to live at the Mission House. Once again it was the beginning of the rainy season, recalling that first journey back to the coast from Kumasi, and his friends felt that he needed every comfort if he were to see the cool weather through. Frail though he became, on his last day, 12 August 1890, he found strength enough to give out a hymn at family prayers, and the one he chose was:

Now I have found the ground wherein
Sure my soul's anchor may remain.

3. The Confluence of Methodist Missions: 1885–1932

During the period 1838–1890, when Freeman was at work in West Africa, the classical pattern of Methodist overseas missions had been established. The main areas had been selected, the emotive adversaries and problems had been defined. Thus, missionaries came home from China talking about the grim effects of foot-binding there; from Fiji came reports of cannibalism; the after-effects of slavery were still being felt in the Caribbean; suttee and caste were part of India's pattern of life, and everywhere 'heathenism' was found with its attendant idolatry and superstition.

The same period saw an immense development in missionary education, so that, for instance, by the middle of the twentieth century almost every African political leader of any note, and nearly all the professional people of that continent, had been taught in missionary schools. There was a parallel growth in medical work. Nursing as we know it was founded by missionaries in China. Fine teaching hospitals grew up in every area served by the Church. It was as a result of their work that Gandhi once said that it was open for anyone to come and care for those suffering from leprosy: it just so happened that only Christians came. On the basis of that dedicated work, and when the use of sulphonamide drugs had been established in the mid-twentieth century, it became possible virtually to eradicate that disease in places where it had been a dreaded scourge. Dr Frank Davey, a Methodist missionary to Eastern Nigeria, was to become a world authority on caring for and curing these patients. It must be acknowledged that one unforeseen result of the medical missionaries' work in teaching hygiene, developing the practice of preventive medicine, and advancing the cause of child-care, has been to accentuate the problem of the world's rapidly increasing population. A third area of public work undertaken by missionaries of the period was the vast and varied realm of what can loosely be called 'social service'. This ranged from redemptive work among young delinquents to improving the stock and methods on the people's farms.

The period also saw the emergence of missionary societies within each of the divided sections of Methodism. Whan, later on, conversations were held in the hope of bringing together the Church of England and Methodism in Britain, it was realized that one characteristic of such a reunited Church would be that it would continue the Anglican tradition of supporting numerous missionary societies – some dozen or so major ones and nearly a hundred altogether. By contrast, every branch of Methodism had followed the pattern of maintaining one single society which was the Department of Overseas Missions of its Conference. When, in 1907, a major reunion of such Conferences took place to form the United Methodist Church, the respective missionary societies were amalgamated too.

Accepting our requirement that to be regarded as missionary societies those amalgamating bodies must exhibit two characteristics – they must have been collective and officially recognized, and they must have been missions to non-Christian communities overseas – they fall for consideration in the following order: the Missionary Society of the Methodist New Connexion (founded 1858–9); that of the United Methodist Free Churches (1861, though we shall note certain work in Jamaica in 1838), and of the Bible Christians (from 1886). These fused in 1907 to form the Missionary Society of the United Methodist Church. Meanwhile, in 1870, the Primitive Methodist Missionary Society had come into being.

All references to the work of these societies and of the W.M.M.S. must be qualified by the reminder that the success of any mission which they initiated depended at least as much upon indigenous lay men and women as it did upon expatriate missionaries. The point is well made in *The Story of the United Methodist Church*, p. 388, just before the editors, Henry Smith, John E. Swallow, and William Treffry, list in chronological order some of the main events in the histories of the three societies which united in 1907:

> NOTE OF RECOGNITION OF THE NATIVE STAFFS
>
> During the quarter century covered by this volume there has been a large and highly devoted company of Native Workers, mainly in China, and in a more limited measure in Africa and Jamaica. Their record is fully set forth in the yearly minutes, but the number of these faithful men and women is so complex and numerous that the exigencies of space unfortunately make it impracticable to set them forth in their order and entirety. It is, however, earnestly desired hereby to chronicle, with sincerest gratitude, the wonderful devotion of all those who have served for Christ's sake their own people in the three continents covered by our Missionary operations. May the God of all grace richly reward the noble band of workers who, mindful of their own brethren and sisters, have aided the advancement of the Kingdom of God and of His Christ.

A sample of similar correctives as regards the work of the Wesleyan Methodist Missionary Society is to be found in an important monograph by A. R. Tippett in *The Christian* (*Fiji 1835–67*), privately printed and published in Auckland N.Z., where the balance between the work of missionaries from Britain and the witness of Fijian lay people is well struck. Speaking of the work of unpaid members he writes:

> But here I must safeguard a point, lest I have created an impression that this work was done by the employed agents only. Let it not be thought that there were not hundreds of ordinary members, just as strong in the faith. It would be difficult at any period, or in any part of Fiji, to find characters who did a better job or manifested greater zeal than Ra Esekaia of Tiliva, Ratu George of Dama, Ilaija Varani of Viwa, to name three obvious examples. These were free citizens, none of them employed agents. These were men of some rank, but they were men who believed that there was a place and work for good Christian chiefs in Fiji – men who were prepared to maintain their civil responsibilities with an applied Christianity. Two of these men died because of these convictions. Their religious experiences were real and in advance of their day.

Expatriate missionaries have never held, or claimed to hold, a monopoly of the right to be persecuted for the Faith that they proclaimed, or of willingness to be faithful unto death.

Apart from their missions to Ireland, Canada, and Australia, which do not properly come into this survey, the missionaries of the Methodist New Connexion were confined to China. For a considerable period of years there had been a 'desire to sustain a direct relation to some heathen people'. It was a shortage of financial resources which had caused their Conference to 'defer action'. There is room for an examination of the theology of such delay. Where does impulsive folly end and faith begin in terms of starting a mission before adequate provision of financial resources can be assured?

Things began to get under way when the M.N.C. Conference, meeting at Hull in 1858, made a firm decision to start overseas work as soon as possible and called for an inquiry as to the most satisfactory place to begin. From then on there was no delay. At Manchester, in the following year, China was selected, and on 18 October two ministers, John Innocent and William Nelthorpe Hall, were commissioned in Woodhouse Lane Chapel, Leeds, so that once again that city saw an important and historic missionary 'first'. In three days they had sailed, and they reached Shanghai on 23 March 1860. Tientsin was chosen as the base for their operations, and subsequent developments were to show what a good choice it was. It is a mercantile city in the north, not far from Peking, with a population at that time of more than half a million and considerable cultural influence over a wide area.

As the historians of the Methodist New Connexion record:[38]

[38] G. Packer (ed.), *The Centenary of the Methodist New Connexion, 1797-1897* (London 1897), p. 127.

> The opening of our first city chapel, standing between a substantial structure called the Drum Tower and an idol manufactory, took place on May 9, 1862. On Sunday, June 1st, in the same year, two native converts were received into Church fellowship by baptism, these being the first fruits of the mission. Additions were gradually made, so that in 1863 we had eleven; in 1864 thirteen, in 1865 thirteen; in 1866 twenty-one, and in 1867 thirteen more. The spring of 1866 was marked by the opening of a large new chapel in a situation very favourable for usefulness.

The year 1881 saw the deaths of two who, in quite different ways, show how the young church was developing.

Miss A. Innocent had been designated as 'Lady Superintendent of the Girls' School in China'. For a while her place remained vacant, until, in 1888, Miss Waller, daughter of the Rev. Ralph Waller, was sent to fill it, and so became the Society's first woman missionary appointed to China in her own right. By 1899 the Women's Missionary Auxiliary had been founded.

Mr Hu, the first Chinese evangelist appointed to Tientsin, who also died in 1881, had given distinguished service for close on twenty years. His outstanding personal qualities and eloquent preaching reinforced another general principle which we have already mentioned, that the evangelization of a people may best be achieved by one of themselves, not only speaking their own language with its proper cadences and nuances, but also using their own thought forms and experience.

Medical Missions under the aegis of the Methodist New Connexion were given their first impetus when J. K. Robson, who had been appointed in 1891, later qualified as a doctor. By 1903 a hospital had been opened at Yung Ping Fu by Dr A. K. Baxter.

So 1907, the year of reunion, saw this branch of the United Methodist Missionary Society bearing the main hallmarks of classical nineteenth-century missions. The following statistics show how the Church in China was growing. In 1897 the M.N.C. is found in that country to be responsible for 89 chapels, 6 missionaries, 82 Chinese preachers, 402 scholars, and 2,092 members, including those on trial. By 1907 there were almost double these numbers: 11 missionaries, and 4,466 members and probationers.

Meanwhile, a parallel course had been run by the United Methodist Free Churches, which had been formed in 1857 by the amalgamation of the Wesleyan Association (begun in 1835) and the Wesleyan Reformers (starting in 1849). In terms of our definition, U.M.F.C. missions began soon after the union, in 1859, though the uniting bodies had earlier roots in Jamaica and West Africa and, like the M.N.C. and for that matter the W.M.M.S., they had long ministered to European settlers abroad.

The pattern of the work in Jamaica was a little complex. In 1838, the year which we have seen to be so significant for Methodist missions, Thomas Pennock, a Wesleyan minister there, joined the Association and carried with him more than 3,000 of his members. In England, a Wesleyan probationer, Kelsham Fullager, himself a Jamaican, seceded at the same time. He was sent to Jamaica to assist Pennock. Very early in their history the constituent parts of the U.M.F.C. accepted the principle of local independence and put it into practice. This decentralization gave the Jamaica Association its own Assembly, which sent and received addresses from its British parent. There is also a contemporary ring about the fact that, at the time of the union in 1857, there was only one compulsory Connexional collection and that it was jointly devoted to the Home and (as it was then called) Foreign Missionary Fund. An additional 'modern' touch is added when we read that this arrangement meant that many other funds in the home Church lacked adequate support as a result of this channelling of gifts into missionary work.

The young church in Jamaica had a stormy passage. By the time of the 1842 Assembly, Kelsham Fullager had died. John Parkyn and Joseph Blythman, who had also been sent to help Thomas Pennock, stayed long enough to see the emancipation of the slaves in Jamaica, and then returned to England. To fill their places, a number of preachers 'in local connexion' were appointed, and Matthew Baxter was sent in 1842. He remained for nine years, but there was an unhappy relationship between him and Pennock, so that as late as 1848 the Assembly was trying to bring them together. Meanwhile, in 1843, Pennock had broken away and had taken the bulk of his members with him. Some of the preachers also seceded, at one time leaving Baxter as the only preacher on the island, and in this divided mood the membership had fallen to 1,237 by 1845.

Fortunately this period of conflict was followed by a time of comparative tranquillity and fruitful colleagueship in which much of the damage was repaired. In spite of a disastrous hurricane in 1880 which destroyed seventeen chapels and drew £1,500 by way of a relief fund from the Connexion, and although there were inevitable disciplinary difficulties due mainly to the fact that before emancipation the slaves had not been permitted to marry, the membership at the time of the 1907 Union had climbed to 3,890. Five years after that Union the whole of the Jamaican work of the U.M.F.C. was transferred to the Methodist Episcopal Church of America.

West African Free Methodism dates from 1859. Once again there was an accession of a sizeable membership, consisting of some 2,300 members worshipping in fourteen chapels and preaching places, who had been in dispute with their parent body. At the Rawdon Street Chapel in Sierra Leone, a division had arisen of a kind that was to afflict the Church in that country for many years to come. The dispute was between, on the one hand, Africans whose ethnic origins were in various West Coast territories and who had been brought back from slavery across the Atlantic to be settled in Sierra Leone, and on the other the indigenous people of the area. The freed slaves left the Chapel in 1844. Being more numerous than the congregation they left behind, they took the name which all had originally borne since 1830: The West African Methodist Society.[39] Anthony O'Connor became their General Superintendent but they looked for white missionary leadership. They turned for guidance to a minister in the Countess of Huntingdon's Connexion, the Rev. J. Trotter, and he, judging that the body whose polity most closely resembled their own was the Free Methodists, advised them to approach that Connexion. Correspondence with Robert Eckett followed, and in 1859 it was announced in the *Magazine* that the decision to amalgamate had been taken. Eckett appealed for volunteers to man these new West African stations, and from five who offered, Joseph New was chosen. A valedictory service was held in the Russell Street Chapel, Liverpool, and on the following day, 24 May 1859, he and his wife started their voyage.

Colleagues joined him at intervals of fifteen months: first, Charles Worboys, and then, in December 1861, James Brown, who had taken a special course at the Borough Road Training School so that he in turn might train African teachers and catechists. In view of the familiar disastrous toll of life taken by malaria during the following years this was a sound policy. New, after writing a series of fascinating and inspiring letters published in the *Magazine*, died after three years of service at the age of twenty-seven. Worboys and Brown were compelled by ill-health to return home, and others died within a few months of their arrival. Then followed the period, which we have already noted in other parts of West Africa, when diminished virulence in the disease, or better understanding of how to cope with it, meant that a number of men were able to endure for longer periods. But because the policy of training African ministers had been put into operation quite early on, by the year of Union, 1907, only two white missionaries were there to share in the pastoral care of 2,510 members.

Up-country work among the Mendi people began around 1883, only to suffer almost immediately from local wars. Premises were destroyed in 1887 and even more seriously in 1898, when the anger of Africans

[39] Soon after the reunion of all the main Methodist Churches in 1932, this Society again seceded and became an all-African independent body. Its membership, between two and three thousand, was numerically little different from what it had been a century earlier.

was directed against all things British because of the abolition of slavery and the hut tax. A number of Africans were murdered, including a minister, John C. Johnson, and two teachers, Timothy Campbell and Theo Roberts. Oliver Beckerlegge[40] describes how Charles H. Goodman (1892–8) almost met the same fate:

> Goodman took refuge, but after being in hiding some little time, he was betrayed and marched to the rebel headquarters in his pants and vest. Dragged before a council, he saw one man go through a dumb show, the only meaning of which was: 'Death!' Goodman burst out: 'You do not know; you do not reckon upon God!' An old man then pleaded that he should not die, amid murmurs of approval from many; a woman took up his case, clasping King Gruburu's knees; and finally the king said in his broken English: 'You do not fight; you teach the children book; you are kind to all women; you mend people who are sick. That is all good; there is no bad in it; you shall not be killed . . . the King will care for you till the war is done.' For days he was kept in a hut in filth and privation, until at last a sub-chief, whom Goodman had nursed some years earlier, brought him clean garments. After three weeks the king panicked, and he and his people fled, taking Goodman with them, now suffering from blackwater fever; but happily a native brought him his Bible, helmet and – quinine! No gift could have been more providential. Gruburu's town was destroyed by a punitive expedition, and Goodman's release demanded. Gradually the chiefs sent in their submission, but Gruburu pleaded that he was too ill to travel, and sent his captive, the sick Goodman, as his plenipotentiary to treat with the English forces! Ingenuously, he asked Goodman when he was coming back again. 'If God wills, when the rains are over', was the reply. Of such stuff were our missions founded! When he finally arrived at the British camp eight weeks after the raid, his sufferings had made such havoc of his health that he was not recognized. The cable telling of his release reached England while the 1898 Assembly was meeting at Lincoln. 'Goodman alive', read the message; and, says Vivian,[41] strong men were moved to tears, and the Doxology was sung.

Backed by the starting of a Foreign Mission Fund in 1858, the formation of a Foreign Mission Committee in 1860, and, a little later, the inauguration of an Annual Missionary Meeting in the Exeter Hall (1865), the United Methodist Free Churches opened up work in two other areas abroad, this time where no other mission had been estab-

[40] *The United Free Methodist Churches: A Study in Freedom* (London 1957), pp. 84f.

[41] See William Vivian, *A Captive Missionary in Mendiland* (London 1899); id., *Mendiland Memories: Reflections and Anticipations* (London 1926), chap. ix: 'Touching Hands with Death'.

lished: in East Africa and in China.

May 1844 had seen the Rev. Dr Johann Ludwig Krapf, the son of a godly German farmer who had been trained by the Church of England Missionary Society, sailing into the harbour at Mombasa. All seemed to be set fair for him to begin work in the interior of Africa. Two months later his dreams had turned to a nightmare. Rosine, his wife, gave birth to a child, but soon both mother and baby were dead. Too ill to notice the moment of her death and only just able to attend her funeral, Krapf wrote to the C.M.S. in London: 'Tell our friends at home that there is now on the East African coast a lonely missionary grave. This is a sign that you have commenced the struggle.' His struggle had certainly begun, and his most valuable contribution, when the time came for him to retire on grounds of health, was the work he had done on various African languages, notably Swahili, and the preparation of a dictionary and a translation of the Bible.

One other important outcome of Krapf's missionary service he could never have foreseen. He published a book in 1860 and called it: *Travels, Researches, and Missionary Labours, during an Eighteen Years' Residence in Eastern Africa.* It came into the hands of Charles Cheetham, who in 1861 was appointed treasurer of Connexional and Mission Funds for the U.M.F.C. For him, the story of Krapf's dedication and courage was a clear call for the U.M.F.C. to enter East Africa. So there occurred one of those decisive moments in Methodist history when Dr Krapf, invited by Cheetham at his own charges, met the Missionary Committee at Lever Street Chapel, Manchester, on a grim November day in 1860. There it was agreed that work in that area should be started. Krapf consented to assist at its initiation, and an appeal for volunteers went out. At that time it was not difficult to catch the ear of church members for such a project. With Livingstone sending home dramatic news about being nearly eaten by lions and revealing the interior, hitherto unknown to Europe, of the fascinating continent of Africa, that continent was very prominent in the contemporary 'media'. From the eight volunteers who came forward, two, Thomas Wakefield and James Woolner, were chosen. They left in June 1861, accompanied by two Swiss young men trained at Basle. So ecumenical was the thinking then: of five who planned to work together, two came from the Basle Mission, one from the C.M.S., and only two were Methodists.

Well-laid as the scheme appeared to be, it went awry. An unhealthy and tedious journey bringing them to appalling conditions turned the Swiss back home. Woolner, after a short period in which they were seeking the best place to begin, became so ill that he too was compelled to return. Krapf helped Wakefield to erect a sectional iron house at Ribé, not far from Mombasa, and then his health gave way and he retired in October 1862. Wakefield was left alone; he stayed for twenty-seven years.

It is interesting to see these and subsequent events through the eyes of an African Christian today. In the Foreword to W. B. Anderson's *The Church in East Africa 1840–1974*, Desmond M. B. Tutu, Bishop of Lesotho, writes of 'this exhilarating story which links us firmly with our glorious and not so glorious past', and says:

> Once Africa got this Gospel, then the liberation struggle was well and truly launched. And when we feel that the Church is irrelevant, as we often must, it is salutary to remember that most of the political leaders of the liberation struggle in Africa received their nurture from Christian missionary institutions and – even more paradoxical and splendidly glorious – most of the leaders of the liberation struggle in Africa have themselves been committed Christians. Yes, these people from overseas brought us something too wonderful for words, even if they brought it wrapped in Western swaddling clothes.

The story of the U.M.F.C. in East Africa up to 1907 becomes one of heroism and grace, though numerically it can hardly be claimed as one of success. One missionary after another succumbed to dysentery and malaria.

Charles New, who in 1863 began his term of service at the very time that news came through from Sierra Leone about the death of his brother Joseph, rejected Ribé as the mission centre and turned explorer to find a more suitable region. 'Let me never think of merging the missionary into the traveller! Let me not be the discoverer of lands unknown, except as it may be necessary to the salvation of souls! Not ambition be my guide – but only Thy glory!' Even so, in 1871, with the help of his servant Tofiki, he succeeded in becoming the first white traveller to reach the shining snows of Mount Kilimanjaro. His account of this event is related in the book he wrote on furlough: *Life, Wanderings, and Labours in Eastern Africa* (London 1874). In his second 'tour', as a period of overseas service was then significantly termed, gravely ill and threatened by a band of African warriors, he appealed to Wakefield for help, but died before he could be reached. At that time, Charles New had been the only Corresponding Member of the Royal Geographical Society apart from David Livingstone.

Even the splendid work of men like New and, later, Thomas Henry Carthew (four years in West Africa and nine in Kenya), or the dramatic escape of Goodman in Sierra Leone, did not make an impact on the home Church like the murder, by Masai raiders in January 1886, of a young couple, John and Annie Houghton. Like Freeman in West Africa, the anchor man while colleague after colleague died or had to return home, there was one in Kenya whose service spanned almost the whole of our period. J. B. Griffiths arrived at Meru in January 1895, and in spite of almost constant attacks of malaria worked there until his death in 1932. At the time of the Union in 1907, this heroic labour could show no more than 404 members in the East Africa District.

The other region where the U.M.F.C. entered 'heathen' territory was in China. Just as Krapf had had a hand in starting the East African mission, Hudson Taylor was involved in this second project. In the first place, his father had suggested the idea to James Everett, and when Eckett heard about it he proposed, in a letter of 1861 to the *Magazine*, that a mission to China be commenced. In view of a generally favourable reaction, Charles Cheetham, who pledged personal financial support, again took the initiative. This time he invited Hudson Taylor to meet and inform the Committee. The outcome was a decision to send two men to Ningpo when the Taiping rebellion had died down. Taylor, for his part, offered to give them instruction in the Ningpo dialect before their departure.

William R. Fuller, whose home was in the London Fourth Circuit, was the first to go. Taylor had given him the promised language lessons, and as an additional preparation he had studied medicine at the London Hospital. With his wife and children he sailed in the summer of 1864. Tragedy overtook the family during the voyage with the death of the youngest member.

John Mara soon followed him, and Frederick Galpin arrived in 1868. He was from the same circuit as Fuller, so illustrating a familiar fact that one man's missionary call has often been another man's missionary call as well. Mara and Fuller were soon in trouble with their health, and this continued although Fuller moved from the trying conditions of Ningpo to a more salubrious station at Chefoo. By 1870 both were back home.

This unpromising start was the prelude to a distinguished period in the missionary history of the U.M.F.C. Frederick Galpin and Robert Swallow, both to be elected President during later service at home, each gave thirty years to China and in 1892 J. W. Heywood began a stint of forty years. In 1882, W. E. Soothill began his outstanding career. Among the many books which he wrote were a hymn-book, a dictionary, and a translation of the New Testament into the Wenchow dialect. Later he was appointed President of the Shansi Imperial University, and then Professor of Chinese at Oxford. In twenty-five years he saw a nucleus of 30 members grow to 200 churches with 30 Chinese ministers, 200 local preachers, and a community of 10,000. At the Union of 1907, the U.M.F.C. reported 20,191 members and supported 30 missionaries.

A third element in the Union was that of the Bible Christians who in Samuel Pollard were to provide one of the most colourful characters ever to leave Britain in the service of a Methodist Church. Six years after they had been founded, in the year of Waterloo, they formed a Missionary Society 'for the purpose of sending Missionaries into the dark and destitute parts of the United Kingdom, and other countries as Divine Providence might open the way'. So the concept of the mission of the Church at home and overseas as *one* was there among the Bible Christians almost from the beginning.

Apparently the young movement did not lack adventurous spirits, and the providential way was opened even to such benighted parts of the country as Kent. What it did lack was funds. This prevented the Bible Christians from sending anyone to non-Christian people overseas until much later in the century. Once again, Hudson Taylor comes into the picture. He, and a lay colleague in the China Inland Mission, Mr B. Broomhall, addressed the Conference in 1884 about a proposed mission to that country. The question as to whether the time had come to start such work had been raised by J. H. Prior as early as 1865 in the *Jubilee Memorial Volume*, and from that time it only needed some great impetus to get the system moving. Now, in the Jubilee Chapel, East Road, London, the powerful advocacy of one who was surely among the greatest missionaries who ever went to China provided that impetus. Hudson Taylor addressed the Conference during one of its morning sessions, and along with Miss Turner, who had spent five years as an educational missionary among Chinese women and children, he spoke at a missionary meeting the same evening. When Thomas Grylls Vanstone, who had been converted in that same chapel only a few years previously, offered to go, decisive action could not long be delayed. It came the following year, 1885, when the Conference, meeting in Bideford, commissioned Vanstone and another young man from a well-known family in the Connexion, Samuel Thomas Thorne, for work in China. At first they were under the wing of the C.I.M., to whom the U.M.F.C. and the Bible Christians owed so much in the vital period when they were just beginning to get established.

Of all the people of many nationalities to whom Methodist missionaries have been sent, the Chinese of the period were perhaps the most cautious and distant.

> The attitude of the Chinese to the foreigner was very similar to their attitude to the spirits of the dead. They were both partly revered and partly feared, because they represented an intangible world beyond their own, great and mysterious, but one that the Chinese were content to know very little about. 'We know you exist but please go away and leave us alone!'[42]

Those words of Elliott Kendall go some way towards an explanation

[42] R. Elliott Kendall, *Beyond the Clouds: the Story of Samuel Pollard of South-West China* (London 1949), p. 2.

as to why so many pioneer missionaries in China found it hard going at the start. They are also a reminder that when the improbable summons to mission comes to a man or woman, a summons which cannot be denied without destroying their inner integrity, it is not a summons to manipulate people but to understand them sensitively.

If progress seemed at first so slow as to be imperceptible to those young people sent to China with the blessing of the 1885 Bideford Conference, it was not for the want of effort on the part of the home Church now that the project had at last been launched. That can be seen from the mere catalogue of events and appointments for the first ten years.[43]

1885 (November 4th) Revs S. T. Thorne and T. G. Vanstone proceed to China
1885–1903 Rev. I. B. Vanstone, Missionary Secretary
1886 Work commenced in Yunnan
1887 Revs F. J. Dymond and S. Pollard proceed to China
1888 First Chinese Church formed
1890 Revs W. Tremberth and John Carter proceed to China
(August 26th) Revd J. Carter died in China
1891 Miss A. Hainge (Mrs S. Pollard) joins Mission staff in China from C.I.M.
(September 23rd) Revd S. T. Thorne died in China
1892 Women's Missionary League formed. Misses E. A. Bailey (Mrs W. Tremberth) and M. M. Cannon, from New Zealand (Mrs F. J. Dymond), first Lady Missionaries sent out from England, commence work in China
1894 Revd E. J. Piper (Australia) proceeds to China
1895 Revs Dr Lewis Savin (first B.C. Medical Missionary) and C. E. Hicks appointed to China

The official chronology from which this list is taken, shows that the same sacrificial giving of men, women and money continued in the following years. Into this diary come three unforgettable dates. The first was at the turn of the century, and the laconic entry reads:

1900 Boxer Riots in China. Christians in grave peril.

The entry for 1900, under the section 'Methodist New Connexion', of the same chronology allows a little cautious expansion:

1900 Boxer Riots in China. Missionaries in peril, many members martyred, and many chapels destroyed.

[43] See the 'Chronology of Foreign Missions', in *The Story of the United Methodist Church*, p. 391: appointments to places like Canada.

Persecution often brings confusion to those of feeble faith, and capitulation to the weak. That is not to deny the fact that it does reveal the high qualities already there in the faithful, to the inspiration and encouragement of us all. For the most part it is this aspect of the effect produced by persecution which is recorded in missionary literature.

The Boxer Riots were directed against the 'Foreign Devils' – missionaries and traders alike. We are able to enter into those events in a unique way through the pages of a book by a Methodist minister who acted as chaplain and interpreter to the British Expeditionary Force which relieved Peking. The book is *China's Dayspring after Thirty Years*, and its author, the Rev. Frederick Brown.[44] Having written in well-deserved praise of the part played in this episode by his colleagues ('Meekness is only strength in repose'; and, quoting a contemporary writer, 'The real hero is the missionary in China'; 'The Church . . . should thank God for the noble army of men and women who have so magnificently given proofs of their devotion to the work committed to their care'), he goes on to say:[45]

> I should like to say a word in praise of the heroic devotion and marvellous fidelity of the native Chinese Christians throughout the Boxer rising . . . Thousands were slain. Most of them could have saved their lives, but would not, at the cost of giving up their faith.

This, Brown claims, is the complete answer to the then current slander about 'rice Christians'. He concluded his book with a prophetic quotation from Dr G. G. Findlay:

> Never in any region of the world has Christendom had before her an open door so great and effectual as that which China is now offering. That door has suddenly been opened by the Unseen Hand, through a chain of momentous international events; it may be quickly and decisively closed.

Elliott Kendall[46] has described how the Boxer Rebellion affected one Bible Christian station: that at Chaotung, where Pollard was holding the line. At first, like missionaries in other parts of China, he took no

[44] Chairman of District, and Officiating Wesleyan Chaplain in the North China Command, he came to be known as 'Brown of Tientsin'. Born in Bishop Auckland and educated at the Quaker School in South Terrace, 'his religious training was received in the Methodist Free Church and Sunday School'. He spoke at the Exeter Hall during the Y.M.C.A. International Conference of 1881. During that visit to London, he heard a call to missionary service, was sent to China, and after two years there was transferred to the North China Mission of the Methodist Episcopal Church. In 1888 he was ordained, and appointed to Wesley Circuit Tientsin. Two years later he opened and became Principal of the first modern school for boys to be opened in that city. Among many other services which he offered to China, he helped found the first T'ieu Tsu Hui (Natural Feet) Society.

[45] Op. cit., p. 189.

[46] Op. cit., pp. 53ff.

action. It seems likely that none of them was aware of the enormity of the coming disaster in which more than two hundred of them were to be murdered. Though the gathering storm was already leaving its wrack of looted houses, burnt-out buildings and innocent victims, they had become used to wild rumours and had come to terms with the thought of sudden death. So for a while Pollard made no change in his pattern of preaching and service to the people, especially in the use of his medical skills. But then a threatening letter was nailed to his door in the night; and next, a Chinese gatekeeper was stabbed almost to death after an evening service, probably in mistake for Pollard. The courage with which the missionaries now continued their normal work, with an air of indifference, was a display which brought out similar courage among the Chinese. Some moved among the villages preaching. Three families which up to then had not ventured to make a public declaration of their faith chose this of all times to burn their idols and follow Christ. Pollard tells how delighted his little boys were with the bonfire.

Then the storm which had been threatening broke. It was in June 1900 that it reached Yunnan. Rioting broke out in Kunming. As the missionaries there fled for protection to foreign consulates, the mob looted and wrecked their homes. At any moment the fury might descend on Chaotung. The Consul sent orders to depart. Pollard called the few Christians together and explained that they were leaving. Some no doubt were afraid, though few showed signs of it. Many were deeply sad. But to the encouragement of all, sixteen begged to be baptized.

With a small escort of soldiers, one of whom was drowned as the party were crossing a river in full spate, they set out on a journey that took them a month. A detour round the dangerous region of Kunming brought them finally into French Indo-China, and we can still share in the relief of Pollard's cry as they crossed the frontier: 'Under the shelter of a foreign flag at last!'

It took less than a year for the worst of the terror to die down, but Pollard returned from this exile alone, since the situation was still judged to be potentially too dangerous for women and children. Even so, an enormous change had come over the scene. The violence of the Boxers had given way to the traditional tolerance of the Chinese people, and his re-entry into Chaotung, complete with banners and fireworks, had all the warmth and excitement of a triumphal procession.

If this, the first of those three unforgettable entries in the Chronology of Bible Christian Foreign Missions, stood for near-tragedy, the second and third covered events that were to bring immense joy and inspiration to the members in China and in Britain alike. They read simply enough:

1904 (July 12th) The first coming of the Miao.

1905 (November 5th) First Miao Church formed. Stone Gateway Mission Station established.

These events prelude a story which subsequently carries us into the period after 1907. So we leave our account of the Bible Christian missions with the report that in 1907 they brought to the Union nine missionaries serving 5,419 members in China.

As we have seen, the formation of the United Methodist Church in 1907 brought under one administration the missions established by the United Methodist Free Churches in South-East China, East and West Africa; by the Methodist New Connexion in North China; and by the Bible Christian Methodist Church in Yunnan, West China. At the time of the Union, the Foreign Missionary Secretaries, as they were then termed, of the respective churches were the Revs H. T. Chapman, G. Packer, and C. Stedeford. The Treasurers were Messrs Robert Bird, J.P., J. Hepworth, J.P., and the Rev. W. R. K. Baulkwill. For three years these officers co-operated while retaining their sectional responsibilities; then, in 1910, the separate missionary funds were amalgamated under the Rev. C. Stedeford as Secretary and Mr W. H. Butler as Treasurer.

Trouble was not long in touching the newly-formed Society. The record is immediately sprinkled with headlines such as:

1907 (April 8th) Rev. S. Pollard brutally beaten by mob. Earthquake in Jamaica. Much damage done to Mission Stations.
1909 Rebellion in Yunnan. Some chapels destroyed.
1911 Outbreak of Chinese Revolution. Work in North and East China greatly hindered.

Within this context appear such entries as:

1907 Pollard opens up mission work among the Nosu.
1910 Conference approves advance to Meru (East Africa).
1912 Meru surveyed by Rev. J. B. Griffiths and Rev. W. U. Bassett. Association with Union Theological College, Peking, established (Rev. G. T. Candlin, D.D., Tutor). Jamaica Mission unites with other Methodist Churches.
1913 Rev. R. T. Worthington and Mr F. Mimmack open Meru Mission. Kopu tribesmen seek missionaries.
1914 Missionary Debt Extinction Fund completed; £28,500 raised. Miao missionaries set out to evangelise Kopu.
(August 22nd) Thomas Mazeras, pioneer native minister, died in East Africa.

So, with Europe entering a war that was to change the whole world and the Christian Church in every nation, we find that that part of it which was becoming at home in China followed St Paul's methods of evangelism, as the Miao converts set out to share their faith with the Kopu.

One of the first effects of World War I on the U.M.M.S., as on all other missionary societies based on Britain, was a drying up of the flow of new missionaries, which until then had enabled vacancies to be refilled and new work undertaken. Indeed the military absorption of manpower meant that some men were drawn away from their stations. This, along with the death of Pollard in 1915 and of Savill and Baxter in 1918, all in China, imposed exacting demands on depleted staffs. At the same time a further anxiety was caused by the alarming rise in prices and in some foreign exchanges, so that expenditure escalated rapidly. One extra area was temporarily added to the territory served by the Society: the direction and maintenance of the German Mission adjacent to its own on Tana River in Kenya was taken over until it could be restored to the German Church in 1925.

For the U.M.M.S., the period between the end of the war in 1918 and the Methodist reunion of 1932 was largely one of recovery and consolidation punctuated by times of regression through political unrest. Thus, 1919 saw the reoccupation of Yunnanfu in West China, where work had been suspended ever since the withdrawal at the time of the Boxer disturbances, and in 1927 Tikonko in Sierra Leone was re-entered after the evacuation caused by the destruction of the buildings in the Mendeland rebellion of 1898.[47] A notable feature in all the Districts of China and Africa was the educational and medical work of the Church, providing schools for children and for the training of native workers, voluntary and paid, and including Bible women. Even these centres, valuable as they were for the life of the local communities, were not immune from political attack and mob violence. So Ningpo College, founded in 1906 under Principal H. S. Redfern, which had enjoyed continuous success and had been built up to a student population of 220, was shattered by the political storm which burst in 1925, and it was some years before it was restored. Redfern returned in 1930, but there were only 100 students after a slow period of growth. A similar pattern developed with regard to Wenchow College: founded in 1903; staff compelled by political turbulence to withdraw in 1926; and buildings restored to use by the Church in 1929. Not inappropriately has the title *A Church Born to Suffer*[48] been conferred upon the Christian family in China. And yet that suffering, and the innate grace and courtesy of the

[47] A unique picture of Methodism in Sierra Leone during the period we are considering here is given in the *Autobiography* of the Rev. Dr Akinumi Pratt, soon to become the first African to be appointed Chairman of the District, and later still the first President of the Methodist Church in Sierra Leone.

[48] Dr John Rose's account (London 1951) of the first century of Methodism in South China (1851–1951).

people of China, have taught the missionaries at least as much as they themselves have given to the Chinese.

Throughout almost the whole of the period in which those branches of Methodism which came together in 1907 were supporting overseas missions, and from then until 1932, a parallel development was going on within the Primitive Methodist Church. Like the Bible Christians, they too began by setting up a 'general missionary establishment' soon after the Connexion had been founded, and they too had to wait for half a century, gathering strength before they were in a position to send men and women to non-Christian areas overseas. Primitive Methodism may be regarded as having started in 1811. The first Missionary meetings of the Connexion were held on 8 July 1821, at Turnditch in the afternoon and Belper in the evening. One of the resolutions that found approval urged the necessity of taking the Gospel 'to the dark and benighted villages of the Peak of Derbyshire', and another asked that there should be 'prayer and supplication for a special blessing upon all missionaries who are labouring in foreign lands'.

The next tiny step was taken in 1837. A shoemaker called Joseph Diboll tried to persuade the Conference, meeting in Sheffield, to sponsor a mission to Africa. It was clear that there would be no immediate practical response, so he offered his services to the Baptist Missionary Society and was accepted. But the idea had been accepted in principle. Diboll's home was in Yarmouth and, in a way that was perhaps characteristic of the Primitive Methodists of that period, the Conference agreed that the Yarmouth Circuit be allowed to open an African mission when it could raise the necessary funds. It is hardly surprising that such a time never came, but the Norwich District, of which the Yarmouth Circuit was part, kept the appeal alive in the Connexion. An African missionary meeting to press the claim was held in 1852 at Swaffham, where James Fuller had made a close study of what was then known of the continent, and at the Jubilee Conference of 1861 the Connexion as a whole finally committed itself to the project. Nearly ten years later, on 25 January 1870, R. W. Burnett and Henry Roe sailed in the *Mangindo* and landed on 21 February at the port of Santa Isabel in Fernando Po.

Even in this tiny island, owing allegiance to Spain and dominated by Roman Catholicism of a type more intolerant than that which Protestant missionaries almost universally meet today, they were not the first members of their Connexion to hold services. Following a pattern which we have found in other parts of the world, a beginning had been made by laymen who were visiting the place in the course of their business. In August 1869, a ship called the *Elgiva*, while trading between Liverpool and the West Coast of Africa, anchored off the island. Her captain,

W. Robinson, and her carpenter, James Hands, were both Primitive Methodists. The resident agent of the firm which owned the vessel needed to have certain repairs done to his own ship, so Hands was sent ashore to do the work. In the evenings and on Sundays he gathered a group who had previously been under the care of Baptist missionaries. They met, as they had done for years, in the house of a loyal and courageous Christian, Mamma Job, and Hands was an immediate success. The little church, which had been looking for a leader, first asked him to stay and be their minister, and when that was seen to be impossible, they wrote a letter to England asking that missionaries be sent. The appeal, reinforced by letters from Robinson and Hands, went to the Liverpool Second Circuit and from them to the General Missionary Committee, who responded by appointing Burnett and Roe. A new chapter in the history of Primitive Methodism had been opened. Some have even compared that first service in Mamma Job's house with the famous camp meeting on Mow Cop.[49] It certainly led on to events in West Africa which, through the next six decades up to the Union of 1932, were a constant source of inspiration and challenge to the home Church.

Even so, there was plenty to contend with. It goes without saying that malaria played havoc with the health of the first Europeans to serve that young church in Fernando Po. How right Aggrey was when he said that the symbol of West Africa should be the mosquito, since it was responsible for preventing white people from settling there. In point of fact it is this factor of health that has produced the great political and social differences between the countries of West and East Africa. The P.M.M.S. too had its martyrs. The first in Fernando Po was R. B. Blackburn. He was followed by M. H. Barron, Mrs D. T. Maylott, Mrs N. Boocock, Mrs H. Buckenham, and the Luddingtons.

To these hazards were added difficulties caused by the Government. An account of the time when William Welford and the members at George's Bay were being harassed reads:

> The schools have been closed, and every indication that the mission premises are used as a place of worship has been removed by order of the government. Singing in the chapel has been prohibited, and all service in the cemetery at the burial of the dead. The missionary was subject to interference and annoyance of the most vexatious kind, and was at last imprisoned on board the pontoon, where he was kept for a month subject to insult and indignity from day to day, and was only released on the interference of the commander of Her Majesty's gunboats, who fortunately visited Santa Isabel. The people were watched as they went to and fro from the meetings, they were insulted by the

[49] *H.M.G.B.*, ii, 304–6.

Romish priests in the streets, summarily fined, dragged to prison, and persecuted in a great variety of ways; still they remained steadfast in the faith. The missionary and his wife were ultimately banished.

The next territorial advance made by the P.M.M.S. in West Africa was attended with the familiar loss of life through illness among the missionaries, but was to lead on to some of the finest work undertaken by the Society. The area was in the south-east of Nigeria. The timing coincided with the Missionary Jubilee of 1893, when it was recalled that half a century earlier the first General Missionary Committee of the Connexion had been appointed and a start had been made upon a colonial enterprise by sending Robert Ward to New Zealand.

The place where it all began was the Old Palaver House at Archibong. Here Robert Fairley and J. Marcus Brown held their first service on 17 December. By 1932 the growth of the Church in Eastern Nigeria was such, numerically, in the quality of its members, and in the value of its services to the community, that the Connexional Editor, Aquila Barber, in a Souvenir volume could claim: 'The wonderful response of the last thirty years furnishes one of the most impressive missionary records of the twentieth century.'[50]

The year 1909 was memorable in that development. By then, the Oron Institute, founded in 1905 under W. J. Ward as Principal, was able to send out its first group of native evangelists. There were nine of them, and two, John Enang Gill and Ben T. Showell, were later ordained into the ministry. C. P. Groves, who later served as Professor of Missions on the staff of the Selly Oak Colleges and wrote a definitive history of the various attempts to found the Church in Africa,[51] took over as Principal at Oron in 1911. Two other outstanding events of 1909 were the opening of the Girls' Institute at Jamestown (with Miss A. Richardson, who was still on the staff at the time of Methodist Union) and the first entry into Nsit country. Here the pioneer was W. Christie, and through his courage and initiative a series of new stations was established. Barber lists them in his description of the missionary pageant of the first three decades of the twentieth century. Names like Ikot Ekpene and Umuahia; Uzuakoli, Port Harcourt and Opobo, were to become familiar in the home Church, as did those of the missionaries who defied heat, humidity and health hazards, with all manner of frustration and fatigue, to become more and more trusted, loved and honoured by the people: Ralph Ladlay (first Principal of the Uzuakoli Training Institute and translator of parts of *Pilgrim's Progress*, whose wife was later to be appointed as one of the Secretaries of Women's Work in the united M.M.S.); Frederick W. Dodds (General

[50] *A Methodist Pageant* (London 1932), p. 192.
[51] *The Planting of Christianity in Africa*, 4 vols. (London 1948–58).

Superintendent of P.M.M.S. missions in Nigeria at the time of the 1932 reunion, who later succeeded George Ayre as Africa Secretary of the M.M.S.); and Herbert L. O. Williams, along with many others.

Medical work at Ituk Mban which in 1932 was just beginning an attack on leprosy that was to become known throughout the world, the Girls' Institute at Ovim, also a fairly recent initiative in 1932, and many churches and schools, were all part of a lively complex. If, as Barber wrote,[52] 'these stations with their outposts are but as points of light in the heathen darkness', they were also 'the only Protestant appeal to a million of people'.

The other regions manned by missionaries of the P.M.M.S. lay much further south and therefore enjoyed, on the whole, a far more healthy climate. The first to be entered was at Aliwal North on the Orange River. Henry Buckenham landed at Port Elizabeth on 5 October 1870, and travelled 300 miles to his station. There he met an Englishman called Lindsay, yet another in the long line of Methodist laymen – residents, traders, soldiers and others – whose appeals to the home Church that missionaries should be sent have been responsible for the development of work which, in a small way, they themselves had begun.

From the start there was steady growth at Aliwal North. Gradually, premises were acquired for preaching services, a Sunday School, an evening school for coloured people and, before Buckenham left in 1875, a purpose-built church and manse. Others took up the work, including J. Msikinya, a coloured minister, so that in 1888 all was ready for the seventeen years of outstanding service given by G. E. Butt. During that period, within an area 150 miles long and 50 miles wide, with eight sub-stations, and where the Gospel was preached in three languages, the educational and spiritual needs both of colonists and natives were served. From these foundations there was built up what the Connexional Editor in 1932 could describe as 'one of our largest and most prosperous missions'.

Henry Buckenham was also in at the start of an arduous mission in South Central Africa. He and his wife, with Arthur Baldwin and F. Ward, sailed from Dartmouth on 26 April 1889. Baldwin looked back on the five years before they reached their objective, Mashukulumbwe-land:

> We have helplessly watched our oxen die until not one has remained. We have been again and again ordered to leave the country; have had our boys taken from us, and all our food supplies stopped so that we should be starved out; in fact, have all the vials of King Lewanika's wrath, brewed by the machinations of a wicked trader, envious of the Chartered Company and the influence the missionaries

[52] Op. cit., p. 192.

> had over the king, poured on our heads; still, Mr. Buckenham never lost heart . . . and that faith, after being severely tried, God honoured by giving us an open door and every facility for entering it.[53]

Buckenham's splendid service came to an end when on the boat coming home, ill and exhausted, he died on 11 July 1896; but others carried on the work. Notable among these were Edwin W. Smith, who in North-Western Rhodesia was to reduce the language to writing, prepare grammars and lexicons, and translate the New Testament, and Dr H. S. Gerrard, known as 'the man who cuts people'. In one month he treated patients from twenty-four villages in an area covering some 2,000 square miles. The varied character of the work done in church, school, workshop and clinic was the outcome of a deliberate policy advocated, during his term as General Missionary Secretary, by John Smith, who was convinced that the complete transformation of the people of Africa required this co-ordinated approach. Nowhere was his policy more successful than in South Central Africa.

The period around 1885 saw one of the most important events in the history of Methodism overseas. The Wesleyan Conference of 1882 had declared that in its judgment the time had arrived for the formation of an autonomous West Indian Conference or Conferences, and directed the missionary committee to prepare and submit a scheme. The committee undertook this task with some apprehension, arising from facts which appear in their annual report for that year:

> Last year we reported the visitation of hurricanes; demolishing buildings, destroying crops, and hurrying whole populations into the miseries of sudden want; this year we tell an even sadder story . . . Yellow fever and smallpox defying all resistance have marched through Barbados, Trinidad, Hayti and Demerara.

The ravages of smallpox among the people of Haiti in particular had been appalling. Among the missionaries in the Caribbean area there were four victims: Cocks, Elliot, Herivel and Mrs Smith of St Martin. Yet they could report that, as far as they could ascertain, there had been an increase in membership. A little later, in 1886, the devastation which these islands suffered was caused by a disastrous failure of the fruit crop resulting in stagnation of trade and the moving out of whole families. In conditions such as these it is small wonder that the report of the W.M.M.S. for 1883, while saying that the committee was engaged in the preparation of a scheme by which authority could be handed over to the West Indian Churches so that they could be 'placed upon a self-supporting and self-governing basis', added that 'the operation is one

[53] B. A. Barber, op. cit., p. 186.

of difficulty and delicacy and will call for the exercise of wisdom, forbearance and generosity'. Such a scheme was in point of fact submitted to the Conference of 1883 and then, for their comments, to the West Indian Districts concerned.

The hope, actually to be fulfilled, was expressed that 'these old-established and wonderfully successful missions will be able to celebrate their Centenary in 1886 under the new régime'. The further hope that 'though for a while they would need help with men and money, at no distant day they will be able to dispense with help as regards both' proved to be far too optimistic. Meanwhile the good work continued. Even after a revolution in which seven thousand people were killed, and in spite of the recent smallpox epidemic, by 1884 it could be reported that the Church in Haiti was beginning to recover.

The British Conference created a West Indian Conference, to meet triennially, with two annual Conferences meeting under it, which were to receive diminishing grants from the W.M.M.S. The Eastern section comprised Districts in Antigua, St Kitts, St Vincent, Barbados and Trinidad, with their neighbouring islands and British Guiana; the Western section was made up of four Districts in Jamaica, the Haiti and San Domingo District, and a mission in Central America embracing Panama and Costa Rica.

In 1885 the missionary committee reported the completion of this transaction by including in their annual report an extract from the Address of the General Conference of the West Indian Connexion of 1884. Its first paragraph sounded a grave note of warning:

> We recognize with devout thankfulness the good hand of God, which has been upon the Churches of these lands from the beginning until now. The general depression of trade makes the present time an unfavourable one for assuming new financial obligations.

Yet there was cause to be thankful. The churches were vigorous and growing. Membership had indeed been affected by what has long come to be the familiar Caribbean tendency towards migrant labour. This time there was an exodus of thousands of workers to the Isthmus of Panama, and yet they reported an overall increase of 182; a total numerical strength of 43,318 full members; 1,812 on trial, and 2,876 in junior classes. Primary education gave them great concern on financial grounds. In the West Conference, higher education had given greater satisfaction. There was a strong home missionary urge, and work had already begun in Panama. They had their eye on Puerto Rico, Guadeloupe, Martinique and Cuba. Plans were already well advanced for celebrating, in 1886, the centenary of work in this, the oldest Methodist mission field.

So began the first brave attempt to grant autonomy to an area first opened up by a Methodist Missionary Society within the terms of our definition. It lasted for nearly twenty years, but at that time, in 1903, the British Conference and the West Indian Churches were reluctantly forced to admit that the step taken in 1885 must be retraced. The third party in the arrangement, the Missionary Committee, had never been convinced that the scheme was viable. When they came to make their report in 1905, they made it clear that in 1885 it had been the British Conference that had thought the time was ripe for Caribbean administrative independence. The Missionary Committee considered that the experiment of creating a West Indian Conference 'was premature, and carried out the measure only under explicit direction of the Conference'.

The scheme never had a hope of being financially sound. Yet when the W.M.M.S. Committee resumed control of the West Indian Missions on 1 January 1904, there were 'no signs of decay in our Churches, but, on the contrary, signs of life and growth. They came back to us with more than 40,000 members, with 3,000 on trial; and have advanced by nearly 1,000 members during the past year.' Coming as they did, appealing in deep distress for the support of the Parent Conference, those Churches posed real problems for the W.M.M.S., which was already in some financial trouble. 'The return of the West Indian Churches revolutionizes our figures. We have talked of doubling our income: we double our membership at a stroke.' Not until well after the reunion of 1932 was a similar grant of autonomy to be made to any District overseas.

The financial embarrassment which brought to an end the first period of Caribbean autonomy was not immediately dispelled when the home Church reassumed responsibility for Methodist work in the islands. Indeed, it was not until the eve of World War I that contributions given in 1913 to the W.M.M.S. Centenary Thanksgiving Fund made it possible to clear away the debts and set the circuits free to do their proper work of evangelism. From then until 1932 that work went forward steadily. There were setbacks. In 1931, just before the Union, Honduras suffered a devastating hurricane which destroyed the capital, Belize. But the first Report of the newly united Society was able to tell how the people were making a magnificent struggle to rebuild their homes and carry on the life of the Church. There were problems – many of them moral problems that arose from the impositions that had been laid on the people when they were slaves. Then they had not been allowed to marry, so it is small wonder that even after emancipation some in the community set up home without taking that prior step. But the Church made its appeal for higher standards, and progress was being made in that respect too. Numerically there was much to be thankful for. At Union, there were 48,500 full members and a total baptized community of 150,000. Of these, 37,000 were in Jamaica, the strongest and most progressive West Indian District. Haiti had been put under the care of the Jamaican Church, and the District also had its outposts on the isthmus of Central America. Wilfred Easton, later to become the Secretary at the Mission House in charge of the Caribbean area but in 1932 one of the younger ministers there, was doing outstanding work with young men at the Coke Memorial Church in Kingston.

With the notable exception of Burma, which had to wait another two years for its first Methodist missionary, the shape of the work under the care of the General Committee of the W.M.M.S. in the third half-century of its history had largely been determined by 1885.[54] In addition to those serving in France, Germany, Italy, Spain, Portugal, Sweden and Switzerland, areas which lie outside the scope of this survey, men and women from Britain were at work in Ceylon, India, China, South and West Africa, and the two Districts which were not included in the scheme for West Indian autonomy: Honduras and Bahamas.

Ceylon, or Sri Lanka as it is called today, had by 1885 two well-developed Districts: Sinhalese in the south and Tamil in the north. They are divided by a belt of jungle and forest which has had a profound effect on the history of the island and of our work there. The Sinhalese come of Aryan stock and by religion are Buddhists. To the north and east the people are mainly Tamils, and they are Hindus by faith. Even in appearance and dress, manner of life and language, these groups are distinct and the missionary approach to them has necessarily been different.

One of the happiest aspects of the work here has been that it has produced distinguished Christians, some of whom have made outstanding contributions to the life of the world Church. Already, in 1885, names like da Silva and Goonawardene appear among the staff. Eventually, perhaps the most memorable of them all was to be that of Daniel T. Niles.

At the opening of our period the Missionary Committee were able to report[55] a second successful year in the island with a large increase in membership, though the cloud which always seems to cover missionary enterprises – lack of money – was causing concern. In the light of subsequent struggles between Church and State over education in the island, the report on the schools is of some significance. It begins with the remark that this work has been carried on vigorously. The comments on such institutions as Wesley College, Colombo, Richmond

[54] For a fuller description of this pattern, see William Moister, *Conversations on the Rise, Progress and Present State of Wesleyan Missions in Various Parts of the World* (London 1869). Since this book was written in 1869, it includes those West Indian Districts which were soon to become self-governing.

[55] Annual Report, 1885, p. 76.

College, Galle and the Girls' High Schools at Colpetty and Kandy sufficiently bear this out. Then comes the ominous news of changes in government policy. Grants to English aided schools were to be reduced to the same level as those for vernacular schools, which was a severe blow to the finances of the mission. A measure which, it was presumed, would work in our favour was the decision to close all government English schools in town. But of greater importance was the new ruling that no child except those who had been vaccinated or had already had smallpox was to be accepted as a pupil in an aided school. In view of the strong prejudice of the country people against vaccination, this was certain to make difficulties for the village schools. There was some irritation in all this, no doubt, some impediment to the progress of the schools; but the hardships were small by comparison with those caused by the government's later interference with curricula.

When it came to summing up the work in Ceylon at the time of the union in 1932,[56] it had to be admitted that, 'In spite of early promise, Ceylon has not been an easy mission-field. The Buddhists in the south and the Hindus in the north have strenuously opposed our work, and have contested every foot of the ground.' When we recall what was soon to come in Germany and Italy, Spain and Japan, the next words in the report gain significance:

> In recent years the strength of the old faiths has been intensified by a Nationalism that represents it as unpatriotic to 'change one's religion'. With the exception of Islam, no religion is presenting such determined opposition as Buddhism to Christianity. Under the influence of reform movements, the Buddhists have copied our methods and borrowed our phraseology. They speak of Buddha as 'our Lord and Saviour', and observe his birthday; they have opened Buddhist Sunday Schools and Young Men's Buddhist Associations. Buddhism has been presented as the national faith . . . Similar movements have taken place among the Hindus in North Ceylon.

Yet there had been real progress towards self-support and self-government. Perhaps with the example of the West Indies in mind, a different method was pursued. In 1932 it was possible to say that about twenty circuits were already absolutely self-supporting. These, which were classed as 'A' circuits, had their own Ceylonese ministers, and received no grants from England. Those circuits which were designated 'B', though steadily advancing towards self-support, still required some assistance. 'C' circuits were receiving considerable help from the Missionary Society, while making varying degrees of progress towards meeting their costs.

[56] *Our Overseas Missions, Past and Present,* described as 'The First Annual Report of the Methodist Missionary Society, Being a Report of the Year 1932', p. 53.

In 1885, the 'other mission Districts in Asia' included those in what was referred to as Continental India. These comprised the Madras District; the Nizam Section (places and work within the territory of the Nizam of Hyderabad, including Hyderabad itself, Secunderabad – with work in Telugu, Tamil, and among the soldiers of the garrisons – and Kureem Nuggur), and the Mysore, Calcutta, and Lucknow and Banares Districts.

The history of Methodist missions in India falls into four periods:

1. For almost half a century the work was confined to the south.[57] During this period, from the inception in 1817 to the Indian Mutiny in 1857, the mistake was made of weakening the effectiveness of expatriate missionaries by distributing them over impossibly wide areas, a policy that too often resulted in frustration and failure.[58] So places like Bombay and Calcutta were occupied for brief periods and then evacuated. During these first four decades of the work in Asia there arose a factor in the life of the home Church which was to have an immense effect on all the stations overseas and particularly those in India. This was the dissension between rival factions which was not finally healed until 1932, and which caused weakness and difficulties enough to make the 'dark forties' a critical time in the Indian missions.

2. The Indian Mutiny of 1857 apparently increased the interest of British Methodism in those missions. The guilty feeling that Christian England had neglected her responsibilities towards the great subcontinent made it easier to recruit reinforcements, so that older stations could be rather better staffed and some new work could be undertaken in Bengal. The high schools at Royapettah and Mannargudi were made more effective and other similar institutions were opened.

There is a further reason for regarding this as a period of development, and one which had important results throughout the whole of the Society's work overseas: the formation of the organization which eventually, indeed at the Union of 1932, came to be known as Women's Work. We have seen[59] that one who had as much influence as anyone in bringing about this memorable beginning was herself a missionary in India. Mary Twiddy, unable to go as a missionary in her own right with the W.M.M.S. or indeed with a number of other societies to which she applied, had eventually been accepted by an inter-denominational group, the 'Society for Promoting Female Education', and sent to

[57] The stations were Madras, Negapatam, Mannagurdi, Trichinopoly, Bangalore, Mysore City, Gubbi and Coonghul.

[58] Obviously this division into periods gives only a rough idea of the times. We still find the Madras District reporting in 1885 what they call 'three important facts which apply equally to all divisions of the Indian field', namely, 'the enormous space which is covered by the Madras District', 'the density of Indian population' and 'the startling paucity of our missionary forces'.

[59] See p. 52, above.

Ceylon. Within a short while of her arrival there she was asked to look after a little boy whose father, Peter Batchelor, a Methodist missionary in India, had recently been widowed. This soon led to an entirely new life for Mary. When the time came for young Percival Batchelor to return to his father at Negapatam, she went with him and within a few months she was married to Peter in the garrison chapel there.

Together, Peter and Mary Batchelor discovered for themselves what a powerful part the missionary's wife could play in offering Christ to India. Often, when her husband went to a village, the men would listen gladly. In part this was, no doubt, owing to their desire to break the centuries-old cycle of hunger, illness, ignorance and sheer grinding poverty which had made their lives such a misery. But for many it was also caused by their disillusionment with their ancestral gods who had clearly proved themselves powerless to help them, and this at the deepest point of their need. As an Indian writer was to put it later, 'I made the pilgrimage to Benares. I washed in the Ganges, and I came away with my sins.' To men like these, the preaching of the Word brought new hope; but what of their wives? Deeply conservative of the old religious ways, and suspicious of anything that would threaten to change them, for all their apparent subjection as less than the dust beneath the feet of their men, they in fact exerted a powerful influence on their families. 'What is needed for the conversion of India,' said one missionary, 'is a new race of grandmothers.' Aggrey, in a different but not entirely dissimilar context, used to say, 'Educate a man, and you educate an individual. Educate a woman, and you educate a family.'

Acting upon this principle, and in line with many another missionary's wife, Mary Batchelor struggled against fierce opposition to start a school for girls. Later, when her own children began to make their inevitable demands upon her time and energies, it became increasingly difficult to maintain both home and school. It only needed one of the children to be seriously ill for them all to be in real trouble. When this happened, as it often did in that region where malaria was endemic, the nearest medical help was two hundred miles away at Madras. The journey had to be endured in a bumpy bullock cart which frequently got stuck in the mud of the so-called road or the soil of the rice-fields they had to cross. At such times Mary had to get out and help to push.

Clearly what was needed was the help of a young woman from England, preferably supported by the women of the home Church. So there came to be written that letter which Dr Hoole presented to the Missionary Committee in October 1858 and which led to the start of W.W. In order to arouse and maintain interest in the work supported by the 'Ladies Committee for the Amelioration of the Condition of Women in Heathen Countries, Female Education, etc.', it was decided that Occasional Papers should be published to give news from overseas and convey requests for help. In the first of these, Mary Batchelor welcomed the new venture and appealed for money and staff in order to start a boarding school. The fact that an epidemic of cholera had left many children orphaned and bereft of all resources sharpened the appeal. The plight of one child in particular, Amurthee, a lovely, lively girl, focused the needs of many who, one by one, were 'adopted' by women's groups in Great Britain.

Mary got her boarding school. The first members of staff appointed to assist her were Mary Scott and her own daughter, now back in India after being at school in England.

> It was an exciting day when at last on May 30, 1860, Mary Batchelor set out to Madras to welcome her two young missionaries. Plans were all ready for their work at Negapatam. But Mary was to discover a disruption of plans which has caused many disturbances in the work of women missionaries ever since! Mary Scott had come out to India, resolved to serve as a single woman, but on September 26 she was married in Madras to the Rev. Robert Stephenson.
>
> So Mary Batchelor and her daughter returned to Negapatam alone, to face their family of twenty-eight boarders, and thirty-three day scholars. Perhaps it was disappointment or perhaps it was overwork that kept her from writing to the Ladies' Committee again. But they did not forget her, and two years later were able to send out at least one who gladly went over to help her.
>
> Then, and not until then, Mary Batchelor left India, her task finished and the Women's Work begun.[60]

3. The third period of Methodist missions in India came some thirty years after the Mutiny. It was a time of expansion which began in three separate areas during the same remarkable year, 1887. The first, which does not strictly fall within the terms of our survey, saw the English work spread westwards from Lucknow to Bombay and Poona, and north-westward to the military centres of the Punjab. The second, which we shall describe later, began when John Milton Brown and W. R. Winston went from Calcutta to Burma, then a predominantly Buddhist stronghold. The third, by far the most memorable, saw the now famous mass movements among the outcaste Malas of Hyderabad and, in 1888, among the Pariahs of the Madras Presidency.

The mass response in Hyderabad has with some justification been claimed as one of the most wonderful movements in the whole history of Christian missions. In 1932 it was possible to say that although it had then continued for forty years it still showed no sign of ceasing. During that time it had spread like wildfire from one jungle village to another. After the first twenty years of this rapid growth it could show a baptized

[60] Pauline M. Webb, *Women of Our Company* (London 1958), p. 31.

community of 16,000; in 1932, after a further similar period, that number had increased to 88,000. At first the response was confined to the Mala outcastes. Then it extended to the Madigas, who were even lower in the Indian social scale.[61] An unexpected feature of the movement was that by 1926 'respectable' villages of higher caste, impressed with the changes in those on the lowest rungs of the ladder, had themselves begun to turn in their thousands to Christ. This reversed the approach which had, at first unsuccessfully, been made in India, and which historically has been the classical model for Christian pioneering missions: make a beginning by effecting the conversion of the ruling class, in the hope that the influence will seep down through every level of the social pyramid.

Just before 1932, movements began in the same District among the gipsy Lombardis and a jungle tribe known as the Ghonds. As the Report of that year emphasizes, this great mass movement was in no sense the response of a mob with all the hysteria that would imply:

> It nowhere consists of great crowds of people, but of little companies of outcaste Christians in more than 600 villages – all under careful supervision and efficient instruction and discipline. They are shepherded by nearly 600 well-trained Indian evangelists, all of whom are married to well-trained Bible-women – our largest band of carefully trained and efficient native workers in the world. There are two boarding-schools (one for girls and one for boys) in nearly every circuit – a total of 22. There are 550 elementary day schools in the villages. There are three large hospitals and 10 dispensaries – most of which have a few beds. There is the leper hospital at Dichpali[62] with 600 patients – one of the largest and finest in all India. And most important of all, the pivot and key of the whole work, there is our great Institution at Medak, with over 300 students being trained to be evangelists by far our largest training institution in the world.

[61] See F. Colyer Sackett, *Posnett of Medak* (London 1951), pp. 50f. From Sackett's account it is clear not only that Posnett regarded the crisis caused by the beginning of the movement among the Madigas as the greatest moment of his missionary life, but also that the claim of these scavengers, who were totally despised even by the outcaste Malas, to be included in the great affirmation, 'God so loved the *world* that whosoever believed in Jesus might be saved', for a while put an enormous strain upon the village congregations. His swift and wise action in sending trained evangelists – 'Emergency Men' – into the areas where they were needed saved the situation. The way in which he arranged for these men to be themselves under the care of selected evangelists was a significant step towards one of his greatest and most inspired achievements – the devolution of authority. It also meant that he had to relinquish his position as Principal of the Institution, to which came a succession of distinguished colleagues who worked with him in all his schemes: Gordon Bennett, Hickman Johnson (later to become India Secretary of the M.M.S.), Robert Howett, Charles Early and Frank Whittaker (later to become a bishop in the Church of South India).

[62] This hospital was later to receive substantial support from Boys' Brigade companies in Britain.

> The work in Hyderabad never 'marks time'; it is always advancing. Last year 2,483 adults and 4,782 children received baptism.[63]

No one made a greater contribution to this unique development in South India than the man who came to be known as Posnett of Medak. In the Conference obituary, Charles W. Posnett was described, with some justification, as 'perhaps the greatest Indian missionary of his generation'. He was the son of a Methodist minister and so went to Kingswood School. There, along with others, he dedicated his life to the service of Christ. As a senior boy he held a Bible class for younger boys. Inevitably, the call to preach, and then to enter the ministry, followed. At Richmond College, which he entered in 1890, he showed himself to be a born leader. Here he offered for overseas service, and after a period of training spent some time gathering medical experience in London hospitals. Then:

> Late in 1892 England was shocked by the total loss off the coast of Spain of the P. and O. s.s. *Roumania*, with almost all of its hundreds of passengers. What stirred Methodism to its depths was the story of the drowning of Mrs. William Burgess of Hyderabad and her children, and the Rev. H. Malkin, a young minister recently appointed to Hyderabad. It seemed to Posnett to crystallise all his past into an urgent call to immediate service. Someone *must* take Malkin's place. So Hyderabad entered into his dreams, and it was not a surprise but the thrilling confirmation of his high hopes when the Conference appointed him to that station. Along with the Rev. H. Highfield, appointed to Ceylon, he sailed in the autumn of 1895 for India on board the s.s. *Golconda*. He spent much of his time during the voyage in prayer, re-dedicating himself to God for service among the outcastes of India, and pleading for power to win them for Christ.[64]

In the first days of his work in India, always a testing time in the life of a missionary, he acquired further equipment for the work that lay ahead by studying Telugu, the language of those around him. Within a year he was able to preach in the vernacular, and was appointed to Secunderabad, where he lectured on Christianity to caste Hindus and Muslims without visible response. It was now that he turned to the 'untouchables': men and women who were regarded as so degraded that if one of them allowed his shadow to fall on the food of a caste person, that food was rendered uneatable and must be thrown away.

Two things drew out Posnett's compassion for these people: their social dereliction and their utter poverty. No one who ever heard Posnett say, 'My dear, they are *so poor*', could ever forget his deep

[63] Annual Report, *The Story of Our Missions* (1932), p. 64.
[64] Colyer Sackett, op. cit., p. 4.

emotional involvement with the people God gave him to care for and elevate.

In 1895 came his appointment to what was then the little village of Medak, where he was to serve until, with typical humility, he retired and left unobtrusively in 1939. From now on, his aim was 'to lay hold of the lowest and by the grace of God to raise them up into a living Church that should command the attention and respect of the Hindu and Muslim world'. This aim was splendidly fulfilled with the completely dedicated co-operation of two colleagues: his sister, and Miss Harris, who shared with him in visiting the villages and healing the sick. As the work opened up, there came the grim affliction of continuous devastating famine followed by lethal attacks of cholera. Ghastly as the effects of this prolonged disaster proved to be, even these horrors became the cause of progress. The famous camp which he set up became a huge training school, and from the desperate need of the cholera patients sprang medical work which continued and developed. When Posnett retired, the Church had been built up from practically nothing to a membership of 140,000.

4. The W.M.M.S. centenary, celebrated in 1913 with its Thanksgiving Fund, marks the opening of the fourth period of Methodist missions in India.[65] The income from that fund made it possible to improve the plant and equipment of schools, colleges, hospitals, and churches. The training of Indian workers received a new impetus, so that although there was little increase in the number of expatriate missionary staff, the church showed an amazing growth. It was in this period that the great mass movement in Hyderabad gained momentum, and a similar one in the Trichinopoly District, after long quiescence, began.

Also in 1913, the Madras Synod decided to send a certain young man to the United Theological College at Bangalore in preparation for what proved to be a remarkable ministry. Paul Rangaramanujam was a Brahmin. The break with his family, which had been inevitable at the time of his baptism, had required enormous courage.[66] That quality, along with immense compassion, was to be demanded in the total self-abasement Paul had to undergo in his work for the untouchables, not least by showing to converted caste Hindus, by his own example, that they must eat with their once-outcaste members.

While he was a student, one of those rare General Synods, which in those days co-ordinated the whole of the Methodist work in the subcontinent, met at Bangalore. Posnett was there, telling about the mass movement in Hyderabad and how he planned to deal with it. W. H.

[65] What was being celebrated was not, of course, the centenary of Methodist missions but of the first missionary meeting in the Boggard House, Leeds, and the setting up of the first District Missionary Society through the initiative of Dr Jabez Bunting.

[66] This took place in 1911: see *Paul Rangaramanujam – Servant of Jesus Christ* (London 1949), by J. J. Ellis, who was Paul's companion in much of his work.

Findlay was present and Dr James Hope Moulton. They knew the story of Paul's home at Mannargudi and his conversion, and spent time with him in his study, but none could have foreseen that he would be the President at the next General Synod thirty years later.

Dr Moulton stayed on to give lectures in the College, so that when the ship in which he was returning home was torpedoed in the Mediterranean and he died from exposure in an open boat, Paul lost a personal friend as well as a great preacher. The days were to come when he himself would go by steamer to England. He made a tremendous impression at the Quadrennial Conference of the British S.C.M. which was held in Birmingham Town Hall in January 1937. The theme was 'God Speaks to this Generation'. The speakers included William Temple, C. F. Andrews, and W. A. Visser 't Hooft. Yet one of the most effective speeches was that on 'God Speaks through India'. 'As we heard of the great movement to Christ in India,' said the Report, 'and the heroism and Christ-likeness of humble folk there, we agreed with Mr Rangaramanujam that here was an unmistakable work of God through His Church.' The General Secretary asked: 'Did you see the majesty of God as our friend Paul Rangaramanujam told us of that simple countryman whose name was Abraham, in the Village of Great Grace?'

This was not Paul's first experience of visiting England. He had been present as one of the two Indian representatives at the Methodist Union celebrations in 1932.

As a result of the Burmese wars of 1852–1885, Burma was annexed to the Indian Empire. Some Methodist work had been done before this among soldiers in the army of occupation. The opening-up of the country made it possible for J. Milton Brown and W. R. Winston to visit Burma in 1887 to see whether a mission could be commenced to the Burmese people. Winston started that work soon afterwards.

From the beginning it was clear that the going would be tough. The Burmese, as opposed to the hill tribes of the Shan Hills and the Lushais of the Upper Chindwin Valley, were all Buddhists. There could be no mass movement among them. The only way forward was by patient approach to individuals, one by one, and by effective work in boarding schools for boys and girls.

By 1932, after nearly half a century of fine service, the statistics spoke eloquently of the difficulties. Nineteen missionaries, seven of them women, had as colleagues four Burmese ministers. This team served a Church with 817 full members and a total baptized community of around 1,700. The Societies lay entirely in the interior of the country: the old kingdom of Upper Burma. The centre was the royal city of Mandalay. In that beautiful town was the strongest Methodist Church in the country, the head of a self-supporting circuit; a Boys' High School with 324 students; a Girls' High School with 211; and what in those days was called a Leper colony – an excellent institution serving almost 300 patients. The prospects among the non-Burman animistic tribes were much brighter, and the 1932 report said that the missionary in the Chindwin Circuit was 'overwhelmed by the opportunities'.

The other great Asian region where missionaries of the W.M.M.S. were serving in the period prior to 1932 was China. At first there was a strong reluctance to enter this field because of financial difficulties. In 1842 a dramatic change had taken place there. The first 'opium war' had ended. It resulted in the Treaty of Nanking which opened the five ports of Canton, Amoy, Foochow, Ningpo, and Shanghai to foreign residents. Opium and the Gospel were able to enter China together, and both were resented as commodities introduced by 'foreign devils'. In those days the Western Powers imposed opium on the people of China, today the police of Western cities like London are trying to cope with a world-wide criminal Chinese organization which trades in millions of pounds' worth of heroin with Mafia-like ruthlessness and efficiency.

The decade following 1842 found Methodism ill-prepared and financially unable to take advantage of this opportunity. Divisions within the home Church produced over the period a fall in income of £18,000. To deflect money into a new area would have meant even further retrenchment than that which had already taken place in such long-established fields as the West Indies. The report of the M.M.S. for the year of reunion remarks with vigour:

> But God Himself forced the hands of the Society. A young Pickering local preacher, George Piercy, felt called to China, and offered himself.[67] The Committee turned him down. Convinced that God was calling him, Piercy worked his passage to China. Landing in 1851, he went up to Canton, the greatest city in Southern China, and attempted to support himself while learning Chinese, and doing what voluntary missionary work he could. God was moving in other hearts; a Richmond College student, Josiah Cox, and a young probationer, William R. Beach, heard the call. The Society's Treasurer, Thomas Farmer, had China laid on his heart, and promised an initial £1,000, and £100 per year towards the cost of a mission. Farmer propounded the theory that a new mission would stimulate a new zeal in the Home Church, and he proved to be right. Cox and Beach were sent out; Piercy was accepted on the field (1852), and all three laboured together in the foreign concession outside Canton. For twenty years the income of the Society steadily increased.

Once again, laymen overseas had played a significant part in persuading the home Church to begin work in a new region. Piercy's conviction

[67] See Moister, op. cit., pp. 124f.

that he should offer for service in China had been clinched by a letter from a group of soldiers stationed at Hong Kong. When, in 1866, he was about to leave Pickering for China a second time, another layman, Joseph Smith, from a neighbouring circuit, acted as chairman of a meeting at which Piercy was presented with 'a purse of gold and a testimonial'. Smith, in the course of his address, said:

> When we remember the circumstances of Mr Piercy's going out: the difficulties that beset him, the cold shoulder that was everywhere turned to him, and recall the steady persevering determination to go despite these, we are led to say: Surely there is an invisible power at work – a Divine power – when we recount the numerous providential interpositions connected with his going, his arrival there, and the great work of preparation going on, so that speedily China was open to Christian missionaries; when we were favoured with reading the letters of our dear friend from which we could see the working of mind and intelligence, the hope and earnest burning love for the souls of these vast millions of China, truly we were impelled to say, 'This is the Lord's doing and it is marvellous in our eyes' . . . we were in error when first we tried to dissuade him from going, and we have now to make public reparation.[68]

That work he was pursuing under immense difficulties. The writer of the 1932 Report ventured the claim that 'in no other mission-field has missionary work had such a troubled career as in China'. Throughout the nineteenth century, anti-foreign emotions, never far from the surface and fuelled by the opium wars, broke out in frequent riots, culminating in the Boxer uprising of 1900–1.[69] Then the whole scene changed. The Chinese deliberately set out to learn from the West, and in this phase, which lasted until the revolution of 1911, the Church made immense headway. After that setback, progress was less rapid, and by the time of the rise of Nationalism and Communism in 1925–26 it seemed as though everything might come to a stop as, in a sense, actually happened a quarter of a century later. In the mid-1920s, Chinese Christians faced intense persecution and many missionaries had to be withdrawn. Another immense change came in 1927 with the expulsion of the Russians and the suppression – for the time being, as events were to show – of Communism. What emerged was the Chinese Church, which had learnt much from its grim experiences and was discovering how to conduct its own affairs. In this period, though missionaries remained and gave support, they were learning to make way for Chinese

[68] *Memoir of Joseph Smith, of South Holme, late of Huggate and Riseborough, Wesleyan Local Preacher; with Records from his Diary; together with speeches and sermons from 1828 to 1898*, pp. 140f.

[69] See pp. 82–4, above.

leadership. By 1932 it was possible to report that Methodist colleges and schools were in the hands of Chinese principals and head teachers; Chinese doctors were taking charge of mission hospitals, with European doctors serving under them, and Chinese ministers were being appointed as superintendents of circuits with Europeans as colleagues.

With little idea of what was to come within the next two decades, that 1932 Report speaks in euphoric headlines about the 'Remarkable Opportunities in the South China District'. The letter of the Chinese members of Synod to the home Church stated: 'This is the Golden Age of evangelism in China.' By contrast, it had been 'a difficult year' in the Hupeh District.[70] Natural disaster had combined with civil war to bring trouble and distress. The people had not recovered from the appalling floods of 1931, and General Chiang Kai-shek was capturing the chief Communist strongholds in the Central China area. Even so, with centres in the three important cities of Wuchang, Hankow, and Hanyang, which have been described as the hub of China, the Church here had a magnificent position, affording a strategic base for the whole country. Wuchang, once the seat of the Viceroy, had three important institutions – Wesley College and two in which the Methodists shared: Hua Chung College and United Theological College. Across the mile-wide Yangtse River, in Hankow, were the Hospital of Universal Love, and the David Hill[71] Blind School, for which the W.M.M.S. was responsible, as well as the great Union Hospital, which was shared with the London Missionary Society. At Hangyang was a girls' boarding school.

Devolution had gone forward swiftly in the Hupeh District during the eight years before Methodist reunion:

	1924	1932
Foreign ministers	17	6
Foreign probationers	2	6
Chinese ordained ministers	5	10

The other W.M.M.S. District in China, that of Hunan, provided a more cheerful prospect at the close of our period. The whole area had remained almost completely impenetrable to foreigners in general, and missionaries in particular, for forty years after all the other provinces had opened their doors. Not until 1902, when the Boxer rebellion was

[70] Under the W.M.M.S. this had long been known as the Wuchang District.

[71] David Hill (*b.*1840, *d.*1895) came from York, and his ancestry brings into prominence three family names closely associated with the mission of the Church: Burdsall, Lyth and Hill. Richard Burdsall was one of Wesley's first preachers. His daughter, Mary, married John Lyth; their oldest son, Richard Burdsall Lyth, was the first medical missionary to Fiji in the cannibal days of Thakombau, the chief who was converted by the dying prayers of John Hunt (see Birtwhistle, *In His Armour*, pp. 93, 189). Indeed, R. B. Lyth was Methodism's first qualified medical missionary. David Hill, father of the son of the same name who became a missionary in China, married Eliza Lyth, who was the eldest daughter of John and Mary. See W. T. A. Barber, *David Hill, Missionary and Saint* (London 1898).

over, could E. C. Cooper and Lo Yu Shan begin there. For nearly a decade the work spread rapidly, but 1911 saw the beginning of a period when the province became a veritable cockpit, with the marching and counter-marching of armies and the capture and recapture of towns, sometimes by bandits. At each capitulation an indemnity was levied to the point where the people's resources were exhausted. A reign of terror, with horrors past all description, was directed against Christians when Hunan fell into Communist hands after the 1926 Nationalist advance upon Hankow. Yet, incredibly, the Church survived. The four years prior to 1932 provided more peaceful conditions, and the District report for that year concluded: 'The successive waves of calamity that have broken over the churches and members in this province during recent years have not succeeded in daunting the spirit of Christ's followers.'

We left our account of W.M.M.S. activity in Africa at the point of Freeman's death in 1890. When the Methodist Churches based on Britain reunited, the total African statistics for the parent body read:

	W.M.M.S. in West Africa, 1932 (*work begun 1811*)	W.M.M.S. in in Rhodesia, 1932 (*work begun 1891*)
Missionaries (*men*)	62	27
Missionaries (*women*)	35	5
African ministers	91	9
Full members	70,000	6,524
Total baptized community	212,000	14,000

Numerically, then, West Africa was by far the largest region which any of the Methodist Societies served. Even in South India, with its dramatic mass movements, the comparable figures were:

	W.M.M.S. in South India, 1932 (*work begun 1817*)
Missionaries (*men*)	79
Missionaries (*women*)	78
Indian ministers	57
Full members	21,800
Total baptized community	132,000

By 1932 the Church in the oldest West African area, Sierra Leone, had developed to the point where all the circuits were staffed with African ministers. Indeed, with the exception of the Chairman, in the

Colony itself[72] all the W.M.M.S. missionaries were women on the staff of a girls' boarding school and a teacher training college shared with the C.M.S. Methodist–Anglican co-operation also worked fruitfully in Fourah Bay College, then affiliated to Durham University and now a university in its own right.

In spite of fine Women's Welfare work, undertaken at the request of the Government of the Gambia, and the devoted service of a small number of missionaries stationed in that colony, which covered only four square miles, the 1932 Report came to the unhappy conclusion that 'we never seem able to throw real strength into this work, and nothing of permanent value has been accomplished; the whole story is one of failure and disappointment'.

A totally different picture was painted of the work on the Gold Coast.[73] There a total Christian community of 115,000 was served by more than 700 churches and 200 other preaching places. The staff of 47 ordained African ministers and 367 evangelists was reinforced by 1,500 local preachers. There were 129 Methodist day-schools employing 479 teachers and caring for nearly 12,000 scholars. Mfantsipim High School for boys with 150 boarders and nearly 100 day boys was, with some justification, claimed in the 1932 Report as 'one of the best schools in West Africa'. The importance of these educational establishments in the developing life of the country is past computation. In addition there was Wesley College for training African workers, at Kumasi, the ancient capital of Ashanti. The Rev. C. Kingsley Williams was seconded to the staff of the government college at Achimota. A distinguishing feature of the District was the existence of highly successful book depots at Accra, Cape Coast, Sekondi and Kumasi. With a steady income over many years from the sale of cocoa to other countries, the finances of this District were in a healthy state and nearly all the circuits had become self-supporting. Only in the last two years before Methodist Union was this stability threatened by a world slump in cocoa prices. Despite local persecution from the still powerful adherents of animism, steady progress was being made. There was little in the way of spectacular mass movements, but the evangelical spirit of the congregations had resulted in small annual increases in membership throughout the region. In 1932 they were reporting 4,588 adult baptisms for the previous year, and over 9,000 under instruction for baptism. There was one exception to the statement about mass movements in the Gold Coast:

In 1920 a strange Ashanti prophet, Samson Opon, arose and like a

[72] The coastal region with full colonial status, as opposed to the up-country areas which comprise the Protectorate.

[73] On 6 March 1957, the Gold Coast became the independent state of Ghana; in 1960, the Republic of Ghana.

> flame of fire went through the forests calling the villagers to turn to God. He carried with him a simple wooden cross as the symbol of his mission, and there can be no doubt that he was mightily used by God. Whole companies of Ashantis responded to his preaching, and within two years our ministers baptised some 10,000 converts who renounced their fetiches and built for themselves little churches in their villages.[74]

To cope with this sudden result of Opon's preaching, so similar in many ways to the one which had begun a decade earlier under the Prophet Harris on the Ivory Coast,[75] the staff, both European and African, was strengthened; so, nearly a century after Freeman had laid the foundations of the Gold Coast Church, a splendid building has been erected, of untold value to the nation.

Another fitting monument to Freeman and his apostolic journeys is to be found in the Western Nigeria District. When he arrived at Badagry in 1842, on his way to Abeokuta,[76] Lagos was still a centre for vigorous slave-trading by the Portuguese and the Brazilians. So it remained until it was captured by a British fleet in 1851. Freeman immediately saw his opportunity and stationed a missionary there, in the town that was later to be the capital of Nigeria. By 1932, a fine Methodist church stood on the site of the old slave market in Tinnubu Square, the head chapel of the circuit and mother church of the District.

One by one the great Yoruba towns were entered. Ibadan, then the largest Negro city in the whole continent of Africa with a population of a quarter of a million, was chosen for the building of Wesley College, where so many ministers, teachers, and evangelists have been trained. Moreover, the control of malaria and health generally, described on p. 20, was bringing an immense improvement in the health of Europeans on the West Coast.

At Ilesha, another large Yoruba town, was built the Wesley Guild Hospital which was to become a world-renowned medical centre. Girls' boarding schools were opened at Lagos and Shagamu. In co-operation with the C.M.S., Igbobi College, a highly successful boarding school for boys, was formed. This was done by transferring to the mainland, where there was ample space for playing fields, the boarding establishments of the Anglican and Methodist boys' schools on the crowded island of Lagos.

At the time of Methodist reunion, the Western Nigeria District had a community of 30,000 with 1,073 adult baptisms in the previous year, and 6,000 under instruction.

[74] *Our Overseas Missions, Past and Present*, p. 38.
[75] See pp. 109–11 below.
[76] See p. 64, above.

Of the two areas in French West Africa, Dahomey[77] and the Ivory Coast, where W.M.M.S. missionaries were stationed in 1932, the former could show little in the way of development, in spite of action by the French more than forty years earlier when they exiled the last Dahomian king and disbanded his once-terrible armies. By contrast, the Ivory Coast could tell one of the most remarkable stories in the whole history of modern missions, that of the Prophet Harris. This legendary figure was matched by a rare investigator, Gordon MacKay Haliburton, in his book, *The Prophet Harris: A study of an African Prophet and his mass movement in the Ivory Coast and the Gold Coast 1913–1915*.[78] This cool appraisal, so much more effective than any partisan approach could be, gives a graphic account of one of the strangest phases of Methodist involvement in West Africa – and of the reluctance of the home Church, for many reasons and over an extended period, to accept full responsibility in spite of that involvement. The bare summary given in the 1932 Report[79] omits many dramatic details such as the selection, by Harris, at each place he briefly visited, of a leader to whom he presented a Bible, telling him to call the converts together every seventh day to pray for the coming of the white man who would expound it. The Report reads:

> Between the years 1913–15, while the nations of Europe were plunging into war, a remarkable African Prophet, William Wade Harris, arose and began to preach. From village to village he passed, proclaiming the simple Message of one God and one Saviour. With fiery zeal he won the hearts of the people. They journeyed long distances through the forests to hear him, and on promising to serve God he baptised them. Certainly more than 60,000 received baptism from him. They destroyed their fetiches and shrines, and at the prophet's bidding built little churches instead. Then the French expelled Harris from the colony, and for ten years these multitudes of earnest but uninstructed people were left to themselves. In their simple, ignorant way they tried to serve their new God as best they could. Then, in 1924, by what men call an accident, we got in touch with them, and they implored us to send them missionaries to teach them about the God they were trying to serve. 'We have waited ten years,' they said. How could we resist such a plea? No other Missionary Society was working anywhere near to help them. So we undertook what we believe was a God-given task. Within a year they gave us 160 churches, and no less than 32,000 were enrolled on our Class-books. It was almost overwhelming.

[77] See p. 65, above.

[78] Published in 1971 by Longman, and based on Haliburton's doctoral dissertation written in the School of Oriental and African Studies of the University of London, and submitted in 1966.

[79] See p. 41.

This account conceals almost as much as it reveals, not so much as regards the character and methods of the Prophet Harris but with respect to the part played by Methodism in the whole episode. This is notably true of the involvement of the Gold Coast Synod as early as February 1915. As Haliburton remarks:[80]

> Among the Methodists certain factors weakened the mobilisation of resources for the task of attracting Harris converts. When, six years later, another Prophet, Samson Opon, appeared in Ashanti, the English missionaries there utilised the most modern forms of transport for control and built up a large Methodist community. Not only were there no modern forms of transport available in Nzimaland at the time, there were no English missionaries either. The one African minister in the circuit had only a handful of trained assistants, and the wonder is that he accomplished as much as he did. The deployment of a larger number of both African and European clergy would have borne permanent fruit. One factor making it difficult to provide European missionaries was the war, another was the Synod politics of the Methodist Church in the Gold Coast.

In brief, the facts are that C. W. Armstrong, after a tour of inspection in Axim in August 1914, had made a report on the Harris movement which was forwarded immediately to London by the District Chairman, William R. Griffin. The W.M.M.S. Secretary for West Africa, William Goudie, was so impressed by this account that he went to the Gold Coast Synod with the purpose of learning more details for use in publicity and fund raising. At the Missionaries' Meeting, Goudie and Griffin clashed over the policy to be followed and Griffin resigned. Lack of clear understanding by the African ministers as to the cause of the dispute, and an ambiguous if not tactless sentence in Goudie's speech at the May Meeting after his return, led them to suppose that he was attacking both their competence and their orthodoxy. In point of fact he was pleading for men to go and help them, understaffed as they were to cope with the enormous opportunity which faced the Church. The result, namely that the mass movement for the time being remained entirely in African hands, was later judged to be unfortunate.

It was not until 1924 that W. J. Platt[81] began to reap the harvest of the Harris movement in the Ivory Coast. That harvest truly was great. In 1932 the Ivory Coast had ten men missionaries of the W.M.M.S., three women missionaries, two African ministers, and 109 evangelists. A training school for evangelists at Dabou was preparing fifty young men for full-time service of the Church, and there was a girls' boarding school there too. The total Christian community numbered 44,000.

[80] Op. cit., p. 151.

[81] Later to be appointed General Secretary of the British and Foreign Bible Society.

The Report might well say that the 'chief task is not the conversion of the heathen, but the Christianising of tens of thousands of people already Christian'.[82] Already some of the Harris converts were slipping away, and nearly a quarter of a century after Methodist Union it was still necessary for an elder statesman of the society to appeal to the Committee that they should not be forgotten. Magnificent as was the work of Platt and his colleagues, the vision of the home Church never matched the immense opportunities which the Ivory Coast provided. From time to time the messages came through from neglected groups: 'Our young people, who never heard the Prophet Harris preach, make fun of us praying week by week for the missionary who never comes, and we older ones, we wait and we die.'

Last among the overseas Districts served by the W.M.M.S. at the time of the 1932 Union which fall to be mentioned in this survey is that of Rhodesia. Wesleyan work began there in 1891, and in the four following decades it had developed so that there were thirty-two missionaries working there, five of them women; nine African ministers shared with them the care of 6,524 members and a total baptized community of 14,000. This was all that remained of the once extensive work in South Africa, since an independent South African Conference had been set up in 1884. This took over the circuits in Cape Colony, Natal, the Orange Free State, Tembuland, Pondoland, and Griqualand. At first, all that was left in the care of the W.M.M.S. was a new mission begun in 1872 in the Transvaal at the time of the gold rush there. In the year before Methodist reunion, this too was judged to be sufficiently mature to be united with the South African Conference. The area entered in 1891, and still under the care of the W.M.M.S. in 1932, was in Southern Rhodesia, notably among the Mashona and the Matabele. The 'economic blizzard' which had hit Britain at the turn of the 1920s and 1930s had not spared many of the Districts overseas, and Rhodesia passed through a specially difficult year in 1932. The financial strain had inevitably led to the curtailment of the work and inability to respond to new opportunities. One of the significant passages in the Report for that year concerned the mission farms and reserves:

> Hitherto an important feature of our work in Rhodesia has been our Mission farms, which vary in size from 1,350 to 10,000 acres. We have ten of them, with a total of 52,000 acres. Most of them were given to us in years gone by by the Chartered Company or the Government. The policy was to settle people upon them in little villages where we could carry on our church and school work without

[82] See Allen Birtwhistle, *In His Armour: The Life of John Hunt of Fiji*, p. 165, where reference is made to Hunt's growing conviction that it required two conversions to bring a man from heathenism into a personal relationship with God – 'one from Heathenism to Christianity as a system, and a second from sin to God'.

interference and where the people would be safe from exploitation. In their day these farms have served a very useful purpose; but their day seems to be passing, and now it is more usual for the Africans to settle on land given to them by Government in the 'reserves'.

In Rhodesia, as in so much of Africa, practically all education was in the hands of the missions. One of the most successful ventures in the District was the establishment of the Waddilove Institution, and in 1932 five candidates for the ministry were being trained there.

While this varied pattern of progress and persecution, development and difficulty, was being woven in the Districts overseas during the period 1885–1932, what was happening at the home base? Surely significant in the light of events which occurred after World War II, when many people from abroad came to live in Britain, was a venture which got under way in 1884: a Chinese mission in London. A house was bought not far from dockland, so that Chinese who lived there and sailors who came into the neighbourhood, especially when the new consignments of tea arrived, could be helped. George Piercy, with his invaluable knowledge of their language, was then in London, and he visited Chinese people in their homes and 'opium dens'. Bible and Tract Societies provided literature. The Gospels and Acts in Cantonese, and Piercy's own translation of *The Pilgrim's Progress*, proved most useful. On average a dozen Chinese visitors a day came to the house, and 4,606 such visits were made in the first year.

The year 1902, in which for the first time the local income and missionary giving of the Districts overseas[83] equalled the whole W.M.M.S. income from Great Britain, saw a remarkable moment in the supreme court of the Church. As the Annual Report for 1903 described it:

> A crowded Conference, in hushed stillness and by a standing vote, pledged itself to the following manifesto:
>
> In the judgment of the Conference, the hour is come for the Wesleyan Methodist Church to adopt solemnly, in the faith and fear of God, a more energetic and aggressive policy with regard to Foreign Missionary work. While rejoicing in manifold and widespread tokens throughout the Connexion of revived interest in the Missionary cause, yet having regard to the growth of the Wesleyan Methodist Church, the increased wealth of its people, and the large number of chapels and halls erected during recent years, the Conference cannot but regard as unsatisfactory and humiliating the fact that for more than a generation the Home income of the Foreign Missionary Society has remained stationary; and recognising also the vast areas of the world still unevangelised, and the unparalleled opportunities

[83] A total of £111,663 12*s.* 11*d.* (see Annual Report, 1903, p. 15).

now presented in all parts of the Foreign Field where the Society's agents are at work, the Conference is strongly of opinion that the Call of God is clear and loud for immediate and continuous advance.

The Conference is convinced that such advance is only possible by such an increase in the spirit of devotion to Christ and of loyalty to His commands as will secure year by year an adequate supply of workers and of funds.

The Conference went on to implement these sentiments by directing that 'on the plan so successfully adopted by the late Revd H. P. Hughes for Conventions during his Presidential year . . . a series of District Conventions for the Deepening of the Missionary Spirit be held in the autumn and winter'. The President, 'himself a returned missionary, heartily consented to preside at these Conventions giving them the foremost place in his official services to our Church'. It would be impossible to over-emphasize the importance to Methodist missions of the influence exerted on their behalf by a long succession of Conference Presidents. By taking the chair at the Society's chief public function at the time of the May Meetings, and presiding over the missionary session in the Conference itself, for very many years the first item of Conference business, they have been able to give the home Church a lead which has at times, like the one just described, been decisive.[84]

Year after year the faithful work at the home base went on, with little expectation of the grim events which were soon to tear Europe apart. In the report presented at the Exeter Hall, London, on 2 May 1904, occurs the statement: 'We are glad to report that in September last the rebuilding of the Mission House was completed in time to welcome within its walls one of the General Secretaries as the President of the Conference.' The building was the one in Bishopsgate, and the President was Marshall Hartley. The term 'General Secretaries', in the plural, requires some explanation to those who are used to societies having but one of these officers. It occurs for the first time in the Revised Rules and Regulations of the Wesleyan Methodist Missionary Society passed at the Conference of 1884. These Rules were printed annually with the Society's report and in 1883 Rule XIII had read:

[84] Nor has their effectiveness been confined to their Presidential year alone. In 1951, the *Methodist Recorder* reported that the given possibility of retrenchment faced the Missionary Committee because of financial stringency, and printed a letter provoked by that report and written by a Past President, Dr Scott Lidgett:

> If we will that the Missions should prosper, as we certainly do, we must enlarge our subscriptions and gifts, as we have been compelled to do in our household expenditure. By all means let us get new subscribers if we can; but this will be quite insufficient. Our subscriptions must match the rise of world prices. This will be costly, but gifts that are not costly are of little worth . . . Let us acknowledge our debt and gladly make this costly gift to the advancement of His Kingdom.

> Four of the Methodist Ministers stationed in or near London shall be appointed to conduct the official correspondence of the Missions, and to perform the other duties of *Secretaries*. The Secretaries shall be expected to devote themselves on the week-days, in general, to the service of the Missions exclusively; being subject, however, to the Rules of the Connexion respecting a periodical change of Station, or formal reappointment to office.

In 1884 this had been replaced by Rule VII:

> The General Secretaries of the Society shall be annually appointed by the Conference in accordance with any regulations which from time to time may be in force touching such appointments.

There were two reasons for the change in terminology. The first was in order to emphasize the principle of *primus inter pares*: no member of what came to be called the Officers' Meeting was to be regarded as over and above his colleagues. The second was to show the collegiate, Cabinet-type responsibility which the meeting carried. All questions which deserved the procedure were brought to the Secretaries for their consideration, and they shared equal responsibility for every decision taken.

The Report for 1905 had important things to say about China. 'Two forms of Christian work specially, though not exclusively, connect themselves in our minds with China: Medical Missions and Christian Literature.' There follows an announcement that the Medical Sub-Committee of the Society had been formed, 'composed almost entirely of medical men', and a separate account had been opened for contributions given expressly for medical work abroad. During the course of the meeting held at the Exeter Hall on 1 May 1905 at which this report was presented, Dr Timothy Richards, one of the speakers, was quoted as having said recently: 'If we do not win China for Christ in the next thirty years we may have to wait for three hundred years.' Ten years after those thirty had expired, all missionaries were expelled from China.

The Report for that same year, 1905, carries the announcement that the new missionary magazine, *The Foreign Field*, had been launched. 'It has taken at once a foremost position in the missionary literature of the Churches . . . Sales already reach 40,000 a month.' Later, this magazine, in the capable hands of its editor, Deaville Walker, was to fulfil all the promise of those early days.

Into this gentle world of steady progress and dedicated service came the war. Printed on paper of steadily deteriorating quality, the annual Reports of the Society described the effects of that conflagration. In 1915 it was said that 'the shock is being felt in the remotest corners of the earth, and is affecting in one way or another the lives of people who scarcely know the names of most of the belligerent Powers'. The Reports go on to speak about the burden of anxiety: banks closed; commerce disorganized; missionaries worried about supplies. As one example of the economies they were compelled to make, building work had stopped. Even so, there was a brighter side: the financial pressure had called forth unusual generosity in the local Churches on the mission field. The wealthy had built churches; the poor had given of their poverty. Undoubtedly the worst aspect was the hindrance to Christian testimony caused by the spectacle of the European, Christian, countries violently at one another's throats. China was asking, 'Why does not your honourable religion prevent European nations from slaying each other?'

In the following year, 1916, 'the strain of war was pressing heavily on practically all fields'. Food prices had risen, so increasing the cost of maintaining such institutions as orphanages and leper refuges. Staff shortages were beginning to tell. The dangers of sea-travel were causing furloughs to be postponed, and Chinese and Indians in particular were becoming increasingly puzzled that Christians could pursue war with such relentless fury.

When the time came to make the Report on 1917 some of the statements from important Districts overseas had not come through, because of wartime delays in the transmission of mails. When at last they did come through, it was to announce that 1916, like its predecessor, had been a year of remarkable advance. The membership figures had increased by 4,292, but the reduction in staff had become really serious.

Under the title 'The Aftermath of the War', a term very familiar in the decade following the Armistice of 1918, the Report of 1919 had surprisingly little to say except on two grounds. The main cause for anxiety seems to have been the Latin countries of Europe, where Methodism was struggling against odds. There was special concern for Italy, clearly at a crisis in her history. The other foreboding was expressed briefly and dispassionately, but it indicated the tip of a shadow that was to lengthen in the coming days: 'Nationalism,' said the Report, 'is inclined to range itself against Christianity.' The remark may rank as one of the most masterly understatements in the whole vast pile of missionary literature.

From the world-missionary point of view, by far the most important single event in the whole period 1885–1932 came right in the middle of it. It was an event which had a profound effect on Churches of all denominations as well as upon their missionary societies: the World Missionary Conference held at Edinburgh in 1910, which gave its name to Edinburgh House, London, the focus of missionary co-operation in Britain ever since. Fifty years after 'Edinburgh 1910' that assembly was still being claimed as 'one of the most creative events in the long history of the Christian Church'.[85] Since then the ecumenical temperature has gone up and down by turn. The slogan so dear to John R. Mott and his colleagues, 'The Evangelization of the World in this Generation', has been somewhat demythologized to mean that they rightly realized that, for the first time in Christian history, modern means of transport and communication made it possible at least to offer Christ to the whole world. The long practice of co-operation, especially at missionary headquarters, because 'organic union' between the denominations seems too far away and difficult, has been found to have its own problems inherent in a Church suffering from 'the sin of our divisions'. But nothing has for long diminished or dissipated the force which was generated in 1910.

One curious sidelight came from what now would seem to be an unexpected quarter. As if to emphasize the apparently stable state of Europe just before the confusion of World War I, a message came from the Imperial German Colonial Office saying that the proceedings were being watched with lively interest, desiring that the Conference 'be crowned with blessing and success', and recognizing 'with satisfaction and gratitude that the endeavours for the spread of the Gospel are followed by the blessings of civilization and culture in all countries'.[86]

Delegates from what we would now call the Third World made a tremendous impact on the Conference. Prominent among these was Cheng Ching-yi, who concisely appealed for two changes: self-government for the Church in China, and an end to denominations there.

The sessions led to a climax with a discussion on the Home Base. Pleas were heard for the better training of missionaries before they were sent abroad. The delegates, considering how the entire resources of the sending Churches could be developed and employed, were reminded that 'God is the ultimate Home Base of Missions'. And in the words of an African proverb quoted by a delegate from that continent, there was a disturbing reminder that we have but one life and one opportunity to prepare for and use it: 'The Dawn does not come twice to awake a man.'

[85] Hugh Martin, *beginning at Edinburgh . . .* (London 1960), p. 3.

[86] W. H. Temple Gairdner, '*Edinburgh 1910*'*: an Account and Interpretation of the World Missionary Conference* (Edinburgh 1910), p. 45.

PART TWO

II

Wesleyan Methodism 1849-1902

HENRY D. RACK

BY 1849, a quarter of a century's dissension within Wesleyan Methodism was coming to a climax symbolized in that year by the expulsion of Samuel Dunn, James Everett and William Griffith and followed during the next few years by the loss of 100,000 members. Subsequent reforms (partly provoked by the agitations) culminated in the entry of laymen into Conference in 1878, which marked a decisive stage on the way towards a Methodism which John Wesley would scarcely have recognized and probably would have disowned. The old Connexion ('the body' as Wesleyans liked to term it) was, in 1849, a surprisingly faithful version of the original movement in institutions, theology and general purpose. In 1902, the year in which Hugh Price Hughes died, the case was different, even though one should not overlook the extent to which the institutions and leadership tended to conserve a past outlook against which influential sections of the Connexion were by then rebelling. The element of conservatism was understandable in view of the habit of rather long-term Connexional appointments for perhaps unduly senior men, running a distinctly centralized organization. The pressures of half a century's development were, nevertheless, decisive in changing the character of Wesleyanism. Its sense of a distinctive position mid-way between Anglicanism and Dissent slowly declined in favour of a closer alignment with the latter; its evangelistic and social concerns were not only shared with other Churches but took forms common to all the Churches; parts of its polity and discipline were modified in ways which made it a little less distinctively Methodist. The influence of society at large – in which Wesleyans increasingly shared and wanted to share – is to be seen not only in changes of organization and thought but also in political, cultural and educational attitudes. Perhaps most important of all were the internal tensions of the body, arising from difficulties inherent in the original Methodist mission. They were fought out in terms of debates about ministry and laity, society and church, the basis of membership, the character and aims of spirituality, as well as in the whole range of relationships with the world outside.

The theme of the present chapter is, therefore, the way in which a particular kind of religious society, organized to serve a particular type of Christianity, was driven, both by the external pressures of a changing society and by its own internal pressures and contradictions, to develop into a body which had altered its character decisively by the end of the nineteenth century. The period from 1849 to 1902 was the time when this process of change became evident, and almost any aspect of Wesleyan Methodism can be used to demonstrate its character. For purposes of analysis, and at the risk of some distortion, I shall begin by describing the relevant features of change in society at large (of which Wesleyanism was increasingly to feel itself an integral part) as a preliminary to describing, with some statistical illustrations, the growth and distribution of the denomination in the second half of the nineteenth century. I shall then discuss and illustrate the relationships of Wesleyanism with the world outside itself; and finally the changing character of its internal life.[1]

1. Religion and Social Change

Behind the very complex political, economic, social, intellectual – and religious – history of England in the nineteenth century lies the fundamental fact of the development of a modern industrial society. To a very considerable extent this development underlies, conditions and provokes changes in almost every aspect of life in the Western world since the eighteenth century, and the Wesleyan fragment of that world is no exception. The situation at the beginning of the half-century we are considering has been summed up as follows:

> Between 1801 and 1851 the population of Great Britain almost doubled, from less than eleven millions to more than 21. The largest towns grew fastest of all, until in 1851 – for the first time in the history of any large nation – half the population was urban.[2]

[1] The lack of modern critical studies of the development of Methodism as a whole in the later nineteenth century has been remedied in part by the recent publication of Robert Currie's *Methodism Divided: A Study in the Sociology of Ecumenicalism* (London 1968), a study which ranges more widely than its title suggests. The manuscript of the present chapter was already completed when Dr Currie's book appeared, and I was gratified to find that on a number of the main topics discussed our analyses followed similar lines. Consequently it did not seem necessary to expand or modify my text, but I have inserted a number of references to *Methodism Divided* in the footnotes.

[2] K. S. Inglis, *Churches and the Working Classes in Victorian England* (London 1963), p. 3.

A large proportion of these were not even accustomed to urban life; nor had town-planning, amenities and government been developed adequately to cope with the population increase. It is in this context that we have to see the changes and conflicts of Victorian England: changes in the class-structure, in political franchise and political parties, in social organization and welfare, in thought and ideals.

The Churches could not be unaffected. There was, first of all, a process which might be described from one point of view as the emancipation of society from church tutelage or from another as the encroachment of secular society and the secular state on the Church. For Anglicanism the shock was particularly severe. Through Ecclesiastical Commissioners and successive Acts of Parliament its resources were redistributed, and disestablishment and even disendowment seemed at times to be a real threat. The repeal of the Test Acts for Dissenters (1828) and for Catholics (1829) was followed during the rest of the century by the progressive emancipation of Dissenters from their underprivileged social status.[3] This had important effects on Nonconformist (including Wesleyan) attitudes: the fight for 'emancipation' was accompanied by, and partly expressed in, the attempt to destroy Anglican privilege as well as to achieve equality for themselves. This may be seen as the religious aspect of the general pressure to reduce the scope of privileged corporations and classes in the nineteenth century in favour of the enlargement of equality and opportunity for the traditionally underprivileged. Changes of this kind gradually reduced the social differences underlying English denominational rivalries and conflicts; but they also broke down the element of self-contained and self-conscious (indeed at times self-satisfied) culture in Nonconformity. The beginnings of this process can be seen in the period under review, but the more immediate results of social change were increased conflict; in the face of state and Nonconformist attacks, Anglicans feared loss of privilege, readily identified with loss of religion itself. Nonconformists were jealous of Anglican privilege but also, as the case of the so-called 'Nonconformist Conscience' showed,[4] tended to try to retain their traditional mores and to enter a wider society by attempting to impose their moral prejudices on society as a whole. Wesleyans were not only affected by these developments but had in addition peculiar tensions of their own, arising out of contradictions between their inherited role as a would-be evangelism and holiness Society and their aspirations and needs as a Church, now a Church with social aspirations as well.

In other respects, too, the Churches were affected by social change, particularly by the problems arising from social and geographical

[3] For details, see W. G. Addison, *Religious Equality in Modern England 1714–1914* (London 1944).

[4] See below, p. 145.

mobility and the plight of the cities' poor. Two connected problems presented themselves: that of social justice in practice and theory, and that of evangelism. The former set of problems was shared with the socially sensitive sections of secular society; in large measure socially-minded churchmen followed, and attempted to modify and Christianize, secular fashions in social thought and action in matters which in any case often required government action. Evangelism was the Churches' own special problem, though the concern about it not infrequently reflects not only a fear of social revolution and an attempt to restrain it but also the need to hold the existing church membership as it moved from country to town, from north to south, from city centre to suburb.

It is in this general social context that we have to endeavour to understand the development of Wesleyanism in these years; it cannot be understood solely in terms of inherent tensions, for these too were conditioned by the development of society. To assess the relative importance and the nature of the interconnection of these forces is always difficult, as may be seen in the explanations given of the Wesleyan splits in mid-century[5] or of the phenomenon of the 'Nonconformist Conscience'. If, as has been said, the Wesleyans in a general way shared these problems and their answers to them with other Nonconformists, one has also to recognize the extent to which they continued to feel and cling to their own sense of a distinctive mission and way of life. Many Wesleyans regarded their doctrines, institutions and peculiar virtues with a self-confidence which to the modern observer verges on the complacent. The age of their leadership, their Connexional structure and the size of their church membership combined to maintain the situation of a self-sufficient culture from which the Methodist public viewed the great world outside; and it is probable that this situation persisted for a longer period and with more force than in the rest of Nonconformity. The world could not, however, be resisted indefinitely; and we shall see plenty of signs of strain and adaptation in what follows.

2. The Growth and Distribution of Wesleyanism

One other essential preliminary is some attempt to describe and assess the size, distribution and composition of Wesleyanism. Here we have an unusually full set of figures based on a relatively precise concept of membership and collected from an exceptionally closely organized religious group. The bare facts of the growth in membership can be stated simply enough:[6]

[5] For example, the political explanations of E. R. Taylor and Maldwyn Edwards.

[6] These figures are drawn from the *Minutes of Conference*, unless otherwise indicated, and are for Great Britain excluding Ireland. The inclusion of Irish figures would depress the proportion of Methodists to the population because of the overwhelmingly Roman Catholic character of that country, which is unrepresentative of Britain as a whole.

1849	348,274
1902	463,225 – an increase of 114,951 or 33 per cent.

In ordinary circumstances, most years in the nineteenth century showed a greater or smaller addition of members until 1906, when the figure of 498,464 was reached. (There followed losses for some years, then a recovery in the 1920s: the maximum was 500,010 in 1931.) The major exception came in the years 1851–5, during which almost 100,000 were lost by disruption and secession. The 1850 figure of 358,277 was not surpassed until 1876.

One must, of course, temper any impression given by these figures with a reminder that they represent a very small proportion of the total population:

1851	Gt. Britain 20,816,351 (excluding Ireland)	Wesleyans	302,209 or 1.4 per cent
1901	36,999,946		454,982 or 1.2 per cent

The proportion of Wesleyan attenders to the church-going population as a whole is naturally more flattering, at least as judged by the only figures available – the imperfect ones of the 1851 Census:[7]

Total Attendances for three services on Census Sunday:	10,896,066
Anglicans	5,292,551
Wesleyans	1,554,528
Independents	1,214,059

(I have included the Independents, i.e. Congregationalists, as the largest body after the Anglicans and Wesleyans. All these 1851 figures are for England and Wales only; the exceptional religious situation of Ireland and Scotland exaggerates the minority situation of other bodies than the Catholics and Presbyterians respectively.)

Total Attendances at one or more services (H. Mann's estimates):	7,261,032
Anglicans (21 per cent of population; 52 per cent of attendances)	3,773,474
Wesleyans (5.1 per cent of population; 12.5 per cent of attendances)	907,313
Independents (4.4 per cent of population; 10.9 per cent of attendances)	793,142

[7] Figures from *Census of Great Britain 1851. Religious Worship: England and Wales.* Report and Tables (London 1853); see also the Report on *Religious Worship and Education: Scotland* (London 1854).

Thus, if Wesleyanism became the largest single English Nonconformist Church, this did not give it more than a moderate proportion of English religious allegiance as a whole. Moreover, the crude figures of increase in the half-century under discussion, together with those for population increase as a whole, might suggest that Wesleyanism's increase failed to keep pace with population increase as a whole, and this might suggest that the increase was largely a product of 'natural' growth rather than of a widening impact on English life; the same may be broadly true of comparable increases at this time in the other English Churches.

It is necessary, however, to look more deeply into the statistics and to ask questions about growth variations within the period in relation both to total population growth and to particular areas. Much work remains to be done here, but useful suggestions have been made by Dr Robert Currie, some of which, with additional material, will now be discussed.[8] Dr Currie points out that the growth rate of Wesleyanism varied considerably in different periods of the nineteenth century; and that in any case the significance of the rate of growth has to be estimated in relation to total population growth rather than simply in terms of crude growth in membership. For example, in 1841 British Wesleyanism had 328,792 members and in 1931 had 500,010 – a growth rate of 51 per cent. But membership figures in relation to the relevant (aged 15 and over) population were 2.79 per cent in 1841, but only 1.47 per cent in 1931 – a clear decline in effectiveness. This decline, seen in terms of the relationship to population increase rate, probably goes back to the later years of the nineteenth century, but was for some years masked by the growth in terms of simple membership figures. In terms of membership growth rate in relation to population growth rate Wesleyanism could in earlier years seem to be achieving wonders: for example, in 1801–71 it was calculated that membership had increased by 287 per cent whereas population had only increased by 155 per cent.[9] But after 1881 this favourable ratio began to decline in relation to population increase rate.

Equally important is the distribution of Wesleyanism (and its rate of growth) in relation to various geographical and social areas, which is an important pointer to its character. Speaking of the late eighteenth and early nineteenth centuries, Dr Maldwyn Edwards pointed out over thirty years ago how Methodism did best in the manufacturing and industrial counties, worst in the purely agricultural. Even then, as he observed, it is necessary to particularize: Wiltshire, Hampshire and Surrey were the weakest of all; yet in Lincolnshire, Leicestershire and other counties of a definitely rural character Wesleyanism did better. Edwards recognized

[8] R. Currie, 'A Micro-theory of Methodist Growth', in *W.H.S. Proc.* (October 1967), 65; and *Methodism Divided*, Chapter 3, for further statistics and discussion.

[9] E. H. Tindall, *Wesleyan Methodist Atlas* (n.d.: *c.* 1873), 46.

that here, as in the 'industrial' areas, the numbers were related to social class: Wesleyanism (unlike Primitive Methodism) was least successful with agricultural labourers; and where it was more successful the success was with craftsmen and artisans.[10] The same writer pointed out that to speak of 'industrial' success also needs qualifications: here again, it was less the industrial proletariat and the very poor who were held than the more independent and rising men. The same conclusion is suggested by Professor Inglis's analysis of the 1851 Census.[11] Abstention from religious worship in that year was most common where the largest numbers of working-class people lived. As between denominations, the Nonconformists as a whole tended to do better than the Anglicans in such areas; and their relative success owed most to the Methodists, especially to the Wesleyans. But this was in the context of all Churches doing much worse in such areas than elsewhere – sometimes as little as one in ten at worship from all Churches combined. London was, no doubt, a special case, but Methodism did particularly badly here, and for once we have the advantage of much more accurate statistics for the end of the century than are otherwise obtainable. The *British Weekly* survey of 1886 gave a total of 1,167,312 attendances; the 1902–3 *Daily News* survey (a more accurate one) gave 1,003,361 in a larger population. Most of the decrease was suffered by the Anglicans, and the Wesleyans were said to have held their own by the effects of the 'Forward Movement' (i.e. the London Missions and Halls).[12] The detailed break-down of denominations shows, however, some significant features. The Wesleyan total is 122,607 (Inner London: 78,139; Outer London: 44,468); the total for all Methodists is 173,117 (105,784 and 67,333). But against this, one can set other Nonconformist totals: for example, figures for all London: 158,913 Congregationalists, 163,052 Baptists; and 167,375 of those who may be broadly classed as 'Evangelicals' meeting with the Brethren or Salvation Army or in a multitude of mission-halls. What is more, the 'main-line' denominations did rather better in Outer than in Inner London; while the Roman Catholics and 'Evangelicals' (except the Salvation Army) did rather better in Inner London. This suggests that the 'main-line' denominations did better in middle-class areas and with a middle-class population, while the less formal and ministerially-centred groups did better in working-class areas (a surmise confirmed by other information). Fur-

[10] Maldwyn Edwards, *After Wesley* (London 1935), pp. 143–8.

[11] K. S. Inglis, 'Patterns of Religious Worship in 1851', in *The Journal of Ecclesiastical History*, xi, No. 1 (April 1960), 74–86.

[12] R. Mudie-Smith (ed.), *The Religious Life of London* (London 1904), p. 293: in Chapter IX there is a comparison at the two surveys. In Mudie-Smith's survey, 'attendances' refer to the numbers at all services; but, calculating the proportion of 'twicers' as 39 per cent, he arrived at a figure of 832,051 individual worshippers out of a total of 1,003,361 'attendances'. In the figures quoted in the text I have used 'attendances'.

ther, it is evident that Wesleyan success was much less marked in London than elsewhere. But it must be added that the Churches as a whole had little comfort from a survey which showed only 1,003,361 'attendances' (and only 832,051 actual 'worshippers') out of a population of 4,470,304.

Mention of these surveys reminds us that Victorian churchmen were not unaware of the limitations in numbers and distribution of church attendance. The 1851 Census had given notice of these problems; and the plight of London was given wide publicity by pamphleteers who worked there in the 1880s. Wesleyan Methodists were also better informed statistically and even sociologically than is often supposed, by certain statistical surveys of the whole or parts of the Connexion as well as by more impressionistic writings. For example, Charles Prest in 1856 used the Census and other information to show how and why Wesleyan strength varied, though more particularly in such rural areas as Surrey, Suffolk, Hereford and Hertfordshire.[13] Similar conclusions could be drawn from the better-known work of W. W. Pocock in his *Sketch of the History of Wesleyan-Methodism in some of the Southern Counties of England*, on which Dr Edwards was able to draw. The picture for rural areas was amplified with minute statistics in a report of the Home Mission Fund on Rural Methodism (mid-1880s), and for the whole of Methodism in E. H. Tindall's *Wesleyan Methodist Atlas*. This last book revealed that there were Wesleyan chapels in just over five out of every nine places in England and Wales; the Rural Methodism survey showed that in southern rural England out of a population of over four million about one-and-three-quarter million might be reckoned as covered by Wesleyan chapels in 2,500 places and touched by proximity in another 500. In 1,500 of these villages there was no other form of Nonconformity; but there were other Methodist bodies in 1,200 non-Wesleyan villages as well as in over a third of the Wesleyan ones. In more than a hundred there were three or four Methodist chapels.

Certainly the full explanation of these facts was not grasped at the time, nor, as we shall see, were the remedies for the decline both of rural and large city centre congregations very effective.[14] It was recognized that Methodism had spread among the kind of population described by Dr Edwards,[15] and that the nineteenth century had seen great increases in population, a drift to the south in the latter part of the century, emigration from country to town and from city centres to suburbs – all of which affected Wesleyanism and perhaps affected it more than other denominations. Dr Currie, in the article and book already cited, has

[13] Charles Prest, *Fourteen Letters on the Home-Work of Wesleyan Methodism, its Sustentation and Extension* (London 1856).

[14] See below, pp. 132ff.

[15] See J. H. Rigg's 'Introduction' to W. W. Pocock, *A Sketch of the History of Wesleyan Methodism in some of the Southern Counties of England* (London 1885).

suggested a further tentative analysis, which runs in part as follows. Methodism had originally been recruited from the population which Anglicanism had failed to reach and in areas where it was weak (e.g. north of the Severn–Wash line). After 1800, Methodist growth in relation to population increase was considerable, but the Wesleyan part of it was slower. This might be explained as due to the newer Methodist groups (e.g. the Primitives) supplementing the growth of Wesleyanism by extending Methodist social appeal to new and poorer groups, and also supplementing the older Methodist geographical coverage. But the mid-century Wesleyan seceders did not grow in the same way: they extended 'laterally' by recruiting from existing Methodists rather than 'frontally' from non-Methodists, and showed little further growth of their own.

After 1881, Methodism generally began to experience a fall in membership in proportion to the population: the obvious reason for this was migration of population of the types already noted from strong Methodist areas. It is suggested, indeed, that Methodists left the north for the south more quickly than the general population, so giving rise to a double problem of empty chapels in the north and scarce resources in the south. The same problems in miniature were repeated between city centres and suburbs.

This analysis may be accepted pending more detailed investigation. It should be added that in social and religious character, as in geographical distribution, one must recognize the way in which the various Methodist bodies not only supplemented but also overlapped each other; there was a slow trend towards a greater homogeneity between the various bodies, which was ultimately to provide a basis for reunion. The middle-class picture of nineteenth-century Wesleyanism and its 'respectability', and antipathy to what the eighteenth century had called 'enthusiasm', can easily be overdrawn. Certain strata and certain areas in Wesleyanism continued to be attracted by revivalism; the ways of rural members often differed little to the outward eye between Wesleyan and Primitive; revivalism, 'perfection' and the use of rural 'lay agents' were combined in the 'Joyful News' mission founded by the Wesleyan, Thomas Champness.[16] All this was often somewhat far removed in spirit from the official leadership, and much depended on accidents of birth, conversion and place. For where men of a certain social and religious type were likely in any case not to be Anglican, it was often a

[16] Some of the characteristics of rough rural Wesleyanism, with a 'revivalist' flavour, may be seen recorded in Benjamin Gregory, *Autobiographical Recollections* (London 1903); his son, B. A. Gregory (an early Wesleyan Oxford graduate), was also rather painfully involved in Wesleyan revivalism; see B. Gregory, *Consecrated Culture: Memorials of Benjamin Alfred Gregory, M.A. Oxon.* (London 1885). For Champness, see E. M. Champness, *The Life-Story of Thomas Champness* (n.d., *c.* 1907). The 'primitive' strain in Wesleyanism is illustrated by men like Peter Mackenzie and Thomas Waugh (see note 32, below).

matter of chance whether the available alternative was Wesleyan or something else. Methodism as a whole had a good chance of recruiting such men because of its large coverage, compared with the rest of Nonconformity. On the other hand, Wesleyanism, like other 'respectable' churches, did not always hold its keener 'evangelicals', as the cases of the Salvation Army and of London tend to show: such found their home in less conventional Churches.

3. Wesleyanism and Society

(*a*) *Finance and organization.* The growth and spread of Wesleyanism posed obvious problems of finance and organization, the development of which shows an eventual shift from the attempt simply to cope with domestic needs to the traditional Methodist notion of its mission to the unevangelized world outside. In coping both with its own expanding and moving membership and with those outside, Methodism, like other churches, was prone to assume that what was needed was simply the extension of its existing system of circuits, churches and ministers to cover the new gaps. There was the greater encouragement to take this view because the system was of relatively recent growth and might seem to have notable advantages over the ancient Anglican system and over the less ancient but still elderly systems of Dissent. The problems of the Connexion might therefore be seen largely in terms of finance for chapel-building and, to a lesser extent, in terms of the support and housing of sufficient ministers; much of the financial history of Wesleyanism in the period reflects such assumptions. Moreover, much that was done amounted to an attempt, first, to relieve the load of debt incurred by societies building chapels on credit which they could pay back only very slowly – a situation aggravated by the decline of many of the societies owing to population changes. Next, money had to be raised to build for areas (e.g. in city suburbs) where the existing Wesleyan population now lived; and also for Connexional projects (e.g. education and ministerial training) which were also mainly services for the existing Wesleyan public. It was only later, and at the end of this list of existing wants, that attention was paid to genuine extension work outside the existing church circle. When 'extension work' is spoken of, one has to examine carefully what was really in mind: very often it merely meant building for existing congregations.[17]

In the first half of the nineteenth century there were two main types of fund. The old Contingent Fund usually had less than £10,000 at its disposal, mainly to support circuits unable to afford ministers and manses without help: there was little it could do to help extensions of any kind. Secondly, there were the various Funds for building chapels.

[17] On the various Funds, see the outline account in *N.H.M.*, i, 437–80, *passim*.

They too were limited in funds and in scope of policy. Much was done locally and not always with official sanction: the purpose of the latter was in any case not so much to implement a policy of planned expansion as to curb the habit of incurring crippling long-term debts.

From the 1850s there was increased activity in the reorganizing of old Funds and the creation of new ones; and much more money was raised centrally for building purposes. One reason was, initially, the need to cope with the results of secession: the Relief and Extension Fund (1853) was to relieve other Methodist Funds which had suffered for this reason. Such needs also stimulated the reorganization of the Chapel Department under its first full-time Secretary (1854). The needs most strongly felt continued to be those of old debts, declining areas, and areas with an increased Wesleyan population lacking chapels. It might seem that the change in title of the Contingent Fund to 'Home Mission and Contingent Fund' from 1856 under the influence of Charles Prest was a pointer in a different direction; but this is misleading. Prest himself spoke and wrote much on 'Home Mission' work and it has already been noted how he made an intelligent use of the 1851 Census and other information to construct a factual analysis of the state of Methodism. It is noticeable, however, that his main attention was directed to the weakness of Wesleyanism in rural areas, and his treatment of London and the cities was more cursory.[18] For such areas of difficulty his basic remedy was more ministers, financed with the help of Home Mission funds, rather than simply more churches. These funds continued to be limited for a good many years longer and they were largely devoted to existing circuits, especially in the country;[19] determined efforts in the cities had to wait until the 1870s and, indeed, the 1880s.

Again, it is significant that the new funds for 'extending' Methodism in particular areas were mainly in terms of shifting and growing Methodist population. There were Funds for Scotland (1867), North Wales (1867), South Wales (1873), and (particularly illuminating) for Watering Places (1861). This last was initiated by the leading preacher Morley Punshon, some of the money coming directly from the proceeds of his preaching and lecturing, but much more from private sources – with debts which were not wiped out for years. The thirteen schemes resulting from the Fund directly reflected changing social habits and Wesleyan participation in them.

The most instructive example of all is the Metropolitan Chapel

[18] See n. 13 above.

[19] By 1866, for example, The Home Mission and Contingent Fund's expenditure was under £21,000, of which by no means all went to strictly 'missionary' work. The portion that did, moreover, was used for such things as financing 'District Missionaries', mainly in rural circuits.

Building Fund (from 1861),[20] which built 78 chapels in twenty years, with a renewed Fund in 1885 when the old one was exhausted. Sir Francis Lycett initiated it and the purpose was to provide large (1,000-seat) chapels in an area where Wesleyanism was noticeably weak. But the rules and the reports of the Fund prove that it did not and could not do much for the city centres, the poor, the unchurched – on the contrary it catered for existing or expected Methodist emigration to the suburbs and other middle-class areas away from the centre. A few church halls and 'iron churches' were built on a smaller and cheaper scale in the poorer areas, in the hope of larger churches later; and the rules were revised to allow 600-seat churches, with the hope of later extension. But the lack of real effort in the destitute areas was illustrated by the Rev. Forster Crozier's recollection of speaking to Lycett just before his death about a destitute region of Southwark, and of Lycett's recognizing that something should be built there.[21]

In 1874 Lycett and Mewburn instituted a 'Fund for the Extension of Methodism in Great Britain', which once again turned out to be largely a measure of consolidation and support of existing work. Its stated object was to increase the resources of the Home Mission and Chapel Departments and the Theological Institution; but it eventually helped about a thousand chapels in the villages and smaller towns.[22] The rest of the proposed work was taken over by the Thanksgiving Fund of 1878.

This[23] had as its stated objects the following: to raise funds to relieve present embarrassment, and to provide as far as possible against the recurring accumulation of debt; also a new branch of the Theological Institution. Apart from a substantial allocation to Overseas Missions, the Fund covered the following projects for Home Work: the training and support of the ministry (Theological Institution; funds for ministers and their families; circuits unable to support ministers);

[20] For the original objects and rules of the Fund, see *First Report of the Metropolitan Wesleyan Chapel Building Fund* (1863), which also gives the location, cost, and some pictures, of the first batch of chapels. Summary reports appear in the *Minutes of Conference* from 1870.

[21] F. Crozier, *Methodism and 'The Bitter Cry of Outcast London'* (London 1885), p. 14. Crozier pointed out that really weak circuits in destitute areas could not meet the Fund's conditions for the proportion raised by local efforts. For the revision of the rules to allow grants for 600- or even 400-seat chapels in 1880, see *Minutes* (1883), pp. 308f. The essentially suburban character of the Fund's work was recognized by J. Hugh Morgan, *Wesleyan Methodism and Destitute London* (n.d., *c.* 1884): Morgan helped to plan the assault on the capital by Missions in the 1880s. Crozier pointed out the need of evangelists as well as of the building of chapels in difficult areas.

[22] In 1878, for example, about 100 chapels were promised help; 63 in villages (*Minutes* 1878, p. 339).

[23] See *Wesleyan Methodist Thanksgiving Fund 1878–9* (1879); *Report of the Wesleyan Methodist Thanksgiving Fund, 1878–83* (1883). The 'thanksgiving' was for the recovery from the secession losses of the 1850s and for the peaceful achievement of Lay Representation in 1878.

education; and buildings. Once again the purposes reflect the extension and consolidation of Wesleyan needs as they then were. The Fund's original target of £204,000 was later expanded to £300,000, and £297,000 was actually raised by 1883.

The last of these special efforts in our period was the Twentieth Century Fund, which was inspired particularly by Sir Robert Perks and raised over a million pounds by 1908. The Fund was similar in character to that of 1878, but the advent of the Central Halls and the new type of city mission they represented were admired by Sir Robert, and money to them meant, on the face of it, an attempt to 'extend' Wesleyanism beyond the limitations observed in the earlier efforts described.[24]

Do the organizational changes of Methodism in this half-century reflect any more drastic change in attitude? The first half of the period saw the Wesleyans pre-occupied with the issues raised by the secessions and by the forces which not only produced them but continued to exercise reformers who stayed in the old Connexion. The series of changes which culminated in the grant of lay representation in Conference and the reorganization of Conference in 1878 into two sessions, Representative and Pastoral (ministers only), were of considerable significance for an understanding of the change in the character of Wesleyanism from its original conception,[25] but may be regarded rather as a reflection of internal tensions, almost (in a sense) backward-looking, than as the result of a pre-occupation with the reform of the structure for the purposes of evangelizing a changing world. Otherwise, Wesleyans seemed content to stick to the traditional apparatus of classes, societies, circuits and districts, served by a travelling ministry moving every three years. Criticism of various features of the system did, however, occur and, so far as the itinerancy is concerned, reflected the experience of tackling nineteenth-century cities with a system developed in the days before the Industrial Revolution and for a Connexion which was not designed to be an independent Church.

The criticisms were that ministers moved too quickly; that they could not be really effective, especially with the un-churched, on the basis of occasional pulpit ministrations for a mere three years. New methods of evangelism seemed called for; but, again, a man could scarcely carry through a new policy effectively in such a short stay. The conservatives[26]

[24] The Fund was raised for 'Evangelistic, Educational, and Philanthropic purposes'; for details, see *Minutes* (1898), pp. 342–7.

[25] Jabez Bunting, indeed, had alleged that he stood for 'the just rights of the laity', and Rigg and Gregory persuaded themselves that 1878 was the logical implementation of the older Wesleyan principles; cf. T. P. Bunting & G. S. Rowe, *Life of Jabez Bunting* (1887), pp. 708f., 713; J. Telford, *Life of J. H. Rigg* (n.d., *c.* 1910), pp. 273ff.; B. Gregory, *Scriptural Church Principles* (1888), ii, 244.

[26] Quoted from *British Weekly*, 8, viii, 1895, by K. S. Inglis, *Churches and the Working Classes in Victorian England*, p. 90.

responded that if the three-year rule were to be abandoned Methodism would collapse – a view which was not without validity, for the change certainly reflected a shift of some importance in the understanding of Methodism. It will be shown in a moment that the changes carried out did not achieve their original objectives, and this suggests that the analysis on which they were based did not go deep enough. At all events the old rule was modified for certain city areas of special mission in the 1880s and more generally relaxed in the 1890s.[27] This was part of the general strategy for specialized missions (to be considered in a moment); and in addition there were attempts to further evangelistic concern and efficiency by encouraging consultation and joint work between existing circuits or at the district level. The use of ministerial or lay missioners detached from normal circuit work pre-dated the Central Hall Movement which began in the 1880s, but these expedients and the Halls themselves tend to illustrate the fact that Wesleyanism still thought in terms of the fundamental soundness of the traditional system, and the traditional use of ministers. The new agencies did no more than supplement the old; there was no overall reorganization, though it is true that the Central Halls were intended to operate in place of existing churches. The fact that it was claimed that they successfully combined a 'mission' with a balanced Methodist 'church' life and that it was hoped eventually to build them up as self-supporting congregations shows, however, the limited nature of the change envisaged.

(*b*) *Evangelism and Home Mission work*. It is time to look at Wesleyan attempts actually or ostensibly aimed not only at areas but also at classes of people whom they were conscious of not ordinarily reaching. Once again the Census of 1851 made them realize more acutely perhaps than others how limited their appeal was. Certainly they were not really a 'working-class Church' in terms of the mass of urban workers; the middle-class nature of Wesleyanism was noted at the time and has been stressed by later writers.[28] The shift of this type of worshipper to the suburbs was recognized, and this, we have seen, was the significance of much of the church-building and of its financial requirements. But they were also uneasily conscious of their (partly mythical, partly misunderstood) 'working-class' past; and they could not escape the equally strong tradition of being a Church based on the concept of an evangelistic society. Following the Report on the Census (published 1854), Conference expressed a concern to 'penetrate the neglected masses

[27] Considerable legal difficulties were involved, and the relaxation was in fact achieved by a legal fiction; see *Minutes* (1893), p. 330; (1895), pp. 323–4; (1896), pp. 321–2; *N.H.M.*, i, 443–6; J. R. Gregory, *A History of Methodism, Chiefly for the Use of Students* (London 1911), ii, 79ff.

[28] But see above, p. 127, and note 16.

of the heathenish population of our large cities' and decided upon 'reviving and sustaining the Home Missionary spirit of Methodism'.[29] This is part of the context in which Prest helped to rename the 'Home Mission and Contingent Fund', but its limited scope in money and work has already been noticed. Indeed, Wesleyans were probably slower and less inventive in their attitude to the devising of fresh evangelistic methods than other denominations. They were hindered by the very success of their original organization; perhaps also by the centralization of the Connexional system and the itinerancy.[30] Meanwhile, other Churches (even the Church of England) took up lay agencies: Spurgeon ran popular services on non-church premises as early as the 1850s; Anglicans of various brands of churchmanship ran 'missions'; Sankey and Moody captivated a section of the Evangelical world; and in a quite different idiom the 'Ritualist' slum-priests were ministering to the very poor.[31]

In fairness to the Wesleyans it should be pointed out that, as was noted earlier, they retained within their spectrum of church allegiance a fair amount of popular Evangelicalism of the 'revivalist' type; but it is also evident that those desiring this kind of religion – essentially less static and less clerical than in the main-line denominations – were in the later nineteenth century[32] looking for it outside the usual channels. The first Wesleyan attempts at a fresh Home Mission effort suggest a harking back to their past, and for that matter a propping up of the failing areas inherited from the past. A body of 'District Missionaries' was instituted in 1858 – fifty-three were operating by 1863 – whose work was to lie in new or declining areas. They were to be ministerial or lay, itinerant or

[29] *Minutes*, xii (1854), 488; Inglis, op. cit., pp. 86f.; see also Charles Prest's 'Charge' as President in 1862.

[30] Charles Booth made some sensible comments on the essentially 'country' rather than city bias in the origins of the Wesleyan organization and on the inhibiting effects of centralized connexionalism: *Life and Labour of the People in London. Third Series: Religious Influences* (1903), vii, 129–38.

[31] K. S. Inglis, op. cit., surveys the whole field, but many ingenious devices no doubt remain to be investigated: for example, some Anglican clergy were able to take regular morning services in business houses, which apprentices were compelled to attend: 'Occasional Papers on London', in *Wesleyan-Methodist Magazine*, 5th ser., xi (May 1865), 446. It is not claimed, of course, that these efforts were very successful in winning the working classes and the unchurched. Spurgeon's congregation was probably middle-class – he was 'the apostle of the grocers', said Lord Rosebery (R. R. James, *A Biography of Archibald Philip, Fifth Earl of Rosebery* (London 1963), pp. 57f.). The 'Ritualists' seem to have attracted people from other parishes, and this was also true of the Wesleyan Missions (see further, below, p. 140 and n. 53).

[32] Thomas Waugh, *Twenty-Three Years a Missioner* (London n.d.), pp. 175f., noted this antipathy to church membership and alleged that the Methodists had lost 100,000 members to undenominational missions during 1875–95; see also the London statistics quoted above, p. 125. 'Revivalism' by the 1880s had not only become more respectable but was felt to be needed in order to counter the attractions of 'Ritualism, Rationalism and Ruffianism' (A. McAulay, in Edward Smith, *An Evangelist's Notebook*, 1880, Introduction).

localized, and they were to support the local Circuits' needs without being bound to normal Circuit work; indeed they were explicitly to refrain from taking part in routine pastoral work. In fact they were sustaining the kind of visitation common in the Methodist past but now taken up in other Churches as well; and they were 'extending' work more in villages than in cities.

It is only fair to add that the weakness of Wesleyanism in a number of rural areas (on which comment has already been made) was aggravated by Primitive Methodist successes there, but even more (for both denominations) by agricultural depression from the 1870s onwards. It could be argued that Methodism continued to have a responsibility in these areas and that some means had to be found to fulfil it. Charles Prest had argued for finance to go to support ministers; more realistically, at a later date, Thomas Champness saw lay agents as essential, ministers being too expensive; and he added the reflection that converting and training young men from the villages might even in the long run help city Methodism, in view of emigration from country to city.[33] Champness founded his 'Joyful News' Mission in Rochdale (1886) with a view originally to training underprivileged men who might then train for the ministry (the Connexion had rejected his idea of doing such preliminary training in the Theological Institution); but he quickly turned to training young local preachers, colporteurs and lay evangelists, with the villages primarily in mind. He therefore helped to maintain the hold of Wesleyanism on a class of men who might otherwise have drifted elsewhere.

But by this time, in the 1880s, the mood of Wesleyanism was changing: like other Churches, it produced some leaders who were more explicitly occupied with the plight of the urban poor and with the narrowed social scope of the main denominations. So Hugh Price Hughes wrote in 1885:

> Methodism has reached the parting of the ways. We must either go back into the obscurity of a class religion, and the impotence of a moribund sect; or we must go forward into the blessed opportunities and far reaching beneficence of a national religion, which preaches the Gospel to the poor.[34]

Such a concern was not the invention of Hughes or even of Wesley-

[33] E. M. Champness, op. cit., p. 234. For the story of the 'Joyful News' and the 'Joyful News Training Home and Mission', see the same work, and an article by H. T. Smart, 'The "Joyful News" Mission', in *Wesleyan-Methodist Magazine*, 6th ser., xiv (January 1890), 12–16. The idea of the newspaper was conceived by Charles Garrett, but Champness in fact ran it on his own responsibility when other backing failed to materialize. He started his Mission out of the profits, and the Conference merely gave its official blessing.

[34] Quoted by K. S. Inglis, op. cit., p. 70. On the 'Forward Movement', see below, p. 139.

anism. The London City Mission for inter-denominational work among the poor, utilizing lay evangelists, had started as far back as 1835; and there were Wesleyan versions of this type of mission in the Metropolitan Methodist Lay Mission (1874) and the Manchester and Salford Lay Mission (1872).[35] These efforts were, it should be noted, purely lay and evangelistic in character; and they merely supplemented existing circuit work. Provoked by circumstances and by examples from other religious groups, some Wesleyan Ministers experienced in city work began to think in terms of specialized city missions which could be led by ministers (preferably on long-term appointments) and replace the conventional church organization in difficult areas. They also came to feel the need of 'social work' (both in a charitable and in a recreational sense), and in consequence this type of mission eventually took the shape of the 'institutional' church, with multifarious social as well as strictly evangelistic agencies within it, which became a feature of city missions in the last quarter of the nineteenth century.[36] Among the Wesleyan pioneers of city mission work of various kinds should be mentioned Charles Garrett, who had helped to found the Manchester and Salford Lay Mission and was appointed to start a Mission in Liverpool in 1875. Peter Thompson started a Mission in East London in 1885; Edward Smith, one in Clerkenwell in 1886; Samuel Collier, the Manchester and Salford Mission in 1886.[37]

At the level of Conference, matters came to a head in 1884 with the appointment of two committees: one was to consider 'Old Chapels in Large Towns' whose congregations had shrunk because 'former seat-holders have removed to suburban districts', although 'around some of these Sanctuaries there are dense populations living in vice and indifference'; the other was on 'Spiritual Destitution in London', to consider the formation of special centres and districts detached from the Circuit organization. In 1885 the former committee reported that

[35] Forster Crozier noted that the Metropolitan Lay Mission had followed the example of the London City Mission, but had few workers and never developed. There are brief reports on the Manchester and London Lay Missions in the *Minutes*. For their methods (conventional evangelistic preaching, visiting, etc.), see *Metropolitan Methodist Lay Mission* (Occasional Paper, October 1874): one article noted the need for such work to make Lycett's chapel building fully effective.

[36] See Charles Booth, op. cit., for details of all denominations in the 1880s.

[37] See R. B. Thompson, *Peter Thompson* (London 1910); E. Smith, *An Evangelist's Notebook* (1880), and especially his *Three Years in Central London: A record of Principles, Methods, and Successes* (London 1889); G. Jackson, *Collier of Manchester: A Friend's Tribute* (London 1923). Collier's Mission was conceived by a group led by H. J. Pope on the demolition of the decayed Oldham Street chapel in 1883; its foundation, it was said, 'marks one of the turning points in the history of modern Methodism. It checked decisively that facile and fatal policy of abandoning the centres of great cities' (G. Jackson, op. cit., p. 38). Hughes's London West Central Mission was only begun in 1887 as part of the plans for a London Mission put forward in 1885, though it has always had a lion's share of the publicity in accounts of the 'Forward Movement'.

declining city churches should be sold only in exceptional circumstances. Instead, they should be adapted to the requirements of the people, that is, they should be converted as nearly as possible into Mission Chapels. There should be more free seats and 'more practical interest should be shown in the domestic and social well-being of the people in the neighbourhood of such chapels'. Ministers appointed should concentrate on these chapels and use lay helpers.[38]

More dramatic and explicit was the result of the London committee in the authorizing by the Conference of 1885 of the 'London Wesleyan-Methodist Mission'.[39] The object was 'to carry the Gospel to such regions of London, and especially of Central London, as are most spiritually destitute and degraded'; and £50,000 was set aside for the purpose. In brief, the plan was to detach special areas and to build and staff Mission premises for them which could include social and philanthropic work. Ultimately they might be restored to Circuit administration when they could once again be worked effectively by Circuits. This special concentration on London was provoked partly by the publicity given to the spiritual and social destitution of London in *The Bitter Cry of Outcast London*, published in 1883, and written probably by a Congregationalist,[40] which is often referred to by Wesleyans and others at the time. According to Hugh Price Hughes, it awoke the Metropolitan churches to their responsibility, first of all in the south London areas with which the book dealt, then in the East End, then (so Hughes said) in the West End where Wesleyans at any rate had done least of all: hence the founding of his own West Central London Mission, for 'the most important sphere of Christian work in the British Empire, and therefore in the world'.[41]

Although Hughes and his Mission have received much of the publicity and credit for the new approach, it was larger than one man or one denomination; a centralized denomination was, however, able to channel more resources and organization than others in this direction. The urban Mission system with its halls and varied ministries was soon

[38] *Minutes* (1884), pp. 281f.; (1885), p. 265; (1887), pp. 361–3. For the origin of the London Committee, see J. Hugh Morgan, op. cit., and Forster Crozier, op. cit.

[39] See *Minutes* (1885), pp. 228–32; (1886), pp. 241–6.

[40] On the book and its authorship, see K. S. Inglis, op. cit., pp. 67ff.

[41] *First 'Annual Report' of the London West Central Mission* (1888), pp. 1f. The 'Imperial' note becomes characteristic of Hughes. He had to justify a mission in an area not commonly noted by evangelists as 'destitute and degraded', at least in a social sense. The complexity of Hughes's aims is revealed in the talk, first, of the area as a great community centre with thousands of young people working there in business houses; next, of the 'influential classes who are significantly called "Society"'; then, of the 'great centre of pleasure ... competing even with Paris ... for all the lusts of the flesh'; and finally, of the general application of Christianity to social life, in terms of concern for the poor but also for public morality. Cf. also *Hugh Price Hughes As We Knew Him* (London 1902), pp. 24ff., for those whom he aimed to reach.

adopted for most large cities after London and Manchester (e.g. Birmingham 1888, Leeds 1889): by 1909 there were forty-one central halls and mission centres which attracted a good deal of wealthy lay support. The reasons for the concern which these missions expressed were more complex than always appears – social compassion, evangelistic concern, but also social and class fears, symbolized by the common conjunction of 'Atheism' and 'Socialism' ascribed to 'the labouring classes'. It has been said that in their developed form the ideal of the missions was 'to embody the redemptive purpose of Christianity in its social as well as its individual aspect, in a way which the old-fashioned chapel could not'.[42] This represents a certain shift from the aims of older city ministers. Charles Garrett and Edward Smith thought primarily in evangelistic terms: social work in the sense of recreation to lure men from the pub, club and music-hall was used by Smith and others; but social charity work they often suspected (except for the church-attached) as breeding pauperism or religious hypocrisy. Collier in Manchester did not originally intend to do much social work – he was concerned with 'evangelism' – and although he soon found himself involved in it extensively he never had any coherent theory of a 'social gospel' kind.[43] Hughes, on the other hand, saw such work as an integral part of his mission and had a 'social gospel' of a kind which will be considered later.

The general lines of policy developed in the missions were as follows. First, long-term ministerial appointments to facilitate a coherent policy. Second, it was hoped that the minister and mission could reach out to the unchurched masses. Third, the setting and conduct of worship was altered to eliminate features commonly held to keep the poor from church: no pew-rents; a 'theatrical' setting with platforms and tip-up seats; popular preaching with choirs and musical items; special services with recruiting by various advertising techniques. Finally, the two kinds of social work: 'cultural' in the shape of concerts, lectures, games and recreation rooms (and hybrids like the Pleasant Sunday Afternoons and Pleasant Sunday Evenings for the People, which combined entertainment with popular religion in which the watchword was 'brief, bright and brotherly').[44] Social relief work included meals, beds, prison

[42] Robert Currie, 'Were the Central Halls a Failure?', in *New Directions* (Spring 1967), p. 21.

[43] G. Jackson, op. cit., pp. 124ff. He did, indeed, see his Mission as improving both on ordinary Methodist church life and on existing evangelical missions by combining evangelical work with normal congregational activities, and by doing the missioning on a grand rather than on a mean and shabby scale. He also thought that Missions should develop their own local Christian communities rather than be 'feeders' to other, more regular, congregations.

[44] These last phenomena were inter- or un-denominational, if not, as some complained, actually diverting people from more ordinary and committed church life. The 'coffee-bar'

work, employment agencies, work for 'fallen women' and so on. It was in this context too that Hughes and Collier used 'Sisters of the People', almost certainly borrowing something from Roman and Anglican models (Hughes even called the head of his group the 'Sister Superior').[45] In both types of social work one should emphasize that Wesleyans were largely borrowing from, and sharing in, ideas common to all socially-minded churchpeople of the time. A specifically Wesleyan flavour came out mainly in the combination of mission methods with ordinary Wesleyan church life (e.g. class-meetings). Hughes and Collier claimed to have married the two and so avoided the weaknesses of either in isolation.

To complete the picture, mention should be made of one special kind of mission which once again is derivative rather than peculiarly Wesleyan in character. This was Scott Lidgett's Bermondsey Settlement (1890).[46] The model for this was the movement originating with Canon Barnett and others who founded Toynbee Hall in 1884. These Settlements varied in their relative emphasis on religious, educational and social work,[47] but in general they were an attempt by middle-class (often public-school, University and professional) men to interest their own class in the welfare of the poor. The novel feature was the concept of a 'resident (lay) gentry' in the Settlement trying to civilize and Christianize the poor, but adding the force of a personal, resident presence among them. The fundamental concept of reconciling the classes owes much to the legacy of F. D. Maurice's teaching on 'co-operation,

---

(name and thing) was in use by missions at least from the 1880s: there is a picture of the London West Central Mission's bar in its *Second Report* (1889; p. 139). Edward Smith prophetically remarked that he did not use them because they were more effective when run privately than when run by the Church; in the latter case they usually lost money and with little result (*Three Years in Central London*, chap. xi). Most of these non-religious devices attracted criticism: see further, below, p. 163 in relation to piety.

[45] The Wesley Deaconess Order proper was, however, founded by T. B. Stephenson, the founder of the National Children's Home and in various ways an architect of the newer, more socially-minded, Methodism: see W. Bradfield, *The Life of the Reverend Thomas Bowman Stephenson, B.A., LL.D., D.D.* (London 1913). Hughes also used a company of young, unmarried men as 'Brethren', some of them living in one of his subsidiary halls for short periods and doing spare-time evangelistic work. This has a faint touch of the 'Settlement' idea, perhaps even more (as in the case of the 'Sisters') of the model of Roman and Anglo-Catholic laymen under 'rule'. But if so, the idea was not developed: the man in charge of them was in any case an old-fashioned 'evangelist', and the men mostly did preaching and visiting.

[46] See an article in *Wesleyan–Methodist Magazine* (January 1890); J. Scott Lidgett, *My Guided Life* (London 1936); R. E. Davies (ed.), *John Scott Lidgett* (London 1937).

[47] See K. S. Inglis, op. cit., chap. 4, for a general account and references. Charles Booth, op. cit., gives accounts of them at the turn of the century. For the mental and social context, which includes the influence of the philosopher T. H. Green, see Melvin Richter, *The Politics of Conscience: T. H. Green and His Age* (London 1964). D. P. Hughes, *Life of Hugh Price Hughes* (London 1904), p. 134, says that Hughes felt Green's influence and thought he had given philosophical expression to entire sanctification.

not competition' and it is significant that Lidgett's theology of the 'Fatherhood of God' is almost entirely derived from Maurice (Hughes drew something from the same source). Lidgett was hampered by having a small Circuit to cope with as well; and he was perhaps missing part of the meaning of the Settlement when he saw it as giving 'additional force and attractiveness to Christian work'.[48]

The vaguely-styled 'Forward Movement'[49] in Wesleyanism, which included the new city mission concept and revised attitudes towards society in general, may be described as an attempt to bring Wesleyanism up to date, to relate it more positively to contemporary thought and society. It manifested itself in a change in theological outlook, method and style of presentation of Christianity. (The terms I have chosen are deliberately vague, in keeping with contemporary usage.) Perhaps the new missions were the most specific feature associated with the 'Movement'; and as such they represent a certain decline in Wesleyan distinctiveness.

How far were these missions successful? Wesleyans then and later have widely considered them to have succeeded in adapting church life to the special needs and problems of the urban working classes; or at least to have stemmed the decline in membership (so a member of the *Daily News* survey of London church life in 1902–3, comparing it with the survey of 1886). Modern students are more sceptical: Professor Inglis[50] concluded, of all these attempts of the Churches to influence and capture the working classes, that they substantially failed – failed because they attempted to change religious habits without changing the social basis on which they rested; those working-class people who were captured succumbed at the cost of adopting middle-class social habits. More recently Dr Currie[51] has subjected the Wesleyan missions to a searching and on the whole convincing analysis, as a result of which he concludes that, so far as social work is concerned, they gave some temporary assistance to a small percentage of the urban poor, but 'remained largely external to the personal experience and needs of the people'. In terms of winning working-class religious allegiance and even of holding or increasing Wesleyan figures of membership, any apparent success turns out on closer examination

[48] Quoted by R. E. Davies (ed.), op. cit., p. 52. Both Hughes, at the end of his life, and Scott Lidgett, in all his theological writing, were influenced by F. D. Maurice's theology of the Fatherhood of God – in strong contrast to the older generation which, in the person of J. H. Rigg (*Modern Anglican Theology*, London 1857), had criticized him severely.

[49] Currie, *Methodism Divided*, pp. 177f., considers that the 'Forward Movement' should be understood less in the context of the crisis of the unchurched masses than in that of the crisis in Methodism at the same time caused by resurgent Anglicanism.

[50] K. S. Inglis, op. cit., Epilogue.

[51] Robert Currie, 'Were the Central Halls a Failure?' (cited n. 42 above), and *Methodism Divided*, p. 211.

to be small and in any case explicable without the help of the new missions.

It would, indeed, be easy to illustrate the attitude of social condescension with which the missioners approached the poor and the 'labouring classes' – an attitude which at times concealed class-fear as well. The work tended to be in terms of work for, or at most with, but scarcely at all through, the poor (i.e. creating a working-class leadership). It is doubtful whether even General Booth succeeded in realizing this last possibility.[52] But this tended to be true of early Socialist groups as well; and even Trade Unionism succeeded best among the working-class élite in 'craft' unions: that élite showed little interest in religion except in rather special cases (connected with Primitive Methodism in particular), just as they turned to the vision of a working-class political party only when the economic or legal position of the Unions seemed at risk and the existing political parties would not do enough for them. Inglis's point about attempting to change religious habits without changing the social basis on which these rested is important. The Churches' attitudes here – even those of their more 'advanced' leaders – were too conservative, and too derivative, to make much impact or to appear more than the reflection of the classes from which most of their membership was drawn. They failed to offer any convincing evidence of rising above these natural limitations and so failed to establish a prescriptive right to prophesy to a society which had clearly ceased to be under their tutelage to any serious degree.

The appeal of the missions, even in strictly and narrowly religious matters, seems also to have been more to established and middle-class than to unattached and working-class worshippers. Certainly the style of preaching had changed in significant respects: from solid evangelical doctrine to less solid pictorial preaching and (in the case of Hughes and others) to broader 'social' themes. There is evidence that this attracted the church-attached looking for a mass congregation with a well-known preacher, neither of which they always found in the suburbs. As Currie says, the Halls became the cathedrals of Methodism and failed to create a city-centre community, though he adds that some of the lesser Halls probably attracted more of the poor.[53]

[52] Despite the inspired vulgarity of their manner and methods, the early Salvationist workers were not from the *industrial* working classes.

[53] It is difficult to be quite certain about this analysis, though a number of contemporary observers do certainly give the same impression. There were complaints that special missions attracted worshippers from the suburbs or from other denominations. Hughes described those who claimed to receive benefit from his early mission services as including M.P.s of both Houses, titled ladies, journalists, actresses, the learned professions, as well as 'the various classes usually reached' (*First Annual Report of the West Central London Wesleyan Methodist Mission*, 1888, p. 8). A special mission of his made converts including 'swells,

One test (which also raises the more general question of how far the Missions held or increased Wesleyan membership) is the significance of their membership figures. The West London Mission rose from 123 in 1888 to 1,357 in 1902; the Manchester and Salford Mission from 93 in 1887 to 3,521 in 1902. However, these figures are partly deceptive – the Manchester Mission 'cannibalized' other churches – and must in any case be seen in perspective. The Connexion as a whole was growing, though at a decreasing speed, so that the Missions could not claim to be responsible for this growth in view of their small part in the whole; other denominations even grew faster without the Wesleyan system. Dr Currie also shows how the more obviously relevant local growth pattern of the South-East suggests that the main explanation for growth common to Mission and non-Mission areas is the general shift of population, including Methodists, to this area.

The Missions, then, in terms of their stated aims to minister to, and capture the allegiance of, the classes and areas alienated from the Church, were really a failure; and in this they resembled most of the other main denominations. It is nevertheless worth considering the possibility that all the special efforts of the later nineteenth-century Churches did succeed in keeping the allegiance of existing church-goers which might otherwise have been lost altogether, and so held up the decline in membership which was to become evident in the present century. Socially, the value of 'first aid' work should perhaps not be dismissed entirely, once it is acknowledged that only structural alterations by the state could really affect the situation fundamentally. More important, perhaps, is the gradual widening of Christian concern – in social matters and in the understanding of Christianity itself. This brings us to an examination of the character and significance of Wesleyan social thought and activity which we have so far observed rather as a facet of the development of the Missions.

---

tradesmen, police, soldiers, footmen' and many young people from business houses (*Third Report*, 1890, p. 95). An observer noted of a 'mission-room' in Manchester of the 1870s (perhaps of the Manchester and Salford Lay Mission) that it had 'little of the "working-man" or "very poor" element': they were mostly small shopkeepers or factory-hands' wives. Another hall he visited did, however, 'fill well with disreputable people' (B. Gregory, *Consecrated Culture*, p. 138). On the other hand, while some critics alleged that Collier's Mission congregations were 'too respectable' and made up of churchgoers, his biographer was able to quote a report in a local paper to the effect that the congregation, in 1893, was made up 'mainly of respectable artisans and their wives and families; present also were many of a lower order, from the ranks of unskilled and unsettled labour' and some from 'the criminal class' in ragged clothes (G. Jackson, op. cit., p. 68). This might, indeed, be taken to indicate a lack of some large section of the working classes.

(*c*) *Political and social thought and action.*[54] I have said that the theoretical and practical problems created by an industrial society in England were the concern of many bodies and individuals, not simply or even predominantly that of the Churches. The last quarter of the nineteenth century saw a certain quickening and intensification of this concern.[55] Britain was now a mature industrial society; the old restraints to free trade had been removed; a new body of regulations had grown up to mitigate the strains and suffering of sections of society. But now more than ever radicals had to face the problems of reconciling individual and collective needs in a society which, socially and politically, was extending privilege, in terms of, for example, education and the franchise, ever further down the social scale in response to the increased bargaining power of the formerly unprivileged classes. At the same time the advantages of being the first industrialized nation were being lost in face of foreign competition, particularly from America and Germany. It is in this increasingly complex situation, with the social tensions which characterized it, that we must view the reactions of Wesleyans, and particularly of the middle-class lay and ministerial leadership which naturally shared the outlook of its class, while as members of a particular religious tradition they felt the pressure of potentially conflicting aspirations.

To take political attitudes first. The view has long been popularized in accounts of later nineteenth-century Wesleyanism that in this period its political complexion changed from 'Toryism' to 'Liberalism', despite the old 'no politics' rule.[56] (Certainly a change is evident in the second half of the century: the 'no politics' rule was less strictly observed; the desire to comment on, and intervene in, social and political affairs, and on some specific issues in particular, on the grounds of religious conviction and of the connection of religion with such matters, became more evident.) If there was no official line on party politics (and this was true of all the Methodist bodies), it is none the less evident that

[54] For a recent survey, see S. G. Checkland, *The Rise of Industrial Society in England 1815–1885* (London 1964), Chapters 2 and 9.

[55] No doubt that rule – slightly relaxed in 1875 (J. R. Gregory, *History of Methodism*, ii, 21) – tended to favour the *status quo* and so had a 'conservative' tendency. The real reasons for it were, however, religious – the preservation of the religious purposes for which Methodism was founded. It was held that it was not the business of Methodism to interfere in politics and social matters as such, unless some specifically religious or moral matter was involved. The general principles just stated need, however, to be examined in relation to specific local and personal examples and in relation to changes in the political situation. See, for example, D. A. Gowland, 'Political Opinion in Manchester Wesleyanism 1832–57', in *W.H.S. Proc.* xxxvi (February 1968), 93ff., for one such situation at the beginning of our period.

[56] For this subject, see the general accounts in K. S. Inglis, op. cit.; Maldwyn Edwards, *Methodism and England: A Study of Methodism in its Social and Political Aspects during the Period 1850–1932* (London 1943); R. F. Wearmouth, *Methodism and the Struggle of the Working Classes 1850–1900* (Leicester 1954).

many Methodists, including a number of leading ones, identified themselves more obviously with the Liberal than with the Conservative Party. But it needs to be remembered that talk of 'Liberal' and 'Conservative' without further qualification is, if anything, even less illuminating for the later than for the earlier part of the century; and that the changes in party character during the century make direct comparisons of the two periods very difficult. The Liberal Party at the end of the century was straining at the seams, and indeed splitting apart, over the Irish and social questions, and the statement that Wesleyans moved from Conservatism to Liberalism could mean a variety of things – it certainly did not necessarily imply a sharp move to the 'left', at least in all respects.

An important element in this Wesleyan political Liberalism was the type represented by such leading Wesleyan M.P.s as Sir William McArthur (1809–87), Sir Henry Fowler (1830–1911; from 1908, Lord Wolverhampton) and Sir Robert Perks (1849–1934).[57] McArthur was a strong Imperialist, who diverged from Gladstone on this question and became a Liberal Unionist over Ireland in 1886. Wolverhampton and Perks stayed with the Liberal Party but were equally clearly on its Imperialist wing: both supported Rosebery and were involved in the Liberal League as Vice-President and Treasurer respectively. They were therefore aligned against Campbell-Bannerman's hesitations over the Boer War – Wolverhampton regarded the war as 'just and inevitable'. Alongside them one needs to consider Hugh Price Hughes and his developing imperialist notions as well as his social reforming activities. The views of these men cannot be held to be identical in all respects – they were not, in any case, members of exactly the same generation. But there is a close association between the sentiments of this kind of Liberal imperialist and a concern for domestic social and class problems. Imperialism was seen partly as an election-winner, partly as an ideal for overcoming class strife, working-class discontent and incipient Socialism. It is no accident that Perks supported Central Halls and that Hughes helped to pioneer them.[58]

The social thought and action of Wesleyanism may be studied from

[57] For their careers in outline, see *Dictionary of National Biography*, and references there given.

[58] Note a significant remark earlier, in the context of the Metropolitan Wesleyan Chapel Building Fund: 'What can save London from the fate of Paris but the maintenance and increase of vital godliness? A merciful Providence has preserved the land from revolution and ruin; but it must not be forgotten that the elements of the vilest Communism are among us' (*Third Report*, 1871, p. 14). The date suggests reflection provoked by the spectacle of the Paris Commune. Edward Smith coupled Secularism and Socialism together in a common contemporary manner (*Three Years in Central London*, chap. V). Sir Robert Perks, like other old-fashioned Liberals, saw Lloyd George's Budget of 1909 as 'Socialism' (quoted by H. Pelling, *Social Geography of British Elections 1885–1910*, London 1967, p. 224). On 'Imperialism' and the 'Forward Movement', see R. Currie, *Methodism Divided*, pp. 179ff.

several points of view: as the emergence of a species of 'Social Gospel' or at least of a practical and theoretical extension of the Gospel into a social dimension, and as a sharing in the work of the celebrated 'Nonconformist Conscience'. On the face of it the two preoccupations might seem to be the same thing, and certainly the moral concern involved in social work often seemed to be channelled into certain narrow preoccupations of a special Nonconformist kind.

In men like Hughes, the Conscience might seem to be a special expression of the general social conscience of the time: that is, a condemnation of such things as gambling, drinking, dancing, the theatre, and a concern for 'social purity' (i.e. the suppression of prostitution – a Wesleyan Committee for Social Purity was set up in 1884). Such concerns, were not, however, exclusively Nonconformist, nor were they of very recent growth; and it might be claimed that they reflected middle-class as much as Nonconformist mores.[59] The most that could be claimed was that the Nonconformists pressed these concerns more strongly than others.

The more positive side of Wesleyan social concern reflects that of the socially-concerned in the country at large. Men might press for legislation to regulate abuses and distress in factories, housing, health and wealth; they might set up church-sponsored social agencies; they might reformulate theology. Hughes and his supporters expounded the social application of Christianity: vice was opposed, but also bad housing and bad industrial conditions; education and municipal reform were positively supported; social service was part of the new Mission technique.[60] 'Let us not only save people's souls but . . . sanctify their circumstances', wrote Hughes in *Social Christianity* (1889). The world, he considered, was not to be seen as a collection of individual souls but as a society, and as a society it must be saved: 'Christ came to save the Nation as well as the Individual' and 'it is an essential feature of his mission to

[59] Teetotalism, for example, spread unevenly from its origins in America and in Preston in the 1830s. The Primitive Methodists took it up quickly and enthusiastically. The Wesleyans were slower and less keen. In 1875 the Wesleyan Methodist Temperance Committee, like its Anglican counterpart, allowed for moderate drinkers as well as total abstainers. The drink problem, like the problems of education and disestablishment, helped to decide political affiliation: the Conservatives came to be seen as the party of the brewers; the Liberals as more likely to support licensing legislation.

[60] For some of Hughes's social concerns, see the West Central London Mission's *First Annual Report* (1888), pp. 7f. The controversy over the standard of living of Wesleyan missionaries in India and their failure to identify themselves sufficiently with the Indian population might also be regarded partly in the light of a concern to bridge the gulf between classes and to help the underprivileged. But of course there was much else involved: racial and Imperial problems, and a challenge to accepted missionary techniques. Hughes and Lunn were lucky not to be expelled over this affair: it led, indeed, to Lunn's eventual resignation, though he believed the official inquiry tended to support some of his criticisms; see H. S. Lunn, *Chapters from My Life: with Special Reference to Reunion* (London 1918), Chapter 8.

reconstruct human society on the basis of Justice and Love'.[61] This was not quite unprecedented in Wesleyanism – very similar sentiments had been expressed by William Arthur in 1859,[62] but the dominance of the social emphasis in Hughes's preaching was a new style for the Connexion, contrasting strongly with the usual 'evangelical' themes, and reflecting more closely the preoccupations of the time.

Hughes made some good points: for example, about the bias in favour of the propertied classes in English law.[63] The trouble was that he lived too much on preacher's rhetoric, and lacked the knowledge in depth which he needed for a less superficial view of society.[64] It is not surprising that he broke with S. E. Keeble, who was reading Marx's *Capital* in the same year as Hughes's *Social Christianity* was published, and who came to regard Socialism as 'industrially-applied Christianity'. He was advocating social studies in the theological colleges in 1899.[65] Lest it should be thought that understanding of society and of the social implications of religion had fundamentally altered Wesleyan attitudes, the following pronouncement of the Conference of 1905 on membership increases after the recent 'revival' should be pondered:

> We believe that such a movement everywhere would solve most of the perplexities over which reformers sigh, and clear away most of the problems of belief which trouble the serious thinkers of our time.[66]

The real significance of the Nonconformist Conscience and the Wesleyans' part in it lies less in attacks on particular vices or in an incipient Social Gospel than in a political direction, mixed not too subtly with religious and moral ingredients. Here we return to a funda-

[61] Hugh Price Hughes, *Social Christianity* (London 1889), p. viii.

[62] 'Have not those who see and feel the importance of first seeking the regeneration of the individual too often insufficiently studied the application of Christianity to social evils? . . . It does not follow that, by spontaneous development, the principles implanted in the minds of the people make to themselves the most fitting and Christian embodiment. . . . Nothing short of the general renewal of society ought to satisfy any soldier of Christ.' – William Arthur, *The Tongue of Fire: or, The True Power of Christianity* (London 1856), pp. 133–4; quoted on the title page of S. E. Keeble, *Towards the New Era: A Draft Scheme of Industrial Reconstruction* (London n.d., *c.* 1918).

[63] Hughes, op. cit., pp. 145ff.

[64] See, for example, the superficial attractiveness of the remark: 'In answer to an employer's question, "What must I do to be saved?", might we not say, "Believe in the Lord Jesus Christ and adjust your wages sheet"?'. Hughes had read Ruskin and Alfred Marshall (*Hugh Price Hughes As We Knew Him*, p. 71), but that was about as far as he went – as is acknowledged by Maldwyn Edwards (*Methodism and England*, pp. 147f.).

[65] For Keeble, see M. Edwards, op. cit., pp. 175ff. and *passim*; *S. E. Keeble: Pioneer and Prophet* (London 1949); and of Keeble's writings especially *Industrial Day-Dreams: Studies in Industrial Ethics and Economics* (London 1896).

[66] Hugh Price Hughes, *Social Christianity*, p. viii, quoted by E. Halévy, *A History of the English People; Epilogue Vol. 1: 1895–1905* (Pelican ed.), iii, 131, n. 2.

mental theme of this chapter: the emergence of Wesleyanism, as part of Nonconformity, from its social isolation and the effects this had on its ethos. The phrase 'Nonconformist Conscience' was probably coined by its enemies and taken up with pride by Hughes and others during the agitation to exclude the Irish leader Parnell from politics because of his involvement as co-respondent in the O'Shea divorce in 1890. On this issue Hughes stated what he took to be a fundamental principle: 'What is morally wrong can never be politically right';[67] and so Parnell must go, even if this ruined Gladstone's slender chances of an Irish settlement, and allowed his government to be replaced by, let us say, Conservative brewers and Anglican advocates of church schools – who also suffered from Hughes's attacks. Whether or not Hughes and the Conscience and its votes for the Liberal Party really ensured the fall of Parnell – certainly much else was involved – the fact remains that Hughes had elevated the moral issue of adultery over the moral issue of justice to Ireland.[68] Or again, consider the Boer War, over which major moral issue the Conscience was hopelessly divided: the majority of Nonconformists favoured the war and the British conduct of it, Imperialism being more important than anything else in this connection. Hughes claimed to follow a moral principle – the saving of the Bantu from Boer domination;[69] but British control of them was unobjectionable. Finally, one should notice the long controversy over church schools which increasingly showed itself to be a drag on educational advance. On this question Hughes slipped once again into rabble-rousing habits[70] and it was evident in this campaign that the desire to demolish the established Church and its privileges was at least as strong as the desire to safeguard Nonconformist consciences and prob-

[67] There is no adequate modern study of the Nonconformist Conscience, but there are some useful pointers in J. F. Glaser, 'English Nonconformity and the Decline of Liberalism', in *American Historical Review*, lxiii, 2 (January 1958), 352–63; some further points will be found in C. Driver, 'The Nonconformist Conscience', in *New Society*, I, xxxix (27 June 1963). For Hughes's connection with the Conscience and an incisive re-interpretation of the phenomenon as a whole, see the study cited below, note 72; and for the connections between Nonconformity, society and politics, see the references in note 71.

[68] Hughes, op. cit., pp. 145–8. For an Irish view of the influence of Hughes and the Conscience in destroying the chance of pacifying Ireland, see Conor Cruise O'Brien, *Parnell and His Party 1880–90* (Oxford 1957), pp. 288, 294.

[69] D. P. Hughes, *Life of Hugh Price Hughes*, p. 557.

[70] Robertson Nicoll (*Hugh Price Hughes As We Knew Him*, pp. 15–17) noted Hughes's 'unbounded faith for years at any rate in public meetings and demonstrations', his love of united action and his over-eagerness to compromise so as to maintain the unity of the associations he worked with. For a very critical view of Hughes as an educational agitator, see J. A. Newbold, *Hugh Price Hughes, M.A., and Wesleyan Methodist Educational Policy* (Manchester Tracts on Education, No. VI, 1889). In another field, Hughes's tale of *The Atheist Shoemaker* (London 1889) hovered on the borderline of fact and fiction, and as a result he eventually required the help of G. J. Holyoake(!) to protect him from the vendetta of the atheist G. W. Foote; see Foote, *A Lie in Five Chapters?* (London 1890) and the *Life of Hugh Price Hughes*, pp. 295–8.

ably outweighed educational interests. Here, however, Hughes's advocacy of the popular Nonconformist line did not reflect Wesleyan official policy in all respects.

In all these issues one may reasonably doubt whether the voice of the Conscience was exclusively Nonconformist, fully representative of Nonconformity, or even as effective politically as its exponents liked to think and claim. Much more serious is its moral quality, which was poor and narrowly conceived, as the examples referred to show only too clearly. To say that in this the Nonconformists shared the outlook of their time and class can hardly count as an excuse, when they claimed the prerogatives of a superior and divinely inspired moral judgment.

What lay behind this phenomenon?[71] The expansion of Nonconformity in the nineteenth century allowed it to make a superficially plausible claim to numerical equality with the Church of England; it had claimed and was obtaining religious and social emancipation; it was socially and religiously in conflict with the established Church in a number of ways. By the 1870s those parts of the Nonconformist middle classes who were interested in such issues as temperance, disestablishment, and the abolition of church schools had failed to gain sufficient political power as promoters of isolated causes capable by themselves of achieving their ends. They therefore had to work with more mixed, more purely political groups if they were to effect anything on a comprehensive national scale. For the ends that Nonconformists had in mind, the Liberal Party was nearest to their views, and in this context Nonconformists did achieve some political influence, though less than they hoped and at a serious cost in lowered moral discernment.

This point of view has been expounded in a particularly telling fashion and with special reference to Hughes and his place in the 'Nonconformist Conscience' in a study[72] by Dr John Kent. The Conscience, he considers, was essentially the manifestation of a social pressure group stating and fighting for its objectives in moral and even religious terms. Given the background of Nonconformity, the situation in which it worked, and the need to work within a political party, there

[71] For this paragraph, see G. Kitson Clark, *The Making of Victorian England* (London 1962), Chapter VI, especially pp. 197–205; H. J. Hanham, *Elections and Party Management: Politics in the Time of Disraeli and Gladstone* (London 1959), pp. 117–24; J. Vincent, *The Formation of the Liberal Party 1857–1868* (London 1966), *passim*; H. Pelling, *Social Geography of British Elections 1885–1910* (London 1967), pp. 431ff. and *passim*; cf. also note 63 above.

[72] John Kent, 'Hugh Price Hughes and the Nonconformist Conscience', in G. V. Bennett & J. D. Walsh (eds), *Essays in Modern English Church History* (London 1966), pp. 181–205. It should be noted that this study is not, and does not claim to be, a complete exposition of Hughes's career and social teaching, and that not all Hughes's attitudes were shared by the Connexion as a whole, nor at the official level. Nevertheless, those who agree with Dr Kent's general diagnosis are bound to consider its implications for the interpretation of Wesleyanism in this period. For a kinder, though by no means uncritical, view of Hughes, see Maldwyn Edwards, *Methodism and England*, Chapter IX.

had to be an appeal to a rather miscellaneous set of ideals which did not always go well together. Dr Kent characterizes them as follows. First, 'Evangelical Pietism': the Nonconformists, having set up standards of social godliness for their own group, tried to keep these standards as they moved into a wider society to fulfil their social aspirations, by imposing their mores on society at large. They also appealed to 'Radicalism': the older middle-class allies of the Nonconformists in the Liberal Party disliked Irish influence in the party, and this may have been as powerful as any purely 'moral' appeal in ejecting Parnell. Such motives also cast some light on the 'morality' involved. Finally, there was the 'Imperialist' appeal, on which something has already been said. The effect of this appeal may be seen in attitudes to the Boer War on the part of many other Wesleyans besides Hughes. The implications of British moral superiority to other races and of a unifying ideal for divided British society often turns up.

In all this, the achievement of power – political, moral or both – for Nonconformity came to bulk larger than the quality of morality and religion. In any case the Conscience failed: it failed as a political force, as an attempt to impose its own vision of life on society at large, or even (in the end) on its own members. A number of reasons may be suggested for this which need not detain us here.[73] In general, the failure reflects a choice between religious institutions with a very limited social interest and the wider life of society in which Nonconformists also wanted to share, whatever the price.

(*d*) *Educational attitudes*. A telling example of the same tensions and not dissimilar decisions may be seen in Wesleyan attitudes to education. The subject is dealt with elsewhere in this volume,[74] but some particular observations on it are required here to illustrate the special problems of Wesleyan society and its ideals, and as a bridge to the theme of the last part of this chapter – the internal changes of the Wesleyan ideal.

The essential point to emphasize in this connection is the way in which Wesleyans proposed to relate themselves to society: were they to create and perpetuate a purely 'Wesleyan' education provided by their Church to sustain a distinctive ethos for their children, or were they to abandon this ideal and risk losing their distinctiveness by seeking their education elsewhere – from non-Wesleyan private sources or, after 1870, from the State? Or were they to do both? That was the problem facing all Churches and educational reformers in this period. Wesleyans for a time wanted to follow the first course; various pressures compelled them largely to follow the second; but tradition, and the existence of a body of Wesleyan schools, influenced them in the direction of

[73] Kent, op. cit.
[74] See chapter VIII.

a limited recourse to the third way. In this, the Connexion followed a more complicated course than the rest of Nonconformity, and the Wesleyan leadership itself was divided for many years. Even when Wesleyan education at the primary level decayed in favour of support for state education, this did not carry the denomination as a whole into such extreme opposition to rate subsidy for church schools as was shown by other Nonconformists.[75] Once again it must be stressed that the passions and policies in this matter reflected the entry of Nonconformity into the main stream of English life and the moral and religious tensions this aroused. On the one hand, they wanted all the benefits and power this conveyed; on the other, their religious and cultural inheritance seemed to be threatened.

In primary education, the Wesleyans had a considerable body of schools of their own which were regarded as an essential support for the work of the chapel; and, despite the doubts of some, they came to accept state aid for these and the Wesleyan Training Colleges. When the state system of primary education began to supplement voluntary education from 1870, the Wesleyans were divided in their attitudes: Rigg and others were prepared to maintain and even to expand the Methodist system, Arthur and others to run them down in favour of state education only; and the issue was further complicated by the problem of religious instruction in state schools.[76] In the end they gave qualified support to the government plans, and by 1891 had accepted three principles: Christian unsectarian schools everywhere; no increased grants without public control; but no national system without religious instruction.[77] Hughes and his supporters would have abandoned all church education in schools or training colleges,[78] but the Wesleyans as a whole never fully accepted this. For one thing, the schools seemed essential as one justification for supporting the colleges, and the latter were a way not only of preserving a Wesleyan contribution to non-Wesleyan society, but also of keeping the teachers Wesleyan.

[75] The best study is M. Cruickshank, *Church and State in English Education: 1870 to the Present Day* (London 1963); see also M. Edwards, op. cit., Chapter VII. There were real problems of conscience, even if these were exaggerated by propaganda: see *Minutes of Conference* (1897), pp. 453–4, for statistics of Methodist children in areas with only Anglican schools.

[76] See Telford, *Life of J. H. Rigg*, pp. 171ff., 321ff.

[77] *Minutes of Conference* (1891), pp. 302–5; and for attitudes during 1902–3, see M. Edwards, op. cit., pp. 123ff. As to statistics, Wesleyan Day School pupils were 42,076 in 1854; the maximum of 180,840 was reached in 1890; in 1902 the number was 160,675 (see *Minutes*). With these figures may be compared the Anglican figures of 1,682,000 in 1890, and 1,886,000 in 1900, by which time the state schools were about to equal them. For Sunday Schools, see below, note 120.

[78] J. A. Newbold, *Hugh Price Hughes, M.A., and Wesleyan Methodist Educational Policy* (note 70, above); Hugh Price Hughes, 'Canon Gregory's Educational Policy', in *The Contemporary Review*, lv (1889), 354–79.

Similar problems arose, and even more acutely for the Wesleyan lay and ministerial leadership, in secondary education. As this also was expanded in the public sector, the long-standing problem of maintaining the Wesleyanism of children while enabling them to keep up their social status became acute. The Church could not maintain enough schools for all their people: the alternatives were, once again, either to deny oneself education or else to get it at the risk of succumbing to a secular or an Anglican and anti-Wesleyan atmosphere. It was evident that parents preferred to take the risk, and therefore in all types of secondary education the Connexion tried to make some provision to save a minority in a Wesleyan version of the appropriate school. The old Connexional schools of Kingswood and Woodhouse Grove (for ministers' sons only) were expanded and modernized.[79] Another group of schools were the 'middle-class' schools – the adjective is significant – for laymen's sons, which began as private ventures responding to social demand and mostly came in the end under Connexional supervision. Increasing demand for these may be seen in the increase in their numbers and in the allocation of funds to them in the Thanksgiving Fund of 1878. At the same time there was talk of the further category of 'lower-middle-class' schools.[80]

Then came the pressure for public-school education. Once again, it was a case of fear for Wesleyanism clashing with social aspiration: the result was the foundation of the Leys School in Cambridge (1875) as a deliberate attempt to create a Wesleyan version of the new-style public school.[81] But it had a further significance in opening up the highest educational level – the Universities – to Wesleyan ambitions; and this produced the now familiar clash of aspirations. Fear of the Universities combined with wistful longings were of long standing. S. D. Waddy had noted: 'A degree adds dignity to a man in the public eye', but he added: 'Few Methodists who go to either university come away Methodists.'[82] Thoughts of Wesleyan university institutions on the American pattern came to nothing; but the issue became acute as the old Universities began to be opened to non-Anglicans from the 1850s, and as other universities were created. Old fears were revived,[83] but the

[79] There was a report to Conference on this in 1872; see also *Minutes of Conference* (1874), pp. 160f. Further evidence of the problem of attraction to the pleasures of the 'world' may be seen in complaints about plays and concerts at the Connexional schools: chess and draughts on Methodist premises were coupled with concerts and plays at the schools in *Information for the Wesleyan Conference* (1882). See below, p. 164, in relation to spirituality.

[80] *Wesleyan Methodist Thanksgiving Fund: Statement and Appeal*, p. 19.

[81] For the Leys scheme, see *Minutes of Conference* (1875), pp. 339–53; John Beauchamp, 'Speech Day at the Leys', in *Wesleyan-Methodist Magazine*, 6th ser., vi (1882), 63–9, explicitly links the foundation with the problem of the loss of young Methodists as I have described it.

[82] This was said in 1845; cf. B. Gregory, *Side Lights . . . 1827–1852*, p. 386.

[83] Lidgett's guardian thought the older universities 'not likely to strengthen, and perhaps likely to undermine' his Methodism; cf. *My Guided Life*, p. 42.

young men were determined to go. The debate followed very similar lines to that in another underprivileged and ingrown Church in the same situation of increasing openness to society – the Roman Catholics.[84] The old exclusive view was reflected in the proposals for a Wesleyan hostel or college for men in Oxford, and for the use of the proposed Leys School for a smilar purpose at Cambridge. Those who knew the Universities opposed the idea, and the proper safeguard came to be seen in terms of the development of chaplaincy work,[85] to which the Thanksgiving Fund of 1878 again made a contribution.

In all this it was evident that, whatever Methodism did or did not do, the pressures of educational and social aspiration would outweigh the desire for 'pure' Methodism regardless of the consequences. The general result was certainly to open Wesleyanism to a wider society and culture, with the consequence of breaking down its sense of particularity. This happened less markedly in the field of ministerial training, which could be kept much more firmly in Wesleyan hands, and in conservative hands at that. It was increasingly felt that both ministers and local preachers must be better educated and trained, to meet the higher education of the congregations. Local preachers were made to undergo examinations.[86] Ministerial training was expanded – there were more men to train in any case – though the curriculum and teaching remained notably conservative.[87] This could not last for ever, and there are signs that the younger men were out of tune with their more cautious elders; nevertheless, the control of the Conference, still dominated by old men, made for theological conservatism to the point at which tutors were haunted by fear of unorthodoxy. One sign of impending change was the increase in ministers with degrees, which included a small number from Oxford and Cambridge who were naturally less dominated by the Wesleyan ethos than the theological college students who had won external London degrees. This category of men were to have an

[84] Cf. the well-known clash between J. H. Newman and Cardinal Manning; Wilfrid Ward, *The Life of John Henry Cardinal Newman* (London 1912), Chapters XXI, XXIV. For an attempt to defend Manning's policy, advocating a more commercial, technical and scientific training for less favoured middle-class boys, see V. A. McClelland, *Cardinal Manning: His Public Life and Influence 1865–1892* (London 1962) – but unquestionably the main problem was exactly parallel with that of the Wesleyans.

[85] Cf. 'Wesleyan Higher Education: University and Secondary' (an article signed: 'H. F.'), in *Wesleyan-Methodist Magazine*, 5th ser., xvii (1871), 343–50; B. A. Gregory, 'Methodism and the University of Oxford', in *City Road Magazine* (November 1871); B. Gregory, *Consecrated Culture*, Chapter 5; and see note 81 above. *Consecrated Culture* poignantly illustrates the nature of the tension between Wesleyan tradition and social and intellectual aspiration.

[86] See *Minutes of Conference* (1893), pp. 435–7; the need had been discussed as early as the 1870s.

[87] More so, perhaps, than in other Nonconformist denominations. I have touched on the character of Wesleyan theology and ministerial training in my *The Future of John Wesley's Methodism* (London 1965), pp. 31–5. For a full account of Wesleyan theology, see Dr William Strawson's chapter in the present volume.

important influence in the next century.[88]

All this shows a desire to play a part in, and win the recognition of, non-Wesleyan society that outweighs the risks felt to a continuing Wesleyanism. Individual cases show this at work, and at the same time the continuing desire to remain distinct, a pride in the Wesleyan virtues and, combining both emotions, a characteristic pride also in the triumphs of Wesleyans in politics, commerce and scholarship, recorded in the denominational journals.

4. Changing Life and Purpose in Wesleyanism

Much of what has been said so far implies and illustrates a process of adjustment in Wesleyanism both to its traditional purposes and character as a holiness society and to the demands of a changing world in which its members were increasingly involved not merely for evangelical purposes but also as ordinary members of the class and culture to which they naturally belonged. It is impossible to say which of these two preoccupations in Wesleyanism, the internal pressures of a holiness society become a church or the external pressures of society at large on the society, should be regarded as cause or effect in the process of change. But in what follows we shall be looking more particularly at the process of inner change which, whatever else it shows, certainly reflects the results of tensions and contradictions inherent in the original Wesleyan position.

(*a*) *Ecumenical outlook*.[89] It has already been observed that Wesleyanism in this period moved away from its conscious middle way between Anglicanism and Dissent. This marked a change both in the self-understanding of the Connexion, and in its understanding of its situation in relation to other Churches.

Two features of Anglicanism helped to shape the stock Wesleyan criticism that the Establishment was riddled with 'Popery and Infidelity' and that Wesleyanism was more than ever justified in its separate witness and in its growing lack of sympathy with its mother Church. The first criticism reflects the results of the Oxford Movement and the growth of Anglo-Catholicism after it. This had a double effect

[88] In 1850 the number of ministers having degrees was 29 (most of them honorary): 1.6 per cent; in 1875 it was 84: 3.5 per cent; in 1900 it was 227: 7.7 per cent. In 1895, the first year in which the university conferring the degree was named, there were 186 men with degrees: from Oxford and Cambridge, 16; from London, 80; from other universities, 55; men with medical degrees, 6; degrees unspecified, 29. In 1900, there were 227 men with degrees: from Oxford or Cambridge, 25; from London, 106; from other universities, 74; men with medical degrees, 8; degrees unspecified, 14. Most of the London degrees were probably external, through the colleges.

[89] For a full treatment of this subject and the motives involved, including the abortive attempts at Methodist Union which are not here discussed, see R. Currie, *Methodism Divided*.

on Anglican–Methodist relations. It sharpened Anglican suspicions of Methodism and added a fresh and more theological dimension to them: more than ever the Methodists seemed lacking in the essentials of a church, as well as being, like all Protestants, unsound in salvation doctrine. On the Methodist side Anglicanism seemed now to have compounded its previous defects by adding the errors and superstitions of Rome to its latent Latitudinarianism and active Calvinism (one naturally falls into this somewhat archaic language, as Wesleyans themselves did). No doubt these developments hastened the decline of the former healing custom of some Wesleyans to communicate (and take part in other rites) in the parish church: by the end of the century Anglican official attitudes on communicating the unconfirmed had hardened from their old laxity or toleration.[90]

As to 'Infidelity', Wesleyans were slower than some Anglicans in absorbing into their religion the results of the intellectual changes of the century. J. H. Rigg's *Modern Anglican Theology*[91] attacked Maurice and various 'broad' churchmen, who were in fact misleadingly classed with Maurice, and this book, like the standard Wesleyan dogmatics of W. B. Pope (1880), reflected a conservative theology which included much that recalled the Anglicanism of an older generation.[92]

On the whole, then, the Anglican heritage in Methodism lessened, a fact symbolized and expressed in the decrease in the former use of the Book of Common Prayer, and in revisions of the Book of Offices in order to eradicate whatever might seem to be suspect of 'Catholicism' (e.g. baptismal regeneration in the Office of Baptism).

At the same time there were increasing signs that the old 'middle way' was being eroded from the other direction by a closer alignment with Nonconformity. Indeed, this helped to alienate Wesleyans from Anglicanism, for that alienation was in part a reflection and result of Nonconformist emancipation in which Wesleyans shared and which sharpened anti-Establishment feeling and the kind of pressures we have seen bearing upon the Nonconformist Conscience. Hughes and others emphasized the solidarity of the Free Churches not only in the face of the Church of England but more positively as a coherent third form of 'Catholic Christianity' alongside Rome and Canterbury; and their efforts in the development of the National Council of the Free Churches and

[90] There were a few survivals of Wesleyans taking Communion at the parish church in the late nineteenth century.

[91] (London 1857).

[92] The modification of this position in, for example, Hughes and Lidgett has already been noticed (above, p. 139). Revivalism, we have seen, as a reaction against both popery and infidelity, tended to break down denominational theological divisions. There is less evidence of any corresponding influence from Anglo-Catholicism; but, for one curious example, we may note that the missioner, Edward Smith, said he used Pusey's *Addresses*, next to the Bible, as 'my text-book in the work of winning souls' (B. Gregory, *Consecrated Culture*, p. 176).

more particularly in the writing of the Free Church Catechism made this clear.[93] But the desire of some for a federal union of the Free Churches was by no means shared by the majority. The Wesleyans, indeed, disagreed sharply with the common Free Church support for disestablishment and for the destruction of church schools, particularly when agitation against the latter expressed itself, in the early years of the present century, in 'passive resistance' to rate-paying.[94] Despite the involvement of a section of Wesleyan opinion in the Nonconformist Conscience, their attitude to the Nonconformist shibboleths just mentioned was often lukewarm.

It is worth observing that by the end of the century some Methodists shared in the occasional signs of ecumenical activity which occur in this period. A concern for the 'home reunion' of Methodism itself gradually becomes evident, partly under pressure from the Methodist Oecumenical Conferences which began in 1881, themselves a sign of the times.[95] Occasional feelers were put out by Anglicans and Methodists, usually in the form of Anglican suggestions for the re-incorporation of Methodism in its mother Church with the possible option of retaining 'society' status within the Church. A more formal approach to the Free Churches on the basis of the 'Lambeth Quadrilateral' of 1888 was rejected by the Wesleyan Conference in 1890 on the grounds that corporate reunion was unnecessary and that in any case the four Lambeth points were inadequate.[96] More realistic were the personal contacts arranged by Henry Lunn's Grindelwald Conferences and through his *Review of the Churches*.[97] On the whole it must be recognized that at this time the Churches felt sufficiently strong to ignore any general need for organic union in defence of Christianity; the social bases of disunity had not yet been sufficiently eroded to encourage union. On the contrary, the Nonconformist Conscience helped to express and encourage continuing separation; the Wesleyans for their part still felt the call for their special witness, and still believed that this witness existed.[98]

(*b*) *Structural change; ministry and laity:* But this was to beg many

[93] See H. S. Lunn, *Chapters from My Life*, Chapter XIII; D. P. Hughes, *Life of Hugh Price Hughes*, Chapter 17.

[94] See above, p. 149, on the schools question. Hughes supported disestablishment: 'the present method of union between the Church and the State tends to make the Church worldly without making the world Christian' (D. P. Hughes, op. cit., p. 483). In the early 1900s Thomas Champness was a 'passive resister' over rate money for church schools; but the Wesleyan Connexion as a whole was much cooler on these questions.

[95] For a short account of these ecumenical developments, see my *The Future of John Wesley's Methodism*, Chapter II, Section 1, 2: pp. 39–50.

[96] *Minutes of Conference* (1890), pp. 302–3.

[97] See H. S. Lunn, op. cit., *passim*; Lunn's work, though useful, was that of an ecumenical eccentric.

[98] See, for example, R. Green, *The Mission of Methodism* (London 1890), pp. 202f.; but see also p. 170, expressing doubts.

questions, not least the degree to which Wesleyanism could claim to be the same kind of religious body that it had originally been, with the same basic aims. The rest of this chapter will be an examination of various aspects of Wesleyan life to test how far this was so.

Something has already been said about structural changes in the Connexion, mainly to meet the needs of mission and pastoral care. One basic change which reflects a change in fundamental standpoint was the process of constitutional reform to give full rights to the laity, culminating in their admission to Conference in 1878.[99] The splits in nineteenth-century Methodism have been variously interpreted (the question is discussed fully elsewhere in this volume),[100] but among the more distinctively religious aspects of these difficulties may be included differences reflecting the legitimate needs of different stages in a religious movement; but also differences reflecting rival views of the nature and purpose of Methodism, which in turn involved differing views of the nature of its ministry. The older Wesleyan view, of which Jabez Bunting was, contrary to popular legend, rather a spokesman than a dictatorial creator, held that the Church required the direction of an authoritative, trained, ordained pastorate which, while it retained lay assistance, had from God the ultimate responsibility for the care of souls and therefore, constitutionally, the right of admission, discipline and exclusion of members. Indeed, the whole Connexion – its doctrine, discipline and administration – was in the last resort under the 'episcopal' care of the ministerial body, corporately in the ministerial Conference and individually at other levels.

Wesleyanism survived the mid-century secessions over this concept of ministry and other, often related, questions. Having survived, it felt able to concede much of what the 'reformers' asked for; and some of those who felt themselves to stand in the old tradition persuaded themselves that 1878 and the earlier reforms were not simply a reluctant concession to the pressure of changing times but a true realization of the tradition, purged of extreme views and the evils of 'political' agitation. Had not Bunting himself claimed to stand for the 'just rights' of the laity?[101] It could be claimed that the retention of a Ministerial Session for some specific purposes and the final sanction for legislation in the (ministerial) Legal Hundred preserved the older concept of ministry; and there were some later occasions when the order of Sessions was changed, with the accompaniment of conflicting arguments as to which order best expressed ministerial oversight.

Even the revised constitution, then, still contained elements which expressed differences between Wesleyanism and other Churches; but

[99] For this, see *N.H.M.*, i, 441ff.; R. Currie, *Methodism Divided*, pp. 157ff.

[100] See also R. Currie, op. cit., Chapter 2, and *passim*.

[101] See above, n. 25.

although it is difficult to trace the stages by which the old 'high' Wesleyan concept of the ministry declined, there is no doubt that this decline took place.[102] The proof lies in the achievement of Methodist Union in 1932 and in the Deed of Union's description of the nature of the ministry which makes it in principle virtually indistinguishable from the laity and therefore aligns it with the general run of Free Church views.

There is certainly a contrast between the Wesleyanism of the earlier and later nineteenth century in the matter of lay and ministerial relationships. For example, it is noticeable in the later period how great is the influence of certain leading laymen over Wesleyan policy and outlook, by virtue of their financial and social resources in the world outside Methodism and the pressure they were enabled to exert within the Connexion as a result, and of the enlarged role allowed them in the new constitution. (One has in mind men like Lycett, McArthur, Wolverhampton and Perks.) As the ministry became more professionalized, it also became less authoritative in its hold on the Church and in the extent to which it controlled the Church's tone – a phenomenon not confined to Wesleyanism. At the same time, the place of Local Preachers became more equivocal. Their status declined as that of the profesional ministry rose in relation to it, although they continued to be indispensable in a Church which did not aspire in theory or practice to providing a minister for each congregation. The power of Local Preachers originally lay in their 'inspirational' quality and their speaking as laymen to laymen. The desire for this quality persisted and was a factor in the hostility to 'high' views of the ministry, or for that matter to the conventionality of ordinary church life. But the desire for 'lay' and for 'inspired' religion in some quarters was more readily met by professional evangelists of the Moody type; ordinary Local Preachers could not compete with them. Neither could they easily compete with the ministers, if what was required was a relatively educated and sophisticated conduct of worship; rather, they seemed a liability in the increasingly education- and culture-conscious late nineteenth century. Hence one finds the development of rules for the training and testing of Local Preachers in biblical and other religious studies.[103]

(*c*) *'Society' and 'Church'*.[104] The fundamental change of which the

[102] See R. Currie, op. cit., pp. 165ff.

[103] See above, n. 86.

[104] On this, see J. Munsey Turner, 'From Society to Church', in *London Quarterly*, April 1963; John H. Chamberlayne, 'Methodism – Society or Church?', in *London Quarterly*, April 1964, and literature there cited, and 'From *Sect* to *Church* in British Methodism', in *The British Journal of Sociology*, xv (1964), 139–49; B. E. Jones, 'Society and Church in Wesleyan Methodism 1878–93', in *W.H.S. Proc.*, xxxvi (June 1968), who notes (p. 138) that the words 'Wesleyan Methodist Church' first appeared on class-tickets in 1893. On the

particular examples we have been discussing are symptoms has been described as that from a 'Society' to a 'Church': an idea which has become popular in recent studies of Methodism with a sociological or ecclesiological flavour, but which had already been expressed in Wesleyan writing of the second half of the nineteenth century, particularly in the context of discussions about Church membership.

This process of development was not new to our period; there are clear signs of its beginning in Wesley's lifetime, and from certain points of view the process was complete long before 1849. That is to say, one may take 'church' to mean a body which has its own independent and self-sufficient life and organization in no way dependent on another body for part of its life. From this point of view Methodism had developed a long way towards a 'church' situation in Wesley's lifetime and fairly rapidly consolidated that situation after his death: the survivals of the reception of communion, etc., in the parish church are therefore largely of personal and antiquarian interest.

But when Methodists began to speak about developing from a Society into a Church they were referring, consciously or otherwise, not only to the process just described but also to something more subtle. Early Methodism could be regarded as a society for the propagation of Christian holiness on a particular doctrinal basis, whose structure and methods were in the last resort determined by the exigencies of this fundamental purpose, and not by some *a priori* notion of what a real 'Church's' structure and ministry 'must' be; and in this lay the real reason for its peculiar position as neither Anglican nor Dissenting in character. Refusing to regard Methodism as a 'church', Wesley did not feel called upon to develop the new theory of the Church which his practice might otherwise have required. Later Methodism clearly was a Church, or rather a group of Churches, in the sense described above – a self-sufficient religious body, and not a dependent society. But, as has often been pointed out, it did retain some important characteristics of a religious society conscious of a special mission and organizing its membership and life with that in view; and its independence of Anglicanism and its increasing size and age confronted Wesleyanism with certain problems which could be characterized in terms of the 'Society to Church' formula. More important than the problem of providing for the organization of an independent church body was the actual nature of that body and the religious ideals for which it was now prepared to stand. It was this question, and not merely the dignity of a self-sufficient 'church', which was at stake in controversies such as that over the basis

---

theological and cultural factors involved, see R. Currie, *Methodism Divided*, Chapter 4. In the discussion in the text above, I by-pass the discussion in terms of 'church' and 'sect' which has been in process since Troeltsch's time, but which presents special difficulties if applied to Methodism.

of membership. A religious society pursuing holiness within a wider Church could insist on membership as membership of the Society, defined in terms of the Class-meeting. Failure to attend Class meant failure to conform to the objects of the Society; expulsion was natural and proper and was not excommunication from 'the Church'. But a Church, it came to be felt, should be for all sorts and conditions of men, providing for varied religious and even social needs by various means. Moreover, if adherence to Christianity is to be the basis of membership for a Church, there can be no insistence that attendance at one particular means of grace – the Class-meeting – should be the criterion of one's Christianity, especially when the Class-meeting was disliked as dull and self-righteous. The decline of effective participation in the Class as the criterion of Methodist membership, despite the long persistence of the formal basis, is an indication of the fact that the original Methodist purpose of a holiness society had been absorbed into a wider, less intense, more conventional view of what Christianity and a Christian Church ought to be.

The formula, 'Society to Church', is therefore rather one way of describing what happened than an explanation of what happened. A better understanding of the situation would require an assessment of the way in which, in any religious group, adherents and their children after the first generation adjust themselves, on the one hand, to the model their group proposes for religion and, on the other, to the aspirations felt as members of society at large. It has already been shown how the latter pressure affected Methodist mores in our period. The pressure for conformity to Methodist standards was affected in two ways: it was weakened in favour of the standards of the world outside; and it was itself lowered both by changing the character of the 'holiness' required by making it more 'social', more 'outward-looking', instead of being primarily a 'religious' experience of concentration on God, and by allowing the organ through which the holiness society had operated – the Class-meeting – to cease to be the central means of Church-fellowship or the effective basis of Church-membership.

This view may now be illustrated by looking first at the controversy over the Class-meeting and Church-membership, and then at the changes in Wesleyan spirituality.

(*d*) *The Class-meeting and Church-membership.*[105] The Class-meeting was the survivor of the various groups through which Wesley had sought to stimulate and channel Methodist aspirations to varying levels of

[105] In addition to specific references in this section I have drawn upon a quantity of books and pamphlets, on the Class Meeting itself and on its relationship to church membership, written throughout the nineteenth century and more particularly during the latter half of the century; see also the discussions in J. C. Bowmer, *The Lord's Supper in Methodism 1791–1960*, pp. 26–9; R. Currie, *Methodism Divided*, pp. 125ff.

progress in holiness.[106] Of all these groups it might be said that they were in trouble almost from the start: Wesley had frequently to purge them and insist on their necessity, just as he had to insist on the necessity for preaching perfection. The Class-meeting proper survived, however, as the basic unit for Methodist fellowship and as the official basis of membership. But by the second half of the nineteenth century there seems to be an increase in the steady stream of writings on the Class, explaining it but also defending it. The tone betrays increasing unease and a sense of defence against criticism.

Two connected problems became explicit. One was the unpopularity of the Class as an institution. The meeting was traditionally conceived as essentially for the weekly exchange of religious experiences with a view to mutual edification and help, under the guidance of the Class Leader. It was not seen, however, merely as one of several means of grace, but rather as the essential and central means by which the Wesleyan sense of being a holy community was expressed and built up. As such, it was intimately connected with the whole local polity of Methodism and so might seem impossible to separate from membership.[107] Critics of the institution pointed to a number of defects: the meeting was dull; the 'experiences' were repetitious; the leaders were inadequate; some people found it difficult to speak in public and yet were forced to try to do so on every occasion. Sometimes complaint was made about the difficulty of mixing various social classes and types of people in one meeting.[108] Remedies suggested by critics and defenders were broadly of two kinds. Those who wished to keep to the basic pattern and intention of the past suggested various practical ways of cultivating adequate leadership, discouraging the repetitive bore, and encouraging the timid. On this view, the necessity of the weekly meeting for the maintenance and extension of experimental religion was still in mind.[109] But there was another view. It seems that no one went so far as to say that the whole meeting should be abandoned: rather, it was suggested that it should change its character and perhaps not be regarded as more than one among several useful means of grace. The

[106] On these varied meetings, see Frank Baker, *H.M.G.B.*, i, Chapter 7. Where 'band meetings' occur in the nineteenth century they commonly turn out to be 'fellowship' meetings rather than perfectionist groups. For a statement of the traditional view of Classes, see, for example, E. Grindrod, *The Duties, Qualifications, and Encouragements of Class-Leaders* (London 1831).

[107] L. H. Wiseman, in *Thoughts on Class Meetings and Their Improvement* (London 1854), Section II (pp. 7ff.), emphasizes the importance of cultivating *communal* Christianity; the Conference Report on the Class-Meeting and Church-Membership in 1889 (*Minutes*, pp. 404–13) emphasized the way in which the Class was an inextricable part of the whole Methodist chain of polity.

[108] So J. H. Rigg, *The Methodist Class Meeting* (London 1865), p. 5.

[109] L. H. Wiseman, op. cit., Section IV (pp. 18ff.), recognized the danger of 'revival' and 'assurance' being looked for instead of (practical) 'fruits'.

Class itself would have a more varied programme: for example, a monthly rotation between an experience meeting, a more general devotional fellowship, a Bible class.[110] These last (on a devotional rather than a critical basis) increased in popularity in any case, but conservatives were clear that none of these modifications were really in line with the purposes of the Class, and where they were used, pains were taken to stress that the new means were to serve the end of eliciting personal conversation. All this meant, moreover, a need for a better-informed leadership and there was a trend to ministerial running of Classes.

What is the significance of these developments? One can certainly see the decline of intensity and interest in religious experience of the traditional Methodist kind. Yet this means, in part, that the Class was the victim of a narrow view of religious experience and of inadequate leadership. Ideally, the skilful leader would have led his Class on from dwelling on the moment of conversion to a more progressive view of the continuing development of the religious life. Lacking the Confessional based on a more or less developed moral theology (though non-Methodists often regarded the Class in this light), Methodists had tended to suffer from the common Protestant imprecision in pastoral care and from unskilled pastoral labour. But there were also the problems of a growing, to a considerable extent hereditary, group becoming more of a comprehensive 'church', less of an intensive 'society'. Hence the demand for meetings which were less intensive and introspective; and, in the end, less specifically 'religious'.

The other major problem about the Class-meeting was the connection between Church-membership and Class-membership, for constitutionally the former was based exclusively on the latter. It is in this connection that one finds a good deal being said about Methodism's change from Society to Church. Without denying the value and necessary continuance of the Class, critics argued that Methodism now in fact included large numbers of people who were members in all but name, but who, by the existing rules, could not be regarded as full members and hold office. On the other hand there were members who did little in the Church and did not even attend their Classes regularly.[111] Here, again,

[110] For examples of these programmes, see F. Friend, *The Methodist Class, the Methodist Church* (Newcastle 1889), and Sister Katherine's Class Meeting in the London West Central Mission (*Second Annual Report* 1889).

[111] As long ago as the 1840s there were complaints that the Class failed to draw in the whole membership of the Church (B. Gregory, *Side Lights*, p. 427). For a clear example of the argument about the change from Society to Church, see J. Willis, *The Class and the Congregation of Wesleyan Methodism* (London 1869). Finance was important here: the faithful non-member was contributing through other than Class channels, and the importance of Class money declined. Some thought that its persistence detracted from the spiritual claims of the meeting. The Class and Church Membership controversy was made more public by the Thomas Hughes case; he was certainly argumentative, tiresome and self-important, but he none the less raised the essential issues. See T. Hughes, *The Condition of Membership*

two solutions were suggested. One was that the old discipline should be revived in all its rigour and the letter of the law enforced, it being agreed that this must be accompanied by a revivification of the Class itself on the lines already discussed.[112] The opposition argued that one should recognize changing times and tastes and change the basis of membership. Logically, what was required – and this was urged by some – was Church-membership on the basis of whatever is regarded as constituting a man a Christian: e.g. a credal and communicant basis. It was urged that the great Bunting himself had foreseen that the Lord's Supper would one day be the mark of membership.[113] One suggested compromise was based on the old practice of giving Communion tickets to 'communicants' who were not yet Class-members – by now a widespread practice. This, it was urged, should be regularized to make two classes of membership: Class and Communicant.

In the late 1880s there was considerable debate about the whole matter; and in 1889 a Conference committee reported its views on the question. It retained the traditional basis of membership, pointing out the way in which the Class was interwoven with the whole Methodist polity and how its vigour might be recovered. But there was one very significant section of the report which underlined what was alleged to be the traditional practice: that ministers were not to insist that failures in Class attendance justified loss of membership. This was to recognize that the old system was really being modified to the point at which in the long run merely nominal Class-membership would suffice and the real basis would be in terms of more general Christian and Church criteria. In line with this was the increasing stress on the reception of people into Church-membership, for which a special service was instituted in 1894.[114] Behind all this one can see at work a relaxation of the original Methodist ideal under the weight of increase of numbers,

in the Christian Church: Viewed in Connexion with the Class-meeting System in the Methodist Body (London 1868; 2nd edn 1873): especially Part I, Chapter 7, on the relation and meaning of 'society' and 'church'.

[112] For criticisms of suggestions that the discipline be relaxed, see B. Gregory, *Autobiographical Recollections*, pp. 256ff.; W. Arthur, *On Class Meeting or Christian Fellowship in Relation to the Constitution of the Church*, etc. (London 1888); J. H. Rigg, *The Causes of Decrease*, etc. (London 1865).

[113] T. Hughes, *A Defence and a Plea* (London 1870), p. 68.

[114] For contrasting views, see A. J. French, *The World in the Church: A Contribution to the Class-Meeting Question* (London 2nd edn 1889); F. Ballard, *The Church in the World: a Further Contribution to the Class-Meeting Question* (London 1889). French wanted to maintain the full rigour of the traditional membership rule, and saw Methodist 'Spirituality' as the only justification for its separate existence; Ballard showed the influence of 'social holiness' ideas. For the Conference Report, see *Minutes* (1889), pp. 404–13. The implications of the Conference Report were pointed out, correctly, by an Australian Methodist observer, whose own Church was experiencing a similar crisis: cf. J. C. Symons, *Wesleyan Methodism: Church Membership* (Melbourne 1890). For the 'Form of Service for Public Recognition of New Members', see *Minutes* (1894), pp. 448ff. An increased concern was also evident at this time for the baptized children of church members.

the diversifying of religious interest, and the pressures of society. The result was to reduce the demands of the Connexion from those of 'experience' to those of 'membership', a process which was, indeed, at work in other Churches at the time but which was particularly significant in changing the peculiar character of Wesleyanism. The nature of the change may be illustrated further by considering Wesleyan spirituality.

(*e*) *Spirituality*. In the second half of the nineteenth century two concerns are evident in Wesleyanism which may usefully be compared with its origins for assessing the nature of its piety. One is the renewal, but also the alteration, of its evangelistic impulse; the other was the social impulse. Taken together, these might be, and have been, regarded as a continuation and renewal of the old holiness mission of Methodism in a form proper to changing times. Two comments must be made on this. One is that both developments were very largely Wesleyan versions of the common preoccupations of 'progressive' churchmen of the time, which reduces any special 'Methodist' significance for them. The other point is more serious. Despite much that has been said to the contrary, it is difficult to regard the Wesleyan brand of social holiness in this period as an entirely satisfactory development of the original Methodist concept, for, as we have seen, it was subject to serious limitations alike in its political, social and moral orientation. There was a very real sense in which these developments corresponded to, and reflected, a turning away from the original religious aims of Methodism and towards ideals and a way of life which made less exacting personal demands.[115]

There was, indeed, another version of holiness which made a certain appeal in some Methodist circles. This was the movement for holiness conventions which began in America and was evident in England from the 1870s, achieving its most respectable and long-lived form in the Keswick Convention. This movement had its more remote roots in the Methodist tradition of 'perfection', including the notion of an instantaneous 'second blessing'. But in the late nineteenth-century context it made an appeal to certain sections of the evangelical public as a quencher of doubts about the strict evangelical gospel by producing apparently convincing evidence of the working of God in a sceptical world. The interest, therefore, was mainly in the general sense of power and presence rather than in any clearly realized moral results – which led, indeed, to some of the usual moral disasters. It is to the credit of Hugh Price Hughes that he discerned this lack of content in the 'holiness', though he saw this mainly in terms of a 'social' lack. In Wesleyanism this type of 'holiness' with 'second blessing' associations appeared most

[115] R. Currie, *Methodism Divided*, pp. 138ff., characterizes the results of all this as 'the Ethic of Community'.

strongly in Cliff College (formerly the 'Joyful News' Training Home), though under Thomas Cook rather than under the founder, Thomas Champness.[116]

The piety commonly practised by Methodists has been studied in outline by Gordon Wakefield[117] in terms of church consciousness, revivalism, family piety and a piety based on preaching. 'Church consciousness' has already been referred to and the form it took was essentially that of the Nonconformist preaching service, relatively infrequent Communion services, and religious meetings of various kinds. The Anglican inheritance declined: Morning Prayer (in the Anglican form or its Methodist adaptation) had probably never been the practice of the majority of Wesleyan churches; nor had the Lord's Supper been the crucial means of grace it was in the Anglo-Catholic tradition. We have seen that that tradition helped to alienate Methodists from their Anglican connections, and this was reflected in such things as the revision of the Book of Offices.[118] Wesleyan borrowings from Anglicanism tended to take the superficial and socially conditioned form of Gothic architecture for chapels as the appropriate shape for a 'church' and a greater stress on 'dignity' in worship.

The special Methodist means of grace persisted in the Class Meeting and Covenant Service, but the Love Feast gradually faded out and the Class itself, as we have seen, became less popular and was supplemented, if not partly supplanted, by more conventional and less specifically Methodist means of grace – the Bible Class and general fellowship meeting, the prayer meeting and week-night preaching services. But a still more significant development became evident: the explicitly religious meeting came to be rivalled by the partly or wholly 'secular' meeting on church premises.

These perhaps appeared first in relation to two problematical groups of people. First, there were those whom Wesleyans were trying to reach by their mixed evangelistic and social activities in the 'institutional' churches and missions. To attract and keep these people it was eventually felt necessary to develop much more diluted religious meetings on church premises; even to allow purely secular activities to keep people away from the dubious delights of pub, club and music-hall.

[116] For Hughes on the Holiness Conventions, see D. P. Hughes, *Life of Hugh Price Hughes*, pp. 105f., 250ff.: Hughes clearly felt he had gone through some kind of 'sanctification' experience in 1875, but he equally clearly felt the lack of a civic and social dimension in the movement later. His own meetings of retirement for his staff were called 'Retreats', not 'Conventions' – the Anglo-Catholic touch once again. For difficulties over 'perfection' at a strictly theological level, see B. Gregory, *Consecrated Culture*, pp. 149f.

[117] Gordon S. Wakefield, *Methodist Devotion: The Spiritual Life in the Methodist Tradition 1791–1945* (London 1966), Chapter 2: 'Nineteenth-Century Modifications'.

[118] See J. C. Bowmer, op. cit., for details. A newspaper description of services at the Manchester Oldham Street chapel in 1871 remarks on Anglican survivals such as the *Te Deum*, taken from a book of chants, in an otherwise 'Nonconformist' type of service.

These activities could be justified as a kind of pre-evangelism, but it became clear that all this and more was to become necessary to attract and keep even the existing Wesleyan membership which (as we have already seen in considering secondary education) wanted to share in the life of the less 'religious' and non-Wesleyan world.[119] This brings us to the other group, which was of peculiar difficulty – children and young people. The concern was partly to evangelize them, partly to keep them in Wesleyanism, partly, no doubt, simply to keep them out of trouble. This generation might slip away unless some special effort was made to give them at least part of what they would get outside, and the means adopted, like the problem they were intended to meet, were, it should be emphasized, similar in general character to those adopted by other Churches – a further sign of the loss of Methodist distinctiveness. The means may be studied in, for example, the statistical and other reports of the Wesleyan Sunday School and allied organizations which proliferated and widened their scope. Finally, there appeared in 1896 the 'Wesley Guild', which was to be 'a Young People's Society, closely linked to the Church, holding weekly or periodical meetings for devotional, literary, and social purposes, and centring around itself various branches of Young People's work' for 'comradeship in the highest aims of life'.[120]

Wesleyanism as a whole was to follow the lead of these trend-setters, for the move towards more mixed and in the end more 'secular' activities on church premises was as much to hold the 'church' as to win the 'non-church' communities, and it may be suggested that here, as in the evangelical efforts of the Missions, the success was rather in holding the former than in winning the latter. (But how many were lost to more 'evangelical' Churches?) Reflecting on all this in relation to the older Methodist tradition, Wakefield[121] correctly states the case

[119] See above, p. 137, and notes, for the devices used by missioners: Edward Smith, we have seen, was dubious about coffee-bars; he also found that reading-rooms did not attract non-churchgoers – they wanted 'sporting' (*i.e.* gambling) papers, and they feared proselytism (*Three Years in Central London*, Chapter XI). Less pragmatic were the objections based on the inherent wrongfulness of secular activities and recreations on church premises, or on the danger of innocent games leading to gambling, drink, etc. (see note 79, above).

[120] *Minutes* (1896), pp. 447–57, gives the complete rules. The Committee from whose work the Guild resulted had been set up explicitly to extend work designed to 'retain' the young people of Methodism and to create an organization utlizing the best points of the numerous youth organizations which had grown up by the 1890s: *Minutes* (1894), pp. 321–2. The growth of these organizations may be seen by a comparison between the situation in 1849, when there were only Sunday Schools and talk of Catechumen Classes, and that in 1902, when, in addition to the Guild, there were 971,223 in Sunday Schools, which had grown steadily throughout the century, and 387,603 in Bands of Hope; plus 47,086 in adult Bible Classes, 17,269 in P.S.A.s, and 107,148 in Temperance Societies: *Minutes* (1902), pp. 482–93.

[121] Op. cit., p. 89. The same lesson could be drawn from other changing characteristics in Wesleyan life – literature, for example. The object of Wesleyan books and magazines originally was to convert, perfect and edify; it continued with the further object of keeping

by saying that the shift from Class Meetings to broader, less explicitly religious meetings shows the confusion of aim in Methodism: was it primarily to enable men to fit themselves for eternal life, or was it a social fellowship as a Christian alternative to 'worldly' groups? The dilemma highlighted by the particular problem of spirituality and its institutional expression runs throughout the various streams of Wesleyan life discussed in this chapter, and constitutes a unifying theme for the period which was to become increasingly evident in the twentieth century.

5. Epilogue (1982)

The manuscript of this chapter was completed in 1968 and since it has not been possible to revise it in the light of later research and reflection, it is necessary to add this epilogue. In 'Wesleyanism and "the World" in the Later Nineteenth Century' (*W.H.S. Proc.* xlii (1979), 39–54), I have added a study of Wesleyan attitudes to culture and recreation. Reflection on this subject also suggested an alternative interpretation of the introduction of recreation into the chapels: that it was not so much (or at least not simply) a capitulation to 'the world' but rather an attempt to confine Wesleyan amusements to the chapel and so to save members from worse things.

Since 1968 there has been some writing specifically on Wesleyanism, and more on later Victorian religion, which provides an essential context for understanding the Wesleyan part of it. The following works will help to expand or correct various parts of the present chapter.

Since no comprehensive work on Victorian Wesleyanism has yet appeared, Robert Currie's *Methodism Divided* (London 1968) may be mentioned once more, since it supplies much useful information even for those who disagree with its ecumenical stance. Statistical material and analysis may now be found scattered through R. Currie, A. D. Gilbert and L. Horsley, *Churches and Churchgoers* (Oxford 1977). The causes and characteristics of Wesleyan growth patterns are discussed in

---

the Wesleyans Wesleyan, and, partly as a result of this, it had to widen its scope to cover more general interests, yet preserving a Wesleyan view of all that passed in the world outside: one might say that all human life was there that was fit to print for the Wesleyan public. *The London Quarterly Review* was founded in 1853 to be a review of a wide field of scholarship, but all the Wesleyan journals were kept to strictly conservative views, especially on biblical criticism, during Benjamin Gregory's editorship (he was more or less forced to retire in 1893 because he had ceased to reflect the views of many ministers: *Autobiographical Recollections*, pp. 439ff.). The decline of all the magazines in the present century reflects not merely declining membership but the decay of a separate 'Methodist' culture, general as well as religious, through assimilation to ordinary society; see also R. Currie, *Methodism Divided*, pp. 131ff.

R. B. Walker, 'The Growth of Wesleyan Methodism in Victorian England and Wales' (*Journal of Ecclesiastical History*, xxiv, 1973, 267–84). What is now known about the social composition of Methodism is analysed and documented by Clive Field in 'The Social Structure of English Methodism: 18th to 20th Centuries' (*British Journal of Sociology*, xxviii, 1977, 199–225). This shows, amongst other things, that the early membership was not among the very poor; and it shows more precisely how it became less so during the nineteenth century.

Social analysis of the Victorian Churches in a longer perspective can be found in A. D. Gilbert's *Religion and Society in Industrial England 1740–1914* (London 1976). Local studies too often remain buried in unpublished dissertations (for example, Clive Field, 'Methodism in Metropolitan London: A Social and Sociological Survey 1850–1920' – Oxford D. Phil. 1974). But some have been published which include material on Wesleyanism in a wider context. Three may be mentioned which illuminate different aspects of the subject. James Obelkevich's *Religion and Rural Society: South Lindsey 1825–1875* (Oxford 1976) includes a rare glimpse of rural Wesleyanism and its class significance. Hugh McLeod's *Class and Religion in the Late Victorian City* (London 1974) shows how the characteristics and appeal of various denominations in London were related to the cultural expectations and conditions of different classes. Stephen Yeo's *Religion and Voluntary Organisations in Crisis* (London 1976) shows how in Reading the difficulties of church work were often part of a more general crisis for 'voluntary' organizations.

The special role of Nonconformity in late Victorian politics and social reform has now been clarified. Stephen Koss's *Nonconformity in Modern British Politics* (London 1975) underlines their limitations and places them in an unflattering light. D. W. Bebbington's *The Nonconformist Conscience* (London 1982) is no less realistic but covers a wider ground and much more perceptively. There is material here on such topics as social reform, imperialism and education. Much of interest about Wesleyanism is included, and the argument of the book gives grounds for modifying some of the severer judgements on the 'Conscience', though the limitations of this kind of campaigning are clearly revealed. He also shows that Wesleyanism retained a good deal of its distinctive position in social and political matters – more so than was allowed in my chapter.

III

The Non-Wesleyan Traditions from 1849

JOHN T. WILKINSON

IN the preceding volume of the present *History* we traced the emergence and development of traditions other than Wesleyan within Methodism and took the movement as far as 1850. What follows now is the completion of the record as far as the Union of 1932, at which time all these traditions became incorporated – with the exception of two bodies, namely Independent Methodism and the Wesleyan Reform Union.

For the Methodist New Connexion the middle years of the nineteenth century were marked by a considerable number of internal improvements in general administration. It was a period of stress owing to the failure of the potato crops in Ireland, but in terms of relief there was a ready response from the Connexion.

An important decision was taken in a scheme for a clearer statement of polity and principles. It was some seven years before the Jubilee Deed Poll was adopted and the constitution of the Conference finally fixed in law. This took the shape of a modified form of Wesley's Legal Hundred, and formed a group of Guardian Representatives consisting half of ministers and half of laymen. Book Room affairs received attention, and preparations were made for a new hymn book: the Conference decided that arrangements should be made for the examination of probationers by a theological committee. Financial schemes for the assistance of the ministry were improved, and Connexional property was protected against fire and loss; the Deed Poll had declared that the religious doctrines of the Connexion were unalterable, but now it was decided that every seventh year a change in polity and discipline could be made with a two-thirds approval by Conference; this revising power was introduced in 1853–54. The suggestion of a change in the name of the Connexion was not favoured. In 1855 a declaration was made of disapproval of all state grants for the endowment of religious institutions. There was a period of strong endeavour to extend aggressive work in more populous centres, and a new department was set up to assist struggling stations. The chief features of the period were the inauguration of missions overseas and the establishment of a college for the education of the ministry.

A new era in the history of the denomination began in 1859 following an inquiry as to the most appropriate sphere for expansion abroad, and at Manchester, China was chosen as the most suitable field. On 18 October John Innocent and William Nettlethorpe were set apart. They reached Shanghai in March and moved north to Tientsin. The first chapel was opened in May 1862. By 1867, some fifteen converts were made and a second mission to China settled at Chur-chi, some 140 miles from Tientsin. The years following brought much hardship; owing to Chinese resentment at foreign incursion property suffered, and later, at Shantung, famine and typhus became menacing, causing the death of a missionary. A further development was the opening up of a Medical Mission in 1884. In 1871 there were eighty-nine chapels, six missionaries, eighty-two native preachers and 2,092 members. Other missions were being maintained. The Canadian mission gathered strength and became prosperous, a policy of consolidation was undertaken, a new chapel was erected and new stations were established. In 1862, Conference agreed to found a mission in Australia and this began in Adelaide, soon to be expanded and extended to Melbourne. This became a frequent cause of concern, and in 1882 the Rev. Dr Ward was sent out to obtain information; in 1887, having regard to the interests of the Gospel rather than denominational credit, it was agreed that the Church at Adelaide should unite with the Bible Christians, and that at Melbourne with the Wesleyan Methodist Mission at Victoria. In 1873 Conference considered the question of Methodist Union in Australia, and in 1874 agreed to an amalgamation; at the time of this Union the Canadian mission had twenty-four chapels, eighty ministers and 8,312 members. The Irish mission was the expression of a solicitude to spread the Gospel in the Province. Although results seemed discouraging considering the money and labour expended, the mission was not without its spiritual usefulness.

As far back as 1832 Conference had favoured the idea of the establishment of a college for theological training, but circumstances had brought constant delay. The financial expenditure was considered to be too great, and there was some fear that a rigid course of theological training might mean a diminution of religious and evangelical zeal. In 1846, the Conference resolved to appropriate part of the Jubilee Fund towards the founding of a college, and in 1856 a committee was appointed to prepare a scheme, but again there was delay. Thomas Firth (1821–60) of Sheffield, the founder of a steel factory and a man of charitable disposition, bequeathed £5,000 to help found a college, and in 1865 the Liverpool Conference opened a subscription list to raise £6,000 for land in the neighbourhood of Sheffield and for the creation of a building. The foundation stone was laid on 25 September 1862, and the college was opened in 1864 bearing the name 'Ranmoor'. It accommodated sixteen students, and its total cost was £9,000, an endowment fund also being created. In 1862 it was agreed that students should remain for a third year or longer.[1]

On the withdrawal of the Canadian mission, the sum previously allotted for its support was given to other missions, and up to one-third of the entire amount was used for the enlargement and strengthening of the denomination in England. The Conference of 1875 considered the revision of the Rules, and the Beneficent Fund was augmented and a Loan Fund created to aid trust property. In 1872 there were 1,555 circuits and mission stations, 271 preachers, 1,303 local preachers, 667 chapels and 30,973 members.

In 1861, an important incident was the resignation of William Booth, the future founder of the Salvation Army, who wished to be free from ordinary ministerial duty and to undertake an appointment as an authorized evangelist of the Connexion. The Newcastle District sustained the proposal, but the Conference would not agree.

By the centenary year of 1897, the end of the New Connexion was in sight.[2] Despite friendly relations with the Wesleyans, its constitutional affinities were closer to the other Dissenting branches of Methodists, especially to the Bible Christians and the United Methodist Free Churches. All this pointed the way to some form of reunion. Ten years after the centenary, this reunion took place.[3] The contribution to that Union was as follows: itinerant preachers 204, local preachers 1,123, members 37,000, chapels 457, scholars 87,741.

During the second half of the nineteenth century the graph of membership for the Bible Christians rose steadily; the overall growth of the denomination by 1901 was recorded as 28,315.[4] The areas of advance were widespread, established at intervals along the south coast reaching

[1] W. Bardesley Brash (ed.), *The Story of Our Colleges* (London 1935), p. 152.

[2] G. Packer (ed.), *The Centenary of the Methodist New Connexion 1797–1897* (London 1897); Cyril J. Davey, *The Methodist Story* (London 1955), pp. 57–68: Chapter 6: 'All Men Have Their Rights: The Story of the Methodist New Connexion'.

[3] *United Methodist Church Minutes* (1907), p. 100.

[4] Two recent books are of definitive importance: (*a*) John Kent, *The Age of Disunity* (London 1966); R. Currie, *Methodism Divided: A Study in the Sociology of Ecumenicalism* (London 1968). Cyril J. Davey, *The Methodist Story*, contains in Part III: 'The Years of Separation, 1800–1932' a useful summary of this period.

from Dorset to Hastings in Sussex, into the Isle of Wight and on to Portsmouth and Southampton. In London the expansion was slow; difficulties were great and it took fifty years for the membership to reach 1,000. In South Wales there was distinct advance, though again the progress was slow in the regions of Cardiff and Swansea. The denomination was largely confined to the south-west and the south coast, but between 1851 and 1894 there were determined efforts to enter other parts. Many attempts had to be written off as failures, but in the north there was success. In almost every case of outreach the initial impulse came through the removal of West-country Bible Christians to the region; but many hopes remained unfulfilled.[5]

For the growth of the denomination there were difficulties through local circumstances, e.g. unemployment in the Southampton Docks or the slackness of the Devon glove trade; the wages of farm-workers were low, and it was they who represented a large portion of the membership; thus there was a limit to the generosity of the members and in consequence the ministry was poorly paid.[6] The Industrial Revolution resulted in great losses to most of the rural societies, and emigration left its mark,[7] the loss of members who had gone to Canada and Australia. It certainly resulted in strong Bible Christian communities overseas, but it drew from the strength of the Church at home.

The problems were many: the missionary expenditure in support of the first missionaries in Canada and Australia was heavy; the founding of the school at Shebbear was a great venture. The Book Room figured as part of the crisis, though signs of prosperity were seen in its removal to London in the 1870s. The Thorne family had kept the business of the Book Room going over the years at great cost to themselves, but it had achieved a good condition by the time that its management was transferred to Frederick William Bourne in 1869. Bourne was the acknowledged leader of the denomination. He took over the offices of Book Steward and Editor in succession to James Thorne. He was appointed secretary of the Missionary Society, and in 1867 became President of the Conference. In 1866 he was appointed Connexional Treasurer. He excelled in matters of administration. His best work as an author was *The Bible Christians: Their Origin and History (1815–1900)*. He was the organizer of the New Century Fund, with a target of £25,000

[5] Thomas Shaw, *The Bible Christians 1815–1907* (London 1965), pp. 59–60, indicates the extent of this outreach in considerable detail; e.g. in Cumberland (1870), Durham (1874), Cleveland (1876), Bradford (1877), Blackburn (1888), Bolton (1889), Birmingham (1894). In 1874 there was a crossing of the border into Scotland, but it proved 'no more than a border raid'.

[6] In 1856 a married itinerant and two children received £1 per week plus a house; forty years later it was less than £2 (Shaw, op. cit., p. 60).

[7] Between 1860 and 1880 one-quarter of the population at Shebbear left the District (Shaw, ibid.).

reached shortly after his death in 1905 (Shaw, op. cit., pp. 67–8). The importance of Shebbear School increased during the headmastership of Thomas Ruddle, who had a breadth of view and an independent pioneering spirit which greatly assisted the enlargement of the school. In 1877 it was renamed Shebbear College. Its success led to the opening of a girls' boarding school at Edgehill, Bideford, in 1884. Under the governorship of William Bryan, the school at Shebbear had from its earliest years its 'theological Faculty', a general course being taken under the headmaster and the theological side under the governor. Here was the early pattern of ministerial study for the denomination. The idea of a theological college was mooted, but the cost was seen to be prohibitive and the approach of Methodist Union made another college unnecessary. Moreover, the type of ministry was rural, with the development of a specialized type of local preacher, most being men of simple faith and experience. In Billy Bray there was an example of 'an eccentric Cornish local preacher whose simple faith could move mountains and whose unbounding energy and quaint and pithy sayings have given him immortality' (see F. W. Bourne, *The King's Son; or a Memoir of "Billy" Bray*, of which more than half a million copies were sold in the author's lifetime; Shaw, op. cit., p. 68). The first preaching places grew from local revivals and sometimes a simple building was constructed at the expense of the evangelist. Farm kitchens, lofts and even a blacksmith's shop were commandeered for preaching purposes. Yet there was a growing demand for a rise in the standard of preaching. Not until 1902 was a local preachers' association formed.

The outreach of the denomination overseas was very considerable. The Bible Christian work in Canada meant that a separate conference was established there in 1854, and in 1883 this joined in Methodist Union with 7,400 members. To the 1850 Conference at home came the request from Cornish farmers and miners who had emigrated there that preachers should be sent to Australia. Within seven years the membership rose to 8,000; the South Australian Conference united with the Methodist New Connexion in 1888; the group in Victoria entered the Methodist Union in 1902, with 113 churches and 2,805 members. A smaller group united in Queensland with the Wesleyans in anticipation of the larger Union of the future.

In New Zealand the Bible Christians entered Methodist Union in 1896, after a separate history of nearly twenty years. In 1865, through the co-operation of the China Inland Mission, the door opened into China, and missionaries sailed up the Yangtze in the next year, to be followed by the advent of Samuel Pollard in 1887. The work proved difficult and seemingly unrewarding: after ten years there were only three small chapels and twenty-eight full members to show for it. But in 1904 Pollard was invited by the Miao tribesmen to visit the country and he found himself 'in the midst of a mass movement to Christianity'.[8]

By the turn of the century, the Bible Christians looked forward to Methodist Union and their leaders – James Thorne and F. W. Bourne – were active advocates. In the period 1863–9 Thorne had tried to achieve Union with the Methodist New Connexion, but the latter suddenly broke off the attempt: financial disparity, despite closeness of polity, seems to have been the reason. Betwen 1894 and 1900 an attempt at negotiation was made with the Primitive Methodists, but finally there came an adverse vote from them. The members of each Church were less keen than their leaders, and Bourne was disappointed. Union with the Wesleyans was not considered seriously till the end of the century, and the Ecumenical Conference of 1901 stressed the desirability of Methodist Union. Bourne said that Union would be possible if 'one single great concession' were allowed, namely the abandonment of pastoral supremacy, which the Wesleyans would not forgo. Reunion with the Wesleyans and Primitive Methodists had to wait for another twenty-five years, but negotiations were opened up with the United Methodist Free Churches and the Methodist New Connexion in 1902, and this 'quickly resulted in the Union of the three demoninations in 1907 and the formation of the United Methodist Church'.[9] To this union the Bible Christians contributed 206 itinerant preachers, 1,515 local preachers, 32,220 members and 22 chapels.[10]

As we have seen, the new denomination, 'The United Methodist Free Churches', came into being in 1857.[11] It was natural that the various Methodist departments and funds should become part of their normal working life, expanding and developing in the new order. In 1842, a Model Deed had been created, and later in 1865 the Reference Deed was framed in order to give the maximum of freedom to the societies.[12] The two features of the new order were 'unfettered representation in the annual assembly' and 'circuit independence in relation to all local matters'. 'Free Representation and Local Independence . . . were the twin foundation stones of their ecclesiastical edifice.'[13]

An important issue in the new denomination concerned ministerial training, though development was slow, not least through the continuing of early prejudices. Although the matter was given repeated consideration, it was not until 1872 that actual steps were taken. A house was found in Stockport and five years later the College moved

[8] Shaw, op. cit., pp. 66–7.

[9] Ibid., p. 75; see also Walter Pollard, *The Life of Sam Pollard of China* (London 1928).

[10] These figures do not include foreign returns.

[11] Cf. *H.M.G.B.*, ii, 318, 322.

[12] Oliver A. Beckerlegge, *The United Methodist Free Churches: A Study in Freedom* (London 1957), pp. 53–4.

[13] Beckerlegge, op. cit., Chapter 4: 'Free'.

to the Victoria Park in Manchester.[14] This college continued to serve Methodism till 1934; there was a close association with the Primitive Methodist Hartley College in the final years. Closely allied with the College development was that of education for the children of ministers, the matter having been considered as far back as 1844; in 1877, Ashville College, Harrogate, was opened.

Another emphasis of this period concerned the advance of the Temperance Movement.[15] In the 1870s a number of memorials in favour of Connexional temperance organizations were sent forward, though the pressures had been stronger before this. The outreach of the denomination was very considerable, beginning with work in Ireland, Wales and Scotland. An early work in Jamaica was carried on with great difficulty and little success; it continued until five years after the Union of 1907, when it was transferred to the Methodist Episcopal Church. Other early openings were made in Australia and New Zealand, and these were followed by important attempts in Sierra Leone (1859) and East Africa (1862), and particularly in China (1864). It was here that the great work of W. E. Soothill, as the first medical missionary, was done. The work was hindered by the Boxer riots, but at Wenchou from slender beginnings a community of some two hundred churches and a similar number of local preachers was created within twenty-five years, with a Christian community. In the year of Union, 4,118 members were recorded in the Chinese missions, with 6,800 on probation.

During this period there was a growing feeling after union; the Ecumenical Conferences in 1881, 1891 and 1901 stimulated the desire. In 1844, Robert Eckett, the first Secretary of the United Methodist Free Churches, took the initative, and an invitation to the Methodist New Connexion was made, but without success. In 1863 the Methodist New Connexion developed under the leadership of Dr William Cooke, and this drew cordial response from the United Methodist Free Churches.

There was a growing readiness to discuss union with liberal-minded Methodists, and in May 1867 there was a conference in Leeds which appointed a Committee to deal with practical difficulties arising from the Deed Poll of the New Connexion and the Foundation Deed of the United Methodist Free Churches. In 1868 the negotiations were terminated by the Methodist New Connexion, and not until the 1901 Ecumenical Conference was there any definite movement; there were

[14] G. G. Hornby, *The Methodist College, Victoria Park, Manchester: A Souvenir* (Manchester 1934); Brash (ed.), op. cit., pp. 148–51, 157–63; for many years J. T. Brewis served as Tutor and Principal.

[15] Beckerlegge, op. cit., pp. 56–7: in the 1840s a group called 'Teetotal Methodists' opened a chapel in Camborne which later became part of the Association: eventually a minister was freed from circuit duties for full-time commitment to the work.

private conferences, and a tentative basis for union was drawn up.[16] A new unanimity in voting took place and a joint committee was created to prepare the main outlines of a constitution for the Quarterly meetings, to which the Bible Christians gave the strongest support. The uniting Conference took place in Wesley's Chapel, City Road, on 17 September 1907; the Deed of Foundation was adopted and also the Model Trust Deed.[17] The sincerity of the Union was emphasized by the decision regarding the election of Guardian Representatives, namely that, although the United Free Churches constituted fifty-four per cent of the contributing membership, it was determined that there should be eight representatives for *each* of the constituting groups. The statement of the United Conference was as follows:

> Whereas the respective annual assemblies or Conference of the Methodist New Connexion, the Bible Christian Church and the United Methodist Free Churches respectively after mature consideration and prolonged negotiations and after ascertaining the wishes of the members of the said Churches or denominations . . . have by large majorities resolved that it is expedient that the said churches or denominations become and form one denomination under the name of the United Methodist Church . . .

The statistical account of the United Methodist Church at this time of Union in 1907 was as follows: 903 itinerant preachers, 6,251 local preachers, 165,502 members, 2,673 chapels, 331,571 scholars.[18]

The Rev. E. Boaden was appointed President of the new denomination and the Rev. George Packer its Secretary. A gavel bearing the inscription 'Primus inter pares' was presented for official use at assemblies. The new Church at once committed itself to the raising of a Thanksgiving Fund of 100,000 guineas for the consolidation of missionary work at home and abroad, including the development of the Deaconess Institute, aggressive work amid the more populous centres, and also an increase in the superannuation and beneficent Funds, and in the endowment of the Theological Institute. Also there came assistance for necessitous local preachers. It was decided to transfer the theological students from Shebbear to the colleges already existing in Sheffield and Manchester, but £2,000 was held in reserve towards a theological college as the new denomination should direct. It should be

[16] Beckerlegge, op. cit., Chapter 6. 'A Dream Comes True'; W. J. Townsend, *The Story of Methodist Union* (London n.d.).

[17] The voting was as follows: 97 per cent, Methodist New Connexion; 86 per cent, Free Methodists; 92 per cent, Bible Christians. Beckerlegge, op. cit., p. 102; *Minutes* (1906), p. 325.

[18] The *Minutes* of the first Conference of the United Methodist Church (September 1907) contain: (*a*) The United Methodist Church Act (pp. 15–35); (*b*) The Foundation Deed Poll (pp. 36–58); (*c*) United Methodist Church Model Deed (p. 67).

noted that in this new United Methodist Church there was to be equal representation of ministers and laymen on its several committees.[19]

With the retirement of Bourne and Clowes, the year 1843 marked an epoch in the development of Primitive Methodism. Administration now fell into younger hands, subtle changes took place in the Connexion and new departures were made.[20] New figures emerged, e.g. John Flesher and John Petty;[21] the Book Room was transferred from Bemersley to London; a special committee took over eleven of the missions in the denomination; there was forward movement for colonial missionary enterprise, and at the end of the period we find fourteen districts instead of seven. The heroic period may be said to have ended.

This period shows the phenomenon of district initiative and predominance; the era of confederated districts had emerged and, with the development of this 'districtism', ministers remained in the same district, and men of mark stamped their individuality on the district where they lived. Moreover, districts acquired special characteristics developed along their own chosen lines, and indeed began a movement which in the end contributed to the general good of the Connexion as a whole.

The Sunderland and Manchester Districts fought for a more thorough equipment of the ministry. In 1850, in the Sunderland District a Preachers' Association was formed, the organ of which was *The Christian Ambassador*, founded in 1856, under the guidance of Colin McKechnie. This was formed for the purpose of directing and stimulating the culture, and in particular the reading, of the ministers. Eventually, in 1879, this became *The Primitive Methodist Quarterly Review*, and was followed by *The Holborn Review*. Similarly in Manchester, James Macpherson assisted the training of the younger ministers.

A separate College was created in Sunderland in 1868, and transferred to Manchester in 1881.[22] Through the munificence of Mr (afterwards Sir) William P. Hartley, Hartley College was built in gradual stages and was eventually capable of taking more than a hundred students.[23] A pivotal decision was the appointment in 1892 of Arthur Samuel Peake, who served on the staff until his death in 1929. Though a layman throughout his life, he became not only the architect of the training of

[19] Beckerlegge, op. cit., pp. 102–3; see Henry Smith, John E. Swallow & William Treffry, *The Story of the United Methodist Church* (London 1932), pp. 7ff.

[20] For these developments, see H. Bickersteth Kendall, *The Origin and History of the Primitive Methodist Church*, 2 vols (London 1906); *What Hath God Wrought* (London nd.); B. Aquila Barber, *A Methodist Pageant: Souvenir of the Primitive Methodist Church* (London 1932).

[21] G. Herod, *Biographical Sketches* (London 1855); see Herod and Kendall throughout, for accounts of these and other leading figures in the new movement.

[22] J. T. Wilkinson, *Hugh Bourne 1772–1852* (London 1952), Chapter 10: 'Mission to America (1844–6)'.

[23] Arthur S. Peake, *The Life of Sir William Hartley* (London 1926).

more than a generation of ministers, but was appointed in 1904 as the first Professor of Biblical Criticism and Exegesis in the University of Manchester, serving also for a considerable period the other Methodist Colleges in Manchester. He gained an international reputation as a biblical scholar – 'Peake's *Commentary*' became a household word – and by his teaching and his books re-shaped ministerial training of the time.[24]

The Hull District inaugurated a process of chapel-building; in 1847 there were 1,400 chapels in the Connexion; by 1867 the number had reached over 3,000, and in the 1870s a further thousand and more were built. Norwich District pressed the claims of overseas missions. As far back as 1837, Yarmouth had sent a scheme to the Conference, and in 1864 it was agreed that part of the Jubilee Fund should be devoted to the formation of a mission in Port Natal, now Durban, South Africa. In 1870, Burnett and Roe went to Fernando Po in West Africa and Henry Buckenham to Aliwal North in Central Africa, later to become the place of the missionary work of Edwin W. Smith, the author of *The Golden Stool* (1926).

It should be noted that a colonial mission had begun as early as 1829, and that Australia and New Zealand were entered in 1844. It was in 1829 that four missionaries, including Ruth Watkins, sailed for the United States.

As its own particular emphasis the Leeds District inaugurated the work of Sunday Schools and for young people.

In the 1870s, the extension of ministerial invitation beyond District boundaries meant the ultimate passing away of 'Districtism' and the growth of the idea of 'Connexionalism'. The era of confederated Districts was over.

The normal structure of a Methodist organization was naturally pursued and there were signs of steady growth. One particular emphasis in Primitive Methodism was the temperance movement.[25] In his later ministry Bourne had stressed the importance of opposition to the drink evil; the subject had been introduced to the Conference as early as 1831, and articles were published on it at the request of Conference. This was re-emphasized at the Conference of 1841, and in 1848 a ministerial Temperance declaration was issued. Literature was widely spread; by 1932 there were nearly a thousand Bands of Hope with some 50,000 members, and 'Abstainers' League' branches numbered 311 with a membership of some 19,000. As time went on, the original concentration on specifically temperance activities gradually expanded the scope

[24] John T. Wilkinson (ed.), *Arthur Samuel Peake 1865–1929: Essays in Commemoration* (London 1958); John T. Wilkinson, *Arthur Samuel Peake: A Biography* (London 1971); Brash (ed.), op. cit., pp. 123–47.

[25] Barber, op. cit., pp. 235–9: 'Temperance Society and Band of Hope Union'.

of its ministry, taking under its direction the promotion of all forms of social redemption. Primitive Methodism had all along had an active concern for the worker and in particular the outcast amidst the prevailing social conditions, especially in rural areas and the mining regions of the north. In the northern areas the trade union movement was largely composed of loyal Primitive Methodists. Attention was focused on the social conditions of London, and pioneers such as James Flanagan and Thomas Jackson in Whitechapel opened up areas of social ministry.[26] In the years following the Union of 1932 we should notice the research work accomplished by Dr Robert F. Wearmouth, revealing the prevailing social conditions.[27]

By the date of its centenary in 1906, Primitive Methodism had come to think of itself in terms of the idea and practice of the 'Church', and beyond a mere Connexionalism. In 1902 the official designation 'Primitive Methodist Church' appeared in the Minutes and on the class-tickets of all the members. It had become possessed of a vital organic life – it had its multitude of gathered societies for the fulfilment of a spiritual idea, its college and schools, its orphanage and social agencies, its numerous committees, increasingly selective, for the appointment of administrators, and an elaborate organization for its evangelistic purpose. It had become a growing force in England.

The divisions in Methodism had become a growing scandal. The main sources of continued separation were at the top level, constitutional differences and, at the lowest, local pride and traditional snobbery.

For a long time reunion had seldom been out of the minds of the leaders. In 1866 a premature suggestion of general Methodist Union was circulating. The non-Wesleyan groups made approaches. Before 1907 there was Methodist Union in Canada, Ireland and Australia, but here at home there were constitutional difficulties not easily laid aside; for instance, the Wesleyan 'Legal Hundred' involved a matter of ministerial autonomy. The United Methodists stood by equality of ministers and laymen; the Primitive Methodists took the position that whoever took the chair at a meeting should be there by courtesy and not by official right; a layman could be President of the Conference, as he certainly could be vice-president. The Ecumenical Conferences strengthened the feeling of unity, and in 1912 the Wesleyan Conference said it was convinced the time had come for some appraisal to be made.

[26] Joseph Arch, *The Story of His Life, Told by Himself* (London 1898); Denis Crane, *James Flanagan* (London 1906); R. W. Russell, *The Life of James Flanagan* (London 1920); Samuel Horton, *From Coal Mine to Pulpit: Life-Story of James Flanagan* (London 1938).

[27] R. F. Wearmouth, *Methodism and the Working-Class Movements of England 1800–1850* (London 1937), *Some Working-class Movements of the Nineteenth Century* (1948), *Methodism and the Common People of the Eighteenth Century* (London 1945), *Methodism and the Struggle of the Working Classes 1850–1900* (London 1954), *Methodism and the Trade Unions* (London 1959).

A Committee was appointed to collect information, and in 1917 a number of leading Wesleyans, Primitive Methodists and United Methodist ministers gathered to discuss the next step. In 1920 an outline scheme of Union was presented to the three Methodist Conferences and in 1922 was sent to the Quarterly Meetings for discussion, though no final vote was to be taken. Discussion was heated and in 1924 the matter was presented in the form of questions. The replies were not unanimous; between two-thirds and three-quarters were in favour, and this proportion was to grow with succeeding years. Three points were mainly at issue: (*a*) finance, (*b*) the ministerial session of Conference, (*c*) the proposed doctrinal statement. The Primitive Methodists and United Methodists were uneasy about (*b*).

The Union took place in London on 20 September 1932. There were 1,708 representatives present and there was no dissentient. After almost a century and a half, divided Methodism was itself one again. Only two Methodist groups stayed out of this Union, namely the Independent Methodists and the Wesleyan Reform Union, all in all about 25,000 members.

The statistics at the time of the United Conference were as follows:[28]

Primitive Methodists: Ministers 1,131; Lay Preachers 12,896; Church Members 222,021; Chapels 4,356.

United Methodists: Ministers 729; Lay Preachers 5,232; Church Members 179,551; Chapels 2,900.

Wesleyan Methodists: Ministers 2,510; Lay Preachers 18,785; Church Members 517,551; Chapels 8,152.

Whilst all the leaders of all the constituent groups eagerly and diligently pursued the cause of Union, a pivotal figure in the situation was that of Dr Arthur S. Peake.[29] Amidst impatience that was inevitable because progress was slow, Peake would again and again indicate the serious and solemn responsibility of deciding to abandon the scheme.[30] He pleaded that if in the end a refusal had come it should not be those of his own (Primitive Methodist) Church who incurred the odium of any adverse vote. He showed great sagacity in framing doctrinal standards; and in expounding the nature and doctrine of the ministry his strong and patient interpretation did more than any other factor to assuage the deep tide of feeling on both sides. Peake's great contribution

[28] Davey, op. cit., p. 165.

[29] Peake had had youthful convictions concerning union in his Oxford days: 'I can never be satisfied till we have gained an organic unity. This unity will never be gained till we consent to sink our differences of belief and make Christ the foundation on which we build . . . For myself I don't care to be called either Methodist, or Church of England or Protestant, or any name except Christian' – from a personal letter.

[30] It should be remembered that at this crucial stage some 800 Wesleyan ministers had signed a manifesto against Union.

was the upholding of patience and goodwill within his own Church.[31] In 1925, a seventy-five per cent majority was required from the denominations, and the Wesleyans fell short of this requirement. After ten years of debate and the drafting of numerous amendments, mostly by Peake himself, in the hope of resolving the differences, a majority of eighty-nine per cent was finally achieved.

As we have already noted, there were two Methodist groups which did not enter into the Methodist Union of 1932, namely the *Independent Methodists* and the *Wesleyan Reform Union*.[32] Their total membership at that time was about 25,000. The larger group, the Independent Methodists, declared their principles firmly: 'The root from which our Church's life springs is the gathered church . . . the Church in which Christ is the centre, the Holy Spirit its life, the discussion guided and activity God-centred. This is what we mean by a sense of High Churchmanship.'[33] At the turn of the century its membership was just over 7,000. It had established a missionary centre including medical work in India. Fraternization with the Wesleyan Reform Union[34] had been going on for many years and seemed to be ripening to union, but did not mature, though links were maintained in the following years. The group became a member of the Federal Council of Evangelical Free Churches. The denomination was very much alive to public questions and was strong in its association with the Christian Endeavour movement. As we have seen, the ministry was open and free, in harmony with the scriptural teaching of the priesthood of all believers, and so was purely voluntary and unpaid. 'We do not recognise clerical titles or designations, or distinctive ministerial dress, as these tend to accentuate distinction between one servant of God and another.'[35]

A three-year course of ministerial training was followed by trial preaching and oral examination. In the 1930s there were 11,000 members. At this period a church was built in Argentina, and similarly two or three churches in New South Wales;[36] also a field-mission in Brazil.

There was a great concern for purity of worship. 'Is not the highest quality for conducting the sacred service (i.e. The Lord's Supper) that of saintliness? May it not rise beyond consideration of "the Ordained and the unordained"?'[37] In 1978 the Connexion had 125 churches and just over 5,000 members and three missions.

[31] To the invaluable leadership of Peake we have the testimony in issues of the *Holborn Review* from Dr W. F. Howard and Dr Scott Lidgett.

[32] *H.M.G.B.*, ii, 323.

[33] James Murray, in *A Short History of Independent Methodism* (Wigan 1905), p. 150.

[34] Ibid., pp. 13, 29; in 1904, a report was presented for specific proposals.

[35] Ibid., p. 41.

[36] Ibid., p. 61.

[37] Ibid., p. 96.

The second group which did not enter Methodist Union in 1932 was the Wesleyan Reform Union.[38] Following the expulsion of 1849, the hope of re-admission still lingered on. The only concern was to achieve reform *within* the Connexion; there was no desire for separation. In 1850 some 400 delegates gathered in Albion Street Chapel, Moorfields, London, and a deputation was appointed to approach the President of the Wesleyan Methodist Conference, who, however, declined to receive them. A document containing proposals for reform had been drawn up, but Conference paid no heed: the expulsion continued. Partly because of the unyielding attitude of the Conference, the 'Reformers' found themselves compelled to consider the setting up of some separate organization. In 1852 came the first step towards independence and the establishment of a denomination. A 'Declaration of Principles' was adopted – the Magna Carta of the Reform Movement. The following elements should be noted. In 1849 the designation of the new denomination was 'Wesleyan Reform Union'. These non-amalgamating Reformers reaffirmed their independence, emphasizing the right of each congregation to choose its own minister, to appoint its local preachers, and to order the administrative affairs of the local Church without interference from any authority. Naturally a number of Methodist usages were retained, yet the Declaration of Principles asserted the autonomy of the Reform Union. The final court was the local Church; circuits were formed on voluntary principles.

The Church did not possess any specific fields of work overseas, but with great charity assisted several missionary societies, in particular that of the China Inland Mission. From its beginning it had expanded its work in connection with the Temperance Movement, and later this developed into wider social responsibilities. There was no further approach to the Independent Methodists on the matter of union, but loosely federal activity continued between the two denominations. As the Wesleyan Reform Union drew near to its Jubilee, disintegrating forces seemed to be at work – whilst still adhering to the constitution and maintaining the principle of the early reformers. There was a growing conviction of the necessity of some measure of central authority, especially in regard to trust properties – the suggestion was made of some kind of Model Deed on which to build a secure structure. This was adopted in 1898. The problems of Independency had to be faced, and at the time of the Jubilee in 1899, a reorganization took place in the direction of connexionalism, Conference being asked to approve this principle on the matter of the ministry. The Wesleyan Reform

[38] *H.M.G.B.*, ii, 323; see *History of the Wesleyan Reform Union*, published by the direction of the Wesley Reform Union Conference, 1896: W. H. Jones, *History of the Wesleyan Reform Union* (London 1952).

Union became a member of the Free Church Federal Council. Although it took no part in the Union of either 1907 or 1932 there was no lack of goodwill. The principal obstacle was *the independency of the church* and this prevented a negotiation committee acting with authority. The early Reformers were proud of Wesleyan Methodism and did not seek or desire a secession. 'The Scriptures are our sufficient authority for the validity of our orders, our liberty of action, our priceless independence; ... we bow to no authority but that of our Lord ... We are one in hope, doctrine and charity with Methodism and our sincere wish is that brotherly love should continue.'[39] Although numbers are greatly reduced, as has been the case of most Churches, the denomination continues (1978), and its present strength is as follows: Church members 4,091; Preachers and preachers on trial 210; scholars 4,041. C.E. Society members 352.[40]

Only very occasionally do the differences we have been considering between the several Methodist traditions rise to the surface; for instance, it may be on the occasion of the sale of a redundant village chapel or in the conversation of folk of the very early generation recalling the past. Perhaps,.as in most cases of corporate union, the greater bodies have tended to maintain a certain dominant influence over the lesser; but the restructuring of Methodism that has taken place in the last ten years or so has been largely a matter of administration and has set Methodism on a new course, with a vision of the future which will eventually ensure the entire disappearance of former denominational differences.

[39] W. H. Jones, op. cit., p. 61.
[40] *Wesleyan Reform Union Year Book* (1978–9), p. 27.

IV

Methodist Theology 1850-1950

WILLIAM STRAWSON

1. The Period 1850–1900

THEOLOGY is the response of the Church to the contemporary situation, and therefore the background of thought is an essential study for a proper appreciation of theology. In the second half of the last century there were many influences which contributed to a lively theological scene. The faith was under attack from philosophy and from the new science based on the Darwinian revolution in biology. John Stuart Mill advanced a most cogent case against the reasonableness of Christianity, developing the scepticism of David Hume, and favouring the positivism of Auguste Comte. Matthew Arnold's thrusts at organized religion were more subtle, and appeared to come from inside the Church, but they were no less threatening than the more direct attacks of Mill. The infamous controversy between Bishop Wilberforce and T. H. Huxley about Darwin's *On the Origin of Species* was the beginning of a long and anxious period in which Christians only slowly admitted that this theory was not necessarily a denial of their faith, and might indeed be used to expound the message of the Bible as progressive revelation. Methodist writers had more to say about this attack on the faith than is generally recognized.

The ecclesiastical situation was also new and provocative. The Roman Catholic hierarchy had been re-established and the claims of Rome were being seriously countered by Evangelicals in the Church of England and in the Free Churches. Within Anglicanism, the Oxford Movement had brought new life to an apparently moribund Establishment, and this movement produced a fresh flowering of theology. It also provoked a response from Evangelical opinion, in which Methodists had an important place.

Methodism itself was in a period of expansion. After the troubles and disruptions of the mid-century, there was a steady and continuous growth in numbers and influence. In the second half of the century the membership of the Wesleyan Methodist Church increased by sixty per cent, 180,000 members being added in that time. This was a Church wide awake to the world around it, as is seen by references in the *Methodist Magazine*, which always reported the proceedings of the British Association, and often contained references to archaeological and scientific discoveries. Furthermore, it was a Church intensely interested in World Mission. The Annual Meetings of the Missionary Society aroused great fervour, and the Methodist people were regularly informed of the progress of Foreign Missions through the 'Missionary Intelligence' of their monthly magazine. Nor was this zeal for the work of God only directed to far-off places. Long before Hugh Price Hughes gave voice to the Nonconformist conscience in the pages of *The Methodist Times*, social concern was being encouraged among Methodists. Price's Candle Company, though founded by an Anglican, was warmly commended as an example of how commercial enterprises should support education and religious work. The Early Closing Association was actively supported, and Methodist ladies were being exhorted, twenty years after the emancipation of slaves in the British Empire, to make this effective by boycotting any slave-produced groceries and cotton.

The words used by William Burt Pope to designate Methodist theology, and continually illustrated in his *Compendium of Christian Theology* (2nd edn 1880) are 'scriptural', 'catholic' and 'orthodox'. This is the hallmark of Methodist theology: the theological assertion of Church status, with the denial that Methodism is a sect. As part of the One, Holy, Catholic Church, Methodists have a contribution to make to ecumenical theology. Methodist theologians wrote Christian theology – not Methodist theology, if this means a truncated version of Christian belief. It is notable that until late in the period little mention is made of Wesley's views, and this is not to be construed as disloyalty to the founder. Rather is it loyalty to the principles he himself adumbrated. For nothing was clearer to Wesley than that he was preaching the full, primitive, scriptural, Christian faith, once delivered to the saints. If Methodist theology is narrow, sectarian and denominational, there is little or none to be found in the nineteenth century. But if it is an expression of the full range of the Christian faith, then there is much of it deserving our attention.

The Methodist Church at this time was an evangelical non-Anglican, or perhaps ex-Anglican, rather than a dissenting Church. That is, the Methodist Church had become aware of its position as a Church whose special relationship was still directed towards Anglicanism, even if it was now mainly concerned with maintaining its position over against the Anglican claims. But Methodism was distinctively evangelical. This explains its missionary zeal, which found expression not only in overseas missions, but in work among the poor and uneducated masses of the growing towns of England. Two great principles largely determined the form and pattern of Methodist theology in this period:

1. *Evangelism*. This means not only special missions, the building of central halls, etc.; but also apologetics – that is, the meeting of the current difficulties and objections to the Christian faith, the response to the attack being mounted by certain philosophers and scientists.
2. *Ecclesiology*. Confronted by the claims of the Church of England, and the growing power of Rome, the Methodist Church found it necessary to work out its own view of the Church, including the doctrine of the ministry and the sacraments. Methodist spokesmen thought that there was a position not represented by either Established or Independent Churches which their tradition led them to adopt.

Two other subjects demand some consideration, but these can be fitted conveniently into this scheme. On the one hand, throughout this period there was a sustained interest in the doctrine of the Atonement. This is a matter never far from an evangelist's thoughts, and we can consider it under our first main division. The other subject which requires attention is the doctrine of the Holy Spirit; this is mainly, but not exclusively, because the Methodist classic on this subject was written in this time; we shall subsume this under the doctrine of the Church, where indeed it properly belongs.

(*a*) *Evangelism*

The Methodist answer to the prevailing scepticism of the mid-nineteenth century appears in many forms. The evident interest in science and all true learning delivers this answer from any charge of obscurantism. The Methodists loved knowledge for its own sake, and were prepared to find it in the most obscure places. Their attitude to rational theism was mainly traditional, and they warmly welcomed the republication of Paley's *Evidences* in 1850.[1] There is a familiar ring about the objections to the Christian faith raised by the secularists when they opened their 'Hall of Science' in 1854. They argued against any future life, and urged greater interest in this life, which is the only one we shall ever know. All prayer or trust in providence is to be rejected, and it is claimed that morality is well able to sustain itself without the aid of supernatural religion. How little modern humanism has advanced on these nineteenth-century secularist views! In reply, Luke H. Wiseman

[1] *Wesleyan-Methodist Magazine* (April 1950), 419.

argued that the Christian is not exclusively interested in the future life. Even if the Christian hope falls short of logical certainty, it is very influential in Christian living. In answer to the objections about prayer, Wiseman elucidates the Christian position. A Christian, he says, certainly must pray, but he must not pray with his arms folded. The secularist position about morality without religion fails to meet the real problems of human conduct, which are that although we know what is right, we so seldom do it; the only power which will give us strength to do the right is Christianity.[2]

William Burt Pope was undoubtedly the outstanding Methodist systematic theologian in the nineteenth century, and we are not surprised to find him often concerned with these apologetic themes. He was keenly aware of the contemporary challenges to the Christian faith, but his stature as an apologist is reduced by his tendency to brush aside extreme atheist arguments without much consideration. When the materialists and positivists say that God is imaginary, this is too much for Pope, who 'has nothing to say to such impiety and scepticism'.[3] But he answers many of the usual arguments of scepticism. Those who venture to criticize Christ's character show that they have not understood the depth of it: Christ faced more than physical death; his struggle was with all the powers of hell. Jesus was more than first among equals; attempts to discredit the Gospels by those who advance a legendary or mythical theory, like the minimizing tendencies of the Tübingen scholars, are resolutely dismissed.[4]

Pope is also aware of the problem of accounting for the existence of God. His approach is comprehensive: the ontological argument in its Cartesian form; the cosmological argument, disregarding the demolition of it by Hume's critique of cause; the argument from design; and the general consensus of view that there is a God – these are all used to support the theist position. But 'the first and best credentials of the existence of a Supreme Being are found in the elements of human nature itself'.[5] Twentieth-century theologians do not have a monopoly of appreciation of man! Yet when all this has been considered, and maybe allowed to give rise to a strong supposition in favour of the hypothesis of God, real belief comes only by the direct witness of the Holy Spirit.

Pope's view of the theory of evolution can be taken as representative of the attitude of most thoughtful Methodists at this time. The theory has opened men's eyes to beauty, and is valuable provided it does not claim to explain everything. 'It is impossible so to state the theory of evolution as to preserve the integrity of the higher element in man's

[2] *Wesleyan-Methodist Magazine* (July 1854), 640f.
[3] *Compendium*, i, 60.
[4] Ibid., 116f.
[5] Ibid., 236.

nature.'[6] Other Methodist scholars such as J. H. Rigg accepted evolution as a process, but denied that it was a cause of anything.[7] Scott Lidgett accepted the theory of evolution and argued that it described the activity of God. He also asserted that it helps theology to appreciate more clearly the truth of the immanence of God.[8]

A notable exception to the typically antagonistic and prejudiced attitude of most Christians to the Darwinian theory of evolution is the work of William H. Dallinger (1841–1909). While Governor of Wesley College, a school in Sheffield, Dallinger published as a Fernley lecture *The Creator and What We May Know of the Method of Creation*. He accepts Darwin's theory without reservation (Darwin is said to have accepted Dallinger's studies in microscopy, which claim to show that 'like produces like' and consequently life cannot be solely evolved from matter). Most of Dallinger's argument is a scientific justification for the idea of cause which he accepted in spite of Hume and Comte. 'The very validity of our mental acts is imperilled, if the congruity of the principle of causality be doubted.'[9] Herbert Spencer's philosophical materialism, with its concept of 'force', is rejected, for 'we cannot supplant the Deity by enthroning force'.[10] Dallinger used his considerable work in microscopy – he was President of the Royal Microscopical Society 1884–7 – to emphasize the basic difference between living and non-living things. This did not so much lead him to assert a single creative act giving rise to life, as to argue that, by whatever method it was effected, life could only come from an Eternal Mind. He was an Idealist, claiming support from Huxley, and opposing Haeckel as well as Spencer.

He also made use of the teleological argument, seeing purpose in the manifold adaptations everywhere evident in nature. His support of the abundant evidence by his own experiments with the long-term effects of changing temperatures on septic germs gives an interesting insight into his scientific ability. His conclusion is that concurrent adaptation rather than final cause is the best defence of theism.[11] Theism is defended by the claim that 'design, purpose, intention, appear . . . to be ineradicable from our view of the creation'.[12]

It has to be admitted, however, that our forefathers rarely fully grasped the challenge to the faith involved in science, especially as expressed in the evolutionary theory. Their concern was more directly with contemporary philosophical systems which claimed to be alternatives to Christianity. The chief opponent in this field was Positivism,

[6] Ibid., 431f.

[7] *Discourses and Addresses on Leading Truths of Religion and Philosophy* (London 1880), p. 24.

[8] *The Spiritual Principle of the Atonement* (London 1897), pp. 330f.

[9] W. H. Dallinger, *The Creator and What We May Know of the Method of Creation* (London 1887), p. 11.

[10] Op. cit., p. 27.

[11] Op. cit., p. 72.

[12] Op. cit., p. 74.

the theory of Auguste Comte which had been popularized in England by Herbert Spencer.

For a thorough critique of Positivism we have to turn to William Arthur, who is now known mainly for his *Tongue of Fire*, to which I shall refer later. William Arthur was one of the outstanding ministers of the nineteenth century. His *Religion without God* (1887) and *God without Religion* (1887) are detailed refutations of the contemporary philosophy which he thought was a great threat to the faith. Not only in their titles, but even more in their substance, they have a peculiarly modern ring and significance.

The system of Auguste Comte is subjected to searching and detailed examination by Arthur. He does not fall into the trap of criticizing popular interpretations of Comte, but goes to the original, and is prepared to recognize the importance of Comte's system of thought. But basically it is atheistic (in this J. S. Mill is wrong, and the French Positivists are right). The worship of humanity in place of God is completely unsatisfactory; humanity is in any case a false abstraction, and a goddess made out of humanity has no significance for ordinary people. Science is supposed to have made belief in God irrelevant, but this substitute provided by Comte is no advantage whatever. A fatherless, futureless humanity seems a strange object of worship![13]

Arthur shows his ability as a philosopher in his discussion of the agnosticism of Herbert Spencer. It is no use Spencer saying that religion is impossible because God is unknowable, for complete knowledge is impossible anyway, and we do in fact accept many notions which we do not fully comprehend. Why should this not also be true of God? In reply to Spencer's view that God cannot be known because he is unique and unclassable, Arthur points out that we do in fact know many unique things. 'Is it not a case of knowing truly, and yet knowing in part?'[14] In *God without Religion*, the scientific rejection of religion advanced by Sir James Stephens is very closely scrutinized. Arthur was no anti-Darwinian: 'If Darwin's view be true, and at the beginning the Creator did breathe into some material forms life and its several powers, then is the existence of God expressly affirmed.'[15] But a world without religion which Stephens describes, would lack counsel, correction or comfort.[16]

This apologetic interest is a rebuke in so far as Methodists have in recent years imagined that their only business is to preach a simple gospel, which often takes no account of the problems and doubts assailing their contemporaries. Methodist thought in this present century can hardly be said to be adequate in this field, and it is all the poorer

[13] *Religion without God*, pp. 154ff.
[14] Ibid., p. 216.
[15] *God without Religion*, p. 200.
[16] Ibid., p. 408.

for not having continued the tradition which was quite strong in the nineteenth century. This glimpse of apologetic interest should remove for ever the false picture of self-satisfied Victorian religion, unaware of the crisis in Christianity. Nineteenth-century Methodists knew what the challenge was, and they bent their energy to meeting it, not only by active and enthusiastic home and overseas missionary work, but also by full-scale attacks on the prevalent atheism and scepticism of contemporary intellectual society.

A Church committed to preaching a gospel of salvation is bound to have much teaching on the Atonement, and nineteenth-century Methodism is no exception. The substitutionary view is nearly always regarded as essential, and indeed was used as a test of orthodoxy. Henry Ward Beecher's *Lectures to Young Men on Various Important Subjects* (London 1851) sold 16,000 copies in America, but for a reviewer in the *Wesleyan-Methodist Magazine* popularity is no substitute for references to redemption in the blood of Christ.[17] Christ died in our stead, not only for our benefit, wrote George Cubitt, one of the early Connexional editors. Yet beneath this orthodox exterior there were many new thoughts being hammered out. Pope boldly expounded in his Fernley lecture for 1871 the theory of the expiatory passion: the God-man died for us; but 'He is not the Substitute of God, but His Representative; and not otherwise our Substitute than as our Representative also'.[18] This is a modification of the substitutionary theory, and it foretokens a tendency to see some truth in other theories. Pope himself thought that there was value in all the main theories, and he considered it was a mistake to be confined to one. Henry Williams, in his 1876 Fernley lecture on *The Priesthood of Christ*, recognizes some truth in the Moral Influence theory, but he mainly expounds a priestly theory which embraces the idea of Christ's heavenly intercession and the priesthood of all believers. Rigg sees in High Anglican views a retreat from true Protestantism, and entirely repudiates any suggestion of transubstantiation. Pope is more positive, in that he recognizes that the satisfactionist view misses the thrill of grace, and in place of this he advances a view of the mediatorial ministry of Christ which emphasizes his humiliation, without accepting the kenotic theory of Christ's nature, which he utterly rejected. This humiliation is completed on the Cross, in which true majesty is revealed; the resurrection guarantees the mediatorial work of Christ, and introduces us to the High Priest who represents us before God. This death of Christ ends the old offerings and is the true antitype of the ancient sacrifices. Perhaps Pope's most significant contribution to this doctrine is his emphasis on love, and the need to appreciate something in all the chief doctrines. It is no exaggeration to

[17] *Wesleyan-Methodist Magazine* (April 1851), 391.

[18] W. B. Pope, *The Person of Christ: Dogmatic, Spiritual, Historical* (London 1875), p. 51.

say of Pope's doctrine of the Atonement that it is more comprehensive than that of his predecessors, largely because it is more biblical; he uses the categories of traditional theories, and prepares the way for Lidgett's comprehensive treatment; yet Pope is not second to Lidgett in his persuasive and eirenical treatment. In some respects there are remarkable anticipations of Vincent Taylor in Pope and, above all, his Atonement doctrine is eminently preachable, full of passionate concern for the whole race of sinful men, for whom he is convinced Christ has died, and to whom this good news must be proclaimed with all the energy the Church can command. The scriptural terms in which this fundamental truth is presented are basically simple – 'Christ as Mediator exhibits in His own Person the Reconciliation between God and mankind, which however required to be wrought out by a Sacrifice of Obedience in life and death, which has propitiated God in respect to sin, and accomplished a Redemption for all men, to be appropriated by the faith of individuals.'[19]

The most notable and extended discussion of the doctrine of the Atonement of nineteenth-century Methodist theology was the Fernley lecture of 1897, *The Spiritual Principle of the Atonement: As a Satisfaction made to God for the Sins of the World*, by John Scott Lidgett. Lidgett himself explains in his autobiography that there was considerable dissatisfaction with the traditional doctrine of the Atonement as it was still being expounded by the Church in the latter part of the nineteenth century. Some notable changes had already come upon the views of the nature of God, who was now thought of more in terms of fatherhood than as the majestic sovereign of Calvinistic orthodoxy and Socinianism. Pope, Lidgett's teacher, had himself contributed notably to this reappraisal in Methodism, and he regarded it as a major triumph when, against the opposition of the aged Dr Osborn, he persuaded the Catechism Committee to define God as 'Our Father', instead of 'An infinite and eternal spirit'. Lidgett saw that the chief obstacle to the full appreciation of this view of God was the current doctrine of the Atonement, and he therefore undertook the task of expressing a view of atonement which was agreeable with the idea of the fatherhood of God. It is extremely important to recognize that he did not abandon the notion of satisfaction; indeed, the very word is used in the title of his book. Unless we remember this, we may easily think that Lidgett was expounding a view of the saving work of Christ which had no place for justice, and no real understanding of the nature of sin. His doctrine is not a form of the Moral Influence theory. For he recognized that the human condition is infected by sin, and in sin man is outside the sphere of life. Sin gives rise to the wrath of God, which co-exists alongside the fatherly love of God, and which issues in divine punishment wider and

[19] Id., *Compendium*, ii, 316.

deeper than human thought can apprehend. So the main issue is how to understand together fatherhood and satisfaction, seeing that satisfaction is not a concept Lidgett can ignore, in the light of the biblical evidence. Satisfaction within the context of fatherhood means forgiveness and restoration, and it has an active quality which is expressed through obedience; applied to Christ, this means that his sufferings arose from his complete identification with man, and his complete trust in God. In particular, satisfaction is effected through the fulfilment of human nature, through Christ who is the head of a new humanity. 'The fundamental condition of fatherly satisfaction is, that it shall satisfy the fatherly by perfecting the filial.'[20] Lidgett thus claimed to present a view of the Atonement which retained the scriptural concepts of sin, satisfaction, wrath and punishment, while at the same time not contradicting the fundamental belief in the fatherhood of God. His application of the theory, in respect of the notion of Christ as the head of a new humanity, is in the direction of social progress towards the ideal of a fulfilled humanity, already embodied by Christ in his incarnation. This was an interesting departure from the individualism and other-worldliness which tended to vitiate the contemporary theories of the Atonement. We must admit that Lidgett did in fact present a better rationale of the Atonement than either the Moral Influence school or the traditional satisfactionist exposition, but it is to be doubted if his theory could provide anything like a satisfactory answer for modern man. His reconciliation between fatherhood and satisfaction is only possible on the basis of the Victorian concept of father, and while Lidgett bears witness to the gracious influence of his own parents, we are bound to ask whether he could have applied this theory in an age when the concept of fatherhood has so radically changed. Perhaps, after all, Pope his teacher was more likely to provide a lasting solution in his insistence on the value of all the main theories, apart from moral influence and over-legalistic satisfaction. But Lidgett's work remains a fitting monument to a man who has been described as the greatest Methodist since Wesley.

The first Fernley lecture, given by Dr George Osborn in 1870 (incidentally, in the borrowed New Connexion Bethesda Chapel at Hanley, because it was too hot to be in the Wesleyan Chapel!), was on the subject of the Holy Spirit. Osborn's short essay expounds the biblical evidence for the orthodox belief in the Person of the Holy Spirit, and shows that his work is in convicting sinners, recalling Christ to our remembrance, effecting our adoption as sons of God, and building up in believers the life of holiness. In the next Fernley lecture Pope emphasized that the work of the Holy Spirit is especially connected with mediating Christ to believers; this connection between Christ and the Holy Spirit is of profound significance for Christian doctrine, and

[20] *The Spiritual Principle of the Atonement*, p. 301.

both Pope and Benjamin Gregory point out the importance of the work of the Holy Spirit in the doctrine of the Church. 'The Church is the organ of the Spirit, and that in its individual members; . . . the Church is a living organism, called into existence, created, shaped, animated, ensouled, actuated, by the Spirit.'[21] It has to be admitted, however, that none of these expositions presents anything novel about the doctrine of the Holy Spirit, and none of them beats at all loudly on the Methodist drum. Robert Newton Young in 1882 did discuss a doctrine dear to the heart of our founder: that is, the witness of the Spirit.

Far and away the most significant and influential book on the Holy Spirit was William Arthur's *Tongue of Fire* (1856). This is a classic exposition of the doctrine of the Holy Spirit, with particular emphasis on the need for the power of the Holy Spirit to revive the Church. At times, the book reaches unusual heights of eloquence, as, for instance, when the interval between the Ascension and the descent of the Spirit is being described. The apostles are depicted waiting for the word 'Go'. Each day they expect the promised gift of the Spirit, and each day they are disappointed; they have been trained by their Master; they have the Gospel, and the world desperately needs it; surely, then, they may begin their work? But no; the Lord said, 'Wait until you receive power from on high'. They dare not go until they are empowered as Christ promised. The book goes on to claim that the promised Holy Spirit did fall upon all, and the signs of his presence are moral power, the development of the life of holiness in every believer, and ability to witness to the Gospel. 'He is an unhappy minister who has to do all the witnessing for a silent congregation.'[22] This holiness is not other-worldly, for reference is made to the need to apply Christian principles to human problems: the social evils condemned include not only intemperance and gambling, but also slavery, class warfare, commercial frauds, bad employers, and parents who raise obstacles to young people getting married and are thereby responsible for the inevitable licentiousness which follows. Nor must this teaching of holiness be concerned only with the life after this; it is intended to be lived out now, for Christian salvation is present salvation.

The lasting impression of this remarkable book is its teaching on a charismatic ministry. The one essential for the work of the ministry is the call of God – 'No training ever did, or ever can, make him a Minister who has no call, no gifts and no power sent upon his soul by the anointing of the eternal Spirit.'[23] But it is not to be supposed from this that Arthur was opposed to training for the ministry. Far from it; he says that the particular subjects needed for this training are the study

[21] Benjamin Gregory, *The Holy Catholic Church, the Communion of Saints* (London 1873), p. 28.

[22] William Arthur, *Tongue of Fire*, p. 81.

[23] Ibid., p. 195.

of the scriptures and practice in the use and development of the gifts needed for the ministry. But still the one essential for which the Church must wait, if needs be, is the call of God. 'Alas,' he says, 'for those whose souls are watched over by unconverted scholars!'[24] Too much emphasis on correctness leads to divine worship which is 'Faultily faultless, icily regular, splendidly null', quoted from Alfred Lord Tennyson's *Maud* (1855). (Arthur's failure to acknowledge his source is partly excused by his speedy recognition of the poem!) But let no one think that this means that lack of ability and training are positive advantages to the work of the ministry. 'The Cross in itself is "foolishness", but Christ never sent fools to be its heralds.'[25]

So Arthur argued that the primary need of the ministry is the power of the Holy Spirit; he believed that the absence of this is our responsibility: 'A Minister can never be responsible for success, but he is responsible for power.'[26] Prayer is the condition of obtaining this power: 'Prayer, prayer, all prayer, – mighty, importunate, repeated, united prayer.'[27] This is indeed one of the essential marks of an Apostolic Church: 'A Church, to be apostolic, must have Ministers powerful in preaching, and members mighty in prayer.'[28]

(*b*) *Ecclesiology*

The Methodist doctrine of the Church in the second half of the nineteenth century was confident that Methodism was a real Church, and could claim her place in the One Holy Catholic Church. These claims were made against the background of the persistent Anglican assumption that the Church of England represented the true and only Church of this land. Bishop Beveridge had asserted in 1679 that the English Church is the same as the primitive Church. So we cannot blame the Methodists if *they* set to work to point out the likeness between Methodism and the early Church. In this task they were encouraged and abetted by the famous Paley, of the *Evidences*, who had said late in the eighteenth century that Methodism most nearly approximated to the primitive Church. Benjamin Gregory's 1873 Fernley lecture is the classic expression of this view. Like the early Church, Methodism is first concerned with the preaching of the Gospel, and with the life of service to God and man which follows from its reception. Organization is a secondary matter and must serve the best interest of the Gospel; the Christian Church is not called into being to set up an organization, but to witness. This implies that no organization can be regarded as essential or normative, and any attempt to define the Church so that

[24] Ibid., pp. 218f.
[25] Ibid., p. 237.
[26] Ibid., p. 257.
[27] Ibid., p. 294.
[28] Ibid., p. 131.

others can be unchurched is repugnant to Methodists. But this does not mean indifference to standards of membership of the Church. Gregory says that 'Heart-experience, shown in character, is the true basis of Church-recognition'.[29] Pope's definition is more theological and sacramental: 'All who approve themselves believers in Christ, and who, whether as adults or as children, are baptized, belong to the external body, and are entitled to all its privileges.'[30] Pope insists that it is wrong to demand full confession of religious conversion before membership can be allowed, but to avoid the Broad Church conception which makes nonsense of the Church by including everyone in it, means of discipline within the Church must be effective. For Methodism, this is found in the class meeting. This is not imposing a new condition of church membership, but the class meeting 'in particular honours the Church's note of external sanctity by admitting freely every anxious applicant on the sole condition that he as a baptized member of the Church of Christ is desirous to flee from the wrath to come and to find salvation in the name of Jesus'.[31]

The emphasis on the class meeting is a notable feature of Methodist ecclesiology of this period. The class meeting represents the vital element of fellowship on which such stress was laid. It provides, says William Arthur, a means of sharing together in the deep things of God, without which Christian fellowship is vain. Rigg asserted that without fellowship the organization would become a cumbrous burden: 'our ancient and essential principle of homely, free, effective mutual fellowship in all that belongs to the life of experimental Christianity . . . even more than the doctrine of justification by faith . . . is the test of a standing or a falling, a living or a dying, Church'.[32] William Slater regarded the class meeting as 'a bulwark of spiritual freedom' – and a safeguard against the horrors of the confessional![33] It cannot be doubted that this characteristic of fellowship is one of the foremost contributions of Methodism to the catholic doctrine of the Church, and Methodists have to ask themselves whether they have rightly used and preserved this precious heritage which their fathers regarded as so important.

The relation with the Anglicans was uppermost in the minds of the Methodists when they thought about Church relations. There was some pressure from the Anglican side for Methodism to return to the fold, a suggestion which was strongly resisted. The idea that because Wesley never separated from the Church of England, therefore Methodists should return to the Anglican fold, is 'eminently fallacious'.[34] The

[29] B. Gregory, op. cit., p. 57.
[30] W. B. Pope, *Compendium*, iii, 278f.
[31] Ibid., iii, 279.
[32] J. H. Rigg, op. cit., p. 129.
[33] William F. Slater, *Methodism in the Light of the Early Church* (London 1885), p. 53.
[34] James Rigg, *The Churchmanship of John Wesley, and the Relations of Wesleyan Methodism to the Church of England* (London 1878), p. 16.

attitude to Anglican – Methodist relations was much influenced by the overbearing claims for apostolic succession put forward by the Anglo-Catholics. 'The genius of Methodism, as now fully organized into a church, and that of Anglican Episcopacy are mutually repellent and exclusive.'[35] But Rigg did not totally reject episcopacy as such. He claimed that 'Methodism's superintendents, chairmen of districts and its presidents give to it some of the characteristics of primitive Christianity'.[36] 'An evangelical episcopacy, even though diocesan, efficiently organized, freed from secular control, and gathering its people into churches, would be a much superior system to that of Independence.'[37] But Rigg was not always consistent when discussing the Church of England – his ambivalent attitude sometimes led him into extreme statements about both episcopacy and Independency. There was a strong conviction, certainly among Wesleyans, that they must seek church unity and not acquiesce in disunity. Rigg had a remarkable knowledge of Anglicanism. He was greatly attracted to that Church, and could conceive of circumstances in which he might 'thankfully accept' her hospitality.[38] With his earlier work on *Modern Anglican Theology* (London 1857), this book presents a fully critical but sympathetic contemporary view of the Tractarian Movement. Later, Rigg's pamphlet on *The Relations of John Wesley and of Wesleyan Methodism to the Church of England Investigated and Determined* (London 1868) provoked Bishop Ellicott of Gloucester to suggest that reunion between Methodism and the Church of England could begin with 'such a recognition of Wesleyan ordination as may open Church pulpits to duly ordained Wesleyan ministers'.[39] But in *Oxford High Anglicanism* Rigg became more open in his criticism of the influence of Pusey and, to a lesser extent, Keble and Newman, on Anglican relations with Methodism: 'Already the influence of the causes I have indicated has gone very far towards alienating the mass of English Methodists from the Established Church . . . The effects of Puseyism go to divide the Church of England itself into two, if not three distinct Churches, as well as to spread religious bitterness and controversy through all classes of the community.'[40] Gregory provided the wisest word: 'All we can do,' he says, 'is to take whatever steps may prepare the way for ultimate organic union.'[41] The High Church view of the necessity of apostolic succession was the chief barrier to this unity, and no progress was possible until Methodists could meet the Anglicans on the basis of mutual recognition; but it is

[35] Ibid., pp. 109–110.

[36] Id., *The Connexional Economy of Wesleyan Methodism in Its Ecclesiastical and Spiritual Aspects* (London 1851), p. 120.

[37] Ibid., p. 137.

[38] Id., *Oxford High Anglicanism and Its Chief Leaders* (London 1895), p. viii.

[39] John Telford, *The Life of James Harrison Rigg D.D. 1821–1909* (London 1909), p. 235.

[40] *Oxford High Anglicanism*, p. 241.

[41] *The Holy Catholic Church, The Communion of Saints*, p. 201.

obvious that, even in these far-off days, the only really live option in church relations was a coming together of Methodism and the Church of England. Gregory in fact favoured the idea of federation, but he could see at that time no prospect of organizational unity, and had to content himself with exhortation to avoid unnecessary divisions. It is dangerous to hazard a guess as to what would have been the reactions of those Methodists to the scheme (1968), but it is certainly fallacious to apply their attitude to the Church of England in the mid-twentieth century, which is so very different in many vital respects.

During this period we see a considerable development of the Methodist doctrine of the ministry. At the beginning, the Wesleyan Methodists were struggling with the problems arising out of the mid-century agitations. The basis of their attitude to the ministry was Bunting's idea that the Conference was a kind of corporate Wesley, from which ministers derived their authority. Ministers were not to be regarded as paid employees of the Church, for they were Christ's stewards and shepherds of the flock. The eventual inclusion of laymen in the Conference did not materially affect the doctrine of the ministry as corporately responsible for the oversight and shepherding of the people of God. This sense of the corporate nature of the ministry was never lost, and was regarded as a safeguard against both Independent individualism and Anglo-Catholic claims about the apostolic succession. These Methodists believed that there was primitive episcopacy in their ministry, functioning through the oversight of Circuit Superintendents, Chairmen of Districts, and the President of Conference. Their objection was not to episcopacy, but to that theory of it which had solidified into the Anglo-Catholic insistence on apostolic succession. They realized that no real unity between Anglicans and Methodists would be possible until this exclusive claim was modified, and they were absolutely against any suggestion of re-ordination for Methodist ministers.

The question of the effect of ordination was discussed by J. H. Rigg in his ordination charge at the Birmingham Conference in 1879.[42] Rejecting any belief in a special grace bestowed at ordination, he claims that the process by which a man is made a minister starts with his call from God, without which he cannot begin; and college training, probation, and the vote of Conference by which a man is received into Full Connexion, are all parts of the divine activity through the Church by which men are appointed by God to the ministry of Word and Sacrament. He does not deny that grace is bestowed through the prayer and laying-on of hands at ordination, but wisely remarks that the sign of this grace having been given is more likely to be a sense of need of further grace than a sense of adequacy and authority. The Wesleyan Methodists achieved during this period a concept of the ministry which

[42] *Discourses and Addresses*, pp. 158–87.

combined the ideas of authority and divine commission with real partnership with the laity in the government of the Church. Is there any other Church which has arrived at a view which has steered so steady a course between the authoritarianism of absolute ministerial control which Anglicans still have, and the low conception of so many 'Free' Churches, in which ultimately the minister is under the dominance of the local congregation who pay him and therefore call the tune?

Methodism in this period continued to be a sacramental Church, but the later tendency to minimize the sacraments can perhaps be partly laid at the door of Rigg, whose interpretation of the churchmanship of Wesley, clearly motivated by a desire to prevent the Anglo-Catholics from claiming Wesley as a High Churchman, seemed to give scholarly support for the view that Wesley dropped his High Church and sacramental views after 1738. In this extraordinary piece of misguided polemic, Rigg seriously underrated the influence of the Brevint treatise on the Lord's Supper, and subsequent Methodist scholarship has shown that in fact Wesley always retained his high view of the sacrament, and linked this closely with his evangelical mission.

For most of this period, Methodists were loyal to Wesley regarding sacramental doctrine and practice. Baptism was accepted as the normal way of entry into the Church; Pope taught that infant baptism effects regeneration; but in adults this is questioned, because the Roman theory made baptismal regeneration a substitute for regeneration by the work of the Spirit at conversion or New Birth. 'The baptism of the children of believing parents is . . . a sign of the washing away of original guilt, and a seal of their adoption into the family of God; a sign of the regeneration which their nature needs, and a seal of its impartation in God's good time.'[43]

The Lord's Supper was equally honoured and used by nineteenth-century Methodists. They were not as ready as John Nelson had been in the previous century to receive the sacrament from the hands of a priest who had falsely witnessed against him and separated him from his family; but they highly valued this means of grace and had a developed sacramental theology. Pope said that the highest expression of the Christian faith in the evangelical sacrifice is thus to partake of the bread of God, and to sup with him: 'The Lord's Supper is spread on the Lord's table: an altar to God, a table to us. Jesus is our great Peace-offering, as well as our Passover.'[44] There is a real presence of Christ in the sacrament, and by this offering we can be sure that the heavenly sacrificial propitiation is made on our behalf; we have fellowship with Christ and his people on earth, and thus we bear our witness to the Gospel of his life and death. The Eucharist signifies and seals the

[43] *Compendium*, iii, 318.
[44] Ibid., ii, 224.

mystical nourishment of Christ; it commemorates the sacrifice of our redemption and the communion which is the badge of our united Christian profession. The constituents, or elements, to be used are 'common bread and unadulterated wine'.[45] And we shall not be surprised, knowing how much the Methodists valued the Lord's Supper, to find that they deprecated the so-called Open Table, and applied the discipline of the class meeting to ensure that those who received these tokens of our Lord's death continue in that fellowship and faith by which alone the benefits of the sacrament could become effective.

A good deal of the spirit of nineteenth-century Methodism is expressed in the words of a little-known author, William Slater:

> Our religion is Christianity or it is nothing; but we do not call ourselves the 'Church' or 'Christians', lest we should exclude, even by implication, those who 'are not of this fold' from the 'flock' . . . We are 'Catholics', for we pray that 'grace may be on all them that love our Lord Jesus Christ in sincerity'. We are 'Protestants', for we deny that there is any authority in Christ's Church higher than His word. We are 'Methodists', for we desire to be 'The friends of all, the enemies of none'.[46]

2. The Period 1900–1950

(*a*) *Biblical studies*

In the field of biblical scholarship Methodism has made contributions which have been recognized far beyond her own borders. A fitting name to head the list is William Fiddian Moulton (1835–1898). Moulton's first notable publication was his annotated translation of Winer's *Grammar of New Testament Greek*, published in 1870. This was described by Bishop Westcott as 'equal to any work which has been done either in England or in Germany on the grammatical criticism of the New Testament'.[47] In this work Moulton set out the principles of textual exegesis which have led to the most enlightened and truthful interpretations. Truth was the objective of all his study: 'For the truth, oh how much may we do.'[48] This meticulous care over detail, together with truly encyclopaedic knowledge, especially of biblical subjects, brought him into the select company of the revisers of the Authorized Version. In addition to his translation work in the New Testament he was largely responsible for the revision of II Maccabees and Wisdom in the Apocrypha, and almost single-handed he produced the Comprehensive Marginal References of the New Testament on which the fuller published references were based. This was a work of comprehensive

[45] Ibid., iii, 328.
[46] Op. cit., p. 161.
[47] W. Fiddian Moulton, *William F. Moulton: A Memoir* (London 1899), p. 107.
[48] Winer, *Grammar of New Testament Greek*, tr. Moulton (London 1870), p. 78.

and exact scholarship, making these marginal references a wonderful storehouse of scriptural interpretation. Moulton's other main works were: *The Commentary on St John*, in the Cambridge Bible for Schools, in collaboration with William Milligan; *The Cambridge Commentary on Hebrews*; he co-operated with Alfred S. Geden in the famous *Concordance*; and he wrote the *History of the English Bible*. This last book was in particular a good example of scholarly accuracy presented in popular form by a true master of the subject. His epitaph in Wesley's Chapel fittingly describes him as one who lived in 'meekness of wisdom'.[49]

James Hope Moulton (1863–1917), the son of W. F. Moulton, did his greatest linguistic work in *A Grammar of New Testament Greek*, Volume 1, *Prolegomena* (1906), which was really the successor to his father's translation of Winer. An entirely new work particularly influenced by recent discoveries in papyri, this *Prolegomena* set out a new approach to New Testament study by insisting that ' "Biblical" Greek, except where it is translation Greek, was simply the vernacular of daily life'.[50] This emphasis on the everyday nature of New Testament Greek brought a freshness to Moulton's interpretations which was very welcome. But it has to be admitted that sometimes his enthusiasm ran away with him, particularly in *From Egyptian Rubbish-heaps*.[51] Perhaps the most notable evaluation of Moulton's grammatical work is contained in a review of the *Prolegomena* by Adolf Deissmann, whose work had greatly influenced him. Deissmann warmly commended the scholarly judgment and lively interest of Moulton's work. His other great undertaking in grammatical research was in collaboration with George Milligan.[52]

Moulton's second specialized field was Zoroastrianism. *Early Zoroastrianism*, the Hibbert Lectures for 1912, is a highly specialized account of Zoroastrian literary sources. *The Treasure of the Magi: A Study of Modern Zoroastrianism* (Oxford 1917), written during his visit to the Parsees in India and published posthumously, is a very clear and readable account of the religion of Zarathustra and the later influences which have contributed to modern Parsism. He regarded Parsism as 'by far the purest of non-Christian religions' and criticized the Edinburgh Missionary Conference for ignoring it.[53] Moulton won the confidence of the Parsees and made a strong appeal to them to return to the pure religion of Zarathustra. He believed that they ought to reassert their founder's missionary zeal, not just to maintain their own community but to offer to their fellow-Indians a religion which was greatly superior to Hinduism. Yet Moulton believed that the true

[49] James 3.13.

[50] *Prolegomena*, p. 4.

[51] (London 1916).

[52] *The Vocabulary of the Greek Testament: Illustrated from the Papyri and Other Non-Literary Sources*, 8 parts (London 1914–1929).

[53] *Religion and Religions* (London 1913), p. 91.

fulfilment of the teaching of Zarathustra is only found in Christ.

> For what India needs, and all the world needs, is not a Teacher, nor even an Example, but a Life . . . Of all the teachers of the Gentiles none has risen higher than Zarathustra: . . . The conspicuous failure of this great religion speaks eloquently of the supreme need of man. Vital energy, not precepts; power, not mere example; grace, not ideals – this is what our Christ gives, what every other messenger of God can only promise through Him.[54]

Moulton showed high appreciation of the work of J. G. Frazer, whose *The Golden Bough* provided a mine of information about primitive religion. This appreciation was no doubt increased by his personal acquaintance with Frazer, and Moulton warned Christians against a negative attitude to Frazer's work, reminding them of the fate of earlier enthusiastic opponents of Darwin. Moulton was a self-styled ultra-Protestant. He admitted to having no interest in matters of ritual.[55] Even the Lord's Supper is to be regarded as a parable signifying our need of constant spiritual nourishment. He had more sympathy with Parsism than with Roman Catholicism or even High-Church Anglicanism, and it is not surprising that his hope in Church relations was for federation. Union was quite unthinkable and would be a wrong step anyway. These views are expressed in two posthumous collections of essays and articles edited by his brother, entitled *The Christian Religion in the Study and the Street* (London 1919) and *A Neglected Sacrament* (see also the *Life of Moulton*, also by his brother). James Hope Moulton was possibly the greatest Greek and philological scholar ever produced by Methodism. As tutor at Didsbury he made a tremendous impression on his students, some of whom, notably Wilbert Howard, carried on his work in grammatical studies. His high standards of scholarly industry and fervent missionary zeal have left a permanent impression on Methodist scholarship.

Wilbert Francis Howard (1880–1952) was a highly skilled student of philology, which together with his studies in the Fourth Gospel is his main contribution to New Testament scholarship. Howard's work in completing the second volume of Moulton's *Prolegomena* deservedly earned for him the reputation of a very thorough and accurate scholar. He completed Moulton's chapter on Aramaisms and Hebraisms and wrote an extensive appendix on Semitisms in the New Testament, displaying in both sections a wide knowledge of the language and background of the New Testament. He did not accept the view which explains the style of the New Testament mainly in terms of Aramaic originals, but found ample evidence of the influence of the Septuagint

[54] *The Treasure of the Magi*, p. 253.
[55] Ibid., p. 136.

in the ordinary language of those by whom and for whom the New Testament was written. He was able to look at the papyrus discoveries from a more detached viewpoint than Moulton, and did not give way to that over-enthusiastic judgement which sometimes makes the work of Moulton very fanciful. *The Fourth Gospel in Recent Criticism and Interpretation* (London 1931) reveals several aspects of Howard's learning and his interest in popular exposition of the message of the New Testament. He proposed three lines of inquiry into the Fourth Gospel. First, he carried through a survey of the interpretation of the Gospel in the past thirty years with great enthusiasm, indicating his familiarity with the notable discussions of German and French scholars, as well as British. Secondly, he considered the characteristics of the Gospel. He was convinced that there is an authentic historical tradition behind this Gospel which makes it at some points superior to the synoptics. His third line of study was to ask what is the permanent value of this book as evidence of the life and teaching of Jesus. While all the Gospels were written from faith to faith, and therefore there is no absolute difference between the synoptics and John, the Fourth Gospel contains the abiding message of the New Testament. If this work on the Fourth Gospel hardly satisfies Howard's own requirement that it should enable preachers to expound the book more effectively, that requirement is more adequately met in a smaller book which is deceptive in its importance. *Christianity According to St John* (London 1943) might appear to a casual reader to be rather commonplace, but to those who know the tremendous background of knowledge which is assumed but never displayed by the author, and the remarkable ability to refer to so many recent and contemporary authors, this little book is a treasure house of deep understanding of 'the Spiritual Gospel'. Almost every line of the book contains the distilled wisdom of one who was an acknowledged authority on this subject. Here is a first-rate example of how the deepest learning can illuminate the Christian message for ordinary people.

Another essay in popular exposition is *The Romance of New Testament Scholarship* (London 1949). This is a biographical study of some of the great names in the history of biblical interpretation. Howard casts his net widely, finding interest and value in the work of Marcion, Origen and F. C. Baur as well as in more orthodox scholars such as Jerome, Lightfoot, Westcott and Hort. There is an infectious enthusiasm about this work, which traces the main outline of biblical interpretation through the centuries. Dr Howard was a man of striking, even dominating personality. His books give the impression of extreme accuracy, and of loyalty to the truth wherever it might lead him. These qualities are seen in his commentaries on *I & II Corinthians*, on *Acts* and *St John*. He was a great lover of the works of Browning and Milton and had a fine sensitivity to style, which gift would have been well employed on the panel of translators of the New English Bible had not his sudden death prevented him from fulfilling this task. He was the inheritor of a noble tradition of classical philology. Perhaps we see in him the last great philologist, at least in Methodism, for there seems now to be a growing awareness that these questions of the minutiae of grammatical forms have been investigated as far as it is profitable to go. When we see the high value of Howard's popular expositions, we recognize that the end-product of this massive scholarship is the enlightenment and encouragement of the people of God. The foundation had been laid, and the building had just begun to rise above ground level when Dr Howard was removed from the scene of his earthly labours. Others have taken up his work, but it is much to be hoped that they will not begin again to do the work which he and others have pursued as far as it is useful to go, but rather be more concerned about the end-product. It has been said of Dr Howard that he was the ideal Christian scholar and gentleman.

The Primitive Methodists had their scholars too, chief among them being Arthur Samuel Peake (1865–1929). Although never ordained, he was largely responsible for the development of ministerial training in Primitive Methodism, and the high standards of scholarship reached by many Primitive Methodist ministers was almost entirely due to his inspiration. His written work was voluminous and far-ranging, and gained for him a deserved reputation as a biblical scholar of the first rank. Dr Henry Guppy, John Rylands librarian, thought that Peake saved the British Churches from a violent fundamentalist controversy. This view of his work certainly places the emphasis on the right spot, for he was a leading exponent of the critical-historical approach to the Bible and exerted great efforts to popularize the scientific view of the scriptures. He was involved in real controversy with the conservatives, who naturally regarded his views as destructive of the value of the Bible. He was often hard-hitting in debate and regarded it as a solemn duty to popularize the critical view of the Bible because only so could Christian theology be saved from obscurantism. His comprehensive but popular statement of his position in *The Bible: Its Origin, Its Significance and Its Abiding Worth* (London 1913) shows him to be a thoroughly readable and sound guide for ordinary people. Peake is best seen as a popular apologist in *Christianity: Its Nature and Its Truth* (London 1908). His approach is a blend of natural theology and an enlightened biblicism. The discussion of the Virgin Birth and the Resurrection shows that Peake was prepared to question the most deeply held convictions of Christian people, but in fact his historical studies led him to accept the historicity of the Virgin Birth and the physical nature of the Resurrection. His attitude to the divinity of Christ and the mystery of the Incarnation shows him to be quite remarkably advanced in thought, and his criticism of the substitutionary theory of the Atonement, in favour of a theory of identification and faith union with Christ, shows that he was alive to the contemporary difficulties raised by the traditional sacrificial and substitutionary theories. This book is surprisingly modern in thought and style and is especially valuable when treating Pauline theology. The basis of Peake's popular apologetics and Bible introduction was his highly specialized work on the Bible. He wrote commentaries on Jeremiah and Job; on Colossians, Hebrews and the Revelation of St John. He spent a great deal of time on the problem of the Servant of Yahweh and the question of suffering in the Old Testament. The volume on the latter subject was the Hartley lecture for 1904. If he had lived longer it is likely that Peake would have produced a full study of the life and teaching of Paul. We have the outline sketch of this in books about the *Quintessence of Paulinism*; *Paul the Apostle*; *Paul and the Jewish Christians*. But of course the work for which Peake is best known is his *Commentary on the Bible*, first published in 1919. The list of contributors gives some idea of the sort of scholarly company he kept, and the standard of colleagueship he could inspire. In its day this commentary was a milestone in the popularizing of critical scholarship, and the recent publication of an entirely new series of articles and commentaries under the same title is but fitting tribute to the first editor. Any estimate of the work of Arthur S. Peake must pay tribute to the tremendous volume and high scholarly standards of his writing. During his lifetime and since, he has been lionized by his fervent admirers, particularly by Primitive Methodists, for whom he was the great doctor without peer or equal among them. He represents a method of Bible study which has an essential place in the development of our understanding of the scriptures, but which is now seen to have serious shortcomings. The enthusiasm for critical and historical study seems to have left too little energy for the more important task of understanding the meaning of the Bible. By the time all the interesting critical questions have been asked, there seems no time left for theology proper. Peake in fact reveals a certain lack of sympathy with systematic theology, and he looks upon systematic theologians as opponents of the critical approach to the Bible. Perhaps W. F. Lofthouse is right in hinting that his work would have been more memorable if there had been somewhat less of it, but it cannot be denied that he made a notable contribution to biblical scholarship and certainly gave to Primitive Methodism a scholarship she could never previously claim.

J. Alexander Findlay (1880–1961) succeeded James Hope Moulton in the Chair of New Testament studies when Didsbury College reopened in 1919. Findlay was a man with a mind of his own, who made a distinctive contribution to New Testament studies; but it is no denigration of him to say that in the influences of J. H. Moulton and

Rendle Harris lies the key to all his writing. He was principally an inspiring teacher, both in ministerial training and in ministers' fraternals, and as a much loved lecturer to laymen at the Methodist School of Fellowship. His scholarship was capable of standing alongside Deissmann, Cadbury, Lietzmann and Windisch, but he made his real mark as a preacher's guide and inspiration. In him the study of the character of Jesus reached its highest point, perhaps revealing the inherent limitations as well as the considerable value of this aspect of biblical study. A vivid imagination sometimes gives startling freshness to his exegesis, but at other times the whimsy produces extraordinary interpretations. It is no disparagement of Findlay to say that he consistently and persuasively expounded a 'Come to Jesus' religion. The phrase needs careful understanding, but it is his own; in his most mature work he states: 'The purpose of the Incarnation was that God might "draw" men to Himself by the flesh-and-blood Jesus . . . "Come to Jesus", not "Come to Christ", is the heart of the Gospel message still.'[56] His first and last love was the study of the life of Jesus in the Gospels. In 1920 he wrote: 'We can reconstruct the biography of this man without difficulty.'[57] Later appreciation of form criticism modified this certainty to some extent, but his whole approach depended upon the conviction that a portrait of Jesus is discernible in the Gospels. In the Gospels we have the portrait of a man, not a collection of ideas and theories about life artificially presented in human form. He recognized the justice of the criticism that some exegesis, surely including his own early work, was too sentimental. It read into the character of Jesus notions which really arose in the exegete's own mind. But the opposite effect was to dehumanize Jesus, to take away the reality of his human life; and this he held rather strongly against some Barthians. He also rejected what he called the Barthian denigration of human nature. But as with form criticism, so with Barthianism, his attitude was far from total rejection. He saw especially in the years just before 1939 that the theology of crisis had much of value to give to the Christian view. It helped him to see the inadequacies of the gospel of the human Jesus and forced him to reconsider and modify, but not to abandon, his belief that the New Testament teaches the natural goodness of man and the general benevolence of God.

Since he is the best instance in Methodist scholarship of this devoted study, it is worthwhile to try to summarize the impression Findlay gives of the life and message of Jesus. Findlay maintains that Jesus belonged to the inner core of true Pharisees, but this did not inhibit him from making trenchant criticism of the domineering arrogance of the Pharisaic party, of whom the pious minority were not typical. Much is

[56] *The Way, The Truth and The Life* (London 1940), p. 259.
[57] *Jesus As They Saw Him* (London 1919–20), pp. 19–20.

made of Jesus' easy relationship with common folk. His sociability is an indication that before we can be in right relation with God we must live in harmony with our neighbour. Jesus lived a life of trust in God and confidence in man's natural goodness. In his early writing Findlay stressed the natural goodness of Jesus and insisted that individually his contemporaries would never have crucified him. The cause was the opposition of the ruling classes. 'Jews' means priests and scribes, not ordinary people. Later events in the world shook Findlay's confidence in man's goodness, but he always insisted that Jesus' message was hopeful and encouraging, not pessimistic or condemnatory. The disciples could not be expected to understand the demand to take up their cross before Calvary. Findlay thought the saying about taking up the cross was really a call to the adventure of loving Jesus, which is all that matters. The true lover of Jesus regards the question about the relation between the Jesus of history and the Jesus of experience as unreal: 'it is just Jesus, the Jesus who comes alive as he pores over the Gospels or thinks of Him as he sits dreaming over the fire at night'.[58] But Findlay did not believe that the centre of the Christian faith was a merely human figure. For one thing, such a figure would be totally inadequate to our need: 'If Jesus be but the noblest of men, we have in the Cross only the most moving of all tragedies; but if He be God, the path of disillusionment, darkening down to despair, leads us, by the only way now open to us, straight into the arms of God.'[59] In the Cato lecture of 1938, *Jesus, Divine and Human* (London 1938), Findlay asserts that the figure of Jesus has for too long been hidden by a series of ecclesiastical images, creeds, Church, Gospel, social witness. His intention is to make plain the central figure of the Christian faith in whom the human is taken up into the divine and the two become one. The experience of Jesus was fully human: this is consonant with the fact that 'Son of man' was our Lord's favourite self-designation. To claim that he was intermittently aware of divine nature is to deny his humanity, for we humans are never self-conscious in the sense in which some have spoken of the filial consciousness of Jesus. We must hold fast to our principle that Jesus was God, but felt himself to be man. As our Lord's consciousness of God and his awareness of the divine presence were the same in principle as ours, if differing in intensity, we can take courage from the way he discovered the will of God. Our course is often directed not so much by any immediate guidance as by the elimination of alternatives. We may be glad to think that it was so with him. But the most important aspect of the divine nature of Jesus is that it alone makes possible the central Christian experience of knowing Christ now. *The* question, he maintained, is 'Do we know Christ?' This

[58] *The Realism of Jesus* (London nd.), p. 180.
[59] *What Did Jesus Teach?* (London 1933), p. 205.

is only meaningful because through death Jesus has made himself available to everyone. Findlay thought that the gospel statement that Jesus gave up his spirit really means that by dying on the cross Jesus let the Spirit go free – which is another way of saying that Jesus is present now with those who love and serve him. There is no doubt that this presence was an overwhelming reality to Findlay, and many testified that he was able to communicate his experience of Jesus to others, especially through his deep knowledge of the New Testament.

Findlay was not only a student of the Gospels, however. His brief book on Paul, *A Portrait of Paul* (London 1935), must surely rank with C. H. Dodd's *The Meaning of Paul for Today*. Findlay's comprehensive New Testament scholarship is most fully displayed in the book *The Way, The Truth and The Life*, in which he says that the key to the meaning of the New Testament is to be found in three ways of expressing discipleship: 'In His Steps'; 'In Christ'; and 'Learn of Me'. Findlay's last book was his Fernley Hartley lecture of 1950, called *Jesus and His Parables*. Especially significant is his insistence that the parables are not religious stories but accounts of real-life situations in which the presence of the Kingdom of God is manifest. What is this but an assertion of secularity? We could do a lot worse than study this volume in our search for Jesus today. Along with this idea of the secularity of the parables he insisted that the New Testament teaches a hopeful view of man. The fundamental belief about man which the Bible from beginning to end is designed to express is that man is made in the image of God and after his likeness. The lesson to be drawn from this is clear: 'Perhaps the greatest thing in the Gospel-story is the proof it gives us that, in spite of everything, God believes in the essential goodness of man's human nature, and so should we.'[60] But there are disappointing features, particularly an inability to see the problems of many people about the reality and meaning of Jesus. Findlay was one of the foremost in his generation in his grasp of the reality of the experience of Jesus. Yet he never really answered the difficulties of those who cannot persuade themselves that this talk is anything more than pious imagination. Furthermore, he seems to squeeze out every drop of meaning from the Gospels until one feels there is nothing left; and this cannot be true, for every generation must find its own meaning from the Gospels. We seem nowadays to need a simpler approach, less speculation, fewer odd theories about background which we know the next scholar will refute. Is there ever to be an end to the multitude of conjectures, interpretations, and explanations? Perhaps Findlay's own complaint about creeds, Church, Gospel and social witness obscuring the face of Jesus can be turned against himself. How can we see the meaning of Christ for today unless we jettison most of Findlay's fascinating, suggestive but

[60] *Jesus and His Parables* (London 1950), p. 142.

highly imaginative reconstruction? No one should underestimate this 'Jesus religion'. Its propounder was a prophet who saw a possible end of organized religion, a man deeply convinced about the practicability of Christianity, who saw himself continually challenged by the Gospel. Who but a true lover of Jesus could have written: 'It is humbling to realise that the only people Jesus denounced were those who, like me, spent the greater part of their time in teaching religion'?[61]

Vincent Taylor (1887–1968) spent a lifetime in active and unceasing study of the New Testament, and probably more than any other Methodist scholar was widely known outside his own Church. In a superficial judgement it might seem strange to place Taylor in the typical 'Jesus religion' school of recent Methodism, and there could hardly be a stranger contrast than that between him and Findlay. Yet Taylor and Findlay are really concerned about the same fundamental issues – the place of Jesus in Christianity. All Taylor's voluminous publications are concerned with the person and work of Christ. This traditional description of biblical and theological doctrine is how Taylor sees his work. By his own standards he hardly qualifies as a theologian: 'Perhaps the final test of the theologian would be his ability to write a tract.'[62] Most of his writing would seem irrelevant to ordinary men, and one wonders what lasting impression it has made even on preachers, for whom supposedly it was intended. But on the level of careful scholarship, the necessary basis for any understanding of the New Testament, Taylor had few superiors in the world, and probably none in his own country. His magnum opus, *The Gospel according to St Mark* (London 1952), the Macmillan Commentary on St Mark, is described by Nineham as 'the great modern English commentary on the Greek text'.[63]

The comparison with Findlay can profitably be pushed a little further. Findlay was much given to imagination, sometimes inspired, often just fanciful. Taylor never once succumbed to this; indeed, I doubt if he was ever tempted that way. Every statement is firmly anchored in the text of the New Testament. Nothing ever diverted him from patiently and resolutely examining evidence. He dissects the Gospels with the cold precision of a surgeon; even when he is discussing the self-consciousness of Jesus, no emotion is allowed to interfere with the scientific accuracy of the microscope. Only very rarely does he permit a little flight of colourful description. Such expressions are so rare that they are mere aberrations in an otherwise uniformly unexciting style. He was a specialist; some would say a narrow one at that. There is much to be said in favour of this. It avoids that extreme diversification which spoilt the work of some of Taylor's most able contemporaries, and it

[61] *The Way, The Truth and The Life*, p. 147.

[62] *Forgiveness and Reconciliation: A Study in New Testament Theology* (London 1946), p. 225, n. 1.

[63] D. E. Nineham, *Saint Mark* (Harmondsworth 1963), p. 12.

enables a man to make a really thorough study of his subject. But on the deficit side has to be reckoned the isolation from ordinary interests which makes the work of reduced significance as a tool for Christian interpretation. The author becomes so obsessed with the minutiae of the subject that he cannot lift his head to contemplate wider horizons. In his discussion of the person of Christ he raises a long list of questions, most of which would seem quite irrelevant to ordinary people. But when we come to the question, 'Was he in fact the Son of God?', after two-and-a-half volumes we are left with the disappointing observation, 'It is still too soon to answer this vital question fully.'[64]

But one thing can be said, without reservation, in favour of this concentration. Maybe it is, as Taylor admits, dusty scavenging work, but it is the sort of foundation-construction which is essential to a stable edifice. Taylor is at his best in this patient, detailed analysis. When he tries to extend his thought into the realms of systematic theology, there is a noticeable stiffness and stubbornness which does not fit in too well with modern ideas of theology as an open-ended debate. But Taylor would be among the first to question the validity of the contemporary fashion anyway.

Vincent Taylor began his work as a student of the Gospels. He thought that their origin and purpose were revealed in reconstructions of the period preceding the writing of the canonical Gospels. In *Behind the Third Gospel*, Taylor set out to test the 'proto-Luke' theory which had been advanced by B. H. Streeter, by a careful study of the relation between the Markan and non-Markan material in the Third Gospel;[65] and the popularization of the theory is almost entirely due to him.

In this study of 'proto-Luke' he comes very near to a full recognition of the importance of the theological purpose of the Gospels. If he had allowed this theological approach to exert its full influence he would have been a better guide to his contemporaries. As it was, the historical question is always uppermost in his thought, to the detriment of all other aspects of the Gospels. In the end, 'proto-Luke' is considered to be so important because it can be claimed as an independent witness to the historical accuracy of the Gospel records – not because it gives a picture of the living experience of Christ in a very early period of faith.

Vincent Taylor was instrumental in introducing the form-critical methods of Bultmann and Dibelius to British readers. His *The Formation of the Gospel Tradition* (London 1933) gives a thorough survey of the methods employed by these radical continental scholars, and vigorously tests the validity of their theories. As an introduction to a point of view hitherto almost completely unknown to British students, this book filled a vital need. Not least among its advantages is that in place

[64] *The Person of Christ in New Testament Teaching* (London 1958), p. 187.
[65] *Behind the Third Gospel: A Study of the Proto-Luke Hypothesis* (Oxford 1926).

of the infelicitous terms 'paradigm' or 'apophthegm', Taylor suggests the infinitely preferable 'pronouncement-story'. Taylor had a deep knowledge of form criticism, and he was ready to acknowledge its valuable contribution to our understanding of the Gospels. He pays handsome tribute to this contribution in the introduction to his *Commentary on Mark*. 'In many important respects the gospel reflects the worship, theology and catechetical interests of a living Christian Church. In spite of its defects form criticism had forced this conviction upon us.'[66] Yet the total impression is not really favourable to form criticism. *The Formation of the Gospel Tradition*, for all its appearance of impartiality, is heavily biased against this approach. We note the heavy sarcasm of the comment about eyewitnesses: 'If the form-critics are right, the disciples must have been translated to heaven immediately after the Resurrection.'[67] Derogatory epithets are liberally scattered throughout all his references to the form critics: 'imagination at leisure', 'violent exaggeration', 'extreme scepticism', etc. He maintained a stubborn refusal to allow the possibility that liturgical, catechetical and apologetic motives could have been determinative of the contents of the Gospels, all this really because he refused to consider any other factor as important as historical trustworthiness. To this nineteenth-century fetish all other considerations must be secondary. It is not too much to say that in spite of his apparent sympathy with, and considerable use of, the method, Taylor seriously misled British scholarship about form criticism. Because of his damning with faint praise, most native New Testament scholars still think of form criticism as a bad smell emanating from Germany: it is fervently hoped that if we don't take any notice, it will go away. A good deal of the deadness and irrelevance of British New Testament study arises from this over-obsession with gospel historicity.

In 1937, Taylor turned, one suspects with a certain feeling of release, from problems of gospel criticism to theology. He was conscious of the need 'to come out into the open', as he put it, 'to investigate some more vital issue . . . and declare the bearing of his tentative results upon the larger problems of Christian belief and worship'.[68] His chosen field of investigation was the New Testament teaching about salvation, and he wrote on this subject his three famous books: *Jesus and His Sacrifice* (1937); *The Atonement in New Testament Teaching* (1940); *Forgiveness and Reconciliation* (1946).

In these three books there is minute and detailed discussion of every conceivable reference to the meaning of the death of Christ in the New Testament. And in the three books there is the fullest statement of

[66] *Commentary on St Mark* (London 1952), p. vii.

[67] *The Formation of the Gospel Tradition*, p. 41.

[68] *Jesus and His Sacrifice: A Study of the Passion-Sayings in the Gospels* (London 1937), pp. vii, viii.

Taylor's doctrine of the Atonement. Undoubtedly this statement provides a good reaction to the sentimentalized views which had become very prevalent in the 1930s. It emphasizes the centrality of the Cross of Christ, and strikes a chord which has always vibrated in Christian thinking about salvation. It is objective, at least in the sense that salvation is seen to be about our relation with God. And it reminds us of the cost of our redemption, while at the same time showing us how we must actively co-operate in Christ's saving deed. Without question the whole exposition has supported the emphasis on eucharistic worship which is one characteristic of ecumenical liturgical growth in our time. It is interesting to notice, however, that Taylor himself was not much impressed by the significance of eucharistic worship, and was often surprised at the use made of his theology by those who had strong sacramental ideas.

But the theory has real deficiencies. From its first introduction discerning scholars such as Lofthouse and Ryder Smith pointed out the ambiguity of the terminology. In the early discussion of the New Testament evidence, Taylor seems to be expounding a sacrificial view – indeed, the title of the first volume, and the way in which he finds ritual references in the most unpromising material, encourage the view that this is a sacrificial view of atonement. But sacrifice is never defined – sometimes it plainly refers to the post-exilic sacrifices, sometimes to the general notion of giving up for others, sometimes to the cost of the whole activity of Christ. Taylor was aware of this, and in his later writing he seems carefully to avoid this dubious terminology. In the end, he designates his theory 'mediatorial', which considerably extends its significance. Indeed, there is a great deal of value in his insistence on Jesus' identification with men, in life and death, not only showing men the way to live, but providing the necessary means of a new relation with God, a relation which must become real for men if they are to be 'saved'. Deficiencies remain, when we look at the problem from where we are: not enough emphasis on love as the key (this, of course, because the New Testament does not emphasize the connection between love and the Cross); insufficient consideration given to the relations between men here and now. It is good to emphasize in these days the need to get right with God; but no acceptable modern view can ignore the equal need to put things right among men.

Taylor completed his theological studies with three books on christology: *The Names of Jesus* (London 1953), *The Life and Ministry of Jesus* (London 1954) and *The Person of Christ in New Testament Teaching* (London 1958). These three works are almost entirely biblical exposition. In the second he attempts the admittedly hazardous task of giving an account of the life of Jesus, and we find his conclusions lacking conviction. The story is colourless if one is honest in excluding episodes which have a questionable historicity, and Dr Taylor was too honest ever to deny his critical judgment. In the second part of the third work on christology we have Taylor's fullest excursion into the realms of historical and systematic theology. The chief interest of this discussion is the modern presentation of the kenotic theory, which Taylor very strongly affirms. It is characteristic of Taylor's method that one feels driven on, almost overwhelmed by the theory, with little or no chance to demur or hesitate. Perhaps this aspect of his writing is most difficult to accept in an age which prides itself on theological exploration.

Taylor was thorough. No effort was too great, no research too laborious to undertake, in order to lay firm foundations for his expositions. This is the value of his work: scholarship of such a standard of accuracy and persistence as few have attained; single-minded devotion to the truth revealed in the New Testament. I can find no evidence that the ever changed his mind about any important issue. Either he was singularly fortunate in the causes he espoused in his youth, or he had a peculiar ability to maintain his position through thick and thin. If his thought seems already seriously out-dated, this is because the climate of theology is changing so rapidly. Whatever the fashion is, we shall always be able to turn to Vincent Taylor if we really want to know what the New Testament teaches. The material is all there, set out with magnificent thoroughness. Whoever differs from him needs to look well to his scriptural evidence. It is perhaps on the interpretation of the evidence that modern theologians find grounds for hesitation.

(*b*) *Systematic theology*

The beginning of the twentieth century marks a new era in Methodist theology, largely because of the work of John Scott Lidgett, whose Fernley lecture of 1897 has already been discussed. There is in Lidgett a new spirit and approach, a new questioning of the old certainties; theology ceases to be mainly a defence of old positions and becomes more critical and forward-looking. The Methodist theology we have so far described was very largely defensive, backward-looking. But Lidgett produced a new attitude which drew much of its inspiration from F. D. Maurice, himself an innovator and radical critic of established theology.

Lidgett believed that the New Testament concept of divine fatherhood, which he used in his idea of a spiritual principle of atonement, far from being sentimental and vague, is inclusive of sovereignty and, indeed, of judgment; holiness and love are uniquely combined in the God and Father of our Lord Jesus. The question is also faced whether the divine fatherhood is obscured or inhibited by ideas of atonement, righteousness, judgment and the like. Lidgett answered this characteristically twentieth-century problem by reference to the fullness of the revelation of the Father in the Son. God the Father takes sin seriously, he provides in Christ a means of overcoming it, for only in righteousness can the fatherhood of God be made eternally secure; there is no contradiction between the religion of the Sermon on the Mount and that of Paul and other New Testament authors.

While he set fatherhood over against sovereignty, Lidgett was far from denying the providential ordering of human life. But he was sensitive to the challenges in the Great War to popular ideas of providence, and thought that these views were fundamentally mistaken in looking for the wrong effects of God's sovereignty. The purpose of God is to forward spiritual values – Lidgett did not hesitate to say this was effected through creative evolution – and he even claimed that the Great War had furthered spiritual values by demonstrating the futility of basing national aspirations on anything contrary to the will of God revealed in Christ. Mankind now faced the unmistakable challenge of Christ; this is a complete demonstration of the sovereignty of God. Lidgett appears to have thought that men would learn this lesson; he himself was to live on to a ripe old age, seeing the world still unable to keep the peace, still not willing to accept the divine ordering of all things for spiritual purposes.

Lidgett's philosophical approach was more favourable to Plato than to Aristotle, whom he considered an unfortunate influence, especially because of the Thomist separation between nature and grace. He used the familiar argument about eternal values subsisting only in ultimate personality to reply to the post-Great War objections to theism; his whole thesis resting upon the claim that beauty, truth and goodness are unquestioned absolute values – an argument which is unstable when its Platonic substructure is removed. His discussion of the use and misuse of anthropomorphisms is more in tune with later thought about the validity of analogy, and he made a very percipient approach to the idea of cause.[69]

His lifetime of residence in Bermondsey gave him a sharpened sense of the need for the social witness of the Christian Church; his zeal was put into action rather than into print, but from several published essays and addresses we can discern the drift of his thought. Sometimes outspoken in condemnation (the House of Lords committed 'an unpardonable offence'[70] in its contemptuous rejection of the Licensing Bill sponsored by the Churches), he believed in state action to put right the social wrongs of the day. He was one of the early advocates of legislation for social betterment, when most Christians still clung to the

[69] *God, Christ and the Church* (London 1927), Chapter 7: 'Anthropomorphism: Its Use and Misuse'.

[70] *Apostolic Ministry* (London 1909), p. 72.

laissez-faire concept which limited Christian social action to personal persuasion and amelioration of individual conditions. Education was equally a lifelong concern of Lidgett; in his Presidential Address to the students of Westminster College, he drew heavily upon the words of his grandfather, John Scott, Westminster's first Principal; his concept of education was strongly influenced by the dictum 'That as good an education should be given to the poor as their children can receive'.[71] He did not believe that education could solve all problems, but he held out before prospective teachers the ideal of developing full personal responsibility and awareness of life in all their pupils.

Lidgett says the promotion of Christian unity was one of his most important activities. His contributions in this direction were notably in the realm of action, as is witnessed by his early leadership in Free Church affairs, his part in the preparation for the Lambeth Appeal of 1920, and his guidance and inspiration in the negotiation for Methodist Union, which culminated in 1932 in his being the first President of the newly united Methodist Church. But in the course of this activity he did from time to time publish some account of the theological basis of his convictions about unity. An essay he contributed to the volume, *Towards Reunion*, afterwards reprinted in his collection entitled *God, Christ and the Church* (London 1927), shows how a proper understanding of the Kingdom of God and its relation to the Church necessitates the view that the Church must be one. Especially it is the function of the Church, as the divinely appointed instrument of the unity of mankind, which requires her own unity. In the same essay he states, and then refutes, the idea of spiritual but not corporate unity, and the theory that divisions in the Church, having arisen through concern for the truth, must necessarily be good, and ought to be continued. He saw the urgency of church unity in the light of the world's need for unity already being expressed in the plans to form the League of Nations; in the evangelistic responsibility of the Christian Church; and in the application of Christianity to moral and social problems. His ecumenical concern was entirely consonant with his intense desire to see the Christian faith applied to political and social issues.

Lidgett was an enthusiastic supporter of the Lambeth Appeal of 1920, which he described as 'the greatest ecclesiastical event since the Reformation'; he was indeed influential in the informal discussions which led up to the Appeal, and his advocacy of it, especially among Free Churchmen, was very persuasive. His essays on the Appeal, on the progress made and the position which resulted (see *God, Christ and the Church*, Part II), are extremely valuable contemporary accounts of the post-Lambeth period of Church relations. Lidgett was emphatic

[71] Ibid., 'The Ideals of National Education', p. 138.

that episcopacy is essential to the real unity of the Church, and he thought that, with proper safeguards and assurances, Free Church ministers were in duty bound to accept the extension of their ministry by being joined to episcopacy.

In his emphasis on the Fatherhood of God and on the nature and unity of the Church, and his pioneering work for the social application of the Gospel, John Scott Lidgett has been very influential in subsequent Methodist literature; by his writing as well as by his activity he may well merit the title of 'the greatest Methodist since Wesley'.

The idea that Methodist theology is 'a theology of experience' may be an inaccurate or misleading description of Wesley's thought; but it is basically true of the systematic theology of Methodism from 1900 to 1932. This theology is centred on the experience of salvation; God is thought of mainly in terms of his redeeming activity, and all other doctrines are subservient to this evangelical concern. It is true that there were some notable discussions of God in himself, so to speak, such as Frederic W. Platt's *Immanence and Christian Thought: Implications and Suggestions* (London 1915), and the references in John Shaw Banks's *Manual of Christian Doctrine* (London 1887) and Maldwyn Hughes's *Christian Foundations: An Introduction to Christian Doctrine* (London 1927) to the nature of God are quite significant. But the main emphasis is on the fact that God is a God who saves. Christian experience is regarded as beginning in conversion; George Jackson's Vanderbilt lectures for 1908, *The Fact of Conversion* (London 1908), are an interesting study of the strains to which traditional ideas were being subjected. The new science of psychology was being applied to religion with apparently disastrous consequences. Jackson boldly used psychological insights to expound the meaning of conversion. While psychology does not explain the fact of conversion, it does supply useful categories by which to describe it, such as 'the expulsive power of a new affection'. This theology of experience can best be illustrated by reference to three books written over a period of thirty years. These theologies of experience are not exclusively concerned with religious experience on a subjective level. They involve the presentation of Christian doctrine from the point of view of Christian experience; they select those aspects of doctrine which are relevant to experience and try to relate religious experience to other facts of life.

Joseph Agar Beet, in *The New Life in Christ: A Study in Personal Religion* (London 1895), examines the way in which man's need is met in the revelation of the Trinity. One of his students remembered Beet as 'an advanced, even dangerous thinker', and there was an occasion when the orthodoxy of his views on human destiny was seriously questioned. The book comes alive when new life in Christ is expounded. This new relation to Christ which comes through faith introduces the believer to a new relation to the moral law, which can now be fulfilled; a new relation to our physical environment which, although often antagonistic to spiritual development, can be used by a Christian for spiritual ends. Life in Christ may be a conflict requiring continual faithfulness, but growth in spiritual things is certainly possible.

In *Spiritual Religion: A Study of the Relation of Facts to Faith* (London 1901), John G. Tasker sets out to show the relation between religious experience and other facts available to human knowledge. Especially, he argues, religion is not against science; those who think it is often wrongly assume that science is the same as materialism. Tasker saw the significance of biological science, and boldly asserted: 'The Darwinian biology has restored man to the place of honour and dignity from which the Copernican astronomy seemed to have dethroned him.'[72] So human knowledge of God is possible; nor can it be denied to be possible on the ground that it is never complete. Knowledge of God is discoverable from nature, but nature is not the same as God, and for a full knowledge we must look to Christ; when we find God in him he sends us back to nature with open eyes. Tasker insists that the true piety of Methodism is not subjective or emotional; it is based upon scripture and the divine ordinances, not merely upon feeling. Yet there are serious inadequacies in Tasker's exposition; no significant place is given to the Church, and his agreement with Wordsworth's view of the Eucharist as 'No sacrifice, but a life-giving feast'[73] reveals a less than satisfactory view of church life. Yet credit should be given to Tasker for his insistence that spiritual religion is not expressed in separation from the world, but in involvement with it. This involvement means the application of the Gospel to social life; by this, future Churches will live or die. This, again, is a necessary refutation of the erroneous notion that a theology of experience must lead to a world-negating attitude.

In *The Christian Experience: A Study in the Theology of Fellowship* (London 1926), C. Ryder Smith set out 'to show that the Christian experience harmonizes with the rest of human experience, and completes it'.[74] The intention is to follow a strictly scientific method, dealing with facts, implicates and postulates. Psychology was the science which Ryder Smith used to illustrate his theme; especially what would nowadays be called social or group psychology, for he was very insistent on underlining the societary aspects of human life. This underlying principle of relationship encourages the view that the divine purpose includes freedom for man to choose, and Christ gives fuller freedom to those who accept his friendship. This conviction about the restoring power of God extends to the natural world; no doubt this world is not

[72] Op. cit., pp. 46–7.
[73] Ibid., p. 156.
[74] Op. cit., p. 10.

what God intended it to be, but perhaps it is in process of becoming that. Here again we touch upon a theology of nature; the work of the Holy Spirit is in art and science as well as in specifically religious realms. All human activity may reflect divine activity, so sociological insights into what man is doing may very well help us to understand what God is doing. Ryder Smith's theology was not esoteric; it answered real questions in a way people could understand. There are two reasons, he says, for believing in God: (1) I know God; (2) I cannot do without him. Theistic proofs, including Kant's moral arguments, belong to the second reason, but they do not play a very significant part. Again, an ordinary man would understand his assertion that because God is personal, he will be influenced by our attitude, and therefore intercession can be seen as a reasonable and natural process.

So these Methodist scholars expounded a theology of experience. It is significant that all three in different ways demonstrated their ability to grasp and expound theological truths in the light of contemporary knowledge. The pity is that all three turned their attention and gave their chief efforts to biblical studies; thus the work they began tended to languish, to a large extent neglected by more than one generation of Methodist scholars. The resulting impoverishment of the theology of experience is apparent both inside and outside Methodism.

(*c*) *Atonement in the twentieth century*

Methodists were more fortunate than perhaps they have ever realized in the appearance on the theological scene of William F. Lofthouse. In 1906, his *Ethics and Atonement* was published; the date is significant, for in this work he advanced ideas about atonement which refuted the old satisfaction theory. Together with his *Altar, Cross, and Community* (London 1921), this book advanced a theory of the way of salvation which even today, sixty years later, seems startlingly fresh and modern. I do not know quite how Lofthouse got away with it less than ten years after Lidgett had been threatened with a doctrinal charge for his much less revolutionary *The Spiritual Principle of the Atonement*.

Lofthouse breaks away from the traditional substitutionary theories by approaching the question from an ethical standpoint. Ethical standards must be determinative of the relation between man and God. These ethical standards are those expressed in the Bible, which are manifestly more advanced than general ethical ideas. The Bible recognizes as virtues such attitudes as long-suffering, kindness, meekness, and so on, which are not natural virtues. But patriotism, justifiable self-assertion and reasonable self-love are not included in the list of biblical virtues. So we have to take notice of the close relation between morality and religion, and to Lofthouse it seems as if morality is determinative of religion. He goes too far when he writes: 'The early writers on

Christianity dwell far oftener on what the Christian has to do than on what has been done for him by his Saviour',[75] but the point is sound; in the Bible morality and religion are indissolubly joined.

The real problem of reconciliation, or restoring right relations, is how contrition may be aroused so that the wrongdoer becomes forgiveable. Clearly Lofthouse, having begun with relations between people, is here thinking of relations with God; but it is necessary to remember that he never separated the two relationships. He has no room for a view of reconciliation with God which leaves out reconciliation among men. The problem being how we can be aroused to contrition, the main emphasis in Lofthouse's interpretation of the work of Christ is that he entered our situation, suffered with us, and thus mediates between God and us by arousing our contrition. An extended illustration which combines the parables of the Prodigal Son and the Rebellious Servant shows how Lofthouse saw the saving work of Christ in terms of identification and persuasion to contrition through ultimate self-offering in death. This involves a complete rejection of any substitutionary theory, which is dismissed as unbiblical, unethical and ineffective.

This view can clearly be criticized for denigrating the value of Christ's death: if it is not a substitutionary sacrifice, is it at all important? Lofthouse replies to this by asserting that even to Paul the death of Christ is not seen as efficacious by itself. 'The value of the death is that it made possible the resurrection.'[76] Many of the New Testament references to sacrifice are really about our self-offering; often the reference to Christ's sacrifice is the basis of an appeal for us to sacrifice ourselves. According to the New Testament, what is required of us is not involvement in questionable ethical ceremonies, but the sacrifice of a broken spirit and a good life. Supremely Christ effects this reconciliation by virtue of his wonderful personality, for as the model of our relation with God is found in communities like the family, so through the persuasion of a gracious person like Jesus we grow into right relationships with a personal God.

Lofthouse's doctrine of the Atonement seems to me to have very great relevance for our present situation. No doubt he did tend to undervalue the concept of sacrifice, which indicates its universal appeal by reappearing from time to time. Incidentally, no one who ever attended the Holy Communion conducted by Lofthouse would have any doubt that a non-sacrificial interpretation of the Eucharist, which he held, could have profound and almost unbearably moving significance. The wonder is that his view seems to have taken so long to influence popular ideas of the meaning of the Cross. This may be in part explained by his limitations as a public advocate; also, the popularity

[75] *Ethics and Atonement*, p. 2.

[76] Ibid., p. 191.

of nineteenth-century evangelical hymns and the general conservative tendency of popular religion no doubt contributed. But it remains a sad commentary on Methodist theology that Lofthouse's views on the Atonement have made so little mark on the interpretation of the Cross.

Maldwyn Hughes, the first Principal of Wesley House, wrote early in the 1920s on *What is the Atonement? A Study of the Passion of God in Christ* (London 1924), continuing the main line of Lofthouse's argument. Hughes was in fact more sympathetic than Lofthouse to the idea of sacrifice, and he sets out the history of the doctrine, although not in a very interesting manner.

A more exciting exposition of the meaning of the Cross is in W. Russell Maltby's *Christ and His Cross* (London 1935). This was the first Cato lecture. Maltby seeks the meaning of the Cross in the total life of Jesus; but in order to appreciate his view of atonement, we have to see it against the background of his concept of Jesus. He told the Copec Conference in 1924: 'There is now within reach of the Church a richer, more reasonable, more universal, and more significant message than we have ever had . . . within our own day the Christian Church has recovered the significance of our Lord's earthly life.'[77] This is the theme of *The Significance of Jesus* (Toronto 1929). The life of Jesus, so confidently known – Maltby says it is surprising how well we know him – reveals the reality of God, his compassion and interest. This life shows us the way to live in the fullness of God's love. The Gospel is the incredible story of God coming near to us in Jesus. Jesus is the one who inevitably draws to himself, and so to God, those who look at him. This is a wonderful message – a message which filled to overflowing such great chapels as Brunswick, Leeds, and the City Temple, London, when Leslie Weatherhead preached it. Many interesting repercussions arise from this Gospel: systematic theology tends to be demoted, for one thing, and a definitely anti-intellectual bias is introduced. Not that Maltby was useless with intellectuals – William Temple said that he was without question the most effective evangelist of students in his day; and many who owed their souls to Maltby became the leading scholars of the Church. But the bias cannot be denied. 'Religion', he says, 'was not given to enable the wise and prudent to complete their intellectual scheme.'[78]

But the more significant feature of this Gospel is that it really contained no specific doctrine of the Cross; or more exactly, its doctrine of the Cross cannot be separated from its message of the life of Jesus. 'He respected as no other has done the sanctity of the human personality, and He died rather than invade it, as He died in order to win it for God.'[79]

[77] *Obiter Scripta*, ed. Francis B. James (London 1952), p. 21.
[78] Cf. *The Significance of Jesus*, pp. 40–1.
[79] Ibid., p. 30.

The death of Jesus is explained, not in terms of divine wrath being appeased, nor as a punishment being exacted; not even as a punishment being borne. It is the inevitable outcome of the sort of person Jesus was, and the sort of people the Jews, and we, are. 'They fought against Him . . . He would not fight; He would not fly: they would not change. So they crucified Him.'[80]

Considered as a doctrine of the Atonement, Maltby's views are disappointing. In so far as he can be classified, he is nearest to the moral influence theory. But the minimizing tendency of that theory somehow does not fit. This is because of the overwhelming importance to Maltby of the reality of Jesus. Along with Findlay and Weatherhead, he had an extraordinary grasp of the reality of Jesus; known in personal experience as the Saviour. As Weatherhead said to Findlay when they visited Maltby on his deathbed, 'I've come to see the master of us all.' The weakness of Maltby's approach is its blatant individualism – a problem shared by all theologies of experience. But it may be that, with all our modern concern for community and social responsibility, there is still not a substitute for that living experience of Christ of which Maltby was such an outstanding exponent and example.

An approach to the subject of salvation which promises to deal more satisfactorily with the proper concern for community which we find lacking even in Maltby is the 'societary concept' of C. Ryder Smith. He deals briefly but effectively with the subject in *The Christian Experience* (1926),[81] and there is a full discussion, mainly of the biblical teaching, in *The Bible Doctrine of Salvation* (1941). The psychological phenomena which emerge from Ryder Smith's study of societary behaviour indicate four conditions which must be fulfilled. The saviour must identify himself with the saved; he must be like him, yet unlike him; he must feel the horror of a sinner's fault more than the sinner does himself; and the one to be saved must be willing. All these conditions are fully met in the life and death of Christ. They are anticipated in the Old Testament struggles after the truth, which come to a climax in the 'prophetic servant' conception. Ryder Smith was a profound student of the Old Testament; his exposition of the meaning of the ritual of the Day of Atonement is not easy to better for clarity, accuracy and insight. He recognizes that the key to the intelligent worshipper's attitude to the sacrificial ritual is thankful obedience. He must thank God who has provided this way of approach to himself, and he must obediently use the means God has provided. But even with this lofty conception of the meaning of sacrifice, Ryder Smith has no doubt that the sacrificial system is a quite secondary source of the New Testament understanding of the death of Christ.

[80] *Christ and His Cross*, p. 72.
[81] Op. cit., pp. 14, 104.

Ryder Smith does not deal much with the perennial problems of Atonement theory, but when he does, he is illuminating and forward-looking. For instance, one old problem is whether salvation is effected by a change in God or a change in man – a problem which we have seen Maltby approach from the angle of relationship. For Ryder Smith there is no doubt that the new relationship involves changes on both sides. That there must be a change in man goes without saying. But equally there is a change in God, if we take the idea of relationship seriously. God is affected by the sinner's return – not only in attitude, but also in activity; for God can now do for his returning child what he could not do so long as the child was estranged from him. This hints at the notion of the suffering of God, but does not develop it.

This exposition of the Atonement is based upon a most meticulous and exhaustive study of the biblical evidence. It is part of the greatness and integrity of Ryder Smith as a biblical scholar that he never systematized the evidence in line with his own theories. But commendable though this is, it leads to tediousness and lack of clear definition, and this becomes increasingly obvious in his other Bible Doctrine books. Excellent as they are as books of reference, they are exceedingly tedious to read as expositions of their themes. In fact, there is much more incisive clarity in *The Christian Experience*, which, if one may say it reverently, is not cluttered up with so many texts! No doubt Ryder Smith regarded the Bible Doctrine books as more scholarly, which in one sense they are. But for an interesting and urgent attempt to present the Christian message to his contemporaries, the early book is far better. Possibly the real import of this is that Ryder Smith was another systematic theologian whose work was vitiated by an over-emphasis on biblical study. No doubt expositions of Bible teaching are nearer to systematic theology than erudite commentaries, which early Methodist scholars ended their days writing. But still these expositions fail to make much impression on anyone, simply because they are not asking our questions; and by not asking our questions, they often fail to give us an answer we will listen to.

(*d*) *The Church*

Methodist teaching on the Church is not an outstanding feature of books written in the first quarter of the twentieth century. This has encouraged some to conclude that Methodist doctrine is really individualistic and subjective. It is true that this doctrine was not so fiercely disputed as at the end of the nineteenth century, partly because episcopal and non-episcopal Churches drew further apart as the Free Church movement developed. But Hugh Price Hughes, the chief Methodist architect of Free Churchism, was accused of 'high church' views in his youth. All his life he preferred liturgical worship, and he helped Dr

Berry to found the Free Church Federation partly to encourage the non-episcopal Churches to appreciate their Catholic inheritance. He distrusted the notion of the 'Invisible Church' because he believed that it encouraged 'ecclesiastical vagrants' to shirk the responsibility of belonging to actual visible Churches.[82] Hughes asserted that the mark of a true branch of the Catholic Church is the presence of Christ through his indwelling spirit, manifested in holy life and fellowship. The whole point of this emphasis on catholicity was that it was being claimed for the Free Churches, and that included Methodism.

John Shaw Banks, whose *Manual of Christian Doctrine* was the standard textbook of several generations of Methodist preachers, had some critical things to say about episcopacy, but he was not uninterested in the Church. He thought that Roman and Anglo-Catholic views were too much based on 'taken for granted', and the New Testament says more about the Kingdom of God than about the Church. He saw no reason for church order to be uniform. Indeed, the unity for which the Saviour prayed is oneness of faith and feeling, and is compatible with its existence in separate communities. 'Unless outward unity is plainly commanded, outward division is no sin.'[83]

Another indication that Methodist theology was never exclusively individualistic is the continual emphasis on fellowship. The earlier Methodist theologians had regarded this as one of the primary marks of the Church. This view was reiterated by A. W. Harrison, in *Methodism in the Modern World*, Chapter VII, 'The Church': 'If there was any distinctive note that Methodism contributed to the doctrine of the Church it was the emphasis that it laid on Christian fellowship.'[84] The importance of fellowship was seen by Wilfred R. Wilkinson, in his *Religious Experience: The Methodist Fundamental* (London 1928), as a more effective way of personal knowledge of God. 'A lone soul may find God: a group of worshipping saints feel and know the presence easily and sooner.'[85] This view is also expressed in terms of man's nature as a social animal by Francis Neil Shimmin in his *Permanent Values of Religion* (London 1914), and even more strongly by Atkinson Lee in *Sociality: The Art of Living Together* (London 1927). Fellowship is the cure for the world's ills, and the way of human fulfilment. Lee thought that separate Churches had been more concerned with a proprietary branding of the sheep than with the building of folds for their nurture and protection. The only answer is 'a World-Church', which he conceived somewhat naively as open to 'all those who admire, respect and enquire after the ultimate values . . . having for its object the worship

[82] Dora P. Hughes, *The Life of Hugh Price Hughes* (London 1904), p. 466.
[83] Op. cit., p. 190.
[84] J. Scott Lidgett & Bryan H. Reed (eds), *Methodism in the Modern World* (London 1929); A. W. Harrison, 'The Church', pp. 139–65.
[85] Op. cit., p. 215.

of deity under the aspects of the great values'.[86]

Yet it has to be admitted that although Methodist writers do not lack interest in the doctrine of the Church, this was not their first interest. Perhaps more quickly than other denominations, Methodists realized the increasing indifference to the Christian faith which has characterized the twentieth century, and they saw the need for an expression of personal relationship with God as the prime need of the time. Even before World War I, F. N. Shimmin wrote: 'The present age is an age of religious indifference.'[87] He did not entirely blame the Church for this state of affairs:

> The Church, aroused by the hostility of some, and alarmed by the indifference of others to her Gospel, has been engaged in a serious and sincere effort to make herself familiar with the teaching of her Founder . . . It is being discovered that what Christ taught is not only different from what the Church has sometimes taught, but even more different from what a professing Christian society believes and practises.[88]

Shimmin was not alone in thinking that too much concern with church organization and authenticity was diverting attention from the central theme of evangelical religion, man's fellowship with God, arising from a sense of forgiveness. Some, indeed, blamed the Churches for neglect of personal religion. Thomas Cook was openly anti-church in his exposition of New Testament holiness, and many 'holiness' writers followed his lead. Samuel Chadwick was a 'high church' Methodist, but he roundly criticized the Churches for missing their opportunity to evangelize the nation after World War I. The Church is too much concerned to save itself, he asserted, to save anyone else. He was opposed to ecumenism because it was becoming the new religion. 'Copec has become the common religion. Lambeth and Methodist union have taken the ginger out of the opposition.'

The holiness movement placed great stress on the work of the Holy Spirit, and insisted that the Spirit must always be seen as superior to the Church. A. Lewis Humphries in *The Holy Spirit in Faith and Experience* (London 1911) took issue with Bishop Gore's interpretation which claimed that bestowal of the Spirit was the exclusive privilege of the bishops of the Church, agreeing with W. L. Walker that this was 'one of the most disastrous mistakes that has ever been made in the history of Christianity'.[90] But Humphries could agree with Gore that 'the church is the special and convenanted sphere of His regular and uniform

[86] *Sociality*, p. 218.
[87] *Permanent Values of Religion*, p. 3.
[88] Ibid., pp. 15–16.
[89] Op. cit., p. 200.

operation, the place where He is pledged to dwell and to work', provided that 'church' means the fellowship of all holy souls, and is not restricted to some particular Christian society.[90]

It is understandable that among Methodists there was considerable questioning of episcopal claims, because biblical scholarship was the most formative influence in Methodist thought in the first half of the twentieth century. A. S. Peake spoke for many Wesleyans as well as for Primitive Methodists in asserting that the Church did not write the New Testament and by replacing the authority of the Church by the Bible, appealing to conscience quickened by the Holy Spirit. It is noteworthy that, in his two most popular expositions of belief, *Christianity, Its Nature and Its Truth* and *The Bible, Its Origin, Its Significance and Its Abiding Worth*, Peake makes no reference to the sacraments, and constantly insists on the supremacy of the Bible over the Church. But J. A. Findlay to some extent redressed this by seeing that in the New Testament the Church is permanently important, not merely a means of establishing a Christian society. In his impressive study of Paul he asserts that Paul was not the rock on which the Church was founded, but rather the Moses who struck the rock. In spite of his profound understanding of the personal element in Christian discipleship, Findlay realized the importance of the Church, and in his later work he foresaw the possibility of a complete collapse of organized religion in the West, but if this happens 'it will only mean that the Churches must die that the Church may be born'.[91]

But biblical studies not only demonstrated the importance of the Church in Christian theology; they increasingly emphasized the theological basis of church unity. Methodists were excited by the Edinburgh Conference in 1910; and the experience of the movement which culminated in Methodist Union in 1932 encouraged them to realize both the difficulties and the necessity of wider union between the Churches. That this wider union should not be based on indifference to the Church, but on full realization of the place of the Church in fundamental Christian thinking, was conclusively demonstrated by Robert Newton Flew in the period immediately after Methodist Union. In *Jesus and His Church* (London 1938), Flew set out the New Testament emphasis on the doctrine of the Church. Using the insights of the contemporary emphasis on the Kingdom of God, he argued that Jesus intended his followers to form a society to carry on his work. The band of disciples is the nucleus of the Church which Jesus founded to be the new Israel, a community bound together by allegiance to Christ, having a message about Christ and a mission to propagate this message to all mankind. These insights into the nature of the Church, Flew showed to be sup-

[90] Ibid.

[91] *The Way, The Truth and The Life*, p. 292.

ported by the teaching of the epistles. Furthermore, this emphasis on the centrality of the Church puts questions about the primacy of Peter and the status and functions of the apostles in their right perspective. Since the publication of *Jesus and His Church* there have been many developments of the theme by theologians of all denominations, but there is no doubt that Flew's work has a pioneer character which has focused the attention of Methodism, and possibly of the whole Church, upon this doctrine which was for so long a neglected part of the Christian message.

The movement towards unity among the Churches has been strongly supported in Methodism, not chiefly because the future of separate denominations seems so insecure, but because it can claim strong biblical support and because it seems to be a necessary prerequisite for the effective proclamation of Christ in the twentieth century. It is no accident that these two convictions concerning the authority of the Bible and the necessity for evangelism have been the strongest influences in Methodist theology in this century. A Methodism which loses interest in ecumenical affairs would be unfaithful to the most formative influences in its tradition. There have been disagreements about schemes of union, and about the place of the ordained ministry in the life of the Church. But important as these are, they are always secondary to biblical revelation and evangelism.

Even a cursory glance at Methodist teaching on the sacraments during the early part of the twentieth century reveals the interesting fact that it was the biblical scholars who mainly were responsible for the ambivalent attitude towards the 'divine ordinances'. J. H. Moulton was an ultra-Protestant when it came to matters of ecclesiology, and to him it was a matter of indifference how Christ's command to eat and drink in memory of him should be carried out:

> When we are dealing with means of grace, the only thing that matters is the grace. If that really comes all is well . . . In the eyes of the angels there is no difference that matters between the devout Roman kneeling before the altar and the devout Quaker feeding on Christ while he eats his supper at home. Our own practice differs widely, but we can thankfully acknowledge that the Real Presence is as sure for each of them as for ourselves.[92]

In the same vein Moulton regarded every common meal as a reminder of the offering of Christ's life. This may be only a commemorative view, but its value depends entirely on who is being commemorated.

> When we are bidden to let every meal remind us that our Lord and Master died for us, to make his offered life the very food of our soul,

[92] *Religion and Religions*, p. 40.

> I find it hard to understand what we could possibly add to the commemorative parable which would enhance its infinite value.[93]

Arthur S. Peake, the great Primitive Methodist 'doctor', gave very little place to the Church or the sacraments in his popular expositions, and when, in 1932, it came to negotiations leading to Methodist Union, it was Peake who was responsible for the clause in the Deed of Union which expressly denies that ordination transmits a priesthood differing in kind from the priesthood of the whole Church. To Findlay the sacraments are 'love tokens'. He favoured a theory of the real presence which saw this reality in the sudden presence of Christ on social occasions. His interpretation of the traditional 'Marana tha' saying was: 'We can imagine that when they met for the common meal, they would look to the empty place, and say, "Our Lord, come back".'[94]

Yet Methodists continued to celebrate the Lord's Supper 'with the greatest simplicity' and 'awesome solemnity', as Wilfred Wilkinson put it. The common custom in Methodist churches was for communicants to walk to the communion table and kneel. Here they 'eat and drink with one longing only, to commune with Christ in His dying'.[95] While the emphasis on the Lord's Supper tended to be strongest among the Wesleyans and the 'established Methodists', 'enthusiastic Methodists' like Brice and Chadwick also greatly valued the sacraments. The link between evangelism and the sacraments was brought out more clearly by J. Ernest Rattenbury in *The Eucharistic Hymns of John and Charles Wesley* (London 1948). It is interesting to note that, even when emphasizing the sacrificial aspect of the Lord's Supper, Rattenbury insists that this does not require a separate priestly order. The whole Church is expressing its priestly character.

> When we affirm the corporate character of the Church; that the Ministry is the instrument of a sacred priestly body and not a substitute for it; that the propitiatory oblations of individual priests are meaningless if not abhorrent – then the importance of priesthood and oblation become intelligible. The Christian Church itself as a corporation is the Priest, not any member of it. Ministers are the instrument of the priesthood.[96]

The researches and views of Rattenbury have been very formative of more recent Methodist sacramental theology, but the suspicions of ordinances and ceremonies which can be merely superficial remain in many Methodists.

[93] Ibid., p. 38.
[94] *The Way, The Truth and The Life*, p. 35.
[95] *Religious Experience*, pp. 223, 227.
[96] Op. cit., p. viii.

(*e*) *Christian perfection*

I have already made the point that Methodist theology is not a different genus from all other theology. But there is one doctrine, Christian Perfection or Scriptural Holiness, which is especially emphasized by Methodists, and sometimes regarded as their exclusive property. It is necessary, therefore, to consider the way in which Methodism in the last century has used and interpreted the doctrine of Perfection, which John Wesley regarded as 'the grand depositum which God has lodged with the people called Methodists; and for the sake of propagating this chiefly He appeared to have raised us up'.[97]

There are two strands of this tradition traceable in Methodist thought. The scholarly, official exposition of Pope, Platt, Perkins and Flew continues the absorbing interest of the doctrine, and seeks to interpret it in the light of contemporary ideas of human nature and responsibilities. The other tradition, equally expounding the biblical roots and Wesleyan emphasis, sees in the doctrine the true basis for Methodist enthusiasm and longing for personal holiness. This tradition, sometimes regarded as the poor relation of the official orthodoxy, has been maintained by the influence of Cliff College and the Holiness Conventions. The authors belonging to this school write directly for the people rather than for scholars and preachers. Among them I shall refer to Thomas Champness, Thomas Cook and Samuel Chadwick.

There is a further point of great interest in the argument that Hugh Price Hughes belonged to both camps and, perhaps more than anyone else, bridged the gap between experience and expression – a gap that has often puzzled and challenged those outside Methodism who sympathize with this doctrine.

Pope's treatment of the doctrine is typically learned and thorough. Although he does not refer to Wesley except in the historical section, he clearly thought Wesley was justified in regarding the doctrine as scriptural. Pope brings out the significance of the work of the Holy Spirit in this aspect of Christian belief and experience. Sanctification is possible and means a real change in the human heart, because the Spirit operates within man's own nature. 'The Spirit's work in us is made our own.'[98] For the same reason, sanctification is total – 'it is of the whole man viewed in all the constituents of his nature'.[99] In all this, Pope is close to Wesley, even though he does not quote Wesley as an authority. But he does advance on Wesley's views, notably in connection with more modern problems. Holiness is 'accommodated' to our finite condition; perfection is a 'probation': that is, it is never absolute, and it can be lost. Pope thought that genuine holiness must be unconscious: 'there is . . . no consciousness more unconscious of self, than that of

[97] Wesley, *Letters*, viii, 238. [98] *Compendium*, iii, 40. [99] Ibid., iii, 35.

perfect holiness and love.'[100] This is really a denial of Wesley's view, that a person can know himself 'made perfect in love', and in certain conditions ought to bear witness to what he knows. In another aspect of his exposition, Pope was more opposed to later developments than to Wesley. He warned against the idea of a second blessing, if this implies the possibility of a higher life than that of faith.

The most telling criticism of this doctrine is that it avoids consideration of ethical responsibility by concentrating on inner experience. Pope is not entirely absolved from the criticism, in that his view of ethical effects is limited to personal response. But he is insistent that only through love can perfection be manifest. Unfortunately, his concept of love is limited by an excess of emphasis on individualism which he shared with all his contemporaries.

The fact that F. W. Platt, a Methodist, contributed the article on 'Christian Perfection' to the *Encylopedia of Religion and Ethics* (1917) indicates continuing Methodist interest, and perhaps leadership, in this doctrine. In addition to a typically orthodox exposition, Platt raises new questions. Is this really scriptural doctrine? Yes, but 'holiness', the biblical idea, has not the same connotation as 'perfection'. Holiness refers to a quality of character, not the achievement of a status; this is firmly rooted in Christ, for he is both the example set before us and the One through whom grace is continually available to those who have faith in him. We can never attain to such holiness as no longer to be dependent on the merits of Christ – this is the answer to Lutheran objections; therefore the term 'sinlessness' is to be avoided, since it inevitably implies an end of the sinner's dependence on Christ. Platt's exposition advances a little, pointing out the corporate as well as the individual aspects of holiness expressed as love.

Harold William Perkins, in his *The Doctrine of Christian or Evangelical Perfection* (London 1927), covers the familiar ground of biblical and historical expositions – incidentally, it is this doctrine, more than any other, which has directed Methodist thinking to historical theology. Perkins suggests 'maturity' as a better modern expression of the biblical teaching, thus anticipating the New English Bible rendering. In claiming that the emphasis of Methodism on obedience in ordinary life is superior to the Roman Catholic teaching on asceticism, he perhaps unwittingly points to the danger of Methodism trying to be both popular and demanding. As Richard Green wrote in 1890, 'Methodism may not be adapted to meet the preferences of the people of this country generally.'[101]

The most scholarly and competent study of this doctrine by a Method ist writer is R. Newton Flew's *The Idea of Perfection in Christian Theology*

[100] Ibid., p. 56.
[101] *The Mission of Methodism* (London 1890), p. 170.

(London 1934). This book inaugurated a new concern in Methodism for spirituality and, by the remarkably wide sympathies of the author, places the Methodist doctrine in the context of Catholic tradition. The biblical exposition arises out of the contemporary emphasis on eschatology and the Kingdom of God, but interprets this differently from the Barthian 'theology of crisis', which was very influential at the time.

Flew was an ardent and convinced follower of the Wesleys, but this did not inhibit his searching criticisms of Wesley's theology. 'The stress on the consciousness and deliberate intention of the agent is the most formidable defect in Wesley's doctrine of the ideal.'[102] He pointed out the failure of the Wesleys to relate perfection to human relations: Wesley's hymns 'do not explore with any success the relations of men with one another'.[103] Flew thought that part of the trouble with Wesley's admittedly logical and spiritual exposition of the divine intention and ability to remove sin is the assumption that 'sin' is something which can be taken out of a man, like a decayed tooth. Flew's deeper psychological understanding of human nature convinced him that this is too naïve and superficial; if this is that 'sin' which Wesley said could be completely removed, then the doctrine of 'freedom from all sin' is not as significant as it appears to be. Furthermore, Wesley's teaching about 'assurance' so easily degenerates into what Ronald Knox called 'salvation by feeling'. This is an unjustifiable criticism of Wesley, but has more than a little truth in it when applied to Wesley's followers. Wesley is partly to blame for this, by his insistence that the experience of full salvation is communicable. 'A man may bear testimony to his awareness of a God who is willing and able to 'destroy the last remains of sin'. He cannot know himself well enough to claim that God has already done it.'[104]

Flew's conclusions are a significant blend of sympathetic criticism and enthusiastic advocacy of Wesley's teaching. He believed that Methodism ought not to neglect this part of its heritage: properly understood, the doctrine of Christian Perfection is one of the important theological contributions which Methodism has to offer to the Ecumenical Movement. The connection between Perfection (or Spirituality) and Ecumenism was undoubtedly firmly established in Flew's mind, and owed a great deal to his wide-ranging knowledge of Catholic spirituality.

The other holiness tradition in Methodism has become closely identified with Cliff College and the now defunct *Joyful News*, both founded by Thomas Champness. His *Plain Talks on Perfection* was published in 1897, and along with J. A. Beet's *Holiness As Understood*

[102] *The Idea of Perfection*, p. 333.
[103] Ibid., p. 340.
[104] Ibid., p. 377.

by the Writers of the Bible: A Bible Study (London 1880) is the foundation of the Holiness Movement in Methodism. Beet's biblical exposition lays emphasis on the real possibility of the gift of holiness, which is only obtained by self-consecration. Beet makes much of the obedience required; but the experience later described by 'holiness' writers is hardly mentioned. Champness, too, emphasizes that holiness implies a high standard of conduct, which cannot be obtained without the aid of the Holy Spirit. The theme of *Joyful News*, in which the *Plain Talks* first appeared, was the constant aim of goodness and love. Neither inward witness nor claims to perfection are as important as earnest endeavour after goodness: 'Let us live high, and talk low. Professing little, let us possess much.'[105]

Thomas Cook based his teaching on holiness on his own experience of sanctification. This emphasis was new, and may be said to have vitiated the doctrine and condemned it in the eyes of modern men, who have become very suspicious of claims based on personal experience. Cook also taught that evil can be totally eradicated: 'Those who are holy have no evil within, consequently no evil thoughts; . . . Christians need not, and do not sin, but capability to sin remains.'[106] While Cook recognizes that holiness means 'spiritual completeness or wholeness . . . not only complete deliverance from all spiritual pollution, but the possession of the unmixed graces of faith, humility, resignation, patience, meekness, self-denial and all other graces of the Spirit',[107] it is more to do with God's gift than with man's endeavour. The conditions for receiving the gift are related to individual 'holiness', which is too frequently expressed in the avoidance of those activities which a narrow sectarianism condemns. Smoking, dancing, drinking and card-playing figure prominently in the list of things prohibited by Cook, as also by later 'holiness' writers.

Samuel Chadwick had a profound influence on the development of the holiness tradition. Not only are national faults roundly condemned – several speakers at the 1928 Whitsuntide meetings at Cliff sounded an insistent note: 'Souls are perishing; the nation is drifting back to paganism, bankruptcy and ruin'.[108] The organized, too respectable Church is also criticized, especially for intellectualism, 'modern' views of the Bible, and failure to seek 'the second blessing'. Theological colleges especially come under attack from Chadwick:

> A ministry that is College-trained but not Spirit-filled works no miracles . . . Some preachers have finished their ministerial training

[105] *Plain Talks*, p. 65.
[106] *New Testament Holiness* (London 1902), pp. 16–17, 22.
[107] Ibid., p. 66.
[108] D. W. Lambert (ed.), *The Testament of Samuel Chadwick 1860–1932* (London 1957), p. 44.

with the confession that they had learned less about their Bibles than about any other subject; . . . Enthusiasm does not often accompany scholarship.[109]

This critical attitude towards nation and Church, together with the youthful excesses and condemnations of the Cliff students, alienated many respectable, middle-class Methodists from this holiness tradition. Yet some of the strictures levelled against this emphasis were manifestly unfair. It is not true to suggest, as many did, that this 'second blessing' approach was a substitute for social action. Samuel Chadwick was as concerned about social problems as Samuel Collier and Luke Wiseman. 'To talk of "the Bread of Life",' he said, 'and the glory that is to compensate in the life to come is impossible.'[110]

This tradition has maintained an emphasis on enthusiasm, evangelism and personal witness which is always needed in the Church. The pity is that when this tradition is allied to obscurantism in theology, conservatism in biblical scholarship, and world-denying negativism in social responsibility, it seems to many to have strayed far outside the path of Christian understanding. Yet the other attitude, now so popular, which sees Christian responsibility solely in terms of the secular application of the Gospel, seems to lack the enthusiasm and zeal so characteristic of the 'holiness' emphasis. We seem to need a fusion of the two traditions – but is this possible? Or are the traditions already so far apart that they can never hope to fuse?

There was one man in Methodism in whom the holiness tradition and social concern were fused. Hugh Price Hughes came into Christian discipleship through the witness of the holiness of a Cornish fisherman. In the early part of his ministry he was actively associated with the Holiness Conventions led by Pearsall Smith, and from first to last he was a zealous evangelist. In fact he combined evangelical zeal and political sensitivity to a high degree. He was a radical holiness man, if ever there was one. The Forward Movement, under his leadership, represented 'the broad, catholic, tender-hearted theology of early Methodism'.[111] But Hughes carried the notion of protest further than most of his contemporaries. He rejoiced to belong to 'the noble army of agitators' and frequently used *The Methodist Times*, of which he was editor, to make open political attacks upon what he regarded as political ills. His political judgment may sometimes have been faulty, but his sincerity in attempting to apply Christian principles to national and international affairs is surely apparent.

Certainly Hughes's radicalism seems not very different from some in

[109] Samuel Chadwick, *The Way to Pentecost* (London 1932), pp. 15–17.
[110] N. G. Dunning, *Samuel Chadwick* (London 1933), p. 80.
[111] Dora P. Hughes, op. cit., p. 165.

evidence today. Speaking of Mrs Besant, the well-known atheist, he said:

> The next best thing to Christianity is atheism, in the form in which it is presented by that noble woman . . . I would rather be in the position of one who has become an atheist through compassion for his fellows, than one who has been so selfish that he has no pity and no love for any one.[112]

If we are to have a full picture of Hughes, we must not ignore his concern for Christian belief, as evidenced in the Free Church catechism which he was instrumental in devising. He was not indifferent to doctine, but he did see the need for political involvement, for zealous pursuit of Christian principles and for personal commitment to Christ. A Church which produced, and never quite managed to muzzle, Hugh Price Hughes ought not to despair of bringing together evangelical zeal and radical responsibility.

3. Conclusion

It has to be admitted that, with one or two notable exceptions, Methodist theology is mainly of interest within the family of Methodism. Methodism has not in fact produced many outstanding scholars, and has depended upon other Churches for leadership in theological matters. One reason for this is that Methodists are never professional theologians. Methodist ministers certainly are all basically circuit men, and even those who are set aside to teach theology in colleges remain in this sense biased towards a circuit ministry; which is as it should be.

Other pressures which have been operative in Methodism in the last hundred years are not quite so acceptable. There has been a very considerable anti-intellectual bias in the emphasis upon evangelism. It has been insisted that evangelism can only be on the basis of a simple Gospel. But if evangelists never tackle the big questions they impoverish people who ought to be growing in Christian thought and action. Furthermore, the idea that Christians ought to be of one mind about everything has not been productive of creative theology. Without proper differences of opinion and discussion there is not likely to be much development of thought. Methodists also have been very much afraid of extreme positions. In the 1930s they were afraid of Barthianism; in the 1940s and 1950s they were afraid of form criticism; in the 1960s they were afraid of 'new theology'. They assume that the safe position is the middle of the road, although their experience of modern traffic ought to disabuse them of this idea. In this period there has also been considerable lessening of interest in spirituality.

[112] Ibid., p. 260.

Modern Methodists have not been a people so earnestly seeking communion with God as maybe some of their friends thought they were, and without that concern for spirituality it is doubtful whether they will ever make much contribution in the world of Christian thinking.

Yet there is much to take heart about in the present situation. If not many great theologians, some of the greatest preachers of this century have been Methodists. The list is very long, and it would perhaps be invidious to mention names, but I doubt if any other Church has produced so many preachers who in their day have gathered in the multitudes, and been able to speak directly to the people. They have preached in varying forms a hopeful, enthusiastic and inspiring Gospel. The great preachers are at the moment in eclipse, but they have been one of the chief glories of Methodism. There is no danger of Methodists going in for too theoretical a theology. But there is every reason to desire that there should be a continual interest, among preachers and people alike, in the great doctrines which have nurtured the Christian people throughout the centuries and still can nurture them.

V

Methodism in Ireland

R. D. ERIC GALLAGHER

1. The Beginnings

Sat. 8 [August 1747].—Finding one of the packet-boats ready, we went on board about eight o'clock in the morning . . . about two in the afternoon the wind sprung up, and continued till near four on Sunday morning, when we were within sight of the Irish shore. . . . Before ten we came to St. George's Quay. Soon after we landed, hearing the bells ringing for church, I went thither directly . . . About three I wrote a line to the curate of St. Mary's, who sent me word he should be glad of my assistance: so I preached there (another gentleman reading prayers), to as gay and senseless a congregation as ever I saw.[1]

JOHN Wesley had come to Dublin and had described his arrival in his *Journal*. Surprisingly enough, his was not the first Methodist presence on Irish soil.

Within months of Aldersgate, George Whitefield had come and gone, apparently without ever having intended to come at all. In October 1738, a gale had forced ships, as the west winds can still drive them, to seek shelter in the bays and estuaries of the Irish coast. On board one of them was Whitefield, eastward bound from Carolina. The ship took refuge in the broad reaches of the Shannon estuary. Whitefield came ashore at Carrigaholt, Co. Clare. An ordained clergyman of the Church of England, a former member of the Oxford 'Holy Club' and friend of John Wesley, he was on his way home after a four-month missionary visit to Georgia. He made his way to Limerick and was welcomed by Dr Burscough, Bishop of Limerick.[2] He then travelled across the midland

[1] *Journal*, iii, 311f.
[2] C. H. Crookshank, *History of Methodism in Ireland* (London 1885–1886), i, 12.

bogs to Dublin, where he preached in two (Church of Ireland) churches.[3] Thus unplanned, but in the providence of God, the first Methodist preacher came to Ireland. His stay was brief, but when he returned to London he gave a glowing account of the welcome he had had from the Irish.

If Whitefield was the first preacher, he was not Ireland's initial contact with the 'Holy Club'. There had been at least two Irish students in its membership. They were sons of Richard Morgan, a senior member of Dublin's Court of Exchequer.[4] Seven years after Whitefield's passing visit, an unnamed 'pious soldier' left the marks of his work and witness on the city. C. H. Crookshank, historian of the first hundred years of Irish Methodism, does not say specifically that the soldier was a Methodist, but the inference is obvious. Also in 1746, the hymn-writer John Cennick, now a Moravian but formerly a Wesley preacher, came to Dublin. His preaching attracted large congregations. He was regarded as a Methodist, and one sermon on 'the Babe wrapped in swaddling clothes' prompted a Dublin priest to dub the Methodists 'Swaddlers'. The name stuck.[5]

Before Mr Wesley's arrival, another fruitful contact had been made earlier in the same year by Thomas Williams. He was a university graduate of magnetic personality and unflagging zeal. Large crowds listened to him out of doors and in a disused Lutheran church in Marlborough Street. This building was destined to serve the Methodists as a preaching place for almost fifty years. Williams sent an account of his work to John Wesley.[6] The time for Wesley's ministry to Ireland had come. He arrived in 1747 and before he died in 1791 he was to make another twenty visits. At one period, he made the journey almost every other year. He spent so much time in Ireland that his English preachers were to complain about his absences. His reply was short: 'Have patience and Ireland will repay you.'[7]

On the second day of that first visit, John Wesley preached again in St Mary's. The curate, Mr Roquier, 'commended his sermon in strong terms',[8] but the *Journal* notes: 'he expressed the most rooted prejudice against lay preachers, or preaching out of a church, and said the Archbishop of Dublin was resolved to suffer no such irregularities in his diocese.'[9]

The visit lasted another ten days. There were already about two hundred and eighty members of Society, 'many of whom appeared to

[3] Ibid., i, 13: St Werburgh's and St Andrew's.
[4] *Letters*, i, 123.
[5] Crookshank, op. cit., i, 13.
[6] Ibid., i, 14f.
[7] Ibid., i, 463f.
[8] Ibid., i, 15.
[9] *Journal*, iii, 312.

be strong in faith'.[10] Among his congregations he noted 'scarcely any Irish'. Wesley here foreshadowed the modern identity problem of Irish Protestants, for he added significantly: 'At least ninety-nine in an hundred of the native Irish remain in the religion of their forefathers. The Protestants . . . are almost all transplanted lately from England. Nor is it any wonder that those who are born Papists generally live and die such, when the Protestants can find no better ways to convert them than Penal Laws and Acts of Parliament.'[11] He also wrote to a friend in London, Mr Ebenezer Blackwell: 'For natural sweetness of temper, for courtesy and hospitality, I have never seen any people like the Irish. Indeed, all I converse with are only English transplanted into another soil; and they are much mended by the removal, having left all their roughness and surliness behind them.'[12] Such and so many were the Methodists of Dublin (and, for that matter, of Ireland) when Mr Wesley first met them.

2. Constitution and Structures

John Wesley held the first conference of his Irish preachers in 1752.[13] Seventeen altogether were held during his lifetime and he presided over most of them.[14] The Conference has met annually since 1792. In the early days, there was a frequent interchange of preachers between the English and Irish Connexions, an arrangement which continued until around 1800 and which gave to British Methodism men of the calibre of William Thompson, the first President of the British Conference after Wesley's death, and the famous Dr Adam Clarke.[15]

Until 1817, a preacher appointed for the purpose by the British Conference presided over the Irish Conference.[16] Since then, the presiding officer has been automatically the British President of the day. This anachronism, undoubtedly pleasing to many, is a cause of mystification to others, who see it as a question-mark, if not a threat, to Irish autonomy. It leaves the President of the Methodist Church in Ireland as Vice-President of his own Conference and without an effective voice in its deliberations except by courtesy and grace of the British President, who, let it be said, is a very welcome and greatly honoured visitor.

Ireland developed similar patterns of Connexional structure and government to England. Conference, District Synods, Circuit Quarterly

[10] Ibid., iii, 314.
[11] Ibid.
[12] *Letters*, ii, 109f.
[13] Crookshank, i, 91; William Smith, *A Consecutive History of the Rise, Progress, and Present State of Wesleyan Methodism in Ireland* (London 1830); *Journal*, iv, 41.
[14] Smith, op. cit., p. 179.
[15] Ibid., pp. 249ff.; Crookshank, op. cit., ii, 109.
[16] Smith, op. cit., p. 180.

Meetings and Society Leaders' Meetings became the courts of the Church. Connexional committees were brought into being and the ministry was and is one of itinerant preachers. Today an eight-year term is the maximum for normal circuit appointments.

Irish Methodism had its schisms and re-unions as well as Britain; they are described later. One outcome of coming together again was the need for adequate regulation of the trusts and properties controlled by the Conference. The result was the Methodist Church in Ireland Act passed by Westminster in 1915.[17] It constituted and incorporated the Trustees of the Church as a corporate body and vested in them the properties, bequests, donations and funds of the Church and its departments. The wisdom and value of this Act have been demonstrated frequently over succeeding years.

Methodist union in Britain had legal as well as other implications for Methodists in Ireland. All Irish Connexional property had hitherto been held on trusts which were 'anchored' to Wesley's Deed Poll[18] of 1784 and to the Legal Hundred (Conference) appointed by that Poll and to which Ireland had the right to appoint ten members. The Act of Union changed all that. Irish Methodism now required a new legislative basis, if its property and legal existence were to be secure. This time, recourse to Westminster was no longer possible. The Government of Ireland Act had set up two separate legislatures, and so two Acts of Parliament were required. They were obtained in 1928, one from the Parliament of Northern Ireland and the other from the Irish Free State.[19] The co-operation of each government is witnessed in the identical wording of the two Acts. (It should be noted that the Free State Act has also an Irish language version.)

A constitution of the Church was drawn up as a schedule to the 1928 Act.[20] It contains among its provisions a statement of belief, the authors of which were the late Professor A. S. Peake and Dr Maldwyn Hughes. The document defines the powers of the Conference and of the various church courts. It maintains the principle of the itinerancy of ministers and it gives the Conference power to alter or amend the constitution. It also, for the first time, makes a formal requirement of the usage that the British President should preside at the Irish Conference.[21]

3. Who and How Many are the Irish Methodists?

Two hundred and eighty members, and all in Dublin – that was the

[17] *Manual of the Laws and Discipline of the Methodist Church in Ireland* (Belfast 1976), Appendix Two: 'The Methodist Church in Ireland Act, 1915'.

[18] Crookshank, op. cit., i, 385–7; *Journal*, iii, 314.

[19] *Journal*, iii, 314ff.

[20] Ibid., iii, 13ff.

[21] Ibid., iii, 22.

strength of Irish Methodism in 1747. In 1980 the circuits returned a figure of 22,449.[22] The total Methodist population in the country is reckoned to be somewhat above 70,000.

Wesley visited every county except Kerry, but his influence was most effective in the areas settled by the English and in the garrison towns. He was less successful with the Scottish settlers. Undoubtedly many Irish Roman Catholics were influenced, to the extent of becoming Methodists, but there was never any mass movement.

In the year of Wesley's last Irish visit, there were 14,010 members of Society.[23] The *Journal* records in its inimitable way his successes and failures, and his observations on Irish life and attitudes. Sectarian rioting broke out in Cork in the summer of 1749, when John Wesley was in Dublin. The affair prompted him to write and publish his famous letter to a Roman Catholic. It is still an apposite and passionate plea for mutual love, understanding and respect.[24]

Ireland has rarely been free from tension and turmoil throughout the years, and in every generation unrest has had its effects. In the latter years of the eighteenth century, the country was simmering with agrarian and sectarian unrest. The Anglican Church was the established Church of the ascendancy. Its bishops were appointed by English statesmen. They were not remarkable for their religious zeal or their pastoral care. A few, like Bishop Berkeley of Cloyne, had a merited reputation for scholarship. Some of the clergy commended themselves to their people; some did not. Oliver Goldsmith could write about the parson 'to all the country dear, And passing rich with forty pounds a year'.[25] He could have written about others whose characteristics were far different.

Behind a façade of quiet all was far from well. The underlying discontent produced secret societies which in their turn were followed by the emergence in 1795 of the Orange Lodges. Everything pointed to the rising which came eventually in 1798. It was a ramshackle affair, but widespread enough to produce fear and panic, especially in rural areas. The itinerant preachers now needed more than the physical strength which had hitherto helped so many of them to survive the damp beds in which they so often had to sleep: they required unusual courage.[26] A French invasion fleet arrived off south-west Ireland in 1796: Atlantic gales saved British rule and Protestant ascendancy. Two

[22] Minutes of Conference (1980), p. 94.

[23] Smith, op. cit., p. 181.

[24] Crookshank, op. cit., i, 49ff., 56; *Journal*, iii, 403, 409ff.; *Letters*, iii, 7ff.; Eric Gallagher, *A Better Way for Irish Protestants and Roman Catholics: Advice from John Wesley*. Published by the Mission Board of the Methodist Church in Ireland (Bangor 1973).

[25] *The Deserted Village*, 141f.

[26] Smith, op. cit., pp. 249ff.; R. H. Gallagher, *Pioneer Preachers of Irish Methodism* (Wesley Historical Society, Irish Branch 1966): this work contains much valuable information on their exertions, etc.

years later, the United Irishmen, a shaky coalition of Irish Catholics and Ulster Presbyterians, took to arms. British soldiers and their Irish establishment allies vied with the supporters of the rising in brutality. Many prisoners, most of them Protestants, taken by the United Irishmen in the Wexford area, were hacked to death.[27] The address of the Irish Conference of 1798 to the British Conference describes the background graphically:

> To attempt a description of our deplorable state would be vain indeed. Suffice it to say, that loss of trade, breach of confidence, fear of assassination, towns burned, countries laid waste, houses for miles without an inhabitant, and the air tainted with the stench of thousands of putrid carcasses, form some outline of the melancholy picture of our times. However, in the midst of this national confusion, we and our people in general, blessed be God! have been wonderfully preserved. Though some of us were imprisoned for weeks by the rebels, exposed also to fire and sword in the heat of battle, carried into the enemy's camp, and plundered of almost every valuable, yet we have not suffered the least injury in our persons! And moreover, God, even our own God, has brought us through all.[28]

Other records would suggest that the Methodists did not escape so lightly.[29] There is no doubt about the reaction of the Conference to the challenge of the rising.

The Conference of 1799 was persuaded to set three of its outstanding preachers apart as General Missionaries.[30] All were outstanding Irish-speakers. The first of them, James McQuigg, was an authority on the Irish manuscripts in the library of Trinity College, Dublin, and was employed for a time by the Bible Society on the translation of the Bible into Irish. Charles Graham became known as the apostle of Kerry. The third, Gideon Ouseley, came from the landed gentry and was to be the best-known of all of them. Their instructions were to go where they pleased, but particularly to the Irish-speakers.[31] The decision to appoint them was not taken easily. Had a less strong-minded man than Thomas Coke, who presided that year, not been in the chair, it might never have been taken at all. William Smith, historian of Irish Methodism from 1747 to 1830, takes up the story:

> At first his proposition was deemed impracticable, and a few only were disposed to support his views. But he had been too much

[27] Crookshank, op. cit., ii, 137ff. Most Irish historians deal with the events of 1798: see especially Thomas Pakenham, *The Year of Liberty: The Great Irish Rebellion of 1798* (London 1972); Robert Kee, *Ireland: a history* (London 1980).

[28] Crookshank, op. cit., ii, 145f.

[29] See note 28, above.

[30] William Smith (op. cit., p. 80) refers to the first-named as McQuige.

[31] Crookshank, op. cit., ii, 165f.

> accustomed to opposition to abandon any plan, which he thought would be for the benefit of mankind, merely because he had not the happiness of meeting with immediate approbation. Persevering, therefore, in his measures, his exertions were, at last, crowned with success, and the Irish Mission was established.[32]

Coke, at all events, was determined that they should succeed. The 1799 Minutes reveal that he also 'procured protections for them from the Lord Lieutenant (Marquis Cornwallis), addressed to all the civil and military authorities in Ireland'.[33] Their appointment ushered in a period of rapid expansion.

The statistics for the next forty years were remarkable: 1800 – 19,292 members of Society; 1814 – 29,388; 1820 – 36,529; 1840 – 42,133; and in 1844 – the highest ever recorded, 44,314.[34] Methodism seemed to have taken strong roots even in the period of the struggle for, and the achievement of, Catholic Emancipation.

But tragedy was about to strike at Irish life, and it was to change its quality dramatically. The potato crop, staple diet of far too many of the peasantry, promised well throughout the summer of 1845. In the early autumn, disease, as unexpected as it was devastating, attacked it. It failed again in 1846, and in each succeeding year to 1849. Death and desolation were everywhere. The British government's handling of the famine was less than generous, and there was an upsurge of nationalist feeling. Emigration was the final blow. The population plummeted from 8,175,124 in 1841 to 6,552,385 ten years later, and it was to continue falling for the remainder of the century.[35] Methodism suffered with the others. A membership reduced to 31,527 in 1850 was down again to 26,790 in 1855. The decline was arrested after 1880. By 1900, numbers had risen to 27,461, but the Home Rule agitation, World War I and the signs of things to come in Southern Ireland kept figures around that level until 1920. In spite of crippling Protestant decline in the South after the partition of the country, numbers for the whole island had reached 31,864 in 1960.[36] By 1980 they were down to 22,449.[37] Secular trends, indifference, defections and a diminishing Protestant population were having their effect. The process was helped by the increasingly costly assessment on circuits, based in part on membership strength. Methodism's persistently unrealistic determination to distinguish those who accept and conform to Society qualifications

[32] Smith, op. cit., p. 168.

[33] Ibid., p. 81.

[34] Ibid., pp. 179f.; Frederick Jeffery, *Irish Methodism: an historical account of its traditions, theology and influence* (Belfast 1964), p. 97; copies should still be available from the Wesley Historical Society (Irish Branch), Aldersgate House, University Road, Belfast BT7.

[35] Kee, *Ireland*, pp. 77ff.

[36] Jeffery, op. cit., p. 97.

[37] *Minutes* (1980), p. 94.

from 'Methodists', and to call only the former 'members', fails to reflect the numerical facts regarding the people called Methodists in Ireland.

4. Schisms and Reunion

Methodism in Ireland succeeded no more than it did in England in coping with schism and defections. Some years after Wesley's death a large number of members withdrew from the Lisburn Society. They joined up with the Methodist New Connexion, founded under Alexander Kilham in 1796.[38] They spread to a number of towns and districts and the witness of some of Irish Methodism's best-known churches, goes back to them. Their chief strength was in the North and they maintained their separate existence until 1905.

More serious was the division which gave birth to the Irish 'Primitive Wesleyans', always to be distinguished from the English Primitives. It arose from the natural desire of many of the Methodist people to receive the sacraments at the hands of their own ministers. There were many hundreds of members of Society with no previous connection with the Established Church of Ireland. Methodism was their natural and spiritual home, and they resented having to go to the parish church for marriages and sacraments. Circuits began to petition the Conference to permit the preachers to administer the sacraments. A number of leading ministers and laymen were strongly opposed to this; they argued that the right to administer the sacraments lay only with those who were episcopally ordained, and further that, as the Church of Ireland was established by law and the King was its human head, it was incumbent on all loyal people to support the parish church. The disputants called themselves 'Primitive Wesleyan Methodists' and they attempted in 1816 to obtain an injunction against the 'Wesleyans'.[39] The courts turned their application down. Efforts were made without avail to reconcile the two sections, and in 1818 the Primitive Wesleyan Society of Ireland began its separate career with a Conference, a Book Room, and all the usual Connexional structures. For more than half a century the two Methodist bodies worked side by side, and often in competition, in towns and even in small villages.

The principal leader of the Primitives was Adam Averell, a man of private means, and of great devotion and ability, who had already made his mark in the Connexion. He was an ordained clergyman of the Church of Ireland, and, under his influence, upwards of 12,000 members seceded from the Wesleyan Conference.

The Church of Ireland was disestablished by law in 1869. This created

[38] Crookshank, op. cit., ii, 146ff.
[39] Ibid., ii, 406f.

a new situation. Emotions had cooled and the Primitives were no longer under obligation to a state church. Increasing numbers of both Wesleyans and Primitives were concerned about the scandal of division. In 1871, the Primitives obtained a private Act of Parliament permitting them to alter their trusts as regards sacraments, and allowing them to join another Protestant Church. Approaches were made from the Church of Ireland, but there was no warmth on either side. They welcomed, however, approaches from the Wesleyans, and entered into conversations with them. Union took place in Dublin in 1879, when forty-six Primitive ministers and 7,838 members joined the Wesleyans.[40] Two important results ensued: laymen were to be admitted as members of Conference, and each division was to drop the adjectives 'Wesleyan' or 'Primitive Wesleyan'.[41] The united Church was henceforth known as the Methodist Church in Ireland.

In 1832 the English Primitives began mission work in Northern Ireland.[42] They erected several chapels and manned them from their Conference. In 1910,[43] however, they decided to bring the operation to an end, and the Irish Conference took over their property at a cost of £2,000.

5. Missioned and Missionary

As we have seen, the Irish Mission was established in 1799. Until 1906, it was funded by the Missionary Society in London, which at the same time received considerable moneys from the Irish Methodists for the support of this work and of missions overseas.[44] Eventually there were twenty-one missionaries working alongside the regular itinerant ministers of the Irish Conference, and many of them, like the first three, preached in Irish. Under this arrangement, 'mission stations' were opened in several parts of the country. The British Conference appointed a Superintendent over them until 1871, when the Irish Conference took responsibility for their oversight.[45] Financial support from the Missionary Society continued until 1906, when a final arrangement was agreed. Under it, Ireland was to support its own mission work and give what it could to the Missionary Society (now the Overseas Division) for overseas work specifically. Ireland benefited from one part of the agreement particularly, in that fifty per cent of the amounts raised annually by 'Juvenile Collectors' was to be devoted to the Irish Home

[40] Jeffery, op. cit., p. 37; *Minutes* (1879), p. 104.
[41] Crookshank, op. cit., iii, 170.
[42] Ibid.; *Minutes* (1878).
[43] *Minutes* (1910), p. 135.
[44] *Minutes* (1906).
[45] *Minutes* (1971).

Mission Fund. The South Derry Mission is today the sole trace on the Irish stations of these mission appointments.

But if Ireland received much, it gave much, in people as well as money. Within Wesley's lifetime, it provided the founding parents of Methodism in America and Canada. Irish Christians have always been missionary Christians. They have sent Christian preachers and teachers overseas for centuries, and Irish emigrants, both Catholic and Protestant, have brought their faith with them to the lands of their adoption.

In 1756 John Wesley reached Co. Limerick and found there a colony of refugees from the Palatinate in south-west Germany.[46] They were good farmers and citizens, but 'having no minister they were become eminent for drunkenness, cursing, swearing, and an utter neglect of religion'.[47] Wesley's preaching to them in German recalled them to a living experience. The Palatines, whose descendants are still to be found in Co. Limerick, became Methodists.

In 1760 a group of these Palatines emigrated to America. Two of them, Philip Embury and his cousin Barbara Heck, both professing Christians, arrived in New York.[48] For some years neither made any great show of Christian witness until Embury, at the instigation of his cousin, began to preach. At first his congregations were small and the rigging loft in Embury's house was enough for their needs. Two years later a chapel was built on the site of the present famous John Street church. It was called by Wesley's name, possibly the first to be so. Barbara Heck's old home still stands, and is the focus of many American Methodists on pilgrimage in search of their denominational roots.

About the same time, another Irish Methodist began to preach in Maryland and gather a class meeting. He was Robert Strawbridge,[49] a converted Roman Catholic from Drumsna, Co. Leitrim, whom Wesley had met in Terryhoogan near Tandragee in Co. Armagh. His work in Maryland was unauthorized by Wesley and was consequently regarded by some as irregular. That notwithstanding, it was blessed by God. 'The Log Meeting House' which Strawbridge built has been claimed as the first Methodist preaching-house on the American continent. Thus by 1766, Methodism had taken root in the North and South of the American colonies; in both places Irish hands had planted it.

Canada's Methodism, under God, also owes its origins to Ireland.[50] In that eventful year 1766, Lawrence Coughlan, a converted Roman Catholic, also from Drumsna, who had become a Methodist preacher in 1756, was ordained by the Bishop of London and sent out by the

[46] Crookshank, op. cit., i, 56f., 110.
[47] *Journal*, iv, 276.
[48] Crookshank, op. cit., i, 142; Abel Stevens, *A Compendious History of American Methodism* (London 1885), pp. 32ff.
[49] Stevens, op. cit., pp. 40ff.
[50] Ibid., pp. 211ff.

Society for the Propagation of the Gospel. He founded there a Methodist Society, but returned to Ireland because of failing health. He was succeeded by John Stratton of Wexford. Two years earlier, Barbara Heck and her husband Paul had left New York for Canada, and they began work near Montreal. They were joined in 1785 by another Irishman, Major John Neal, and later by James McCarty, who was kidnapped and murdered by French settlers.

The records of the Overseas Division in London bear witness to the contribution of Irish pioneers in Methodism's mission to Wesley's world parish. When Thomas Coke made his memorable plea in 1813–14 for missionaries to go with him to Ceylon,[51] two of the six volunteers were from Ireland. They were James Lynch and George Erskine. Coke died on the voyage; Lynch and Erskine landed in Ceylon, and after a time they were permitted to work in India. Lynch was the founder of Methodist work in Madras. Other pioneer missionaries from Ireland may be mentioned. Their names include those of William Hammet[52] (1786) in St Kitts and Jamaica, and John Stephenson[53] (1799) in Bermuda. James McMullen,[54] also Irish, was the first Methodist missionary to Gibraltar.

Irish Methodist missionaries continue to serve with the Wesleyan Methodist Missionary Society, and their work ranks high in its annals. One outstanding name among many may be mentioned. It is that of William Arthur, author of *The Tongue of Fire*.[55] He was born in Co. Antrim in 1919 and offered for the ministry in 1837. Jabez Bunting, the serving President, recognized the young man's potential. He asked for him to serve in India. Arthur eventually arrived in Mysore, where his labours and achievements were to be long remembered. Eye-trouble brought him back to England, and in 1851 he was appointed secretary of the Missionary Society in London. His death in 1901 brought a legendary story to its earthly end.

Mention of William Arthur is a reminder that Ireland has made important contributions to the work of British Methodism. The appointment of William Thompson as first President of the British Conference[56] after Wesley's death has already been recorded. Henry Moore was ordained by Wesley, was one of his trusted friends[57] and was an executor of his will. He was President in 1823–4. Adam Clarke[58] (1760–1832) was a native of Co. Derry and was called out by Wesley. His extensive

[51] Smith, op. cit., p. 101; Crookshank, op. cit., ii, 372.
[52] Crookshank, op. cit., i, 421.
[53] Ibid., ii, 145.
[54] Ibid., ii, 253.
[55] Ibid., iii, *passim*.
[56] Ibid., ii, 38.
[57] Ibid., ii, 420f.
[58] Ibid., ii, *passim*; R. H. Gallagher, *Adam Clarke: Saint and Scholar* (Wesley Historical Society, Irish Branch 1963).

scholarship and humble piety marked him out as one of the great men of Methodist history. His Bible Commentary was in use in America until very recent years. James Creighton, a Church of Ireland curate, became a Methodist preacher and was appointed to Wesley's Chapel, London.[59] He acted with Wesley in the ordinations for America in 1784. And there are many others whose names are written in the Lamb's Book of Life.

6. Relations with the British Conference and other Churches

Irish Methodists today are given their place, and they take it easily, in the comity of ecclesiastical life, inside and outside the country. The Conference is, of course, autonomous, but it has links going back to the days of the Legal Hundred[60] with the British Conference. The somewhat ambivalent anachronism regarding the Presidency of the Conference has already been noted. The arrangement is claimed to be a recognition which is due to whoever may be John Wesley's successor for the time being in the Presidential chair. It is a strange logic which claims that his successors in the Irish and British chairs must always be one and the same person. Each year the President brings his 'companions' with him. There are five of them: four – two ministers and two lay representatives – are nominated by him, and the fifth is the British Vice-President of the day. All have voting rights. In return, Ireland sends the four back to the British Conference as part of the Irish delegation. In their turn, they have as companions the Irish Vice-President, his designated successor and his predecessor, and four others – two ministerial and two lay – elected by the Conference.

There the formal Conference links end, but not so the other contacts. There are Irish representatives on the Overseas Divison, on the Division of Social Responsibility, and from time to time, by invitation, on other British committees. British ministers are frequently invited to preach in Irish pulpits, and in recent years there has been a marked increase in Irish visits to Britain. The British Hymn Book and sections of the Service Book and the old Book of Offices are used in Ireland, and there is a wide readership of the *Methodist Recorder* and books from the pens of British Methodist authors.

Ireland has its own experience of Church Union discussions. Since 1963, discussions of one kind or another have been going on with the Church of Ireland and Presbyterians. The joint negotiating committee approved a Declaration of Intent which was followed in 1973[61] by a draft scheme for union. It provided for an episcopally governed

[59] Crookshank, op. cit., i, 375.
[60] Ibid., i, 386.
[61] *Minutes* (1973): Report of Inter-Church Relations Committee.

Church in the historic tradition. Reaction from the Churches was muted and lacking in enthusiasm. Since then, the discussions have proceeded slowly. Each Church seems content to await some new development from outside itself. Meanwhile, Methodists wonder what will happen to them if British Methodism in its covenanting for unity takes episcopacy into its system. Episcopal Presidents ordaining Irish preachers will cause no less interest and perhaps controversy than did Dr Leslie Davidson, in a previous generation, on his Presidential visit to the Pope. Presidents do not always remember that their actions have real implications for the other Conference over which they must preside before their year of office comes to an end.

Ireland plays a full part in ecumenical activity. The Conference has never hesitated to join inter-Church Councils. Away back in the last century, it was sending its representatives to the Methodist Ecumenical Conferences, the precursors of the World Methodist Council. When the time came, there was no hesitation about joining the United Council of Christian Churches and Religious Communions in Ireland (now the Irish Council of Churches), the British Council of Churches and the World Council. Since 1948, Irish Methodism has provided two chairmen of the I.C.C.[62] and a Vice-President of the B.C.C.[63] Several have been seconded to serve with the W.C.C., the B.C.C., the I.C.C. or some of their agencies. Dr Charles Ranson was General Secretary of the International Missionary Council and first Director of the Theological Education Fund.

Though decisions were taken easily to join these ecumenical bodies, dispute and controversy were rampant during the 1970s regarding involvement with them. To date, the Conference has withstood all attack and criticism on these issues. Over the same period, there has been a marked thawing in Irish Catholic–Protestant relationships. Methodists played a leading part in this development, which had hitherto been regarded as impossible. The first co-chairman[64] of the important Joint Group of Catholics and Protestants to advise the Churches on their role in Irish society was a Methodist minister and others have been prominent in similar bodies.

7. Ministry and Training

Wesley looked for more than a warmed heart in his preachers. Willingness to learn and study was essential, and from Ireland he called some who combined passion and scholarship to an outstanding degree. Any list of early obituaries is evidence of that. For instance: 'Andrew Blair

[62] Harold Sloan and R. D. Eric Gallagher.
[63] R. D. Eric Gallagher.
[64] R. D. Eric Gallagher.

discovered a strong inclination to reading and study: he preferred conversing with books to all other gratifications.'[65] There were Irish linguists like Graham, McQuigg and Ouseley, or scholars like Adam Clarke and Thomas Walsh,[66] 'the best Hebrew scholar he [John Wesley] had ever met'.

And yet, despite this honourable tradition, Ireland was slow to recognize its responsibility for the training of its ministry. It had no theological institution of its own until 1868, when the Methodist College, Belfast, opened its doors as a day and boarding school, and made provision as well for training students for the ministry. Prior to that date, those who did receive formal theological training were sent to institutions of the British Conference.

The erection of the new College changed all that. The adjoining Queen's College, now the highly regarded Queen's University of Belfast, enabled students to work for and obtain degrees from the National University of Ireland. After 1868, the great majority of accepted candidates were sent for theological training and always to Methodist College.

Welcome, however, as the new provision was, the dual arrangement of school and theological college wrapped up in one was bound to create difficulty and tensions. It certainly did so. The headmaster of a growing school did not take kindly to interference from an over-all ministerial President, no matter how eminent he might be as a theologian.

The inevitable separation came shortly after World War I. A suitable building was acquired in the same neighbourhood. School and Theological Departments were separated, and the Methodist College Act of 1928 of the Northern Ireland Parliament gave legal recognition to the separate existence and endowments of what is now Edgehill Theological College.

The opening of the new institution enabled the Conference to insist that in future all accepted candidates should be sent for training, and provision was made for assisting those who wished to pursue university courses. With the eventual abolition of the previously acceptable, but nevertheless pernicious, tendency to send some young men to circuit for a year or two before going to college, all candidates are now sent for training on acceptance.

Enlightened leadership from successive early Principals, Dr Alexander McCrea, Dr William L. Northridge and the Rev. Ernest Ker, forged closer links with the neighbouring Presbyterian College, now Union College. Their successors and their colleagues now form part of a combined faculty and teaching body. Though the Colleges remain as

[65] Smith, op. cit., p. 263.
[66] Ibid., p. 249.

separate institutions, there is agreement on 'who teaches what'. Appropriate timetabling and the propinquity of the two colleges to each other and to the university enable the students of each college easily to take their lectures where they may be given. By agreement, each Church appoints to its teaching staff only those with sufficient academic qualifications to ensure their recognition by the university as teachers or lecturers in degree courses. Thus, many students in successive generations have obtained university degrees or diplomas in theology while taking their ministerial training. Meanwhile, educational requirements have been raised for intending candidates, so that most students now qualify for entrance to university courses.

Advantages from this arrangement with the Presbyterians and the university are self-evident. It has nevertheless come in for occasional criticism from those who fear the influences of Calvinism and other tendencies, or who object to any curtailment of the Church's freedom to appoint whomsoever it wishes. Whatever merit there may be in these arguments, the joint faculty has enabled succeeding generations of students, whether married or single, male or female, to know each other better and to be taught by a better qualified staff than either Church could have made possible of itself.

8. Education

If there was delay in the provision of theological training, it was a different matter with day schools. The involvement of Irish Methodism with education is of long standing and its record is honourable. An essential part of the strategy of the Irish Mission set up in 1799 was the emphasis on the erection of schools. By 1826 there were twenty schools with 1,412 enrolled children in the day-school section and almost nine hundred Sunday scholars.[67] An extract from the 1826 missionary report says:

> . . . the schools connected with the missions, which are under the care of pious and qualified schoolmasters, have been conducted with great regularity throughout the year, and the effects produced by them, upon the morals of the children, and the neighbourhoods in which they are situated, have been, in many instances, great.[68]

Adam Clarke added significantly to the number, especially in the north-east of the country. By 1865 there were forty-eight mission schools and fifty National schools under Methodist control and a training college for teachers located in Dublin.[69]

[67] Ibid.
[68] Ibid., pp. 171f.
[69] Jeffery, op. cit., p. 70.

The educational provisions of the new Northern Ireland Government in 1922 began to render church primary schools no longer necessary, and population changes in the South have made most of the Methodist day schools redundant. It has been another matter, however, as far as secondary education is concerned.

In 1845, the Wesleyan Connexional School was opened in Dublin by a group of Methodist laymen. Many eminent persons, including George Bernard Shaw, were among its early pupils. Its premises were soon too small, and it was replaced by Wesley College in 1879.[70] It has been a most successful school and has done much to cater for the educational needs of young people from all over the Republic. In recent years, the Governors took a courageous decision to transfer the school from its down-town site at St Stephen's Green. Wesley College is now located both beautifully and strategically in the southern outskirts of the city. The erection of a brand-new school at a staggering cost was by any standards not only courageous but imaginative in the extreme. The developments in the new buildings since its opening by the late President de Valera have amply justified the faith of the Governors. Wesley is an institution of which any Church could be proud.

The rapid growth of the city of Belfast in the middle of the last century called for the erection of a large secondary school and, as we have seen, Irish Methodism met the challenge with the opening of Methodist College[71] in 1868, with the legendary William Arthur, on loan from England, as first President and Principal. Almost from its inception, the College played a leading part in Northern Ireland's educational scene. Since 1945, its accommodation has been transformed and increased out of all recognition. Recent additions have included an extremely beautiful Chapel of Unity, used every day, and a magnificent Sixth-Form Centre. This latter provision has made the College the envy of most other schools. The total enrolment of the College and its two Preparatory schools is well over 2,000. One significant development in the government of the College took place in the 1960s. The Conference agreed to a change in the composition of the Board of Governors from the former membership of twenty-one persons appointed by the Conference to a Board of twenty-seven, nine of whom are now the nominees of the Minister responsible for Education. This change has made possible much greater financial assistance from the Government.

One other educational initiative by the Irish Conference must be mentioned. The flight from the land, rural mixed marriages, and the need for scientific training in agricultural methods, prompted the Conference, at the instigation of a number of laymen inspired and led by the late Rev. Wesley McKinney, to launch Gurteen Agricultural College

[70] *Minutes* (1879), p. 70; *Manual of the Laws and Discipline*, p. 214.
[71] *Minutes* (1868), p. 10; *Manual*, pp. 215ff.

in 1947.[72] After initial difficulties, each year has seen land improvement, increasing modernization, and more and still more application of modern training techniques. Gurteen is one of the greatest contributions the Church has made to rural Ireland.

9. A Caring Church

In 1765–6 a Home for Widows was established in Dublin. Before the end of the century there were also a Free School, an Orphan School for Girls, and a Strangers' Friend Society.[73] To this day the Irish Minutes carry references to two of these institutions. The Orphan School[74] was still in existence until, well within living memory, the property was sold and a Trust Fund created to be operated by Wesley College and so fulfil the purposes of the original school. It is reported on annually by the Wesley Governors. The Home for Widows[75] has continued without a break, though not in the same buildings. It is managed by a committee appointed by the Conference, and its entry in the Minutes always carries the sub-title: 'founded by John Wesley in 1766'.

Thus, early on, Irish Methodism put into practice something of Wesley's concern for practical religion. The concern has lasted through the years and has never been so evident as recently. The City Mission concept was taken from England during the nineteenth century, and work of this kind was started in Belfast, Dublin and Londonderry.

The Belfast Central Mission, based at the city's Grosvenor Hall, has provided and pioneered a new concept in residential accommodation and adjoining sheltered dwellings for senior citizens. Since World War I, it has maintained a children's home. Between the wars, it accepted responsibility for, and amalgamated with, a home run by the Methodist Orphan Society,[76] and moved to a magnificent site on the Co. Down coast not far from Belfast. In recent years the home has been completely modernized and is recognized as one of the best of its kind by the statutory authorities, with whom it works closely. There is also a residential holiday home and conference centre, the history of which goes back to the early days of this century. The Grosvenor Hall premises were used on a number of occasions, in the early phases of the civil unrest, to provide refuge for displaced families. The Mission was entrusted with the disposal of large sums of money and emergency relief during the same period. The Superintendent was appointed to a small committee handling the huge Innocent Victims' Fund provided

[72] *Manual*, pp. 226ff.
[73] Smith, op. cit., pp. 242ff.
[74] *Manual*, pp. 285ff.
[75] Ibid., pp. 288ff.
[76] Ibid., pp. 282ff.

by the British Government. He was also a member of the Northern Ireland Prime Minister's Peace Conference in 1969.

The North Belfast Mission has made a virtue out of necessity. Its first home in the north of the city was a building, 'Salem', taken over with other New Connexion premises in 1905. For many years it carried on very successful social and evangelistic work in Great George's Street. Recently urban redevelopment and new road works forced it to move to the densely populated new housing area of Rathcoole on the northern outskirts of the city. The compensation received for the acquisition of its buildings has enabled it to provide purpose-built accommodation that will still be appropriate in the twenty-first century. The Mission runs a large and efficient Home for Senior Citizens in Belfast, and has for many years provided children's summer holidays.

The work of the Dublin Central Mission also began in premises formerly in the control of one of the break-away bodies, the Primitive Wesleyans. Its story is one of outstanding success. Here again a virtue has been made of necessity. The depopulation of the inner city forced an amalgamation of the congregation with that of the city-centre church at Abbey Street. The Mission has since opened near by a new social service building which is catering in a new way for many of the city's social problems. This venture and the residential provision for old folk have done much to provide caringly where help is needed most. At the same time, as a by-product, the name and reputation of Methodism have been greatly enhanced among the majority community.

The Londonderry Mission has also made a worthy name for itself in the wider community. Again, use was made of former Primitive Wesleyan property to house the venture when it started. The witness and work of the Mission have meant much in a city which has suffered more than most from unemployment and civil unrest. When the Superintendent, the Rev. James Williamson, was transferred in 1980, he was accorded a civic reception by the Mayor and City Council in recognition of his ministry in the city. But the Missions have had no monopoly of human concern. The 1960s and 1970s saw a healthy determination to cater for the well-being of young people. Many Churches participated in the youth service and made good use of statutory help in the provision of buildings, equipment and leadership. There has been involvement in the Churches Youth Council and in the outreach of the Youth Secretaries appointed by the leading Churches, including the Roman Catholic Church. The Youth Department set up by the Conference immediately after World War II was not only a studied attempt in evangelism. It was evidence of a caring Church.

Team ministries have emerged and have opened up new possibilities in social and community work of a type undreamed of in former years.

10. Communication

Wesley believed in both the spoken and the printed word. Ireland has been slow to see the full potential of the latter. True, the Irish Methodists have rarely been without such journals as the *Methodist Chnrch Record*, the *Wesleyan Magazine*, various forms of the *Irish Christian Advocate* or, in latter years, the *Methodist News Letter*. But they have never seen their way to encourage or facilitate the publication of new books from the pens of their own people. Indeed, all the Irish Protestant Churches have suffered in this respect, all of them probably having depended to a large extent on the publishing facilities, such as they have been, of the Church of England, the Church of Scotland, and British Methodism. This failure has cost Ireland dear – new thought relevant to Irish problems has not been encouraged, and all the Churches have been the poorer. Even a Lecture Trust Fund to make possible the dissemination of literature from Irish authors relevant to Irish problems, from British publishing houses or from the growing number of smaller Irish publishers, would have helped.

The recent emergence of Christian Journals Ltd, Belfast, under the direction of an Irish Methodist minister, Wilbert Forker, on secondment to the Templeton Foundation, has done something to meet this need. His impressive list of titles includes books by a number of Irish authors, with a few Methodists among them. But more is needed.

11. The Ministry of Reconciliation

Many with no axe to grind have been good enough to say that when the history of Northern Ireland in the 1970s comes to be written, the Methodist Church will emerge with less discredit than other Churches. True or false, the statement indicates that the record of the Church at least merits attention.

Like every other Irish Church, Methodism is influenced by its environment. It has been subjected to all the pressures and the inadequacies, many of them almost intolerable, that have affected all the Churches. It too has among its ministers and members those who have only 'tunnel vision' and have not seen all that the Gospel stands for. They may not have been as enlightened as their critics could have wished, but in a remarkable way most of them have remained, within the parameters of their insights, loyal to the fellowship of their Church.

More, however, needs to be said. It is arguable that during the period 1920–70 none of the Irish Churches was sufficiently sensitive to issues and evils that prevented many, North and South, from living the good life. In addition to the chronic problems of unemployment, bad housing, tuberculosis and underdevelopment, there were social and political issues and evils about which little was said or done by any of the Churches. All the makings of civil unrest and violence were just under the surface, even if they were not immediately visible. Methodism cannot escape the word of judgment set against all the Irish Churches for their failure to understand and interpret the economic, social and political implications of biblical teaching. It could be argued that they have not even yet begun to understand.

Notwithstanding this failure, in 1966, before the Northern Ireland Civil Rights Movement had been born, the Irish Conference issued a biblically based and reasoned call to the Irish people.[77] It recognized the urgent need for abolishing all forms of discrimination, of eliminating violence and working for reconciliation. Succeeding Conferences issued similar statements.

Individual Methodists have been involved in the many peace movements and organizations. The Church played a full part in the Churches' Peace Campaign in the winter of 1974. An Irish woman, member of a Belfast Methodist congregation, won the first World Methodist Peace Prize.[78] There were two Irish Methodists[79] in the small and courageous group of Irish Churchmen who in 1974 sought out the Provisional I.R.A. at Feakle, to plead with them to call off their campaign of violence. In times of crisis, Methodist voices have frequently been sought and listened to with great attention and respect on both sides of the divide. There was prominent Methodist participation in the production of the historic 'Violence in Ireland' report commissioned by the Roman Catholic Church and the Irish Council of Churches.

All of this reflects great credit on a small Church, but one must ask if that Church and its members have been as courageous and resolute in the search for reconciliation as they might have been. Official statements are not enough, if they are not backed up by resolute attempts to carry out their recommendations. Methodism, with the other Churches, has yet to face fully the issues of leadership and of the need for the prophetic voice. The Church and the community have reason to be grateful for the courage of ministers and members alike in some of the most dangerous areas. Much of the work has been carried on in extremely difficult circumstances. Shooting and rioting have taken place outside church doors immediately before and after church services. One city-centre church has suffered from the effects of bombs exploding in the immediate vicinity on more than twenty occasions. In spite of all this the work went on. More serious has been the movement of populations arising from either urban redevelopment or sectarian intimidation. This is now a major factor in the Church's strategic

[77] *Minutes* (1966).
[78] Miss Saidie Patterson, MBE.
[79] Dr Stanley Worrall and Dr Eric Gallagher.

thinking, especially in the North Belfast area. Some congregations with long and honourable traditions are now facing decisions which must sooner or later result, in every case, in loss of status, and in some cases, in disappearance.

12. Reflections

Three final comments may be allowed. What has been written may suggest to some that Irish Methodism is shrinking, too traditional and lacking in vision. That conclusion would be too superficial. The General Mission, born in the despair of 1799, belies any attempt to write off the work of the Holy Spirit. Its successor in the Special Evangelistic Agency, and a new insistence, by the General Secretary for Home Missions,[80] on the evangelistic responsibilities of District Home Mission Committees, justify the refusal to write 'Ichabod' at the end of any account of the Church's work in this century. The second comment has to do with the Youth Department, which in recent years has dramatically broken new ground. Many may regard its demands on the Church's budget and general assessment as excessive. They are mistaken. Inspiring leadership[81] in the Department is bringing new life to the Church. The Youth Evangelism Teams are now a firmly established part of its witness; they leave a refreshing influence on the life of many circuits, and are producing a new brand of candidates for the ministry. Finally, there is the contribution of the charismatic and lay witness movements. Both are controversial, and it could be argued that each is in danger of producing forms of irrelevant or superficial religion. There is, however, evidence that, with adequate awareness of the need for sound biblical teaching and insights, both these movements can be used in awakening the Church to the pressing challenges of the rapidly approaching twenty-first century.

In the providence of God, Ireland's Methodists may well be able to contribute something of worth to the developing witness of Christianity in their native land. That something may be greater than their numbers would suggest. If they can, under God, do just that, they will be worthy successors of the founding fathers, who made their landfalls on Irish soil more than two hundred years ago, and of the people called Methodists 'in the Connexion founded by the late Rev. John Wesley, A.M.'

[80] Edward R. Lindsay.
[81] From John D. Knox and his successor, J. Winston Good.

VI

Methodism in Wales

GRIFFITH T. ROBERTS

When John Wesley first visited Wales, in October 1739, he had no intention of forming societies of his own in the Principality. He had come, so he informs us, 'upon a pressing invitation, some time since received', an invitation which had undoubtedly been extended to him by the Welsh revivalist, Howel Harris. The two had first met at Bristol four months previously. Harris admitted that he had had 'some prejudice' against Wesley, because he did not hold the Calvinistic doctrines of Election and Perseverance, but, having heard him preach, his 'prejudice against him fell away' to such an extent that he warmly invited him to visit Wales at his earliest opportunity. Harris himself had been 'converted' in the spring of 1735, and ever since then the Revival in Wales had been steadily gathering momentum, under his own leadership and that of Daniel Rowland, a Cardiganshire clergyman. The fact that a Calvinist like Harris should invite an Arminian like Wesley to visit his people need cause no surprise. At that time Wesley himself was at Bristol, eagerly continuing the work begun there by another Calvinist, George Whitefield, and had gone there at Whitefield's own invitation. The two men had agreed to set their theological differences to one side, and to concentrate on preaching salvation. The success of the revival was more important in their sight than the solution of doctrinal problems. It was in the same conciliatory spirit that the invitation to Wales was given and accepted. During that first visit Wesley preached from such texts as 'The Son of man is come to save that which is lost', and 'Believe in the Lord Jesus Christ and thou shalt be saved'. One of Harris's converts, who heard him preach more than once during the course of his journey, found it difficult to believe that he was an Arminian, so studiously did he avoid controversial topics. He had come to Wales, not to introduce a new sect into the country, but to strengthen the hands of Howel Harris and his fellow-workers.

The next twelve months, however, proved to be critical months in the history of the Methodist Movement, and it became increasingly difficult to preserve peace in the societies. By November 1740, when Charles Wesley first visited South Wales, the tension between the Calvinists and the Arminians had increased significantly. At one service, when Harris himself was present, a 'gentleman' challenged Wesley to speak to Harris, since he had been sent for 'to disprove his errors'. Wesley refused, saying: 'I am unwilling to speak of my brother Howel Harris, because, when I begin, I know not how to leave off; and should say so much good of him, as some of you could not bear.' Nevertheless, during the following months, Charles Wesley and Harris became increasingly estranged from each other, and at the end of June 1741 the breach became complete and, to all appearances, permanent. As a result of these controversies the Religious Society at Cardiff decided to adhere to the Wesleys and thus became the first 'Wesleyan' society in Wales.

Thenceforth there would be two kinds of Methodists in Wales. The vast majority would be the disciples of Harris and Rowland and their helpers, Calvinistic in doctrine and to a very large extent Welsh-speaking. It was during the second half of the nineteenth century that they began in earnest, and in the face of considerable opposition, to form English-speaking churches. They are the people who are nowadays known as the Calvinistic Methodist Church or the Presbyterian Church of Wales. The other Methodists would be the disciples of John Wesley, Arminian in doctrine, and until 1800 to all intents and purposes English-speaking.

The personal estrangement between Harris and the Wesleys lasted for only a few months; before the end of the summer of 1741 they had been reconciled, and for the rest of their lives remained close friends. There came a time in the early 1750s when Harris's Calvinistic friends, almost without exception, turned against him, but his friendship with the Wesleys remained unimpaired throughout the years. After his reconciliation with the Wesleys in September 1741, Harris made many attempts to bring the two Movements together into one body, but without success. Many reasons could be suggested for this failure, such as the language barrier and doctrinal difficulties, but we must remember that the two Movements, however much they resembled one another, had sprung from two separate Revivals. Harris's people and Wesley's people were (and still are) known as Methodists, but the Welsh Methodists trace their origin to a conversion experienced at Talgarth church in 1735, and Wesley's people to a similar conversion experienced in Aldersgate Street in 1738. Of all the Welsh leaders, Harris alone was in constant touch with the Wesleys and felt any real eagerness for a union of the two Movements. It is significant that even the Calvinistic Methodists of England and Wales eventually went their own separate ways, although they had had for some time a united Association, with Whitefield as President and Harris as his deputy.

What Harris did achieve, however, was a large measure of agreement on policy. The basic principle which was to be their guide was expressed at the Bristol Association of January 1747, attended by John Wesley and four of his preachers: 'We all agreed that wheresoever we might occasionally preach among each other's people, we would endeavour to strengthen rather than weaken each other's hands, and particularly to labour to prevent separation in the Societies.' Since the previous year, 'Wales' had appeared as a circuit in the *Minutes* of Conference, and arrangements were made for Wesley's preachers to visit the country regularly, but it is not clear what efforts were made to form societies there. The object of the Bristol agreement was to prevent the preachers of both parties, but particularly of the Arminian party, from disrupting societies of the opposite persuasion. In 1745, the Conference had agreed to 'make a trial, especially in Wales and Cornwall, of preaching without forming any Societies', and although three years later this was condemned as a general policy, it was possibly continued in Wales for many years.[1] If so, the danger of disrupting non-Wesleyan societies may have been greater than it would have been if the Preachers had concentrated on setting up and nurturing purely Wesleyan ones.

One fact, at least, is fairly obvious: the number of Wesleyan societies in Wales in the 1740s was small. In 1748 there were societies at Cardiff, Fonmon, 'Lanmais, &c.' (presumably Llanmaes) and 'Lamission' (probably Llanishen), and the following year we read of three other societies, at Bedwas, Llanwynno and Llantrisant. All seven places were in east Glamorganshire. We know that the Wesleys had preached in other districts in Wales – in the Builth area, for instance, and in Anglesey – but apparently without forming any societies in those areas. It is certain that no attempts were made to form societies in Anglesey: Wesley had been content to preach in those places where the Calvinistic Methodists had already been established, and his only intention had been to support them. Reading between the lines, one gathers that there were some people in the Builth area, including Marmaduke Gwynne, Charles Wesley's future father-in-law, who were not completely satisfied with the Calvinism of Harris. The preaching of John and Charles Wesley may have brought them some comfort, but there is no evidence to suggest that Wesley attempted to form any societies in the district, so close

[1] Under 25 August 1763, there is a cryptic entry in Wesley's *Journal*: 'How much preaching has there been for these twenty years all over Pembrokeshire! But no regular societies . . .' If Wesley was referring to his own preachers, they were covering a wider area than historians have realized from 1743 onwards.

to Howel Harris's own home. From one point of view, we might say that the six or seven societies in east Glamorganshire could not be regarded as much fruit to ten years' work in Wales, but we must always remember that Wesley had never intended to compete with Harris and his people. They were the people who had begun the work and who knew the language of the people. Wesley had enough work to do in England and amongst people who could understand his preaching without the aid of an interpreter.

After 1750 we know very little of the work in Wales for more than a decade. Harris had retired to Trefeca, rejected by his own people, and his papers throw hardly any light on the history of Methodism during that period. Wesley, for his part, seldom visited the Principality during those years: four journeys through Wales to or from Ireland, two specific visits to South Wales and two to North Wales, between 1750 and 1760. The second visit to South Wales (in 1758) took him as far as Swansea and Neath, where there was some prospect of forming societies, which suggests that the work had not been completely at a standstill during those years, but that progress had been small and slow.

In 1761, however, Thomas Taylor was sent to labour in South Wales. He was only twenty-three years old, and Wales was his first circuit. Young and energetic, he infused new life into the work, and introduced Methodism into new areas in the Gower peninsula and Pembrokeshire. The journeys which Wesley took to West Wales, at fairly regular intervals from 1763 onwards, reflect the change caused by Taylor and his successors. Before long, South Wales was divided into three circuits: Pembrokeshire, Glamorganshire and Brecknockshire; membership figures slowly, but fairly steadily, increased, and new chapels were opened at places like Carmarthen, Haverfordwest and Pembroke. 'Wesleyan' Methodism had at last been fairly firmly established in Wales.

We must not, however, over-emphasize the growth of the Movement in Wales, even during the latter years of Wesley's life. At the time of his death he had only about 600 members in the whole of South Wales, and a handful in the North. As early as 1759 he had made a short visit to Mold in Flintshire, and there had been a society in that town from 1762 at the latest – the first, as far as we know, in North Wales. Before the end of the century a few more societies had been formed in the north-east fairly near to the English border, and served by those Preachers stationed at Chester. A new circuit was also formed in mid-Wales, based on Welshpool – a sign that Methodist influences had been spreading northwards from Brecon and westwards from the Shrewsbury area along the Severn valley. The establishment of English-speaking Methodism came about, therefore, in two ways. In the south it was the result of the deliberate policy of stationing Preachers in the area. For many years this policy was not very energetically pursued, partly to avoid trespassing on the territory of Howel Harris and his friends,[2] and partly through lack of Preachers who could preach in Welsh. Nevertheless, small though they were, the South Wales societies were, in the main, the fruits of the labour of Wesley's Preachers stationed in the area. The North Wales societies, on the other hand, were the result of the penetration of Wesleyan influence from across the border, from such centres as Chester and Shrewsbury. Like other influences throughout the centuries, this influence also came along the coast and the river valleys, and could make little headway beyond those areas where a substantial number of people could understand the English language.

In both North Wales and South Wales the Wesleyan societies were almost entirely English, although Henry Lloyd had for years been preaching 'mainly in Welsh'. There is evidence, however, that some members of these societies would have preferred Welsh-speaking ones had they been available, but as they had been converted under the ministry of John Wesley's Preachers, they could find a spiritual home only in a Wesleyan environment. But Welsh Wesleyan Methodism did not exist in any formal sense before 1800, although the ground had been prepared for its coming for some years.

For many years during the latter part of the eighteenth century, Richard Harrison had been preaching regularly in Welsh in many places in the north-east, but had not attempted to form a society anywhere except at his home in Northop, where he was 'leader'. About 1787 a society was formed at Denbigh, through the efforts of Evan Roberts, who had joined the Methodists at Liverpool. This society was mainly, if not exclusively, Welsh, and Roberts had great difficulty in securing regular preaching in Welsh – or indeed in any language – since the Chester Preachers felt that it was futile to preach in English to an almost monoglot Welsh congregation, and no Welsh preachers, apart from Richard Harrison, were available. Evan Roberts appealed directly to Wesley himself for a Welsh preacher, but Wesley had none he could send. Then in 1798–9 the Chester Preachers decided to make a similar appeal to the leaders of the Connexion. Towards the end of 1799, Edward Jones of Bathafarn, near Ruthin, who had been converted at Manchester, returned home, invited Wesleyan preachers to visit the district, and formed a society at Ruthin.

The needs of Wales had been discussed by the Conference of 1800, but no decision was reached on the matter until Thomas Coke, himself a native of Brecon, secured the appointment of Owen Davies and John Hughes to work in North Wales. Four years later, Coke explained how he had been convinced, during his journeys through North Wales to Ireland, of the need of itinerant preachers for that part of the country,

[2] This factor would decrease in importance after 1750.

preachers who could preach in Welsh. We should remember that neither Calvinistic Methodism nor indeed the older Nonconformist denominations had, at that time, become a significant influence in the life of north-east Wales, to the extent they had become in South Wales and indeed in south Caernarfonshire and Anglesey in the North. We can thus understand Coke's eagerness to send missionaries to those parts of North Wales which had not as yet come under 'evangelical' influences, as understood by a Methodist. So it happened that in 1800, for the first time, a Welsh-speaking circuit, Ruthin, appeared in the *Minutes* of the Conference. Owen Davies was given 'an unlimited commission to form a new Circuit'. Neither he nor his young colleague was a fluent Welsh-speaker, but they began without delay to proclaim the Gospel, as it was understood amongst the Methodists, throughout North Wales. In 1801, John Bryan, a fluent Welsh-speaker, was received as a Preacher on Trial and stationed in North Wales, and year by year the team was strengthened by new recruits, many of whom were eloquent and influential preachers.

The first few years were years of rapid growth, in North Wales to begin with, and from 1805 onwards in South Wales as well. By 1809 there were 5,826 members in the Welsh-speaking circuits, and a goodly number of chapels had been opened. Soon after his coming to North Wales John Hughes had written in his diary: 'The Calvinists will no doubt oppose us . . .' and after a short period of friendliness they did so. The peaceful days when John Wesley and Howel Harris were at the helm had now receded into a dim and distant past, and more militant men were in control. In 1745, the *Minutes* of the Conference had stated that the truth of the Gospel lies, 'as it were, within a hair's breadth' of Calvinism and Antinomianism, but the nineteenth-century controversialists, on both sides, tended to exaggerate the differences between Wesley's doctrines and those of Harris. There is no doubt that many people welcomed the Wesleyans because of their doctrines, but it is also true that many Calvinists found the doctrine of Election a very comfortable doctrine. The early nineteenth-century controversies probably enlightened the minds of many, but they also left behind them an aftermath of bitterness, which persisted throughout the century and did nothing to enhance brotherly love.

It was certainly one of the aims of the early leaders of Welsh Methodism to teach men the truths of the Gospel as they understood them. Hence their active support to Sunday schools for both adults and children, and their eagerness to publish books, pamphlets and periodicals. At an early stage in their history they published their first hymn-book, *Diferion y Cyssegr* (1802), edited by John Hughes. In January 1809, the first number of the monthly magazine, *Yr Eurgrawn Wesleyaidd*, appeared; it is still being published – although it now appears quarterly – and is the oldest extant Welsh magazine.

The main intention of Coke, however, had been to evangelize Wales, and the early fathers regarded themselves primarily, not as theological teachers, but as proclaimers of good tidings. In that respect their work for years was markedly successful. But after the successes of the first decade, there followed some years of disappointment and frustration, and for nearly another decade the annual return of membership showed a steady decline. Whatever were the initial causes of that decline, the attempts made by the Conference to deal with the crisis proved unfortunate. Attempts were made in South Wales between 1814 and 1817 to amalgamate the English and Welsh societies, only to be met with hostility on both sides. At Brecon, the English party went so far as to lock the chapel against the Welsh Preachers, and one can easily imagine how much hard feeling was caused by their action. The policy of amalgamation was finally abandoned in 1817, but the very word became a term of opprobrium amongst South Wales Methodists for generations, and must have added to the difficulty of dealing realistically with the ever-changing bilingual situation in the Principality. During the same period, Conference withdrew a large number of ministers from the Welsh work and transferred them to England, among them some of the leaders of the mission, men like Owen Davies, John Bryan, Edward Jones, David Rogers and others, thus permanently impoverishing the life and witness of the circuits.[3] The circuits which felt the effects of these changes most keenly were in north-west Wales, which accounts for the weakness of Methodism in Gwynedd as compared with the north-east to the present day.

These changes, together with a later reduction in financial aid, deferred the recovery of Welsh Methodism for some years, and perhaps made a full recovery impossible. The decay had set in before Conference intervened, but Welsh Methodists tended to ascribe the blame for all their failures to Conference, and that at a time when the confidence of Methodists in their supreme court was being assailed from other directions as well. After 1817, however, Welsh Methodism began a slow process of recovery, which continued without interruption until 1830, when the movement had to face the gravest crisis in all its history.

Some of the secessions which had occurred in British Methodism from 1797 onwards had not been without their influence in Wales, but that influence had been felt mainly amongst the English-speaking branch. The Bible Christians, for example, had arrived in South Wales by the early 1820s, if not earlier. These early quarrels, however, had occurred in England. What Wales had felt were their repercussions coming across its borders. Welsh-speaking Methodists had not been unaware of some of these controversies, and a Welsh secession, under the

[3] John Hughes had gone over to the English work some years previously.

leadership of Thomas Jones, had occurred in Liverpool in 1818. Jones and his friends aligned themselves with the Independent Methodists of England, and tried to persuade some Methodists in North Wales to break away from orthodox Methodism. In that way, at least, they had prepared the ground for the great upheaval of 1831, and there is some evidence that Thomas Jones himself was directly responsible for that upheaval.

The 1831 secession was largely due to a revolt of some local preachers, mainly in Caernarfonshire and Anglesey, against the Methodist discipline and practice. The leaders claimed that 'the Churches should receive a greater variety of preaching', both ministerial and especially lay, by a more frequent interchange of preachers between one circuit and another. In order to achieve that end, it was suggested that a meeting be held in North Wales to station preachers for 1832, 'to which every circuit should send a local preacher and a leader', but at which the attendance of the ministers was to be optional. It is not surprising that the seceders were bitterly critical of the ministers and of the Conference, causing great bitterness on all sides at the time, and in many quarters a distrust of the Connexional principle which persisted for generations.

The new movement formally came into being on 6 October 1831, when seven Anglesey 'reformers' were expelled from the Connexion by the Quarterly Meeting. In a short time, Methodists from Caernarfonshire and other parts of North Wales joined them. The signs were that a comparatively strong denomination would soon be formed, leaving the parent body considerably weakened. The 'revolt' itself was purely Welsh in origin, but the seceders soon joined similar bodies in England – first the Independent Methodists and later the Wesleyan Methodist Association. Its main strength was always in the north-west, but it had a few societies also in Denbighshire, Merionethshire, Flintshire, and even as far south as Aberystwyth and Carmarthen. The early zeal of the 'reformers', however, soon gave place to despondency, largely owing to financial problems. Before 1840, many of the strongest seceding churches had returned to the parent body, thus breaking the backbone of the revolt. In time, other churches joined other denominations, or else returned to the orthodox Wesleyans. The fact that many of the churches submitted to Conference because of economic pressures was disconcerting: they did not return because they had been convinced of the rightness of the Methodist constitution. Hence many of the leaders, either at the time or later, sought a spiritual home in other churches. As a separate denomination, the 'Minor Wesleyans' (as they were popularly known) were insignificant, but their indirect influence was considerable. The upheaval checked the growth of orthodox Wesleyanism and engendered considerable prejudice against its method of government.

When the Reform Movement of 1849 arose, however, it found little support amongst the Methodists of North Wales. When the leaders of that Movement visited the Bethesda–Tregarth district (in Caernarfonshire) in 1854, an area which had been one of the strongholds of the 'Minor Wesleyans', they failed to win any supporters. This may have been due to the superior debating abilities of the superintendent of the circuit, Thomas Aubrey, but also to the fact that the revolt of 1831 had proved so futile. It was only in South Wales, an area almost untouched by the troubles of 1831, that the 1849 Reformers found sympathetic listeners.

In 1828, the Welsh-speaking circuits had been grouped into two Districts: the North Wales District consisted of 4,155 members; the South Wales District of 3,026. Thirty years later, the increase in membership in North Wales had been three times as large as it had been in the south, despite the fact that the Industrial Revolution had transformed the face of the south-east. Welsh-speaking Methodism had always been stronger in the north than in the south. It had been easier for it to gain a foothold there, because (as I have already explained) the other Free Churches had not taken a firm hold of many parts of the north, whilst in the south they had all the advantages on their side. Nevertheless, one cannot help feeling that Welsh Methodism failed to respond adequately to the challenge of the South Wales valleys at the time of their most rapid development in the nineteenth century. A considerable proportion of the blame belongs to the leaders in the north, who should have sent some of their ablest men to the valleys when a door was being opened wide to them. The mission of John Evans (Eglwysbach) to Pontypridd came rather late in the day, but one of the significant things about that mission is the fact that many Welsh Methodists were blind to the importance of such an enterprise and tended to be critical of it.

Meanwhile, with the rapid influx of people from England, the English-speaking circuits were making steady progress and were responding to the challenge of the times. In South Wales some of the pioneers of industrialization, such as Thomas Guest and Richard Crawshay and others whose names are prominent in industrial history, were enthusiastic Methodists. Their example and active support contributed considerably to the growth of English Methodism in South Wales. Moreover, a large number of the workers who flocked to the valleys had been members of society in their native areas, and they brought their religion with them to the factories and the mines. In the south-east, new chapels were built and new circuits formed to cater for the spiritual needs of the teeming crowds of immigrants. In 1800, the Cardiff circuit, for instance, was only four years old, having been carved out of the Swansea circuit. It had two ministers – an ordained minister and a probationer. In 1900, there were five English Wesleyan circuits in the city with fourteen ministers, not to mention the Welsh circuit and those circuits belonging to other branches of the Methodist family. The rural South Wales which John Wesley knew had changed beyond all recognition and especially the south-east, and his people were to be found in all the industrial towns and most of the villages of Monmouthshire, Glamorganshire, east Carmarthenshire and adjoining areas.

Industrialization had not taken place to such a marked extent in the north, but there also the old order was passing away. A new circuit was formed at Wrexham in 1803, from which the Oswestry circuit was formed sixty years later. In 1747, John Wesley had great difficulty in finding anybody in the Caernarfon district who knew enough English to direct him on his way to Anglesey, but less than a century later the Caernarfon–Bangor area had been sufficiently Anglicized to justify the formation of an English circuit there. The growth of places like Rhyl, Colwyn Bay and Llandudno occurred later, but, thanks to men like Frederick Payne, Methodism kept pace with that growth and established strong and flourishing churches along the North Wales coast.

When the Welsh missionaries came to Wales in 1800, the movement they represented was not well known in the Principality, and for many generations the Wesleyans were regarded as a semi-alien breed. From about the middle of the nineteenth century onwards, however, it has become gradually more a part of the life of Welsh Wales. To some extent it has developed its own machinery of government, whilst remaining under the ultimate control of the British Conference. In the late 1850s Welsh Home Mission Funds and Welsh Chapel Loan Funds were formed in the Welsh Districts, which gave the Synods a large measure of autonomy in those fields. We have already referred to the interest of the early fathers in the publication of suitable literature for their people. In 1887, a new building was erected at Bangor to house the Welsh Bookroom. In 1897, a fund was launched to enable suitable candidates for the ministry to receive part of their training at the University of Wales, and it is difficult to overestimate the benefits the Church received from contacts made at the University between its future leaders and those of other Churches. In 1899, the Welsh Assembly was formed, mainly as a consultative body, binding the Welsh Districts together, but it became also a visible sign that Welsh Methodism existed as an entity to some extent separate from the Conference. Its legislative powers were actually very small, and confined to such concerns as the administration of the Bookroom and kindred matters, but to members of other Churches the Assembly, with its President, was the symbol of a denomination which could stand side by side with other denominations.

In many matters Methodism aligned itself increasingly with the other

Nonconformist denominations. The early fathers were, generally speaking, Tory in politics and largely Anglican in their sympathies. It was probably the influence of the Oxford Movement, regarded by many as Popery in disguise, that began to turn the minds of Welsh Methodists away from their original loyalties, but for a considerable time they were regarded with some suspicion by the more radical denominations. Many Wesleyan leaders, for instance, could not agree with other Nonconformists on educational matters, and their uncompromising attitude to the more radical seceders of 1831 and 1849 branded them as reactionaries. But before the end of the century the majority of the Welsh Wesleyan 'hierarchy' were probably Liberal in politics, and supported such causes as the Disestablishment of the Church of England in Wales as fervently as the leaders of the other Free Churches. Their full participation in those movements supported by all the Nonconformist bodies was a considerable help to bring them out of their isolation into the life of the nation.

In other directions their contribution to the life of Wales was small. The nineteenth century was not notable in the history of Welsh literature, for instance; but it is not without significance that hardly a single 'Wesleyan' made any important contribution to literature. Their interests were almost wholly confined to the fields of biblical and theological studies, and even in those fields they made their contribution in the pulpit rather than in the press. The Movement was blessed throughout the century with great preachers, the greatest of whom, perhaps, was John Evans of Eglwysbach. The movement came to Wales as an evangelical mission, and so it remained, to a very large extent, from 1800 to 1900.

I have endeavoured to trace, at least in outline, the history of Welsh and English Methodists. They were part and parcel of the same Church, and Welsh-speaking Methodists were proud of their links with the Connexion at large. The monthly magazine, *Yr Eurgrawn Wesleyaidd*, kept them informed of movements in England and overseas, and regularly reported what the Conference debated and decided. The Welsh Wesleyans did not lack interest in the mission-field, and contributed men and money to the work overseas. They were not a parochial people, nor were they narrowly nationalistic. Nevertheless very few links were forged between the English and the Welsh sections of Methodism in Wales. The two lived and grew in almost complete isolation, and sometimes in mutual suspicion. Both might have benefited from a larger measure of fellowship and co-operation. But perhaps they did not particularly feel the need of one another. On the whole, apart from some periods of decline, both sections were gaining strength and influence from one generation to another, and were full of hope and expectation for the future.

They did fall on periods of regression and depression, it is true, but those were mainly of short duration. Great revivals, like those of 1859 and 1904–5, brought new life to the churches and rekindled their hopes. The twentieth century was to bring problems undreamt of in the previous century, but those belonged to the future. As we leave the Welsh and English Methodists of Wales at the end of the nineteenth century, we leave them as a people who could look back on their history with gratitude and a considerable measure of pride, and who looked to the future with eagerness and expectation.[3]

[3] This chapter covers only the period up to 1900.

VII

Methodism in Scotland

A. SKEVINGTON WOOD

It was in the spring of 1751 that John Wesley first ventured across the border into Scotland. He had been invited by an army officer, Captain Gallatin, who was then stationed at Musselburgh. It hardly seemed a propitious project: both his brother Charles and his friend George Whitefield expressed their misgivings.[1] A Scots mist concealed the landscape as he and one of his itinerants, Christopher Hopper, made for the quaint little firthside town. The visit only lasted two days and included a quick trip to Edinburgh.[2] But it was long enough for the worthies of Musselburgh to be impressed by Wesley's preaching and beg him to remain. They even offered to provide a more suitable auditorium than the school which had been hurriedly brought into use. Wesley, however, was committed to his itinerary and could only promise to arrange for his colleague to return. A week later Hopper did so and, in his own words, 'This was the beginning of a good work in Scotland.'[3]

What prompted Wesley to take a step which he must have known might well lead to the formation of Methodist societies in a land where Presbyterianism was so strong? Clearly, he regarded Gallatin's approach as a providential call. Beyond that, William Myles believed that Wesley wanted 'to make a stand against the overflowing of Arianism

[1] Thomas Jackson (ed.), *The Journal of Charles Wesley* (London 1849), ii, 91–2; *The Works of George Whitefield*, ii (London 1771), 420–1; Wesley, *Letters*, iv, 295.

[2] Wesley, *Journal*, iii, 522–3; *Works*, xiii, 299.

[3] Thomas Jackson (ed.), *The Lives of Early Methodist Preachers chiefly written by themselves*, i (London 1865), 206; David Wilson, in *Methodism in Scotland: A Brief Sketch of its Rise, Progress and Present Position* (Aberdeen 1850), p. 7, conjectured that Methodism was first introduced into Scotland by Dr John Memyss, who moved from Wrexham to Aberdeen about 1747; but he joined the congregation of an evangelical minister, John Bissett, and it was only after the latter's death in 1756 that, on a visit to London, Memyss urged Wesley to send a preacher. Hopper eventually arrived in 1759 (*Journal*, iv, 449n.).

and Socinianism in that kingdom'.[4] The Scottish Church had been torn by theological controversy. John Simson, Professor of Divinity at Glasgow, was accused of teaching Arian views similar to those expressed by Samuel Clarke, whose treatise on *The Scripture-Doctrine of the Trinity* (London 1712) had caused such a commotion in England.[5]

It is unlikely that Wesley intended to cast himself in the role of another Athanasius by entering the lists to engage in direct controversy, although he inherited his father's suspicion of Arian deviations.[6] Nor did he propose to wage verbal warfare against the entrenched Calvinism of the Kirk by pressing the claims of Arminian doctrine. This was what Whitefield feared, but Wesley reassured him: 'I will give them no provocation to dispute; for I will studiously avoid controverted points, and keep to the fundamental truths of Christianity.'[7] In so doing, nevertheless, Wesley would make a positive contribution towards stemming the tide of error and unbelief which had aroused his concern.

Another factor must have encouraged him to involve himself in the Scottish scene. Revival had already begun to manifest itself, at first quite independently of what had been happening in England. By the year 1745 the awakening in the Highlands, which started under the ministry of John Balfour at Nigg, had reached a climax.[8] Meanwhile, Whitefield's visits to Cambuslang in 1741 and again in 1742 had touched off a work of the Spirit which was to spread elsewhere along the Forth–Clyde valley and into Perthshire. Wesley knew of these stirrings, and they may have influenced his ultimate decision to cross the Tweed.

He was to pay twenty-two visits to Scotland between 1751 and 1790.[9] He usually travelled in the spring when the weather was apt to be indifferent. His main objective seems to have been to establish societies in the principal cities of Scotland. He went regularly to Edinburgh, the capital, and found a friend and ally in Dr Alexander Webster, minister of the Tolbooth Church, who was Moderator of the General Assembly in 1753. It was in Edinburgh, too, that Wesley met D'Arcy, Lady Maxwell, the widow of Sir Walter Maxwell, fourth baronet of Pollok. She joined the Methodist society whilst still remaining a communicant member of St Cuthbert's Church. Lady Maxwell supported Wesley in Scotland as Mary Bosanquet and Lady Mary Fitzgerald did in the south.

[4] William Myles, *A Chronological History of the People Called Methodists* (Liverpool 1790), p. 57; cf. George Smith, *History of Wesleyan Methodism* (London 1865), ii, 71.

[5] John H. S. Burleigh, *A Church History of Scotland* (London 1960), p. 290.

[6] *Journal*, vii, 28; viii, 90; cf. Martin Schmidt, *John Wesley: A Theological Biography*, i (Eng. tr. London 1962), 45.

[7] *Letters*, iv, 295.

[8] John MacInnes, *The Evangelical Movement in the Highlands of Scotland 1688 to 1800* (Aberdeen 1951), p. 156.

[9] The visits may total twenty-three if we include Wesley's journey through the south-west in 1767 on the way to Portpatrick and Ireland (*Journal*, v, 201).

Perhaps even more significant was his contact with Dr John Gillies in Glasgow. It was he who invited Wesley to the city in 1753. Gillies was for fifty-four years the distinguished minister of the College Church, the confidant and biographer of Whitefield and the historian of revivals in Scotland. As Dugald Butler put it, 'to Wesley he was a kind of Scottish Fletcher of Madeley'.[10] He shared Wesley's own catholicity of spirit and did much to demolish the barriers of prejudice which might have impeded Wesley's usefulness in Scotland. When he was offered the pulpit of the College Church, Wesley commented: 'Who would have believed, five-and-twenty years ago, either that the minister would have desired it or that I should have consented to preach in a Scotch kirk?'[11]

It was not until 1761 that Wesley reached Aberdeen. Here he sought permission to preach in the grounds of Marischal College, but because of rain he was given the use of the Hall.[12] Later the Principal, the Very Reverend Dr George Campbell, together with faculty members and magistrates, came to hear him. A society was already in existence and as a result of Wesley's preaching the membership increased from forty to close on ninety.[13]

It must not be supposed, however, that Wesley restricted himself to the major cities of Scotland. There were in fact few towns which he did not include in his itinerary. Invariably he was well received. 'Oh what a difference there is between South and North Britain!' he wrote. 'Every one here at least loves to hear the Word of God; and none takes it into his head to speak one uncivil word to any for endeavouring to save their souls.'[14] On the other hand, Wesley sometimes complained that whilst his Scottish congregations were politely attentive, they also appeared to be unmoved by his message.[15]

Despite the favourable reception accorded to him, Wesley was well aware that Methodism made far less headway in Scotland than in England. Statistically speaking, its growth was unimpressive. Nevertheless, Wesley's overall impact on the existing Church was considerable and lasting. 'If the John Wesley of Scottish history founded no extensive organisation on Scottish soil, the John Wesley *in* Scottish religion has been an influence of the deepest and most pervading kind,' concluded Butler. 'In Scotland, assuredly, Wesley's work has been a victory; the spirit of his movement within the Church has been an expansive force.'[16] The full effect was not apparent until the beginning of the next century under leaders like Andrew Mitchell Thomson and

[10] Dugald Butler, *John Wesley and George Whitefield in Scotland* (Edinburgh 1898), p. 123.
[11] *Journal*, iv, 63.
[12] Ibid., iv, 450.
[13] Ibid., iv, 451.
[14] Ibid., v, 75; cf. vii, 387.
[15] Ibid., vi, 19–20, 499.
[16] Butler, op. cit., p. 221.

Thomas Chalmers. In this development the mark of Wesley is unmistakable, in the realms both of belief and practice. As Professor J. H. S. Burleigh recognizes, 'His influence was the quite general one of preparing the way for the Evangelical revival of the nineteenth century.'[17] Nor must it be forgotten that, so far as we know, Wesley was a pioneer in introducing the singing of hymns into the worship of the Scottish Church.

We can hardly speak of Wesley apart from his helpers. This is especially true in the case of Scotland. 'It cannot be gainsaid that the establishment of Methodism in Scotland was due, not so much to the frequent visits of Wesley himself, as to the toil and travail of his preachers,' acknowledged Swift.[18] The hardships they endured are well-nigh unimaginable. Thomas Taylor confessed that Scotland subjected him to severer tests than he had yet known in his ministry.[19] Matthew Lumb found 'everything disagreeable to flesh and blood except the kindness of the people'.[20] Jonathan Crowther told Wesley: 'No man is fit for Inverness circuit, unless his flesh be brass, his bones iron, and his heart harder than a stoic's.'[21]

The most successful of these early preachers were themselves Scots. They understood the people in a way which was hardly possible for their English colleagues. They had shared the deprivations and disturbances of a troubled period. Outstanding amongst them was the Highlander, Duncan McAllum, whom Wesley nicknamed the 'north star'.[22] David Wilson referred to 'his almost apostolic labours'.[23] He spent nineteen years of his ministry in the Aberdeen and Inverness circuits and regularly preached four times a Sunday – twice in English and twice in Gaelic. It is recorded that,

> when his congregations were not equal to his expectations, and when other means failed to increase them, he announced that he would preach from any text that might be named to him, a *tour de force* that appealed to the tastes of his critical sermon-loving Scotch hearers.[24]

But McAllum did not stand alone. We can do no more than mention Duncan Wright, who brushed up the Gaelic he spoke as a boy in order

[17] Burleigh, op. cit., p. 295.

[18] Wesley F. Swift, *Methodism in Scotland: The First Hundred Years* (London 1947), p. 12,

[19] R. Spence Hardy, *Gleanings in Methodism to be Rescattered in Scotland* (Edinburgh 1857), p. 257; T. Jackson (ed.), *Early Methodist Preachers*, v (London 1866), 37.

[20] Hardy, op. cit., p. 257.

[21] MS autobiography; cf. Luke Tyerman, *The Life and Times of the Rev. John Wesley, M.A., Founder of the Methodists*, iii (London 1871), 507.

[22] Cf. *Wesleyan-Methodist Magazine* (September 1834), p. 717; *City Road Magazine* (1875), pp. 560ff.

[23] Wilson, op. cit., p. 14.

[24] Cf. Wesley F. Swift, *The Romance of Banffshire Methodism* (Banff 1927), p. 29.

to preach Christ to eager Highlanders;[25] Peter Mill, from Arbroath, an indefatigable itinerant who, when his toenails were loosened under the strain of constant walking, would tie them on with a piece of sheep's wool;[26] Robert Dall, born in Dundee, who once tramped over six hundred miles to and from a mission;[27] and Alexander McNab, a Perthshire man, adjudged by Dr Webster to be an even greater orator than the famous Hugh Blair.[28]

Other helpers came from south of the border and proved their mettle. Christopher Hopper has already been mentioned as Wesley's companion on the pioneer visit to Scotland. In 1759 he undertook an extensive tour including Leith, Dundee, Aberdeen and Peterhead. Within the next two years he twice covered the same ground and could report that 'the work of the Lord prospered in our hands' and that there was now 'a fair prospect of a great harvest in North Britain'.[29]

Although the Methodist witness in Scotland began in Musselburgh, a society was not formed there until some years later.[30] The first Methodist cause to be officially established in Scotland was at Dunbar. It was founded by soldiers. Some of John Haime's converts in the dragoons, who had fought at Dettingen and Fontenoy in the War of the Austrian Succession, were stationed at Dunbar and soon hired a room for prayer and Bible study. Eventually a number of local citizens joined them, so that when Wesley arrived in 1757 he 'found a little society, most of them rejoicing in God their Saviour'.[31] According to Thomas Rankin, first President of the American Methodist Conference, who was a native of Dunbar, the society there dated back to 1755, although an article in *The Haddingtonshire Courier* places it even earlier.[32] The chapel, which Wesley described as 'the cheerfullest in the kingdom', was probably opened in 1770.[33] It is the oldest surviving Methodist building in Scotland. The octagon at Aberdeen, no longer in use, was the first Methodist chapel to be erected (in 1764).

During Wesley's lifetime only eight chapels were opened. Other congregations met in premises that had been either hired or bought, such as the disused malt-kilns at Elgin, Inverness and Newburgh; the hall

[25] T. Jackson (ed.), op. cit., ii (London 1866), 127.
[26] Swift, *Methodism in Scotland*, p. 41.
[27] A. N. Cass, *Methodism in Dundee 1759–1959* (Dundee n.d.), p. 10.
[28] *D.N.B.*, lx, 114.
[29] T. Jackson (ed.), op. cit., i, 211.
[30] Ibid., v, 156.
[31] *Journal*, iv, 218.
[32] T. Jackson (ed.), op. cit., v, 156; *Haddingtonshire Courier*, 1 May 1914. This is said to be 'at least six and probably nearly ten years before Wesley's first visit', i.e. in 1751 or 1747. Abel Stevens, *The History of the Religious Movement of the Eighteenth Century, called Methodism* (New York 1878), i, 183, claimed that Wesley found the society prospering twelve years later, implying that it was started in 1745; but Rankin's evidence appears to be decisive.
[33] Swift, op. cit., p. 46; *Journal*, v, 368.

above the vaults of a former Franciscan nunnery at Dundee; and the room in the Meal Vennel at Perth. When Wesley died in 1791 there were 1,179 members in Scotland, with sixteen preachers.[34] It might seem a meagre harvest after such heroic efforts.

One reason why the expansion of Methodism in Scotland was so slow in the early years was that a particularly crippling doctrinal controversy threatened to wreck the good work. Hopper referred to it as a period when Christians spent their 'time and strength about the meaning of words, instead of promoting the fear and love of God'.[35] It arose from the protest of Dr John Erskine, minister of Greyfriars Church, Edinburgh, and a highly respected Evangelical leader, against Wesley's Arminian theology. In republishing James Hervey's *Aspasio Vindicated* (Edinburgh 1765), Erskine chose to insert a caustic preface of his own in which he not only assailed Wesley's doctrine as blending 'with some precious gospel truths a medley of Arminian, Antinomian, and enthusiastic errors', but also impugned his character by accusing him of deceitfulness in forbidding his preachers in Scotland to deal with polemical topics.[36] Wesley refused to be drawn into an unseemly dispute. He wrote to Erskine and then went to see him in an attempt to achieve a reconciliation, but with no success. 'I love and reverence him,' Wesley confessed to a correspondent, 'but not his doctrine.'[37] No doubt Erskine would have said the same about Wesley. But the damage had been done and the spread of Methodism was seriously retarded. In 1770, Willielma, Viscountess Glenorchy, an intimate of Lady Maxwell, who had opened a chapel in Niddry's Wynd, Edinburgh, where Wesley's preachers were regularly welcomed, separated from Methodism and joined the Calvinistic cause. It was little short of a miracle that Wesley's societies in Scotland survived this upheaval.

It was in an attempt to consolidate the position that Wesley was led in 1785 to take what Swift called 'an important, decisive, and, indeed, a despairing step' in ordaining three of his most experienced preachers for the ministry in Scotland.[38] Eight more were added by 1788. Was this merely a measure to prevent the collapse of the Scottish work under the strain of theological controversy, or did Wesley actually intend to inaugurate a distinct Methodist Church in Scotland? There is some evidence to suggest that the latter may have been the case. David Wilson, reviewing the situation in the middle of the last century, regretted that what he regarded as Wesley's own plan had been set aside by a Conference resolution in 1793, when the recognition of ordained

[34] *Minutes*, i (1791), 252; there was one supernumerary preacher also.

[35] T. Jackson (ed.), op. cit., i, 211.

[36] *Eleven Letters from the late Rev. Mr. Hervey to the Rev. Mr. John Wesley* (Edinburgh 1765), preface, p. 6; for Wesley's reply, see *Works*, x, 346–57.

[37] *Letters*, v, 91.

[38] Swift, op. cit., p. 56.

ministers and the wearing of gown and bands were dropped.[39] He claimed that Wesley had founded the Methodist Church in Scotland, conformed in externals to the established Presbyterian Church of the country, with a metal communion token as a badge of membership. Within this framework the salient features of the Methodist societies were retained. Wilson considered that a separate Scottish Conference should have been set up. If this was indeed what Wesley meant, it is curious that there is no reference to it in any of his published writings.

Wilson was not the only nineteenth-century observer to take the view that the development of Scottish Methodism had been seriously impeded through the reversal of what was considered to be Wesley's own scheme. 'Had the arrangements of our venerated founder regarding Scotland been faithfully adhered to and efficiently carried out the direct effects of the system would in all probability have been much more extensive,' insisted a contributor to the *Wesleyan-Methodist Magazine* in 1849.[40] But instead, every effort was made after Wesley's death to assimilate Scottish to English Methodism. Membership had risen steeply from the time of Wesley's decision to ordain ministers for Scotland, and this increase continued until 1819, when the total reached 3,786.[41] From that year, however, a decline set in, and by 1826 the figure had fallen by more than a thousand. Both Adam Clarke and Jabez Bunting advocated withdrawal since the finances were on the verge of bankruptcy. An over-ambitious programme of chapel building, carried out by Valentine Ward, a District Chairman in Scotland for thirteen disastrous years, had largely contributed to this abysmal state of affairs. The situation was eventually retrieved, however, and a limited number of societies maintained. But ground had been lost at a time when an expanding population provided wider opportunities for outreach.

As the Shetland Islands belong geographically to Scotland, we must note how Methodism started there, even though a separate District emerged almost at once. In June 1822, Duncan McAllum's son, Daniel, then stationed in the Edinburgh circuit, visited the societies already pioneered in the Shetlands by a lay missionary, John Nicolson.[42] McAllum reported to the Conference that the spiritual oversight of the population numbering 25,000 could not be effectively maintained by the twelve parish ministers placed there by the Church of Scotland and that an extension of the Methodist witness appeared to be justified. A few Congregational and Baptist causes had been established following an evangelistic tour undertaken by James Haldane in 1799. He had been brought over by a group of Shetlanders who were influenced by reading Wesley's sermons and *Journal*. They had originally invited Dr Thomas

[39] Wilson, op. cit., p. 10.

[40] *Wesleyan-Methodist Magazine* (January 1849), p. 74.

[41] *Minutes*, v (1819), 36.

[42] *Wesleyan-Methodist Magazine* (November 1835), p. 861; *W.H.S. Proc.*, xxxviii, 137–8.

Coke to conduct the mission, on the advice of the Methodist District Chairman. Because of this link, the first Methodist preachers regarded themselves as continuing Haldane's 'Society for the Propagation of the Gospel at Home'.

John Nicolson had been a bombardier in the Royal Artillery and was converted in London under the ministry of the Methodists. In 1819 he returned to his native Shetland filled with evangelistic zeal. Two years later he could claim that he had formed a circuit covering thirty miles which he managed to get round once a month. He laboured single-handed and was eventually compelled to ask for help from Joseph Benson at the Conference office in London. It was in response to this appeal that McAllum was sent to inspect the station, and by the autumn of 1822 two preachers officially appointed by the Conference arrived in Lerwick. One was John Raby, who had served in the Caribbean. The other was a fiery Cornishman, Samuel Dunn, who was later involved in the Fly Sheets controversy. When Nicolson died in 1828, there were four circuits in a separate Shetland District with over a thousand members. Adam Clarke, who was President of the Conference when the project was launched, directed the Shetland mission with remarkable vigour and discernment during the last ten years of his life. He constantly urged the preachers to uphold a distinctive witness not only in evangelism and fellowship, but also in agitating for social reform.

The development of Methodism in the Shetlands, considerably more rapid than on the Scottish mainland, owes much to the influence of these pioneers. At present, Methodist membership is approximately one-fifth of the Church of Scotland total, representing a substantially higher proportion than on the mainland.

Clarke was responsible, too, for initiating Methodist work in the Orkneys. Dunn was sent there in 1825, and in 1834 John Knowles responded to a call from the fishermen of Stronsay. As a result, a circuit was constituted with two preachers, one of whom was soon transferred to Wick on the mainland. Little progress was made, however, and eventually the declining societies were handed over to the Free Church of Scotland after the Disruption of 1843.

It was in 1826 that the Primitive Methodists extended their influence north of the border. Four years previously, a Christian philanthropist in Scotland had begged William Clowes to hold an evangelistic mission. Unfortunately the letter was mislaid, and Clowes did not respond.[43] Had he been able to do so, Primitive Methodism might have got off to a better start than it did. As it was, the lead was given by the Sunderland circuit, which sent two missionaries to Edinburgh.[44] Thomas Oliver

[43] H. Bickerstaffe Kendall, *The Origin and History of the Primitive Methodist Church* (London 1906), ii, 208.

[44] *Primitive Methodist Magazine* (1878), p. 629.

and Jonathan Clewer went on foot to save the coach fare. They stood in the Grassmarket, where so many martyrs had confessed their faith during the Scottish Reformation. After they had sung the hymn, 'Arise, O Zion, rise and shine', Oliver preached from a strikingly apposite text in II Kings 9.11 – 'Is all well? Wherefore came this mad fellow to thee?' Soon they were able to rent a room, previously used for weaving, and gather a society. Their strategy was in terms of house-to-house visitation. Within three months, over seven hundred families were approached. Both Thomas Chalmers and Thomas Guthrie adopted this method in the scheme of parochial oversight and mission which they later introduced.[45]

The newborn society quickly ran into trouble, however, when its superintendent left the Connexion, taking the preaching room and the majority of members with him. Two more ministers appointed from the Sunderland circuit also seceded, and it seemed that the Primitive Methodist witness in Scotland was stillborn. 'What shall we do for Edinburgh?' Clowes might well ask.[46] John Flesher was sent and, in spite of the setbacks at the start, the cause eventually recovered and the Victoria Terrace chapel was opened in 1861. Alloa and Dunfermline were missioned from Edinburgh in 1838, though not with conspicuous success.

Shortly after the pioneer project in Edinburgh a work began in Glasgow.[47] James Johnson was commissioned by the Carlisle circuit and preached on Glasgow Green beneath the Nelson monument. Within a few months the Primitive Methodist society grew to over a hundred members and the Lyceum Hall was hired for services. It is said that an admission fee of twopence was charged to prevent overcrowding. Before the first chapel was built in Suffolk Street the congregation moved to the Mechanics' Institute.

The cause in Glasgow had not been in existence for so much as a year when Johnson called for volunteers to evangelize Paisley.[48] The eager recruits marched from the Broomielaw to sing the gospel in Jail Square. An intensive campaign of visitation and open-air meetings led to the formation of a thriving society, which eventually found a regular home in the Philosophical Hall, known for the next forty years as the 'Ranters' Kirk'. It was here that a young servant girl, Bella McNair, learned to love the lively hymns that were used at the services and to sing them as she went about her household duties. She was overheard by one of the sons of the family. 'They acted upon my religious nature like the quickening influence of spring,' he testified, 'and evoked in my heart strong

[45] Kendall, op. cit., ii, 206.

[46] Ibid., 207.

[47] Joseph Ritson, *The Centenary of Glasgow Primitive Methodism 1826–1926* (Leominster 1926), pp. 5–8.

[48] Ibid., p. 29.

yearnings after God and goodness.'[49] When he asked about them and the church she attended, Bella invited him to the services. It was thus that Colin Campbell McKechnie was introduced to Primitive Methodism and quickly entered the ministry which he was to adorn for so many years. He became the littérateur of the denomination, associated with the founding of the *Christian Ambassador* (later, the *Quarterly Review*), which he edited for over forty years.

It is disappointing to discover that, after such a promising start, Primitive Methodism in the Glasgow area soon declined sharply. By 1846, numbers had dropped to a mere twenty-one. Analysing the reasons for this lapse, a writer in *The Primitive Methodist World* placed his finger on a significant factor.

> In the abundant zeal for souls the early missionaries neglected to provide a home for the converts they had made. They developed the power to obtain converts, but lacked the ability to retain them. They were allowed to drift away, or become members of other churches, for want of a building of their own in which to dwell. Halls, lofts, shops and other places may do as a starting place, but never as a permanent abode for God's people, and will never be considered (especially in Scotland) as churches.[50]

James Johnson came to Dundee in 1835 and, at the request of the congregation he had built up, remained until his death in 1864. Anecdotes which survive about 'Ranter' Johnson suggest that he preached 'Wesley's own "old, coarse Gospel", enlivened by a command of the local vernacular'.[51] On the day he died he followed his usual Sunday routine in summer, consisting of an 8 a.m. open-air meeting before delivering three sermons to his own congregation. His obituary notice is revealing:

> Sprung from the labouring class, he devoted the whole of his time to the promotion of the highest welfare of that class. Day after day he was to be found labouring like a city missionary among the outcast of the population.[52]

On Johnson's death his society, which had never been formally affiliated to the Primitive Methodist Connexion, voted to join the Wesleyans.

The beginnings of what in 1907 became United Methodism can be traced back in Scotland to the early nineteenth century. Until recently it was assumed that the Methodist New Connexion had no work north of the border, but the investigations of Dr Oliver A. Beckerlegge have

[49] Kendall, op. cit., ii, 140.
[50] *The Primitive Methodist World*, 24 May 1883.
[51] Cass, op. cit., p. 18.
[52] Quoted, ibid., p. 19.

shown that such was not the case.[53] From 1810 onwards, Scotland figured in the *Minutes* of the M.N.C. In that year it was recommended that a preacher should be allotted to Glasgow and Paisley when one was available. No immediate steps were taken, but by 1814 the tabular returns listed a society with one preacher, two local preachers and seventy-five members. Succeeding *Minutes* included directions about an exchange of preachers, first with Alnwick, then with North Shields, and finally with Bangor in Ulster. From 1818 onwards, the Scottish extension was associated with Ireland.

In that year, too, the East Clyde Chapel was opened in Glasgow with the help of a grant from the Home Missions fund. In 1827 the membership reached its maximum figure of 123 in three societies. No doubt this increase was due to the Leeds organ case which in England led to the emergence of the Protestant Methodists. The increment to the Methodist New Connexion in Glasgow was short-lived, and soon the membership fell to only thirty, the preacher was withdrawn, and the chapel closed. By 1834 the cause had disappeared from the survey in the *Minutes*.

Further societies, however, and conceivably the remnant of the Glasgow M.N.C. membership, joined the Wesleyan Methodist Association, formed in 1835 following a dispute in the Wesleyan Church about the foundation of a Theological Institution without adequately consulting the rank and file. Next year the Protestant Methodists joined the Association and the first annual Assembly was held in Manchester. Three ministers from Scotland were in attendance. Robert Anderson represented Edinburgh, whilst J. C. Kennedy and D. K. Shoebotham were sent by the 'Scottish United Methodist Churches'.[54] It would appear that these Churches had resulted from earlier secessions and had now agreed to join the Association. The evidence of later stations indicates that the Scottish United Methodist Churches stand for Paisley and Dundee, and that these places, together with Edinburgh, constituted the origins of Free Methodism in Scotland.[55]

Glasgow, Johnstone, Dumfries, Aberdeen, and Kilmarnock were afterwards added, but there were never more than six causes at any one time. Although their stations were listed in the *Minutes* and their ministers recognized by the Wesleyan Methodist Association, the Scottish Churches had their own Assembly to which the Association sent representatives.[56] The difficulty experienced by local authorities in classifying this latest offshoot of Methodism is reflected by the entries in the Paisley *Directory*. Here J. C. Kennedy's congregation is successively

[53] *W.H.S. Proc.*, xxix, 160–1; cf. xxviii, 96, 122.
[54] Oliver A. Beckerlegge, *The United Methodist Free Churches* (London 1957), p. 77.
[55] Ibid.
[56] Ibid., p. 72.

denominated as 'Dissenting Wesleyan Methodists', 'United Methodists', and 'Congregational Methodists'.[57] D. K. Shoebotham's society in Dundee, however, described itself as Independent Methodist. Finally it seceded in 1840, 'not wanting in anything to be subject to the Assembly of the Free Methodists'.[58] It survived as a Congregational church until the second decade of the twentieth century.

Our main purpose within the limits of a brief survey has been to trace the origins and early development of Methodism in Scotland. Its subsequent history can only be mentioned in closing. During the second half of the nineteenth century there was some advance, especially in the Wesleyan Church. In 1856 the membership had slumped to just over 2,000, and in an impassioned plea for drastic action Peter Prescott took the view that 'its condition, hovering between life and death, is such as must be terminated, and will, at no distant day, terminate itself, unless vigorous and effectual measures be resorted to for its renovation'.[59]

A period of considerable improvement followed, and by 1870 the membership had almost doubled. The rate of increase was now higher than in England, and new causes were started in a number of places.[60] Even before this more general advance, Alexander Patrick and a band of local preachers went out from Airdrie to conduct open-air and cottage meetings in the towns and villages of central Scotland. We hear of similar efforts elsewhere. Finance was still a major problem, however, and as a step towards consolidation the Relief and Extension Fund for Methodism in Scotland was launched in 1866. As the title implies, the ultimate objective in view was that outreach might be encouraged and the growth of the Church promoted.

It was out of a concern to evangelize the rapidly expanding urban population that the Scottish Central Halls were established. The first of these was opened in Edinburgh at the turn of the century. The initiative had been taken in 1888 when George Jackson, a young minister only a year out of College, was sent to pioneer the enterprise. Services were held in the Albert Hall in Shadwick Street, but soon its capacity of 600 was overtaxed. The Synod Hall of the United Presbyterian Church, holding 2,000 people, was hired and quickly filled. There the Edinburgh Mission remained until the Central Hall at Tollcross was built in 1901. Some of the means employed to reach the unchurched were strikingly novel at the time. Amongst them was a Sunday afternoon Men's

[57] *W.H.S. Proc.*, xxix, 99.

[58] Cass, op. cit., p. 16.

[59] Peter Prescott, *The Case of Scottish Methodism Impartially Considered* (London 1856), p. 6; the decline is also deplored and analysed in Thomas L. Parker, *Methodism in Scotland* (Knottingley 1867). The membership in 1856 was 2,143, excluding Dumfries (*Minutes* xiii (1856), 276).

[60] J. Robinson Gregory, *A History of Methodism: chiefly for the use of Students* (London 1911), ii, 127.

Meeting, where to his surprise Dr Marcus Dods, Principal of New College, found no fewer than 1,200 present, 'a solid bareheaded mass, waiting to hear about the Resurrection of Christ'.[61] Even more out of the ordinary was a Saturday night temperance public house. Missions were soon started also in Glasgow and Paisley – the latter as a result of a remarkable revival in a society on the point of extinction.

The Primitive Methodists shared in this expansion. In 1888 the Scottish Circuits became the North British District and enjoyed a measure of autonomy. Advance was particularly marked in Glasgow where membership rose sharply, new chapels were built, and the circuits grew to four, each with its own programme of extension.[62] In Edinburgh a forward movement was led by Samuel Horton, who had been dispatched by the Conference to halt the decline at Victoria Terrace. Consequently new premises were acquired and renamed the Livingstone Hall, after the famous Scottish missionary.[63] No United Methodist Free Churches remained.

Meanwhile, relations between Methodists and other communions had grown more cordial. The imaginative evangelistic strategy which had produced such impressive results commended itself to the Church of Scotland in particular. It was now recognized that Methodism had a valid contribution to make to the religious life of the country. Cooperation with other Churches became more common, and pulpit exchanges were arranged with mounting frequency. A joint Methodist Council was set up prior to the union of 1932, when the total membership stood at 11,997.[64] At present, the Methodist Synod in Scotland is engaged in multilateral conversations, although it has rejected a scheme for formal union with the Church of Scotland.

It is not to be supposed, however, that Methodism in Scotland has no distinctive contribution to make to a reunited Church. It has largely retained the essential features of Methodism, whilst at the same time adapting itself to its national setting. Its worship and discipline clearly reflect its provenance. In spirit and outlook it is patently Methodist. Its membership is not mainly recruited, as might be conjectured, from English immigrants or discontented Presbyterians, but is predominantly indigenous. With the development of neighbourhood churches, this is even more noticeable today than in the past. Scottish Methodism shares with Christians of other communions in the rising tide of concern for the welfare of the nation as such – for Scotland is not merely a region – but this involvement is not necessarily to be interpreted in terms of political nationalism.

[61] Marcus Dods (ed.), *Later Letters of Marcus Dods, D.D. (1895–1909)* (London 1911) p. 140.

[62] Ritson, op. cit., pp. 21–37.

[63] Kendall, op. cit., ii, 516–18.

[64] *Uniting Conference Agenda* (1932), p. 180.

Writing just before Methodist Union, S. Wilcox Stocker, the Wesleyan Chairman, insisted that 'our Church will never take the place it ought in Scotland until it fits in more definitely with Scottish life'.[65] Current trends suggest that Methodism in Scotland will increasingly integrate with its ecclesiastical and sociological environment as it shares in ecumenical ventures.

[65] *Methodist Magazine* (1928), p. 71.

VIII

Education

F. C. PRITCHARD

THIS chapter must start with John Wesley himself, for education was implicit in his evangelical technique. From his early days at Oxford he took a practical interest in education in its widest sense, and it is significant that the agenda of his first Conference in 1744 opened with the questions 'What to teach?' and 'How to teach?'[1] Reading was important because the Bible had to be studied by congregations as well as by preachers, and many of them could not read, still less write. Wesley was a pragmatist.

His educational memorial is of course Kingswood School, which opened in Bristol in 1748 and moved to Bath just over a hundred years later. It was a project, as Wesley himself recorded, on which he spent more time and thought and patience than on any other, and, in the years that have followed, his school has sent forth a steady stream of former pupils into community service: the ministry, teaching, the medical and legal professions. It has been the model and inspiration for other Kingswoods and Wesley Colleges in other parts of the world. Kingswood is in fact more than a memorial to John Wesley; it is a vital part of the Methodist Church in nurturing scholarship and service in a manner worthy of its founder and it bears the imprint of Wesley's rational mind and of his organizing ability. Wesley has been pilloried in some quarters for his narrow, strait-laced views on child mentality, and for the seemingly harsh and unimaginative discipline on which he insisted. In assessing such criticism, however, one needs to remember the eighteenth-century background of immorality and ill-discipline against which the original school was set.[2] Wesley had read educational theory, he had seen schools at work; but he was essentially a practical man, and

[1] *Minutes of the Wesleyan Conference* (1862), i, 1.
[2] *H.M.G.B.*, i, chs. 1–2.

his evangelical work compelled him to experiment and extemporize. In founding Kingswood he followed two guiding principles: provision of sound religious training, and control of pupils so that they would be insulated against everything that might vitiate that training. 'Our design,' he said, 'is with God's assistance to train up children in every branch of useful learning.' In this process the pupils had to be guarded against vice in general and from idleness and effeminacy in particular. It was to be 'a Christian family'. Only boarders were admitted, and they had never to leave the school from the beginning of their course until they left for good.[3]

There is little direct evidence, but it is tempting to see in the conduct and organization of early Kingswood a reflection of Wesley's friend, Philip Doddridge, Principal of the Dissenting Academy at Northampton. Although Wesley was an Anglican clergyman, his school at Kingswood was directly in the tradition of the Dissenting Academies with their strongly religious, though Nonconforming, emphases and their enlightened views on school curricula which combined a thorough knowledge of the Greek and Latin classics with the realism of contemporary thought and experience. Another of their features was a close relationship between general education and theological training. These academies were, after all, the only centres in which Dissenting ministers could receive specialized training. It was directly following that tradition, therefore, that John Wesley in 1749 held a residential course at Kingswood for seventeen of his preachers: an early answer to the oft-repeated Conference question, 'Can we have a seminary for labourers?' Wesley himself was never forgetful of the need for theological training, and his chief method of supplying the need was his careful preparation and distribution of extensive reading matter, a work about which he certainly consulted his friend at the Northampton Academy.[4] Always he insisted that his preachers should *know* the foundations of their faith. Two years before that first Conference, Wesley had opened the Orphan House at Newcastle-upon-Tyne as 'a place of worship, a school for orphans, a refuge for the injured and oppressed, and the theological institution of his preachers', where they received instruction in the efficient discharge of their preaching and pastoral duties. He also established libraries in London and Bristol for the preachers, libraries which included works on divinity, philosophy, history, poetry, the classics, and Hebrew. He had faith in his colleagues' will to learn, and not without justification did he claim, when he heard them attacked as ignorant

[3] For Wesley's own description, see his *Short Account of Kingswood School: Works*, xiii, 283–9; *Plain Account of Kingswood School: Works*, xiii, 289–301; *Remarks on the State of Kingswood School: Works*, xiii, 301–2; and see also A. G. Ives, *Kingswood School in Wesley's Day and Since* (London 1970).

[4] *Letters*, xi, 67, 151–2; *Journal*, iii, 206, 236n., 244–5. L. Tyerman, *The Life and Times of the Rev. John Wesley, M.A. Founder of the Methodists*, i (London 1870), 515–18.

men, that in biblical knowledge his preachers were inferior to none. Nor did he think only of theological training. He was an educator of all who had the will to learn, and insufficient credit has been given to him as one of the first editors of school textbooks. During the early years of Kingswood School nearly half the textbooks used were edited by Wesley himself, and such blind reliance was placed on their value that when in 1812 the second Methodist boarding school was opened, it was largely these textbooks which were prescribed for use.

In 1775 John Fletcher wrote to Wesley suggesting that Kingswood School become an institution for the education of preachers. Nothing more was heard of the suggestion, though in 1782 John Newton formulated a scheme for establishing such an institution on the lines of a Dissenting Academy for men who at the end of their course would be prepared to serve as clergy either in the Anglican Church or in the Churches of Dissent. The training of men for the ministry was early in the mind of Wesley's followers.

In founding Kingswood School, however, Wesley's primary concern was the education of boys. In his plans for that school can be seen the influence of the Dissenting Academies and reflections of what he had seen among the Moravians, but most of all what he had learned from his own mother. It was from Susannah Wesley and his own upbringing in the large family at Epworth that he inherited his practical approach to problems and his recognition of a need for strict discipline. Any group of people, young or old, living together in close proximity, must learn the art of cohabitation; the larger the group, the stricter had to be the rules. He saw this on board ship going to Georgia; he heard it expressed clearly in the long letter he received from his mother when he asked her advice on the education of children.[5]

Kingswood was not Wesley's only educational enterprise. He recorded his concern at 'the abundance of children' for whom there was no moral, mental, or spiritual training. A school was part of the community at the London Foundery; there was the Orphan House at Newcastle; the educational value of fellowship and mutual instruction in the band meetings was recognized, as it was even more later in the class meetings. Wesley was the first to experiment with a parent–teacher association; his publication of the *Christian Library* was another aspect of the enlightened teacher; his dispensaries for the sick and injured revealed his recognition of the importance of physical well-being in spiritual development. Religion for Wesley was an inherent part of ordinary life, but education was necessary to help others share that view and live life to the full.

Educationally, the period that followed his death was a dark one. By his own widespread and frequent contacts with his preachers Wesley had kept alive a spirit of inquiry and sound learning, but, with his

[5] *Journal*, iii, 34–9.

influence removed, learning tended to become too narrowly confined to the reading and exposition of the Bible, and there was a serious lack of cultured minds who could see the Bible against the background of the ancient classics. This was the concern of men like Adam Clarke, and Jabez Bunting was one of those who came to share that concern. If Methodism was to continue to be an evangelical force, it must be led by men in no way inferior intellectually to other church leaders. Directly from this concern came later the theological colleges; indirectly came the foundation of a second school to provide for the sons of preachers in the North what Kingswood was providing in the South. On 8 January 1812 Woodhouse Grove School was opened, and Methodism had its second boarding school.[6]

At that time there was more concern with the education of the preachers themselves than with that of their sons. In 1805 Jabez Bunting wrote:

> I am no friend to Colleges or Academies: but I do think that some regular, systematic plan ought to be adopted with respect to the young Preachers, during their four years of probation, which, without interrupting their pulpit labours, would make them more accurately and thoroughly acquainted with Divinity as a science, and qualify them for more extensive and permanent usefulness.[7]

He saw that unless preachers were trained, Methodism could not advance beyond a certain point, and he believed that first-rate potential scholars were being wasted through lack of opportunity for training. That was the view of Adam Clarke also. He recognized that many preachers educated themselves, but their scholarship lacked the inspiration of tutors and the stimulus and competition of other minds. In 1806, therefore, he asked at the Leeds Conference for information about a plan for improving young preachers. The plan was produced and distributed the following year to district meetings. 'We want,' he said, 'some kind of seminary for educating workmen for the vineyard of our God, as need not be ashamed. We need without delay to get such a place established, either at Bristol or London.'[8]

The plan was not to materialize till thirty years later, for Methodism at that time was suspicious of higher education and especially of any place that might be labelled 'college'. Nevertheless, views were changing. Some people were becoming fearful of the rapidly increasing population in industrial centres, with the resulting vagrancy and vice; others

[6] J. T. Slugg, *Woodhouse Grove School: Memorials and Reminiscences* (London 1885); H. W. Starkey, *A Short History of Woodhouse Grove School* (Bradford 1912); F. C. Pritchard, *The Story of Woodhouse Grove School* (Bradford 1978).

[7] Thomas Percival Bunting, *The Life of Jabez Bunting, D.D.* (London 1859), i, 259.

[8] W. Bardsley Brash, *The Story of Our Colleges 1835–1935: A Centenary Record of Ministerial Training in the Methodist Church* (London 1935), p. 26.

were realizing the horror of a society which allowed women and children to work in mines and mills with all the attendant exploitation; others, following Wesley himself, believed in the brotherhood of man and were courageous enough to act on their belief. So came the Factory Acts, though it is a shock to realize how late in the nineteenth century the evils of child labour still persisted. One problem was the sheer weight of numbers. Wesley had felt the problem, but it had grown far worse by the nineteenth century, and it was this which largely accounted for the enthusiasm which greeted the educational schemes of Andrew Bell and Joseph Lancaster. There was, further, a strong suspicion of state direction in education. Other European countries were experimenting with and establishing firm policies of education, but Britain liked state direction and streamlining of education no more then than some people do today, and so the voluntary systems of education proposed by Bell and Lancester and their imitators were enthusiastically adopted, and out of the interest (and the acrimony caused by the unfortunate and almost accidental rivalry of the two men) there came the 'National Society for Promoting the Education of the Poor in the Principles of the Established Church throughout England and Wales'. This adopted the ideas of Lancaster, was inspired by the church loyalty of Mrs Sarah Trimmer and Dr Herbert Marsh, and was under the (unpaid) superintendence of Andrew Bell! That was in 1811. Three years later, after considerable difficulty with the now arrogant Joseph Lancaster, the committee which had sponsored his scheme restyled itself the 'British and Foreign School Society'. The Church had begun a real attempt on a voluntary basis to tackle the problem of illiteracy. The Methodist Connexion had to take its share of responsibility.

In fact the problem of illiteracy was not so acute in Methodism. The Sunday schools had done much to obviate that, while the very force of evangelism had impelled converts to pass on to others the good they had come to know.[9] It seems strange that Wesley himself did not more actively introduce Sunday schools, regarding them, as he did, as 'one great means of reviving religion throughout the nation'.[10] Perhaps he felt they could safely be left to develop, for there was abundant evidence of popularity and success. Though Wesley himself took little direct action, the Methodist Connexion did much, having a pioneer in Miss Hannah Ball, who had started a Sunday school in 1769 eleven years before Robert Raikes began his great work, and developing them especially in the densely populated areas of the North, where everything possible had to be done to get children off the streets and to check the immorality and depravity which were becoming so acute a problem. It was indeed to combat these evils rather than to spread the Gospel

[9] See also *H.M.G.B.*, i, 25, 67; ii, 101–4.

[10] *Journal*, vii, 236n.

that Sunday schools came to be established so widely. One aspect of the movement which would have delighted Wesley was the free association between Anglicans and Methodists in regard to premises and teachers during the early years of the nineteenth century. An interesting social relationship developed also through the meeting of employee and employer on equal terms each Sunday in teaching their classes. Children's books began to be published, modelled on those written by an early Sunday-school teacher already mentioned, Mrs Sarah Trimmer; libraries were provided in some schools and were used by adults as well as children; experiments were tried in methods of teaching. In fact, as Sir James Kay-Shuttleworth, first Secretary of the Committee of Council on Education, later said, 'The Sunday school was the root from which sprang our system of day schools.'

This is very true, for the scope of the Sunday-school curriculum grew from reading and writing to include matter usually associated today with day schools, and in the first half of the nineteenth century there were many Methodists who disapproved of such mental expansion on Sundays. However, at least they saw to it that the core of instruction was the Gospel and the Christian faith, and it was only when the wider instruction become too evident that the Methodist Conference showed concern. Back in 1808, thirty-nine years after the first Methodist Sunday school had been opened by Miss Hannah Ball at High Wycombe, the question had been asked in Conference, 'What can we do for the spiritual benefit of the children of our people?' To which the reply was given, 'Let the good old custom of holding a children's service once a week be revived in every town, and wherever it shall be found practicable; and let all Preachers turn their serious attention to this important subject.'[11]

Twelve years later this earlier Minute was referred to again. By that time a number of independent Sunday schools had appeared, and Conference felt it imperative that such schools should operate in close connection with the chapels: an outlook paralleled in this century when people believed that youth clubs, to be most effective, should be organized in close association with the Church. Conference in 1820, therefore, reiterated its view that preachers should make themselves responsible for the oversight of Sunday schools and should ensure that their pupils attended public worship each Sunday.

There was at first considerable confusion of aim. Some Sunday schools were administered by laymen and the local clergy were excluded, others were administered by the local parish church; in some the aim was the propagation of the Gospel, in others it was wholly secular. There was no standard policy, and in 1827 'General Principles and Rules to be observed in the management of Methodist Sunday

[11] *Minutes* (1862), cxi, 31–2.

Schools' were printed in the Minutes of Conference, and each school was required to be connected with a particular chapel. Four years later Conference went further when it saw in the Sunday schools the appropriate means of introducing boys and girls to the Christian faith and of bringing them into Methodist membership. From that time onwards, for at least a decade, with a clear aim in view, Methodism found its chief educational outlet in its Sunday schools.

It was during that decade that a clearer view of education as a whole was coming into focus. Kingswood School had become a household name in preachers' homes, Woodhouse Grove was beginning to be known in the North, the Missionary Society was a growing channel of educational enterprise, the ebullient Jabez Bunting was outspoken on the problem of an uneducated ministry, and the need for trained teachers as well as preachers was beginning to be recognized. When the time came for Methodism to take a more active part in education, it did so on a broad front, and it will be well to consider separately the various ways in which it expressed itself.

During the early years of the nineteenth century one voice persistently pressed the claims of child education – that of Samuel Jackson. He had no easy task. The Bill proposed by Lord Brougham in 1820 by which parish clergy were to be required to provide education for the children of Nonconformists as well as Anglicans caused sufficient interest for it to be rejected. It was not until 1833, when the passing of the Reform Act in the previous year was giving food for thought and the government set aside £20,000 for the building of schools for the poorer classes, that Conference was asked for its 'sentiments with regard to the formation of weekday schools in connection with our Societies'.[12] The sentiments were somewhat nebulous, but a paternal blessing was given to those Societies able and willing to organize what was at last becoming regarded as a valid branch of evangelical work: education; and in 1836 Samuel Jackson's work was recognized when he, together with Richard Treffry and William Atherton, was asked to prepare a report on Sunday *and other* schools for presentation at the next year's Conference.

Even in those days schedules and returns were not dealt with as punctually and accurately as could be wished, and the resulting report was known to be inaccurate. It did show, however, that there were at least 3,339 Sunday schools with 59,277 teachers and 341,442 pupils; that twenty-five per cent of the chapels had no Sunday school, and that there were nine weekday schools for infants and twenty-two for older children. The report ended: 'What we wish for is not merely schools but *Church* schools; which, being systematically visited by the Preachers, may prove doors of entrance into the Church of God: not merely education, but an education which may begin in an Infant School and end in

[12] Id., vii, 297.

Heaven.'[13] Conference received the report and appointed a committee to implement such recommendations as were practicable. So began the Wesleyan Education Committee, whose manuscript Minutes from 1837 to 1841 make it clear that the primary aim of day- and Sunday-school teaching was religious, and that therefore it was the duty of the Methodist Connexion to provide schools for its own people.

Equally it had been realized by this time that preachers must receive some training to fulfil their calling, for they were no longer as well educated as many of Wesley's own preachers had been. The Connexion had grown, congregations were better read; it was essential that preachers should also be well-read and in no way inferior in intellectual standard to those of other denominations. In 1834, Conference agreed to the establishment of a 'Theological Institution'. An old Dissenting Academy at Hoxton was rented, a resident Governor (Joseph Entwisle) was appointed, and in January 1835 the first students (described as 'inmates'!) arrived.

Unfortunately this step forward was marred by controversy, resulting in the expulsion of Samuel Warren from the ministry, and the compromise appointment of Jabez Bunting as 'President' of the Theological Institution. The one good feature of the controversy was the testing of the legal framework of the Wesleyan Connexion and the resounding victory when the Conference was deemed a fit body to deal with its own judicial problems.

The gathering together of ministerial candidates at Hoxton revealed a disturbing fact which links with what was said earlier about general education: many of those students lacked the educational foundation on which theological training could be built. To meet this need, the former home of Isaac Watts at Abney House, Stoke Newington, was offered as a 'preparatory branch' of the Theological Institution to provide the needed general education, and it continued in use till 1843 with John Farrar as Tutor and Governor.

Such mingling of general education with theology was a feature of early ministerial training. Soon after the opening of the West of England Proprietary Grammar School (later Queen's College) at Taunton in 1842 a number of young men among the pupils were beginning their training for the ministry, for the school was 'a Collegiate Institution' of the University of London. Similar mingling of general and specialized education was also seen at the Bible Christian Shebbear College and at the Primitive Methodist Elmfield College, York. With the necessity for this foundation of general education at the bottom went a widening of the work at the top, and students at Hoxton extended their purely

[13] The full report is printed in the Annual Report of the Wesleyan (later Methodist) Education Committee (1889), pp. 114–18. This fiftieth Report also gives a survey of the first fifty years of the Wesleyan Education Committee's work.

Methodist training by attending lectures at King's College, which had opened in 1829 in the Strand, London. So was taken the first step in an ever closer working relationship between theological colleges and a neighbouring university.

The success of the Wesleyan Centenary Fund organized in 1838 as a practical measure of thanksgiving made possible an expansion of theological training along the lines which experiment at Hoxton and Abney House had made clearer, and it was decided to open two new branches of the Theological Institution, one in London and the other in Manchester, £55,000 (later increased) being allocated for the purpose. The London branch was to have been opened first, but it happened that a suitable manor house was offered for sale in Manchester, and in 1842 Didsbury College came into being. Thus 'the old ship', as it came affectionately to be entitled, was launched with a complement of thirty-six students (seven of them transferred from Hoxton).

A year later, a fine estate became available near London, and Richmond College was born, though care was taken to call it 'the Richmond branch of the Wesleyan Theological Institution', so suspiciously was the word 'college' still regarded. Richmond will always symbolize Methodism's responsibility for a world parish. In 1863 the Missionary Society raised a Jubilee Fund of £180,000, part of which was to be spent on a centre for training missionaries. The Society, instead of building anew, took over the Richmond estate, and between 1868 and 1885 only students preparing for overseas work were received there. Such segregation was not a good arrangement, as Hugh Price Hughes was courageous enough to point out while still a student, and after 1885 ministerial candidates received their training in any one of the colleges, no matter which the field of future service.

Meanwhile the government too was feeling its way tentatively towards a more effective organization of national education, and was thereby coming into conflict with the branches of the Church and their rigid denominational loyalties. It early realized that any system of education depended on a steady stream of trained teachers. So did Methodism. 'The masters and mistresses employed should be truly converted to God, and zealously and habitually devoted to Him. They should also be competently instructed in one or other of the approved systems of popular education,' pronounced the Wesleyan Education Committee.[14] When, therefore, in 1839 the Government Committee of Council on Education proposed to establish a teacher-training college in which all denominations were to share in providing instruction, one might have expected support from the Church. But the day of the 'Agreed Syllabus' had not dawned, and the idea of Anglicans, Roman Catholics, and

[14] Ibid., p. 118.

Nonconformists on a common educational footing was abhorrent to each denomination. The resulting outcry nearly caused the downfall of Lord Melbourne's government.

But there was whole-hearted agreement over the need for a steady supply of trained teachers. The monitorial systems of Bell and Lancaster had been in general use long enough for their defects to be seen, and it had become recognized that teachers must be trained for their profession as fully as ministers or doctors. Since Methodism objected to this training being given as a combined operation by all the Churches, it had to train its own teachers. David Stow had already earned fame and favour by his teacher-training institution and methods at Glasgow, and in 1839 the Wesleyan Education Committee advertised for 'at least three young men' prepared to offer themselves for training there. Money was scarce, and it was felt that a small nucleus of Methodists trained in this way could provide peripatetic teachers and organizers to tour the schools of the Connexion and train others: an idealistic blend of the monitorial and institutional method! This embryonic scheme was made possible by the Centenary Fund already referred to, from which £5,000 had been set aside for Wesleyan day schools. The response, at first disappointing, gathered momentum, and by 1851 a total of 334 teachers (90 of them women) had been trained. The wastefulness of this method of training, however, has been revealed by a study of the Register kept by the Committee, on which an article appeared in *The Times Educational Supplement* in 1954 showing that only about thirty per cent of Wesleyan teachers trained in any one year were still teaching ten years later, some teaching for less than five years.[15]

It was facts like these, frustration and sheer lack of money, which explain the slow beginnings of Methodist education in the first half of the nineteenth century, and these were as instrumental in creating difficulty as were the rivalry between clergy and laity and the involvement in ecclesiastical and party politics referred to earlier in this *History*.[16] But signs of growth were there. In 1841 Conference approved a plan drawn up by the Wesleyan Education Committee, and it is an illuminating comment on the times that it was felt necessary to state categorically that Methodist day schools were started not in self-defence but in fulfilment of a religious duty:

> The educational movement in our body partakes of the same general character with that which now animates the whole country on the important subject of training up the youthful population of the land; and leads to the best hope that if enlarged facilities can be afforded to the Committee they may, from year to year, become increasingly

[15] Op. cit., p. 1089.
[16] *H.M.G.B.*, ii, 239–46.

> efficient in spreading abroad through our whole Connexion the blessing of a sound Scriptural education.[17]

No Society was considered to be doing its duty properly unless it was helping to provide religious education for its youth.

In 1843 a man whose name is inseparable from Methodist education became President of the Conference, John Scott. He had inherited Samuel Jackson's concern for education, and more than any of his contemporaries he saw the possibilities in terms of Christian mission. Under his chairmanship a meeting of ministers and laymen from all parts of the country was convened, and unanimously adopted the plan he proposed: to build seven hundred day schools in the following seven years. The government was still floundering in its educational policy, but was coming to recognize voluntary effort, and was now prepared to help denominations by financial grants where such grants were acceptable. John Scott was supported by the President of the Theological Institution, Jabez Bunting, who told Conference, 'It is well worth our while to push day schools. Let us establish day schools. Let us go to it at once!'[18] Possibly he was remembering why Abney House had been deemed essential. This was voluntary effort on the part of Methodism led by John Scott, but suddenly, in 1847, he changed his view on voluntaryism and upset many of his friends as a result. Dr J. H. Rigg, who was later to become so influential in Methodist education, was then a young supply minister in London, and years later he told the story of what happened behind the scenes.[19] John Scott had called another meeting of leading Wesleyans to consider the plans which the Committee of Council were formulating for national education. William Arthur, who through residence in France knew more about State involvement in education than most Methodists, had been invited to attend as an observer and he took with him his young friend, J. H. Rigg. Speaker after speaker, led by Samuel Jackson and W. M. Bunting, supported voluntary effort and opposed State interference, but the more that was spoken on these lines the more difficulties became apparent, for all knew that they could not depend on Methodism as a whole for support in educational schemes of their own. Then John Scott was called from the room to speak with Lord Ashley (later the Earl of Shaftesbury), who had come specially to clarify certain points which he knew were upsetting the Wesleyans, on whose support he relied in his work on the Factory Acts. When, after a long and confidential talk, John Scott returned to the meeting, he persuaded those present to give qualified support to the government plans and, in the words of the Resolution

[17] M.E.C. (1889), p. 24.
[18] Benjamin Gregory, *Side Lights on the Conflicts of Methodism* (London 1899), p. 352.
[19] This is the incident referred to in *H.M.G.B.*, ii, 63, 76, 239, 245.

framed a little later for Conference, 'not to offer any further Connexional opposition to the scheme embodied in the Minutes [of Council]'.[20]

This did not mean that the Methodists relinquished their own efforts, however, and though the building target previously set was not reached, there was a great surge forward. As the number of schools increased, so did the problem of staffing them. It was to solve this problem that Westminster College was opened in 1851. The project had been mooted in 1844, and by 1847 a site had been found. It was no accident that this was in the then drab surroundings of the Westminster slums. It was to the abundance of illiterate children that the founders looked and, though a site had been offered in a more salubrious neighbourhood, they deliberately chose the slum area. As John Scott said, they did not wish their potential teachers to be spoilt in training and, by a lengthened residence away from the dwellings of the poor and among the attractions of 'superior life', to become disinclined and unfit to undertake the arduous and self-denying duties of school teachers.[21]

At first the College catered for men and women, but as education extended its scope, another college was called for, and in 1872 Southlands College was opened for the training of women teachers, Westminster becoming an all-male college. It was Westminster men who did much to create the National Union of Teachers, three of whose general secretaries have been Westminster men, but perhaps the most notable feature of this College in the past century has been the variety of education served by former students: not only in primary and secondary education but in the prison and Borstal service, in the National Children's Home, in the schools' inspectorate, in local authority administration, in universities and higher education, in this country and overseas. Matthew Arnold, as an inspector of schools, saw much of the College during its first thirty years. He was an outspoken critic of nonconformity, as he showed in his *Culture and Anarchy*, but he paid sincere tribute to what he found at Westminster College where the training of teachers, he said,

> is studiously addressed to form in them habits of right feeling and of good conduct as well as of correct thinking; to develop in them a spirit of peaceableness and affectionateness; the spirit of teaching for the good of others as well as for their own livelihood . . . This is the spirit which, I truly believe, those who conduct the Wesleyan training institution do their best to develop and promote.[22]

[20] James H. Rigg, *Wesleyan Methodist Reminiscences: Sixty Years Ago* (London 1904), Chapter 13: 'Still in London – An All-Important Committee', esp. pp. 113–14. See also H. F. Mathews, *Methodism and the Education of the People 1791–1851* (London 1949), pp. 135–7.

[21] F. C. Pritchard, *The Story of Westminster College 1851–1951* (London 1951).

[22] M. Arnold, *Reports on Elementary Education 1852–82*, pp. 237–8.

By the second half of the nineteenth century Methodism's responsibility for education was generally recognized, and this was showing itself, as we have seen, in Sunday schools, day schools, the training of teachers, and the training of ministers. Inevitably it must appear that it was the Wesleyan section of Methodism which played the greatest part in this awakening responsibility. It did, but it would be wrong to assume that other sections played no part at all.

One of the most interesting contributions came from North Devon, where the small but vigorous Bible Christian community grew up among illiterate but thinking farming people. Their illiteracy did not last long. They taught themselves to read, and for long hours after their day's agricultural work was done, they pored over the Bible, laboriously spelling out words by candlelight. If only a school could be started so that their children might be spared the double labour which the adults had to undergo! That was the thought ever-present in the mind of Samuel Thorne, one of the early Bible Christian preachers, who, like John Wesley earlier, had realized that scriptural holiness demanded education. In 1834, just when interest in education was taking practical shape elsewhere, a small boarding school was opened in their home at Prospect House by Samuel Thorne and his wife. It would probably have been a passing enthusiasm had not Samuel's brother James recognized the urgent need of education not only for youth but for future ministers. He realized that private enterprise could not meet the need in that rural locality and that the Bible Christian community must assume responsibility. He infected others with his views and in 1841 a Company was formed to finance and administer 'the Bible Christian Proprietary Grammar School'. So began Shebbear College, and there too were combined a school for boys, a training ground for preachers, and a teacher-training centre. This school played a considerable part in extending the Christian witness in Australia. A sister school was opened for girls at Edgehill College, Bideford, in 1884. Both schools are members of the group of boarding schools under the Methodist Board of Management to which reference will be made later, and their stories are told by Richard Pyke.[23]

Nor was education forgotten in Primitive Methodism and the United Methodist Free Churches. Hugh Bourne taught in a day school at Harriseahead in 1802 and a favourite dictum of his, 'Take heed of the children', sowed seeds among his followers, though for some time there was suspicion lest education be too worldly. By the mid-nineteenth century the Primitive Methodists and the United Methodist Free Churches, partly because of lay influence, had their schools for elementary education up and down the country, though there was no attempt

[23] Richard Pyke, *The Story of Shebbear College* (1953); *Edgehill College: 1884–1934* (London 1934).

to establish an educational system, finance proving an insuperable obstacle. In 1849 the Primitive Methodist Conference recorded: 'We have three kinds of Connexional schools and one kind in prospect: Sabbath, day, and night schools; the one in prospect is designed for the education of preachers' children.' This prospect was realized in 1864, in the opening of Elmfield College, York, later to be closed and incorporated in 1932 with Ashville College, Harrogate, which was the chief secondary school of the United Methodist Church. In 1882 another boarding school was opened at Quinton, near Birmingham, as Bourne College, but it failed through lack of financial support. The Sunday, day, and night schools were entirely the business of local societies, and there was no attempt, as in the Wesleyan body, to formulate an educational policy from the centre.

This lack of central purposive pressure also showed itself in ministerial training in the non-Wesleyan branches. There was reluctance to segregate potential ministers for special training lest they lost 'the common touch'. With them too the idea of 'college' was suspect, but as the nineteenth century passed there was a gradual breaking down of suspicion about higher education, as there had been earlier about elementary education, and there were pioneers. As early as 1835 Thomas Allin, a minister of the Methodist New Connexion, boarded a few students in his own home and supervised their studies for future work in the ministry. Twenty years later the possibility of a theological institution was proposed, and in 1857 the decision was taken to found one, though it was not until 1864 that Ranmoor College was finally opened at Sheffield.

For the Primitive Methodists, Elmfield College provided not only a school but a training centre for preachers, and paved the way for the opening of a theological institution in Sunderland in 1868, where Wesleyan experience repeated itself, and the one-year course had to include basic education as well as more specialized training for the ministry.

We are running ahead of the chronology of this chapter, but it may be well to continue dealing with ministerial training in the non-Wesleyan branches of Methodism at this point. By the 1870s the success of Wesleyan ministerial training and the increase of better-educated congregations showed the necessity for proper ministerial training everywhere. Finance was still a major difficulty but wealthy and loyal laymen were appearing. Such a man was Thomas Firth, who had made possible the opening of Ranmoor College. Another was William Beckwith, who made possible the opening of a second Primitive Methodist college in Manchester in 1878. Even as late as that, however, despite the work of James Travis, a Primitive Methodist minister, there was no whole-hearted support for ministerial training, and it was not until 1888 that the debt on this latest venture was finally cleared by general contributions. It was yet another layman, Sir William Hartley, whose generosity and business acumen enabled this College to become firmly established as a centre of inspiration to the whole Connexion in a more enlightened evangelism, for it was he who was largely responsible for persuading Dr A. S. Peake to leave his position of academic distinction at Oxford and give his genius to the College at Manchester which, after extensions in 1906, was appropriately named Hartley College.

Manchester was regarded as a good centre for ministerial training, partly owing to the strength of Methodism in that area so that students could get practical experience for their future work, and partly because of the presence of Owens College (later the University of Manchester), already famed for its broad and unsectarian spirit. So the United Methodist Free Churches were also interested in that city. When the need for ministerial training first began to obtrude itself, the suggestion had been made that a system of in-service training should be used whereby candidates for the ministry should board with circuit ministers who would supervise study and provide practical experience in the work of the ministry. This idea was still in the minds of many when in 1872 a house in Stockport Road was rented and a minister set apart as Theological Tutor. Four years later three more houses were bought, and Victoria Park College came into being. With the Union in 1907, the United Methodist Church thus had two colleges, one in Sheffield and one in Manchester.

We have been tracing trends and noting positive steps forward, but much of Methodism's best work in the educational field has been done almost unconsciously! The spirit of Methodism itself engendered a desire to read and write, there was a methodical self-imposed discipline, and a sense of mission compelled communal service. It was no accident that it was largely from nonconformity, infected by this self-educating spirit of service, that the Chartists and Trade Union pioneers appeared, men who had learned their rhetoric in chapels and class meetings. That had been going on all the time. Formal education caught on more slowly, though there was no lack of individuals prepared to experiment. At first in favour of the voluntary principle, from the middle of the nineteenth century Wesleyan Methodism was prepared to support the State so long as its actions could be approved, but remained as ready as ever to criticize if necessary; and in 1860 it became necessary. It is ironic that the chief criticism came from the man who had persuaded his friends to depart from the voluntary principle: John Scott.

The government was understandably worried about the increasing cost of education, and to save money the Secretary of the Committee of Council, Robert Lowe, introduced his notorious system of 'payment by results', less critically known as the Revised Code, which could only have the effect of lowering standards of education. Already many of the Methodist elementary schools carried instruction beyond the normal curriculum of the three R's. They were, in fact, developing into higher grade schools more akin to the later secondary schools. The blindly mechanical method of inspectorial examination proposed would stop the provision of instruction above a basic minimum, and that would hit hardest the poor, whose need was greatest. Here was an early example of 'the Nonconformist conscience'! The Wesleyan Education Committee protested direct to the Lord President of Council. John Scott, then Principal of Westminster College, toured the country, encouraging teachers, school managers and ministers to disregard the implications of the latest measures, and to maintain the high standards of education that Methodism had reached, to *educate* and not merely instruct. He pointed out their responsibility in an address to Westminster College students and others:

> The children of your schools . . . are not machines. They may, and probably will, have to work; but they are the children of *men*. We wish you to have a just conception of man, *as man*, – a thorough sympathy with human feelings, human interests, irrespective of worldly conditions. Is a child less rational, less capable of intellectual and moral improvement, of living an orderly, creditable, and useful life in society, of serving God and ensuring a blissful immortality because his parents are poor?[24]

It was the first but by no means the last time that Methodism voiced its Nonconformist conscience in upholding high standards, and by that time those in charge of Methodist education had a clear conception of their aim: the inculcation of religious truth among all sections of society, the preservation of individual liberty in matters of faith and worship, the training of men and women as Christians. To quote John Scott again, 'As long as the Wesleyans pretend[25] to give education to the poor, they will give them an education which it will be worth their while to receive.'[26]

The Revised Code came to an end in 1870 with W. E. Forster's Bill aimed at making elementary education available for every child in the land, and ensuring that every child took advantage of it, School Boards being set up to implement the Act which was only passed with some difficulty. It was a compromise solution of an increasing problem. On the one hand the Government recognized its duty to provide education, thus making an end of the *laissez-faire* policy so marked earlier in the century. On the other hand it recognized its inability to finance and

[24] M.E.C. (1861), Appendix, pp. 51–2.
[25] John Scott was using the word in its older sense of 'claim'.
[26] Ibid., p. 55.

supervise that duty. So the Government decided to support the voluntary principle embodied in denominational schools, inspection being undenominational, and religious liberty guaranteed by a conscience clause. The Act was greeted, at least in private, with some relief by Methodism, which had continued to compete in the supply of schools and teachers with Anglicans and Roman Catholics only with difficulty because it too lacked adequate finance. Experience had left no delusions about the defects of the voluntary denominational system. A few Methodist schools were immediately transferred to the newly created School Boards, though the Wesleyan Education Committee persisted in its efforts to supply more, and it was indeed in 1873 that it showed its greatest numerical strength: 912 schools. After that the number began to drop as more schools were handed over to the School Boards, though the average attendance in the Methodist 'voluntary' schools increased by twenty-five per cent during the period 1870–83, and it was publicly acknowledged that Methodist schools were among the most efficient in the country. From 1870 onwards, however, the official policy of Methodist education came more and more to favour state provision of schools, provided always that there was freedom for the individual to be instructed in the Bible and to study it unimpeded by sectarian influence.

In 1890 a special Education Committee presented its considered and tried policy: to maintain schools wherever possible, but to support the Government in establishing schools in all parts of the country to ensure the availability of unsectarian Christian teaching for every child, for it recognized the difficulties of single school areas where, despite the conscience clause, there was still the possibility of intolerance and oppression. In the years that have followed, this policy has sometimes been questioned, for it has resulted in an apparent diminution of interest in elementary education, if statistics alone are considered, but the stark fact remained that schools could not be provided, still less maintained, without money. It must be remembered, too, that though the official policy of Methodism did not change until 1961, official state policy has changed considerably, and the gradual handing over of responsibility for elementary education has increased Methodism's responsibility for the training of Christian teachers and ministers to ensure sound leadership. There was also the problem of what we now know as secondary education.

Before dealing with that, however, we must record another notable contribution that Methodism has made to education in its widest sense. In 1869 Dr T. B. Stephenson rescued twenty boys from the streets of London, following directly in the tradition of John Wesley, who started an orphanage at Newcastle. In 1873 Dr Stephenson was seconded from circuit work to give all his time to the orphanage he had founded. That work has developed not only along normal lines of child-care, but has pioneered social education with a steadily growing emphasis on the concept of the family as the true educator: a principle now evidenced by the omission of the word 'orphanage' from the title 'the National Children's Home'.[27]

A history of this sort inevitably has much to say about official policy, relationships between church and state, and the material facts of money and building; but these matters depend on human personalities behind the dreams and accomplishments. The drive, the business acumen, the cultural mission, the sacrifice which have made the educational and evangelical strength of Methodism emanate from men and women. Money from official sources has always been scarce, but men have won over others by the strength of their convictions, wealthy laymen have been influenced by the sacrifice of impoverished clergy. Nowhere is this better seen than in the histories of Methodism's schools and colleges.[28] Reading these stories, one realizes that bricks and mortar, necessary as they are, matter little; it is the men and women who dwell among them who are all-important, personalities who have developed their own gifts for the benefit of others. John Scott's words quoted above typify Methodism's view of education, and over sixty years later his grandson, Dr John Scott Lidgett, echoed them when, at a conference of ministers and laymen held in 1927 to stress the importance of ministerial training, and to consider ways of making the need more widely recognized, he said, 'The supreme question is not that of church buildings, but of the character, capacity, and equipment of the men who minister in them.'[29]

The decade from 1870 was one of increasing Methodist involvement in higher education, with Dr J. H. Rigg largely instrumental in shaping Methodist views and achievements. There was the inquiry into the education of ministers' children, by that time girls as well as boys, forced upon the authorities by financial difficulties; there was pressure to allow laymen's sons to share in the highly successful education which Kingswood and Woodhouse Grove were providing; there was the opening of the Leys School as a deliberately constructed bridge between Methodist education and the universities.[30] The strong feelings and cross-currents of thought are well seen in the report of a special committee appointed in 1877 to consider the whole question of Wesleyan education *other than primary*.

This apparently sudden emergence of interest in secondary and higher education had in fact been developing for some time. By the second half of the nineteenth century many Methodists could legitimately label

[27] A. A. Jacka, *The Story of the National Children's Home* (London 1969).
[28] See *H.M.G.B.*, iv: Bibliography.
[29] W. B. Brash, op. cit., p. 114; the full text is quoted on pp. 114–16.
[30] Derek Baker, *Partnership in Excellence* (London 1975).

themselves 'middle-class', and that phrase was much used without the self-conscious overtones associated with the phrase today. The Methodist emphasis on a close relationship between the spiritual and the material had helped to create wealth in the prosperous nineteenth century; by 1870 there was a consciously widening culture accompanied by the means to pay for it. For reasons already shown elsewhere in this *History* there was a strengthening of sectarian differences. Parents wanted a good education for their children but were reluctant to seek it in Anglican and other non-Methodist schools. Methodism, committed to supporting the state in primary education, had good reason to echo Matthew Arnold's cry, 'Organize your secondary education!'

The second half of the nineteenth century had seen a number of far-reaching Royal Commissions on education, the first of them significantly dealing with the older universities. That Commission of 1850 to inquire into the state, discipline, and revenues of Oxford and Cambridge was followed by the Newcastle Commission in 1858 dealing with primary education, by the Clarendon Commission in 1861 dealing with nine leading schools, and by the Taunton Commission of 1864 dealing with schools not covered by the previous inquiries. Action began to follow, recruitment for the Civil Service was opened to all by examination, and Methodists no longer found themselves barred from university education and the highest offices. Long before this, Methodism had attempted to provide a university substitute, again following the tradition of the Dissenting Academies, and Wesley himself had seen Kingswood in this role.[31] Queen's College, Taunton, and Wesley College, Sheffield, were affiliated to the University of London, and Methodism had pioneered a number of higher educational centres overseas. This liaison grew and showed itself in the close relationships which developed between theological and teacher-training colleges and the universities.

It was an age, as we see it now, of narrow loyalties and fierce competition. Other denominations and even commercial companies were busily founding schools: the Woodard schools for Anglicans, the Society of Friends for Quakers, Congregational schools for Independents, Benedictine and Jesuit schools for Roman Catholics. Competition was not merely a matter of 'keeping up with the Joneses'; it involved religious convictions.

The extension and increasing efficiency of primary education had done much to awaken cultural interests, and nowhere was this more clearly seen than in Methodism. Official reports spoke of the manner in

[31] Three Old Boys (i.e. A. H. L. Hastling, W. Addington Willis, W. P. Workman), *The History of Kingswood School, Together with Registers of Kingswood School and Woodhouse Grove School, and a List of Masters* (London 1898), Section I, Chapter 8: 'The University of Kingswood'.

which Methodist primary schools were giving an education far in advance of the average primary school so that, long before the State set about organizing secondary education, Methodism was providing it. The Hadow Report of 1926, looking back to this period, said:

> A considerable number of the pupils [in Wesleyan schools] remained after the age of 11, and in addition to reading, writing, ciphering, and scripture lessons, received instruction in English, grammar, geography, history, elementary science, hygiene, and singing. Some of the Wesleyan schools in rural areas had an agricultural bias, with lessons in mensuration, land surveying, book-keeping, and agriculture. In the same way, some of the Wesleyan urban schools had a slight commercial bent.[32]

But it all needed organization, as J. H. Rigg made clear:

> In order to meet existing wants and duly to complete the educational arrangements for Methodism it is not only desirable to provide for such higher education as is contemplated by the Cambridge scheme [Foundation of the Leys School], but also to promote the establishment in various parts of the country of Methodist Middle-Class Schools, so organised as to furnish suitable instruction and on moderate terms.[33]

The centenary year of John Wesley's death, 1891, provided a fitting occasion for a review of all aspects of Methodist enterprise. The ministry had long been proud of its Kingswood School, modelled as it was by Wesley himself on the Dissenting Academies of the eighteenth century and on the University of Oxford, and certain distinctive features had emerged. It drew its pupils from all over the 'world parish' and sent them out again to the same parish to spread the Christian witness; it had never underestimated the value of scholarship; in the changing circumstances of succeeding generations of masters and boys it had kept clear before itself the two commandments stressed by Jesus Christ and summed up as they are in the School motto: 'Ad gloriam Dei optimi maximi et ecclesiae et reipublicae usum'.

Kingswood School was typical of much that was good in the organization of Methodism, but other schools were appearing with similar aspirations and girls' education was no longer disregarded. In an age when sex-equality is the law of the land it is difficult to realize the revolutionary changes which have taken place in less than a century. Methodism has played its part in these changes. Its schools for girls were little different from any other girls' schools, but the success of Laleham under Hannah Pipe (supported as she was by Edward Thring

[32] Op. cit., p. 7.
[33] M.E.C. (1874–5), p. 74.

of Uppingham and W. B. Pope of Didsbury College) evidenced a spirit of emancipation coupled with discipline and a sense of responsibility which influenced other schools, and led directly to the foundation of new ones. There was no lack of candidates for Southlands College. When the city missions began to appear towards the end of the nineteenth century, with their manifold social services, the special role of women became apparent, and men like John Scott Lidgett are remembered among the male pioneers who saw women's place in communal life in a new light. T. B. Stephenson's fame rests largely on his foundation of the National Children's Home, but he should also be remembered as one of the two men who showed the need for deaconesses. He in the Wesleyan and T. J. Cope in the United Methodist Free Churches founded Deaconess Orders. With Union, the two Orders fused into the Wesley Deaconess Order, and the work of training and organizing their service was centred at the College in Ilkley, which opened in 1902 with sixteen students.

In education generally, however, the problem confronting Methodism was: secular or Christian? If the latter, then it still had to be denominational. It was estimated in 1878 that there were at least 7,000 boys who would be sent to Methodist secondary schools if places could be found for them, and although schools for girls were still not considered so essential there was growing enlightenment.

The appointment of the Bryce Commission in 1894 to consider the whole question of secondary education focused attention. The Wesleyans were invited to provide information and the resulting report presented a more impressive picture than many had dared expect. There were two Connexional boarding schools for ministers' children; six middle-class boarding schools for boys, five for girls; five proprietary schools; one Public School; and an unknown number of private schools widely differing in scope for both boys and girls.[34]

Not included in the report were the two Irish schools at Belfast and Dublin, the Primitive Methodist Elmfield College at York, the Bible Christian Shebbear College for boys and Edgehill College for girls, the United Methodist Ashville College, Harrogate, and a number of schools of similar type in Australia, New Zealand, Africa, and Ceylon, where the missionary, the teacher, and the doctor, often educated in one of the Methodist schools, sought to spread the Gospel in a practical manner.

The Bryce Commission's Report revealed the muddle and overlapping that existed in English education. It did make clear, however, that future planning, though distinguishing between primary and secondary education, must view it as one whole; that there must be

[34] For more detail, see F. C. Pritchard, *Methodist Secondary Education: A History of the Contribution of Methodism to Secondary Education in the United Kingdom* (London 1949), pp. 295–7.

decentralization, and that an independent body of educational advisers must be established. It took care to reassure interested parties that there would be no undue interference with schools already doing sound work. Legislation was obviously imminent, and Methodism was awake to educational needs and dangers as never before. It was uneasily aware that Roman Catholics and Anglicans had never subscribed wholly to the idea of state-administered education and that they were not only holding firmly to their own schools but were increasing their number. When, therefore, a Bill was drafted which offered financial assistance to schools without accompanying it by a condition of adequate representative management, the special committee set up by Conference to watch Methodist educational interests objected violently. Nor did the Bill find greater favour elsewhere; it was therefore withdrawn, but other measures were clearly to follow.

It was at this time that Robert Morant emerged as the architect of twentieth-century educational administration. In 1902 he introduced a new Education Bill which dealt with primary, secondary, and higher education as a single whole, and for the first time made the state (through County and County Borough Councils) responsible for the entire range. It proposed to abolish the School Boards and to substitute local education authorities which would control both Board and Voluntary schools at primary and secondary level; all of them were financed from the rates. The managers of voluntary schools were to continue to be responsible for religious instruction, the previous conscience clause being retained. Thus the 'Dual System' came into being.

The proposals caused an explosion to which all religious denominations contributed. At the time it must have been impossible for all but a few to see in true perspective. In retrospect it is obvious that decisive, constructive measures had to be taken by the Government, that the piecemeal methods of the nineteenth century had to be relegated to the past to which they belonged, and that all stages of education had to be considered as one whole. The School Boards had worked successfully in some areas; they had failed miserably in others. What upset Methodists, and indeed Nonconformists generally, was that rate-aid was to be given to all schools. 'To him that hath shall be given' had a bitter taste for a denomination which had deliberately given up some of its possessions. Few Methodists had J. H. Rigg's clear vision of the whole field or were prepared to pay a denominational price for better secondary education. Some, like Scott Lidgett and Hugh Price Hughes, saw too many merits in the proposed Bill to oppose it wholly, though the former with his intimate knowledge of London's schools regretted the overthrow of the School Board framework. A mass meeting was called to protest against the Bill. Grievances were undeniable.

G. A. N. Lowndes has summarized them in his *Silent Social Revolution*:

> In 12,000 out of 14,000 denominational schools conducted by and in the interests of a single denomination, 8,000 to 9,500 of them being the only schools available in the district, 700,000 Methodists and perhaps 500,000 other Nonconformist children were either being compelled to make themselves conspicuous by withdrawal from religious instruction or to run the risk of petty proselytisation. They could add that so far from seeking to end this injustice the Government were proposing to perpetuate it by compelling the parents to support it out of the rates, thus incidentally relieving the squire, the parson, and the richer inhabitants of the parish from the burden of its support. Moreover, they could show that although the Government could not produce a single precedent where rate-payers had not a controlling voice in the management of a fund derived from the rates, the proposals in the Bill would ensure that the two representative managers appointed by the Local Authority would be in a permanent minority. Worse still, in any one of these 14,000 schools no head teacher could be a Nonconformist and few Nonconformist children could hope to become pupil teachers without accepting Anglican baptism.[35]

That mass meeting was unanimous in opposing the Bill. A deputation waited on the Prime Minister to tell him so, and a leading Nonconformist minister, Dr John Clifford, led a passive resistance movement pledged to refuse payment of rates in support of education; Methodists were among those who went to prison for their refusal.

Official Methodist policy did not support such extreme measures, but did oppose the Bill, supporting the Liberal party in doing so. Nevertheless, the Bill passed into law, and English education was committed to development along new lines. On one point especially Methodism made itself abundantly clear: it would not tolerate an educational system that was purely secular. It was because of such a stand that a Bill to transfer voluntary schools to local education authorities was withdrawn in 1906; that another proposing the withdrawal of rate-aid from voluntary schools and their transference to local education authorities ('contracting out', as it came to be known) was withdrawn in 1908; and that a third similar attempt proved equally unsuccessful.

Amid the welter of confused voices raised in angry altercation a unifying body came into being in 1903 to supervise, improve, and coordinate all matters relating to the extension of Methodist secondary education. It took some time and much argument to persuade the newly constituted Board of Education to recognize the legal status of this body, but eventually the 'Board of Management for Methodist

[35] Op. cit., pp. 84–5.

Residential Schools' was accepted as the legal governing body of certain schools, and this Board was empowered and indeed required by the Board of Education to delegate powers to a local board of governors for each school. This arrangement continues today. Each school had complete freedom of action so long as it remained a school, but the Methodist Board of Management was in the background, sometimes as a rubber stamp, occasionally as a needed goad, most often as an avuncular holder of the purse-strings! It must be noted, however, that neither this Board nor the Connexion now finances any of the schools it helps to administer.

Since Methodism had accepted government grants for primary education there was no logical reason why it should not accept similar grants for secondary and higher education; but these could be obtained only on certain conditions. Already the 'company' schools founded in the late nineteenth century compared unfavourably with the state schools which began to appear after 1902. They produced no dividends for ploughing back into capital development nor for their shareholders, who were therefore not unwilling to relinquish their responsibilities and liquidate their companies when they realized that grants could be obtained only for schools not carried on for even nominal profit. It was recognized, too, that curricula had to be revised, that buildings, equipment, teaching staff, and fees had to compete with those of other denominations and the new state schools. This was the first task of the newly created Board of Management.

This focusing of attention on secondary education came at an opportune time, in that a substantial sum of money became available from the Connexion itself. Twenty years before, the Thanksgiving Fund to commemorate the association of ministers and laymen in the administration of Wesleyan Methodism had set aside £14,000 to settle debts incurred by the Education Committee. Later a further £10,000 had been given to settle some of the secondary schools on a firmer basis, while £34,000 had been given to the Theological Institution. At the end of the century another thanksgiving fund had been raised: the 'Twentieth Century Fund'; and the growing interest in education was signified by the granting of £200,000 from it in support of education. This century started therefore with the winding up of school 'companies' and the preparation of schemes for carrying on their schools as Trusts under the administration of the Board of Management, property being vested in the Secondary Schools Trustees.

By that time Methodism by its very spirit and organization had become a reading, studying denomination. The life, training, and curriculum of the two teacher-training colleges at Westminster and Southlands were reviewed to meet new opportunities and challenges. Only fifty years before, special theological training for potential ministers had been regarded by many with deep suspicion on the grounds that evangelical zeal might be diminished or extinguished altogether. All that had changed. The course of study in theology and kindred subjects had been widened and deepened in the light of current research and a more enlightened reading of the Bible. It was true that tutors still had to struggle sometimes with students who lacked a general education as in the days of Abney House, but it was being more and more accepted that men offering for the ministry must have reached a certain academic standard and then should have two years' intensive training in a college. Wesley College, Headingley, had been opened in 1868, the first purpose-built Wesleyan theological college – Didsbury and Richmond had grown up around older properties – and within a year of its opening was free from debt. At that opening, two speakers alluded optimistically to another college planned for the Midlands, though in fact it was not until 1881 that Handsworth College opened at Birmingham, memorably in that it opened debt-free.

The 1914–18 war saw work in schools and colleges marking time or coming to a halt altogether. Students and tutors in the theological colleges joined the armed forces or went back into circuit while the buildings were used for other purposes. Richmond College was occupied by a dwindling band of Westminster College students whose corporate life was maintained by the Principal, Dr H. B. Workman, largely by correspondence during the time his own buildings were occupied by the Australian Expeditionary Force. Richmond reopened as a theological college in 1920, Didsbury, Handsworth, and Hartley having reopened the previous year. It was not until 1930 that Wesley College, Headingley, reopened. Ranmoor College remained closed, and the ministerial training of the United Methodist Church was concentrated at Victoria Park, which had reopened in 1919 with sixteen students of three different years and one tutor. It was an impossible state of affairs, and Hartley College went to the rescue with tutorial help. For fifteen years that co-operation between the two colleges continued, leading to one of the most helpful results of the 1932 Union, when they merged to form Hartley Victoria College in 1934.

That spirit of co-operation was typical of a broadening outlook generally. In the schools the introduction of an 'Agreed Syllabus' of religious instruction in Cambridgeshire in 1924 was a notable step forward. The days of the enthusiastic amateur, whether in evangelism or in more secular matters, were ending, and it was fully recognized that men and women who felt called to teach or preach must be adequately trained. The Methodist Study Centre, started in 1927, was typical of the new outlook. It was a correspondence college intended primarily to help Sunday school teachers, Youth Club leaders, Local Preachers and others to serve better by a planned course of study in the Bible and other foundations of Christian faith. Valuable as it was as an instructional centre, it also played a small but effective part in Methodist fellowship, for among its members were the deaf and others who through no fault of their own were barred from normal association with their fellows. Through letters and study they were made to feel that they belonged. This was but one of the ways in which that leader of thoughtful youth, Dr Russell Maltby, brought meaning and friendship into the lives of the young in heart, for it was largely his wide-ranging view and planning which brought together in that Study Centre a number of different interests.

Methodism was no longer conscious of intellectual inferiority, and nowhere was this better seen than in ministerial training. Until the changes wrought by the 1914–18 war it was broadly true to say that the aim of the Theological Institution was to train ministers for their everyday work; but from that time, largely owing to the outstanding scholarship of men like A. S. Peake and W. F. Moulton, who laid foundations, there has been a determined attempt to make a worthy Methodist contribution to biblical and theological scholarship. Methodism showed leadership in the new intellectual requirements as in more traditional evangelical mission. Men like Scott Lidgett, A. W. Harrison, C. W. Andrews, Ryder Smith, T. H. Barratt, and W. F. Lofthouse had come to regard ministerial training as the greatest need for Methodism at that time. This advance was typified by the opening of Wesley House, Cambridge, which is in effect a post-graduate theological college.

The project was largely due to two laymen who themselves had not had the benefit of a university education: Michael Gutteridge and William Greenhalgh. In 1921 a house was rented from Cheshunt College and there Dr Maldwyn Hughes made his home and the nucleus of a college. In the following year, thanks to the interest and friendship of Bernard Manning, Jesus College sold to Methodism a plot of land in Jesus Lane, and building started. Wesley House was completed in 1926, its setting in the life of the University of Cambridge giving the men resident there the opportunity to mingle with some of the finest minds in the country and to be challenged by the conflicting currents of modern thought. It was Dr Maldwyn Hughes who steered the scheme to success as, thirty years later, one of his sons was to steer the scheme for the removal of Westminster College from London to its new home at Oxford.

Though the foundation of Wesley House epitomized the intellectual aim of ministerial training, the aim was not concentrated there to the exclusion of the other colleges.[36] The conference of ministers and

[36] In fact, while Wesley House established and maintained a very strong academic tradition, it was the other colleges which led the way in working out the implications of the broader view of ministerial training which began to emerge shortly after World War II. For these developments, see pp. 386f. below.

laymen already referred to (p. 289) made clear the need for both an intellectual and a practical approach to ministerial training. On the one hand, scholarship and skill in communication were needed to help Methodists to worship God with the whole of their minds, and to explain the faith which they held; on the other hand, there was the need for training in the pastoral office and in administration. These considerations led to the instituting of a fourth year of college training, and, later, to clinical training in circuit under selected superintendents. Probation work was now to be related more directly to a teaching and preaching ministry, and to pastoral and administrative duties in the context of changing circumstances.

Scholarship and research depend on intellectual exchange; and more generous endowments were needed to ensure the continuing influence of first-rate minds among tutorial staffs in all the colleges, together with better libraries and facilities for private study. Above all, there was now a strong conviction that each college ought to have a chapel as a focal point. These needs had been appreciated by Dr John H. Ritson, a former scholar of Balliol College, Oxford. He saw the way to put matters on a better footing, and he showed others how; it was largely through his efforts that, despite the growing economic depression of the time, £250,000 was raised to supply the deficiencies. As a result, by 1932 there was a chapel in every college, and professorial chairs were endowed at each which served, and still serve, the purpose of relieving the Methodist Church of some financial strain, commemorating benefactors, and enabling colleges to keep abreast of current research and scholarship. Links with neighbouring universities have become ever closer. In 1929 the cumbersome term 'Theological Institution' was dropped. A 'Ministerial Training Committee' was set up, with (from 1934) a whole-time Secretary responsible for supervision of all training from candidature to ordination.

Westminster College shared in this facing of intellectual challenge. Since 1891 there had been the occasional graduate as a student, but in 1930 began an experiment. Potential teachers were accepted for a four-year course, the first three years being spent in reading for a degree at the University of London, the fourth at Westminster in reading for a teacher's Diploma. At the same time a Students' Union started, and the college became as well-known on the games field as it was in other places. In fact, in Methodism, as elsewhere, the 1930s saw the emancipation of the student. It was a time of enlightenment in striking contrast to the spartan imprisonment and narrow views of earlier days, and it owed much to the statesmanlike vision and firm diplomacy of college authorities. The spirit of the men trained in Methodist theological colleges speaks for itself all over the world; the spirit of the men and women trained at Westminster and Southlands noted by Matthew

Arnold in the nineteenth century has persisted, indeed developed, so that a leading educationist, Professor W. O. Lester Smith, was moved to write, 'The Wesleyan movement has exercised an educational influence altogether out of proportion to the number of its schools because of the good quality of the men and women teachers trained at its colleges.'[37] By 1932 the Methodist Education Committee was giving much attention to the secondary schools which fed the colleges.

They needed attention. The social and other changes caused by the war, coupled with the expansion of State schools, had made it apparent that Methodist schools could survive only if they competed successfully with schools outside the Connexion in making a distinctive contribution. Kingswood School may be taken as an example.

The headmastership of Alfred Barrett Sackett from 1928 to 1959 opened an entirely new chapter in Kingswood's history. Discipline and the morale of the School had reached a low ebb during the difficult days of the war and its aftermath. Discipline at least had been restored by the stern and often unpalatable methods of Sackett's predecessor, H. A. Wootton. Sackett built on that foundation and transformed the whole character of the school from a rather narrowly enclosed seminary into a progressive Public School open to the best cultural influences and using the most liberal educational methods of his day. He was much helped by a team of young masters, many returned from the battlefield, so that a new pupil-and-teacher relationship began. Sackett and his colleagues imparted to the school a distinctive flavour by their patient and determined attempt to bring the best out of every boy individually, whether his bent lay in academic pursuits, artistic expression, or making things with his hands, without in the least diminishing the family spirit and community loyalty which had so strongly marked the school ever since Wesley's day. But perhaps Sackett's most noteworthy achievement was to hold constantly before his staff and boys the ideal of an education made truly Christian by seeing all studies and interests as the exploration of God's creative and redemptive activity, and by offering them in worship to him through Jesus Christ.

A. B. Sackett was not the only outstanding head of a Methodist school in that generation. It had at last been realized that a school was a business as well as a community, and that the maintenance of fees at a low level was not the best way to progress. No one realized that more clearly than Dr H. B. Workman, Secretary of the Methodist Education Committee. He was largely responsible for the founding of two new schools: Hunmanby Hall for girls and Culford School for boys, both of which owe much of their success to the work and vision of their first heads, Miss F. A. Hargreaves and Dr J. W. Skinner.

[37] W. O. Lester Smith, *To Whom do Schools Belong?: An Introduction to the Study of School Government* (Oxford 1942), p. 56.

Methodist Union in 1932 increased the amount of school property and with it the volume of problems, for many of the buildings were old and quite unsuited to the renovation, extension, and development foreshadowed in the Hadow Report on the education of the adolescent. The very compliments paid to Methodist education in that Report made bitter-sweet reading in the light of the obvious impossibility of doing in the twentieth century what had been done in the nineteenth. The number of primary schools steadily decreased as they were handed over to local authorities, but that did not mean a loss of Methodist interest. It did mean a realization that the role of teachers trained in Christian education was becoming even more important. In 1932 there were 124 primary schools in Methodism. Most of them, because of their age, had become junior schools – in contrast to the nineteenth century when Methodist schools had tended to move upward in academic status. It was a curious position: no denomination wanted to see the state control of education which existed on the continent of Europe; the government needed the help which voluntary education had provided; each denomination watched with jealous care lest another received an undue proportion of state aid which might foster sectarianism. Fortunately these sectarian problems have lessened with the broadening influence of ecumenism.

Just as 1932 marked the start of a new chapter in the history of the Methodist Church, so it may be said to mark a new phase in the history of education in this country, for thinking and planning were already moving towards the milestone of the 1944 Education Act which saw the Churches at last advancing more in step with each other. While the Methodist Church retained some of its primary schools, especially in the North-West, its boarding schools grew in numerical and academic strength.[38] Until 1932 the story could be summed up in the words of Dr A. W. Harrison, then Principal of Westminster College, Secretary of the Methodist Education Committee, and, when he died in 1945, President of the Conference:

> The attitude of Methodism to education has been wavering and uncertain. At times there has been real devotion to the cause of education, and in all parts of the world great and flourishing Methodist educational institutions have been built up; at other times there has been an inclination to regard the State as the generous foster-mother, to whom this great responsibility should be left, with the pious hope that State education will be based on the main principles of the Christian religion; at other times, or in other circles, education has been either suspect or neglected by a fervent evangelical Church

[38] Statistics provide some evidence of growth. Number of pupils in 1908: 418; in 1937: 1,788; in 1959: 5,333.

which did not regard that as one of its main concerns. Wesley himself had no such hesitations.[39]

The future is more than ever imponderable as history moves into the age of comprehensive education, of rampaging inflation, and increasing dependence on the state. The Church will conceivably need both to leaven the state system and to be itself a great educational institution in the widest sense, with its emphasis on standards of excellence and the education of the whole personality in the environment of the time.

[39] A. W. Harrison, *The Methodist Church: Its Origin, Divisions, and Reunion*, p. 208.

IX

Methodism in England 1900-1932

J. M. TURNER

1. A Profile of Wesleyanism

It can be argued that it was World War I which marked the end of the Victorian Age, yet presages of change were occurring in the generation before.[1] In 1900 Max Planck broke the chains of classical Newtonian physics to formulate the quantum theory of energy. In Switzerland, in 1905, Albert Einstein set out his special theory of relativity, in 1901 wireless telegraphy spanned the Atlantic and Daimler produced an automobile. In 1903 a motorized flying machine took flight at Kitty Hawk. The Second Industrial Revolution was well under way, dominated by steel, oil, electricity and later by synthetic materials. The British Empire covered one quarter of the globe with 400 million inhabitants, but the U.S.A., Germany and Russia were already threatening its hegemony. There were also ominous signs of a breakdown of social cohesion typified by the Taff Vale dispute of 1901 and its aftermath, the militant women's suffrage movement, unrest in Ireland and a threatened breakdown of the norms of parliamentary government itself.

In this period English Nonconformity appeared outwardly strong and confident.

> It is probable that Nonconformity reached its height of political power, was most representative of the temper of the English people, round the beginning of this century . . . But in the generation that has passed since the great Liberal landslide of 1906, one of the greatest changes in the English religious and social landscape has been the decline of Nonconformity. Partly that decline has been due to the

[1] Cf. Barbara W. Tuchman, *The Proud Tower: A Portrait of the World before the War, 1890–1914* (London 1966).

> general weakening of the hold of Christianity on the English people, partly it has been due to the comparative irrelevance of the peculiarly Nonconformist (as apart from Christian) view of the contemporary world and its problems.[2]

The Methodism of the period before 1932 needs to be seen against that realistic judgement sharpened by Dr Kitson Clark when he affirms:

> The Protestant Dissenters have never had their moment at the centre and in consequence their great men, their domestic crises, their varying beliefs have little troubled the ordinary historian. Indeed, one might almost say that historians have cared to know little more about Dissenters than that they normally voted Liberal and that they could on occasion when appropriately stimulated evince strong moral indignation which might have political results.[3]

More recently sociologists have found religious deviance more fascinating.

What was the contribution of Methodism to English religion, society and politics in this period? Is it the case that Methodism, as we know it now, owes more to the period between the Liberal landslide of 1868 and that of 1906 than it does to the years between the evangelical conversion of John Wesley and the 'painless extraction' of Methodism from the Church of England at the end of the eighteenth century?

Late Victorian Methodism shared the naïveté and at times truculent optimism of the age typified in thinkers as diverse as Herbert Spencer and Lord Acton. This was the era which Bishop Wickham[4] called 'the years of religious boom', though this was somewhat of an illusion which the wisest minds in the Free Churches were aware of long before World War I.[5] Hugh Price Hughes said:

> We Christians, when we unite our forces, are simply irresistible. Let us, then, in the name of God and humanity, combine heartily to abolish Slavery, Drunkenness, Lust, Gambling, Ignorance, Pauperism, Mammonism, and War. After that is done, we shall not have much difficulty in settling all our theological and ecclesiastical differences . . .[6]

[2] D. W. Brogan, *The English People: Impressions and Observations* (London 1943), p. 121; cf. John Kent, 'A Late Nineteenth-Century Nonconformist Renaissance', in Derek Baker (ed.), *Renaissance and Renewal in Christian History* (Studies in Church History xiv) (Oxford 1977), pp. 351–60.

[3] G. Kitson Clark, *The Making of Victorian England* (London 1962), pp. 23–4.

[4] E. R. Wickham, *Church and People in an Industrial City* (London 1957), chapter 4.

[5] William Bradfield, *The Life of the Rev. Thomas Bowman Stephenson* (London 1913), pp. 275ff.; R. Martin Pope, *The Life of Henry J. Pope* (London 1913), p. 250.

[6] Hugh Price Hughes, *Social Christianity* (London 1889), p. xiii; cf. *London Quarterly Review*, lxxii (July 1889), 376–7.

Hughes believed, as did many Methodists, that the future was with their Church.[7] Methodism and Catholicism were for him the only churches of the future, and rational man would favour the former. When Hughes preached at the opening of the Leeds Mission in 1898, he could afford to lambast the Roman Catholics in the morning and the Anglicans at night.[8]

The Forward Movement in Methodism was the last great attempt to reach those alienated from all the churches. The great mass of the working class, whom no church, not even Primitive Methodism, had really touched at a deep level since the Industrial Revolution, manifested nevertheless much vaguely evangelical folk-religion through the pervasive influence of the Sunday School Movement.[9] Henry J. Pope, Charles Garrett, Samuel Collier, Hugh Price Hughes and others, who were the pioneers of the Forward Movement, saw clearly that the Wesleyan itinerant system, with its compulsory three-year cycle, was inappropriate to the style of work needed to reach the estranged and needy masses not only to save people's souls but to 'sanctify their circumstances'.[10] This was the time when *The Bitter Cry of Outcast London* of 1883,[11] William Booth's *In Darkest England and the Way Out* (1890), and Charles Booth's pioneering surveys *Life and Labour in London* (*c.*1902) had revealed the divided state of the richest nation on earth. Charles Booth in London (and Rowntree in York in 1901) revealed that thirty per cent of the population were living below an adequate subsistence level. More than half of the children of working men were in this condition, which meant forty per cent of the children in England. In York, infantile mortality was 94 out of 1,000 live births in the middle classes but no less than 247 per 1,000 among those in poverty.[12] In 1898 measles alone carried off 13,000 folk.[13] Drunkenness was a fearful social evil and for six shillings one could buy thirty-one pints of beer in 1901! A ministry was needed to offer the Gospel to mind and body. The basis of the Forward Movement was to provide centres of evangelism and social amelioration, the sacrament and the soup-ladle hand in hand, with a minister at the head of the enterprise who could remain long

[7] Even W. L. Watkinson, in *London Quarterly Review*, xci (1899), 343ff.

[8] *Leeds Mercury*, 23 September 1898; cf. Robert Currie, *Methodism Divided: A Study in the Sociology of Ecumenicalism* (London 1968), p. 181.

[9] Richard Hoggart, *The Uses of Literacy* (London 1957), pp. 79ff.; K. S. Inglis, *Churches and the Working Classes in Victorian England* (London 1963), p. 331; Hugh McLeod, *Class and Religion in the Late Victorian City* (London 1974), pp. 32, 54; David Martin, *A Sociology of English Religion* (London 1967), p. 27.

[10] Hughes, in *Methodist Times*, 6 August 1885, p. 505.

[11] Andrew Mearns was the author. There was a reprint in 1970. Valentine Cunningham, *Everywhere Spoken Against: Dissent in the Victorian Novel* (Oxford 1975), p. 81.

[12] P. Laslett, *The World We Have Lost* (London 1965), pp. 200ff.; note the clear definition of poverty given by Rowntree.

[13] Laslett, op. cit., p. 221.

enough to be a social (and often political) force in the neighbourhood.[14] This was the basis of centres like St James's Hall (ancestor of Kingsway Hall), the Manchester Mission and the Central Hall in Birmingham under Luke Wiseman (1858–1944) – scholar, evangelist and musician[15] – and later Benson Perkins (1881–1975)[16] and Noel Hutchcroft (1888–1949).

What were the characteristics of the Central Hall?[17] First, evangelistic preaching[18] of a simple and powerful type, though tinged often enough with the kind of scholarship which enabled Samuel Chadwick (1860–1932) to preach through the Nicene Creed and W. B. Pope's *Compendium* to his congregation in Leeds[19] and to introduce the innovation of Passiontide services.

All centred on the preacher; the hall was his throne and this was still the age of the great platform orator. Worship was all too easily subordinated to preaching save for congregational singing and choral performances which did much to diffuse popular musical culture. Preaching was designed to secure a verdict. Charles Hulbert recalls how he would carefully record all the verdicts for Christ in his notebook and would deem a service a failure if there were none.[20] He also repeatedly stated that his headquarters was a 'hall', not a 'church', and woe betide if it became one! Just before his death, J. Ernest Rattenbury recalled his observations on the style of 1900.

> The great difference between congregations then and now is the difference between a sense of guilt and a sense of doubt.[21] Guilt is like tinder which blazes when the spark of emotion is applied to it. Doubt is like a rust which can only be removed by careful polishing.

It is important to note that great missioners like Wiseman and Chadwick always backed up their preaching with Bible studies and class meetings. Growth in discipleship was as vital to them as conversion. Leeds Mission, indeed, organized classes in theology, N.T. Greek, domestic economy and cricket!

Secondly, a social witness of a basically individualistic style despite

[14] A good example was Lax of Poplar; cf. W. H. Lax, *Lax – His Book: The Autobiography of Lax of Poplar* (London 1937).

[15] R. G. Burnett et al., *Frederick Luke Wiseman: A Commemorative Record* (London 1954).

[16] E. Benson Perkins, *So Appointed: An Autobiography* (London 1964).

[17] G. Sails, *At the Centre* (London 1970).

[18] R. Martin Pope, op. cit., pp. 239–41.

[19] John A. Broadbelt, in W. Bardsley Brash and Charles J. Wright (eds), *Didsbury College Centenary 1842–1942* (London 1942), p. 115; Norman G. Dunning, *Samuel Chadwick* (London 1933), p. 89.

[20] Kenneth Hulbert, *Passion for Souls* (London 1959), pp. 32ff., 95; E. C. Urwin, *Henry Carter, C.B.E.: A Memoir* (London 1955), p. 18; J. Ernest Rattenbury, *Evangelism: Its Shame and Glory* (London 1932), chapter VI: 'The Practice of Evangelism'.

[21] Cf. Donald Soper, *The Advocacy of the Gospel* (London 1961), p. 18.

avowals of collectivism.[22] Hugh Price Hughes in his treatment of Parnell reveals a paradox at the heart of dissent: Churches which consider themselves gathered from the world seeking to impose their brand of morality on society in the form of drink legislation, anti-gambling laws, strict Sunday observance and other symbols of respectability, and sometimes obscuring the underlying causes of social evils. Hughes's boast has a hollow ring about it:

> Sir Charles Dilke defied the Nonconformist Conscience and is a political outcast to this day. Mr Parnell despised the Nonconformist Conscience, and so doing destroyed himself and his party. Lord Rosebery ignored the Nonconformist Conscience for the sake of a racehorse, and the whole world sees the result.[23]

We may appeal from Hughes drunk to Hughes sober, for in 1894 he had uttered a warning which echoed that of R. W. Dale of Birmingham, which Nonconformity failed to heed.

> We must not allow our Churches to be identified with party politics, and in the twentieth century party politics will not be Whig or Tory, Liberal or Conservative, but Collectivist and Individualist. Woe to the Church that commits itself either to the Collectivist or to the Individualist side![24]

We shall ask later whether the belated Methodist stress on teetotalism drove a wedge between the Church and the working class, or whether it was a means of bringing middle class and workers together, helping to produce a viable and peaceful society,[25] at the same time pointing towards a more collectivist ordering of society. This would exemplify T. H. Green's dictum that the state should remove 'hindrances to freedom', of which drink was most certainly one.[26]

A third feature was what Dr Tudur Jones[27] has called the 'fellowship of activity', the creation of cultural or semi-cultural interests around the church or hall building, which can be seen either as a broadening of

[22] Cf. John Kent, in G. V. Bennett and J. D. Walsh (eds), *Essays in Modern English Church History* (London 1966), viii: 'Hugh Price Hughes and the Nonconformist Conscience'; Maldwyn Edwards, *Methodism and England: A Study of Methodism in Its Social and Political Aspects during the Period 1850–1932* (London 1943), chapter 9: 'Hugh Price Hughes'; D. W. Bebbington, *The Nonconformist Conscience: Chapel and Politics 1870–1914* (London 1982), chapter 3: 'The Problems of Society'.

[23] Editorial in *Methodist Times*, 15 October 1896, p. 705.

[24] Letter from Rome, October 1894, in D. P. Hughes, *The Life of Hugh Price Hughes* (London 1904), p. 473n.; cf. A. W. W. Dale, *The Life of* R. *W. Dale of Birmingham* (London 1905), p. 649.

[25] Brian Harrison, *Drink and the Victorians: The Temperance Question in England 1815–1872* (London 1971), pp. 93, 296, 311, 353, 395, etc.; Harold Perkin, *The Origins of Modern English Society 1780–1880* (London 1969), chapter 9: 'The Rise of a Viable Class Society'.

[26] T. H. Green, *Lectures on the Principles of Political Obligation* (London 1895), p. 209.

[27] R. Tudur Jones, *Congregationalism in England 1662–1962* (London 1962), p. 295.

the Church's outreach or as a creeping secularization of the Church's life. The Pleasant Sunday Afternoon Movement,[28] the Band of Hope, Bright Hours, were means of bringing folk within reach of the Gospel in a non-churchly atmosphere. The 'Institutional Church', as it came to be called in the other Free Churches, was a marked feature of this period. Dr Hugh McLeod,[29] in a recent analysis of London Church life at the turn of the century, sees in the Brotherhood Movement a kind of 'new informal Protestantism', and suggests that 'the words "PSA" symbolised all that was original and fresh in Nonconformity'. Mudie-Smith's survey of 1904 had come to the same conclusion. Certainly an analysis of Methodism in this period would be incomplete without a stress being put on the role of organizations like the Wesley Guild (in Wesleyanism) and the Young People's Society of Christian Endeavour more especially, though not exclusively, in the other Methodist Churches. There young folk learned to pray, to set their thoughts in order, to debate, to question, and not least to meet their marriage partners!

Theologically the Forward Movement was moving away from the old orthodoxies. Hugh Price Hughes was not a great thinker but an orator with all the dangers and glories of a church whose chief intellectual activity was preaching and which easily substitutes declamation for argument and perorations for scholarship.[30] Hughes, nevertheless, was a high churchman in the classic Wesleyan tradition.

John Scott Lidgett (1854–1953) was the shrewdest theologian of the period in Methodism – the one Methodist thinker to take Frederick Denison Maurice's view of Christ as the Head of the human race rather than John Wesley as his starting point.[31] Hughes paralleled Lidgett to some extent – his high churchmanship revealed itself in his attitude towards William Booth and the Salvation Army. 'They do not even make proper provision for the sacraments specially ordained by our Lord, and that is fatal.'[32] His exclusion of the Unitarians from participation in Free Church Federalism by a deliberate assertion of the deity of Christ in its title deeds was a similar assertion of orthodoxy. Yet there was at the turn of the century a dichotomy in Methodist theology. 'It seemed as if Free Church ministers had either to compromise with the evolutionary spirit of the age, or to ignore it altogether.'[33] Those like Campbell Morgan or Dinsdale Young (1861–1938), for long minister

[28] For the P.S.A., see Inglis, op. cit., pp. 79–85; *Minutes of Wesleyan Conference* (1895), p. 380. For Christian Endeavour, see Francis E. Clark's article in *Encyclopedia of Religion and Ethics*, iii, 571–3. For the Wesley Guild, see L. E. Ingram, *Fifty Years for Youth* (London 1945).

[29] Hugh McLeod, op. cit., p. 65.

[30] Gordon S. Wakefield, *Methodist Devotion: The Spiritual Life in the Methodist Tradition 1791–1945* (London 1966), p. 83.

[31] Rupert E. Davies (ed.), *John Scott Lidgett: A Symposium* (London 1957), pp. 83–6.

[32] D. P. Hughes, op. cit., p. 630.

[33] Horton Davies, *The English Free Churches* (London 1952), p. 183.

of the Central Hall, Westminster, who chose the latter path, ran the risk of irrelevancy, while those who sought to integrate theology with the claims of modern science were dubbed modernists, as moderates like J. A. Beet (1840–1924), and George Jackson (1864–1945) found to their cost. Methodism suffered, as did all basically non-liturgical[34] Churches, from the inadequacy of the theology of the period, though there were few in Methodism whose position was as extreme as that of R. J. Campbell of the City Temple, whose 'New Theology' of 1907 revealed a great rift in Congregationalism.

The weakness of the churchmanship of the period was a decay of discipline. Bishop Leslie Hunter, a sympathetic critic of his own father's generation of Freechurchmen, pointed to a loss of discipline among the successors of the Puritans.

> The sad decline in the vigour of Free Church worship seems to have dated from the passing of the Puritan Sabbath, for it left Free Churchmen with no other discipline of worship. It all became too easy among the middle classes. Morning church after a late breakfast; none of the discomfort of kneeling when you got there; apart from hymn-singing, which tended to become more and more sentimental, no vigorous call to participate in a liturgy of the people. Little demand, and so slackening response.[35]

Perhaps Hunter's strictures are as applicable to the Wesleyanism of watering-place and suburb as to the Missions. The long debate concerning the place of the class meeting in the definition of Methodist Church-membership continued in this period.[36] In contrast to Hunter, Newton Flew[37] claimed that as late as 1928 it was estimated that 'half the London members of the Wesleyan Church met regularly in class'. The warning signs were clear enough, for the Victorian façade of religious consensus had begun to crumble long before the Queen's death.[38] In Methodism the change showed itself in a new, broader and vaguer sense of commitment to the local society and a decline of the sense of corporate holiness which had characterized earlier periods of Methodist history

[34] I.e. Churches which do not use responsive set forms as a norm of worship. The basic late-Victorian 'preaching service' was clearly of this free category.

[35] Leslie Stannard Hunter, *The Seed and the Fruit: Christian Morality in a Time of Transition* (London 1953), p. 79.

[36] Currie, op. cit., pp. 125–31; Henry D. Rack, 'The Decline of the Class-Meeting and the Problem of Church-Membership in Nineteenth-Century Wesleyanism', in *W.H.S. Proc.*, xxxix (pt 1, February 1973), 12–21. *Wesleyan Methodist Minutes* (1889), Appendix XI: pp. 404–13; (1894), pp. 218ff.; (1908), pp. 105, 355, 574–90; George G. Findlay, 'Church Membership in Wesleyan Methodism', in *London Quarterly Review*, cxi (April 1909), 213–32.

[37] R. Newton Flew, 'Methodism and the Catholic Tradition', in N. P. Williams and C. Harris (eds), *Northern Catholicism* (London 1933), p. 523.

[38] Hugh McLeod, op. cit., p. xi.

as well as a tendency to perpetuate rather than break down the class distinction which marked Victorian Methodism.[39]

The Forward Movement has had its sharp critics in recent years.[40] There was social aggression as well as aggrieved morality in the Nonconformist Conscience, and signs of an attempt to manipulate the Liberal party for sectarian ends. We need also to point out that no succeeding generation has achieved more in mission to mass industrial man, and we need to ask whether the inculcation of habits of self-respect, responsibility and desire for justice for others is in any way to be denigrated.

Much of the ethos of the Forward Movement spilled over into the Methodism of the conventional circuit. The ordinary chapel became the institutional church.[41] Its impact on a younger generation was ambivalent. Thus Lord Birkett, who lapsed from Wesleyanism, said:

> My mother and father, they were Wesleyan Methodists and I suppose one would say that they were very, very, devoted people. I shall always be grateful for my home life and for the chapel life to which they led me. My knowledge of the Authorized Version and the hymns of Wesley and Watts are certainly some of my very greatest possessions, and at the most formative period of my life I shall never cease to be grateful for the training I had in religious things.[42]

Professor Basil Willey describes his grandmother's home:

> We Wesleyans were a chosen people, and we Willeys a subsection thereof, rather more chosen than the rest, and under a special obligation to keep ourselves unspotted from the world. 'The world' meant almost everybody else – certainly all who smoked, drank, swore, played cards, went to theatres or dances, wore evening-dress, and 'went nowhere' on Sundays.

Of his place of worship he says:

> I do not believe that in church I ever heartily prayed, or repented, or felt any promptings towards a changed life; still less did I experience there any feelings of awe, mystery or communion with the unseen.

[39] John C. Bowmer, *Pastor and People: A Study of Church and Ministry in Wesleyan Methodism from the Death of John Wesley (1791) to the Death of Jabez Bunting (1858)* (London 1975), p. 254.

[40] John Kent, in Bennett and Walsh (eds), op. cit., pp. 182, 187, 204; Stephen Koss, 'Wesleyanism and Empire', in *The Historical Journal*, xviii, No. 1 (March 1975).

[41] For examples of typical church programmes, see David M. Thompson (ed.), *Nonconformity in the Nineteenth Century* (London 1972), pp. 246–8; Charles Booth, *Life and Labour of the People in London*, Third Series: Religious Influences, vii, chapter IV: Illustrations, §3 Wesleyans (pp. 195–207), §4 Other Methodists (pp. 208–33); cf. Stephen Yeo, *Religion and Voluntary Organisations in Crisis* (London 1976).

[42] H. Montgomery Hyde, *Norman Birkett: The Life of Lord Birkett of Ulverston* (London 1964), p. 573.

Respectability, rather than reverence, was what filled the air of the Edwardian pseudo-gothic building, with its walls of new red brick exuding patches of salty white crystals. The hymns, unless the tune happened to be one of our favourites such as 'Gopsal' or 'Wrestling Jacob', were something to be endured, not sung (my father, I noticed, never sang); the Te Deum, when it occurred, was a penance (I knew what my father thought of it because he used to sing, with suppressed vehemence, the last word only – 'confounded'); the prayers, especially the 'long' prayer, were embarrassing because in their approach to the Almighty the Methodist ministers of those days commonly used a tone of easy familiarity, as of the leader of a deputation interviewing a trusted but perhaps not too well-informed chief. The sermon was the thing: it was the centre-piece and *raison d'être* of the whole performance. Upon this I knew that my father's closest and most critical attention would be fixed and upon this I knew that we should have his detailed judgments over the Sunday dinner afterwards.[43]

This was clearly the ethos of a denomination 'suffering from too close inbreeding, and the disabling traditions, already out of date, which sprang up after the death of Wesley'.[44] A more critical generation was to widen its horizons or burst out of this little world altogether typified by the description of his adolescent spiritual struggles by Dr Peter Fletcher[45] in *The Long Sunday* which parallels Professor Willey. Once a year his parents' church would have its 'Mission' – 'Sankeys' would replace the more sober Methodist Hymn Book. Every attempt would be made to induce 'conversion'. The result for the sensitive young Fletcher was the end of Christian observance. For others, no doubt, it was the Church of England. What happened to Peter Fletcher was a reflection of a great change in Nonconformity stemming from the Education Act of 1870 and the end of dissenting disabilities. For many the chapel was no longer the centre of the whole of their existence. There was a shift from a close-knit to a more broad-based community.[46] Dr Robert Moore[47] has recently shown the breakdown of the old style of Methodism in County Durham. His observations can be paralleled by the researches of Dr David Clark into a Sheffield suburb,[48] where he differentiates between the 'locals' and the 'cosmo-

[43] Basil Willey, *Spots of Time: A Retrospect of the Years 1897–1920* (London 1965), pp. 37, 47; cf. Hugh McLeod, op. cit., pp. 135ff.; M. K. Ashby, *Joseph Ashby of Tysoe, 1859–1919: A Study of English Village Life* (Cambridge 1961), pp. 220–6.

[44] J. Ernest Rattenbury, in Brash and Wright, op. cit., p. 102.

[45] Peter Fletcher, *The Long Sunday* (London 1958).

[46] Sociologists, following F. Tönnies, would talk of 'Gesellschaft' and 'Gemeinschaft'.

[47] Robert Moore, *Pit-men, Preachers & Politics: The Effects of Methodism in a Durham Mining Community* (Cambridge 1974), pp. 124ff.

[48] David B. Clark, 'Local and Cosmopolitan Aspects of Religious Activity in a Northern Suburb', in David Martin and Michael Hill (eds), *A Sociological Yearbook of Religion in*

politans': those whose life is bounded by chapel, work, home and local community, and those who, through social, spatial and cognitive mobility, through education or work or marriage, have wider horizons and consequently less local loyalty. Dr Hugh McLeod,[49] working on several London regions, shows that it was working-class people, both within and outside the Church, who were more prone to be 'locals' or, as he puts it, were more prone to both 'secularism and parochialism'. For the products of the new education and the opening of the older universities to Nonconformists, Bernard Lord Manning's verdict on the period was accurate:

> Nonconformity as it was presented to and embraced by them was a sturdy, severe, somewhat crude affair, morally bracing but aesthetically weak and intellectually nondescript.[50]

Deeper currents were, however, flowing in Methodism, with possibilities of renewal. Methodism owes a great deal of its spiritual life to its theological colleges, since many of its ministers owed their culture and general learning, as well as theological and pastoral expertise, to their college. College tutors have had a place in the Church's life quite different from their comparatively low status in the Church of England. In 1900 all was not well[51] – the colleges were the seminaries of an inbred denomination with little attempt to move on to the frontiers of theological thought. Change was, however, heralded by scholars of a new type – William Fiddian Moulton (1835–1898) was the first, at Richmond College, to initiate critical biblical study, followed by his son James Hope Moulton (1863–1917) at Didsbury, a scholar with an international reputation both in Hellenistic Greek and Zoroastrianism. The loss of Moulton, through enemy action, in 1917, followed by the death of Charles L. Bedale, another brilliant young scholar, next year, was heavy. Moulton was paralleled in Primitive Methodism by Professor Arthur S. Peake (1865–1929), whose arrival in 1892 at what became Hartley College, Manchester, was a crucial step in the process of transforming the training of the ministry in his Church.

Britain, iii (London 1970), 45–64; iv (London 1971), 141–59; David B. Clark, 'Community, Membership and the Church', in John Kent and Robert Murray, S.J. (eds), *Church Membership and Intercommunion* (London 1973); cf. Robert K. Merton, *Social Theory and Social Structure* (Glencoe, Ill. 1957), chapter 10: 'Patterns of Influence: Local and Cosmopolitan Influentials'.

[49] Hugh McLeod, op. cit., pp. 61–88; also 'White-collar Values and the Role of Religion', in G. Crossick (ed.), *The Lower Middle Class in Britain 1870–1914* (London 1977), pp. 15–95.

[50] Bernard Lord Manning, 'Some Lapsed Dissenters', in *Congregational Quarterly*, April 1951.

[51] George G. Findlay, 'The Higher Education of the Minister', in *London Quarterly Review*, xcv (January 1901), 108–32; 'The Better Education of the Ministry', in *London Quarterly Review*, xcviii (July 1902), 97–118.

Following World War I, new thinking and styles of training were required, pioneered by John H. Ritson (1868–1953), Balliol scholar and Bible Society Secretary who, as Treasurer of the Theological Institution, induced a group of notable benefactors like T. R. Ferens, Edmund S. Lamplough, Michael Gutteridge and William Greenhalgh to endow theological chairs and equip college chapels.[52] In 1921, a house belonging to Cheshunt College in Cambridge was rented, with H. Maldwyn Hughes (1875–1940) and six students beginning what was to become Wesley House in 1925 through the purchase of land from Jesus College, where B. L. Manning was bursar. Hughes remained as Principal, with R. Newton Flew (1886–1962) as his colleague from 1928. Each college developed links with its neighbouring university so far as was possible. In 1927 it was noted that too few ministerial candidates had previously received higher education, a sign of a cultural lag in the Church which was partially overcome by the 'Methodist Society' Movement stemming from the work of W. H. Beales at Cambridge and Harold Roberts at Oxford in the early 1930s.[53]

Methodism has never had party colleges of the Anglican type, which has meant that no candidates for the ministry have been able to escape the rigours of critical methods in biblical and theological studies. The other positive benefit was the ability of men of differing styles of churchmanship and spirituality to work together and realize how much they had in common. Samuel Chadwick's régime at Cliff College, intended to equip laymen with evangelistic and theological skills, though owing a good deal to the holiness tradition, was also firmly Methodist with a happy, almost Franciscan style of spirituality. A. E. Whitham (1879–1938), who was later one of the founders of the Methodist Sacramental Fellowship (1935), was not dissimilar, though with more of a sacramental and mystical streak.

These varying emphases sought institutional shape in the group movements which inevitably follow and produce spiritual renewal in Methodism.[54] A diet richer than that provided in Wesley Guilds was found in the School of Fellowship and for ministers in the Fellowship of the Kingdom,[55] with focal points in annual conferences at Swanwick, the Mecca of ecumenists and renewers alike. The spiritual leader of this

[52] W. Bardsley Brash, *The Story of Our Colleges 1835–1935: A Centenary Record of Ministerial Training in the Methodist Church* (London 1935), chapter IX: 'Re-opening of Three Colleges – The Coming of Wesley House', chapter X: 'A Great Crusade', esp. pp. 119–20; Gordon S. Wakefield, *Robert Newton Flew 1886–1962* (London 1971), pp. 75ff.

[53] Brash, op. cit., chapter X: 'A Great Crusade'; *Wesleyan Methodist Minutes* (1927), p. 90; *Agenda*, pp. 233–4; (1928), *Agenda*, pp. 239–54; *Minutes*, pp. 249–51.

[54] Cf. Gordon S. Wakefield, op. cit., chapter 2: 'The Young Minister'; *Methodist Devotion*, chapter 3: 'Twentieth-century Trials and Hopes'.

[55] The publications of the School of Fellowship and the Fellowship of the Kingdom from 1920 onwards provide a useful barometer of Methodist spirituality among ministers and intelligent layfolk.

movement was William Russell Maltby (1866–1951), Warden of the Wesley Deaconess Order, aided by J. A. Findlay (1880–1961), T. S. Gregory (1898–1975), who became a Roman Catholic, R. N. Flew, and the young Leslie Weatherhead (1893–1976), who were able to combine a rich catholic spirituality with an intense concern to follow the 'historical Jesus' as he had been revealed to them by the Protestant biblical scholarship which they had studied. The influence of this style of liberal evangelicalism (paralleled in Primitive Methodism by the Hartley clubs) was very great upon ministry and intelligent laity alike.

Methodism was thus becoming more heterogeneous both in its social composition and its theological outlook, yet with a quite clear commitment at many levels to a style of evangelism which distinguished it both from the other Free Churches and from Anglicanism in its Evangelical form. It is here that men as diverse as Professor J. H. Moulton, W. H. Lax, ministerial mayor of Poplar, and Samuel Chadwick would be at one. Thus, Moulton puts prime stress on the doctrine of Conversion. 'We should be forced to drop the name of Wesley if we were unfaithful to that ideal.' He follows with,

> the doctrine of Experience – that for every man the greatest of all reasons for believing is his own power to say, 'Once I was blind, but now I see.' With it stands the doctrine of Holiness – the declaration that nothing less than perfect love to God and man can ever satisfy God's claim upon us, . . . These were the three great doctrines that Wesley rediscovered; and it is on the strength of our unwavering hold on them that we remain Wesleyans today.[56]

W. H. Lax, speaking to King George V, said: 'The Methodist Church, sir, is a loyal Church.' But secondly he stressed that it stood for the 'great evangelical message of conversion', and thirdly the 'absolute necessity of rendering service to the community'.[57] The theological tension within Methodism this century has been between *that* ideal and its fulfilment in a new generation whose religious experience may follow other modes, and the fact that many 'local' Methodists would have put forward as *their* belief system a much more behaviour-centred theology, owing perhaps more to late Victorian respectability than to the experience of the brothers Wesley.[58]

[56] James Hope Moulton, *A Neglected Sacrament: and Other Studies and Addresses* (London 1919), pp. 20–1.

[57] W. H. Lax, op. cit., p. 192.

[58] Robert Moore, op. cit., chapter 4: 'Village Methodism – I', esp. p. 119. Dr Moore uses the dimensions of religious commitment set out in Charles Y. Glock and Rodney Stark, *Religion and Society in Tension* (Chicago, Ill. 1965), and in Rodney Stark and Charles Y. Glock, *American Piety: The Nature of Religious Commitment* (Berkeley, Cal. 1968), pp. 20ff., to show the style of theology prevalent in the Durham coalfield among Methodists.

Three further matters need to be set out as elements in a profile of early twentieth-century Methodism: its declining numbers, its changing geographical distribution, and its sociological composition.

A number of sociologists, notably Dr Bryan Wilson and Dr Robert Currie, have recently propounded the thesis that what they call 'ecumenicalism' is an organizational response to adverse conditions. Churches which cease to advance frontally begin to advance laterally, seeking union with other groups, since in union lies strength.[59] The theory may be vulnerable,[60] while much of the hard evidence lying underneath it is much more intractable. It can be shown by the use of membership figures that the late Victorian years saw an inexorable slowing of growth in all the Methodist groups when seen against a rise of population.[61] A comparison of membership and population figures reveals the danger of the 'years of religious boom' argument for 1850–1900. It was the *previous* fifty years which had the greatest growth of Methodists in proportion to the population. This was clearly seen by leaders like Hugh Price Hughes and Luke Wiseman. Ageing of membership in proportion to the total, and disproportionate to the population around the chapel, is also a feature of this period. If consideration is given to the fact that late-Victorian and Edwardian congregations had many adherents, the fall away in numbers in the Methodist community may be even more ominous, a pointer to which is the fall in the numbers of registered Sunday School children.

Geographically, the distribution of Methodism reveals a gradual shift from the predominance of the North to the South. Thus, in 1801, Wesleyanism was dominated by the West Riding which provided 17.3 per cent of the total membership, with Lancashire running close with 10.4 per cent. In 1901, the pre-eminence of the West Riding had been eroded, though it still showed 12.9 per cent with Lancashire 12.0 per cent. Middlesex and London showed 7.7 per cent, compared with 4.1 per cent in 1801. After 1880 the 'new' Methodist areas grew at disproportionately high rates compared with the old strongholds, much of the change being due to migration.[62] The building of chapels shows

[59] Bryan R. Wilson, *Religion in Secular Society: A Sociological Comment* (London 1966), esp. chapter 8: 'The Clergy and Ecumenicalism'; Currie, op. cit., chapter 3: 'The Dynamics of Ecumenicalism'.

[60] Bryan S. Turner, 'The Sociological Explanation of Ecumenicalism', in Charles Leslie Mitton (ed.), *The Social Sciences and the Churches* (Edinburgh 1972), Chapter 20; D. Thompson, 'Theological and Sociological Approaches to the Motivation of the Ecumenical Movement', in Derek Baker (ed.), *Religious Motivation* (Studies in Church History xv) (Oxford 1978), pp. 467–79.

[61] Compare the tables and graphs in Currie, op. cit., pp. 87, 90, 91, 95–6, 99–100; cf. also Currie, 'A Micro-theory of Methodist Growth', in *W.H.S. Proc.*, xxxvi (pt 3: October 1967), 65–73; E. R. Wickham, op. cit., chapter 4; Owen Chadwick, *The Victorian Church*, ii (London 1970), 218–38; *Minutes of Wesleyan Conference* (1918), pp. 22ff.; Alan D. Gilbert, op. cit., pp. 30ff.

[62] Currie, *Methodism Divided*, p. 104; Charles Booth, op. cit., Third Series: *Religious Influences*, iii, chapter VI: Illustrations, §5 Various Opinions, etc., pp. 215–16.

the same pattern, with a large proportion of new Wesleyan buildings in the London area. Primitive Methodism suffered similar distribution changes. In the mid-Victorian period the growth points are Lancashire, Norfolk, Cheshire, Yorkshire, Lincolnshire and the North-East. In the later nineteenth century there is greater growth in London, the South-East, the Thames Valley and the South Midlands. The leakage of members due to migration was greater than in Wesleyanism, which had more viable societies in the South of England. It is possible in the light of the work of Currie and Dr J. D. Gay to make a tentative generalization.[63] In the eighteenth century Wesleyanism often grew in the gaps of Anglican pastoral coverage. The story is complicated by rural social patterns which no longer applied in the late nineteenth century,[64] but geographical variations in the Church of England's ability to maintain a close-knit pastoral oversight as shown in the Isle of Wight, Cornwall or the West Riding, were clearly a prime factor (though not the only one) in Methodist expansion.[65] In the early nineteenth century the newer Methodist groups tended to grow in the gaps of Wesleyanism. Later in the century, the distribution of Methodism began to change, resulting in an accelerated decline in the North and in rural areas,[66] and increased growth in the South, even in the south-eastern areas previously called 'the Methodist desert'.[67] This pattern of change must not be exaggerated, however, since as late as 1961, apart from Devon, Cornwall and the Isle of Wight, the main strength of Methodism lay in the northern half of the country – north of a line from Worcester to the Wash.[68] During the twentieth century, Methodism's strongest societies have tended to be found in the suburbs of large cities in which the Church becomes a focus reflecting the prevailing middle-class norms, and provides the residents and their children with an anchor point in a sea of social change.

The number of Methodist members and their geographical distribution is far easier to determine than the social composition of individual Methodist churches, and even obvious sources such as marriage registers and lists of trustees' occupations can be misleading. Certainly the old 'Wesleyan' pattern of celebrating rites of passage in the parish church lingered on into the twentieth century, combining with non-theological factors concerned more with photography than sociology. Methodism has boasted very few who 'wore coronets and prayed'.

[63] Currie, 'A Micro-theory . . .', p. 73; cf. John D. Gay, *The Geography of Religion in England* (London 1971), pp. 144ff.; chapter 8: 'The Methodists'.

[64] For rural patterns, see Alan Everitt, *The Pattern of Rural Dissent: The Nineteenth Century* (Leicester 1972).

[65] Gay, op. cit., pp. 158–9.

[66] See the 1959 Report to Conference on Rural Methodism.

[67] Gay, op. cit., pp. 304–16: maps of Methodist distribution.

[68] Ibid. p. 165: map on p. 311.

There has always been a notable and generous group of 'self-made' businessmen of the type who supported Jabez Bunting[69] and who, as we have seen, assisted John H. Ritson's ministerial training renaissance in the 1920s. These men supported the Twentieth Century Thanksgiving Fund[70] to provide (in addition to support of Missions and bodies like the National Children's Home) 'a building in London . . . large . . . central . . . monumental', which provided in the Westminster Central Hall a suitable headquarters for a great Church. The Ranks – father and son – and Lord Mackintosh of Halifax can typify this breed of Methodist – wealthy, generous, with an engaging homespun piety.[71] The link between the Ranks and modern mission is a remarkable if ambiguous chapter in our history. The new professions created by the Industrial Revolution have been well represented in Methodism. H. H. Fowler, Lord Wolverhampton (1830–1911), was not only the first Methodist, but also the first solicitor to enter the Cabinet.[72] His friend, Sir Robert Perks, the Vice-President of the first uniting Methodist Conference in 1932, was the typical Wesleyan political layman. Below these wealthy men lay a great army of petty clerks – Methodism had many Mr Pollys in its vestries – schoolteachers, shopkeepers and petit bourgeois who gave Methodism its middle-class ethos. Below them was the highly significant group whom we can call the 'Labour Aristocracy', men of skill and ability who by dint of hard work and thrift pushed themselves into the lower-middle-class groups, and often provided the leadership and drive not only in Methodist chapels but in trade unions, friendly societies and the early Labour Party at constituency level, and who may well have played a crucial role in providing an element of stability and conciliation in English working-class politics.[73] Lower in the scale again was the great mass of working men whom no Church, not even Primitive Methodism or the Salvation Army,[74] reached in any great numbers, though many workers were to be found in their chapels and citadels which were certainly working-class in ethos. Very much more local study, such as that of Dr Hugh McLeod in London, Margaret Stacey in Banbury and Bishop Wickham in Sheffield, is needed before more generalization can be risked, though the picture of the Methodist chapel culture given sympathetically by Robert Moore in *Pit-Men, Preachers &*

[69] W. R. Ward, *Religion and Society in England 1790–1850* (London 1972), p. 97.

[70] Currie, *Methodism Divided*, p. 181; for the use of the Fund, see E. Benson Perkins, 'Twentieth Century Fund', in Nolan B. Harmon (ed.), *The Encyclopedia of World Methodism* (Nashville, Tenn. 1974), ii, 2381–2.

[71] R. G. Burnett, *Through the Mill: The Life of Joseph Rank* (London 1945).

[72] R. C. K. Ensor, *England 1870–1914* (London 1936), p. 305n.

[73] Harold Perkin, op. cit., chapter 9, esp. pp. 393–5; E. J. E. Hobsbawm, *Labouring Men: Studies in the History of Labour* (London 1964), chapter 15: 'The Labour Aristocracy in Nineteenth-century Britain'.

[74] E. R. Wickham, op. cit., pp. 131–4: 'The Boom in Primitive Methodism in Sheffield'; J. D. Gay, op. cit., pp. 150–4.

People can probably be paralleled in many Northern communities in the early twentieth century.[75]

This profile reveals a Church entering a new century confident and yet at the same time unsure of itself. The organic union of Methodism was in the offing, with each group seeing it in different terms. The smaller bodies among which union began were aware that their size was insufficient for either growth or dynamic mission. They needed to overcome losses by migration, they needed an adequately paid and equipped ordained ministry, they needed capital for expenditure on building schemes and publishing enterprises. The acute pressures towards organic unity came first in the liberal Methodist groups, though it is clear that the most theologically aware minds in Wesleyanism and Primitive Methodism such as Hughes, Lidgett and Peake had far wider horizons than the small world of Methodism.[76] To their vision and its accomplishments and failure we now turn.

2. The United Methodist Church 1907–1932

In 1878, lay representatives were admitted to the Wesleyan Conference, a fundamental change which, despite a continuing Pastoral Session, made union between Wesleyanism and the more liberal Methodist bodies possible. 'Once Conference is made a mixed assembly, the function of a collective Pastorate is destroyed and it becomes something quite different, a legislative rather than an episcopal body.'[77] Nevertheless, the union negotiations first of all produced a regrouping of Free Methodism in the United Methodist Church of 1907.[78]

Abortive attempts to unite the Methodist New Connexion and the United Methodist Free Churches (1868, 1890) stemming from William Cooke's initiatives of 1863, the negotiations following Hugh Price Hughes's 'Olive Branch of Peace' of 1886, a possible M.N.C.–Bible Christian union (1870), and a similar union of Primitive Methodists and

[75] Robert Moore, op. cit., chapter 6: 'The respectable Methodists and the old Liberalism', and for occupational status and social mobility, see his Appendix IV. For rural areas, see J. Obelkevich, *Religion and Rural Society: South Lindsey 1825–1875* (Oxford 1976); also C. D. Field, 'The Social Structure of English Methodism', in *British Journal of Sociology*, xxviii, No. 2 (June 1977), pp. 199–225; 'A Sociological Profile of English Methodism 1900–1932', in *Oral History*, iv, No. 1 (Spring 1976), pp. 73–95.

[76] Robert Currie, op. cit., p. 89.

[77] The word 'episcopacy' is used in the sense of 'episcope' or 'oversight': John C. Bowmer, op. cit., p. 167.

[78] W. J. Townsend, *The Story of Methodist Union* (London n.d.), is the standard account; cf. also William Redfern, 'Unions and Reunions Effected', in *N.H.M.*, ii, 445–82; Currie, *Methodism Divided*, chapter 7: 'The Origins of United Methodism'; Robert F. Wearmouth, *The Social and Political Influence of Methodism in the Twentieth Century*, chapter 5: 'The Making of Methodist Union'. For the wider union of 1932, cf. John Kent, *The Age of Disunity* (London 1966), chapter 1: 'Methodist Union'; Currie, op. cit., pp. 248–9; John T. Wilkinson (ed.), *Arthur Samuel Peake: A Biography* (London 1971), pp. 59–79.

Bible Christians (1899) had foundered by the turn of the century. The Primitive Methodists began to see themselves as the possible begetters of a large liberal Methodist Church, but sociological objections were masked by constitutional difficulties.[79]

The Methodist Ecumenical Conference of 1901, held at Wesley's Chapel, gave stimulus to new negotiations. T. B. Stephenson made clear that 'any serious further advance spells *union* and nothing else'.[80] The *Methodist Times*, under its editor Hugh Price Hughes, appealed to the smaller groups to wait for a Wesleyan initiative.[81] William Redfern and David Brook of the U.M.F.C. emerged as the ministerial leaders of a movement for the union of the liberal Methodist groups supported by Sir Robert Bird, a symbolic opportunity being provided by the Jubilee of the United Methodist Free Churches in 1907.[82] The threat of a larger church with an anti-Wesleyan approach alarmed some Wesleyans like R. W. (later Sir Robert) Perks, who attempted to push a union scheme with the M.N.C. in 1904, a move condemned by J. S. Simon[83] as a discourtesy and strongly opposed by the still active J. H. Rigg. 'To invite a minor body to separate itself from the Committee [for union between the smaller groups] and join with them would be an utterly unheard-of and unworthy proposal.'

The long-standing opposition of certain elements in the M.N.C. to union with the U.M.F.C. broke down at this point,[84] and alleged U.M.F.C. fears of ministerial dominance in the M.N.C. gave way to compromise on the vexed question of ministerial chairmanship at meetings[85] and the power of Conference to levy money from the circuits. Voting for the union scheme, which was an amended version of the scheme of 1890, was overwhelming both at Quarterly Meeting and Conference level.[86] Only two U.M.F.C. circuits, one M.N.C. and one B.C. circuit, voted against union, and when the union took place only one U.M.F.C. circuit seceded, for a period of three years.[87] Union, no doubt, had different perspectives for the groups involved. For the Bible Christians this could be some protective against leakage of members from their south-western fastnesses; for some Free Churchmen like

[79] W. J. Townsend, op. cit., pp. 137, 180–6.

[80] Ibid., pp. 135–6.

[81] *Methodist Times*, 4 September 1902, p. 644.

[82] Cf. William Redfern, *Modern Developments in Methodism* (London 1906).

[83] W. J. Townsend, op. cit., p. 234; cf. Oliver A. Beckerlegge, *The United Methodist Free Churches: A Study in Freedom* (London 1957), pp. 101ff.; *Methodist Recorder*, 28 July 1904, p. 8.

[84] Currie, op. cit., pp. 245–6; *Minutes* (Methodist New Connexion) (1905), p. 35.

[85] Currie, op. cit., p. 247; Oliver A. Beckerlegge, op. cit., p. 102; *Minutes* (United Methodist Free Churches) (1905), p. 39.

[86] For the figures, see W. J. Townsend, op. cit., p. 228; chapter xiii: 'Final Voting in Circuit Meetings'.

[87] W. J. Townsend, op. cit., p. 253; Henry Smith, John E. Swallow and William Treffry (eds), *The Story of the United Methodist Church* (London 1932), p. 25.

William Redfern it was a fusion of liberal Methodist forces which could lead to negotiation from strength with the Wesleyans. 'A strong democratic Methodist church' would be the harbinger of renewed Methodism, with a constitution free of Wesleyan sacerdotalism. 'In the meanwhile, let all liberal Methodists come together, confident that by their own organic union they are making the larger reunion of Methodism to be, sooner or later, inevitable.'[88] Free Methodism thus sought a 'superdenomination'[89] within the framework of the Methodist Church with sufficient strength to support an adequately trained ministry, capital for expansion typified by the Twentieth Century Fund parallel to Perks's Million Guineas scheme in Wesleyanism, to publish Connexional literature (the *Free Methodist* had anticipated union in 1902!) and to exercise political influence. The new denomination was inaugurated at Wesley's Chapel in September 1907.

Constitutionally, this Church retained much of the system of the Methodist New Connexion. Free Methodist commitment to Wesley's teaching was displaced by a liberal biblical position. 'The Scriptures of of the Old and New Testaments through Divine Inspiration *contain* a revelation of the Will of God to man and furnish a sufficient rule of faith and practice.' Provision was made for a decennial revision of the doctrinal basis – a more liberal position than the doctrinal clauses of the 1932 union. The sacraments[90] were described, quoting Kilham, as of 'divine institution and perpetual obligation' – a phrase taken up into the larger scheme of 1932. In the new Constitution, largely based on the 1890 scheme, Guardian Representatives were an M.N.C. method of providing Conference with a measure of continuity, and Conference itself had greater power over the circuits than was ever the case in Free Methodism, with the ministers being granted an *ex officio* chairmanship of all local meetings. Numerically the Church of 1907 brought together 79,948 U.M.F.C. members, 37,009 from the M.N.C. and 32,202 Bible Christians.[91]

The Bible Christians brought into the wider Church a virile rural community, often frankly in financial straits, which had in the past provided difficulties regarding union.[92] Shebbear College (1841), under its outstanding headmaster Thomas Ruddle (1839–1909), which had acted as a theological college as well as a boys' school, and Edgehill College for Girls (1884) were institutional gifts of the Bible Christians.

[88] William Redfern, op. cit., pp. 163–4.

[89] Currie, op. cit., p. 86.

[90] For the Constitution and Doctrines, see Henry Smith et al., op. cit., chapters 3 and 4. The phrase about the sacraments is from the Foundation Deed Poll of 1907, and derives from the 1797 Methodist New Connexion Constitution; cf. *N.H.M.*, ii, Appendix E: 'The United Methodist Church Act, 1907'.

[91] For full statistics, see *N.H.M.*, ii, 549.

[92] Thomas Shaw, *The Bible Christians 1815–1907* (London 1965), p. 74; see p. 58, for its membership distribution.

Outstanding in leadership was Richard Pyke (1873–1965), who was President of the United Methodist Church in 1927 and of Methodism in 1939. The majority of its membership was to be found in the south-west, in the Isle of Wight, along the south coast, and in Kent.

The United Methodist Free Churches were much less homogeneous than the Bible Christians. This church included the great centres of the disruptions of the 1840s and 1850s typified by chapels like Baillie Street, Rochdale, and George Street, Burton upon Trent, which were more like strong Congregationalist churches than Wesleyan societies. The balance of its membership was in the north.[93] Institutionally it brought the theological college at Manchester, Victoria Park,[94] and a Deaconess Institution (Bowron House),[95] which was later merged at Ilkley with the Wesley Deaconess Order. Ashville College at Harrogate (1876) provided a boys' public school for the north to complement Shebbear in the south-west. Notable laymen included Sir James Duckworth (1840–1915), one of the two lay Presidents of the U.M.F.C., and outstanding in ministerial leadership was David Brook (1854–1933), who was chairman of the Union Committee of his church from 1921 to 1932 as well as chairman of the interdenominational committee. A notable scholar was W. E. Soothill (1861–1935) who, after years in China, became Professor of Chinese at Oxford.

The Methodist New Connexion had always remained a comparatively small Church with a Constitution more akin to Wesleyanism than the other Free Methodist bodies. It had its college in Sheffield (Ranmoor) largely financed by the generosity of the Firth family who were notable in both steel and education in that city. J. S. Clemens (1857–1929) was Principal at the time of union[96] and the college remained in use until 1919 when final amalgamation with Victoria Park was effected. The strength of this Church lay north of a line from Stoke to Nottingham, especially in industrial Yorkshire and Lancashire.

United Methodism was in some ways a bridge Church, bringing into a wider cultural context those groups of Methodists who had sought to work out a genuine democracy in church affairs. The influence of the patriarchal style of layman who often benevolently dominated United Methodist (and Primitive Methodist) societies is an interesting example of what might now be called 'auxiliary ministry'; for such men were often enough pastors, preachers and financial benefactors with all the perils of this sort of power and all the local benefits also. This tended to be seen by Wesleyans as something of a threat to good order, and was

[93] Oliver A. Beckerlegge, op. cit., pp. 92–7: maps of membership distribution.

[94] Henry Smith et al., op. cit., pp. 40ff., 141ff.; G. G. Hornby, chapter XII: 'Victoria Park and Ranmoor Colleges', in Brash, op. cit.

[95] Henry Smith et al., op. cit., pp. 121f.

[96] G. G. Hornby, in Brash, op. cit., pp. 152–6.

met with a lack of sympathy which was sometimes hurtful as well as a denial of what union was supposed to be about.

3. The Primitive Methodist Church 1900–1932

Primitive Methodism, having begun as a revivalist movement in the Potteries, had grown steadily in numbers throughout the nineteenth century, though not without considerable tension.[97] It spread, often by the individual initiation of revivals, along the Trent Valley with successful and lasting work in the East Riding, centred on Hull, and then northwards in Durham and southwards through Lincolnshire into East Anglia. By the time of the 1851 Census, it was clearly the second largest Methodist group and remained so until union. The Connexion was largely rural in character, and can be seen as part of the 'revolt of the field' – the challenge of the agricultural workers for a place in the sun. Joseph Arch, the founder of the Agricultural Workers' Union,[98] was for years a Primitive Methodist, as was Sir George Edwards (1850–1933), who in *From Crow-scaring to Westminster* described himself:

> With my study of theology, I soon began to realize that the social conditions of the people were not as God intended they should be. The gross injustices meted out to my parents and the terrible sufferings I had undergone in my boyhood burnt themselves into my soul like a hot iron. Many a time did I vow I would do something to better the conditions of my class.[99]

Edwards was not converted to Methodism until 1869, but he had many precursors – men who found their ability to speak and think and debate in the chapel or who combined their theology often enough with radical politics. The anti-sacerdotal nature of the smaller Methodist bodies provided a first-rate mechanism for selecting leaders and radical camp followers. The political transformation of a non-aggressive sectarian into a 'labour sectarian' under the pressure of social agitation was common. Primitive Methodism was much nearer than Wesleyanism to the proletarian groups. An analogy might well be drawn between them and the Anabaptist sects of the Reformation period which appealed to the

[97] The massive history by H. Bickersteth Kendall, *The Origin and History of the Primitive Methodist Church*, 2 vols. (London 1906), can be supplemented by the same author's *History of the Primitive Methodist Church* (London 1919); B. Aquila Barber, *A Methodist Pageant: Souvenir of the Primitive Methodist Church* (London 1932), and chapter III: 'Primitive Methodism', in A. W. Harrison et al., *The Methodist Church: Its Origin, Divisions, and Reunion* (London 1932). For a clear geographical analysis, see Gay, op. cit., pp. 150–4.

[98] Cf. M. K. Ashby, op. cit., esp. pp. 6, 45ff., 79ff.; Alan D. Gilbert, op. cit., p. 171; Nigel Scotland, *Methodism and the Revolt of the Field* (Gloucester 1981).

[99] George Edwards, *From Crow-scaring to Westminster: An Autobiography* (London 1957), p. 36; Robert F. Wearmouth, op. cit., p. 176; Pamela R. Horn, *Joseph Arch (1826–1919): The Farm Workers' Leader* (Kineton 1971).

displaced peasants and the disoriented urban poor – groups which, rootless and cast out from traditional society, found identity in the total solution of a revolutionary millenarianism.[100] For such folk the close-knit life of the chapel, with the maximum of democracy, gave purpose and meaning to a grim existence. 'The chapel gave them their first music, their first literature and philosophy to meet the harsh life and cruel impact of the crude materialistic age.'[101]

Primitive Methodism had considerable success in large villages, especially the colliery type as in County Durham. Its urban successes were more limited, though in great centres such as Sheffield and Sunderland,[102] it reached further down into the lower social strata than any of the large denominations, even if its numbers were never large. By the end of the century much of the economic, social and even religious impetus of Primitive Methodism had begun to wane, though in the areas of its strength it represented a style of dissent with not only a large proletarian percentage of members, but an almost Pentecostal style of worship with an authentic participation of the congregation quite different from Wesleyanism.[103]

The turn of the century saw an increasing church consciousness in Primitive Methodism. The Thanksgiving Fund of 1892, the Chapel Aid and Church Extension Fund (1900), enabled new building schemes to be carried out, the title 'Church' rather than 'Connexion' appearing on class tickets in 1902. In 1912 the Hymn Book of 1886 was given a supplement, a collection which catches the somewhat exuberant and romantic atmosphere of Edwardian Methodism. Primitive Methodism had its Forward Movement, though inevitably on a smaller scale than that of Wesleyanism, but Thomas Jackson's Whitechapel Mission and the work of James Flanagan in Southwark, including the establishment of a Sisters' Settlement and Training Home, were notable.[104] A fitting Headquarters for the denomination was acquired in Holborn Hall in 1912.[105]

The debt of a Church which was never rich to the beneficence of Sir William Pickles Hartley (1846–1922)[106] was very great. Hartley, an

[100] See E. J. E. Hobsbawm, *Primitive Rebels* (Manchester 1959), chapter VIII: 'The Labour Sects'.

[101] Jack Lawson, *A Man's Life* (London 1944), p. 69.

[102] E. R. Wickham, op. cit., pp. 131–4; Geoffrey E. Milburn, 'Tensions in Primitive Methodism in the Eighteen-Seventies; and the Origins of the Christian Lay Churches in the North-East', *W.H.S. Proc.*, xl (pt 4, February 1976), 95.

[103] For a description of Primitive Methodist worship, see John Briggs and Ian Sellers, *Victorian Nonconformity* (London 1973), pp. 35–6; J. Obelkevich, op. cit., chapter V: 'Primitive Methodism'.

[104] William Potter, *Thomas Jackson of Whitechapel: A Record of Fifty Years of Social and Evangelistic Enterprise* (Liverpool 1929); B. Aquila Barber, op. cit., pp. 197–201; Robert F. Wearmouth, *Methodism and the Struggle of the Working Classes 1850–1900*, pp. 164–8.

[105] H. Bickersteth Kendall, *History of the Primitive Methodist Church*, p. 152.

[106] Arthur S. Peake, *The Life of Sir William Hartley* (London 1926).

astute and theologically aware jam manufacturer, saw the need for proper education of the ordained ministry and was largely responsible for the Manchester College (renamed Hartley College in 1906), which could boast of being 'the largest denominational training College in the land'.[107] Without doubt Hartley's astutest move was to bring the Oxford-trained Arthur S. Peake to Manchester in 1892. It was Peake who moulded the theological outlook of a whole generation of ministers, many of whom came into the wider Methodism of 1932. Peake was only twenty-five when he began his work at Manchester. Primitive Methodism took the risk of employing so young a man (and a layman too!), a policy followed up later with the appointment of Atkinson Lee, another layman, to teach philosophy in 1908. Hartley made Peake's books, including the famous *Commentary* of 1919, available to Primitive Methodist preachers, a benefaction which made critical scholarship widely known and not feared.[108] Peake was the first non-Anglican to hold a divinity chair in an English university,[109] and as editor of the *Holborn Review* from 1919 made it one of the best theological periodicals of its day. Other notable Primitive Methodist scholars included A. L. Humphries (1865–1950), W. L. Wardle (1877–1946), H. G. Meecham (1886–1955) and more recently the late N. H. Snaith and J. T. Wilkinson.

Institutionally, Primitive Methodism was not as strong as Free Methodism. Elmfield House, York, from 1865 onwards provided a Connexional boys' school until 1932, and from 1885 Bourne College, Quinton, in Birmingham – another small public school. In much of its central organization, Primitive Methodism paralleled Wesleyanism, though it is notable that enthusiasm for the temperance cause was more widespread. The Anti-cigarette League also revealed an awareness of another social evil. In youth work the Young People's Society of Christian Endeavour had a full-time secretary from 1898 onwards. Although many individual Primitive Methodists were active in politics, the official pronouncements of the Church tended to the pietistic, stemming from Hugh Bourne's dislike of 'speeching Radicals'.[110] In 1908 the Primitive Methodist Social Service Union was recognized by Conference, and in 1924[111] there were Conference resolutions on

[107] H. B. Kendall, op. cit., p. 149; W. Bardsley Brash, op. cit., chapter 11: 'Hartley Primitive Methodist College'.

[108] John T. Wilkinson (ed.), *Arthur Samuel Peake 1865–1929: Essays in Commemoration and Selections from His Writings* (London 1958), p. 12.

[109] John T. Wilkinson (ed.), *Arthur Samuel Peake: A Biography*, p. 69.

[110] G. T. Brake, *Drink: Ups and Downs of Methodist Attitudes to Temperance* (London 1974), chapter 7: 'Temperance in Primitive Methodism'; Robert F. Wearmouth, *Methodism and the Working-Class Movements of England 1800–1850* (London 1937), p. 212; Bryan S. Turner and Michael Hill, 'Methodism and the Pietist Definition of Politics: Historical Development and Contemporary Evidence', in Michael Hill (ed.), *A Sociological Yearbook of Religion in Britain*, viii, 159–80.

[111] G. T. Brake, op. cit., p. 74; *Minutes of Primitive Methodism* (1924).

housing, unemployment, education, gambling, rodeo exhibitions, Royalty and the Turf, and one supporting the C.O.P.E.C. resolutions with a typical rider:

> All social conditions, economic or industrial, national or international relations are widely acknowledged to be dependent primarily upon a change of heart in the individual.

1907 saw the centenary of 'the day's praying on Mow Hill'. The Connexion could boast an increase in 1905 of 4,638 members (the largest since 1833), which may have been an echo of the Welsh Revival, but a slow decline in numbers related to population marked the last generation of Primitive Methodism. What features of Primitive Methodism were notable in the early twentieth century?[112]

First, a close kinship with the other Free Churches which was made clear in World War I in the association of Primitive Methodism with the United Methodists and 'Orthodox Dissent' in chaplaincy work involving fifty chaplains. There was also a much more wholehearted support of Free Church Federation than was to be found in Wesleyanism.

Secondly, an attempt to work out within a Connexional framework a great deal of local and district autonomy. The legacy of the 'Districtism' of the mid-Victorian years was the District Meeting occupying a week-end. This was a Conference in miniature – much more of an intimate fellowship than Conference itself. Recognition of ministers had been a feature of the District Meeting – a more Anglican feature than the centralized ordinations of Wesleyanism! Perhaps the union of 1932 missed an opportunity here of regional development, for the post-1932 Synod became much more a business meeting than a sharing of spiritual insights.

Thirdly, a view of ministry which may have had more relevance in an era of economic depression. At the local level the minister was a 'travelling' preacher as distinct from a 'local' preacher. He had a different function, but ordination was not deemed to confer on him any gifts not available to other preachers. The minister was first among equals and was respected as such.[113] At his request a layman could preside at the Lord's Supper and in one-man circuits[114] two or three local preachers of wisdom and experience would be entrusted with this privilege, if need arose. This was a mode of auxiliary ministry in which even some Anglicans now see merit.[115] At Connexional level a layman could become President of Conference, though only Sir William Hartley attained this distinction in 1909. No doubt there was a streak of

[112] See *Methodist Recorder*, 9 October 1952: Hugh Bourne Centenary Supplement.
[113] A. Victor Murray, ibid., p. vii.
[114] See John Kent, op. cit., p. 7.
[115] Anthony E. Harvey, *Priest or President?* (London 1975), esp. pp. 37–54.

anti-clericalism and a persistent Quaker element here,[116] which Wesleyans disliked, though may not have understood.

Fourthly, Primitive Methodism bore a steady witness to the value of free worship, which is acknowledged as a valued part of the Methodist tradition. In the Book of Offices of 1936[117] the call to extempore prayer came from Primitive Methodist sources, a call echoed in the 1975 Methodist Service Book. Clear guidance concerning the conduct of extempore prayer at Holy Communion might have been of more value than the Alternative Order of Communion manufactured for the 1936 Book of Offices.

Primitive Methodism, guided by Sir William Hartley, avoided long, term investments.[118] This had the effect, at times, of producing burdensome chapel debts, as circuits paid their immediate dues before clearing property debts. It also gave an air of poverty to a largely working-class Church, though in days of inflation a church of givers rather than savers has its merits. Following union, much of the distinctive ethos of Primitive Methodism disappeared through social change and also owing to the unconscious tendency of Wesleyan norms to prevail in the larger Church.

When Churches unite, they bring together not so much doctrines and liturgies as people. Primitive Methodism brought into the wider union men and women who combined a genuine piety of a simple, Quaker-like style, a concern for social righteousness and social justice. Typical is Jim Simmons,[119] a member of the 1945 Attlee Government, who espoused Primitive Methodism, teetotalism and an idealistic brand of socialism which avowedly owed more to Methodism than to Marx. R. F. Wearmouth has shown the number and quality of such men in the early Labour Movement and in local politics, especially in the north-east, though his picture is tinged with romanticism. More recent research has widened the perspective. The contribution of Primitive Methodism was clearly of considerable importance.[120] Men like Thomas Burt (1837–1922)[121] of the Miners' Union and a Liberal M.P., Charles

[116] Geoffrey Nuttall, *The Puritan Spirit: Essays and Addresses* (London 1967), chapter 20: 'Early Quakerism and Early Primitive Methodism'.

[117] W. E. Farndale, in *Methodist Recorder*, 9 October 1952; J. C. Bowmer, in *London Quarterly and Holborn Review* (October 1966), pp. 268ff.

[118] I owe the point to the late Dr Norman H. Snaith.

[119] Jim Simmons, *Soap-Box Evangelist* (Chichester 1972), pp. 2, 102, 142, 156, 172, 174.

[120] Sidney Webb, *The Story of the Durham Miners (1662–1921)* (London 1921), pp. 22–4; Robert F. Wearmouth, *Methodism and the Struggle of the Working Classes 1850–1900* (Leicester 1954), chapter 7: 'Methodism and Trade Unionism', esp. pp. 175–207; cf. A. R. Griffin, 'Methodism and Trade Unionism in the Nottinghamshire–Derbyshire Coalfield, 1844–90', *W.H.S. Proc.*, xxxvii (pt 1, February 1969), 2–9; Pamela R. Horn, 'Methodism and Agricultural Trade Unionism in Oxfordshire: the 1870s', *W.H.S. Proc.*, xxxvii (pt 3, October 1969), 67–71; Colin P. Griffin, 'Methodism in the Leicestershire and South Derbyshire Coalfield in the Nineteenth Century', *W.H.S. Proc.*, xxxix (pt 3, October 1973), 62–72.

[121] Robert F. Wearmouth, *The Social and Political Influence of Methodism in the Twentieth Century*, pp. 82ff., 245.

Fenwick (1850–1918),[122] another 'Lib-Lab' M.P., who went directly from coal-face to Parliament, William Straker (1855–1941),[123] successor to Burt as leading official of the Northumberland Miners' Association, were never afraid to mix their piety and their politics.

John Wilson (1837–1910)[124] was another radical Liberal M.P. who had served as the Chairman of his County Council. Peter Lee (1864–1935), of whom it was said: 'In the chapels of Durham County, from one end of it to the other, Sunday after Sunday, he preached the Gospel'[125] – coal-hewer, checkweighman, miners' agent, County Councillor and alderman, magistrate and M.P. – was the typical Primitive Methodist politician.[126] We must note that some of the men whom Wearmouth lists lapsed from their Methodist allegiance and made their socialism their religion. Certainly a fissure developed, especially at the time of the General Strike of 1926, which had the effect of producing alienation between Church and political party which has widened since. Primitive Methodism, even if seen as an interim faith, played the role of a midwife in the painful birth of modern English Socialism out of all proportion to its numerical size. The ministry of Primitive Methodism was recruited from men who knew proletarian life in the raw and who shared depression and poverty with their people. To the Methodist Church of 1932 Primitive Methodism brought 222,021 members (including African members), 1,131 ministers, 12,896 local preachers, 4,356 buildings and 277,792 Sunday school children.

4. The Methodist Church of 1932

The motivations of the proponents of Methodist Union were somewhat like those of British liberal Imperialists – a blend of triumphalism and idealism. A wider union, with Wesleyan initiative, was mooted in 1913.[127] No doubt the impact of World War I then acted as a stimulus – the era of the League of Nations was also the period of the Lambeth Resolutions of 1920 and the idealism and hopefulness of the advocates of union. A. S. Peake[128] stated clearly the reasons for union and his sentiments were echoed by strong personalities like Sir Robert Perks (1846–1934) and Aldom French in Wesleyanism, and the veteran David Brook in United Methodism.

[122] Ibid., p. 85.
[123] Ibid., pp. 87–91.
[124] Ibid., pp. 115–18.
[125] Jack Lawson, *Peter Lee* (London 1936), p. 194; Robert F. Wearmouth, op. cit., pp. 126–7, 225.
[126] Jack Lawson, *A Man's Life*; for a picture of the north-east at this time, see esp. chapter 10: 'Little Bethel'.
[127] *Minutes of Wesleyan Conference* (1913), p. 97.
[128] Leslie S. Peake, *Arthur Samuel Peake: a Memoir* (London 1930), pp. 162–85.

Peake saw union as following the Will of God stated in the New Testament. It is interesting that at a time when Federal unity was popular and espoused by astute thinkers like P. T. Forsyth and J. H. Moulton,[129] Methodists like Peake[130] and Lidgett consistently advocated the corporate reunion not only of Methodism but of Christendom. Secondly, union testified to the fact that Methodists were at one at the deepest level. It is fatal for a Church to 'coddle its denominationalisms and erect prejudices into principles'.[131] Social change had eroded distinctive emphases especially in new areas.[132] Thirdly, the taunts of the world outside the Church are justified if the Church remains divided. Evidence is rarely provided for this, though it flows from the New Testament conception of one people of God. Fourthly, evangelism would receive a fresh impetus. This was widely accepted in Methodism as a cardinal reason for union, and men like George Eayrs (1864–1927) and Sir Robert Perks had visions of a new impetus and the setting up of chapels in village areas,[133] with a consequent recapture of the power rapidly vanishing from the Free Churches. 'One powerful Church might make the forces of evil tremble, where now they are unmoved by the thin piping of contending sects.'[134] Fifthly, the movement towards union tied in with a centripetal tendency in all departments of life. Methodist union is thus linked not only with the League of Nations but with the movement towards large monopolies in industry. 'Christian unity is their definite charge from God, as the League of Nations is the definite charge for the nations.'[135] Methodist union was then seen as the first step towards the reunion of Christendom. The Church of England – this was the aftermath of the Lambeth Appeal of 1920 – would rather negotiate with one Methodist Church than with three. We might add that many saw in union a means of increasing the numbers of Methodists, a consequence of the losses in membership of the period up to 1919 and barely offset by the increases of the 1920s Ecumenism is much more than a response to decline,[136] but this aspect of it cannot be ignored – and it can be linked with the cultural changes already noted which made denominational niceties and total commit-

[129] Cf. P. T. Forsyth, *Lectures on the Church and the Sacraments* (London 1917), pp. 29–70; James Hope Moulton, op. cit., pp. 9ff.

[130] *Primitive Methodist Leader*, 29 April 1920, pp. 273–4. Address to the National Free Church Council 1928, printed in John T. Wilkinson (ed.), *Arthur Samuel Peake: A Biography*, pp. 143–59.

[131] Cf. J. Scott Lidgett, in *N.H.M.*, ii, 417ff.

[132] Currie, op. cit., p. 108.

[133] Ibid., pp. 183, 193.

[134] Ibid., p. 188, cited from J. Ernest Rattenbury, *Christian Union and Methodist Fusion* (London 1921), p. 8; *Methodist Leader*, 23 June 1927, p. 394; *Primitive Methodist Leader*, 27 November 1924, p. 776; E. Aldom French (ed.), *Evangelism: A Re-interpretation* (London 1921), p. 11.

[135] *Methodist Recorder*, 2 January 1919, p. 3.

[136] Currie, op. cit., pp. 14, 85–103; Bryan R. Wilson, loc. cit.

ment to chapel culture irrelevant to increasing numbers of Methodists.

On the other hand commitment to denomination, to chapel culture and to the social divisions which had previously been factors in Methodist divisions were still brakes on swift union and even more on its local consummation after 1932.

> Unionists were caught in a peculiar dilemma. On the one hand, if union was to make Methodism 'a greater evangelistic force throughout the country', the rationalization consequent upon closure of overlapping chapels was essential. On the other hand, if they advocated closure of chapels as the main plank of their programme, the union movement was doomed. . . . The purpose of union was to close the chapels; the price of union was to keep them open.[137]

The next generation in its zeal for efficiency sometimes forgot the great role of the chapel in providing the primary group necessary for depth in Christian discipleship. This was a cruel dilemma for Methodism.

The difficulties were at first thought to be basically constitutional, the greatest obstacle being the continuance of a Pastoral or Ministerial Session in Conference. The small groups of opponents in Primitive and United Methodism made this their main objection. To permit a Pastoral Session was a major concession by the liberal Methodist Churches, barely compensated by the lay Vice-Presidency and the end of the 'Legal Hundred'. In the event the basic scheme of 1920 was hardly altered.[138] The difficulties arose over matters of doctrine, and the final statement on doctrine was a patchwork as complicated as the documents of the Revolution Settlement of 1688–9![139]

The points at issue were the nature of the ministry and the sacraments and the way in which the doctrinal standards of the new Church were to be expressed. There was also a strong feeling on the part of some Wesleyan ministers, led by J. E. Rattenbury (1870–1963) and laymen like Sir Henry Lunn and Sir Kingsley Wood, that the dilution of Wesleyan principles by the outright dissenting sentiments of the Primitive and United Methodists would make a further union with Anglicanism difficult, if not impossible.[140] A parallel can be seen in the opposition of some Anglicans to the 1963 scheme on the grounds that it would make ultimate reunion with the Church of Rome more difficult. On the

137 Currie, op. cit., pp. 197–8; cf. John Kent, op. cit., pp. 40–1.

138 For the various schemes A, B, C, D, see, respectively, *Minutes of Wesleyan Conference* (1920), pp. 72ff.; (1922), pp. 68ff.; (1924), pp. 70ff.; (1926), pp. 70ff.; for the Model Deed, see *Minutes* (1926), pp. 104ff.

139 George Macaulay Trevelyan, *The English Revolution 1688–1689* (London 1938), chapter 5: 'The Revolution Settlement'.

140 J. Ernest Rattenbury, op. cit., pp. 27–31.

other hand, some of the liberal Methodists feared a sacerdotal view of the ministry and a moving away from the Free Churches. If some Primitive Methodists feared sacerdotalism, some Wesleyans feared a view of the ministry which demeaned it to the position of a 'paid agency', a lingering legacy of the Disruption of 1849; behind this, no doubt, lay a fear of loss of status by the ministry. A great deal of credit must be given to A. S. Peake for drawing the sting of these Wesleyan fears and giving his own Church a consistent sense of direction. Peake pointed to the value of a Pastoral Session and repudiated a grovelling view of the ministry in the smaller Churches.

> I repudiate with hot indignation . . . the opinion that we value it so lightly . . . Be it ours to have a high doctrine of the ministry just because we have a high doctrine of the Church; to regard the ministry not as possessed of any priesthood which it does not share with the laity, but to recognise that that priesthood finds its fittest organ and most intense expression in the activities of those who are wholly dedicated to its service. If anyone thinks of a grace different in quality, which is not the possession of the whole priestly body, I repudiate this as wholly at variance with the New Testament teaching on the Church. And in this I rejoice to believe that the vast body of Wesleyan opinion is with me.[141]

Peake could rightly claim that his views were similar to those of the Wesleyan G. G. Findlay (1849–1919) as expressed in *The Church of Christ as set forth in the New Testament* (1893). The Wesleyan opposition was clearly hampered in its criticism by the fact that the older Wesleyan view of the pastoral office had by now been replaced both theologically and practically by a representative view of ministry, the view which came to be laid down as a norm for the United Church in 1932. When union had been consummated, W. F. Howard (1880–1952) made clear the debt of all to Peake:

> There were not a few on our side who feared that the two smaller churches, in their traditional dislike of clericalism, would hold in too light an esteem elements in our usage which our own experience has shown to be of the utmost value in the development of a strong and healthy churchmanship. . . . If re-united Methodism holds up to the world in its teaching about the Body of Christ the noble doctrine

[141] *Primitive Methodist Leader*, 8 June 1922, p. 356; *Methodist Recorder*, 8 June 1922, p. 5; 15 June 1922, p. 14 (letter from J. E. Rattenbury); *Methodist Times*, 22 June 1922, pp. 4–5. For a careful analysis of Primitive Methodist support of, and opposition to, Union, see John T. Wilkinson (ed.), *Arthur Samuel Peake*, pp. 165–71; also *Primitive Methodist Leader*, 19 February 1920, p. 121; 9 November 1922, pp. 715–16; 10 April 1924, pp. 233–4.

which Paul sets forth in the Epistle to the Ephesians, we shall owe this more to Dr Peake than to any other man.[142]

Recent studies of the union negotiations by Robert Currie, John Kent and J. T. Wilkinson[143] give the detailed and tortuous story of the ten-year-long debate. We can only try to interpret the main features of a matter which largely absorbed the energies of Methodism during that decade – in itself a factor which is not unimportant, like the similar absorption in the 1960s with union with the Church of England.

The Wesleyan Committee of 1913, with Aldom French (1868–1962) as Secretary, was overshadowed by the War, though it drew up in the first place a Questionnaire on the doctrine and polity of the various groups, and later, in October 1917, a set of twenty-eight questions for the other denominations to answer.[144] Possibilities of a reunion of the Free Churches and of Wesleyanism with the Church of England were being mooted at this time.[145] In January 1918 representatives of the three major Methodist denominations met to discuss the union of Methodism. A scheme for union was quickly drawn up and the changes made after 1920 were in the area of doctrinal definition and the matter of lay presidency at the Sacraments.

The Non-Wesleyans, led by Peake, clearly wanted a liberal definition of doctrine. Peake himself would have preferred the elimination of references to Wesley's *Notes on the New Testament* and *Sermons*, since Wesley was an outmoded exegete.[146] The phrase, the 'evangelical doctrines' for which Methodism has stood from the beginning . . . as generally contained in Wesley's Notes on the New Testament and the first four volumes of his Sermons was acceptable 'subject to the Divine Revelation recorded in Holy Scripture',[147] a phrase which could be interpreted in a liberal direction and placated those who desired freedom of critical inquiry. Opposition in Primitive Methodism and United Methodism was significant, but never large enough to hinder majority voting.[148] In Wesleyanism the opposition which came to be called the 'Other Side' claimed the support of nearly one-third of the Wesleyan ministry in 1920 and by the time of the publication of its official manifesto in April 1922 was very formidable indeed.[149]

[142] *Holborn Review*, 1930, p. 32; for Scott Lidgett's comment, see pp. 38–9.

[143] Currie, op. cit., pp. 248–9; John Kent, op. cit., chapter 1; John T. Wilkinson (ed.), op. cit., pp. 165–72; for a parallel in Scotland, cf. Rolf Sjölinder, *Presbyterian Reunion in Scotland 1907–1921: its background and development* (Edinburgh 1962).

[144] Currie, op. cit., pp. 250–2, cited from Minutes of the Wesleyan Methodist Union Committee, 17 October 1913 – 18 December 1919.

[145] Currie, ibid.

[146] *Primitive Methodist Leader*, 19 February 1920, p. 121; John T. Wilkinson (ed.), op. cit., p. 167; John Kent, op. cit., pp. 21–2.

[147] Later altered to: 'based upon . . .'.

[148] John T. Wilkinson (ed.), op. cit., p. 169; Currie, op. cit., p. 264.

[149] *Methodist Recorder*, 27 April 1922, p. 15: the Manifesto against Union; Currie, op. cit., pp. 259–65.

The effect of the opposition, besides the delay in effecting union, was a tightening of the doctrinal clauses which were built into the Deed of Union. Peake and Scott Lidgett were largely responsible for the much more comprehensive clauses of 1925–6: 'The Methodist Church ... ever remembers that in the Providence of God Methodism was raised up to spread scriptural holiness through the land by the proclamation of the Evangelical Faith.' Methodism – this was a concession to the Wesleyan high churchmen – was stated to 'claim and cherish its place in the Holy Catholic Church which is the Body of Christ. It rejoices in the inheritance of the Apostolic Faith and loyally accepts the fundamental principles of the historic creeds and the Protestant reformation' – a phrase so loose as to be positively misleading. Scott Lidgett himself gave his interpretation of these principles as 'Justification by faith, the completeness and all-sufficiency of our Lord's sacrifice and priesthood, the direct access of all believers to God through Him, expressed as the priesthood of all believers'.[150] Some contemporaries might have added the right of private judgement in the interpretation of Scripture, and few[151] realized that Calvinists would have *their* interpretation of such principles. The statement is typical of an age of theological imprecision.

On the doctrine of the ordained ministry the principle of representation generally acceptable in all three Churches came to be strongly expressed: 'The Methodist Church holds the doctrine of the priesthood of all believers and consequently believes that no priesthood exists which belongs exclusively to a particular class or order of men.' The minister is the theological and pastoral expert, the full-time representative with no apparent ontological difference from laymen. This statement owed much to Peake and reflected also the Wesleyan statement on church membership of 1908 which clearly bore the stamp of G. G. Findlay.[152]

From this statement it was logical to bring into the new Church not only the *practice* but the *principle* of lay presidency at the sacraments, which had never occurred in Wesleyanism and was strongly opposed by J. E. Rattenbury and the 'Other Side'. For Peake, this was a necessary way to secure regular eucharistic worship in rural areas. The final compromise of 1925 was to place the onus on the Quarterly Meeting, which could nominate laymen to preside at Holy Communion, such persons to be granted 'dispensations' by Conference to preside in their own circuit. The United Methodist leader David Brook[153] could see

[150] Cited from Lidgett's Inaugural Address of 1932 by R. Newton Flew, in Williams and Harris (eds), *Northern Catholicism*, p. 528; cf. *The Nature of the Christian Church according to the Teaching of the Methodists* (London 1937), pp. 31ff.; *The Senior Catechism* (London 1952), p. 29.

[151] Cf. John Kent, op. cit., p. 33.

[152] *Wesleyan Methodist Minutes* (1908), p. 575; cf. Scheme C: ibid. (1924), p. 70.

[153] John Kent, op. cit., pp. 34–5; Currie, op. cit., p. 280.

this as a guarantee of the equality of ministerial and lay presidency despite the clear indication of the overriding element of necessity, and the normality of ministerial presidency. Even J. E. Rattenbury[154] could not contravene this, as he could only use the 'order, not orders' argument. The old Wesleyan pastoral doctrine was no longer a viable option.

Scheme 'D' (1926) was the final scheme to be voted upon despite an attempt by some of the 'Other Side' to delay union by an interesting scheme of 'unificaiton by stages' involving a fusion of departments and the encouragement of local unions, with union complete by 1938. The scheme propounded for Anglican–Methodist union by E. L. Mascall and C. O. Buchanan in *Growing Together* was a parallel attempt at union by stages. Neither scheme took seriously the Connexional system of Methodism or the overall *episcope* of Conference.[155] In 1925 it had been required that a seventy-five per cent vote was necessary for union with any other denomination. This was not achieved until 1928. By this time Rattenbury could not bear the responsibility for delaying union, the 'Other Side' virtually collapsed, and on 27 July 1928 the Pastoral Session of the Wesleyan Church achieved precisely the seventy-five per cent vote needed to allow the Enabling Bill to go forward which provided for full organic union in 1932.[156]

The Methodist Church Bill was passed in 1929,[157] providing the necessary legal basis for the new Church. Each denomination held its final Conference in the summer of 1932, with the Uniting Conference assembling on 20 September 1932 at the Royal Albert Hall, when the Deed of Union was signed in the presence of the Duke and Duchess of York. John Scott Lidgett was elected President, Sir Robert Perks Vice-President and Robert Bond Secretary – all three from the Wesleyan Church. In terms of statistics the United Church brought together 517,551 Wesleyans (in Great Britain), 222,021 Primitive Methodists and 179,527 United Methodists. The ordained ministry consisted of 2,510 Wesleyans, 1,131 Primitive Methodists and 729 United Methodists with 18,785 Wesleyan local preachers, 12,896 Primitive Methodists and 5,232 United Methodist local preachers.[158]

As we have seen, Methodist Union was attended with great hopes, yet there were no illusions in the minds of men like Aldom French

[154] J. Ernest Rattenbury, op. cit., pp. 26, 38–9.

[155] Currie, op. cit., pp. 281–2.

[156] Ibid., p. 286; for the strange story of the vote, see Rupert E. Davies, *Methodism* (London 1962), p. 152; the missionary referred to was C. K. Williams.

[157] The Bill is printed in part in *The Constitutional Practice and Discipline of the Methodist Church* (London 1974), pp. 3ff.; for the Deed of Union and the Model Deed, see ibid., pp. 39ff.

[158] The story of the Uniting Conference and its aftermath can be found in R. Newman Wycherley, *The Pageantry of Methodist Union* (London 1936).

about the decline of Methodist membership.[159] Although there were consistent increases through most of the 1920s, attributed to a revival of aggressive evangelism, with Wesleyanism just touching the half-million mark at Union compared with 450,000 in 1900, this absolute increase needs to be seen against a rise of population. Certainly the United Methodists could not claim that union had brought any great renewal of the Church – in fact it had fewer members of society and more societies per minister in 1932 than it had in 1907, and a decline overall of nine per cent.[160] On the other hand, there is not a scrap of evidence that independent groups would have fared any better. The somewhat triumphalist approach typified by Sir Robert Perks was still-born before 1932.

The Union was a merger without the teeth which a commercial or industrial merger would have had. The price of union was non-interference with the circuits in the first stage. Methodist union was consummated at a time of declining commitment to institutional Christianity which made the problem of 'redundancy' worse than it might have appeared in an age of chapel-going.[161] In the higher echelons of the Church the union was smooth and beneficial – colleges, schools, departments were united easily, an outstanding example being the partnership in Temperance and Social Welfare of E. C. Urwin (United Methodist) and H. Carter (Wesleyan). Four denominational Weeklies in 1932 were finally amalgamated in the virtual monopoly of the *Methodist Recorder*, though this was in no way an official organ of Conference but an independent journal. At local level it soon became obvious that Methodist union had provided no really new ideas about church organization, but rather an uneasy compromise, with very little experimentation.[162]

> The sequel of Methodist union is a warning against the assumption that . . . the unification of ministries and of central departments will be sufficient to guarantee effective union where it really matters, where the Christian meets the non-Christian.

It must be admitted also that Wesleyanism brought to union an ageing leadership – Lidgett and Wiseman, for instance, were well beyond the peak of their intellectual agility – and the general leadership of the United Church before World War II tended to lack vigour, drive, or new ideas.

[159] Cf. *Wesleyan Methodist Minutes* (1918), p. 25. For varied interpretations of the statistics, see Currie, op. cit., pp. 85–111; Robert F. Wearmouth, *The Social and Political Influence of Methodism in the Twentieth Century*, chapters 4 and 5; John Kent, op. cit., pp. 4–5, 17–20.

[160] Currie, op. cit., p. 299.

[161] For a reflection upon redundancy typical of the 1950s, see Eric W. Baker, *Fathers and Brethren: The Doctrine of the Ministry and Other Issues* (London 1959), pp. 7–8; but note also Robert F. Wearmouth, op. cit., p. 78.

[162] John Kent, op. cit., pp. 15, 17.

5. Methodism and the Wider Ecumenism 1900–1932

Sir Ernest Barker once argued that

> apart from any question of their relative numerical strength it may be said that the general relations, the general balance, and the general interaction of Anglicanism and Nonconformity have been a cardinal factor in English life and development for over three centuries.[163]

This was still true in the Victorian age, which saw on the one hand a militant Dissent[164] seeking equality and asking deep questions about the relevance of any Establishment in a democratic society, and on the other the pervasive influence of the Oxford Movement on all the Churches, at once 'an opposition to Nonconformity and an expression of Nonconformity'. Paradoxically, the Oxford Movement drove a deep wedge between Anglicanism and Dissent, but also indirectly produced what can be called a recovery of a Catholic doctrine of the Church among the main-stream dissenting groups, which found its first expression in the movement for Free Church unity[165] and theological expression in the ecclesiology of William Burt Pope and the catholicity of Hugh Price Hughes and Scott Lidgett.

At a time when sociologically the Free Churches were tending to lose their cohesion[166] – it was possible after 1886 for a Dissenter to be a Unionist like Joseph Chamberlain – the Churches began to come together. Even the Congregational Union in 1895 claimed: 'The time has gone by when any order of churches can flourish simply by its polity.'[167] This Union held a joint Congress with the Baptists in 1886. Two years later the Lambeth Conference set forth the Lambeth Quadrilateral[168] as the Anglican terms for corporate reunion, though its original purpose had been somewhat different, and in 1892 the first Free Church Congress[169] was held in Manchester. Methodist initiatives are seen in the publication of *The Review of the Churches* in 1891 onwards, originating with Henry S. Lunn (1859–1939) and Percy Bunting, and the fruitful and creative Grindelwald Conferences initiated by Lunn in 1891–6 which brought together churchmen of all kinds who had previously

[163] Ernest Barker, *Britain and the British People* (London 1942), p. 24; cf. p. 90.

[164] Owen Chadwick, op. cit., i (London 1966), 2; Bernard Lord Manning, *The Protestant Dissenting Deputies* (Cambridge 1952); Alan D. Gilbert, op. cit., chapter 7: 'Church and Chapel in Denominational Relationship'; John Munsey Turner, in *Epworth Review*, January 1976, pp. 56–64.

[165] David M. Thompson (ed.), op. cit., p. 7.

[166] Ibid., pp. 11ff.

[167] Cited ibid., p. 227.

[168] Alan M. G. Stephenson, *Anglicanism and the Lambeth Conferences* (London 1978), p. 84.

[169] For the early negotiations, see E. K. H. Jordan, *Free Church Unity: History of the Free Church Council Movement 1896–1941* (London 1956), chapter 2: 'Vision of the Fellowship'. D. W. Bebbington, op. cit., chapter 4: 'The Free Church Council Movement'.

never met as individuals.[170] Hugh Price Hughes and Scott Lidgett were involved from the beginning in the Free Church unity movement and contributed greatly to it. Local Free Church Councils sprang up after 1892, notably in Birmingham, despite the grave misgivings of R. W. Dale,[171] who feared alignment with one political party. The fully organized National Council of Evangelical Free Churches, on a representative basis, met in 1896, with Hugh Price Hughes as President.

Hughes[172] made clear what Free Church unity meant for him.

> The unit of this movement is not the individual Christian but the Church. Therein it differs *toto caelo* from the Evangelical Alliance, which is merely a fortuitous concourse of Evangelical individuals who meet together occasionally to say that they love one another.

Denominational representation was to wait until the federation movement of the 1910s. We are, he claimed, 'Catholic high churchmen' – hence the refusal to admit the Salvation Army and the Unitarians – but this was expressed in a triumphalist fashion.

> We are Free Evangelical Churchmen. Above all, we are Churchmen. We are in truth, High Churchmen, and the highest of all Churchmen, so high that we could not think for a moment of allowing any politician to appoint our ministers or any parliament to manipulate our creed . . . We are not one in the Pope. We are not one in the Crown. But we are one in Christ. The Roman Catholic stands for the supremacy of the Pope, the Anglican Catholic for the supremacy of the Crown, and the Scriptural Catholic for the supremacy of Christ.

This rhetorical stance spilled over into Liberal Imperialism: 'We represent an immense majority in the British Empire, and an overwhelming majority in the English-speaking world.' Hughes did not espouse an anti-Anglican stance except on the issue of Establishment and ritualism, which he saw as a revival of 'extreme medieval clericalism', though he makes clear that the Free Churches must see that England, 'the land of civil and religious freedom, the land of gospel light shall never sink to the degraded level of Spain.' The Free Church Movement should and could lead the Churches to a deepening of spiritual life, to evangelism of the vast unchurched majority. This policy was set out in the Free Church catechism of 1899 which was approved of at key points by

[170] Ruth Rouse and Stephen Charles Neill, *A History of the Ecumenical Movement 1517–1948* (London 1954), pp. 338–44; R. Tudur Jones, op. cit., pp. 332–3; cf. E. K. H. Jordan, op. cit., pp. 21–5; Henry S. Lunn, *Chapters from My Life: with Special Reference to Reunion* (London 1918), chapter 12: 'The Grindelwald Reunion Conferences'.

[171] A. W. W. Dale, op. cit., p. 649.

[172] John Briggs and Ian Sellers, op. cit., pp. 168–71: extracts from Hughes's presidential address; David M. Thompson, op. cit., pp. 240–4; cf. G. F. A. Best, 'Popular Protestantism in Victorian Britain', in Robert Robson (ed.), *Ideas and Institutions of Victorian Britain* (London 1967), esp. p. 138.

Charles Gore and heavily criticized by the conservative Wesleyan theologian Marshall Randles (1826–1904) and practised in the simultaneous mission to London of January 1901 followed soon after in the Provinces by missions in which the Wesleyan evangelist Gipsy Smith played a leading part.[173] Revival and political agitation coincided in this period.

As we shall see, the Free Church Council was divided and then adopted a mediating role in the Boer War.[174] It was sucked into the education battle between Church and Dissent after the promulgation of the Balfour Act of 1902, and, except for Welsh Disestablishment, saw none of its political causes totally espoused by the Liberal Party. In this period Scott Lidgett emerged as the supreme diplomat and was instrumental in preventing total identification of the Council with political party cries.

During World War I, when co-operation between all the Churches grew very greatly, not least in the chaplaincy service, the Baptist J. H. Shakespeare (1857–1928)[175] began to adumbrate a United Free Church of England as a first stage to full corporate reunion with the Church of England including the acceptance of episcopacy. 'Denominationalism is a decaying idea – it certainly does not commend itself to a nation in a socialistic age, nor to the very people upon whom its success depends.'[176] The first step for Shakespeare was some form of Federation, an approach which had the support of the leading Free Church theologian of the day, Peter Taylor Forsyth, and is not to be dismissed too easily as 'reunion without repentance'.[177] Scott Lidgett, who, like Shakespeare, saw a further goal of union, had said earlier:

> Where there are no differences our watchword must be union; where they are comparatively slight, federation; where they are more serious, yet not destructive of the fundamental agreements of Christianity, co-operation in order to defend and promote the supreme interests and applications of our common Christian life.[178]

[173] E. K. H. Jordan, op. cit., chapter 4: 'Mission to England'; Gipsy Smith, *His Life and Work, by Himself* (London 1902), chapter 29: 'As the National Council's Missioner'; Stephen Koss, *Nonconformity in Modern British Politics* (London 1975), pp. 41–5; Alan D. Gilbert, op. cit., pp. 192ff.; D. Ben Rees, *Chapels in the Valley: A Study in the Sociology of Welsh Nonconformity* (Denbigh 1975), pp. 152ff.

[174] E. K. H. Jordan, op. cit., pp. 72–5; chapter 5: 'A Conscience on Education'; chapter 6: 'Religion and Politics'; D. W. Bebbington, op. cit., chapter 6: 'The Role of Britain in the World'.

[175] Ibid., chapter 7: 'Towards a United Free Church'; J. H. Shakespeare, *The Churches at the Cross-roads: A Study in Church Unity* (London 1918).

[176] *Free Church Year Book 1916*, pp. 1–24: Shakespeare's Presidential Address.

[177] Cf. P. T. Forsyth, op. cit., esp. chapter 6; Lesslie Newbigin, *The Household of God: Lectures on the Nature of the Church* (London 1953), p. 22; Reginald Kissack, *Church or No Church?: A Study of the Development of the Concept of Church in British Methodism* (London 1964), pp. 96–102.

[178] J. Scott Lidgett, *Apostolic Ministry: Sermons and Addresses* (London 1909), pp. 15–16.

Shakespeare's dream was not to be fulfilled in its entirety. The Wesleyans were lukewarm on the whole issue, despite the advocacy of Scott Lidgett, Sir Robert Perks, J. S. Banks, and Arthur Henderson. In July 1918 the Wesleyan Conference decided to defer the proposals for a year,[179] Sir Robert Perks withdrawing his support of a year before. The Federal Council of the Evangelical Free Churches was inaugurated in October 1919, without benefit of Wesleyans, though they took their place in 1920 and provided a Moderator in 1923–5 in the inevitable Scott Lidgett! Henceforward two Free Church bodies ran on parallel lines before constituting the Free Church Federal Council in 1940. Free Church Federation did not bear out the enthusiasm of J. H. Shakespeare and P. T. Forsyth and did little to bring the Free Churches into formal union, for not until 1972 did the most obvious union, that between the Congregational Churches and the Presbyterian Church of England take place.

Nevertheless the Free Church Council provided a valuable clearing house in negotiations with the Church of England. If the late nineteenth century saw the Free Churches growing together, the gulf between Dissenter and Anglican was as great as ever. J. H. Rigg (1821–1909), who was representative of much Wesleyan opinion, and by no means anti-ecumenical, could say: 'The genius of Methodism, as now fully organised into a church, and that of Anglican Episcopacy are mutually repellent and exclusive',[180] and maintained that there was then no party within Methodism who 'have felt the slightest concern as to union with the Church of England'.[181] Cultural isolation, as well as the Oxford Movement, must not be overlooked here. 'Speaking generally,' said J. H. Moulton,[182] 'our Church stood nearer to the Church of England than it did to other Methodist communities, not to speak of the older Dissenting Churches. The Oxford Movement has changed all that . . .' Biographies[183] reveal that in many parishes churchmen and Methodists simply did not meet, and the battles of Dissent for equality, contested at each ditch by the Church of England, had added fuel to the bitter fires. Anglican initiatives concerning corporate reunion can be found before the Lambeth Conference of 1888[184] – for example, cooperation between Anglican and Free Church scholars in propounding a Revised Version of the Scriptures. Hort[185] regarded it as 'the

[179] *Wesleyan Methodist Minutes* (1918), p. 82; E. K. H. Jordan, op. cit., pp. 134–5.

[180] J. H. Rigg, *The Churchmanship of John Wesley, and the Relations of Wesleyan Methodism to the Church of England* (London 1886), pp. 114–15.

[181] Ibid., p. 14.

[182] James Hope Moulton, *A Neglected Sacrament*, p. 15.

[183] Cf. M. K. Ashby, op. cit., p. 6.

[184] Geoffrey F. Nuttall and Owen Chadwick, *From Uniformity to Unity 1662–1962* (London 1962), pp. 331–42.

[185] Arthur Fenton Hort, *Life and Letters of Fenton John Anthony Hort* (London 1896), ii, 139.

beginning of a new period in Church history'. In this enterprise W. F. Moulton, the Wesleyan Headmaster of the Leys School, played a notable part. Indeed, a kind of ecumenical movement was growing up which moved right across denominational barriers as in the Oxford School of Theology in the days of Hatch, Sanday, Fairbairn, Cheyne and Bartlet. Free Churchmen were not guilty of 'cultural aggression' when they moved their Colleges, such as Mansfield or Manchester, to Oxford, or when Methodism opened Wesley House at Cambridge. This was a recognition of new freedoms both of theological scholarship and of theological sharing. Methodists like James Hope Moulton and A. S. Peake were scholars known and respected far beyond their denominations. The World Christian Student Federation, the missions of Moody and Sankey, often underestimated in their widespread personal consequences, the impetus of the Edinburgh Missionary Conference of 1910, which many see as the real beginning of the modern ecumenical movement, are all factors in the impulse towards ecumenism.[186] After World War I the mood of idealism and new Christian brotherhood, forged in the trenches, was caught up by the Lambeth Conference of 1920 in its 'Appeal to All Christian People'.[187]

The Appeal begins by acknowledging 'all those who believe in our Lord Jesus Christ, and have been baptized into the name of the Holy Trinity, as sharing with us membership in the universal Church of Christ which is His Body – a phrase reflecting the theology of A. C. Headlam's recent Bampton Lectures with their clear assertion of schism being within the Body of Christ.[188] A noble vision is presented of a 'Church, genuinely Catholic, loyal to all Truth, and gathering into its fellowship all "who profess and call themselves Christians", within whose visible unity all the treasures of faith and order, bequeathed as a heritage by the past to the present, shall be possessed in common, and made serviceable to the whole Body of Christ'. Anglican norms for unity are laid down again in advance – the Scriptures 'as the record of God's revelation', the 'sacraments of Baptism and the Holy Communion', the Apostles' and Nicene Creeds and a 'ministry acknowledged by every part of the Church'. It is made clear that this implies the Episcopate, but, 'It is not that we call in question for a moment the spiritual reality of the ministries of those Communions which do not possess the Episcopate. On the contrary, we thankfully acknowledge that these ministries have been manifestly blessed and owned by the

[186] Ruth Rouse and Stephen Charles Neill, op. cit., pp. 318–24; and esp. p. 341, for the role of the American Methodist layman, John R. Mott.

[187] Printed in G. K. A. Bell (ed.), *Documents on Christian Unity 1920–24* (Oxford 1924), pp. 1–5; cf. J. G. Lockhart, *Cosmo Gordon Lang* (London 1949), chapter 23: ' "An Appeal to all Christian People" '.

[188] A. C. Headlam, *The Doctrine of the Church and Christian Reunion* (London 1920), pp. 219–20; cf. also T. A. Lacey, *Unity and Schism* (London 1917).

Holy Spirit as effective means of grace.' This is a reversal of the classical Augustinian position, '*Ubi Christus, ibi ecclesia*.' Anglican bishops would willingly accept wider commissioning from fellow Christians, but, 'It is our hope that the same motive would lead ministers who have not received it to accept a commission through episcopal ordination, as obtaining for them a ministry throughout the whole fellowship. In so acting no one of us could possibly be taken to repudiate his past ministry.' This was a vain hope and displayed almost incredible theological clumsiness, despite the grace of the Appeal in general.

The Free Church Council[189] responded to the Appeal in September 1920, issuing a full statement in May 1921, by which time the Presbyterian P. Carnegie Simpson emerged as the Free Church spokesman. Three main issues were set out as: 1. recognition of Churches, 2. episcopal ordination, and 3. spiritual freedom. The blunt question is asked: Are non-episcopal Communions part of the Church of Christ and their ministries ministries of Christ's Word and Sacraments? Concerning episcopacy it is made clear that re-ordination is quite unacceptable. Any recommissioning must be clear in intention. 'To begin to build a union in the Church of Christ on a conscious ambiguity is not, it seems to us, to build in God's name and in God's way' – a matter of debate still in the 1963 Anglican–Methodist scheme. The Free Churches made their individual responses.[190] The Wesleyan response of July 1922 was the longest, and it clearly accepted three sides of the Quadrilateral; but on church government it made the point sharply that, 'The proposal to make episcopal ordination an essential part of the scheme of union, if it be interpreted as implying re-ordination, could not be accepted by those who believe themselves to be already ministers in the Church of God', nor could any fellowship be abrogated with other non-episcopal groups.

Methodists on the Free Church Committee set up in response to the Appeal were W. T. Davison (1846–1935), H. Maldwyn Hughes, J. Scott Lidgett, Walter H. Armstrong (1873–1949), A. S. Peake and T. Nightingale (1867–1934). On the joint Anglican–Free Church Committee, set up at Archbishop Davidson's initiative, Scott Lidgett and Peake clearly played a substantial role.[191] The Anglicans attempted to clarify statements about the ministry in a Memorandum of 6 July 1923.[192] Words like 'valid' or 'invalid' relating to ministries ought not to be used; it is said that Anglicans regard these ministries as 'being within their several spheres real ministries in the Universal Church . . . Yet

[189] G. K. A. Bell (ed.), op. cit., pp. 118–42.

[190] Ibid., pp. 107 (Primitive Methodism, June 1921), 108 (United Methodism, July 1921), 109–15 (Wesleyan Methodism, July 1921; July 1922).

[191] Ibid., p. 155.

[192] Ibid., pp. 156–63.

ministries, even when so regarded, may be in varying degrees irregular or defective', and certainly episcopal ordination was required in Anglican eucharists. The Free Churches in September 1923[193] made plain that for them this took away in practice what had been granted in theory and rightly pointed to Anglican practice before 1662 in this matter. The nub of the negotiations lay here, and a second Anglican Memorandum in June 1925[194] made clear that 'spiritual efficacy' does not necessarily imply due authority. Granting of 'authority' by a bishop or ordination *sub conditione* is put forward as a way out of the impasse. This position was clearly unacceptable to most Free Churchmen.[195]

Methodist contributions to this somewhat disappointing series of Conferences and resolutions were notable for the statesmanlike approach of Scott Lidgett, who looked beyond minutiae to the great vision of the Church given in Ephesians,[196] and the ironic approach of A. S. Peake, whose Presidential address to the Free Church Council of 1928, 'Pray for the Peace of Jerusalem',[197] was perhaps the finest Methodist contribution in this period. Peake saw reciprocal authorization as necessary to a united ministry, but rejected re-ordination. Episcopacy is accepted as the probable norm of ministry in a United Church. 'To an episcopacy which would be constitutional and not prelatical' there would be no objection, provided that 'no theory of episcopacy as of the essence of the Church is demanded'. To the Free Churches Peake gave a warning: 'Free Churchmen may make the mistake of the Bourbons, if forgetting that all life involves development, adjustment to environment, they insist as a matter of principle on retaining their organisation in its traditional form.'

The original Free Church replies to the Lambeth Appeal made clear difficulties over Establishment and over the safeguarding of Reformation principles – though these were not clearly defined, as was the case also with the Deed of Union of 1932. The former issue was highlighted by the Prayer Book controversies of 1927–8 and the subsequent policy by which bishops exercised their *ius liturgicum* to enable the technically illegal 1928 Prayer Book to be used. Carnegie Simpson in a famous

[193] G. K. A. Bell (ed.), op. cit., pp. 164–9; cf. N. Sykes, *Old Priest and New Presbyter: Episcopacy and Presbyterianism since the Reformation with especial relation to the Churches of England and Scotland* (Cambridge 1956).

[194] G. K. A. Bell (ed.), *Documents on Christian Unity: Second Series* (Oxford 1930), pp. 77–86.

[195] Ibid., pp. 108–10 (Primitive Methodist reply, June 1926), 110–12 (United Methodist reply, July 1926).

[196] For a typical Wesleyan statement of this period, see J. Scott Lidgett, 'New Testament Principles', in J. G. Simpson (ed.), *The Lambeth Joint Report on Church Unity* (London 1923), pp. 86–104; cf. W. F. Lofthouse, 'Wesleyan Methodism and the Anglican Church', in H. A. Wilson (ed.), *The Anglican Communion: Past, Present and Future* (London 1928), pp. 422–34.

[197] John T. Wilkinson (ed.), *Arthur Samuel Peake 1865–1929: Essays in Commemoration* (London 1958).

phrase thought this solution at the least 'hardly cricket',[198] and most Free Churchmen would have endorsed the remark of Bernard Lord Manning about the Church of England receiving the benefits of Establishment but objecting only when the shoe pinches, as over the Prayer Book. 'The situation was not new; the relation of Parliament to the Established Church had always been indefensible; but it was denounced as wicked only when it became unpleasant.'[199] The Prayer Book Controversy may lie behind the failure of the Lambeth Conference of 1930 to push forward the initiatives of 1920, a matter of deep regret to leaders like William Temple,[200] though exchanges of pulpits and occasional acts of Communion by people cut off from their own Churches was encouraged by Convocation in 1932 as well as limited Intercommunion in schools and colleges where no Free Church services were held.

The debate of the 1920s, though inconclusive, had at least laid down the lines for future approaches. The Church of England was also concerned in probes towards both the Roman Catholics (as in the Malines Conversations) and the Orthodox. There were also deep disagreements within the Church of England represented by A. C. Headlam and O. C. Quick on the one hand and Charles Gore, Frank Weston and C. H. Turner on the other.[201] The ecclesiologies of Augustine and Cyprian were still alive. In the Free Churches there was sharp division between Lidgett, Peake and Simpson and the redoubtable Baptist T. R. Glover,[202] who deplored studied ambiguity: 'If re-union depends on artificial fog, I for one am for daylight, for straight thinking, and straight speech' – a stance not without relevance for the breakdown of the Anglican–Methodist Conversations in the early 1970s, when Dr C. K. Barrett and Archbishop Fisher opposed the scheme from similar premises about ambiguity. A unifying feature in the 1920s discussion was the influence of some of the disciples of William Sanday – A. C. Headlam, J. V. Bartlet, and A. S. Peake – Anglican, Congregationalist and Primitive Methodist, who revealed at key points a notable

[198] P. Carnegie Simpson, *Recollections: Mainly Ecclesiastical but Sometimes Human* (London 1943), p. 91; cf. E. K. H. Jordan, op. cit., chapter 13: 'The Free Churches and the Revised Prayer Book'.

[199] Bernard Lord Manning, *Essays in Orthodox Dissent* (London 1939), p. 202; J. M. Turner, *Journal of U.R.C. Church History Society*, i, No. 5 (May 1975), pp. 131–3.

[200] F. A. Iremonger, *William Temple Archbishop of Canterbury: His Life and Letters* (London 1948), p. 460.

[201] Ronald C. D. Jasper, *Arthur Cayley Headlam: Life and Letters of a Bishop* (London 1960), p. 154; Cuthbert Hamilton Turner, *Catholic and Apostolic: Collected Papers* (London 1931), pp. 273–315.

[202] *Daily News*, 15 December 1923, p. 6; cited in E. K. H. Jordan, op. cit., p. 173; cf. H. G. Wood, *Terrot Reaveley Glover: A Biography* (Cambridge 1953), pp. 152ff.; Terrot Reaveley Glover, *The Free Churches and Re-union* (Cambridge 1921); A. M. Ramsey, *From Gore to Temple* (London 1960), p. 121.

unanimity of stance which has been taken up again by the Churches Unity Commission in their report of January 1976.[203]

6. Methodism, Social Life and Politics 1900–1932

The General Election of 1906[204] is often depicted as a Nonconformist triumph, since at least 157 M.P.s in the new parliament bore Free Church labels. To some it seemed as if the days of Oliver Cromwell were back again. Free Church optimism was not, however, justified. Scott Lidgett (like A. J. Balfour) was right to state: 'The most momentous of recent political events has been the organization of a distinctive Labour Party in Parliament.'[205]

Methodism has never been politically monochrome. There was, no doubt, great support for Liberalism as the party which represented the non-Anglican, non-landowning elements in the local and national community. The role of political Dissent through strong family connections in cities like Birmingham and Manchester is clear, though the consensus was breaking down by 1900. Methodism clearly retained a strong Conservative element represented in 1900 by W. L. Watkinson (1838–1925), Marshall Hartley (1846–1928) and F. W. Macdonald (1842–1928). The Home Rule split of 1886 may have marked the final frustration of any real possibility of the total manipulation of the Liberal party by Nonconformity. Joseph Chamberlain, indeed, stated to Sir Robert Perks (then M.P. for Louth) in 1902: 'You Nonconformists[!] made a great mistake in 1886 when they followed Mr Gladstone and refused to listen to me. Had they supported me, they would have had Disestablishment long ago. Now they have got nothing.'[206] Chamberlain's petulant outburst came after the Boer War had revealed political division in Nonconformity, paralleling those in Anglicanism and the Labour Movement alike over this issue.

Hugh Price Hughes took an Imperialist line following politicians like Perks and H. H. Fowler.[207] Perks and Hughes sought a moratorium on discussion of the Boer War in the National Council of Evangelical Free Churches.

[203] The contribution of these men to the Faith and Order Conference at Lausanne in 1927 was also considerable. C. H. Turner and Frank Weston, however, were also pupils of Sanday!

[204] I am taking the *lowest* figure here; Koss gives 185. Cf. David M. Thompson, op. cit., pp. 1, 17; N. J. Richards, *Journal of Ecclesiastical History*, xxiii (January 1972), 51; Stephen Koss, op. cit., pp. 73–5, 228.

[205] John Scott Lidgett, op. cit., p. 188; cf. Robert Blake, *The Conservative Party from Peel to Churchill* (London 1970), p. 170.

[206] Cited in David M. Thompson (ed.), op. cit., p. 224; cf. J. F. Glaser, in Harold T. Schultz (ed.), *English Liberalism and the State* (Lexington, Mass. 1972), pp. 43–53.

[207] Stephen Koss, 'Wesleyanism and Empire', in *The Historical Journal*, xviii, No. 1 (March 1975).

> The War, Home Rule, and all topics on which we are not agreed, should never be touched. The one great peril of the moment is the perpetual attempt to drag such burning questions into our midst. Our business is to keep to the deep theological and ecclesiastical issues on which we are agreed.[208]

This approach is what an earlier generation of Wesleyans would have called the 'No politics' rule – whereby moral issues like slavery or the Bulgarian Horrors could be discussed, but not party political issues, though the distinction is not always clear. In the same letter Hughes condemned

> pestiferous whitewashing of one of the most cruel and mendacious military oligarchies that ever enslaved black men and outraged white men.

This stance could easily be linked with the Liberal Imperialism of Rosebery which Hughes clearly espoused.[209] On the other hand, it is sometimes forgotten that the Free Church Council, while silent in 1900,[210] was able in 1901 at Cardiff to present a united front, and later produced a manifesto embodying John Clifford's six-point peace plan.[211]

If the Boer War divided Free Church political opinion[212] – the 1901 Manifesto had its critics – three other issues tended to bring Free Churchmen together. These were the Education Bill of 1902, the problem of Chinese Labour in South Africa, and drink legislation, all of which had more unifying power than attempts to reconcile the old liberalism of 'peace, retrenchment and reform', and the old radicalism of liberty, arbitration and anti-militarism, with Liberal Imperialism.[213]

The Education Bill of 1902, which R. C. K. Ensor[214] ranks 'among the two or three greatest constructive measures of the twentieth century'

[208] David M. Thompson (ed.), op. cit., p. 245; D. P. Hughes, op. cit., p. 573 (letter to Henry Lunn: 12 February 1900).

[209] Stephen Koss, *Nonconformity in Modern British Politics*, p. 31; note also H. C. G. Matthew, *The Liberal Imperialists: the ideas and politics of a post-Gladstonian élite* (Oxford 1973).

[210] John Kent, in G. V. Bennett and J. D. Walsh (eds), op. cit., p. 181.

[211] E. K. H. Jordan, op. cit., pp. 72–6; James Marchant, *Dr. John Clifford, C.H.: Life, Letters and Reminiscences* (London 1924), pp. 145–53. But cf. R. Tudur Jones, op. cit., pp. 335–6; D. W. Bebbington, op. cit., pp. 123–4.

[212] Cf. A. J. P. Taylor, *The Trouble Makers: Dissent over Foreign Policy 1792–1939* (London 1969), p. 98. Henry Pelling, *The Origins of the Labour Party 1880–1900* (Oxford 1965), pp. 187–91, shows the complexity of political divisions here.

[213] John Kent, op. cit., p. 195; for a local situation, cf. Robert Moore, op. cit., chapter 8: 'Methodists in Action: Three Political Case Studies'.

[214] R. C. K. Ensor, op. cit., p. 355; cf. Bernard Lord Manning, *The Protestant Dissenting Deputies*, pp. 355–67.

for England and Wales, was designed to secure a greater measure of secondary education. The Act replaced the School Board System of 1870 with Local Education Authorities. Church schools would be rate-aided instead of tax-aided. Nonconformist opposition centred on the single-school areas, of which 5,600[215] were solely Anglican in type, and on religious tests for teaching staff, as well as criticism of the new rating system sloganized in Clifford's battle cry: 'Rome on the Rates'. Clifford's position seemed to some Anglicans to be dangerously near to an apologia for secularism.[216]

Wesleyanism was in an ambivalent position, having its own system of Day Schools with 160,787 children attending 750 day schools.[217] Leaders such as Scott Lidgett were never happy about the possibilities of a fighting alliance between the National Free Church Council, the champions of the old School Boards, and the Liberal Party. A joint meeting of the Wesleyan Education Committee and the Committee of Privileges laid down policy guidelines.[218] Lidgett sought to prevent a total identification of the Free Church Council with the Passive Resistance Movement and was successful – the Passive Resisters, who did not by any means include all Free Churchmen, formed their own powerful pressure group.[219] This had limited Wesleyan support,[220] but was supported by the Primitive Methodists who, in rural areas, were more subject to discrimination.

The Liberals were pledged to bring in a new Bill, but Mr Augustine Birrell's Bill of April 1906, with its thorny clause four on Roman Catholic schools, and its virtual abolition of the 'Dual System', so bringing all schools under the L.E.A.s, failed entirely to meet the Free Church case while arousing powerful Anglican opposition.[221] This was not assuaged by the later abortive McKenna Bill of February 1908, which included 'contracting out' clauses for denominational schools.

[215] For extracts from parliamentary debates, including a major speech by Sir Robert Perks, see David M. Thompson (ed.), op. cit., pp. 250ff.; D. R. Pugh, *Journal of Ecclesiastical History*, xxiii (July 1972), 224; D. W. Bebbington, op. cit., chapter 7: 'The Education of the People'.

[216] John Neville Figgis, *Churches in the Modern State* (London 1913), Lecture II: 'The Great Leviathan'; *Antichrist and Other Sermons* (London 1913), p. 266.

[217] *Wesleyan Methodist Minutes* (1900), p. 458; for official policy, see ibid. (1891), pp. 302–5; cf. Maldwyn Edwards, *Methodism and England*, pp. 121–6.

[218] *Wesleyan Methodist Minutes* (1902), p. 112; ibid. (1906), pp. 9–11. Cf. Rupert E. Davies (ed.), *John Scott Lidgett*, chapter 4: 'The Educationist'.

[219] Eliza M. Champness, *The Life-Story of Thomas Champness* (London 1907), pp. 302ff.; L. S. Hunter, *John Hunter, D.D.: A Life* (London 1921), p. 190; H. G. Wood, op. cit., pp. 64ff.; A. H. Dodd, 'The Nonconformist Conscience', *Hibbert Journal*, xxxvi, 223.

[220] *Wesleyan Methodist Minutes* (1903), pp. 115–17; Stephen Koss, op. cit., pp. 51–4.

[221] D. R. Pugh, loc. cit.; N. J. Richards, loc. cit.; Stephen Koss, op. cit., p. 84; G. K. A. Bell, *Randall Davidson Archbishop of Canterbury* (London 1952), chapter 29: 'The Education Controversy, 1906–1908'; Marjorie Cruikshank, *Church and State in English Education: 1870 to the Present Day* (London 1963), chapter 5: 'The Liberal Bills, 1906–8'.

Even if a prominent Wesleyan, Walter Runciman (1870–1949), was appointed to the Board of Education, the Liberals clearly were not prepared to fight the House of Lords and the Establishment on a battleground chosen by the Nonconformists.[222] Disenchantment with the Liberal Party may well date from this period. The last great confrontation of 'Church' and 'Chapel' ended in defeat for militant Dissent.

Scott Lidgett's position was representative of much Wesleyan opinion: 'We will continue to strive for a completely national system of education set entirely free from denominational tests and interests.'[223] Education should be in the hands of the state for reasons not of efficiency but humanity. This is 'a civic and not an ecclesiastical concern'.[224] There must be protection of conscience but no room for sectarianism. Provision should be made for the training of character in a definitely Christian civilization. The demands of the people for the Bible in the schools should be respected; likewise respect should be shown to the spiritual mission of the Churches, though they are to be restrained from trespassing on ground that is not theirs. Methodism avoided the 'hard' approach of Clifford, who saw no room for 'associations' between the state and the child, and its stance pointed the way to the continuance of the 'Dual System' in a modified form up to and including the Act of 1944.[225]

More unitive for the Free Churches was the issue of 'Chinese Slavery'.[226] A decision of February 1904 permitted the mine-owners of the Rand to import indented Chinese coolies in order to supply a lack of labour following the Boer War. Nonconformists were here highly sensitive to slavery, to possible miscegenation, and to the spread of drunkenness, not to speak of 'nameless practices' in the all-male compounds. The system was brought to an end in 1907. The Licensing Bill of 1904, which Lord Blake coolly calls 'a notable effort to bring sense and order into the jungle-like obscurity of the British laws on drink',[227] provided another rallying point with the Liberals pledged to amendments in the Bill of 1908. Scott Lidgett, as President of the Wesleyan Conference, when news came of the probability of the rejection of the measure by the Conservative bloc in the House of Lords, telegraphed the Marquis of Lansdowne. He stated that if this Bill was rejected with-

[222] John Scott Lidgett, *My Guided Life* (London 1936), pp. 171ff.; Stephen Koss, *Nonconformity in Modern British Politics*, pp. 38–99; D. W. Bebbington, op. cit., pp. 141–52.

[223] John Scott Lidgett, *Apostolic Ministry*, p. 71.

[224] Ibid., p. 250; for an Anglican view, see E. A. Knox, *Reminiscences of an Octogenarian 1847–1934* (London 1934), chapter 10: 'The Birmingham School Board, 1897–1903'.

[225] Richard Austen Butler, *The Art of the Possible: The Memoirs of Lord Butler, K.G., C.H.* (London 1971), chapter 6: 'The Education Act'; cf. M. K. Ashby, op. cit., pp. 205, 228f., for the controversy in a local setting.

[226] G. K. A. Bell, *Randall Davidson*, chapter 26: 'Chinese Labour, 1904–6'; Robert Blake, op. cit., pp. 172–4; R. C. K. Ensor, op. cit., pp. 376–9.

[227] Robert Blake, op. cit., p. 174.

out proper discussion, this action by the House of Lords 'would never be forgotten or forgiven by the Wesleyan Methodist Church'. This was a political threat which Lidgett felt was justified at the time, though this method has not been repeated.[228] Lidgett could say:

> The Conference has lived to see the day when the whole of its own resolutions and demands are embodied in a Bill before Parliament. The Government has accepted the mandate of the Christian Churches and of the friends of temperance instead of hearkening to the wire-pullers or trembling before a mighty and cruel monopoly.[229]

In 1905 the Bible Christian Conference had called upon the nation to 'shake itself free from the incubus of a Government dominated by the priest and the publican'.[230] The temptation was to see the Drink Trade as more than a social evil – part of a whole network of organized devilry.

> For the Liberal party's radical and nonconformist tail, the great landowners, the legal system, the Anglican church, the London clubs, the armed services, the magistrates and the great London brewers were constituents of a great Leviathan which obstructed social and political progress.[231]

Teetotalism was a platform which, in the early twentieth century, united most of the Free Church ministries and a large proportion of the laity. William Bradfield (1859–1923), Warden of the Wesley Deaconess Order, was a notable non-abstaining Wesleyan.[232] Teetotalism also symbolized a mildly collectivist view of the state and the status of respectability among the 'Labour Aristocracy', which went far to cut off Methodists among this group from the world of the Working Men's club and the public house.[233]

The drink issue was not isolated from other social problems by the social thinkers of Wesleyanism like Scott Lidgett, W. F. Lofthouse, S. E. Keeble or Henry Carter,[234] but there was an ominous predictability about annual Conference statements (1905–1914) of a negative character concerning drink and gambling.

In the Temperance (i.e. teetotal) Movement there was always tension

[228] John Scott Lidgett, *My Guided Life*, p. 240.

[229] John Scott Lidgett, *Apostolic Ministry*, p. 21; cf. p. 69.

[320] *Bible Christian Minutes* (1905), cited in G. T. Brake, op. cit., p. 92.

[231] Brian Harrison, op. cit., p. 29; cf. Stephen Mayor, *The Churches and the Labour Movement* (London 1967), p. 354.

[232] G. T. Brake, op. cit., p. 49; Maldwyn Edwards, op. cit., p. 107.

[233] Hugh McLeod, op. cit., pp. 13–15, 59, 157.

[234] See The Manuals of the Wesleyan Methodist Union for Social Service: *The Citizen of Tomorrow* (London 1906); *The Social Teaching of the Bible* (London 1909); cf. E. C. Urwin, *Henry Carter*, pp. 47ff.

between moral persuasion and the use of the legislature, with prohibition, or at least 'local option', as the ultimate goal. The former stance was upheld in Methodism by the Band of Hope Movement (beginning in 1847) which had 426,041 members in Wesleyanism alone in 1901, with all the appearance of a popular youth movement with a tendency to equate pledge-signing with response to the gospel. The Young Abstainers' League, pioneered by Henry Carter, comes into the same category.[235] The legislative approach (Carter's slogan was 'elevate, educate, legislate') stems from the founding of the United Kingdom Alliance of 1853 pledged to secure 'the total and immediate suppression of the traffic in all intoxicating liquors as beverages'. Methodism threw its weight belatedly behind moral persuasion, but it could be argued that by 1920 its official stance had moved much nearer towards that of the Alliance.[236]

The Balfour Licensing Act of 1904 seemed to many Methodists, by its compensation clauses for lapsed licences, to create a vested interest in licences, and there was clear support for the 1908 Bill which would have given greater discretion to magistrates and brewster sessions. Support for the Bill was gathered in 610,000 Methodist signatures,[237] and there was a clear feeling of betrayal when the Lords threw the Bill out. Power – for the drink trade was thought of as an aristocratic interest – should be taken from 'these unworthy Lords'.[238]

During World War I, excess drinking was seen to be a national problem. Lloyd George could even state: 'We are fighting Germany, Austria and Drink; and, as far as I can see, the greatest of these three deadly foes is Drink.'[239] King George V abstained 'for the duration'. The Government set up a Central Control Board to deal with the drink problem. Henry Carter (the extremely well-informed and able Wesleyan Temperance Secretary) swung round, as a member of the Board, to support of state control on the lines of the Carlisle experiment, but

[235] *Wesleyan Methodist Minutes* (1900), p. 465; G. T. Brake, op. cit., pp. 29, 36ff. (the League), 65–6, 78, 97ff.

[236] *Wesleyan Methodist Minutes* (1873), pp. 193–4; (1874), p. 452; (1877), pp. 418–19; (1899), pp. 325–6. *Methodist Recorder*, 1 August 1901, pp. 10–11. For useful summaries, see Maldwyn Edwards, op. cit., chapter 6: 'Methodists and the Temperance Problem'; G. T. Brake, op. cit., chapters 3–10.

[237] E. C. Urwin, op. cit., p. 23.

[238] S. E. Keeble, writing in the *Methodist Times*, 3 December 1908, p. 963; cf. G. K. A. Bell, op. cit., pp. 598–602: Lidgett–Davidson correspondence.

[239] *The Times*, 30 March 1915; cited in Henry Carter, *The Control of the Drink Trade: A Contribution to National Efficiency 1915–1917* (London 1918), p. 50; E. C. Urwin, op. cit., p. 34; cf. Stuart P. Mews, 'Urban Problems and Rural Solutions: Drink and Disestablishment in the First World War', in Derek Baker (ed.), *The Church in Town and Countryside* (Studies in Church History xvi) (Oxford 1979), pp. 449–76; Michael E. Rose, 'The Success of Social Reform? The Central Control Board (Liquor Traffic) 1915–21', in M. R. D. Foot (ed.), *War and Society* (London 1973), pp. 71–84.

never won complete support for this position in Methodism.[240] In 1917 the Wesleyan Conference declared that the

> manufacture and sale of intoxicating liquor for beverages is definitely opposed to the best interests of the State and to the Kingdom of God; and recommends our people everywhere to work and pray for the total and permanent prohibition of the common manufacture and sale of alcoholic drinks.[241]

Prohibition, in its American form, was supported in 1919,[242] as was the Nine Point Programme of the Temperance Council of the Christian Churches which had been founded in 1915.[243] This made demands for Sunday closing, control of clubs, local option and restriction of licences.

The last great teetotal effort in Wesleyanism was led by J. Alfred Sharp (1856–1932)[244] in 1921 with the clear aim of a 'dry Britain'; but both the methods and objects had a somewhat dated air about them. Henry Carter played a lively political role in the advocacy of the moderate Licensing Bill of 1921 restricting drinking hours, and of the 1923 Bill restricting the sale of drink to those over eighteen years of age.[245] He sat also on the Royal Commission on Licensing in England and Wales set up in 1929, the Report of which was given measured support by Conference in 1932, although concern was expressed that its proposals were not radical enough on Sunday closing.[246]

The legislative harvest of the Temperance Movement was meagre, and we must ask whether this concentration on one problem was a reflection of a style of Nonconformity which would no longer impose its standards on the Liberal Party, let alone the nation. There was certainly a tendency for diagnoses of social evils to conclude that drink, gambling and thriftlessness rather than bad housing, unemployment and soul-deadening working conditions were responsible for the misery and degradation of the poor.[247] Was this the ethic of the 'self-made man', reflecting his strengths and weaknesses, his principles, his prejudices, his insight and his blind spots? It is, however, easy to criticize the inherent intolerance of the Temperance Movement, with its

[240] E. C. Urwin, op. cit., p. 39; G. T. Brake, op. cit., pp. 47ff.

[241] *Wesleyan Methodist Minutes* (1917), p. 91; cf. ibid. (1916), pp. 591–4: Appendix VI: Abstract of the Report of the Temperance Committee.

[242] Ibid. (1919), p. 60 §9; (1918), p. 64.

[243] E. C. Urwin, op. cit., p. 43: The Nine Points; G. T. Brake, op. cit., pp. 50ff.

[244] *Wesleyan Methodist Minutes* (1921), p. 57 §11; Brake, op. cit., pp. 53, 54ff.; E. C. Urwin, op. cit., pp. 56–7.

[245] E. C. Urwin, op. cit., pp. 50–3.

[246] *Wesleyan Methodist Minutes* (1932), pp. 34–7; G. T. Brake, op. cit., pp. 61ff.; E. C. Urwin, op. cit., pp. 70ff.; cf. Henry Carter's booklet, *The Nation Surveys the Drink Problem* (London 1932).

[247] Gambling (including the innovation of Premium Bonds) was condemned in 1916, 1921, 1925 and 1928. H. F. Lovell Cocks, *The Nonconformist Conscience* (London 1943), pp. 36–9; Robert Moore, op. cit., p. 119.

'Good Samaritan' ethics, and to underrate the social evil of alcoholism even if this is now rightly seen within a wider social context.[248]

The Nonconformist Conscience, it has been said, won its last major political victory on the issue of the right of Dissenters to be buried in their parish churchyard,[249] unless we except the Disestablishment of the Church in Wales,[250] which was on the Statute Book in 1914, and the suppression of the Wells–Johnson fight in 1911.[251] The Muhammed Ali of the day was set to fight Bombardier Wells. Luke Wiseman asked the Birmingham Watch Committee to ban the showing of the film of the earlier American contest involving Johnson, while Samuel Chadwick hailed F. B. Meyer (1847–1929), Secretary of the Free Church Council, as a 'modern Telemachus',[252] when Churchill banned the fight.

'It is broadly true that it was only when most of the religious societies, Anglican and non-Anglican, could agree to fight together on a moral issue that British society was much impressed.'[253] Free Churchmen, and to a lesser extent Methodists, could feel somewhat betrayed by the Liberal Party in the period before World War I. The years after 1906 were years of disappointment and frustration for Free Churchmen.[254] Some Methodist voters were now turning to the Conservatives, others to Labour, breaking free of Liberal patronage. It was ironic for the Nonconformist Conscience that the first avowedly Nonconformist Prime Minister, David Lloyd George, although perhaps the most inspired and creative British statesman of the period, was also 'the first prime minister since Walpole to leave office flagrantly richer than he entered it, the first since the Duke of Grafton to live openly with his mistress'.[255]

The Nonconformist Conscience, seen positively as a concern for minorities, was active in the War when A. S. Peake identified himself with the struggle for the humane treatment of conscientious objectors

[248] For other viewpoints in this period, see Henry Carter, *The English Temperance Movement: A Study in Objectives* (London 1933); *The Church and the Drink Evil: A Challenge to Christian Citizenship* (London 1922); Joseph Rowntree and Arthur Sherwell, *The Temperance Problem and Social Reform* (London 1899); *Alcohol: its Action on the Human Organism* (H.M.S.O. 1924).

[249] P. T. Marsh, *The Victorian Church in Decline: Archbishop Tait and the Church of England 1868–1882* (London 1969), p. 262.

[250] P. M. H. Bell, *Disestablishment in Ireland and Wales* (London 1969), chapter 7: 'Welsh Disestablishment: The Bills'.

[251] Stuart P. Mews, 'Puritanicalism, Sport, and Race: A Symbolic Crusade of 1911', in G. J. Cuming and Derek Baker (eds), *Popular Belief and Practice* (Studies in Church History viii) (Cambridge 1972), pp. 303–31; R. Tudur Jones, op. cit., p. 326.

[252] William Young Fullerton, *F. B. Meyer: A Biography* (London/Edinburgh 1929), p. 121.

[253] Cf. John Kent, in G. V. Bennett and J. D. Walsh (eds), op. cit., p. 182.

[254] Stephen Koss, op. cit., pp. 106ff.; J. F. Glaser, in H. T. Schultz, op. cit., p. 52; D. W. Bebbington, op. cit., chapter 8: 'The End of the Conscience'.

[255] A. J. P. Taylor, *English History 1914–1945* (Oxford 1965), p. 74.

after the Conscription Acts of 1916.[256] Peake's position, and that of S. E. Keeble in Wesleyanism, has to be seen as a minority position in the Free Churches, whose leaders, like J. H. Shakespeare, John Clifford and even P. T. Forsyth, saw the War as a fight for Christianity against paganism, of right against might, of liberty against cruel tyranny, for humanity against the wiles of the Devil. This unexpected War, foreseen by prophetic figures like John Neville Figgis but not by politicians like Winston Churchill,[257] called for the soul of the English Churches and found it wanting. The Report of 1919, *The Army and Religion*, endorsed the thinking of a generation of chaplains who had experienced not only the great gulf separating the mass of working men from the Churches, but the abysmal despair in the soul of Western man.[258] The numerical effect of war is difficult to determine, for the War, while disruptive, does not appear to have been followed by any mass exodus from church membership.[259] Certainly Methodism made great efforts to re-establish itself after the decimation of a generation of young men. There was a lack of prophetic witness in any genuine sense, which revealed the hollowness of much Nonconformist political activity. Political Nonconformity became moribund despite Lloyd George or perhaps because of him.[260] 'Whereas the Church of England might survive, and even prosper from, identification with the nation in arms, such identification

[256] John T. Wilkinson (ed.), *Arthur Samuel Peake: A Biography*, pp. 152–5; Michael S. Edwards, *S. E. Keeble* (London 1977), pp. 38–44; Stephen Koss, op. cit., chapter 6: 'The Impact of War'; Robert Moore, op. cit., pp. 199ff.; David A. Martin, *Pacifism: An Historical and Sociological Study* (London 1965), chapters 5–9; Stuart P. Mews, 'Neo-orthodoxy, Liberalism and War: Karl Barth, P. T. Forsyth and John Oman 1914–18', in Derek Baker (ed.), *Renaissance and Renewal in Christian History* (Studies in Church History xiv) (Oxford 1977), pp. 361–75. For another Free Churchman's dilemmas, see Nathaniel Micklem, *The Box and the Puppets (1888–1953)* (London 1957), pp. 58–9. For the general effect of war on the Churches, see Albert Marrin, *The Last Crusade: The Church of England in the First World War* (Durham, N. Carolina 1974), pp. 157–63; Clyde Binfield, *So Down to Prayers: Studies in English Nonconformity 1780–1920* (London/Totowa, N.J. 1977), chapter 11: 'Christ's Choice of a Battlefield?'; Alan Wilkinson, *The Church of England and the First World War* (London 1978).

[257] John Neville Figgis, *Antichrist and Other Sermons*, p. 31; A. J. P. Taylor, *The Trouble Makers*, p. 106; cf. Nathaniel Micklem, op. cit., pp. 54–5; Albert Marrin, op. cit., p. 67; Stuart P. Mews, 'Kikuyu and Edinburgh: The Interaction of Attitudes to Two Conferences', in G. J. Cuming and Derek Baker (eds), *Councils and Assemblies* (Studies in Church History vii) (Cambridge 1971), pp. 345–59; Alan Wilkinson, op. cit., chapter 1: 'The Coming of War'.

[258] General Accounts: Arthur Marwick, *The Deluge: British Society and the First World War* (London 1965); E. L. Woodward, *Great Britain and the War of 1914–1918* (London 1967); for two recent accounts, see F. W. Dillistone, *Charles Raven* (London 1975), p. 410; F. R. Barry, *Period of My Life* (London 1970), p. 56. F. B. Macnutt (ed.), *The Church in the Furnace* (London 1917), gives contemporary evidence; see also Alan Wilkinson, op. cit., chapter 7: 'The Army and Religion'; chapter 10: 'Faith and War'.

[259] For local disruption, see M. K. Ashby, op. cit., pp. 288ff.; Robert F. Wearmouth, *The Social and Political Influence of Methodism in the Twentieth Century*, pp. 46–54.

[260] Stephen Koss, op. cit., pp. 140–215: an important recent study of the role of Lloyd George.

did violence to the genius of Nonconformity.'[261] The complexities of the decline and collapse of the Liberal Party have a fascination of their own.[262] Even if it is an exaggeration to speak of the 'strange death of liberal England' before 1914, clearly after 1918 the Liberal Party no longer held the allegiance of the bulk of Methodists, and while Isaac Foot might be a survival of the ethos of a previous era, Arthur Henderson was the precursor of a new style of politics which was to hinge on class much more than on religion.

Can we now make any generalizations about the contribution which was made by Methodism to the political life of this period? The prevalent mood was a seeking after a form of limited Collectivism which would replace the worst aspects of the *laissez-faire* politics of earlier Liberalism. The search for a new ethic would bring together earnest supporters of the Liberal Party itself and those who were on the radical wing. Some of these desired the kind of social welfare expressed in Lloyd George's social policy, others espoused Socialism in the more technical sense of the nationalization of the means of production, distribution and exchange.[263] Ordained ministers like Samuel E. Keeble (1853–1946) and J. Ernest Rattenbury, politicians of the style of Arthur Henderson (1863–1935) and Philip Snowden (1864–1937),[264] who owed much to Keeble, shared a common non-Marxist collectivism. Henderson, indeed, as Labour's first Foreign Secretary was greatly respected for his espousal of arbitration and liberal internationalism reflecting the idealism of his religious creed. The contribution of Methodists to the politics of the left was often of a conciliatory rather than a class-warfare style, an attitude which began to break down in the industrial unrest leading up to the General Strike of 1926. It may be an exaggeration to claim that the Labour Party is more Methodist than Marxist[265] (though Blatchford complained of '"lily-livered Methodists" who controlled the I.L.P.').[266] It is also undeniable that Methodism produced the idealism behind many Labour leaders, even if their intellectual stimulus came from secular sources. The 'lapsed Methodist' is a common socialist phenomenon also!

[261] Trevor Wilson, *The Downfall of the Liberal Party 1914–1935* (London 1968), pp. 27–8; Robert Moore, op. cit., p. 216.

[262] See Trevor Wilson, *The Downfall of the Liberal Party 1914–1935* (London 1966); J. A. Thompson (ed.), *The Collapse of the British Liberal Party: Fate or Self-Destruction?* (Lexington, Mass. 1969); George Dangerfield, *The Strange Death of Liberal England* (London 1936).

[263] Samuel H. Beer, *Modern British Politics: A Study of Parties and Pressure Groups* (London 1965), pp. 137–40, 144–9.

[264] Robert F. Wearmouth, op. cit., pp. 246–53.

[265] The phrase is usually attributed to Mr Morgan Phillips.

[266] *The Clarion*, 3 December 1892, cited in Henry Pelling, op. cit., p. 174. For changes in the Labour Party after World War I, see Ross MacKibbin, *The Evolution of the Labour Party 1910–1924* (Oxford 1975).

Recent research has suggested a modification of Elie Halévy's thesis, that Methodism was a key factor in producing the stability of Victorian England,[267] in the direction of the view that religion (especially in its Dissenting form) provided a means of avoiding overt class-conflict by producing a *modus vivendi* between middle class and worker.[268] Methodism served the working class by producing leaders with a capacity for sustained organizational dedication and a high degree of personal responsibility.[269] After the War, as class conflict grew sharper under the pressure of economic depression, Methodist attitudes were more and more pushed aside as politically irrelevant,[270] though at another level it is perhaps no coincidence that the last three speakers of the House of Commons have been Methodists.[271] Methodists tended to be men in whom the habits of thrift, frugality and enterprise had been inculcated – the great age of the 'Methodist Societies' in the universities in the 1945–1960 period was a direct consequence of a passion for education and social betterment in the previous two or three generations of Methodists in which the gap between 'Labour Aristocracy' and the middle class had greatly narrowed. This basically individualist ethic, including temperance and an abhorrence of gambling, fits into an ethos of hard work, exactness and responsibility, producing a highly disciplined, self-controlled person willing to train his mind in critical thinking and his voice in harmony singing.[272] This is basically liberalism in a classic sense rather than socialism, though it had its effect on the Labour Party. English socialism is a river into which have flowed many tributaries[273] – secularism from Tom Paine onwards, the idealism of Ruskin, Morris and George, the thinking of Marx, the Christian Socialism stemming from Ludlow, Maurice and Kingsley, the later Christian Social Union and the particular style of religious idealism contributed by Methodism. Perhaps we might call this a secularization of evangelical Arminianism.

We have spoken of a basic individualism and pietism running into a moderate form of Collectivism. In 1900, if many Methodists were Liberal in outlook and voting habits, increasingly there was a tendency to follow the Collectivist style of Liberalism deeply influenced by T. H.

[267] Elie Halévy, *History of the English People in 1815* (Harmondsworth 1938), iii, 9f.

[268] E.g. Harold Perkin, op. cit., chapter 9; Brian Harrison, op. cit., p. 395; Robert Moore, op. cit., pp. 11, 26.

[269] E. P. Thompson, *The Making of the English Working Class* (London 1963), p. 433; Robert Moore, op. cit., pp. 189–90; D. Ben Rees, op. cit., pp. 148ff.

[270] Robert Moore, op. cit., pp. 202–13. For Wales, see D. Ben Rees, op. cit., pp. 184ff.

[271] Dr Horace M. King (now Lord Maybray-King), Mr J. Selwyn B. Lloyd (the late Lord Selwyn-Lloyd) and Mr George Thomas.

[272] Robert Moore, op. cit., p. 116; C. P. Griffin, in *W.H.S. Proc.*, xxxix, 70.

[273] E. J. E. Hobsbawm, *Primitive Rebels*, p. 128; Harold Perkin, op. cit., pp. 261–70; Stephen Mayor, op. cit., chapter 4: 'Christian Socialism', and, on the Independent Labour Party, pp. 308–14.

Green's political philosophy and actualized politically in the social policies of Lloyd George. The Methodist contribution was a deep ethical concern sometimes expressed in a basically conservative style, by which we mean that there was little desire for a fundamental change in social order. Hugh Price Hughes in his writings and especially in the *Methodist Times* advocated a much more articulate collectivism, though he, like Scott Lidgett, was never a Socialist in the technical sense. S. E. Keeble's summary of Hughes was not far from the mark: 'Hugh Price Hughes had re-actionary tendencies which came out with fearful force at times. But on the whole, he has been the leader of the progressive forces in Methodism and Nonconformity.'[274]

Keeble, whose *Methodist Weekly* was much more socialist in a proper sense, represents a small but highly articulate group within Wesleyanism whose main instrument was the Wesleyan Methodist Union of Social Service with a magazine, *See and Serve*, running from 1906 to 1917 and setting forth new styles of Christian citizenship. The leading members were Keeble himself, W. F. Lofthouse (1871–1965) and later Henry Carter (1874–1951). A direct comparison can be made with the Christian Social Union led by men like Scott Holland and Charles Gore in the Church of England, though some of the more radical Anglican socialists were highly contemptuous of Nonconformity.[275] Keeble's own writings, like *Industrial Daydreams*, were backed up by Symposia – *The Citizen of Tomorrow* (1906) and *The Social Teaching of the Bible* (1909), which made use of most of the scholarly minds of the Methodism of the day. On the further wing of this group was the 'Sigma Club' of 1909,[276] which included among its members J. E. Rattenbury, A. W. Harrison (1882–1946), Henry Carter, H. Maldwyn Hughes, W. F. Lofthouse and J. H. Moulton. Some of these men were also associated with the Free Church Socialist League.[277]

This group did not convert Methodism to Socialism, but forced the Church to concern itself with social welfare policy and with international affairs, a clear foreshadowing of the Christian Citizenship Department of more recent years. Other notable Methodist socialists were Peter Thompson (1847–1909), who took over the Old Mahogany Bar and was the leader of the London East End Mission;[278] D. B. Foster (1858–1949),[279] the erstwhile Wesleyan preacher in Leeds who gave up

[274] Cited in Maldwyn L. Edwards, *S. E. Keeble: Pioneer and Prophet* (London 1949), p. 57.

[275] Maurice B. Reckitt (ed.), *For Christ and the People* (London 1968), p. 74.

[276] Maldwyn L. Edwards, op. cit., pp. 67–8; Michael S. Edwards, *S. E. Keeble: the Rejected Prophet* (Chester 1977).

[277] Peter d'A. Jones, *The Christian Socialist Revival 1877–1914: Religion, Class, and Social Conscience in Late-Victorian England* (Princeton, N.J. 1968), pp. 348–9.

[278] R. G. Burnett, *These My Brethren*, chapter 3: 'Peter Thompson'.

[279] Peter d'A. Jones, op. cit., chapter 8: 'Organized Protestant Socialism', pp. 403–12; Robert F. Wearmouth, *Methodism and the Struggle of the Working Classes*, pp. 217ff.; Foster's relationship to Wesleyanism was one of disillusionment, and became tenuous.

affluence to live on an artisan's wage and was Labour Mayor of Leeds in 1928, and E. J. B. Kirtlan (1869–1937), a member of the Social Democratic Federation, a *rara avis* among Methodists, who wrote *Socialism for Christians* (1907), demanding total collective ownership of all national resources.

Keeble's Fernley lecture of 1921, *Christian Responsibility for the Social Order*, was a fine Methodist preparation for the Conference on Christian Politics, Economics and Citizenship (C.O.P.E.C.) in Birmingham[280] in 1924, at which Methodist participants included W. F. Lofthouse, W. R. Maltby, Henry Carter, Benson Perkins, S. E. Keeble and Ryder Smith. The Conference proved to be a splendid witness to an awakened Christian social and economic conscience. F. W. Dillistone[281] goes so far as to maintain: 'The Copec report could well be regarded as a blueprint for the Welfare State which was before long to be established in Britain', and many of its recommendations have been embodied in the legislative programmes of post-1945 governments, though this may be somewhat of an exaggeration. Bleak years of depression came in between.

[280] COPEC Commission Reports, 12 vols. (1924); S. E. Keeble, '*COPEC*': *An Account of the Christian Conference on Politics, Economics, and Citizenship* (London 1924); Michael S. Edwards, op. cit., pp. 45ff.; E. R. Norman, *Church and Society in England 1770–1970* (Oxford 1976), chapter 7: 'Christian Politics, Economics and Citizenship 1919–1924'.

[281] F. W. Dillistone, op. cit., p. 120; S. E. Keeble, op. cit., p. 3.

X

Since 1932

RUPERT DAVIES

As Rupert Davies has naturally omitted to refer to his own notable contribution to the life of the Church in this period, his fellow-editors add that he has written not only on church history and on Christian education, but also on the nature of authority, both in the Continental Reformers and in the more recent age of doubt. As a devoted ecumenist, he has served on numerous Methodist, bilateral and ecumenical committees and commissions in tireless efforts to promote the unity of the Church.

AFTER the sober but fervent celebration of Union in the summer of 1932, the Methodist Church set out on its way rejoicing and full of hope. One of the major obstacles to the fulfilment of Methodism's evangelistic mission had been removed, and the others could be tackled by the wisdom, eloquence and zeal of the various sorts of Methodist, now happily united and co-operating. Superfluous chapels could be closed, Circuits could be amalgamated, energies and financial resources could be concentrated on the clear and effective proclamation of the Gospel, now that they were no longer required for the maintenance of redundant denominational structures. And the need for the Gospel was more urgent than ever, for the aftermath of World War I, so far from heralding a spiritual revival among the people of Britain, had led to an even greater preoccupation than before with material prosperity among all classes; and meanwhile a new challenge to what Methodism stood for – and she had not forgotten her social and international concern while she put her own house in order – came from the steady growth in the number of unemployed and the misery which attended it, from the collapse of Wall Street and the economic fever which followed it, from the turmoil of Germany, and from the threat to the peace of the world in the Japanese invasion of Manchuria.

Surely Methodism had been reunited, in the providence of God, to meet just such a time as this, and by God's grace it would meet it with the Gospel, the hymns of Charles Wesley, and the witness of social Christianity to God's intention to build a new society, free from injustice and war.

The feeling of optimism was somewhat tempered by the decrease in the number of Church members which was noted in 1933, and by an equivalent shrinkage in the number of Sunday School scholars, rightly regarded by many as a more serious loss for the future of the Church. But it lasted, with modifications, until the bicentenary, on 24 May 1938, of the conversion of John Wesley. The title of the itinerant exhibition of 'Methodistica' which brought the message of the anniversary to chapels everywhere was 'How Great a Flame', with its reminiscence of the opening line of the Wesley hymn which contains the verse:

When He first the work begun
  Small and feeble was His day:
Now the word doth swiftly run,
  Now it wins its widening way;
More and more it spreads and grows
  Ever mighty to prevail;
Sin's strongholds it now o'erthrows,
  Shakes the trembling gates of hell.

But a few months after the bicentenary, world events shattered this mood of confidence in the ability of Methodism to redeem the multitudes and help to create a new order. The mood has never returned.

The hard facts of the post-Union period give every excuse for pessimism. The numbers of members of the Methodist Church in England and Wales fell from 817,429 in 1932 to 557,249 in 1974, and the proportion of Church members to each 1,000 of the population from 27 to less than 15. During this period, the only years that showed an increase was considerably accelerated; a loss of over 20,000 was reported 1950, 1951, 1953, 1954 and 1955. From 1961 to 1970 the pace of decrease was considerably accelerated; a loss of over 20,000 was reported in 1967, and the total loss for the ten years was 103,529.[1] From 1970 the decrease slowed down. There were equivalent losses in the ranks of Local Preachers and Sunday School scholars. In 1933 there were 34,948 Local Preachers (33,526 men, 1,422 women); in 1973, 17,291

[1] Church Membership returns are now published triennially, not annually. The Conference of 1969 instituted a Community Roll, 'in which the names of all those who are within the pastoral care of the local church shall be recorded'. In 1974, the number on this Roll stood at 1,429,103.

(13,208 men, 4,083 women).[2] In 1933 there were 1,297,953 children in Methodist Sunday Schools, in 1974 there were 332,129. Nor is it possible to ignore the comparative numbers of men offering themselves for the ordained ministry. In the years which immediately followed Union, the number tended to exceed 200. In 1970 it had dropped to less than 50. After that year it increased somewhat, mostly because of the advent of women.

Hopes in other spheres also remained unfulfilled. One of the obvious advantages of Methodist Union was the chance to rationalize Methodist work by reducing the number of chapels in use, and amalgamating circuits. In some areas this double process began fairly quickly and proceeded at a reasonable speed. In others, no movement of any sort was discernible for several years, and when something began to happen, it was often due, not to the pure desire to facilitate and further the preaching of the Gospel, but to the painful fact that the retention of this or that chapel had become financially impossible. By the middle of the 1950s 'redundancy' was recognized as a running sore in the body ecclesiastical, absorbing energies and resources which were badly needed in the new areas of urban growth, making impossible the sensible deployment of the ministry, and breaking the spirit of many young and not so young ministers who entered a Circuit with all kinds of plans for an enterprising future, only to find that they were forced, on weekdays as well as Sundays, to serve chapels which ought to have been closed long ago, and that no amount of argument about the misuse of manpower and the needs of the Gospel would shift trustees who were determined to keep 'their' chapel open. In due course the Conference had to take to itself special powers to override the local trustees under certain conditions, but it has been understandably reluctant to use them, and the problem rumbles on. Sheer opposition to change as such, nostalgic attachment to a building where the family has worshipped for several generations, a half-consciousness that to close a chapel is an admission of defeat for the Gospel and the Church, a not unworthy conviction that the 'Methodist witness' must still be made in

[2] Here also there has been a steep decline since 1961. The Rev. John Stacey, Secretary of the Local Preachers' Department, has suggested in a letter to the writer of this chapter that, apart from the general disenchantment with institutional religion, the operative causes for the decline in the number of local preachers are the theological doubts now prevalent, which men and women think that they ought to resolve before beginning to preach; the fear among the young of a 'triumphalist' pretension to 'know the answers'; the widespread rejection of preaching as a method of communication; and the still current notion that a local preacher is only a second-class replacement for a minister. He adds: 'The disposal of preachers throughout the country hinders recruitment. In the suburban areas where we have many competent young people, they do not offer because there is little work for them to do. In the country, where the need is desperate, people are given far more work than is reasonable in view of their other commitments.' Yet this last, geographical, reason must have operated almost as much before Union as after.

that particular neighbourhood, plus the defiant refusal, in some cases, to allow the 'Wesleyans' to have it all their own way and close down the chapel of the 'Primitives' and the 'United Methodists', have combined to create and perpetuate this unhappy situation, and even the natural process of human mortality does not do as much as one might expect to diminish it.

During the years of numerical decrease, therefore, the ratio of chapels to members has remained absurdly high, and has given the impression that the Methodist Church is even weaker in numbers than it actually is. For the steady decrease in numbers many explanations can be given. It is ludicrous to ascribe it to Union in itself. Between 1907 and 1920 the Wesleyan Methodist Church had lost 35,000 members, the Primitive Methodist Church 5,000, the United Methodist Church 9,000. The Wesleyan Methodists regained a large proportion of their losses between 1921 and 1928, but these years proved to be the last ones to show an increase of any importance.[3] It is beyond question that, Union or no Union, the number of Methodists who claimed Church membership was on the way down. There were a few secessions when Union took place, but not enough to affect the general trend. Nor can it be seriously argued that the united Church is notably inefficient, except in the matter of redundancy. Indeed, since the other Churches in Britain have suffered much the same order of losses as those of Methodism, there is no need to seek for some deficiency peculiar to Methodism in order to account for the losses in her case; nor would it be possible to find one.

It is much more satisfactory to say that, whereas until about 1910 the social, cultural and economic forces at work in Britain provided a favourable context for the growth in influence of the Protestant forms of the Christian religion, and Methodism, with several other Christian communities, was swimming with the tide, this gradually ceased to be the case after 1910, and ever since then Christianity in general and, for our purposes, Methodism in particular has had to battle against the prevailing climate of life and opinion. For instance, throughout the nineteenth century and into the twentieth, the churches and chapels of English Protestantism provided the social and educational groupings which met the needs of large numbers of people who had no chance of further education beyond the 'primary' level, or of entertainment apart from the kinds frowned upon by the Puritan conscience of the country. Since then, the opportunities of education for all at every level have steadily grown, and the entertainment industry has made good the other deficiency (and has 'liberated' or 'debauched' – according to one's

[3] J. H. S. Kent, *The Age of Disunity*, pp. 4–6. Dr Kent says: 'The years 1921–8 turned out to have seen the last flicker of expansion of modern Methodism.'

point of view – the national conscience in the process). In 1910 a 'religious' or 'spiritual' (though not necessarily Christian) explanation of natural events, like harvests and wars, was widely acceptable, even to those who did not actually take part in religious activities. But in the modern period people have come more and more to suppose that only a 'scientific' explanation of anything beyond their immediate control can be considered, and that such an explanation necessarily rules out religion. This does not make Western man less superstitious; but it does make him less amenable to the normal presentations of Christian truth, even when they are in accord with scientific discoveries.[4]

But is the formidable decrease in the number of Church members, and of people associated in one way or another with the activities of the Methodist Church, to be equated with the decline of that Church as a community of Christian and would-be Christian people? It may be that historians and journalists have been somehow induced by sociologists and others to fasten too greedily on one particular criterion of the health of a Church – the criterion of numerical strength. It is an easy one to employ, but there are others, more elusive and more significant. The rest of this chapter will be largely devoted to applying some of these criteria to the Methodism of the last four decades.

Has modern Methodism experienced a development in its understanding of the Bible, the Christian Faith and its own heritage? Ever since the time of Wesley, as readers of this *History* will know, there have been individual Methodists of sufficient distinction to entitle them to play an active part in the progress of Christian scholarship, though the Anglican near-monopoly of the older Universities, and the inability, and sometimes the unwillingness, of the Methodist Church to set its scholars free from the insistent claims of teaching and administration have until recently often prevented them from actually doing so. A very great change has come over the scene in the last half-century, largely because of the admission of Methodists to teaching posts in the newer universities, and even in Cambridge itself, but also partly because the theological agencies of the Ecumenical Movement, notably its

[4] R. Currie, *Methodism Divided*, in a chapter on 'Methodism and Ecumenicalism' full of astonishing inaccuracies, makes the probably true statement: '... denominational growth rates fluctuate over time in such a way as to suggest that they are influenced by factors external to the denomination. Mere improvement of the material or spiritual efficiency of the organization would not necessarily result in a higher growth rate, since the "evangelization opportunities" afforded by the denomination's social context might change adversely. Conclusions about ecumenicalism [*sic*] and mission cannot be drawn from the fact that both the United Methodist and the Methodist Churches suffered very severe losses. These may be due to adverse changes in evangelization opportunities rather than adverse changes in the ability of the organization to utilize these opportunities' (p. 298). Since Mr Currie does not believe that the slightest good comes from 'ecumenicalism', it is perhaps significant that he does not blame the decrease in the numbers of Church members on the achievement of union.

Faith and Order Department, have asked for and obtained the participation of British Methodists in work on an international scale.

It was the New Testament scholars of Methodism whose books first began to appear on non-Methodist bookshelves, chiefly those of A. S. Peake, Wilbert F. Howard,[5] Vincent Taylor and C. Leslie Mitton; a new generation looks also for the work of C. Kingsley Barrett and Morna Hooker-Stacey.[6] The biblical-ecumenical writings of R. Newton Flew[7] continued the Methodist intrusion first made by H. B. Workman into the long-maintained Anglican preserve of church history. Partly, no doubt, as a direct fruit of the Barthian revolution in theology, Philip S. Watson and above all E. Gordon Rupp have forced the insular theologians and church historians of Britain to pay attention to the Continental Reformation. In some fields, notably those of the Old Testament (except for the work of W. F. Lofthouse, C. R. North, Norman H. Snaith and George W. Anderson), systematic and pastoral theology (except for the writings of Frederic Greeves) and the philosophy of religion, it cannot be said that Methodists do more than hold their own, or even always that they do that; but the general situation is that British Methodist scholars are now accepted as honourable members of the commonwealth of Christian learning, nationally and even internationally.

Methodist Union, followed by a succession of Methodist bicentenaries of every sort, encouraged a spate, not yet exhausted, of Methodist re-writings of Methodist history, mostly concerned, of course, with the eighteenth century. In fact, hardly any historical personage from outside the New Testament has attracted to himself in modern times so many books, dissertations, essays, chapters and articles, at every level of scholarship and its substitutes, as John Wesley. These innumerable writings have tended to fall into two classes: those, far too often smacking of hagiography, which depict early Methodism as incomparably superior to any other form of Christianity at the time of its origin (though it may be admitted by the authors that since then other denominations – under the influence of Methodism, no doubt – have managed to make up some of the lost ground); and those which offer a critical study of the best, the worst and the mediocre in Methodism as

[5] Howard by no means confined himself to biblical scholarship and the training of ministers. During the forties and early fifties of the century he held a position of recognized pre-eminence in the Conference because of his statesmanlike qualities.

[6] W. F. Flemington's *The New Testament Doctrine of Baptism* (1953) takes rank as an important contribution to biblical theology.

[7] Flew's greatest, though not his most widely read, work of scholarship was *The Idea of Perfection in Christian Theology* (1934). This considerable Methodist achievement in the field of spiritual history was followed by A. Raymond George's *Communion with God in the New Testament* (1953) and Gordon S. Wakefield's *Puritan Devotion* (1957). As an example of Methodist writing on the spiritual life, J. Neville Ward's *The Use of Prayer* (1968) is outstanding.

a contribution to the future unity of the Church Catholic. The first sort has tended to encourage in Methodists that undue preoccupation with the affairs of Methodism which members of other denominations do not fail to notice and point out. The second sort – including the works of Maldwyn L. Edwards, E. Gordon Rupp, Frank Baker[8] and John H. S. Kent – has helped to make it really possible for Methodists to enter into the life of the larger Church, and for non-Methodists to appreciate the value of Methodism past and present.

Another criterion of a Church's health is the influence of its well-informed members on the intellectual life and the educational movements of their time. In 1930 in Oxford, there was one Methodist Professor (of Chinese – W. E. Soothill) and one Methodist Fellow of a College (a notable classical scholar – E. E. Genner). There were twenty-eight members of the Wesley Society, which was then limited to men, and a few other Methodist undergraduates, men and women. In Cambridge and London, the situation in regard to both students and teachers was somewhat better; this was also true of the provincial universities. But, all in all, the number of potential leaders of thought in the Methodist student-groups was inconsiderable, and these few people could scarcely be expected by anyone greatly to affect the life of the Church.

But the small group in Oxford was cared for and led, just before and just after Union, by Harold Roberts, who convinced his hearers of the intellectual integrity of Christianity and invited them to share in the exploration of Methodist spirituality. Many of them responded with zeal and diligence. Not surprisingly, several who studied at Oxford during his time came later to occupy positions of leadership, both lay and ministerial, both theological and administrative, both in the Church and beyond it. In Cambridge, at about the same time, Harold Beales was the guiding personality in the formation of the 'Cambridge Group Movement' (to be sharply distinguished from the 'Oxford Group Movement', later called 'Moral Rearmament'). Teachers and students, town and gown, men and women, came together in group meetings, retreats, exchanges of correspondence, and in visits to Methodist churches up and down the country. They were responding to the question posed by Harold Beales, among others: 'Is the full, rich, evangelical experience available to everyone?', and were seeking to give substance to an affirmative answer. The movement was eagerly taken up by London University Methodists, and spread through the Methodist student world. The groups which were formed bore as close a resemblance to the original Class Meeting as anything else to be found in the modern Church. The beneficiaries of the Movement were destined,

[8] General Editor of the Oxford University Press edition of *Wesley's Works* in 34 volumes, which began to appear in the second half of the 1970s.

like the members of Harold Roberts's group in Oxford, to be among the Church's leaders at many levels, not least in the field of education.

In the period after Union the number of Methodist students grew steadily, and after World War II, with the immense increase in the availability of University places for the non-affluent, very rapidly indeed. The intelligent and hard-working members of the class in society to which most Methodists belonged could now afford to give their sons and daughters the education which they would have been so well able to use themselves. Although the tendency for well-educated Methodists to graduate for social and cultural reasons to the Anglican or agnostic establishment by no means ceased, there is little doubt that since the War the 'learned' professions have received far more Methodists than ever before, or that Universities and Colleges, and most notably secondary schools, contain more teachers from Methodism than the size of the Church would lead the observer to expect. Outstanding in every aspect of these matters has been the contribution of Charles A. Coulson, whose writings and lectures on 'science and religion' were fiercely discussed in universities and sixth forms for two decades. Herbert Butterfield has performed a similar service in the matter of 'Christianity and history', and Basil Willey in his eighteenth-century studies; Russell Hindmarsh had begun to build a further bridge between science and theology before his early death.

Meanwhile, Methodism's own educational institutions – its theological colleges, its Colleges of Education (Westminster at Oxford, Southlands in Wimbledon), its few primary schools, its dozen or so boarding schools, and most notably Kingswood School under the headmastership of A. B. Sackett from 1928 to 1959[9] – have been largely free from the cramping effects of ecclesiastical control, and have sent into the world a very respectable quota of humane and liberal-minded Methodist citizens *ad gloriam Dei optimi maximi et ecclesiae et reipublicae usum* (Wesley's motto for Kingswood).

A further criterion is the growth and depth of social awareness in the Methodist community, for it is the besetting sin of smaller, non-established religious bodies to renounce responsibility for the life of society at large, on the ground that they cannot influence it very much anyway, and to subside into their own concerns, while frowning heavily at some of the popular pleasures which their principles compel them to forgo. There had been a vigorous group in each of the three uniting Churches which maintained the best traditions of its communion by reminding it of underlying social problems. But the majority of Methodists in all the three Churches were sensitively aware of only two social problems, drink and gambling. That these had posed,

[9] A. G. Ives, *Kingswood School in Wesley's Day and Since* (London 1970), pp. 207ff.; John Walsh (ed.), *A. B. Sackett: A Memoir* (London 1979).

and continue to pose, very urgent social dilemmas, no one with any knowledge of industrialized England at the end of the nineteenth century and the beginning of the twentieth will wish to deny,[10] but the Methodists had got them out of proportion so badly that they failed to see other yet more monstrous evils staring them in the face in their own country and abroad. It has been the serious responsibility of the Temperance and Social Welfare Department (happily renamed the Christian Citizenship Department in 1949 and later renamed again the Division of Social Responsibility) of the united Church to open their eyes to the implications for Christians of unemployment, war, unbridled nationalism, racial discrimination and oppression, homelessness and world poverty without diminishing their legitimate concern with the private vices of drunkenness, drug-addiction, gambling and sexual licence. The Department has done this with conspicuous success under the leadership of Henry Carter, E. C. Urwin, Edward Rogers and Kenneth G. Greet; and for many years now each successive Conference has been asked to pass judgment on the social, economic and international issues most pressing at the time of its sessions. Perhaps also the Department and its leaders have done something to destroy the persistent public image, never correct and now wildly inaccurate, of the typical Methodist as a rabid and humourless teetotaller who mistakes abstinence for Christianity. Moreover, the British Council of Churches could not easily dispense with the help given by Methodist research and active involvement in its studies of social, national and economic issues.

To the British public at large, Methodist social and political witness was for many years personified in Donald (later Lord) Soper; in fact, it seemed that in the minds of the majority he was a kind of perpetual president of the Methodists. This is easily understandable. His beautifully lucid exposition of Christian democratic Socialism in the Press and on radio and television, as well as in Hyde Park and on Tower Hill, commanded an attention which no other ecclesiastic of his day succeeded in gaining – though it also tended to conceal the depth of his personal, sacramental Christianity. For all of the width of his public commitments, he is essentially a single-minded Methodist Christian. In the 1960s and early 1970s Colin Morris emerged as the most 'political' Methodist, both as a personal adviser to President Kaunda and as an outspoken champion of the Third World. It is notable that, whereas Donald Soper based many of his arguments on a dynamic pacifism,

[10] The author remembers visiting Dr Fink, a Roman Catholic Professor of the University of Tübingen and a priest, who owned a wine cellar of vast extent and remarkably high quality, and who could not understand the Methodist distaste for excellent wines and spirits – until he learned of the personal and social disasters caused by alcoholic indulgence among the people of industrial England to whom it had been the special mission of Methodism to communicate the Gospel.

Colin Morris was not willing to condemn violence in the interests of justice. His preaching, like Soper's, was recognizably orthodox. In the higher councils of the World Council of Churches, as it turned some of its attention after 1968 to the liberation of the oppressed, Pauline Webb brought the fire of Methodist social zeal to the Programme to Combat Racism – as well as to the fight against sexism. And Philip Potter, the third General Secretary of the World Council of Churches, was trained for the Methodist ministry at Richmond College, Surrey.

But this is not to say that Methodists had finally deserted the Toryism of their founder, though most of them were Liberals during the period of Liberal power, and when the Conservatives gained a majority in the General Election of 1970, the number of Methodist M.P.s fell steeply, climbing again with the victory of Labour in 1974.[11] No precise figures are available, but it is probable that the majority of middle-class, middle-aged Methodists are mildly Conservative, though on the left wing of the party, with a certain residual infusion of the Liberalism which once dominated the Free Church scene. Socialism is strongest among the young, lay and ministerial.

We come to a yet more important criterion. How far and how profitably has Methodism been engaged in the Ecumenical Movement at its various levels? But before we attempt to answer this, we must justify in principle the use of this criterion. After all, the heyday of Methodism undoubtedly occurred when it was separate from all other forms of Christianity, and had every intention of remaining so. If the 'ecumenical' criterion is applied, except in the loose sense of 'being the friends of all and the enemies of none', we shall have to conclude that Methodism at its strongest entirely failed to satisfy it; it does not seem, therefore, to be a very useful criterion of health. Furthermore, it might be argued that Methodism turned to ecumenism in order to restore its failing fortunes; if that be so, ecumenism would seem to be, not a sign of health but a therapy for sickness. These two contentions, however, fall to the ground when it is remembered that the original impetus to ecumenism belongs to a time before Methodism, or any other Church, was conscious of declining strength. This impetus was double, as is well known: it was compounded of the realization that in the areas of overseas missions the Churches acting singly and separately were exceedingly unlikely, for all their strength, to make a successful inroad into the vast territory of paganism (as it was then called; 'other faiths', as we should now say); and of the discovery, precipitated by the growth of interdenominational Bible Study and the steady emergence of the Faith and Order Movement after the Edinburgh Conference of 1910, that obedience to the New Testament requires the search, not just for

[11] There have recently been three successive Methodist Speakers of the House of Commons – Horace King, Selwyn Lloyd, and George Thomas.

cooperation, but for organic unity.[12] It is true that, since the Churches have seen the decline in their size and influence, many Christians have urged the need for ecumenism for the sake of strength, but the original and continuing rationale of ecumenism is biblical, theological and evangelistic. It cannot be wrong, therefore, to test the health of Methodism by asking how fully it has obeyed the imperative of Christian unity.

As early as 1908, John Scott Lidgett, who was later to be the first President of the Conference of the united Church, set out what he held to be the ecumenical role of the Wesleyan Methodist Church:

> Where there are no differences, our watchword must be union; where they are comparatively light, federation; where they are serious, yet not destructive of the fundamental agreement of Christianity, cooperation in order to defend the supreme interests and applications of our common Christian life.[13]

It could fairly be said that Methodists came more and more to accept this programme after World War I, and Methodist Union was the implementing of its first section. There was not much progress beyond this point before World War II (though the Lambeth Appeal of 1920 had been widely welcomed by those who were even then prepared to look beyond their own borders); for the apparent back-tracking of the Lambeth Bishops when they met in 1930 had helped to remove any sense of urgency from the subsequent discussions between Anglicans and Free Churchmen, and many Methodists were still not very eager for progress to be made. World War II showed to many people, at least for the time being, the irrelevance of many factors which divided the Churches from each other, and the announcement of the inauguration of the Church of South India, in the formation of which Methodists had played a leading and constructive part, and of the meeting of the First Assembly of the World Council of Churches in Amsterdam, brought the old ecumenical warriors smartly to their posts. This time they were reinforced by a younger generation of Christians, many of them trained in the Student Christian Movement, to whom the necessity for Christian unity was self-evident, and the search for it their most exciting adventure.

Meanwhile, in November 1946, Geoffrey Fisher, Archbishop of Canterbury, had preached his famous Cambridge Sermon on Christian Unity. In this he called on the Free Churches of Britain to achieve

[12] This is not the view of Currie, who says (*Methodism Divided*, p. 316): 'Close examination of the process of reunion shows that in advanced societies ecumenicalism is the product of an ageing religion. It arises out of decline and secularization . . .' But Mr Currie, here as elsewhere, shows himself unaware, or contemptuous, of any theological dimension to religious movements.

[13] Rupert E. Davies (ed.), *John Scott Lidgett*, p. 196.

intercommunion with the Church of England by 'taking episcopacy into their systems', and he indicated that the Church of England would welcome this approach to the perennial problem of the ministry. It is clear that he did not at this juncture contemplate the organic union of the Churches, though he did, in fact, recommend it in at least one later utterance. There is no doubt that the Sermon inaugurated a new era of Church relations, or at least inter-Church conversations, and a new and fruitful set of ideas had been set in train. Fisher's contribution to the matter needs to be remembered, in view of his later, post-retirement utterances and letters to *The Times*, which repudiated the notion of organic union, and could easily lead to the suspicion that he became an enemy of the very cause which he, at one time, did so much to promote. The fact simply is that Christian thought on the ecumenical issues, in his own Church as in others, had moved some distance on from his original idea, while he himself, with some variations, had remained loyal to it. This is the common fate of pioneers!

Free Churchmen of many kinds now met with Anglicans to work out the implication of the proposal, and duly produced *Church Relations in England*,[14] which set out those implications without formulating any actual scheme for closer unity, and went on to show that the next steps forward could best be taken by launching conversations between individual Churches and the Church of England. In the event, no Church in England felt able and ready to take this step except the Methodist Church. though the Church of Scotland involved itself in equivalent conversations (which, alas, came to nothing in the end). The Conference of 1955, by an overwhelming vote (there were two contrary votes, and none neutral), resolved to accept the invitation of the Church of England to engage in bilateral conversations. Harold Roberts, Principal of Richmond College, was appointed leader of the Methodist delegation, consisting of nine ministers and three lay people (including one woman, the Vice-Principal of the Deaconess College, Dorothy Farrar).

But this is not to say that there had been uninterrupted progress in ecumenical relations since Archbishop Fisher's Sermon. Fisher, in the interest of better understanding, asked three groups, one of Anglo-Catholics, one of Evangelicals, and one of Free Churchmen, to answer in print a series of questions about Church, Ministry and Sacraments. The first publication to appear was the one that issued from Anglo-Catholic sources, under the title of *Catholicity*,[15] and this contained a strange and apparently perverse (but, in fact, merely ignorant) travesty of Protestant and Free Church doctrine (which it was not invited to handle anyway). Newton Flew, the Principal of Wesley House, Cam-

[14] (London 1950).
[15] (London 1947).

bridge, and leader of the Free Church group, which had not yet started its work, was impelled to ask his colleagues to join him in a veritable *apologia pro vita evangelica*. This appeared as *The Catholicity of Protestantism* under Methodist editorship;[16] it drew most profitably on the theological scholarship of Philip Watson and the historical insight and knowledge of Ernest Payne, Secretary of the Baptist Union. There is no doubt that this small but closely-packed work of polemical ecumenism helped greatly to clear the air, and to rid it finally of several illusions about the Free Churches cherished for long years in Anglican minds. It is possible, however, that the misunderstandings so patent in *Catholicity* began the sad process of disenchantment with Anglicanism which beset the mind of Newton Flew in his last years – sad, because he had worked so constructively and at so profound a level for the cause of Anglican – Methodist rapprochement for many decades.[17]

Conversations between the Church of England and The Methodist Church: An Interim Statement appeared in 1958. It shows considerable evidence of a growth in understanding between those who were taking part in the Conversations, and marks some very significant steps forward. Above all, it contains this sentence: 'In the course of our discussions, we have been led with impressive unanimity to the conviction that nothing short of organic unity, whatever form it may take, should be our final goal.'[18] With this sentence, the Report catches up with Archbishop Fisher's proposals, which were directed towards intercommunion only, and proceeds to march ahead of them. Ways of reaching the 'final goal' are considered. The 'South India method' (by which certain Methodist ministers would be consecrated as bishops, all Methodist ministers recognized as ministers of the United Church, and all *future* ordinations of Methodist ministers would be episcopal, but nothing further would be done, so that intercommunion might be incomplete at first, but would gradually grow into completeness) is decisively rejected for this country, though its suitability for India is not questioned. Then for the first time a *two-stage* method of attaining organic unity is adumbrated; this, it is stated, would mean that for the first stage certain Methodist ministers would be consecrated as bishops and that all future Methodist ordinations would be episcopal, but also that there would be a unification of the ministries from the outset. Thus there would be full intercommunion, and union would follow in due course.[19] The Report seeks at some length to make the 'taking of episcopacy into their system' acceptable to Methodists, and explicitly says: (*a*) 'We wish to make it plain that taking episcopacy into the

[16] (London 1950), edited by R. Newton Flew and Rupert E. Davies.
[17] See Gordon S. Wakefield, *Robert Newton Flew* (London 1971), pp. 241–3.
[18] Op. cit., p. 41.
[19] Ibid., pp. 40–2.

Methodist Church would not mean taking episcopacy in the precise form in which it appears in the Church of England today'; and (*b*) 'We wish to make it abundantly plain both that the Church of England form is not the only form of episcopacy in the Anglican communion, and that we by no means regard the Church of England form as the ideal'.[20]

The approval of this Report by the governing bodies of both Churches sent the Conversations off to a good start on the second phase of their explorations, and in 1963 the *Report of the Conversations* appeared. It may fairly be said that there was nothing of substantial content which is new in this document; the suggestions contained in the Interim Report are amplified and worked out in considerable detail, and under the heading 'Theological Considerations' a strong case is made out for the contention that there is sufficient theological agreement between the two Churches for union to be possible and desirable. Some of the doctrines and practices ascribed to the Methodist Church by the Report were not immediately recognized by some Methodists as characteristic of Methodism as they knew it, and there is no doubt that the flavour of 'High Methodism' to be discerned in its pages complicated the discussion of Anglican–Methodist Union in the Methodist Church during the next few years.

Of greatest immediate importance and practical interest were the proposals for the service of unification, now re-named, of deliberate purpose, the 'Service of Reconciliation', which was to inaugurate 'Stage One', the stage of intercommunion. In the draft the 'Declaration of Intention' states that,

> we are met together today in order that, after our long years of separation we may be reconciled to one another as brethren in our Father's house, to pray that he will join in one the ministries of our two Churches, and to seek that full and free communion in things spiritual which we believe to be His will. In the union of ministries neither of us wishes to call in question the reality and spiritual effectiveness of the ministry of the other Church . . .

After Thanksgiving and Repentance comes the Reception of the ministers and members of each Church by the ministers and members of the other Church; and here was the nub of the proposals, for it was, of course, the reconciliation of the ministries that had afforded to the drafters their greatest difficulty.

The solution propounded rests on the valid theological judgement that the meaning of a rite of laying on of hands is to be found in the prayer which immediately precedes it. The prayer which was to come just before the laying of Methodist hands on Anglican heads contains the sentence: 'Renew thy blessings already given and pour out thy Holy

[20] Ibid., pp. 39, 43.

Spirit upon them for the work of a minister in thy Church'. The prayer preceding the imposition of hands on the Methodist ministers has this: 'Renew thy blessings already given, and upon these thy servants do thou pour out thy Holy Spirit to endue each according to his need with grace for the office of priest in the Church of God.' The small difference was meant to be significant, for whereas no Methodist casts doubt on Anglican orders, there are Anglicans who cast doubt on Methodist orders. Thus the prayer for the Methodists, while it in no sense required to be understood as an 'ordaining' prayer, and Methodists in general were expected to reject such an interpretation, could be understood as 'ordaining' by those who wished to do so; and because of this wording the rite provided the *materia* of ordination in the minds of those who were looking for it.[21] But the main purpose of the whole ceremony was to leave the matter of the ministry in the hands of God, with the prayer that he would give to both Churches in their reconciliation a ministry adequate for his purposes and recognized without scruples by Christendom at large.

The Report was signed by all the Anglicans who had shared in the Conversations, and by eight of the twelve Methodists. The dissentient Methodists, who contributed a minority statement, included Kingsley Barrett, who had joined the Conversations in 1959; the other three also came from non-Wesleyan Methodist antecedents.

The ensuing debate followed lines which should have surprised no one. In the Church of England, controversy was muted, perhaps because many Anglicans tacitly but naïvely concluded that the Methodists were rejoining the Church of England; but the Conservative Evangelicals began fairly soon to criticize the scheme, on the grounds that Methodist ministers should simply be accepted without any question, but also, it may be suspected, because an Anglican–Methodist union portended a revision of the Establishment on which Evangelicals relied for their security within an otherwise, they held, non-Evangelical Church. In Methodism, Kingsley Barrett, with the other three dissentients from *Conversations between The Church of England and The Methodist Church* (London 1963), led the theological opposition, arguing that the imposition of episcopal hands on Methodist ministers could not mean anything but ordination, and that the insistence of the Report on episcopal succession flouted the New Testament doctrine of the ministry. Quite a different kind of Methodist opposition, though sometimes clothed in theological terms, came from many ministers and laymen who cherished folk-memories of Anglican arrogance and now feared an Anglican take-over; they were, in fact, sturdy Nonconformists, by temperament and conviction, and refused to recognize the Anglican change of heart which the Ecumenical Movement had brought

[21] Ibid., pp. 42–7.

about. Harold Roberts and his colleagues who had signed the Report tirelessly toured the country to explain that the theological objections rested on a failure to see the openness of the Service of Reconciliation to more than one interpretation, including a sound Methodist one; and that the non-theological objections had been rendered out-of-date by the genuine desire of the Church of England, not to absorb the Methodists, but to enter into a creative reconciliation with them. The organization calling itself 'The Voice of Methodism', and other organizations, were formed to counter the arguments and proposals of the ecumenists, and the atmosphere in the Church was not free from accusations of bad faith.

After two years of controversy, for the most part gradually turning into reasonable discussion, the matter came to the first point of decision. In the summer of 1965 the Anglican Convocations and the Methodist Conference registered their approval in principle by commanding majorities, and a new joint Commission was set up to deal with outstanding questions and work out detailed proposals. Once again the Methodist chairman was Harold Roberts. The new Commission brought out its interim report as *Towards Reconciliation* in 1967. The report gave a positive answer to the question once again put, whether there was really enough common ground in the matter of doctrine for the Churches to come together; it revised the Service of Reconciliation in the light of certain criticisms; it also included the first draft of the new Ordinal which was to be used by both Churches during Stage One and by the united Church thereafter.

This document was well received by Methodists in general, and was felt by many to contain doctrinal reassurances needed by those who did not take the 'High Methodist' position; it certainly increased the volume of Methodist support for the scheme of union. Some Anglicans of the Anglo-Catholic persuasion, on the other hand, now began to feel that too many concessions had been made to Methodist and Evangelical 'Protestantism' and that too wide a latitude in doctrine had been offered to radicals in both Churches. These people were partly reassured by the appearance in 1968 of the revised new Ordinal,[22] which speedily gained the warm approval of all schools of thought, while its Preface contained an agreed doctrine of ordination.

Later in 1968 the *Scheme*[23] was published in its final form, and the stage was set for the decisive debate. The 'Voice of Methodism' and its allies rallied their forces. The Conservative Evangelicals deepened and carefully organized their opposition, and a new party of opposition emerged in the Church of England, led by the Bishop of Willesden

[22] *Anglican–Methodist Unity:* I, *The Ordinal* (London 1968); *Towards Reconciliation: The Interim Statement of the Anglican–Methodist Unity Commission* (London 1967).

[23] *Anglican–Methodist Unity:* II, *The Scheme* (London 1968).

(Graham Leonard), an earlier supporter of the scheme, to denounce its contradiction of Catholic principles – but willing, nevertheless, to join forces with those who opposed the Scheme for entirely opposite reasons. In both Churches, the great central body of ministers and members remained firm in their support; nearly all the diocesan bishops of the Church of England, including both archbishops, came out strongly in favour, and as the various courts of Methodism recorded their constitutional votes, it was seen that the higher the court, the larger was the likelihood of a majority in favour.[24]

On 8 July 1969, the Convocations of the Church of England (meeting together in London) and the Methodist Conference (meeting in Birmingham) debated and voted simultaneously. It was agreed that a seventy-five per cent majority in both Churches was necessary if the matter was to be proceeded with. The Methodist vote was announced first – nearly seventy-eight per cent in favour. Few who were present in the Methodist Conference will forget the tension of expectancy as the minutes ticked by until the Anglican vote was announced – nearly sixty-nine per cent, and insufficient for the purpose.

The archbishops and the bishops – except those few bishops who had voted against the Scheme, some at the last moment – with a great body of clergy and laypeople over the whole country, were filled with deep disappointment and compunction. Members of the minority which had triumphed in most cases concealed their joy, but sometimes with difficulty. There was nothing that the Methodist Conference could do, except ratify in 1970 the vote of 1969, as it was required to do to make the decision binding; this was done by an increased majority.

At the end of 1970 the government of the Church of England was transferred from the 'clerical' Convocations to the lay-and-clerical General Synod; and in February 1971 the matter came before the new body. It was deferred until July for an Anglican–Methodist Working Party to make some clarifications. Thus clarified, the Scheme was approved in principle in July by a vote of sixty-five per cent, and referred to the Diocesan Synods, also lay-and-clerical, for their judgement. The date of 3 May 1972 was fixed for the final vote, and a majority of seventy-five per cent was again laid down as necessary for the Scheme to be implemented. In spite of the continued support of the bishops, and of the great majority of central Churchmen, and a most

[24] Fifty-five per cent of the members of the Quarterly Meetings voted in favour; all the District Synods in England did so, often with very large majorities. The voting in the Quarterly Meetings has given rise to the charge made by opponents of the Scheme that the people at the 'grass roots' were 'steam-rollered' by the 'establishment'. But it has been reliably conjectured that the attendance at many Quarterly Meetings for the occasion was artificially inflated by those who were opposed to change but did not usually attend the Meeting; and those who voted in the Synods were, so far as the laymen were concerned, those whom the Quarterly Meetings had sent there as their responsible leaders.

moving appeal by the Archbishop of Canterbury, Michael Ramsey, the alliance between Evangelicals and Anglo-Catholics depressed the majority well below the needed seventy-five per cent, and slightly below the sixty-nine per cent of the previous occasion.

In Methodism, the main result of this failure was a certain numbness, followed by a slightly feverish preoccupation with denominational affairs. There was an admirable absence of bitterness among those who could have maintained that the Church of England had 'led them up the garden path'. But no one knew what the next step was, and for a time few steps of any sort were taken. An Anglican–Methodist Liaison Commission was set up, and this body encouraged local ecumenism by promoting the establishment of a Consultative Committee for Local Ecumenical Projects. There were faint stirrings in Anglican and Methodist ecumenical quarters when it was seen that the Congregational Church and the Presbyterian Church were about to form the United Reformed Church. An unofficial conference of interested and influential persons from as many denominations as possible, meeting at Christ Church, Oxford, launched the idea of talks designed to find out whether serious conversations could begin again, and when these 'talks about talks' took place, it was found that the way was open for the appointment of a Churches' Unity Commission on which all the mainstream Churches in England, including the Roman Catholic Church, were willing to be represented.

In 1976 the Commission produced Ten Propositions, the thrust of which was to suggest a covenant whose signatories would recognize each others' members and ordained ministers, practise full intercommunion, and engage themselves to seek further ways of expressing the 'visible unity' which they had reached. The Churches were asked to make a definitive response within a specific period, and they in their turn asked for several clarifications. The Methodist response in general was favourable but muted; many Methodists professed themselves, although still in favour of unity itself, weary of constant negotiations and discussions about unity; yet on the decisions of the Churches whether or not to enter the Covenant suggested, and on the acceptability of the Covenant that will have to be drawn up, depends for this century the hope of the visible unity to which the Methodist Church stands committed.

Ecumenism, as Methodists would be the first to claim, is not simply a matter for high-level negotiation and argument. It is not fully operative unless it is also applied locally to the relations of congregations and people with each other. The Nottingham Faith and Order Conference of 1964 initiated a great amount of local activity in areas where it had not yet started – certain cities, like Sheffield and Bristol, had given the lead long before – and developed what was already going on. The apparent imminence of the Anglican–Methodist decision gave a fillip to many local congregations, and the repeated failure of the Church of England to approve the Scheme – ascribed by some to the Holy Spirit, by others to less exalted influences – paradoxically enough, gave a further fillip. Those who had opposed the Anglican–Methodist Scheme wished to show that they were none the less in favour of Christian unity and those who had supported it were keen to press on with what they knew to be right. The Shared Churches Act of 1969, together with the backing given by the British Council of Churches, and by bishops and Chairmen of Districts, to 'Areas of Ecumenical Experiment', where several things could be tried which were normally against ecclesiastical regulations, carried further the cause of local ecumenism. But it remains true that local activity of this kind needs the background of agreed union between the Churches, and without it tends, sooner or later, to die the death of all church life which receives no general direction. There could, just possibly, be an exception in this case, in view of the strong resolve of many younger Christians to have the unity of Christendom whether the Churches agree to it or not; if they do not agree, it is often said, so much the worse for the Churches!

A current which has flowed all the while directly across the stream of ecumenical advance is the World Methodist movement. This had some significance in 1881, when the first 'Ecumenical Methodist Conference' met, for the two largest communities which had arisen from the work of John Wesley, the British and the American, were now talking with each other for the first time since their separation at the end of the War of Independence. The Conference and its successors for fifty years consisted largely of speeches, but they brought the leaders together, and opened up the prospect of an eventual meeting of minds. In 1947, in Springfield, Massachusetts, the movement once again seemed on the verge of becoming important, and in Oxford in 1951 practical plans were made for exchanges and interchanges of various sorts; a permanent and potentially effective organization was formed, with E. Benson Perkins, who had conducted the affairs of the Chapel Department during the difficult post-war years, and Elmer Clark, one of a small group of mostly Southern American enthusiasts, as co-secretaries. It was the hope of nearly all the British Methodists who participated in these affairs, notably Harold Roberts, that the Council and its Conferences would enable Methodists from everywhere to make the best possible contribution to the world-wide Ecumenical Movement. But a few of the British participants were thinking in terms of building a World Methodist Church, and it is now clear that these were the terms in which a large number of the keener American participants were also thinking. As a result there has been constant conflict between the advocates of growth towards the union of Churches and those who wish to retain denominational independence (with goodwill towards all). The United States provides the majority of the active leaders, and because of this and of the generosity of the American Methodist Church in providing so much of the essential finance, the British version of ecumenism has rarely prevailed.[25] Moreover, there has been a tendency towards Anglo-American dominance in the affairs of the Council, although a partial reform of the constitution in Denver, Colorado, in 1971 gave more effective representation to the Churches from the Third World. The Dublin Conference in 1976 showed some inclination towards a more comprehensive ecumenism, though this has still to be worked out in terms of policy.

Not surprisingly, World Methodism, in spite of its potentialities, has never come to count for much in British Methodism, though the exchange of pastors across the Atlantic, the holding of conferences by the World Federation of Methodist Women, World Methodist Youth, Methodist 'theological educators', and Methodist liturgists, and the quadrennial Oxford Theological Institute, have conferred many fringe benefits on Methodists of all nations. The World Methodist Council remains at present a consultative body, and could provide a useful forum for all Methodists. If the attempts of its American leaders to turn it into an operational organization, with an ambition to direct the policy of its autonomous member-Churches, are renewed and pressed, disintegration of the movement could easily follow.

World Methodism has, however, provided a useful channel through which a fresh stream of ecumenism can flow. After the Second Vatican Council, the Roman Catholic Church was ready and willing to engage in bilateral conversation with other Churches on doctrinal matters. Because of the character of the Roman Catholic Church, these conversations had to be on a world scale. The representatives of the World Methodist Council, meeting with Roman Catholic representatives, have produced statements on Eucharist and Ministry and have begun to prepare one on Authority, and British Methodists have played a considerable part in the formulation of these.

It is time to turn to another criterion of the health of modern Methodism. To what extent has it taken part in the international and inter-confessional movement for liturgical renewal? Until about 1960 there was no evidence of any impact, and it took all the patient and scholarly enthusiasm of Raymond George, Principal successively of Wesley College, Headingley, and Richmond College, Surrey, to awaken the Conference, through the Faith and Order Committee, to its responsibilities and opportunities. The Committee was empowered in that year to draw up a complete revision of the 1936 Book of Offices, which

[25] As it did, perhaps, in Oxford in 1951, when the title of the Council became 'The World Methodist Council' (instead of 'The Ecumenical Methodist Council').

had been produced in an earlier liturgical atmosphere, partly liberal, partly traditional Anglican, and in the event obtained permission to produce an entirely new set of main services which embodied the ideals of the modern Liturgical Movement. The new services were authorized for an experimental period, and the Committee received many comments and criticisms from congregations and individuals before setting out on the final revision; but the new linguistic style – straightforward English, avoiding both the established language of traditional liturgy and the ephemeral speech-forms of the 1960s and 1970s – and the combination of the eucharistic and baptismal structures of early liturgy with modern insights concerning relevance and the Church's mission, survived in the final revision intact. The influence of this vigorous reform on Methodist worship up and down the country was slow to show itself, and in many Circuits at first no change from the conjunction of the simple form of service sometimes known as a 'hymn-sandwich', and the 1936 liturgy, with the emphasis on the former, was noticeable. Yet the 'Sunday Service' (the new eucharistic office) and the new orders of Baptism, Reception into Full Membership (or Confirmation), Burial and Marriage steadily won their way, and in the next ten years a total transformation of liturgical worship may well have taken place. At the same time, the Methodist concern for spontaneous worship, long canalized and stereotyped, has found new expression in experimental worship of all kinds, some, indeed, somewhat bizarre. On this double development, liturgical and free, the future strength of Methodism may depend, for the descent into dreariness of much that passes for worship has alienated more people of every age than can possibly be calculated, and the resurgence of living worship may help to bring them back. The new *Methodist Service Book*, containing the main new liturgical services, was officially authorized in 1975.

Nor has the call for hymnodic renewal been neglected. In 1969 a supplement to the *Methodist Hymn Book* appeared under the title of *Hymns and Songs*, containing a number of contemporary and almost contemporary melodies and hymns, some of them of an admittedly transient character, but many of them destined for a long and useful life.

Many friends and critics of Methodism would claim that the next criterion which we employ is by far the most important of all – what success can it show in evangelism, in the sense of bringing men and women from outside, or nearly outside, the Church to the knowledge of Jesus Christ as their Saviour and Lord? Yet it may not be right to attach quite so much importance to this criterion, since, as we have seen, the Methodist Church has operated during the period under review in a social and mental climate highly inimical to evangelism; it is certain that evangelists and evangelistic methods which would have registered a great access of members to the Church in the early part of this century have no hope of doing so today. This does not necessarily mean that the Church is lacking in zeal and spiritual progress, or the evangelists in sincerity and power. Nevertheless, the future of a Church which makes no recruits to its ranks from those outside its immediate sphere of influence is likely to be one of increasing introversion. There have been many campaigns and missions, on a local or a national scale, designed to appeal to the 'man in the street' – the 'Christian Commando Campaigns' of the period just after World War II inspired by Colin Roberts, and the World Methodist 'Year of Evangelism' (1953) and Call to Evangelism (1971 and 1976) being the most spectacular examples; in the 1930s, and to some extent later, teams of students and theological students descended on many towns with the object of manifesting the appeal made by the Gospel to young and lively-minded people. But the results of all this, in terms of additions to the membership of the Church, have so far been negligible. Nor have those Methodists who have associated themselves with the highly organized, lavishly financed and widely publicized missions of Billy Graham any substantially greater success to report.[26]

Those, however, who are convinced that evangelism is the life-blood of Methodism have not been daunted by ill-success, and the recent rise and spread of the Charismatic Movement, which has attracted many ministerial and lay Methodists by its emphasis on the invigorating power of the Holy Spirit, has given them new heart. Yet, in spite of constant reappraisals, many theoretical and practical questions remain unanswered.

In consequence, attention has shifted in many places from campaigns of evangelism to the concept of the Church, not least in the form of the local congregation, as continuously engaged in mission – 'mission' being thought of as a word of less limited connotation than 'evangelism', and as including everything done by the Church in its locality as an act of service to men and women and to the community at large. This concept has been recommended in theory and practice in many areas of Methodism by members of the Methodist Renewal Group,[27] most of them, at the time of joining the Group, young ministers profoundly dissatisfied with many forms of the Church's thought, life and activity, but wholly committed to the task of bringing the Gospel home, in word and deed, to the people of this age – an age which they were, perhaps, the first in Methodism to recognize as secular in all its

[26] All evangelism and work for advance needs considerable finance. Methodism owes a great deal in this respect to the Trusts endowed by Joseph Rank and to the personal generosity of his son, J. Arthur (Lord) Rank.

[27] Later merged with the Anglican 'Parish and People Movement', the 'Friends of Reunion' and other bodies, into 'ONE'.

ways. No striking success has attended their efforts, but at least there is now a much greater number of local congregations devoted to standing by the people of their neighbourhood in their various needs than ever before in the history of Methodism.

Presiding over the evangelistic efforts of Methodism for more than a decade, first as minister of the Central Hall, Westminster, then as General Secretary of the Home Mission Department, was the commanding personality of W. E. Sangster. He was well aware of the change in the intellectual climate, and did his best to adapt the language of evangelism to the understanding of the new age. He was among the first churchmen to recognize the approach of the 'permissive society'. Perhaps he was the last of the orotundly eloquent preachers of Methodism, and he had a great following to the end.

In the period spanning the 1920s and 1930s, the preaching of W. Russell Maltby, for many years Warden of the Deaconess Order, to students and to people with similar interests, was second in influence only to that of William Temple. Maltby's theology could be described as 'liberal', but his chief emphasis was certainly on the personal relationship of the Christian believer to Jesus Christ.

Leslie Weatherhead, who with Donald Soper and W. E. Sangster completed the trio of Methodist preachers known as such to the non-Methodist public, was an evangelist of a different sort. He was one of the first to use the new psycho-therapeutic techniques in the interests of the Gospel, and for a quarter of a century and more, with a mastery of words which enabled him to touch the heart-strings and appeal to the imagination, he presented Jesus as the great healer of mind and spirit. His message did not change very much with the changes in public taste, but he continued to exercise a personal magnetism which helped him to be the spiritual counsellor of a large public and many individuals.

The final criterion of Methodism's health which needs to be used is the nature and extent of its response to the challenges presented by the rapid development of contemporary society. This response, taken all round, has not been negligible. As soon as World War II was over, the nation cried out for a vast increase in the facilities available to youth, thinking, rather pathetically (as it turned out), that this provision would reduce the incidence of crime, irresponsibility and ignorance. Methodism's reply was the foundation of the Methodist Association of Youth Clubs, conceived and directed by Douglas Griffiths, and this has certainly done more than most organizations to achieve the desired result.[28] It became clear at the same period that women were about to

[28] In the inter-war years, James Butterworth, by his work at the First Clubland Church in South London, anticipated many of the ideas about the service of youth which later became orthodox.

take a much fuller part in business, political, educational and social life than ever before. The Churches gave only a slight lead in this direction, and Methodism responded only slowly to the lead given by others. But women Local Preachers[29] and Church officials steadily increased in numbers, and the movement for the ordination of women was active in the 1950s, powerful in the 1960s and successful in the early 1970s.[30] The Women's Fellowship, which had begun with the efforts of a few kindly and able women to infuse life and meaning into the innumerable Women's Meetings in the Church, was transformed in the 1960s into a movement which captured the loyalty and informed the minds of many in the great company of serious-minded and conscientious women who form the backbone of any Church, and certainly of Methodism. Moreover, it entered the field of Young Wives' Groups in a big way, and cleared the ground for what may be the biggest area of evangelism that the modern world is likely to afford. Yet it has not entirely succeeded in convincing Methodists at large of the equal ability and essential role of women in the life of the Church, and in this respect a great deal still needs to be done.

More than half of the laity in the Church are women. The men have been much less willing to organize themselves, but the 'Westminster Laymen' (largely masculine) did much to re-formulate the role of the laity for the 1950s and 1960s.

In common with all large organizations, secular and religious, the Methodist Church in the 1960s came to be conscious of top-heaviness, and excess of expenditure in administration. It had already ceased to be the case that a few families with long and noble Methodist traditions exercised an influence disproportionate to their size; but the power and influence which had once tended to gather into comparatively few hands were still not spread widely enough, and there was some discontent among the younger ministers with the continued dominance of the old. Rationalization, reform and economy were in the air. So local and Connexional 'restructuring' claimed and occupied the attention of many preparatory committees for several years, and was in due course introduced. Its effect was to reassemble the many and various 'departments' of the Church into seven 'divisions' corresponding to the natural areas of the Church's work – Home Mission, Ministries, Education and Youth, Social Responsibility, Overseas Missions, Finance, and Property; to cut down the size of committees and the frequency of their meeting, at every level; to bring together the leaders (that is, most of

[29] See pp. 363f. above.

[30] The Ministerial Session of Conference finally approved the scheme for the ordaining of women, under, as far as possible, the same conditions as men, in 1972. This decision was postponed several times previously in order to avoid prejudicing the conversations with the Church of England.

the active members of the old 'Leaders' Meeting') and trustees of the local society into the Church Council, with its various committees; and to set up a kind of cabinet to oversee the general policy of the Church under the title of the President's Council. The President's Council came into existence in the autumn of 1971, as a foretaste of the new order, and the Connexional, District and Circuit reorganization was brought into effect in orderly succession thereafter.

The new system has not escaped criticism. At the Circuit level, the reduction of the Quarterly Meeting to a twice-yearly Circuit Meeting has led to the crowding of business, and at the Church level too few people have found themselves serving on too many committees. The President's Council, it is said by some, gives too much weight to the heads of the Divisions.

To the growing alienation of society in general from the Church and from traditional Christian principles, Methodism has responded by reconsidering its educational policy in relation to its own boarding and day schools, its Colleges of Education,[31] its Sunday Schools, its adult members, and its ministers in training.[32] These measures have the overruling purpose of preparing its representatives to go into the community with a mature understanding of the Christian Faith. The blueprint for the reform of the Sunday School was contained in 'The Way Ahead', the work of a special commission, published by the Youth Department in 1961. This was effectively followed up by a thorough exploration of the 'experiential' methods of religious education powerfully advocated by Douglas Hubery, and then by the issue, in concert with the other Free Churches, of annual series of Sunday School Notes, entitled 'Partners in Learning', which embodied the principles behind these methods. These were later revised in order to include more biblical material.[33] The Board of Lay Training, under Pauline Webb, had to carve out for itself the appropriate ways of educating the laity – rather surprisingly, since it has presumably been the duty of ministers to educate the laity from time immemorial.

The training of the ministry entered a very troubled patch of its history in the late 1960s. On the one hand, a great advance had been made, and was being consolidated, in the employment of modern educational methods and the gradual abandonment of the idea that an

[31] In the nationwide reduction of Colleges of Education from 1975 onwards, Westminster College, Oxford, survived as a separate entity, and Southlands College, Wimbledon, as a constituent part of the Roehampton Institute of Higher Education.

[32] On general educational issues, the Conference of 1970 approved a forward-looking statement called 'Christian Commitment in Education', thus fulfilling an overdue obligation to its many representatives in the teaching profession. The Laybourn Report of 1973 cast a searching light on the principles and practice of Methodism's own boarding schools.

[33] The educational and child-care policy of the rapidly expanded National Children's Home has similarly kept well abreast of modern developments.

academic, or semi-academic, training, in the Bible (preferably in the original languages), church history, and systematic theology, together with a strict devotional discipline, and a little pastoral and homiletic instruction, was all that was needed. Psychological, sociological and more directly practical subjects had been introduced, without, of course, displacing the old, except that much less time was spent in attempting to master Hebrew and New Testament Greek. The students spent far more time than of old within the actual context of Methodist circuit life and in acquiring some knowledge of hard contemporary realities. Moreover, the entry of married students, with their families, had widened the community life, and eliminated many restrictions on freedom now thought to be irksome. But, on the other hand, progress was constantly hampered by economic and other problems arising from the shortage of candidates for the ministry, by steeply rising costs, and by frequent and meteoric changes in Conference policy about the closure and location of Colleges. In addition, the failure of the Anglican–Methodist Scheme impeded the development of ecumenical theological training just at the time when both wisdom and economic factors demanded it.

The actual course of events must have been extremely puzzling even to the most sympathetic observer. In 1967, Wesley College, Headingley, Leeds, was united with Didsbury College, Bristol, to form Wesley College, Bristol, and this arrangement, though painful to many, proved successful. In 1971, Handsworth College, Birmingham, was merged with the Anglican foundation of Queen's College to form the new Queen's College, which has turned out to be the only truly ecumenical College so far in Britain. In 1972, Richmond College, Surrey, with its long traditions, not least in scholarship and missionary training, disappeared. Meanwhile the Conference seemed entirely unable to decide between Wesley College, Bristol, and Hartley Victoria College, Manchester, as the final candidate for closure. Hartley Victoria College was rich in associations with Northern Methodism and Manchester University, but its buildings needed immense expenditure to be made suitable for modern purposes; Wesley College was closely associated with Bristol University, was housed in buildings recently designed and erected with modern needs in view, but its local and regional connections were not quite so deeply ingrained as those of Hartley Victoria. Both had modified traditional training by a flexible approach. Feelings ran high on both sides throughout the ministerial section of the Church, and many laypeople were also passionately involved. In the end the Conference of 1972 decided by a narrow majority – the vote by show of hands was a tie and a further vote was taken by ballot – to close Hartley Victoria and develop Wesley.

Since then, to the advantage of all, including the women students who entered the Colleges in 1973, matters have progressed peacefully, although the impact of the 'new' ideas of the 1960s may have declined. Wesley House, Cambridge, which was untouched by the turmoils which afflicted others, is part of an ecumenical consortium. In Manchester a Methodist and a Baptist College co-exist in the same building, and the name 'Hartley Victoria' is thus preserved.

New concepts of ordained ministry were much canvassed in the late 1960s, and that of 'ministers in the sectors' was gradually put into effect. Since there are large 'sectors' of human life which fall entirely outside the scope of ordinary ministerial activity, such as the social services and national education, it was thought proper, after anxious debating, to send ordained ministers into them to work there for their living, but to do so as ordained ministers carrying out the mission of the Church in all ways open to them. This was seen to need the most careful scrutiny of those who were to be sent and of the work they would be employed to do; and the Conference laid down that they were still as far as possible under the authority of the Conference and required to play as full a part as they could in the life of the Circuit in which they resided. The controversy aroused by this new notion was not allayed by its being put into effect, but the 'sector ministry' seems now to have come to stay, though the name is liable to change.

It is a sad fact that after World War II and the financial crises which followed it, shortage of money came more and more to overshadow all other problems and far too many opportunities. This has led the Church to rely too much on the generosity of wealthy individuals; and, more seriously still, to adjudge the merits of projected enterprises, not by their value to the real purposes of the Church, but by their financial implications. The Methodist Stewardship Organization, emphasizing that all a Christian's resources, and not his money only, are called to be at the service of his Lord, did a great deal to halt this process in local Societies. But the reduced number of Church members have not been able to contribute enough to keep up with the steep rise in prices, and the financial prospects of the Church must give cause for great concern into the foreseeable future.

The nearest approach to a permanent office in the Methodist constitutional system is that of the Secretary of the Conference, and it is also at the policy of the holders of that office that we must frequently look for the response of Methodism to the demands of the age. The office has been held by four men between 1932 and 1982. Robert Bond incarnated the courteous firmness and mild autocracy of the old-style Wesleyan Superintendent. Edwin Finch stood for the unobtrusive but inflexible government of Methodist affairs by the well-thought-out principles and practice of the Methodist constitution. Eric Baker came out into the open and made himself known to the people of Methodism far more than his predecessors had done. By swift and far-sighted decision, by clarity of utterance, by accessibility to every minister and member, by wholehearted approval of ecumenical development, by supremely competent administration, and by sage and self-effacing advice to each successive President (though with personal reservations about the ordination of women), he kept the spiritual and material fabric of Methodism in working order for two decades. It is a well-grounded truism that with his retirement in 1971 an age came to an end.

His successor, Kenneth Greet, has made an even greater impact on the Church outside Methodism than Eric Baker; within Methodism he is known for his leadership in ecumenical affairs, his continuance of competent administration and his courteous affirmation of Methodist values, both old and new. He has become the spokesman of Methodism in a way that used to be reserved to Presidents in office and, in the mind of the Press, to Donald Soper.

Much of his time during his first quinquennium of office was necessarily spent, with many advisers, legal and other, on the formulation, presentation and defence of the Methodist Church Bill which became law in 1976. Methodist Union was made legally possible by the Methodist Church Act of 1929. In various respects its provisions needed to be revised in the light of changed circumstances, as well as of more recent legal enactments. In 1932, the doctrinal clauses of the Deed of Union which was prescribed by the Act were declared unalterable (though of course what Parliament had enacted, Parliament could alter). This provision was desirable at the time in order to guarantee to each of the uniting Methodist Churches the impossibility of changes in the doctrinal basis of agreement. In the 1970s it was no longer needed, and its presence was an affront to those who believed that the Church's teaching should be under its own authority and not that of the state. So the new Bill provided for the alteration of the doctrinal clauses if the Church as a whole, after a statutory period of checks and consultation, wished for it. The buildings of Methodism, under the old Act, were held by local Trustees for the purposes of the Conference, though the Trustees were sometimes under the mistaken impression that they had the ultimate right of disposal. The Trustees had usually acted in conformity with the wishes of the Church and Circuit whose buildings they managed, but sometimes they had maintained a dogged and effective resistance to them, and to change of any sort. The new Bill transferred the power of management in each case to the Church Council, of which the former Trustees, if they lived in the neighbourhood, were for the most part members.

A small group of ministers and laypeople believed the supersession of the Trustees to be contrary to justice, and the alterability of the doctrinal clauses to be dangerous to the Methodist gospel (perhaps suspecting that 'modernist' and 'High Church' innovations were contemplated). It obtained large sums of money from unidentified sources to conduct a campaign of opposition, and the Church was put to similarly large expenditure. Both Conference (almost unanimously) and Parliament (strongly) rejected the objections, and the Bill became law in 1976.

Methodism, since Methodist Union, has experienced many changes, some forced upon it, some actively and consciously willed by its leaders and people. These changes have affected not only its outer structures, but also the inner life of its members, in a Church in which every member is offered a position of responsibility. Many of the changes have been in the direction of assimilation to other Churches, as other Churches have been assimilated to Methodism, and of a greater openness to influences and ideas from the world outside Methodism; many have been designed to preserve and strengthen its distinctive characteristics. The result so far, it can be argued (but also, presumably, disputed), has been to maintain the essentials of Methodist teaching and spirituality (though not always at a deep enough level), while dispensing with many of the formulae and activities in which they used to be clothed, and to fit the Methodist people in some measure for the reciprocal sharing of spiritual treasure with other Christians.

What Methodism will become in the future does not depend, under God, on Methodism alone, but on the pattern of ecumenical relationships that the last years of the twentieth century will witness. If continued separation from the Church of England and the other Churches of the country is forced upon it, then the application of the criteria suggested by this chapter to the present life of the Church makes it necessary to ask this question about its future: will its inner resources be sufficient to save it from gradual decay? But then, of what denomination in Britain does this question not have to be asked?

INDEX

References located only in a footnote are indicated by the addition of *n* to the page number.

The following abbreviations, arranged alphabetically, are used:

BC	Bible Christian
IM	Independent Methodist
MNC	Methodist New Connexion
PM	Primitive Methodist
WM	Wesleyan Methodist
WI	West Indies
WMMS	Wesleyan Methodist Missionary Society